W9-CMN-761

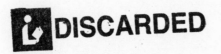

SPENCER PERCEVAL
THE EVANGELICAL PRIME MINISTER
1762–1812

To

BARBARA AND KATHLEEN GRAY

Frontispiece

Spencer Perceval

(*from the portrait by Sir W. Beechey*)

Spencer Perceval

The Evangelical Prime Minister

1762-1812

by

DENIS GRAY

MANCHESTER UNIVERSITY PRESS

Published by the University of Manchester at
THE UNIVERSITY PRESS
316–324, Oxford Road, Manchester 13

Printed in Great Britain by Butler & Tanner Ltd, Frome and London

CONTENTS

LIST OF ILLUSTRATIONS

PREFACE

I BEGAN work on the life of Spencer Perceval in the autumn of 1948 and completed it in the autumn of 1961. For the first four of those thirteen years, I was able, as a post-graduate research student, to devote myself fully to the work. For the remaining nine years, I had to rely on such free time as I had as a tutor in adult education.

Thirteen years may well seem too much to have been spent on a little-known politician whose entire parliamentary career lasted only a little longer than this, and whose period in high office was over in five years. I first became interested more in the times of Spencer Perceval than in his life. Too many standard works on the period seemed to flit lightly from the death of William Pitt to the battle of Waterloo, as though the one event followed hard on the heels of the other, instead of being separated from it by nine years of world war. When Spencer Perceval first entered the cabinet in 1807, Great Britain had been at war with France for fifteen years and yet eventual victory seemed as far off as it had ever been. Napoleon was at the height of his power in Europe and Great Britain was left without a single major ally on the continent. The British economy showed increasing signs of strain and many observers soon began to doubt both the soundness of our inconvertible currency and our ability to continue for much longer to finance a major war effort. By the time of Perceval's death in 1812, the pattern of Wellington's eventual victory in Spain was clear, while Napoleon had been forced into preparations for his final and fatal invasion of Russia.

In the history of British political organisation the period seemed to pose several important questions. What effect had the long domination of the younger Pitt and of Fox on the existing structure of politics? How had ministers maintained a parliamentary majority, however precarious, in face of the fragmentation of 'Mr. Pitt's Friends' and of the continuous process of economic reform? How important a political role did the ageing and ailing George the third still play in the last years before his final attack of insanity?

A little work on the period soon convinced me that all these issues led to a study of the life of Spencer Perceval, for it was Perceval who, at first as chancellor of the exchequer, and then as first lord of the

treasury, had managed in the face of immense difficulties to finance
Wellington's armies in the Spanish peninsula. It was also Perceval
who, in spite of the strongest parliamentary opposition and a virtually
uninterrupted series of political crises which might have broken even
the most powerful of ministers, still carried on the business of the king's
government in the house of commons. This double feat seemed to me
ample reason for writing the biography of a man whose life has been
largely ignored since Sir Spencer Walpole's study of him, published
in 1874.

Finally, as my work continued, I became increasingly absorbed with
the personality of Perceval and with the drama of his life. His fervent
evangelicalism made him, in many ways, a herald of the victorians.
The little black-suited prime minister, with his sabbatarianism and his
distaste for fashionable pursuits, was an odd leader of Regency
England. He had, throughout his life, to make his own way in the
world for perhaps no other British prime minister has had less financial
backing than did Perceval as a young man. When he married Jane
Wilson, after a remarkable elopement, he took her to live over a
carpet shop in Bedford Row. He had to support her, and their twelve
children, out of his earnings from the bar: his political career cost
rather than earned him money. He is one of the very few lawyers to
have reached the highest office in British politics and he remains the
only one who has ever been both solicitor or attorney-general and
prime minister. Above all he is the only British prime minister to have
been assassinated. Had that not happened at a time when he seemed
destined for many more years of political power he must surely long
since have been rescued from an unmerited neglect.

Denis Gray

195, Damson Lane,
  Solihull

ACKNOWLEDGEMENTS

My first thanks must go to those tutors who supervised my work during a long and peripatetic post-graduate career. Dr. Stanley Hardy of the university of Birmingham patiently bore both my first and worst blunders and my failure to appreciate fully the merits of William Huskisson. Mr. Philip Styles gave me constant encouragement, kept gently prodding me to finish my work, and always seemed to believe, in spite of the passage of years, that eventually I would. Professor Robert Greaves of Bedford college, university of London, accepted me as a member of his seminar on administrative history at the institute of historical research and first encouraged me to tackle the treasury papers. Above all, I am indebted to the late Sir Lewis Namier whose scholarship was matched only by his kindness. My tutorials with him were an unparalleled and unforgettable lesson in the art of non-violent demolition.

I have to acknowledge the gracious permission of Her Majesty the Queen to make use of material from the George III and Regency papers at Windsor. Mr. David Holland and the late Mr. Dudley Perceval kindly allowed me access to the Perceval papers before they were deposited in the British museum. The earl of Harrowby made available both the main series of the Harrowby papers and the papers of Richard Ryder. Lieut.-Col. A. H. Spottiswoode helped me by putting the Herries papers at my disposal. I have, in the first section of the bibliography, expressed my thanks more fully to them all.

I have also to acknowledge the co-operation of those people who have helped in providing illustrations. I am indebted to Mr. W. T. Fehsenfeld for the frontispiece of this book, to the late Mr. Dudley Perceval for plates 1a and 1b, to the London county council for plate 2a, and to the controller of H.M. stationery office for plate 2b. The Mansell collection provided plate 3; Mr. F. W. Eyles kindly allowed me to reproduce plate 4, while the dean and chapter of Westminster abbey gave permission for the inclusion of plate 7. I am also indebted to the national portrait gallery both for permission to include plate 5 and for all the advice kindly given to me by Mr. J. F. Kerslake, the assistant keeper. Mr. T. L. Jones of the university of Manchester press has given me the most generous help in all stages of the preparation of this book.

I am greatly indebted to the publications fund of the research committee of the university of Birmingham for their generous contribution towards the cost of publication.

Finally I give my best thanks of all to my wife, who not only spent many hours making transcripts of documents, but who, for more than a decade, has managed to live with Spencer Perceval as well as with Denis Gray.

CHAPTER ONE

LITTLE P.

THE Honourable Spencer Perceval, the eleventh living child and seventh son of John, second earl of Egmont, was born in Audley Square, London, in the morning of Monday, 1 November 1762.[1] The order of his birth is more significant than its exact date, for the second son of a second marriage had little hope of inherited wealth. Throughout his career he had to rely on his abilities, bolstered only by such help as his family's social and political connections could afford him. When, in later life, political opponents taunted him as an impecunious and upstart lawyer, he could point to the authorised version of his family's history, contained in that 'remarkable document of human vanity', the *History of the House of Yvery*. This two-volume work, first published in 1742, was compiled, with suitable professional aid, by the first earl of Egmont. Noble blood and military glory are as Castor and Pollux in this type of family chronicle. The Perceval saga was traced back to 'Robert, Lord of Breherval, Montinney and Villoris Vastatis', the son of 'Eudes, sovereign Duke of Brittany, and Lord of the stoutest fortress in all Normandy'. Successive generations of Percevals were found fighting for William (and a grant of English land) at Hastings; following Strongbow into Ireland; winning a knighthood for bravery on the field of Crecy; dying at Bosworth after political knavery; and deciphering Spanish despatches for Lord Burleigh.[2]

It is unfortunate that nearly all of this, though accepted by contemporaries, was but an 'impudent fiction'. The authentic history is far less remarkable. The first Perceval to achieve any sort of distinction was Richard, son of George, the owner of Tykenham and Sydenham in Somerset. This Richard, a servant of Sir Robert Cecil, took part in the investigations into the Gunpowder Plot before selling his land in England and going to Ireland as registrar for the court of wards.

[1] F. A. Crisp, *Fragmenta Genealogica*, vol. IV, p. 73. The family Bible gives the exact time of Spencer Perceval's birth as 'half an hour past seven o'clock in the morning'.
[2] Spencer Walpole, *Life of Spencer Perceval*, vol. I, pp. 1–4.

Richard's son, Philip, succeeded to the office and did so well out of it that he came to own large tracts of land in both Somerset and County Cork. He was knighted by Lord Wentworth in June 1636, but during the Civil War supported parliament as commissary-general in Ireland and as M.P. for the Cornish borough of Newport. Sir Philip was sufficiently famous to be buried at the public expense, which was just as well, since his preoccupation with politics had much reduced the family estates. The second baronet, John, decided that politics and estate management did not mix. He sold all his property in Somerset, and devoted himself to the care of that which remained in Ireland. Such peaceful pursuits stood him in good stead at the Restoration, when Charles II confirmed his baronetcy and admitted him to the privy council. Thereafter, the Percevals settled down as undistinguished Irish country gentry until Sir John, the fifth baronet, used his political career to gain social advancement. From 1703 to 1715 he sat in the Irish house of commons as member for Cork County and in 1717 was created an Irish baron. Five years later he was a viscount, and after seven years at Westminster as whig M.P. for Harwich, he attained an Irish earldom. The second earl, 'a youth of extraordinary sense and character', inherited his father's taste for both antiquarianism and politics. He is said to have written two political pamphlets by the age of nineteen; was elected an F.S.A. in 1736; and after holding a number of political offices, received an English peerage in 1762, under the genealogically doubtful title of Baron Lovel and Holland. In politics he was an ardent 'King's Friend' and hoped to restore feudal society in England.[1]

The second earl married twice. By his first wife, Katherine Cecil, daughter of the fifth earl of Salisbury, he had five sons and two daughters. His second, Catherine Compton, bore him first a son, Charles George, then two daughters, Mary and Anne. Spencer, the second son, was followed by Elizabeth, Henry, Frances, and Margaret, all born at two-yearly intervals between 1763 and 1769. This numerous brood of children spent their childhood in the manor house of the village of Charlton in Kent, where Spencer was christened. He had four sponsors—Sir John Rushout, his great-uncle, a governor of Harrow school, and the fourth baronet in a family of Flemish descent; Lady Elizabeth Drummond, his maternal aunt; the seventy-five-year-old Dorothy, widow of John Howe, first Lord Chedworth; and his uncle,

[1] Hist. MSS. Comm., *Introductions to the Egmont MSS.*, vols. 1 and 2, and to the *Diary of the Second Earl of Egmont*, vol. I.

Spencer Compton, later the eighth earl of Northampton, from whom the child took his christian name.[1] During Spencer's infancy the earl of Egmont was first lord of the admiralty, and the perquisites of office extended to the youngest generation. At the age of one year and ten months the 'Honourable Spencer Perceval Esquire' received notice that, 'in consideration of the good and faithful service already performed', he had been granted the second reversion (in succession to his eight-year-old brother, Charles) to the sinecure of registrar of the high court of the admiralty.[2] Unfortunately the earl did not survive to make further provision for his younger sons. In 1770 he died suddenly at his town house in Pall Mall and was buried in the family vault of the parish church of St. Luke's, Charlton, where, two years later, he was joined by his children, Henry and Anne, both victims of a 'sore throat'.[3]

In 1774 Spencer entered Harrow, where he remained until the age of seventeen. The school had just passed through a major crisis, for in the year that Spencer's brother, Charles, had first taken up residence, the scholars had rioted against the election to the headmastership of Benjamin Heath, formerly a master at Eton. This had ended in the stoning of a governor's carriage and the secession of one master and forty boys to form a rival school at Stanmore under the popular Dr. Samuel Parr. But the Percevals, probably because of their family connection with the Rushouts, remained faithful to the original foundation. Heath soon proved to be a successful head, quickly restoring both the discipline and the numbers of his pupils. In place of the ancient ceremony of shooting for the silver arrow he inaugurated school speech days. Charles Perceval had been a spectator at the final archery event when an unskilful competitor had the misfortune to pierce a local barber's instead of the bull's eye.[4] A scholar's life at Harrow in the late eighteenth century was not particularly arduous. Lessons certainly started at seven in the morning, and included two hours' work before breakfast. But, in all, formal study occupied only about five hours a day, the morning and afternoon being broken up into three short periods of work, varied by regular prayers and

---

[1] *Complete Peerage*, vol. IX, p. 686, and vol. III, p. 156; L. B. Namier, *Structure of Politics*, vol. I, p. 131.

[2] This grant, dated 30 July 1764, is now in the Hulton library of Harrow school. Whitbread described the duties of registrar as requiring 'little more abilities than were sufficient for counting the money from its emoluments into his own pocket'.

[3] *Gentleman's Magazine*, 1772, p. 391.

[4] P. M. Thornton, *Harrow School*, p. 175.

free hours.[1] Beyond these communal prayers the school made little provision for religious instruction.

Joseph Drury, who later succeeded Heath as headmaster, was severely handicapped by having 'no pulpit of his own from whence to deliver the teaching which experience bade him impart'. Instead the school attended Harrow parish church where a 'rustic, battered gallery' at the west end accommodated the upper school while 'another stifling and cavernous gallery was hitched into the north aisle for the lower boys'.[2] Nor was the service, in the days before Cunningham became the incumbent, likely to be very inspiring.

Perceval's career at Harrow was academically successful. He won many prize books, became a school monitor in his final year, and formed two life-long friendships. The first of these was with Matthew Montague, nephew and adopted heir to that 'Queen of the Blues', Mrs. Elizabeth Montague. The second was with Dudley Ryder, heir to the peerage of Harrowby. Ryder, although always handicapped by poor health, was reported by the headmaster to be 'by far the best scholar I have ever been concerned with' and 'some of his late compositions are very wonderful. . . .'[3] Young Perceval, under Drury's careful tuition, made equally good progress. 'My mind naturally recurr'd to those early times', wrote Perceval's old tutor in June 1812, 'when my venerated friend used to attend on my instruction; and full well can I recollect, with what temper and patience he bore erasures of his favourite passages in his compositions; with what intense perseverance he labour'd to acquire accuracy; and with what delight his countenance beam'd, when originality of thought, and purity of diction ensur'd praise and confirmed the distinction he had attained among his contemporaries.'[4] Hard work and singleness of purpose were his cardinal virtues. He decided to 'confine his views chiefly to classical composition and a critical knowledge of those authors, whether historical or poetical, from whom he might derive literary treasures best suited to his purpose'. With this end in view, he overcame the temptations of 'desultory reading' which could only 'vitiate his taste and confuse his ideas'. Drury, who got on well with the boy, was full of admiration for such self-control, 'rarely found in lively parts in early youth'.

[1] P. M. Thornton, *Harrow School*, p. 191.

[2] *Ibid.*, p. 206; J. H. Overton and E. Wordsworth, *Christopher Wordsworth, Bishop of Lincoln*, p. 84.

[3] *Croker Papers*, vol. II, pp. 373–4; J. T. Perceval to Croker, 6 Sep. 1840; *Journal of Miss Berry*, vol. II, p. 395; Harrowby MSS., vol. VII, fol. 67.

[4] Perceval MSS., J. Drury to Sp. Perceval, 17 June 1812.

Perceval left school in 1779 with, wrote Brougham, 'no information beyond what a classical education gives the common run of English youths'. He remained, however, throughout life a staunch old-Harrovian. 'I feel', as he once rather pompously expressed it, 'there is something in early acquaintance which predisposes to good inclinations and friendship whenever persons are afterwards in any degree approximated or connected.'[1]

It was Cambridge, rather than Harrow, that did most to mould his character. He entered Trinity college and matriculated in January 1780, three years after his brother Charles had gone down with an honorary M.A. At first a Mr. Collier acted as his tutor, but later he had more contact with the celebrated wit, William Lort Mansel, and with the Italian scholar, Thomas Mathias, who was probably both his personal friend and his private tutor. Under their tuition he won the college declamation prize for English and took an honorary M.A. in 1782.[2] The university at this period was hardly a centre of religious life, and Trinity was notable for its opposition to 'enthusiasts'. According to Gunning, there were, at the end of the century, only two or three out of the eight seniors of the college whose characters could pass muster. In 1779 John Venn was refused admission solely because he was the son of the evangelical rector of Yelling. Twenty years later a Trinity undergraduate witnessed parties begun 'in the endeavour to make each other drunk', for hard drinking at Cambridge was almost as prevalent 'as it was in county society'. 'A young man', wrote Charlotte Elizabeth, 'could not with impunity be a Christian at either of the Universities.'[3] Fortunately, Perceval always gloried in opposing popular opinions. He made the empty gesture of applying for admission to White's (for there is no evidence that he ever used the club) and then identified himself with the yet small group of Cambridge

---

[1] Perceval MSS., Sp. Perceval to Lord Redesdale, 7 Jan. 1804. Among Perceval's contemporaries at Harrow were two evangelicals, Thomas Gisbourne and Thomas Grimstone, the future seventh earl of Elgin (of the Marbles' fame), and Harry Calvert, later adjutant-general to the forces. Among those who were to sit in the 1807-12 house of commons were C. P. Yorke, William Chute, Scrope Bernard, John Calcraft, Christopher Codrington, Lawrence Dundas, Lord Euston, A. H. Eyre, William Wickham and (most curious of all) G. L. Wardle (W. T. J. Gun, *Harrow School Register, 1571-1800*).

[2] Croker, *loc. cit.*; W. W. R. Ball and J. A. Venn, *Admissions to Trinity College, Cambridge*, vol. III, p. 269. Perceval's most notable contemporaries seem to have been Richard Porson, later regius professor of Greek, and Charles, 2nd earl Grey.

[3] H. G. C. Moule, *Charles Simeon*, pp. 9 and 65; J. H. Overton, *The English Church in the 19th Century*, pp. 222-3.

B

evangelicals.[1] Isaac Milner, a fellow of Queen's, was then rector of St. Botolph's; William Farish was a fellow of Magdalene; Trinity Hall boasted Joseph Jowett as a tutor; while Dr. William Cooke at Queen's had young Charles Simeon in his charge. It was Cooke who, in 1782, wrote the Latin ode 'Ad Percevallum':

> Hail! Youth, most worthy to engage,
> The lessons of th' Athenian page,
> Of Athens self the love;
> Whom learning's venerable host,
> Their truest, noblest son might boast,
> In academic grove.[2]

Perceval was undoubtedly studious; perhaps, for most tastes, he was a little too serious-minded. A young student who could insist on paying the salary of an office to the defeated candidate (because he had forgotten to cast a promised vote) may sound too good to be true.[3] But there was a lighter side. Famed for his 'guileless, guiltless jokes', he was constantly to be found in 'gay humour's train'. Long afterwards, one of Perceval's sons told Croker that it was at a college supper that Spencer (while still an undergraduate) first met Pitt, but this is surely overstressing the debt to Cambridge.[4] The university developed his love of literature, added to the number of his friends, and made him an evangelical.

> Still as thou art for ever be,

---

[1] A. Bourke, *The Betting Book of White's Club, 1743–1878*, vol. II, p. 69 of members' list.

[2] Walpole, on the authority of Miller, attributes the ode to Ward, a fellow of Trinity (vol. I, p. 10). The original Latin version is in the Perceval MSS. The English version and attribution to Cooke can be found in the *Northampton Mercury*, 16 Jan. 1819.

Isaac Milner (1750–1820), mathematician, divine and friend of William Wilberforce. He later became dean of Carlisle and vice-chancellor of the university of Cambridge.

William Farish (1759–1837) later became Jacksonian professor of natural and experimental philosophy.

Joseph Jowett (1752–1813) went on to be professor of civil law.

William Cooke (d. 1824) was the professor of Greek who edited Aristotle's *Poetics*.

Charles Simeon (1759–1836). Influential evangelical leader and one of the founders of the church missionary society.

[3] *Public Characters, 1809–10*, p. 505.

[4] Croker, *loc. cit.*

wrote William Cooke in farewell:

> And whether fate to thee assign,
> A seat where England's statesmen shine,
> In proud ambition's sphere,
> Or favouring stars thy footsteps guide,
> To holier joys—the loved fire side,
> The wife and prattling line,
> Granta (thou'lt say) to thee in truth,
> In studious love I gave my youth,
> In head and heart I'm thine.

In fact lack of means rather than 'favouring stars' guided his foot-steps after he came down from Cambridge. There was no money for the usual grand tour of Europe, although he may have visited relations in Ireland. Within a year he had entered Lincoln's Inn, where he remained until February 1786. In the interval he lost his mother, who in her widowhood had been created Baroness Arden in her own right. 'My poor Mother', wrote Perceval to Dudley Ryder, 'was taken with a slight cough in the end of last August—but it was nothing; and so it continued nothing not only in her own opinion, but was so apparently to every body else till the beginning of November when she grew rather worse and was forced to come to town for advice, and though she was frequently a little better she was never well afterwards.' [1]

Charles, already an M.P., became Baron Arden in the Irish peerage and the Percevals decided to economise by ending their lease of Charlton House. It was while he was still a student at the Inns of Court that Perceval also joined the *Crown and Rolls* debating society. This club, which took its name from a public house in Chancery Lane, was confined to M.P.s and to actual or potential barristers. Meetings were held every Monday evening at which young Perceval was a regular speaker. Dudley Ryder, Charles Yorke (another contemporary at Harrow), Nicholas Vansittart, the future chancellor of the exchequer, the Canningite, William Sturges Bourne, John Singleton Copley (the first Lord Lyndhurst), and James Scarlett, a future chief baron of the exchequer, were all members. During debates at the *Crown and Rolls*

---

[1] Harrowby MSS., vol. VIII, fols. 144-5, Perceval to Dudley Ryder, undated, but endorsed 'June 1784'; *Records of Lincoln's Inn—Admissions*, vol. I, p. 505. For the suggestion of the visit to Ireland, see Perceval MSS., Dudley Ryder to Sp. Perceval, 9 Sep. 1783—'there was, I remember, a time when you were obliging enough to write me a long history of an expedition you made into Ireland . . .' Perceval's mother died at Langley in Buckinghamshire on 11 June 1784. She was fifty-three years of age.

Perceval spoke on a wide variety of subjects. He resisted a motion to codify the common law, but agreed that a true report should not be a libel. He urged the retention of the usury laws but condemned the Clandestine Marriage Act. He supported the Test Acts, insisted that no nation had the right to interfere in the internal affairs of another, and, in a particularly vigorous and sensible speech, argued that parliament should seek to balance the competing interests of agriculture and industry.[1] All his speeches were read from carefully-prepared drafts. Forthright and unsubtle matter was presented in a style always artificial and frequently involved. He sounded as if he were addressing a judge rather than a debating society for at the *Crown and Rolls* Perceval was clearly practising for the bar rather than for the house of commons.

By 1786 he was ready to begin his legal career. He took his brother's old chambers 'at no. 20 in Field Gate Court and Kitchen Garden Row, two stories high' and attached himself to the midland circuit.[2] At first he attended the quarter sessions at Northampton, Nottingham, and Leicester with more enthusiasm than success. Money and clients were so scarce that expenses had to be constantly watched. He hired 'Mr. Sturt's horse' instead of buying his own, and while at Northampton he lodged with Joseph Edge during the whole period of the quarter sessions for a very reasonable sum. While travelling from one town to another he would make a note of the shilling spent on his dinner at a wayside inn, or of the florin which covered both supper and breakfast, of the sixpenny tip to the chambermaid and the hostler, and of the cost of the oats for his horse.[3] Fortunately, as early as 1787 the interest of his relatives, the Comptons, gained him the office of deputy recorder of Northampton, the salary of which played a big part in balancing his precarious accounts. His main failing was a lack of self-confidence and an 'excess of modesty, which, at that period, almost amounted to timidity'. He had, moreover, to compete with such formidable barristers as Romilly, Vaughan, Ascough, and Bramston.[4] But if he failed to gain briefs, he soon won the respect of his friends.

---

[1] The drafts of Perceval's speeches are in the Perceval MSS. For details of the *Crown and Rolls* society, see Mackintosh, vol. II, p. 280.

[2] *The Black Book of Lincoln's Inn*, vol. IV, p. 36.

[3] *Anonymous Memoir*, p. 5; Bills in Perceval MSS. C. M. Atkinson and J. E. Mitchell in *The Life and Principles of Sir Samuel Romilly*, say Perceval 'soon became the favourite and delight of the bar' (p. 37).

[4] *Victoria County History, Northamptonshire*, vol. III, p. 15; *National Adviser*, 16–20 May 1812.

Samuel Romilly found him a young man 'with strong and invincible prejudices on many subjects', who had read little (a poor reward for his efforts at Harrow) and who was 'of a conversation barren of instruction'. Yet 'by his excellent temper, his engaging manners, and his sprightly conversation he was the delight of all that knew him'.[1] In January 1786 he dined in a small company at Rainham with his old school companion William Chute. Afterwards, Windham, the principal guest, noted in his diary, 'Perceval is a young lawyer, and from his quickness and acuteness likely, I should think, to be some time or other a distinguished man'.[2] Sir Walter Scott later quoted as an example of George Ellis's discrimination that, at first meeting, he saw in Perceval a man who 'with the advantages of life and opportunity, would certainly rise to the head of affairs'.[3] For several years, however, Perceval was well content to keep his head above water.

His vacations were mostly spent at his brother's new home at Charlton, where the manor house now belonged to Sir Thomas Wilson, an old soldier who had served at Minden and had sat in the house of commons as one of the members for Sussex. When Charles and Spencer re-visited their old home, they found that Sir Thomas's three daughters added to the attractions of the place. Charles fell in love with Margaretta Elizabeth, while Spencer courted her younger sister, Jane. Unfortunately, although the brother's inclinations were similar, their means were quite different. Charles was an Irish peer, a lord of the admiralty, tolerably wealthy and with the prospect of a considerable fortune when he became registrar of the high court of the admiralty. He and Margaretta were married in the private chapel of Charlton House on 1 March 1787.[4] The less fortunate Spencer had little to

---

Sir Samuel Romilly (1757–1818). Law reformer and solicitor-general in the All the Talents ministry.

Sir John Vaughan (1769–1839) ultimately became justice of the common pleas.

James Yorke Bramston (1763–1836) was later a convert to Roman catholicism and became a Roman catholic bishop.

Ascough was described by Romilly as 'possessed of a large property' and yet as following his profession 'with as much ardour as if his subsistence had depended upon his success'. He died, while still a young man, of consumption.

[1] Romilly, *Memoirs*, vol. I, p. 91.

[2] *Diary of William Windham*, p. 71.

William Windham (1750–1810), statesman who served in the cabinet under both Pitt and Grenville.

[3] Scott, *Journal*, vol. II, p. 215. George Ellis (1753–1815), author, friend of Sir Walter Scott and founder, with Canning, of the *Anti-Jacobin Review*.

[4] Crisp, *Fragmenta Genealogica*, vol. IV, p. 73.

recommend him to a prospective father-in-law. He was poor, and his intended bride was only eighteen years' old. Sir Thomas Wilson refused his consent, and the young couple waited patiently for happier times. For three more years Perceval attended to his business on the midland circuit without achieving any great success, until, in July 1790, Jane came of age and Spencer became a commissioner of bankrupts.[1] Equally important was Arden's succession to his admiralty sinecure, for Charles and Spencer had always been the fondest of brothers, and, in an emergency, the proceeds of the court of admiralty could easily support two families. On 10 August Jane and Spencer were married at East Grinstead, Sussex.[2] Walpole, rejecting the tradition of an elope-ment through a drawing-room window of Charlton House, insists that Sir Thomas Wilson decided to accept a marriage of which he did not approve. Yet if Sir Thomas did send his daughter on holiday knowing that she was to marry Perceval, it is strange that Jane managed to arrive at the altar dressed in her riding clothes. Whatever share Sir Thomas took in the affair, he soon accepted the *fait accompli*. 'You, I am sure, will be pleased to hear', wrote Spencer to Dudley Ryder, 'that Mrs. P. and myself have been to Charlton, on Sir T[homas]'s invitation, and were received with all the kindness and warmth that a very affectionate parent (as he certainly is) could bestow on his daughter. He also has told me that he will make up her fortune, just what it would have been had she married with his consent, and was not satisfied till he made us repeatedly assure him that we were convinced we had his full forgiveness.' 'In short', concluded the ecstatic Spencer, 'every everything that I could have wished and much more than I could have expected, has concurred to make the step I have just taken the happiest and most prosperous event of my life.'[3] The match was certainly happy, but it was scarcely immediately prosperous. As Jane's dowry was a frozen asset, the couple returned to London to live in lodgings over a carpet shop in Bedford Row. £21 was spent at Messrs. Christie and Barrow on one great celebration in port and sherry, after which they settled down to a sober and regular delivery of Kirkman, Brittleston, and William's beer.[4]

---

[1] *Gent. Mag.*, 1790, vol. II, p. 674; *Royal Kalendar*, 1791, p. 172.

[2] *Gent. Mag.*, 1790, vol. II, p. 764. Jane Wilson, who was born on 7 July 1769, was just twenty-one years of age and Perceval thirty at the time of their marriage.

[3] Walpole, vol. I, p. 12; Harrowby MSS., vol. VIII, fol. 146, Perceval to Dudley Ryder, undated but endorsed 'August 1790'.

[4] Bills in Perceval MSS.

(*a*) Spencer Perceval, aged 30

(*from Anthony Cardon's engraving of a miniature by Miles*)

(*b*) Jane Maryon Wilson

(*from a miniature by Andrew Plymer*)

PLATE I

The grant in April 1791 of the sinecure of surveyor of the meltings and clerk of the irons (worth a little over £100 a year) helped, but did not solve, Perceval's financial problems.[1] In the same month Spencer published anonymously *A Review of the Arguments in Favour of the Continuance of Impeachments notwithstanding a Dissolution*. Neither the cumbersome title nor the 123 learned pages of this pamphlet were likely to make it a best-seller. It was intended as an answer to Professor Edward Christian's *Examinations of Precedents and Principles* and discussed, with a wealth of illustrative material, the effect of the 1790 dissolution on the impeachment of Warren Hastings. 'We have perused this pamphlet', ran the notice in the *Monthly Review*, 'with singular satisfaction; and we have no hesitation in declaring it to be the most clear, candid, and masterly discussion of the subject that has yet fallen under our notice.' [2] Encouraged by this success Perceval produced in the following year, again anonymously, *The Duties and Powers of Public Officers with respect to Violations of the Public Peace*. This essential handbook for all good anti-Jacobins gave concise legal definitions of libel, unlawful assembly, sedition, and treason, as well as outlining the powers of magistrates, sheriffs, and private citizens in detecting and denouncing such crimes.[3]

It was, however, the outbreak of war with France and Pitt's repressive policy at home which first gave a fillip to Perceval's legal business. As junior counsel for the Crown he read the indictments at the trials of Tom Paine in 1792 and of Horne Tooke in 1794. Then attorney-general Scott sent him to Knutsford to lead a prosecution for publishing Paine's *Rights of Man*. Perceval handled the case with such skill that thereafter he became almost the midland deputy to the attorney-general. He was, in Cobbett's contemptuous words, Scott's 'understrapper'—'a short, spare, pale-faced, hard, keen, sour-looking man with a voice well suited to the rest'. Slowly, overcoming his earlier diffidence, he began to build up an appreciable private practice.[4]

The extra money was soon badly needed. On 23 October 1791 Jane

---

[1] *Gent. Mag.*, 1791, vol. I, p. 391; *Royal Kalendar*, 1794, p. 199.

[2] *Monthly Review*, Jan.–April 1791, p. 448.

[3] This pamphlet is not mentioned by Walpole but a copy in the Perceval MSS. is endorsed 'By Hon. Spencer Perceval'. The copy in the British museum is also attributed to him.

[4] Cobbett, *Regency and Reign of George IV*, p. 124; Howell, *State Trials*, vol. XXII, p. 357 and vol. XXV, p. 1. Perceval gained great credit for his handling of the defence of George Thomas of Brackley (Northamptonshire) on trial for forgery (*National Adviser*, 16–20 May 1812).

Perceval gave birth to her first child, a daughter, who was given her mother's name. In the following year there arrived a second girl, Frances, and in February 1794 a third, Maria. Their first son, Spencer, was born in 1795. When only a few days old he developed a serious and very painful disorder in his bowels. Doctors, nurses, and even his parents thought him on the point of death. Spencer wrote a special prayer; Jane and he joined in saying it, 'and by the blessing of God our boy was restored to us'. In the following year Jane bore another son, Frederick James, and then a third, Henry. 'I assure you', wrote Perceval to his brother-in-law, that the happiness of children 'is as great as anything in this world can produce'.[1]

After the birth of their second child the Percevals decided that they could afford to move from Bedford Row. Although their lodgings there had been convenient in many ways (they were near the proprietary chapel of St. John's, then a centre for London's evangelicals), it was not the place to rear a large family. They chose as their first house 59, Lincoln's Inn Fields, which had previously belonged to Baron Parry, and formed half of the old Lindsey House, originally built by Inigo Jones for Robert Bertie, first earl of Lindsey. A surveyor reported that it was in good condition, newly decorated throughout, and advised a bid of £4,550, a large sum for Perceval whose income by 1795 was just over £1,000 a year.[2] Arden did all he could to help, for, after a near miss in 1791, he succeeded, three years later, in persuading Chatham to accept Spencer as counsel to the admiralty. The basic salary was only £100 a year, but as a sign of government favour it was worth much more. Ministers, particularly Henry Dundas, began to throw out hints of a political career, all of which were politely ignored. As long as Jane continued to bear children, her husband was in no position to sacrifice a reliable, if moderate, income at the bar for the hazards of politics.

In the spring of 1794 (when the fear of French invasion first became acute) Perceval joined the Volunteers. He became a mounted trooper in the fashionable Light Horse Volunteers, a corps commanded by Colonel Charles Herries, which included in its ranks the duke of Montrose, the earl of Leicester, Richard Ryder, William Dundas,

[1] Walpole, vol. I, p. 83; Perceval MSS., Arden to Perceval, 20 July 1794; *Royal Kalendar*, 1798, p. 131; Perceval MSS., copy by Spencer Perceval junior of a paper written by his father on 11 Mar. 1800; *Gent. Mag.*, 1796, vol. II, p. 969; Perceval MSS., Perceval to Thomas Walpole, 3 Oct. 1804.

[2] *Gent. Mag.*, 1794, vol. I, p. 276; Overton, *op. cit.*, pp. 79–80; *The Estates Gazette*, 13 Nov. 1909; Perceval MSS., H. Cockerel to Perceval, 24 Oct. 1792.

(*a*) Lindsey House, Lincoln's Inn Fields

(*b*) Charlton House, Greenwich (1607)

PLATE 2

Nicholas Vansittart, and Charles Abbot.[1] The government, however, soon decided that Perceval could be more usefully employed than either trailing round the midland shires or parading in Hyde Park. In September 1795, Thomas Pelham, the chief secretary in Ireland, told Pitt that he wished to retire. The earl of Camden, then lord lieutenant, proposed his own nephew, Robert Stewart (later Lord Castlereagh), as his successor, but neither Pitt nor the duke of Portland, the home secretary, was convinced that he could overcome his 'Irish prejudices'. They nominated instead either Thomas Steele or Perceval. Unfortunately Steele's health was bad, and Camden preferred 'the willing Perceval to the driven Steele'. He insisted that the offer should be made as a choice 'between his prospects at the bar and the fame he may possibly acquire by a political pursuit, together with the certainty which I think I can offer him of a reversion . . . and if he determines in favour of coming here, he will come heartily and seriously intending to make the situation he will fill his constant study whilst he is here and his road to future political importance'.[2] Pitt made the formal offer on 2 January 1796 and enclosed a letter from Lord Spencer, the first lord of the admiralty, urging Perceval not to refuse because of 'misplaced diffidence'. On the following day Perceval sent off his reply. He was, he wrote, flattered by the prospect of an office 'so vastly beyond what I could have imagined would ever have been submitted to my choice. . . . If I had no interests to consider but my own, I should not from any private motive hesitate to accept it.' But the responsibility of his family ('already considerable in number, and in all human probability, likely to be increased') forced him to remain in his profession. 'For myself I could be easily satisfied; for my family I could not . . .' Even if Pitt was prepared to make an offer which would provide for his wife and children (the original proposal did include 'some provision of a permanent nature') Perceval would

[1] P.R.O., Bosanquet MSS., 30/3/23 and 30/3/2.

James Graham, third duke of Montrose (1755–1836), held minor offices under Pitt. He eventually became lord chamberlain.

George Townshend, earl of Leicester (1755–1811), also held various minor offices under Pitt before becoming lord steward of the household.

Richard Ryder (1766–1832) later became home secretary in Perceval's cabinet.

William Dundas (1762–1845) sat in the house of commons from 1796 to 1831 and was secretary at war in Pitt's second ministry.

Nicholas Vansittart (1766–1851) a supporter of Sidmouth who eventually succeeded Perceval as chancellor of the exchequer.

Charles Abbot, first baron Colchester (1757–1829), was Speaker of the house of commons from 1802 to 1816.

[2] P.R.O., Chatham MSS., 326/42–48–50.

still refuse. He felt that such terms 'would be so much too great for any service I could render to the public, that you could not grant them with any degree of credit to yourself, or indeed without the imputation of inexcusable profusion of the public money'. His determination not to go to Ireland was 'absolutely insurmountable'.[1] He decided instead to press his claims for a silk gown and wrote to Pitt on 24 January asking for permission to approach Lord Loughborough. 'I am encouraged to think,' he confessed, 'from what the Chancellor said to me near a twelve month ago, that he would not be unwilling to attend to an application from me. . . .' In fact, Loughborough had forgotten the hint and thought there were already too many K.C.'s on the midland circuit, 'but', he admitted, 'I have so strong a persuasion that your talents require only the opportunity of being more displayed to be admired that . . . I shall have great pleasure in submitting your application to His Majesty.' Finally at a meeting of the council of Lincoln's Inn, held on 26 February 1796, Perceval was elected a bencher of the Inn.[2] After ten years' work on the midland circuit, the thirty-four-year-old barrister had successfully established himself in his profession.

[1] Perceval MSS., Pitt to Perceval, 2 Jan. 1796 and Perceval to Pitt, 3 Jan. 1796. For full text see Walpole, vol. I, pp. 20–5.

[2] P.R.O., Chatham MSS., 326/166, Perceval to Pitt, 24 Jan. 1796; Perceval MSS., Lord Loughborough to Perceval, 24 Jan. 1796; *Black Book of Lincoln's Inn*, vol. IV, p. 66.

CHAPTER TWO

AN ODIOUS EVANGELICAL

SYDNEY SMITH once wrote of Perceval that he had 'the head of a country parson, and the tongue of an Old Bailey lawyer'.[1] Unfortunately Smith's two greatest phobias were religious enthusiasts and Pittite politicians: Spencer Perceval was both. This is perhaps one of the reasons why his personality has never emerged from the shadows. A lawyer, a strict conservative, and an evangelical does not seem a prepossessing mixture. Yet he was in fact personally one of the most attractive figures of his age. Physically his most striking features were his size and his complexion. It is impossible to say exactly how tall he was, but nearly everyone who met him comments on his smallness. Eldon called him 'little P', while Sheridan was inspired to one of his happiest impromptus—

> I, the chance poet of an idle hour,
> With thee in verse will battle, when George Rose
> Shall hate employment and demand repose;
> When Trotter shall the prince of lies outfib,
> And Spencer Perceval shall challenge Cribb.[2]

He was unusually pale and only emphasised it by habitually dressing in black. Smith called him the 'sepulchral Spencer Perceval' or the 'sallow Surveyor of the Meltings'.[3] Judging by the few existing portraits of him it would be difficult to say that he was good-looking, for his mouth was ugly and too wide for his small round face. Lord Holland thought that, except when he smiled, he looked very like Robespierre.[4] He was naturally cautious and distrustful of innovation,

---

[1] *Letters of Peter Plymley* (ed. E. G. Heseltine), p. 7.

[2] Quoted in Treherne, *The Rt. Hon. Spencer Perceval*, p. 22.

George Rose (1744–1814), a politician and pamphleteer who was almost continuously in one office or another from 1777 to 1812.

Alexander Trotter was the paymaster who mingled public accounts with his own and was a witness at the impeachment of Lord Melville.

Tom Cribb (1781–1848) was the heavyweight boxing champion of Great Britain.

[3] *Letters of Peter Plymley*, p. 35.

[4] Holland, *Memoirs of the Whig Party*, vol. II, p. 215. Thomas Fletcher described him as 'a small slender man of a pale complexion with an intelligent

thinking too little respect was paid to the wisdom of the ages. 'I am sorry to say', he once told fellow-members of the *Crown and Rolls*, 'that we live at a time when to be unprecedented and paradoxical is to have no mean title and pretentions to support, no inconsiderable recommendation to favour—when men adopt opinions as they choose their dresses, according to the mode of the hour; when nothing is followed but what is fashionable and nothing esteemed fashionable but what is new . . . and I must own that I am old-fashioned enough to think, and hardy enough to avow the thought, that this age, enriched as it ought to be by experience, and wise as it is in its own conceit, is not the only age in which wisdom has shewn herself to man; that there have been in former days, men who could think, who could act, who could reason, who could legislate, who could profit by the experience of those who preceeded them; and were not disinclined to study, nor unable to protect, the interests of that posterity which now with so much gratitude condemns them.' ¹ Such an attitude could easily lead to mere bitterness and despair, and at times of crisis Perceval certainly felt the temptation. 'If it were desirable to preserve anything of our ancient and venerable establishments,' he once wrote, 'it could only be effected by making a stand against every fresh attempt at innovation': 'there is no being sure', he told a friend, 'of anybody in these times'.² But generally he remained sanguine. 'My criticism of life', he assured his brother-in-law Redesdale, 'like Horace's of poetry leads me to say *"ubi plura nitent in carmine, non ego paucis offendar"*.' ³

He had both the virtues and the vices belonging to an evangelical. Roberts chose him as 'the model of a Christian gentleman', a man 'not resting in the formal profession, or a lifeless orthodoxy, but illustrating the Gospel by his public adoption of its verities, and his practical submission to its precepts. . . . He might be said to have been Christianity personified.' ⁴ Wilberforce thought his generosity unbounded; 'I don't mean merely in giving away money, but in a much higher and larger sense.' What spare money he had he gave away gladly and, as far as possible, anonymously. As soon as he moved

---

and pleasing expression of countenance' (quoted in C. R. Fay, *Huskisson and his Age*, p. 378).

¹ Perceval MSS., draft of speech at the *Crown and Rolls*.

² *Parl. Deb.*, vol. VIII, p. 124; Rose, vol. II, pp. 489–91.

³ Perceval MSS., Perceval to Redesdale, 7 Jan. 1804. The quotation from Horace's *De Arte Poetica* has been translated by Conington as—'But when I meet with beauties thickly sown, a blot or two I readily condone'.

⁴ William Roberts, *The Portraiture of a Christian Gentleman*, pp. 169–70.

to Lincoln's Inn Fields he told the local parish clerk to relieve such poor people as he saw fit and send the bill to him afterwards. Anthony Rosenhagen, one of Perceval's private secretaries after 1809, was regularly making allowances out of the Perceval family budget—£20 a year to a Mrs. Wegg, and another £20 to a Mr. Dickinson, as well as paying for the schooling of one of his children. When a Mr. Stoddart, a Northamptonshire clergyman, was found to be ineligible for an office which had been promised him, Perceval regularly paid him the amount of the salary out of his own pocket.[1] He had little time for some of the most fashionable pursuits of his day, thinking that both gambling and hunting were wrong in principle and were a waste of money. 'Lord Sefton gives up the Quorn Hounds,' he wrote to Thomas Walpole. 'This is nothing to you, but it is an event to the sporting gentlemen. If nobody takes them up it may save the pockets of some young men, as many have been ruined there.'[2] Richard Ryder, having hurt himself in a fall from his horse, got a long lecture instead of sympathy. 'You are no more fit to be trusted on horseback than a child. . . . I dare say your accident was occasioned either by the folly of your riding a-hunting, or the still greater folly of riding as madly as a hunter, without the same excuse. If it happened in hunting, it is too bad for a man of your sense, age, and understanding to be such a dolt as to follow other people's pleasures, for you have too good sense to suffer it to be your own.'[3] But this was nothing compared with Dudley Ryder's offence in losing £800 at faro. 'The Pharaoh banks are so many traps set for all the birds they can catch —you are wary or you are strong; you risk only the loss of an ornamental plume, or an overgrown talon; but a weaker race dash headlong into the heart of it, and expose at once their liberty and life to its grasp. . . . Only suppose that instead of having flung these £800 into the sink of a Pharaoh-bank, you had distributed them in equal shares to 80 poor housekeepers. . . . Now do but think over and over again of the number 80. How many units go to make that sum, 80 families with suppose only 4 to a family—320 fellow creatures—think of it a little in its detail, of widows, orphans etc. raised from a pinching state of penury to a comfortable existence.'[4]

<hr />

[1] J. S. Harford, *Recollections of William Wilberforce*, p. 18; Perceval MSS., A. Rosenhagen to Mrs. Perceval, undated (after 12 May 1812). Perceval was a keen supporter of the Shoreditch Refuge for the Destitute (*Courier*, 12 Feb. 1812); *Sun*, 8 Aug. 1810.   [2] Perceval MSS., Perceval to Thos. Walpole, 10 Oct. 1804.
[3] *Ibid.*, Perceval to Richard Ryder, 24 Nov. 1806.
[4] Harrowby MSS., Perceval to Dudley Ryder, Jan. 1793.

His evangelicalism affected his public as much as his private life. He always wished to make adultery a punishable offence and never wavered in his support for the abolition of the slave trade. He normally refused to see legal clients on a Sunday, and although in cases of particular urgency he did dispense with this rule, he always postponed the consultation until after evening service.[1] In later life he even once put off the re-assembly of parliament so that members should not be forced to travel over the week-end. His fervent sense of religion compelled him to rebuke the Commons for their 'discreditably thin' attendance at divine service on the anniversary of Charles I's execution, and, as prime minister, he persuaded the treasury to stand the cost of distributing 'suitable' religious books to sick and wounded soldiers, to grant a yearly annuity of £100 for life out of public funds to missionaries in North America and the West Indies, to repair Whitehall Chapel so that it could seat the King's Guard during services, and to reform the system of appointing army chaplains at the sacrifice of considerable treasury patronage. The Percevals daily said family prayers together, and after becoming prime minister, Spencer wrote a special prayer for Divine Guidance in his efforts. 'My charge', he wrote, 'is great and my strength little.' [2] Like many of the 'weaker vessels among the evangelicals' he was a keen student of biblical prophecy. 'It has been a study,' he once confessed, 'which in a very superficial way I have pursued for some time, with what profit I know not, but certainly with the greatest entertainment to myself.' [3] He was a great admirer of the works of William Hales, and himself wrote six anonymous letters in defence of prophecy to the *Orthodox Churchman's Magazine*.[4] Yet he was, in spite of his evangelicalism, a very orthodox Anglican. Liberal Anglicans like Dr. Herbert Marsh were sometimes tempted to denounce him as a 'fanatic' while dissenters often thought of him as 'a High Church bigot'. Perceval took both

---

[1] *National Adviser*, 20–23 May 1812.

[2] R. I. and S. Wilberforce, *The Life of William Wilberforce*, vol. III, pp. 397–8; Windsor MSS., 14021–2, Lord Hawkesbury to George III, 9 Dec. 1808; 14889–90, Perceval to George III, 20 Jan. 1810; P.R.O., T27/66/243, T29/95/312, T29/111/475, T29/108/68–74; Perceval MSS., Porteus, bishop of London to Perceval, 29 Feb. 1808.

[3] *Ibid.*, Perceval to R. Bosanquet, no date.

[4] Overton, *The English Church in the 19th Century*, p. 182; Perceval MSS. Perceval wrote in his letters to the *Orthodox Churchman's Magazine*, 'I have been so forcibly impressed with the advantages to be derived to the world from making that study a more general pursuit, that, if any observations of mine can have that effect, I am persuaded I cannot perform a more useful work for mankind.'

charges with perfect good humour. 'I am rather glad', he wrote to his former tutor, Dr. Mansel, 'to have what the lawyers call a sort of set off—and vanity is alert enough to hail the two charges as a proof of moderation.'[1] Certainly he was far removed from methodism, although not quite far enough to avert the wrath of Sydney Smith.

Unlike many contemporary evangelicals he held a perfectly clear and logical view about the church. He completely rejected the liberal and dissenting doctrine (admitted by many first generation evangelicals) that any society professing belief in Christ is a church in itself, and clung passionately to the church of England as established by law. In her name he bitterly opposed Roman catholic emancipation, in her interests he framed his education policy, and for her good he tried to introduce many measures of reform. 'He is', said Grattan once at an opposition dinner, 'a bigot in religion, which is to be disapproved, but there is sincerity in what he does and upon such a subject, when that is the case, allowance is to be made.' Allowance has, however, rarely been made. 'He was', said Holland, 'a bitter persecutor of such political and religious principles as he without much painful inquiry or dispassionate reflection disapproved. . . .' 'His religious feelings were mingled with so much bigotry,' wrote the *Edinburgh Review*, 'that he was quite incapable of viewing the claims of the Catholics with the eye of a statesman. He felt against their faith all the zeal of a sectary. . . . He thought his cause was the cause of heaven; the Irish priests think the same of their cause. All bigots and fanatics in all ages have been of the same opinion.'

During his early days in politics he relied, perhaps, too much on the opinions of his fiery brother-in-law, Redesdale, particularly on Irish questions.[2] But by the time the first catholic petition was presented in the spring of 1805 he had formed his own views on the relations between church and state. His speech in the Commons on 13 May was the most important he ever made on the issue of emancipation. Some members had in the debate used a variant of the 'Natural Rights' argument; religious questions were solely between God and each man's conscience. Any legislature was tyrannical that imposed forfeiture of civil rights, exclusion from office, or other penalty on those whose religious views differed from those adopted by that legislature. 'Dissenters', replied Perceval, 'had every right to full and

---

[1] Perceval MSS., Perceval to Mansel, 6 Feb. 1812.
[2] Holland, *Further Memoirs of the Whig Party*, p. 132; *Edinburgh Review*, July 1812, p. 29. For Redesdale's influence see chapter 5, pp. 51–2.

perfect toleration in the exercise of their religion', but they had no natural right to political power. The nation, through parliament, had a full and unquestionable right to give political power and office to such persons and on such terms and conditions as it judged 'most expedient to the general security of the Constitution at large'. If parliament believed that people professing certain religious opinions were a threat to any part of that constitution, then it was its duty to exclude them from such offices and authority which might facilitate their designs. Hostility to the established church was alone sufficient to evoke this ban, for, as Croker once put it, Westminster abbey was part of the British constitution. Other supporters of emancipation argued that, although under certain conditions the nation had the right to apply tests of fitness to hold office, such a right arose out of necessity and ceased with it. By the early nineteenth century, they contended, all necessity for tests against Roman catholics had ended, for catholicism was no longer a danger to the state. The real threat, answered Perceval, had never been the Pope as an individual, but the Pope as an instrument of a great power hostile to Great Britain.[1] The Pope, he thought, was now Napoleon's puppet: 'a poor old man dragged with so much degradation to Paris to play so painful a part in an impious farce'. Yet the Roman catholic church might use French conquests to spread its doctrines. Although it had been argued that the age was too enlightened to permit the spread of catholicism, Perceval saw too much indifference among the upper classes and infidelity among the lower to accept this conclusion. Again it was claimed that the extension of catholicism was not dangerous because it was 'just as useful a bugbear for the vulgar'. This, replied Perceval, was to degrade and make nonsense of all religion. Finally, supporters of emancipation argued that parliament had removed so many disabilities that it was unjust to retain the rest.[2] Two answers were given by Perceval to this. Any further concessions which admitted Roman

---

[1] Perceval returned to this point on 4 Mar. 1807 in a speech on the report stage of the grant for Maynooth College. 'The revolution in France and its consequences have shaken to its foundations the Roman Catholic religion in Europe; have degraded the supreme head of that infallible church into the lowest and most abject sycophant, the most subservient vassal and instrument of the bloodiest and most unexampled tyrant who ever trampled on every principle of right, of morality, and religion' (*Parl. Deb.*, VIII, 1079; Perceval MSS. draft of speech). For a similar version of the argument, see *Quarterly Review*, Nov. 1809, pp. 303–6.

[2] The Roman catholics were excluded from sitting in parliament and could not be appointed to the following offices: lord lieutenant, keeper of the seal, lord high treasurer, chief justice of king's bench or common pleas, lord chief baron or

catholics to parliament and allowed them to hold high political, legal, and military offices, to take part in local government and to present to church livings would endanger the church of England and so endanger the welfare of the state. Furthermore, even these reforms would not, as many imagined, finally satisfy the Irish catholics. No concession suggested in the 1805 petition would affect the catholic 'lower orders'. The petition by itself would mean a seat in parliament for Lord Fingall and a troop in the Guards for Mr. Bryan. As the catholic leader, Cornelius Keogh, put it, 'to satisfy the people of Ireland, there must be means adopted which the poor man will feel in his cabin'. This meant a change not merely of men but of the total system of government, the abolition of tithes, the annulling of all corporate bodies and 'the resumption of the immense misapplied revenue of the intrusive church'. It was to avoid change on this scale that Perceval wished, as he told Wilberforce, 'to let the Roman Catholic know that he has got as much as a Protestant Parliament can give him, and that he must be contented'. 'I will not shrink', he ended his speech against the 1805 petition, 'from the false imputation of bigotry. . . . I therefore oppose the present motion. I oppose it not because I suspect the loyalty or impeach the morality of the petitioners; not because I am unwilling to conciliate the Roman Catholics, and to give them satisfaction, if that were possible; not because I do not earnestly desire to tranquillise Ireland; but because I am absolutely convinced that the measure proposed . . . would not effectually conciliate them . . . [but] would necessarily and immediately lead to and encourage other demands.'[1] In the existing circumstances Perceval opposed any new concession, but he always denied that his opposition

---

chancellor of the exchequer, judge in four courts or of admiralty, master of the rolls, secretary of state, Irish secretary, privy councillor, king's counsel, sergeant, attorney- or solicitor-general, master in chancery, provost or fellow of Trinity College, Dublin, postmaster-general, master and lieutenant general of the ordnance, commander-in-chief, or general on the staff. They were also excluded from the offices of custos rotulorum or governors of counties, sheriff, mayor, bailiff, recorder, burgess or other municipal office. No catholic could act as guardian to a protestant and catholic priests could not act as guardians at all. Catholics could not normally bear arms, or present to a church living. Finally the pecuniary qualification to act as juror was higher for catholics than for protestants (*Edinburgh Review*, Oct. 1807, p. 121).

[1] For a full text of Perceval's speech of 11 May 1805 see D. M. Perceval, *The Church Question in Ireland* (London, 1844); Wilberforce, vol. II, pp. 17–19; Cornelius Keogh, *A Commentary on the Grenville Manifesto* (London, 1810). Many of Perceval's arguments were suggested in a letter from Redesdale of 25 Nov. 1804 (Perceval MSS.).

c

to emancipation was eternal. In the debate on the Union in 1801 he had hinted at eventual emancipation, and, speaking on the 1808 petition, he begged 'to be distinctly understood, that if there should be such an alteration in the affairs of the world, or in the nature of this religion itself . . . then, consistently with what I have done and am now doing, I may assent to the propriety of adopting some measure for the purpose of granting what the Catholics may then seek'.[1] For the present he concentrated on fostering the Irish establishment 'for the gradual diminution of papal error' by trying to solve the tithe problem, build glebe houses, and oppose future unions of parishes. He consistently fought all attempts to increase the grant to Maynooth, the training college for Roman catholic priests, claiming that it played a predominant role in saving catholicism from 'ruin and extinction'.[2] His attitude to protestant dissenters was far more liberal. Thus when Sidmouth, in 1812, tried to revise the Toleration Act in a way offensive to the dissenters, Perceval received and treated their deputations with great courtesy and successfully opposed Sidmouth's bill in parliament.

Where the interests of the church of England were concerned Perceval also played a much more constructive role, and was indeed the first politician to attempt to alter the distribution of church property since the outbreak of the French Revolution.[3] 'I must do Mr. Perceval the justice to say,' wrote Cobbett in the *Political Register*, 'that he is the only member of Parliament that I know of, who has spoken upon the subject of non-residence in suitable terms.'[4] Sir William Scott's Non-Residence Bill of 1802 had, *inter alia*, extended the period of permitted absence from one to three months and given the bishops power to excuse any clergyman from residing within his parish. Perceval, then attorney-general, opposed both clauses in debate, but failed to carry the House with him.[5] The following year Scott introduced a Stipendiary Curates Bill which would have compelled non-resident clergy to pay an adequate salary to the curate left in charge of the living. The bill, hotly opposed by pluralists and unpopular at Oxford, was twice rejected and finally abandoned by Scott himself. Three days later Pitt assured the Speaker that Perceval, 'who was

---

[1] For the 1801 speech see chapter 4, pp. 43–4. For the 1808 speech see *Parl. Deb.*, XI, 624.

[2] Perceval MSS., draft of cabinet memorandum (undated, but probably 1810).

[3] For Sidmouth's bill see Pellew, pp. 38–62 and Add. MSS., 38246, fol. 341; 38247, fols. 50, 82, 84, 102, 163, 176, 185, 201, 244 and 248.

[4] *Political Register*, 25 July 1807.

[5] Wilberforce, vol. III, pp. 49 and 102.

not so easily intimidated', had agreed to sponsor the reform.[1] At the end of April 1805 Perceval introduced a bill giving bishops power to enforce residence in all livings under £400 a year and, when the living exceeded that sum, compelling the rector to pay his resident curate a minimum of £200 a year. For once Perceval felt the frustrations of a reformer. The opposition, to its discredit, bitterly attacked the bill, Porchester denouncing it as 'unprincipled, incoherent, and wicked'. It was, he assured an astonished Perceval, 'founded upon the antient jacobin principle'. In the end the bill was mangled and lost in the Lords.[2] On 14 April 1806 Perceval tried again, this time from the opposition benches, with even less success. During the debate on the second reading Sir John Wrottesley moved the bill's rejection while the indefatigable Porchester warned the House that 'it was a serious thing to degrade and destroy so large a portion of the middle classes of the people'. Wilberforce did his best to support Perceval, but when Fox himself proved hostile, the bill was lost in a thin House by 25 votes to 13.[3] Even Mansel, Perceval's old tutor, joined the opposition. 'The University', he wrote, 'is in considerable agitation about your bill.' The vice-chancellor found it alarming that Perceval proposed to pay curates in proportion to the value of the benefice instead of in proportion to the value of their services, 'according to which rate all clerks and assistants are usually paid'. Curates, it was argued, would forget 'old connections of kindness' with their rector and readily desert him to serve in a more lucrative neighbouring living.[4] After this rebuff Perceval decided to bide his time. There was, he realised, no hope of success while the Talents remained in office, but he had no intention of conceding defeat. 'If the attempt is given up by me,' he told Mansel, 'there is no chance that my objects will ever be obtained at all, as no other person is likely to pursue them but myself.'[5]

As soon as he had settled into office under Portland he returned to the attack. In the spring of 1808 his third bill proposed that, in cases of non-residence, the curate should be paid one-fifth of the value of the living, provided he did not receive more than a maximum of £250

---

[1] Colchester, vol. I, pp. 545–6. Lord Harrowby calculated that in 1807 no less than 4,113 out of 7,167 livings worth more than £150 a year were held by non-resident clergy and, by 1808, that 2,438 out of 3,997 livings with a stipend of under £150 a year were non-residentiary (*Substance of a Speech of the Earl of Harrowby delivered in the House of Lords, June 18 1810.* London, 1811).
[2] *Parl. Deb.*, IV, 5 and 612, and V, 154 and 737.
[3] *Ibid.*, VI, 741 and 922–7.
[4] Perceval MSS., Mansel to Perceval, 25 Apr. 1806.
[5] *Ibid.*, Perceval to Mansel, 30 Dec. 1806.

a year. In order to rally opinion he published a pamphlet explaining the aims of the bill. His ideal, he wrote, was to see a resident officiating minister of the church of England in every parish in the kingdom. 'I confidently deny that his mere duty is to read prayers, to preach a sermon, to christen, to marry and to bury.' He must be an example to his parishioners and a source of charity and so 'rescued from that contempt to which, under a state of indigence, he is inevitably exposed'.[1] Again the opposition rallied against reform. Porchester, continuing his personal vendetta against the bill, reached new heights of extravagance. It was, he claimed, 'the most unconstitutional that was ever submitted to the consideration of Parliament'. He saw Perceval as 'the organ of a secret influence behind the altar', seeking to introduce 'a system of rigorous puritanism, the unfailing source of unconquerable bigotry and rancerous persecution'.[2] In the *Edinburgh Review* and in his *Letters of Peter Plymley* Sydney Smith sank to cheap and irrelevant sneers.[3] Rarely can so threadbare a case have been argued with such vehemence. During the committee stage in the Commons Creevey talked of 'this system of robbery' and compared the bill with 'the worst acts of the worst period of the French Revolution'. It took Burdett himself to surpass even this nonsense. 'Poverty', he declared, 'had hitherto been the badge of honour of religion.' Perceval, by enriching curates, sought to alienate them from the masses. He ended by exhorting the 'gentlemen of England' to rally to the cause of nonresident clergy, 'this defenceless portion of the community'. In spite of such hysteria the bill passed the Commons, only to be defeated without a division on its third reading in the Lords.[4] All a discouraged Perceval could do was submit the facts of clerical poverty to the king

[1] Perceval, *A Letter to the Rev. Dr. Mansel*, London, 1808, p. 21; Perceval MSS., Perceval to Mansel, 14 Apr. 1808. Abbot, the Speaker, undertook to distribute the pamphlet 'to my most influential Oxford friends' (Perceval MSS., Abbot to Perceval, 20 Oct. 1808). *The Sun* (14 Apr. 1808) welcomed the bill as likely to increase the 'active zeal' of the establishment, 'and thereby check the growth of Methodism, which has prodigiously increased within the last few years'.

[2] *Parl. Deb.*, XI, 54; Hist. MSS. Comm. *Dropmore MSS.*, vol. VIII, p. 199. 'I most heartily wish this bill success', wrote Cobbett. 'Mr. Perceval has always been respected by me on account of this bill: and his persevering in it through all situations . . . . This, indeed is a step in the way of a *real* reform' (*Political Register*, 16 Apr. 1808, p. 597).

[3] Heseltine, *Letters of Peter Plymley*, p. 15; *Edinburgh Review*, Oct. 1808, pp. 26–34. Smith began his article with the famous sentence—'The poverty of curates has long been a favourite theme with novelists, sentimental tourists and elegiac poets'.

[4] *Parl. Deb.*, XI, 835–41, 877, 958 and 1135.

and recommend a grant of £100,000 a year for four years to raise all livings to a minimum of £50 a year.[1]

In many other less spectacular ways, Perceval showed his zeal for church reform. In 1811 he produced the first plan for building churches in the new industrial towns, although, because of financial difficulties, the idea was not presented to parliament until after his death.[2] He did much to further missionary work and to support the newly formed Bible Society. Early in 1808 he was largely responsible for defeating an attempt by the East India company to restrict missionary work within its territory. 'Mr. Perceval', wrote a grateful Wilberforce, 'has stood our friend.'[3] When Raymond Johnson, the evangelical missionary, returned from New South Wales, Perceval, after reading an account of his work, gave him unsolicited a living worth above £200 a year.[4] He was also one of the earliest and keenest supporters of the claims of the church of England to control popular education, playing a decisive role in founding the church's National Society in opposition to the Lancastrian Society. In the winter of 1810 Joseph Lancaster visited Northampton and persuaded a town meeting to set up a school 'in which bigotry and intolerance should have no share'. Perceval, when approached by the mayor, refused his support. Instead he helped the bishop of Durham to draft the original circular to all Anglican clergy calling for the establishment of the National Society and used his influence with the post office to secure its distribution. Moreover, after an appeal from Manners Sutton, the archbishop of Canterbury, Perceval persuaded the Prince Regent to withdraw his earlier patronage of Lancaster in favour of Bell's Madras system. It was Perceval's most important and least happy intervention in educational problems.[5]

Above all Perceval worked very closely with his fellow evangelicals, the Saints, particularly on colonial and slavery issues. His first meeting with James Stephen followed immediately upon the publication in March 1807 of the report on the commercial state of the West Indies.[6]

[1] Windsor MSS., 14435-7, Perceval to George III, 25 May 1809; *Annual Register*, 1809, p. 344.

[2] Harrowby MSS., vol. 18, fol. 315, Sir John Nicholl to Perceval, 7 Sep. 1811.

[3] Wilberforce, vol. III, p. 359. Perceval also supported the missionary cause when the East India company's charter came up for renewal in 1812 (Wilberforce, vol. IV, p. 13).

[4] Wilberforce, vol. III, p. 458.

[5] Perceval MSS., George Baker to Perceval, 27 Nov. 1810; bishop of Durham to same, 27 Aug. 1811; archbishop of Canterbury to same, 23 Aug. 1811.

[6] *Parl. Deb.*, IX; *Parl. Papers*, LXXXI; Perceval MSS., Stephen to Perceval, 17 Aug. 1807.

In November he and Perceval worked out a scheme for giving religious instruction to all negroes hired by the government, in spite of opposition from local governors and army commanders. 'Unhappily for the negroes', wrote Stephen, 'the West Indians whom you see here in the house of commons, or in private circles, are a very different kind of animal from those who govern slaves in our islands.'[1] Early in 1808, after Stephen and Wilberforce had complained of evasions of abolition, Perceval became a founder-member of the African Institution, which aimed at safeguarding the Abolition Act.[2] The British alliance with Spain and Portugal spurred the Saints to further efforts. In the summer of 1808 Stephen, recently returned to parliament through Perceval's influence, urged that we should offer to restore Trinidad in exchange for a Spanish pledge to end their slave trade. But although Wilberforce and Zachary Macaulay brought similar pressure, all Perceval could do was to send special instructions to British officials in Trinidad and at Demerara to put down illegal slave trading.[3] A year later, after prompting from Stephen, Perceval persuaded the admiralty to agree to use naval vessels to put down illegal slavers by patrolling the coast of Sierra Leone.[4] Still the Saints were not satisfied, but the tottering Portland ministry was too preoccupied with its own problems to bother about the West Indies. In April 1810 Stephen even threatened to apply for the chiltern hundreds unless the cabinet sponsored a slave registry bill for Trinidad. He never doubted, he wrote, Perceval's own zeal for the cause, but abolitionists had long suspected the good faith of some of the new prime minister's colleagues.[5] On 15 May Wilberforce decided to introduce a private members bill and was hurt when Perceval cut short his attempt to explain the bill's provisions in the House.[6] With more enthusiasm than discretion, the Saints kept up their pressure on the harassed minister. In September 1810 a special West Indian commission was instituted with instructions from Perceval to investigate all alleged evasions of abolition. At first Stephen had wanted Babington, Zachary Macaulay, Henry Thornton, and Wilberforce to be members, only to be reminded that many of Pitt's Friends would object if the commission were packed with Saints. Wilberforce

---

[1] Perceval MSS., same to same, 30 Nov. 1807.

[2] *Ibid.*, same to same, 13 Jan. 1808; Wilberforce, vol. III, pp. 348 and 360.

[3] Perceval MSS., same to same, 17 July 1808; Wilberforce, vol. III, pp. 372 and 382.   [4] Perceval MSS., same to same, 9 Aug. 1809.

[5] *Ibid.*, same to same, 19 Apr. 1810.

[6] Wilberforce, vol. III, p. 445; Perceval MSS., Wilberforce to Perceval, 29 Apr. 1810.

then suggested Lansdowne, Grenville, Grey, Whitbread, and Brougham, until Perceval protested that it would be even worse to pack it with members of the opposition.[1] Finally, Stephen demanded the immediate recall of Hislop, the governor of Trinidad, for his treatment of freed negroes.[2] Had Perceval agreed every West Indian in the Commons would have voted to bring his government down. What the abolitionists failed to see was that the prime minister was going as fast as his own survival permitted; at times, admitted Wilberforce, the more fiery Saints were inclined to be 'unjust towards so staunch an abolitionist'.[3]

Perceval's spotless private life was one of his greatest assets in his later political career. In society he was 'easy, cheerful, playful and unassuming' and never lost his delight in a good hoax.[4] He set a new standard in fair-dealing and candour in politics, even at times to the detriment of his own interests. But it was on his family life that his friends loved most to dwell. His constant devotion to Jane and pride in his children, his piety and his honesty endeared him to the rising commercial and middle classes. Like George III, Perceval shared and expressed their standards. The splendour of Carlton and the wit of Holland House could not outshine the good sense and sobriety of a man who joined in all his children's games, 'was beloved without a sensation of fear, and was never so happy as when playing in the midst of them'. He was one of the first public figures in the nineteenth century to illustrate the importance of being earnest.

> Such was his private, such his public life,
> That all who differ'd in polemic strife,
> Or varied in opinion with his plan,
> Agreed with one accord to love the man.[5]

---

[1] P.R.O. T29/108/127; Perceval MSS., Stephen to Perceval, 24, 25, and 28 Sep. 1810.   [2] Perceval MSS., Stephen to Perceval, 20 Sep. 1810.

[3] *Ibid.*, Wilberforce to Perceval, 26 Apr. 1810. In April 1810 Perceval wrote to the foreign secretary, Wellesley, urging him to bring pressure on the Spaniards 'as a point of feeling private and national as much as upon higher principles even of humanity, justice, benevolence, and religion' to abolish the slave trade. This was not, however, to be made a *sine qua non* of further aid 'considering the state of mistaken prejudice on that subject' (Add. MSS., 37295, fol. 274).

[4] *Anonymous Memoir*, pages not numbered. James Stephen once suggested the dropping of propaganda leaflets on France by balloon. 'I thought the scheme', he wrote to Perceval, 'too open at first sight to ridicule to be hastily suggested to a grave politician, much more to one so good at a hoax as yourself' (Perceval MSS., Stephen to Perceval, 6 Aug. 1809).

[5] *Universal Sympathy or The Martyr'd Statesman*, Anon. poem, 1812.

CHAPTER THREE

MEMBER FOR NORTHAMPTON

THE borough of Northampton had, in the late eighteenth century, a well-deserved reputation as one of the most tumultuous parliamentary constituencies in the country. In 1768 the earls of Northampton, Halifax, and Spencer are said to have spent £250,000 on a single election, while Spencer threw in the complete contents of his cellar. The result strained the finances of all three families. The Spencers decided in future not to interfere in borough elections, Halifax was forced to sell his estates in the county, and the eighth earl of Northampton retired for life to Switzerland in order to economise.[1] But his son, Lord Charles Compton (who was returned as senior member and who held his seat in 1790), carried on the family interest. All householders not in receipt of poor relief had the right to vote for the town's two members, and, in the 1790's, three political groups competed for their support—the Comptons at Castle Ashby, the closed corporation, and a group of local whigs. They were so evenly matched that no single interest could control both seats. Not even a Compton-corporation alliance could easily eliminate the third party, for the local whigs had a strong hand to play. Their leader, Edward Bouverie (a son of Lord Radnor and the owner of Delapré Abbey), was generally respected as 'an upright, assiduous, and independent man'.[2] His supporters rallied under the cry of 'the independence of the borough' and were organised into an 'Independent Electors Club'.[3] In 1790 Bouverie won the second seat and thereafter usually voted with Fox in the house of commons. Northampton politics had thus reached a stalemate. Either all three local interests could continue to put forward candidates (and leave the issue to be settled by the second votes) or Castle Ashby and the corporation could decide not to contest the second seat.

The situation was further complicated when the party struggle

---

[1] *Complete Peerage*, vol. IX, p. 686. Halifax sold his Northamptonshire estates to Sir Robert Gunning (Farington, vol. III, p. 111).

[2] Markham and Cox, *Records of the Borough of Northampton*, vol. II, p. 509.

[3] *Northampton Mercury*, 20 Aug. 1796, 31 May 1800, 20 Nov. 1802, and 25 June 1803.

extended to municipal affairs. Under the existing borough charter the Northampton corporation consisted of the mayor, aldermen, bailiffs, and a common council of forty-eight members. In practice, the aldermen had come to control the common council and had left it with so little real authority that the local whigs decided to refuse to accept election to it. This policy of boycott soon proved so effective that by 1791 the common council had been reduced to nineteen members. Only rapid and effective action could defeat what had become a threat to the continued existence of the corporation. The charter prescribed fines in cases of refusal to serve, but this raised two serious legal questions. Were the provisions of the charter secure enough to withstand a case in court of law, or should the aldermen use some other authority to justify their fines? And could defaulters be fined more than once (or even annually) for refusal to attend? Perceval was asked, as deputy recorder, to give an opinion on both issues. He strongly advised caution and conciliation. If new elections were held, less obstinate members might be elected; those who persisted in nonattendance could then legally be fined. As an alternative he suggested an appeal to the court of king's bench for a mandamus to compel attendance. If the court agreed to issue a summons, the opposition would probably collapse, or if the court refused to do so, then the judges would at least advise the corporation what further action it could legally take.[1] Consequently new elections were held (probably under the threat of a mandamus), but three staunch whigs still held firm and accepted the appeal to king's bench. They admitted that they would have been bound to serve had they been legally elected. In fact, they argued, their election was not legal, because it lacked the required absolute majority of the common council of forty-eight. They also challenged, on similar grounds, the election of the mayor. The verdict threw Northampton into an uproar, for the court upheld the defendants plea, declared the corporation to be incapable of legally electing any new officers and, consequently, to be in a state of dissolution.

The corporation immediately petitioned for a new charter to be based on the provisions of the old while the opposition argued that there should be a town meeting to frame the new clauses. The whigs, therefore, decided to call a great meeting of their supporters, which had to be held in the shire hall as the mayor refused them the use of the town hall. A committee was set up to oppose the re-creation of the

[1] The town clerk endorsed the case, 'Mr. P. refused to take his fee of 3 guineas which I offered him'.

old closed corporation and a petition, said to contain 500 signatures, was got up to be presented by Bouverie to the king. For a while feeling in the town ran high as both parties used the usual inflammatory handbills.[1] Yet the struggle ended in complete victory for the corporation. Bouverie's petition had so little effect that, in November 1795, the opposition committee decided to disband rather than oppose individual clauses in the new charter. On 6 April 1796 Lord Compton, John Hall (the mayor), John Markham (a local attorney), and Perceval arrived by coach with the charter. All the adherents of Castle Ashby and of the corporation gathered to cheer the party while the crowd unharnessed the horses and dragged the coach through the centre of the town. Before the leading citizens retired to the Peacock Hotel for a dinner at the corporation's expense, Perceval had time to make a short speech. 'You are all townsmen living under the same laws,' he told the cheering crowd, 'neighbours interested in the same common good; protected by the same chartered rights. Therefore let me ask you all to live together as neighbours and friends, forgiving and forgetting anything that might interrupt the peace, the good-neighbourhood of the town, and remembering nothing but what you may all recollect with mutual congratulation, and satisfaction, and joy. Let the new charter which unites you all as freemen be the bond of harmony, union, brotherhood, and friendship.'[2]

The speech was moderate and sensible. It was probably also a bit of shrewd electioneering, for on the following day the earl of Northampton died in Switzerland, Charles Compton took his seat in the Lords, and Perceval was invited to contest Northampton in the Castle Ashby interest. At the first meeting of the corporation held under the terms of the new charter, Perceval received the freedom of the borough and a fee of one hundred guineas, which he promptly donated to the local infirmary.[3] On 26 April he was publicly adopted as a candidate in the shire hall, his election address appeared on the thirtieth, and the by-election writ was issued on 1 May.[4] As a general election was due that summer there was no opposition. By 9 May Perceval was thanking his new constituents in a speech 'received with the most distinguished applause'. He afterwards entertained 200 of the principal inhabitants at an 'elegant entertainment' at the Angel Inn. Many loyal and con-

---

[1] Markham and Cox, vol. II, pp. 22–4.
[2] Perceval MSS.; Markham and Cox, vol. I, pp. 152–4.
[3] *Ibid.*, vol. I, p. 154, and vol. II, p. 319; *Northampton Mercury*, 16 July 1796.
[4] *Ibid.*, 30 Apr. 1796.

stitutional toasts were drunk before the day concluded 'in the most harmonious and convivial manner'.[1]

The harmony, however, did not last long. Within a fortnight, and even before the new member had time to take his seat, Northampton was taking part in the general election. All three connections put forward candidates. The earl of Northampton's agent, Thomas Scriven, directed Perceval's campaign, the cost of which was met by the earl. Edward Bouverie represented the 'independent electors', while William Walcot junior of Oundle (a J.P. and a lieutenant in the Northampton-shire yeomanry) was supported by the corporation.[2] All three candidates published their election address in the *Northampton Mercury* on 21 May. Four days later the customary show of hands was taken from the hustings and declared by the mayor to be in favour of Perceval and Walcot. But Bouverie's supporters, convinced that Hall's decision reflected his wishes rather than his arithmetic, demanded a poll. This remained open from the twenty-fifth to the thirtieth. 'The contest is warmly disputed', reported the *Mercury*, 'and the friends of the different parties all seem confident of success.'[3] Perceval's tactics were simple. He refused to be drawn into any formal alliance with Walcot against Bouverie, concentrated on making himself agreeable to all parties, and fished for as many second votes as possible. He had given all the usual donations to local charities, and had even so far overcome his prejudices as to buy 'a hunting saddle compleat with bridle' for his horse and 'a pair of thistle breeches and two pairs of flannel drawers' for its cautious rider.[4] Bouverie's main hope lay in persuading electors to cast only a single vote for himself. His supporters therefore circu-lated handbills calling for 'plumpers' which Perceval denounced as an unwarrantable interference with the freedom of election. 'In the course of my own canvass thro' the town,' he claimed, 'I have carefully avoided asking for plumpers, and even when they have been offered me by my friends, as has frequently been the case, I have always declared that I wanted but one vote, and wished my friends to dispose of the other as they pleased. I should have thought it inconsistent with the professions of neutrality which I have uniformly made to have done otherwise.'[5] He had also to warn his supporters against

[1] *Ibid.*, 14 May 1796.
[2] Perceval MSS., Thos. Scriven to Perceval, 24 Oct. 1796; *Northampton Mercury*, 19 Nov. 1796 and 28 Jan. 1797.
[3] *Ibid.*, 21 and 28 May 1796.
[4] Bills in Perceval MSS.
[5] Perceval MSS., draft of speech.

over-confidence. There was a rumour that he had so many promises of votes that his re-election was quite certain, but Perceval was very concerned with the extent of his majority. He had recently been returned 'by almost the unanimous voice of the town' and so would feel 'much hurt were I to find that the numbers of my friends in so short a period had been much diminished'. By 28 May his worries were nearly over. At the end of that day the state of the poll was:

Perceval 658   Bouverie 448   Walcot 441

'I consider', admitted Perceval, 'that I may now fairly state to you that I have succeeded.'[1]

He had been attacked throughout the campaign as a lackey of Castle Ashby. He was the Compton candidate and was proud of it as there was no reason to deny or excuse the family's interest in borough elections. 'This influence, gentlemen,' he told electors from the hustings, 'does not depend upon the usual sources. They have no tenants whom they can command, no dependents whom they may control, but many grateful and affectionate friends of whose support they may be assured.' Those who sought to destroy this attachment 'would reform us out of the best dictates of our nature and the proudest virtues of our heart'. [2] Henceforth the real interest lay in the struggle between Bouverie and Walcot for the second seat. 29 May was a Sunday, during which both candidates rallied their supporters for the final struggle on the thirtieth. Bouverie, with his slender lead of seven, was worried by a report that Perceval had decided to turn over his remaining votes to Walcot. The corporation, meanwhile, was sparing neither 'pains nor expense' for militia men who had votes had been brought from as far as Bristol to support Walcot and 'every effort was tried with bad votes'. Therefore Bouverie repeated his call for 'plumpers': on no account should one of his supporters give his second vote to Walcot. Meanwhile his rival professed to be quite confident and urged his well-wishers to vote early on the Monday.[3] The poll finally closed on that day and the result announced as:

Perceval 720   Bouverie 512   Walcot 474

'The independence of the town', wrote a whig observer, 'proved

[1] *Northampton Mercury*, 28 May 1796.
[2] Perceval MSS. The Compton family was reported as being 'very amiable and most agreeable neighbours'. The family's finances were in 'a very good state' (Farington, vol. III, p. 111).
[3] *Northampton Mercury*, 28 May 1796; Markham and Cox, vol. II, p. 508.

superior to all.' [1] In fact it was probably Perceval's refusal to abandon
his pledge of neutrality that decided the issue. In all a record total of
991 electors voted. Of these Perceval polled 14 single votes, shared 467
with Walcot, and 243 with Bouverie. Bouverie got 263 'plumpers'
while Walcot got none.[2] The defeated candidate asked his friends not
to sign the return as he intended to petition against the result. He had
lost, he claimed, because certain electors who had pledged their votes
to him, 'basely and dishonestly ranked themselves against me'.
Bouverie was at a loss for words to express his gratitude, but Perceval
never suffered on that account. The contest, he said, had cost a great
deal of time, energy, and money. He had certain things to complain of,
and many more to lament, in the conduct of his rivals. Yet he did not
regret the contest. 'For the manner in which some of my friends have
thought proper to conduct it, it has given me the opportunity of making a very important discovery—enabling me to distinguish between
those who are really my friends and may be relied upon when they are
wanted, and those summer sunshine friends which lend their votes of
acclamation, and voices of applause, when the sky is clear, and the
prospect around is cheerful, but which in a change of season are not
to be found.' [3]

As soon as Walcot had second thoughts about a petition, the victors
began to arrange their election 'treats'. Many of Perceval's 'respectable
friends' wished him to choose the same day as Bouverie; the less
respectable (who had voted for both) naturally preferred the chance
of two free dinners. In the end Perceval gave his at the Angel and
invited the magistrates and the earl (who paid the bill). Bouverie held
his two days later at the George. Then Perceval closed his campaign
with a donation of £100 for poor relief. He became M.P. for Northampton as *locum tenens* for the infant son of the ninth earl. He was the
Castle Ashby candidate, supported and financed by the Compton
family 'yet when possible', confessed his agent, 'you would, I know,
satisfy all'.[4]

It was Perceval's first and last contested election during the sixteen
years in which he represented the borough. He was returned, together
with Bouverie, at the general elections of 1802, 1806, and 1807 as well

---

[1] Markham and Cox, vol. II, p. 508.
[2] Poll Book for the Northampton election of 1796. Members of the corporation
voted as follows: Perceval 72, Walcot 48, Bouverie 22.
[3] Perceval MSS.; *Northampton Mercury*, 30 May and 5 June 1796.
[4] Perceval MSS., Thos. Scriven to Perceval, 24 Oct. 1796; *Northampton Mercury*, 5 Nov. and 17 Dec. 1796.

as on the three occasions when he had to seek re-election after accepting office in the government.[1] Throughout that period he served Northampton well, taking pride in representing 'an extremely numerous body with as extended and popular right of election as any in the country'. He gave generously to local charities, became patron of the Northampton Grand Musical Festival, and acted as steward at the Northamptonshire races. He is also supposed to have used his influence to secure army contracts for the Northampton shoe makers.[2] Yet he never thought of himself as bound to serve merely local interests. When the town's woolstaplers petitioned him to oppose a clause in the Act of Union which allowed the export of British wool to Ireland, he promised to attend the debate 'to weigh as well as I can all that is said on both sides and to support or oppose the proposition according to my judgement'. As member for Northampton, he wrote, 'I shall conduct myself in the way most conformable to my duty which compels me to attend to the interests and wishes of my constituents, but at the same time not to forget the general advantage of the Empire.' [3]

[1] *Parl. Papers, H. of C., 1878 (Members of Parliament)*, vol. II. In 1810 Bouverie was succeeded by William Hanbury of Kelmarsh, who also voted with the opposition in parliament. Hanbury, whose father inherited the estate of the last Viscount Bateman, was born in 1780 and educated at Eton and Oxford (*Northampton Mercury*, 13 Oct. 1810; Farington, vol. II, p. 166).

[2] *Northampton Mercury*, 23 Aug. 1806 and 8 Sep. 1809; Markham and Cox, vol. II, p. 487; *Victoria County History, Northamptonshire*, vol. III, p. 15.

[3] Perceval MSS., John Baker to Perceval, 25 Apr. 1800 and Perceval to Baker, 28 Apr. 1800.

CHAPTER FOUR

WAR AND THE CONSTITUTION

PERCEVAL entered the Commons on 27 September 1796 a confirmed
party man, and at first his presence there generated a great deal more
heat than light. He was for the constitution and Pitt; he was against
Fox and France. Before parliament was prorogued in the following
July, he probably spoke at least five times: on 13 December (on the Austrian subsidy), twice on 19 May (against Combe's motion for peace and
Fox's for the repeal of the Treason and Sedition Acts), on the twentieth
(during a debate on the Nore mutiny) and on the twenty-sixth (against
Grey's motion on reform).[1] He read all his speeches from carefully
prepared drafts, and together they summarise most of the important
points of his early political beliefs. He might have started on a false
note by devoting his maiden speech to welcoming peace negotiations
if Pitt had not (at the last minute) changed his mind about asking
him to second the Address. That honour went to Sir William Lowther
and Perceval waited a further ten weeks before first addressing the
House.[2] He began with a panegyric on the constitution and a violent
tirade against Fox. The leader of the opposition had charged Pitt
with deliberately seeking to undermine the constitution by advancing
a subsidy to Austria without first consulting parliament. Perceval
decided to retaliate in kind, for to him Pitt was 'the immediate instrument under providence raised up for our deliverance from those calami-
ties which have spread over Europe'.[3] Therefore Pittite and patriot
were synonyms. 'Indifference to the honour and dignity of Englishmen as a nation,' he told the Commons, 'and to the constitution as
the guarantee of their continued prosperity was at all times unworthy

---

[1] Only the least important of these, that of 20 May, was reported (*Parl. Hist.*,
vol. 33, p. 810). The other four are taken from drafts in the Perceval MSS. The
debates in which they were spoken may be found in *Parl. Hist.*, vol. 32, pp.
1297–1347; vol. 33, pp. 594–613, 613–639 and 644–734.

[2] P.R.O., Chatham MSS., 166, Perceval to Pitt, 25 Sep. 1796. Three drafts of
Perceval's intended speech may be found in the Perceval MSS.

William Lowther, first earl of Lonsdale (1757–1844), was William Wordsworth's patron.

[3] Perceval MSS., draft of speech.

of English bosoms.' [1] Yet the constitution was threatened by Napoleon abroad (that 'satyr in disguise') and by whigs and reformers at home. Its chief glory lay in its 'wholesome balance' between the extremes of popular and royal power. The whig tradition of 1688, argued Perceval, was now the common heritage of all parties, but they still could not agree on an authorised interpretation. Was it the Crown or the mob which threatened to upset the balance? 'I know indeed,' continued Perceval, 'that the right hon[ourable] gent[leman] and his friends state that they believe the dangers of this period to impend from the Crown. But I know likewise that the great majority of this House, and a great majority of the people of this country, instructed by the miseries which they have witnessed in a neighbouring country, from the delusions of popular opinion, from the plausible fallacies of democratic theories believe that the danger to the constitution of this country . . . arises from that spirit of democracy, which the right hon[ourable] gent[leman], if he does not actively inspire it, at least very considerably enflames both by his language in this House, and out of it.' [2] The Foxite case centred on the growing influence of the Crown, both in parliament and throughout the country. It was futile for government supporters, like George Rose, to draw up lists of places and sinecures which had been abolished. The constant rise in government expenditure, due mainly to the war, was undeniable and it was quite impossible, as the *Edinburgh Review* later argued, 'that money can be spent without creating an influence—without giving the purchaser an authority over the dealer'. Perceval saw the real answer. 'I would oppose in the other scale the weight the people have acquired by the increase in wealth, the extension of knowledge, the speedy communication of all political topics and all political events. . . . I don't believe there ever was a period in the history of this country, when the enlightened knowledge, the wealth, the strength, the character of the people more directly and powerfully influenced and controlled the measures and opinions of the Government.' [3] That tendency had gone far enough; firmness in domestic affairs and resolution in the conduct of the war could now

---

[1] *The Senator*, vol. XIX, p. 470.

[2] Perceval MSS., draft of speech.

[3] George Rose, *Observations Respecting the Public Expenditure and Influence of the Crown*; *Edinburgh Review*, Apr. 1810, pp. 188-97; Perceval MSS., draft of speech. 'I don't know', said Perceval when interrupted by opposition shouts, 'whether gentlemen fancy they will frighten me by their vociferous "hear hear". If they do, I can assure you they mistake the tone of my nerves.' For posthumous comments on Perceval's maiden speech see *Gent. Mag.*, June 1812, p. 589.

alone avert chaos. The naval mutinies and Hoche's raid on Bantry Bay had shown how close we were to disaster. But though, continued Perceval, the Bank had been forced to suspend cash payments, our credit was not impaired. When whig defeatists concentrated on our setbacks by land, Perceval stressed our successes at sea. Rivoli was a serious blow and the French landing in South Wales a worse shock, but Nelson had won at Cape St. Vincent. Unrest at home could, and must, be checked by repressing the disaffected minority. Thus the Treason and Seditious Meetings Acts, although not 'measures good in themselves', were 'a remedy for an existing evil, called for by the pressure of circumstances of the time, and required of the wisdom of Parliament for the suppression of impending mischief and danger'. They were 'a temporary sacrifice of one of the means of constitutional security for the preservation of that constitutional security itself'.[1] Grey's Reform Bill (introduced just before the prorogation) was a blow aimed at the roots of the constitution. Perceval was not content simply to denounce Grey's 'speculative improvements' because they were opposed by a majority in the country. The counting of heads was, he thought, a jacobinical device; Perceval's approach was qualitative not quantitative. Although some of those who favoured reform might be 'respectable' citizens, the majority were the disaffected who would be satisfied by nothing short of revolution. They were the Universal Suffrage men, those who followed the doctrines of Tom Paine, the members of the Corresponding Societies and of the Constitutional Information Society. 'Are they', Perceval asked the opposition, 'the sort of people you would like the constitution to conciliate?' 'Sir,' he continued, 'I admire gentlemen gravely getting up and telling you they love the British constitution and then proposing to alter so completely, so radically, and so entirely such an important branch of that constitution as the whole House of Commons.'[1]

Attendance at Westminster at first absorbed only a small proportion of Perceval's time, for his profession still came before politics. As soon as parliament was prorogued he travelled to Warwick to handle his first major case as senior counsel for the Crown. On 15 August John Binns (an agent of the London Corresponding Society) was charged with sedition for having urged a Birmingham audience to 'be ready to shed blood' in the cause of annual parliaments and household suffrage. Perceval, handicapped by a poor brief, was as conscientious as usual. Romilly, who defended, was brilliant. The jury returned a

[1] Perceval MSS., draft of speech.

D

verdict of 'not guilty' and received a special letter of congratulation from the Corresponding Society.[1] Perceval was, however, slowly making his way in his profession. Five months previously he had rented Belsize House, Hampstead, the property of Philip Stanhope, earl of Chesterfield. He heard of it through David Rees, a Holborn lawyer and a former companion on the bankruptcy commission, who had the unusual distinction of following his term on the commission by three years in the Fleet prison for debt. Consequently he had been forced to sub-lease Belsize to Thomas Richardson, a cooper of Tower Street, London. The Percevals had their lease from Richardson; it cost them £250 in the first instance, but a great deal more to make the house habitable. For Belsize, a rambling old place, was never popular with the family.[2] 'I have in a humble way,' confessed Perceval to his brother-in-law, 'a sad morbid turn for spending money in alterations and improvements even of such a miserable hole as this from whence I now write, where when all that is, that can be done, I have but a leasehold interest and could hardly get a gentleman who would succeed me.'[3] The Percevals did their best to improve the place, making a special effort with the grounds. They planted elms, chestnuts, sycamore, plane trees, limes, sweet bays, spruce, larch, and Portuguese laurel, while the garden bloomed in purple and white lilac, jasmine, and honeysuckle. Into the kitchen garden went May Duke cherries and Moor Park apricots, white and red figs, greengages, nectarines and peaches, raspberries, gooseberries and Alpine strawberries, asparagus and a hundred artichokes.[4] But, in spite of all their efforts, Belsize was never a success. It was cheap and that is about all that could be said for it.

When parliament re-assembled on 2 November 1797 many of its

---

[1] Howell, op. cit., vol. XXVI, pp. 595–652; Veitch, The Genesis of Parliamentary Reform, pp. 329–30. The trial was originally fixed for the spring. Perceval had travelled to Derby in May and had written three letters to Jane from that town. They all began 'My dear' and then continued with a full draft of his intended speech for the prosecution (Perceval MSS.).

[2] Deeds in Perceval MSS.; Royal Kalendar, 1791, p. 172.

[3] Perceval MSS., Perceval to Redesdale, 4 Dec. 1802. Belsize House stood on a site once occupied by an Elizabethan mansion. It was described by Wroth as 'a large plainly-built house' (The London Pleasure Gardens of the Eighteenth Century, pp. 189–92) and by Brewer, writing in 1816, as a 'handsome modern edifice' (London and Middlesex, vol. IV, p. 205). It later became 'a place of popular amusement' and was finally demolished in 1852.

[4] Perceval MSS., Daniel Greenwood of Kensington nursery to Perceval, bill dated Dec. 1798 to May 1799. Brewer (London and Middlesex, vol. IV, p. 205) commented particularly on the beauty of the grounds which were approached from the Hampstead road through a long avenue of trees.

leading members were absent. Burke had died in the previous July
while the majority of the Foxites had decided to secede after the defeat
of Grey's scheme for reform. The war continued to go badly, in spite
of the victory at Camperdown, and Pitt was hooted in the City after
proposing to treble the assessed taxes on inhabited houses, windows,
male servants, horses, and carriages. Even Fox returned to Westminster to oppose increased taxes and to prophesy that it would lead
to 'the immediate destruction of our trade, to the annihilation of our
fortunes and possibly to the loss of liberty to our persons'. 'Nothing
short of a total reform of our late system,' he argued, 'nothing short
of our reverting to the principles of our constitution, to the popular
maxims of our ancestors, can save us from utter ruin.' Members of the
opposition had repeatedly failed to persuade the House to accept this
advice; therefore they had ceased to attend.[1] It was a weak defence of
a mistaken policy, and it moved Perceval to fury. Yet, as he had no
opportunity of making an immediate reply, he was forced to wait until
the debate on the third reading of the Assessed Taxes Bill, which began
on 3 January 1798.[2] One of the first speakers that day was Sir Francis
Burdett who, like Perceval, was new to the Commons.[3] He refused to
support the granting of supplies for 'this disgraceful war' and its
'infamous system of corruption'. The French had set us an example
in frugal government; the British people would soon demand that
we should follow it. On the following day Perceval answered both
Fox and Burdett in the longest speech he had yet made in the House.
Burdett had complained that the bill would enable Pitt 'to carry on a
war against liberty'. 'If the present war was a war against liberty,'
replied Perceval, 'it was that species of liberty against which, he trusted,
we should ever bear arms—it was against the importation of French
liberty into England.' [4] At that very moment the French Army of
England was camped on the shores of the English channel. Even before
we had entered the war the French had ruined their own economy by
a reckless financial policy. But it was against Fox and his recent
secession that Perceval devoted most of his arguments. 'Sir, nothing
can be clearer', he said, 'than that the times we live in are times of the
greatest danger; and that there necessarily arises a call upon men of

[1] *Parl. Hist.*, vol. XXXIII, pp. 1066-89 and 1100-41.
[2] *Ibid.*, pp. 1146-1274.
[3] Perceval represented almost 1,000 electors; Burdett, the radical, paid £4,000
for one of the duke of Newcastle's pocket boroughs (M. W. Patterson, *Sir
Francis Burdett and his Times*, vol. I, pp. 38-9).
[4] *Parl. Reg.*, vol. IV, pp. 564-639.

every description to exert the utmost of their abilities with the utmost integrity in discharge of their public duties. . . . And of all the symptoms which alarm my mind for the fate of the country, there is none more striking than the new course which is taken by the patriots of the present day to obtain the good opinion of the public.' Fox argued that his absence from the Commons was a matter on which he owed responsibility to no one, but he had more than his conscience to satisfy. He was in public life 'and if it be at all time that the abilities of great men are in some sort the property of the public, I see no right that they can have to subtract them from the public service'. It was even worse to argue that the opposition withdrew because their policies were constantly outvoted. If they really thought such policies essential for the safety of the realm, it was their bounden duty as patriots to keep on recommending them, however great the discouragements. Only if their real aim was self-advancement could they justify secession. Fox had then put forward the 'monstrous and indefensible' principle that if the opposition stayed at Westminster to point out minor faults in the government's measures, they would only delay the discovery of their inherent folly. It was best that bills should be passed unaltered so that the public could quickly see how bad they were. Was this the argument, claimed Perceval, of a man who prided himself on seeking the happiness of the people and the good of the country? 'His end was the happiness of his fellow subjects; his means the overthrow of the present ministers; but in the eager and heated pursuit of these means he has lost sight of the end for which he desired it, and is now ready to sacrifice that very happiness which he first pursued.' The Foxites now had a new party cry—'Evil be thou my good!' Finally Perceval dealt with Fox's call for reform. 'What then is this total, radical and fundamental reform of the whole system, which is the price we must pay for the Hon[ourable] Gent[leman's] assistance?— a phrase certainly sufficiently general and in my mind most dangerous and alarming. But what is it, and what does it mean? The R[ight] H[onourable] G[entleman] is fertile in explanation when any phrase that he has adopted seems to be rather too strong for the public ear and too highly seasoned for the public taste. And perhaps this ingenuity and adroitness may be exercised upon this very phrase. Perhaps we shall hear that the total reform of the whole system means an alteration only in some of its parts; that a radical reform meddles only with the branches and the trunk, and has no concern with the roots; and that the fundamental reform leaves the foundations entirely untouched.' In this case no explanation could undo the damage, for every reformer in the country, 'be his plan ever so wild, let it reach to whatever extent of revolutionary violence, and subversion, but he must find in these words . . . countenance for his opinions and encouragement to hope for his assistance and co-operation in the prosecution of his designs to their most dangerous extremities'.[1]

The speech established the new member's reputation in debate. 'Perceval's speech was incomparable', reported Granville Leveson-Gower. 'I never saw the Opposition so stung as they appeared to be by his remarks. . . .' Both Sheridan and Fox himself attempted to reply, but with little success, and in the division which followed, Perceval acted as a teller for the majority. Even Pitt was full of praise for his young supporter. 'Our last debate (to my great joy)', he wrote to Mornington, 'produced a speech from Perceval, which was in all respects one of the best I ever heard; and was an attack upon Fox pointed and galling enough to have drawn forth one of Grattan's warmest encomiums. It certainly sent him home very sick to his supper. Since this effort we have heard nothing of him. . . .' [2]

Nor for the rest of the session was much heard of Perceval. He probably made two short speeches on the Land Tax Redemption Bill and three on the Irish rebellion of 1798. Only the last of these was in his best style, which he seems to have reserved for attacks upon Fox.[3] But ministers had already recognised his worth. In May 1798 Pitt fought a duel with Tierney and chose Dudley Ryder as his second. While on their way to Putney Heath, Ryder introduced the delicate subject of Pitt's successor. 'Whom', he asked, 'did he consider capable of filling his situation in case the country should have the misfortune to lose him?' Pitt's reply must have surprised even Ryder. 'He thought Mr. Perceval was the most competent person, and that he appeared the most equal to Mr. Fox.' [4] Two months later the place of solicitor to

[1] Perceval MSS., draft of speech.
[2] Granville, *Private Correspondence of Lord Granville Leveson-Gower*, vol. I, p. 193; *House of Commons Journal*, 1798, vol. 53, p. 174; Lord Rosebery, *Pitt*, p. 205. In his report to the king, Pitt referred to Perceval's speech as 'most spirited and masterly' (Windsor MSS., Pitt to George III, 5 Jan. 1798).
[3] Perceval MSS., drafts of speeches. None of the five was reported but the debates may be found in *Parl. Hist.*, vol. XXXIII, 1360 ff., 1487 ff., and 1513 ff.
[4] This anecdote can be found in the *Anonymous Memoir*, p. 8. Later Ryder himself told it to D. M. Perceval, who published it in his pamphlet *Remarks on the Character ascribed by Col. Napier to the late Rt. Hon. Spencer Perceval*. Pitt's answer is certainly surprising, but as Ryder was hardly the sort of man to have invented it and Pitt's words are too precise to suggest a misunderstanding, there seems no reason to reject it. Jane Perceval always maintained that Pitt had said

the ordnance became vacant through the death of the former Wilkite, Sergeant Adair. Cornwallis had almost decided to give it to his own secretary, Vernon, when Alexander Ross mentioned Perceval's name. At first there was some doubt as to whether a barrister was eligible, but Cornwallis immediately wrote that, if it were possible, 'I will certainly give it to Mr. Perceval, whose character and great abilities are well known to me, although I have not the pleasure of his personal acquaintance'. Consequently in August Perceval was notified of his appointment to a place (worth £300 a year) which he did not even know existed and which, he wrote, 'had I known it, I certainly should not have expected it to be given to me'.[1]

During the following session Perceval appears to have spoken only three times. On 11 December he opposed Tierney's motion asking the ministry not to enter into any engagement 'which may prevent or impede a negotiation for peace'; on the thirty-first he wound up the debate for the government on the third reading of Pitt's Income Tax Bill; and on 9 May 1799 he spoke in favour of Abbot's Forfeiture for High Treason Bill.[2] In the short fourth session he did not speak at all, but in the fifth he made five speeches, three of them important. The first, in support of the war against France, dealt particularly with the future of Napoleon after the *coup d'état* of Brumaire. 'I do not believe', said Perceval, 'that this Corsican adventurer, brought into the situation as he has been, can continue possibly to hold it. I do not believe that a nation, who have now for some years been enthusiastically devoted to a representative government, will contentedly acquiesce in that tyranny which is founded on the very destruction of all idea of representation and gravely kiss the rod of that usurper who has dis-

---

of her husband, 'That young man will be leader of the House some day' (Walpole, vol. I, p. 51).

[1] C. Ross, *The Correspondence of Marquis Cornwallis*, vol. II, pp. 377 and 384. Major-General Ross's friendship with Perceval probably began because Mrs. Ross was the daughter of Sir Robert Gunning of Horton, Northamptonshire (Lady Lewis, *The Journal and Correspondence of Miss Berry*, vol. II, p. 330 and see above chapter 3, page 28, footnote 1). The notice of Perceval's appointment as solicitor to the ordnance is in the Perceval MSS., R. H. Crew to Perceval, 22 Aug. 1798. Walpole (vol. I, p. 54) states that Perceval was also appointed solicitor-general to the queen. His authority is one of D. M. Perceval's transcripts of his father's letters. But there is no record that Perceval ever held the office.

[2] Perceval MSS., drafts of speeches. Only the second of Perceval's speeches was reported (*Parl. Hist.*, vol. XXXIV, pp. 1–23, 73–108, 131–48, and *Parl. Reg.*, vol. VII, p. 496). The other two debates may be found in *Parl. Hist.*, vol. XXXIV, 26–73 and 1067 ff. Perceval spoke a second time on income tax on 17 Apr. 1800 (*Parl. Reg.*, vol. XI, p. 222).

missed their representatives by an armed force.'[1] Seven days later he again wound up for the government, this time on Sheridan's motion for an inquiry into the duke of York's handling of the expedition to Holland. Thereafter he confined himself to the A, B, C—adultery, bread, and catholicism. He joined his fellow evangelicals in supporting Lord Auckland's bill for the better prevention of adultery. After this was rejected, he attempted to defeat a private divorce bill filed by a woman because 'there was certainly not the same ground for a wife to apply for a divorce for adultery that there was for a husband. . . . It would open the door to divorce in every case where the parties disagreed, for as there was not the same degree of guilt attached to a man who committed adultery as there was to a woman, it would be easy by a little collusion between the parties, to effect a separation.'[2] On bread he proved himself independent and a good free-trader by voting against the ministry. In an attempt to check rising prices Hawkesbury introduced a measure to set up a London Incorporated Society for the manufacture of flour and bread. Perceval supported the second reading 'though he doubted much the soundness of the principle'; he hoped to see the bill amended in committee. But when it emerged unaltered for its third reading, he opposed strongly. It was 'impolitic', 'unwise', and 'most unreasonable'. It would do nothing to lessen the existing scarcity because its provisions would not come into effect for two years, and when they did, they would only set up a monopoly with the power 'to grind and oppress the public, when, and to as great a degree as they should think proper'. The ministry had accused millers and bakers of profiteering without producing 'a single tittle' of evidence. In the division he acted as a teller for the 'noes', who ran the government to a single vote.[3] Then the debates on the Irish Union brought him back to the grand theme of the British constitution. The prospect of one hundred Irish M.P.s at Westminster was not pleasant. 'I look forward not without anxiety,' confessed Perceval, 'not to say alarm to the possible effect which may be produced. I don't like any alterations in these walls.' Beyond this he favoured the scheme. The

---

[1] Perceval MSS., draft speech. The draft, which is incomplete continues—'I do not believe that that nation, which has for so many years been enthusiastically pursuing the idea of liberty, will be contented to receive a Government containing it itself . . . .' Walpole (vol. I, p. 71) prints a version of his own composition.

[2] Perceval MSS.; *Parl. Hist.*, vol. XXXV, 301–25, and *Parl. Reg.*, vol. XV, 631–2.

[3] *Ibid.*, vol. XII, 123 and 256–60. He repeated this view in a debate on the bread shortage on 7 Dec. 1801. 'The way to produce competition in a trade was to have as few restrictions as possible upon it' (*Parl. Reg.*, vol. XVI, 373).

state of Ireland was so bad that the removal of their legislature to the calmer atmosphere of Westminster would be a great improvement. He even hinted at eventual emancipation. 'Not that I entertain a hope,' he said, 'that this or any other measure, within the reach of human wisdom or prudence to devise, can operate like a charm, at once to settle the disturbed state of the country; but that, by removing the influence of some of its worst evils, by diminishing, perhaps, the necessity for keeping alive the political distinction between the Catholic and the Protestant, and by thus giving to them all the full blessing of the British constitution, which they at present do but imperfectly enjoy, that the most sanguine hopes may naturally be entertained that the best and surest foundations would be then laid, not only for the permanent connection between that country and this, but also for the internal security, tranquillity, and prosperity of that island.' [1]

It would be easy to make too much of this cautious liberalism. His second speech on the subject (in support of Mildmay's Monastic Institutions Bill) revealed a different approach. It was 'the spirit of the Catholic persuasion to make as many converts as possible—indeed it was the principle of every religion to a given extent, but emphatically so of the Catholics'. Therefore, while we could expect refugees in this country to show their gratitude to us, we ought not to be surprised if they expressed it by trying to convert us to catholicism. Nor ought we to be angry 'for they believed that they could not obtain for us a greater blessing than to make Catholics of us all'. He would not say a word against toleration; 'there was not in England a man who had more esteem for it than himself'. Indeed he did not wish to see 'the hair of a man's head hurt on account of his religious opinions'. Yet, in spite of this, we must be on guard against catholic zeal, 'since it was inconsistent with the spirit of our constitution'.[2] Always his early speeches returned either to the war or the constitution. The constitution was glorious and unchanging; but to many there was a growing feeling that the war was as inglorious as it was unending.

The Percevals own main worries were still financial. By 1800 Spencer's total income was about £2,600 a year, of which £1,800 was earned at the bar. But over £400 a year went in direct taxation alone, while the rent for Belsize and the coal bill accounted for another £210.[3]

[1] Perceval MSS.: *Parl. Hist.*, vol. XXXIV, pp. 406–9, and *Parl. Reg.*, vol. VIII, pp. 32 ff. The version printed by Walpole (vol. I, p. 81) is not accurate.

[2] *Parl. Reg.*, vol. XII, pp. 171–2.

[3] Income figure from Walpole, vol. I, p. 83; figures for taxes and expenses taken from receipts and bills in Perceval MSS. Details of his tax payments for

On the rest he had to support a wife and seven children, for Jane had given birth to two more sons, Henry and Dudley Montague. Although there can have been little money to spare, they did their best to keep up appearances. They had a large carriage with Thorpe, the coachman, and liverymen in 'breeches of scarlet pluch', a butler, and a gardener. As his family grew too large for 59, Lincoln's Inn Fields, Perceval was forced to buy number 60, thus reuniting the old Lindsey House.[1] It was probably the happiest period of Perceval's life, for, in spite of his profession and politics, he still had a good deal of leisure, most of which was devoted to Jane and the children. Frequent child-bearing had weakened Jane's health, much to her husband's concern. She had in fact become an authority on confinements, and gave detailed instructions to her sister-in-law on the management of children. 'You will', she wrote, 'excuse my taking the liberty of giving advice, and will recollect that it comes from an experienced matron.' And after the event, Spencer expressed his wife's pleasure that 'her good advice has been anticipated, 'tho', he was forced to admit, 'she does not fully approve of the senna'.[2] Their own 'dear brats' gave little trouble. Spencer, the eldest son, was now 'a hearty child between four and five years old'; Jane was nine, Frances eight, and Maria six. Their father would call at George Grosvenor's perfumery warehouse in Chancery Lane to buy them 'a large doll to dress and undress complete' and received in return ivory carved 'in imitation of Roman shells', which he insisted on having set.[3] He also continued to spend time on the study of prophecy, especially after he found that his future brother-in-law, Thomas Walpole, shared his enthusiasm. Together they made calculations on the probable end of the world and decided on 1926. After a close study of the Book of Revelation Perceval concluded that Napoleon could be identified as 'the woman who rides upon the beast, who is drunk with the blood of the saints, the mother of harlots' but it was less easy to tell whether the Pope

---

1799 are—income tax £262 1s. 8d.; highway rate £15 18s.; house and window tax £14 2s.; inhabited house tax £11 5s.; male servants £16 10s.; fourwheeled carriage tax £9 12s.; horse tax £9 12s.; dog tax 18s.; stamp 4d. Total £339 19s. 4d. In addition he paid about £17 poor rate in the parish of St. Giles and St. George, Bloomsbury; £15 12s. 10d. on his town house in pursuance of an Act for enclosing, cleaning, and adorning Lincoln's Inn Fields; and about £30 poor rate at Hampstead.

[1] Perceval MSS., Perceval to Redesdale, 4 Dec. 1802.

[2] *Ibid.*, Jane Perceval to Thos. Walpole, undated (Oct. 1805) and Perceval to same, 5 Oct. 1805.

[3] *Ibid.*, household bills and Perceval to Thos. Walpole, 10 Oct. 1805.

was 'the beast with seven heads' or just one of the heads. He even
suspected that the French Revolution might be a divine instrument
for the destruction of Roman catholicism. 'If you will take up your
map', he wrote, 'and look at the countries where the French power and
opinions have made their greatest impression, I think you will be of
opinion that they have been raised up by Providence for the overthrow
of the popish superstitions; for except with some few exceptions, which
may have been permitted to prevent this object of God's Providence
from being too strikingly apparent, you will find their progress most
destructive where the popish superstitions most prevailed.' [1] When
Sir Sidney Smith checked Napoleon before Acre, Perceval published
an anonymous pamphlet (based on part of the eleventh chapter of
Daniel) proving that Napoleon's fall would date from that event.[2]
But in the meantime he continued his annual subscription to the Light
Horse Volunteers. He may even have taken part in that great parade
on Clapham Common before the royal family when the corps assembled in new hussar jackets and white leather breeches with their hair
'powdered and greased, six inches long, close to the head' and wearing
two holsters, one for a pistol, the other for 'a handkerchief or anything
else'.[3] Even with such aids it is doubtful if the little lawyer made a
very impressive-looking soldier. He soon found, however, that he
no longer had the time for many parades.[4] In October 1800 his old
university chose him as their counsel, and within four months Pitt
was out of office and Perceval was acting for the defence in a far more
important cause.[5]

[1] Perceval MSS., Thos. Walpole to Perceval, 10 Oct. 1806 and Perceval to R.
Bosanquet (undated). Walpole married Perceval's sister, Lady Margaret, at St.
George's, Hanover Square, in Dec. 1803 (*Gent. Mag.*, 1803, vol. II, p. 1253).
[2] *Observations intended to point out the Application of a Prophecy in the eleventh
Chapter of the Book of Daniel to the French Power* (1800, printed by E. Cox and
Sons, Great Queen Street, London).
[3] Colchester, *Diary*, vol. I, pp. 114–15.
[4] P.R.O., Bosanquet MSS., 30/3/23. Perceval resigned on 30 July 1803. He
afterwards acted as honorary treasurer to the corps.
[5] Perceval MSS., Perceval to Mansel, 25 Oct. 1800; *Gent. Mag.*, 1800, vol. II,
p. 1282.

PLATE 3

The Court of King's Bench, Westminster

CHAPTER FIVE

COUNSEL FOR THE DEFENCE

On 23 February 1801 Perceval paid £48 in fees to the Crown office in chancery and became solicitor-general in the Addington administration.[1] It was ironic that so staunch a Pittite should have entered office as his hero left it, but Pitt had fallen on catholic emancipation, the one issue on which he and Perceval did not agree. Nor, at first, did membership of the new government mean estrangement from Pitt, for the ex-minister though out of office was still in power. He thought of Addington as his protégé and canvassed his friends to accept cabinet places. Only Grenville and Canning refused, but their loss, combined with Pitt's own absence from the treasury, seriously weakened the government front bench, particularly in the Commons. There Addington had, for sixteen months, only one cabinet college in Hawkesbury, the foreign secretary. Castlereagh accepted the board of control in July 1802 and a seat in the cabinet that October, and Charles Yorke was promoted from the secretaryship at war to the home office in the following August. As neither of them was much use in debate, there was a golden opportunity for the young solicitor-general to make his reputation as an orator. He was allowed, as the son of a peer, to refuse the customary ex-officio knighthood. In the spring of 1802 he succeeded Law as attorney-general: ' 'I have hopes', wrote Wilberforce in his diary, 'Perceval will still prove a blessing in a high station'.[2] The immediate blessing was to the Perceval family finances. In order to be able to devote more time to politics, he transferred his practice from king's bench to chancery; within a year his fees had more than doubled and reached almost £10,000 by 1804. The benchers of Lincoln's Inn elected him treasurer of their society, and for the first (and only) time in his life he felt free from private financial worries.[3]

Politically his period of office under Addington was far less comfortable. It took him a long time to accept the necessity for the peace of

[1] Receipt (23 Feb. 1801) in Perceval MSS.
[2] Romilly, vol. II, p. 136; Wilberforce, vol. III, p. 46.
Edward Law (1750–1818) later became, as Lord Ellenborough, lord chief-justice of England.
[3] Walpole, vol. I, p. 89; *Black Book of Lincoln's Inn*, vol. IV, p. 93.

Amiens, and he never approved of its terms. Throughout the summer of 1801 Hawkesbury had been secretly negotiating with the French plenipotentiary, Otto, who had originally come to London to arrange an exchange of prisoners of war. The foreign secretary, handicapped by a little bad luck and a lot of bad diplomacy, made a sorry mess of the British case. He allowed himself to be bullied, by the threat of an indefinite continuation of the war, into signing the preliminary treaty on 1 October, one day before the news reached London of the surrender of the enemy army besieged at Alexandria. The number of concessions made to the French came as a great shock to Perceval. Glenbervie, who met him at a party dinner on the 24 October, noted that he looked 'far from elate', but when Pitt assured the company that he 'most cordially' approved of the peace, Perceval was persuaded to hide his own views, at least in public.[1] Only to his closest friends did he confess his misgivings. The surrender of most British colonial conquests did not worry him, for he was never an imperialist. Colonies, he argued, were a 'source of expense and weakness', not of strength. His objections were to the clauses promising to return Malta to the Knights of St. John and the Cape of Good Hope to the Dutch, for the loss of these military bases would leave us at a disadvantage when the war was renewed. Even before the preliminaries were ratified he was convinced that the peace could not last. The weakness of the Turkish empire would give Napoleon the opportunity and the excuse to renew his attack against Egypt, 'and I suppose we shall not endure that, and then to war again'. The peace of Amiens, he grumbled, had left Europe 'in a state which no Englishman could fail to deplore', and he was not happy to remain a spokesman for the government that had signed it.[2] Yet he had little sympathy for the ill-assorted opposition. Fox, in his famous speech at the *Shakespeare*, seemed to recommend the treaty because it was favourable to the French: Perceval thought that 'very abominable' and 'a statement as disgraceful and as little English as can be uttered'. Napoleon was still 'a usurper, who is trampling upon every idea, principle, and feeling of liberty' while Fox's attitude would 'let down the English character, exalt the French, and encourage rebellion as much as any United Irish or English Jacobin

---

[1] Glenbervie, *Diaries*, vol. I, p. 270. Sylvester Douglas, Baron Glenbervie (1743-1823), sat in the house of commons from 1795 to 1806 before becoming first chief commissioner of the land and forest department.

[2] Harrowby MSS., vol. VIII, fols. 149-50, Perceval to Dudley Ryder, 25 Oct. 1801.

could wish'. Windham and his followers at least saw the real danger to the country, but were too violent and intent on defeating the government. The Canningites were even worse, concentrating on bitter personal attacks on Addington and on manœuvring Pitt into opposition.[1] Until they succeeded the government was comparatively safe against an opposition crammed with talent but starved of effective leadership. In fact, judging from the evidence in the published debates, Perceval's political duties as solicitor-general were light. Only five major speeches by him are recorded for the session of 1801—three in defence of government repression in Ireland and two on the disputed election of the radical cleric Horne Tooke.[2] In the following year he advised the cabinet on the prince of Wales' petition of right (claiming arrears of revenue from the duchy of Cornwall) and spoke against the prince's case in the House.[3] But his promotion to the attorney-general-ship and the general election of 1802 (in which he was returned un-opposed for Northampton) quickly brought him to the fore. When parliament re-assembled in November it seemed clear that the peace of Amiens would soon be broken and very doubtful that the govern-ment would long survive the peace. Perceval spoke well in the debate on the navy estimates, but better still once the war with France had been renewed. On 3 June Patten's resolutions censuring the cabinet for declaring war were overwhelmed by 275 votes to 34. But Pitt, urged on by Canning, ominously proposed passing to the orders of the day, and, after being heavily outvoted, left the House before the main division.[4]

Fortunately for the ministry the outbreak, on 23 July, of Emmet's rebellion in Ireland temporarily diverted attention from party politics at Westminster. The rising itself was not markedly different from the usual run of Irish rebellions: if anything it was worse planned and less effective than most. Yet the brutal murder of Lord Kilwarden outraged English opinion and confirmed all Perceval's growing prejudices against Roman catholicism. The rising also broke out at a time when it was becoming vital that Perceval should re-assess his own political

---

[1] Perceval MSS., Perceval to Arden, 16 Oct. 1801; Perceval to Redesdale, 4 Dec. 1802.

[2] *Parl. Hist.*, vol. XXXV, 1049, 1284, 1342–1401, and 1527; *Senator* (Second series), vol. II, 858; *Parl. Reg.*, vol. XV, 65.

[3] Perceval MSS.: *Parl. Hist.*, vol. XXXVI, 438 and 441; *Parl. Reg.*, vol. XVII, 387.

[4] *Parl. Hist.*, vol. XXXVI, 1043 and 1570; Rose, vol. I, p. 464; Perceval MSS., draft of speech against Patten's resolutions.

position. While Addington clung to the treasury and Pitt took the waters at Bath, there was a spontaneous loosening of party discipline. The terms 'Pittite' and 'Foxite' no longer covered all the major issues in dispute. Fox had at least kept his small band together, but Pitt's friends sat on both sides of the House as long as their leader sat uneasily on the fence. Even the circle of Perceval's closest advisers failed to agree on a common policy. Arden backed the ministry and became a privy councillor and master of the mint (an appropriate place for one who had made a fortune out of politics); Mansel wished to see Pitt return to power; Richard Ryder, Perceval's next door neighbour at Lincoln's Inn Fields, followed Canning into opposition.[1] For a time Perceval seems to have fallen back on the advice of Sir John Mitford under whom, in the past, he had often acted as a junior in state prosecutions. It was Pitt who had persuaded Mitford to resign as attorney-general in order to succeed Addington as Speaker, an office which he disliked and for which he was eminently unsuitable.[2] So in January 1802 Mitford was raised to the English peerage as Lord Redesdale and sent to Ireland to succeed Clare as lord chancellor. In the following June he married Perceval's sister, Lady Frances, taking her back to Dublin just in time to have their honeymoon interrupted by Emmet's rebellion.[3] Eldon, who gave Perceval the first news of the insurrection, thought that Lord and Lady Redesdale had been assassinated with Kilwarden. After that shock Perceval asked his sister to write every day, which she did even when reduced to filling her letters with sketches of the pikes issued to the Dublin Volunteers. On 25 July the Irish government suspended habeas corpus and proclaimed martial law, much to the satisfaction of the entire Perceval family. 'Don't you wish', wrote the timid Lady Elizabeth to Jane, 'they would suspend the Habeas Corpus Act in England immediately and (proclaim) martial law upon the very first insurrection in any quarter?' But by the end of

[1] P.R.O., Chatham MSS., 155, Mansel to Pitt, 27 Feb. 1801.

[2] Perceval MSS., Redesdale to Perceval, 6 May 1804—'W. Pitt was the man who prevented my retiring when he quitted his office, and almost entreated me to take the office of Speaker, which of all offices was the one I had the least disposition to take'.

[3] *Gent. Mag.*, 1803, p. 595. Redesdale's appointment, said Eldon, was 'the greatest boon that has been conferred on Ireland' (Twiss, vol. I, p. 401). Perceval first became friendly with Mitford when he acted as junior counsel to him at the trial of Horne Tooke in 1794. For Emmet's rebellion see E. B. Mitford, *Life of Lord Redesdale*, pp. 95 ff. Robert Emmet (1773-1803) visited Paris and interviewed Talleyrand and Napoleon in 1802. He was arrested and executed after the failure of the 1803 uprising.

the month the Irish rebellion was over: 'altogether', wrote Lady Redesdale, 'it was such a time that I pray God I may never experience anything like it again. . . .' [1]

Her husband added long accounts in his usual heated manner, calling for the most savage repression and blaming almost everyone except the lord lieutenant and himself.[2] Ireland, he insisted, needed a strong man and honest government, the eternal cry of frightened reactionaries. Irish affairs were still controlled by an English junta, led by Castlereagh, who disliked the lord lieutenant and so did all he could to lessen his authority. Lord Hardwicke was treated like an old lion, 'kicked, buffeted, and insulted by everyone'; legislation affecting Ireland was approved by parliament before he had even heard of it; and the duke of York frequently ignored Irish claims to army patronage. Redesdale could see no one (except himself) who had either the ability or the authority to tranquillise the country. Foster and his numerous relations had usurped vast power, almost as great as that of Melville in Scotland, but they used it for their own not the public good. Pelham, the home secretary, knew as much about Ireland as he did about Tibet, while Pitt was 'so short-sighted, so pitiful a politician' on Irish questions. The government must put down the irregular armies which terrorised all loyalists and cease to deal with venal Irish politicians. 'Honesty and truth', wrote Redesdale, 'are two words which seem to have no place in the Irish vocabulary.' [3] The agitation for Roman catholic emancipation had been fostered by the weakness of English statesmen, for it was misguided sympathy not repression that had caused the unrest. 'The philanthropists happily helped them forward; and the Burkes and the Wilberforces . . . have contributed their share.' Redesdale himself published a virulent *Letter to Lord Fingall* (the most moderate of the catholic leaders), warning Irish protestants that once they conceded catholic emancipation they would themselves become a persecuted minority. And he reminded Perceval that if the Irish establishment fell, the church of England would be weakened, for under the Act of Union the two were united. 'The question', he concluded, 'is not now merely a question of religion. It

---

[1] Perceval MSS., Lady Redesdale to Lady Elizabeth Perceval, 26 July 1803; same to Jane Perceval, 26 July, 2 and 3 Aug. 1803.

[2] *Ibid.*, Redesdale to Perceval, 26 July, 16 Aug. and 12 Dec. 1803.

[3] *Ibid.*, Redesdale to Perceval, 27 Nov. 1802, 29 Aug. and 20 Oct. 1803, 4 Nov. and 3 Dec. 1804. John Foster, Baron Oriel (1740–1828), was the last Speaker of the Irish house of commons and served as Irish chancellor of the exchequer both before and after the Union.

is a question of property; a question of existence.'[1] Week after week Redesdale scribbled his long letters from Dublin, denouncing all who suggested the slightest concessions to Roman catholicism: it was a complete correspondence course in religious hysteria. Yet Redesdale did not change Perceval's views. He merely confirmed them. The series of letters was begun at Perceval's invitation and, as early as August 1803, the attorney-general was known in the Commons as one of the most violent of ultra-protestants.[2]

When parliament re-assembled in November 1803 the country was prepared for immediate invasion. Perceval heard that Christmas day had been fixed for the sailing of the French army, but that a storm had delayed preparations. 'In this country,' he told his brother-in-law, 'we begin to think the suspense of expectation worse than the attempt, and there are more wishes expressed for their making than for their delaying it.'[3] Throughout the winter and the following spring he was busy drafting proclamations for the suspension of court sittings, for imposing martial law, and for arranging the business of the Bank in case London should be occupied by the enemy. In the House he spoke boldly for the tottering government, defending the renewal of the Irish Martial Law Bill and the cabinet's policy on home defence.[4] So great was the pressure of business that he began 'trespassing on the Solicitor's devotions on Sunday' and found little time to spare for his family. Consequently Jane (who never liked Belsize House) brought her children to live with their father in Lincoln's Inn Fields. There, on 10 December 1801, she had given birth to her eight child, a daughter who was christened Isobella. In February 1803 she presented Spencer with another son, the ill-fated John Thomas, and on 11 March 1804, with a daughter, Louisa. It was a wonder, confessed Lady Frances, that 'Spencer is not quite knocked up with all his fatigues'. But Jane's recovery after the birth of Louisa was slow. She decided that London air did not agree with the children, particularly with the eight-year-old Frederick, always a delicate child, and so took her brood, looking 'so very pale', back to Hampstead.[5]

[1] Perceval MSS., Redesdale to Perceval, 17 May and 23 Oct. 1803, 11 and 20 Mar. 1804.
[2] Ibid., Perceval to Redesdale, 4 Dec. 1802; Parl. Reg., vol. III, 1055; Walpole, vol. I, p. 144.   [3] Perceval MSS., Perceval to Redesdale, 27 Dec. 1803.
[4] Ibid., draft proclamations (23 Jan. 1804) and copies of precedents; P.R.O., Chatham MSS., 166, Perceval to Pitt, 2 Apr. 1804; Parl Deb., vol. I, 299.
[5] Perceval MSS., Lady Redesdale to Jane Perceval, 2 Aug. 1803; Perceval to Mansel, 26 Feb. 1803; same to Redesdale, 16 Mar. and 28 Aug. 1804; Gent. Mag., 1804, p. 277. John Thomas Perceval was placed in a lunatic asylum in December

Perceval himself stayed in town and prepared for the critical session of 1804, when the government had to face the united opposition of Pitt, Fox, Windham, and Canning. The contest was too unequal to last long, but, until the cabinet gave way, Perceval touched heights in debate which he never equalled again until the Regency crisis of 1811. He may have been criticised 'in high company' as 'a little man with a little mind', but no one thought to question his courage. His talents, wrote Brougham, 'sparkled with peculiar brightness. His dexterity in any great or any personal conflict; his excellent language, always purely but uneffectedly English . . . his attention continually awake and his spirit ever dauntless, gained him the greatest reputation as a great and powerful debater.' [1] On 23 April Fox, supported by Pitt in 'a long speech of great hostility towards the administration', moved for a committee on national defence. Addington left it to Perceval to sum up for the ministry, and he spoke so 'uncommonly' well that the motion was defeated by 256 to 204. The minority included Pitt, Canning, Rose, the Dundases, and Wilberforce, Fox, Windham, Creevey, and Sheridan: against such forces, wrote young Horner, 'nobody conceives that the Doctor can any longer remain at the head'.[2] Already Redesdale had long lost faith in the cabinet and wished to 'see our old friend again in office'. Since October 1803 he had been urging Perceval to consider what his own financial position might be if the government collapsed, but the attorney-general remained loyal to his chief to the end. When, on the 25 April, Canning made one of his usual bitter attacks on the falling prime minister, Perceval 'much to his honour' insisted on making 'a warm and feeling' defence of him.[3] Moreover the attorney-general had refused, just before parliament re-assembled, an offer of the vacant chief justiceship of the common pleas, together with a peerage. 'I think', wrote Redesdale on the twenty-sixth, 'you have done right'. Three days later it seemed very doubtful

---

1832, was released in the following October and married 'quite out of his station in life'. Five years later he fell foul of the home office for distributing pamphlets 'calculated to inflame the lower orders' (P.R.O., H40/40 Rob. Stedman to home office, 20 June 1838).

[1] Farington, vol. II, p. 182; Brougham, *Statesmen*, vol. I, p. 248 and vol. II, p. 58.

[2] *Parl. Deb.*, vol. II, 233, and draft of speech in Perceval MSS.; Colchester, vol. I, p. 494; Pellew, vol. II, p. 271; Horner, vol. I, p. 250. Francis Horner (1778-1817) a politician best remembered as chairman of the 1810 bullion committee.

[3] Perceval MSS., Redesdale to Perceval, 27 Oct. 1803; Wilberforce, vol. III, p. 154.

if he had, for Addington told the Speaker that he had decided to resign and Pitt began his attempt to form a coalition ministry with Fox. Had it succeeded Perceval was determined 'not to have anything to do with them'; he would, he told Abbot, accept the chief justiceship of Chester, a dignified and lucrative retreat.[1] But the king soon killed the idea of a coalition and Pitt sent Perceval's old friend, Harrowby, to ask him to stay in office. 'Certainly,' answered Perceval, 'if things were as I conceived them to be upon three points; first that Mr. Fox was to have nothing to do with the Government; second that there was to be no criminatory retrospect on Addington's Govern[men]t; and thirdly that there was to be no support to the Catholic Question'.[2] Grenville, refusing to accept such crippling terms, stayed in opposition with Fox and left Pitt to carry on as best he could with a cabinet majority of be-ribboned lumber. Canning might have increased the level of cabinet ability, but was out of favour because of his violence in opposition to Addington. The best of the ministers were Hawkesbury, the home secretary, Melville at the admiralty, and Castlereagh, who was soon promoted from the board of control to the war and colonial office. Harrowby accepted the foreign seals until he was forced to retire through ill-health: then Pitt could find no more suitable successor than Mulgrave. In January 1805 Addington patched up his quarrel with Pitt and accepted a peerage and the lord presidency of the council. The reconciliation pleased Perceval without appreciably strengthening the government.[3] In fact it barely survived the session of 1805, during which the opposition impeached Melville for gross misappropriation of naval funds and Addington (now Viscount Sidmouth) resigned after a dispute with Pitt over rights of patronage. Perceval was a frequent and usually an effective speaker. During the debate on Fox's motion for a committee on the Roman catholic petition he made one of the greatest speeches of his career and he co-operated enthusiastically with Wilberforce and James Stephen in their efforts to end the slave trade.[4]

By the close of the session Pitt's strength was failing and only the king's stubbornness prevented his making overtures to the opposition.

---

[1] Perceval MSS., Redesdale to Perceval, 26 Apr. 1804; Colchester, vol. I, p. 502. According to Pellew (vol. II, p. 253) Redesdale himself had the first refusal of the common pleas.

[2] Perceval MSS., Perceval to Redesdale, 10 May 1804.

[3] *Ibid.*, Perceval to Redesdale, 17 Dec. 1804.

[4] Wilberforce, vol. III, pp. 216 and 231. For Perceval's speech on the Roman catholic petition see chapter 2, pp. 19–21.

In October the enemy's navy was overwhelmed at Trafalgar: in December Napoleon routed the Austrians and Russians at Austerlitz. 'When and where', wrote Perceval to his brother, 'will it please God to put a stop to this Scourge? That it will so please him, I cannot feel a doubt—but the when and the where are in his hands.' [1] By the time parliament met again Pitt was on his death-bed: early in the morning of 23 January he died. 'It is', wrote Perceval to Redesdale, 'now over.' 'On what is to follow from this event . . . I have no means of furnishing you with any information. In my humble opinion the state of parties renders the attempt of forming a government out of the remains of the present totally impracticable; and therefore the true wisdom seems to me to point out the necessity of the King's immediately sending for whatever person in the Opposition he may think unexceptionable, and making the best arrangements which he can by means of him.' [2] At Pitt's funeral Perceval was chosen to carry the banner of emblems. Wilberforce tried to raise a fund by private subscriptions to pay Pitt's debts, but had little success. Only Perceval 'with a large family, and a moderate fortune', at once offered £1,000 which he could ill-afford to spare. Loss of office soon made his personal financial position even worse, for though the king tried to keep the Pittites in power he failed to persuade the cautious Hawkesbury to accept the treasury. When Eldon journeyed to Windsor to resign, conscious that he had done his duty 'to God, his King, and every individual on earth', he was asked to lay his seals of office on the sofa. 'I cannot,' said the king, 'and I will not take them from you. Yet I admit you cannot stay when all the rest have run away.' [3]

As the government's law officer Perceval is usually remembered for the part he played in prosecuting Despard, Peltier, and Cobbett.[4] But, except where religion or patriotism was at stake, he showed surprising liberalism in his legal decisions. He listened to Bentham's views on the transportation of criminals to New South Wales and sponsored a bill

[1] Perceval MSS., Perceval to Arden, 28 Sep. 1805 and same to same (undated).
[2] *Ibid.*, Perceval to Redesdale, 23 Jan. 1806.
[3] Rose, vol. II, p. 257; Wilberforce, vol. III, pp. 248-9; Campbell, *Lives of the Lord Chancellors*, vol. VII, p. 189.
[4] *State Trials*, vol. XXVIII, pp. 346 and 529, vol. XXIX, pp. 1 and 502; Walpole, vol. I, pp. 98-105 and 118-25. His peroration in the Peltier case was often recalled in May 1812—'There is something so base and disgraceful, there is something so contrary to everything that belongs to the character of an Englishman, there is something so immoral in the idea of assassination, that the exhortation to assassinate this or any other Chief Magistrate would be a crime against the honourable feelings of the English law.'

to alleviate the worst horrors of the passage.[1] On labour and trade union questions he steadfastly refused to identify the interests of the government with those of the employers. Two of his decisions were particularly important in limiting the interpretation of the Combination Acts of 1799 and 1800, under which it was declared an offence for workers to form any association in order to secure an increase in wages. The difficulty of enforcing the ban lay in getting sufficient legal evidence of the existence of a trade union. Workers willing to inform on their comrades could be offered rewards and assured of protection. But the payment made often had to be greater than the real value of the information received, as operatives who had once betrayed their colleagues could rarely find work again in the same district. A less expensive and more reliable method of collecting evidence was for local magistrates to seize the papers of suspected union organisers: its weakness was the risk incurred by magistrates of having legal actions brought against them whenever they failed to find incriminating evidence. In July 1802 Perceval advised the home secretary that he ought not to give magistrates any general promise of indemnity, but 'to appraise them that the justification of what they may do . . . will depend on what they find and with the warning to leave such a measure to be adopted or not rather upon their discretion than the express advice of His Majesty's Government'.[2] Two years later the London boot and shoe manufacturers petitioned the home office to begin a government prosecution of their employees for forming an illegal union. Although the evidence submitted was, in Perceval's opinion, sufficient to secure a conviction, he strongly advised against granting the petition. For if the ministry intervened in one trade dispute it would soon be called to do so in others. There were, he argued, always complaints on both sides, 'and the impartiality of Government would be awkwardly tested if, after undertaking a prosecution at the instance of the masters, against the conspiracy of the journeymen, they were to be applied to on the part of the journeymen to prosecute the same masters for a conspiracy against their men.'[3]

Like many other evangelicals Perceval, although a fervent supporter of the abolition of the slave trade, took little interest in the fate of child factory workers at home. The only time he spoke on the subject in the Commons was during the debate on Sir Robert Peel's Cotton

[1] Add. MSS., 33543, fols. 663, 665, 667, 691; 33544, fols. 4, 6, 44, 46, 52, and 64.
[2] P.R.O., H.O., 48/11/68.
[3] Yonge, vol. I, pp. 166–9.

Manufacturing Apprentices Bill. He then supported Wilberforce in urging that the act should be extended to cover all child labour employed in the trade. Unless this were done, he argued, masters would hire pauper children for short periods instead of training apprentices. 'The very fact of the extension being opposed by manufacturers,' he told the Commons, 'on the ground that it would be prejudicial to their interests, was, with him, a reason why it should be extended. It was a proof that they possessed powers over the free labourers, which ought to be restricted.' [1] But members were not convinced, and, in the end, all Perceval would do was to submit his opinion 'to the judgement of those who were better informed'.

[1] *Parl. Reg.*, vol. XVIII, 458–9.

CHAPTER SIX

PITT'S FRIENDS IN SEARCH OF A LEADER

'THIS seems to me', wrote Huskisson as Pitt lay on his death-bed, 'like the end of all things; what further trials and misery await us God only knows.' [1] He was not left long in doubt, for when Grenville made public the list of his coalition ministry it was seen that none of Pitt's Friends was included. The cabinet consisted of 11 members, of whom 4 (Fox, Grey, Erskine, and Petty) belonged to the old opposition, and an equal number (Grenville, Spencer, Windham, and Fitzwilliam) to the new. The Sidmouth connection was represented by its leader and by Ellenborough, while Moira acted for Carlton House. What had become, asked the Pittites, of Grenville's opposition to the 'principle of exclusion'? Apparently it did not extend to 'the most respectable party in the country'.[2] Pitt's Friends were out of office, but did it follow that they were in opposition? Many of their leaders disliked the idea, especially as the war was going so badly. Mulgrave hoped for 'moderation on all sides', Camden insisted that he was the last person who wished to oppose, while Castlereagh agreed that to do so immediately they lost office would be 'unpolitic and unbecoming'. Stanhope was certain that to go into systematic opposition 'would only insure our destruction'.[3] But it was difficult to see how Pitt's Friends could remain united if they were to be neither in office nor in opposition. Was it wise, or even possible, to aim at 'the preservation of Mr. Pitt's connection'? Canning was not alone in burying his political allegiance in his leader's grave. Rose felt himself 'completely left alone' in politics, and decided to judge all future issues by 'what Mr. Pitt would have been likely to have wished me to do if he had been alive'.[4] Although this might serve as a rough guide for individual conduct, it was no basis for a party programme, since there was no guarantee of finding a commonly accepted interpretation of a dead leader's

---

[1] Melville, *Huskisson Papers*, p. 59.
[2] *Hist. MSS. Comm., 13th Report, Part 7, Lonsdale MSS.*, p. 204. See also Perceval MSS., Perceval to Redesdale, 20 May 1806.
[3] *Lonsdale MSS.*, pp. 160, 163, and 164; Perceval MSS., Castlereagh to Camden, 7 Feb. 1806 (copy).
[4] Rose, *Diaries and Correspondence*, vol. II, pp. 261–2.

wishes. Camden thought it best to bury Pitt, honour his memory, and all go their own ways. Then, objected Castlereagh, they would certainly all blunder into opposition. No one thought it would be easy to keep the connection together; many agreed that it was 'in vain to hope that it can be completely accomplished'. The tragedy of the group was, as Carrington put it, that it had lost its leader 'and with its leader everything'.[1] There was no hope of forming an opposition based on public principles. For what (besides their name) peculiarly distinguished Pitt's Friends as a group? All parties, except a few extreme Foxites and radicals, now accepted the war, although they differed on the best way of fighting it, reform no longer seemed a live issue, and the catholic question cut across most group divisions. All they had, as the irreducible minimum for continued unity, was veneration for Pitt's memory and distrust of Fox. 'Upon every measure', wrote Romilly, 'they talk of the opinions and plans of Mr. Pitt: or, in their language, the great statesman whose death the nation finds every day more reason to deplore. There is nothing very formidable in all this; and it surely is not very encouraging to a party to have no leader but one who is dead. . . .' Pitt's Friends were, of all political groups, the least fitted for systematic opposition, for as long as the Talents appeared to retain the confidence of the king organised opposition ran counter to their basic principles and, moreover, exposed them, at a critical stage in the war, to the charge of being unpatriotic. Their best course, as Perceval told Richard Ryder, was to try to maintain their unity in order 'to preserve a retreat to Lord Grenville from his new friends, or a retreat to the King from both.' [2]

The memory, even of a Pitt, was hardly in itself sufficient to keep a group of mainly young and ambitious politicians together for long. In 1806 Canning and Hawkesbury were both only thirty-six, Castlereagh was thirty-seven, and Perceval forty-four years of age. The first three had long experience of office. Hawkesbury had already been both foreign and home secretary, Castlereagh had served at the war and colonial office, while Canning had first entered junior office in 1796. Now they had not even a monopoly of Pitt's memory, for both Grenville and Windham sat on the government front bench. Fox's death in the autumn of 1806 further lessened the chances of continued

[1] Malmesbury, *Diary*, vol. IV, p. 350.

[2] Romilly, *Memoirs*, vol. I, p. 163; Perceval MSS., Perceval to Richard Ryder, 20 Nov. 1806. Cobbett dismissed the opposition contemptuously as 'three or four clerks turned out of the treasury' (*Political Register*, 17 Jan. 1807).

unity. Even contemporaries began to admit that it was becoming increasingly difficult to apply old party labels to the existing political scene. 'All the ancient distinctions of whig and tory,' wrote one observer, 'of loyalist and democrat, have been melted down and disappeared.' [1] As politicians were no longer under the same compulsion to become Pittites or Foxites, they had far greater opportunities of changing their allegiance without incurring the charge of apostasy. In such a situation the best cement was defence of office; the opposition tended to break into molecules if not into atoms.

In this predicament Pitt's Friends fell back on what to them was the natural structure of politics. It seemed indecent for those 'more peculiarly anxious for active political situation' to take the initiative in holding the connection together. 'But there are', wrote Castlereagh, 'many men of great station in the party who are entitled to take a lead in such a case.' [2] Canning explained to Lowther that what Pitt's Friends needed was those 'who shall consent to lend their names, influence and character to give weight and consistency to the connexion which we have in view'.[3] Ability, it seemed, was not an essential qualification. It was a unique situation, for the connection Pitt's Friends sought to build was entirely artificial, and was in great measure later responsible for the fiasco of the Portland ministry. Instead of a peer attracting followers by kinship, self-interest, electoral influence, or ability, they, the potential followers, consciously sought for a suitable figure-head. Fortunately some of the group remembered that in this great auction Grenville was one of the bidders. If they delayed their choice too long, he might snap up the best bargains by dangling the prospects of office before the ambitious Canning and the impecunious Perceval. On 8 February, therefore, Castlereagh and Perceval called on Canning to discuss future tactics. The meeting was surprisingly successful as both visitors accepted Canning's thesis that it was best to limit the power of the Foxites by trying to strengthen Grenville's position in the cabinet. Hawkesbury and the great majority of the group's supporters in the Lords agreed with this policy. The only important dissentient was Eldon.[4] But no progress was made in choosing a leader in the Commons. Canning told Rose that he would accept neither Castlereagh nor Hawkesbury, although he agreed (with-

[1] *Politics and Public Men, 1812,* p. 4.
[2] Perceval MSS., Castlereagh to Camden, 7 Feb. 1806.
[3] *Lonsdale MSS.,* p. 167.
[4] *Ibid.,* p. 165; Add. MSS., 42774, fol. 209, Eldon to Rose (undated); Rose, vol. II, p. 311.

out enthusiasm) that Charles Yorke or Perceval 'ought to do tolerably
well'.[1] It was a clear indication that Canning did not regard either as
a serious competitor. This pre-occupation with personal rivalries
hampered Pitt's Friends throughout. In parliament they inspired
neither confidence in themselves nor respect in their opponents. 'I hear
rather of grumbling', wrote Grenville, 'than of formed opposition.' [2]
Spurred on by Perceval, they rightly opposed the decision to include
Lord Chief Justice Ellenborough in the cabinet. Yet no previous notice
of the motion was sent to Bathurst, Camden, Chatham, or Long, with
the result that the group's leaders declined to divide in the Lords and
were overwhelmed in the Commons by 222 votes to 64.[3] Their liaison
was so poor that Eldon claimed he never knew what was happening
in the Commons until he had read his newspaper.[4] After their first
experiment in the division lobbies, therefore, they decided to speak as
much and as long and to vote as little as possible. In these tactics
Perceval excelled. He spoke at least sixty-nine times during the session,
often with great effect and nearly always with considerable wit. He
was supported so ably in these wearing tactics that Sheridan suggested
in despair that the Talents might distribute the burden of listening to
unending speeches by attending in relays.[5]

Beyond this there was little novelty in the methods used by the
group in parliament. They relied largely on the stock arguments of all
eighteenth-century oppositions by criticising the details of government
legislation (in which methods Perceval had the advantage of professional training) and by declaiming against jobbery and excessive
treasury interference in elections. Perceval did particularly well at
Sheridan's expense after the 1806 Westminster contest.[6] Yet the only

[1] Rose, vol. II, pp. 262–4.
[2] *Journal of Lord Auckland*, vol. IV, p. 276; *Parl. Deb.*, vol. IX, 808. 'I don't
think', wrote Arthur Wellesley in Feb., 'that this government can last very long'
(Wellington, *Despatches*, vol. III, p. 1).
[3] *Parl. Deb.*, vol. VI, 342. Wilberforce and Babington voted with the opposition (*Lonsdale MSS.*, p. 169). Perceval's correspondence with Ellenborough is
printed in full by Walpole (vol. I, pp. 183–8). The earl of Essex wrote that the
fiasco resulted from the lack of leadership—'no such leader exists, but everyone
who wishes to be so and knows he cannot, forms his own plans and acts upon it.
One stays away, one opposes and one supports, and thus none act together'
(*Lonsdale MSS.*, p. 175). Bathurst reports the decision to avoid dividing
(*Bathurst MSS.*, p. 53). Romilly, vol. II, p. 134.
[4] Add. MSS., 42774, fol. 209.
[5] Harris, *History of the Radical Party in Parliament*, p. 84. By June Perceval
was already talked of as 'the ablest man' in opposition (Farington, vol. III,
p. 246).
[6] *Parl. Deb.*, vol. VIII, 83 and 234.

time they really worried the government in parliament was when they opposed Windham's military plans. On this issue they had the inspiration of defending one of Pitt's own measures and the assistance of blundering tactics by Windham. Early in March the army estimates were introduced for a period of only two months in order to give Windham time to perfect his plans. A month later he gave the House a general outline of his views: Pitt's Additional Services Act was to be repealed, the principle of short terms of army service introduced, and the Volunteers largely replaced by a more efficient local defence force. Whatever the merits of Windham's proposals, they found no favour at the horse guards. The prospects of royal support invigorated the opposition. 'The King and the Duke of York', Bathurst told Harrowby, 'are very much displeased, particularly the latter; as he remonstrated against the plan of limited service, and they promised to reconsider it; and then gave notice of the motion without again speaking to him.' [1] Consequently the opposition hit back by moving for the production of any reports in favour of short enlistments received from military officers, while Perceval asked for an account of all sums issued for the service of the Volunteers since the outbreak of the war. [2] On 17 April a bill was introduced to repeal the Parish Quota Act but this did not become law until 13 May. In the meantime the secretary-at-war had been forced to bring in additional army estimates for another month, and Pitt's Friends rallied all their supporters to resist the repeal of the Additional Services Act. 'A more incompetent Government', wrote Perceval to Redesdale, 'for the detail of business, I believe, was hardly ever seen.' [3] There were long and angry debates on the second reading of the repeal bill, and in committee the opposition divided 125 strong. Windham's short service proposals went through in the form of an amendment to schedule A of the Mutiny Act, but Perceval delivered one of his longest and best speeches against the Chelsea Hospital Bill, while the Training Act was given a very rough passage in committee. [4] Nothing similar was attempted in the Lords, where, given a resolute opposition, the bill to repeal the Additional Services Act might have been defeated.

The very prospect of success sobered certain of the group's leaders. Bathurst confessed that he was 'one of those who deprecate the

[1] Harrowby MSS., main series, vol. 9, fols. 135 ff., Bathurst to Harrowby, 4 Apr. 1806; *Parl. Deb.*, vol. VI, 21.
[2] *Parl. Deb.*, vol. VI, 652 ff., 777, 790, and 840.
[3] Perceval MSS., Perceval to Redesdale, 20 May 1806; *Lonsdale MSS.*, p. 182.
[4] *Parl. Deb.*, vol. VII, 479, 622, 825, 845 and 854.

exertions which must be made to produce such a majority, from being persuaded that no Government could be formed (fit for this country in its present situation) without any acknowledged leader, and with Lord Grenville and Mr. Fox united against it'.[1] Portland held similar views, and even Perceval was, at heart, a defeatist. In public he inveighed against the Talents as a ministry 'of splendid pretence and pitiful performance', gratuitously announcing that he would never join so heterogeneous a government. In private the trumpet sounded an uncertain note. 'But still they have, and I think they must have, the Government,' he confessed to his brother-in-law, 'for I don't see how, till they fall out amongst themselves, any Government can be found which could do without them, or stand against them.' [2] By the end of their first session in opposition Pitt's Friends were in real danger of disintegration. As Castlereagh had feared from the beginning, they had split into three 'intolerant sects'—the enragés, who thought only of getting back to office; the moderates, who had few clear aims at all; and the deserters, who would rather take office under Grenville than earn it by defeating him in the division lobbies. Political dinners did a little to rally the group, but they too easily became gatherings of one or other of the cliques. Canning gave regular fortnightly dinners at White's to his own little group, which was reported to include Bourne, Rose, Lord Binning, Mildmay, Robert Dundas and 'eight or ten more'.[3] Malmesbury maintained contact with the sympathetic of the royal dukes and acted as confidential adviser to Portland, while Sturges Bourne managed the opposition press.[4] But there was little heart

---

[1] Harrowby MSS., vol. IX, fols. 72 ff., Bathurst to Harrowby, 2 June 1806.

[2] Perceval MSS., Perceval to Redesdale, 20 May 1806.

[3] *Lonsdale MSS.*, p. 180. The Canningites were already an organised group. Rede writes of Canning in 1806 that he 'showed, instantly, the determined spirit of opposition, and now felt, that, as Mr. Pitt was no more, the hopes of his party rested on himself' (p. 172). Professor Aspinall believes that the Canningites would have emerged as a separate group even before 1801 had it not been for Canning's devotion to Pitt. He lists the Canningites in 1807 as Bagot, Lord Binning, Blachford, Sturges Bourne, Col. George Canning, Dent, Ellis, Lord Fitzharris, Greenough, Huskisson, Joliffe, Holt Leigh, Lord Granville Leveson-Gower, Sir Henry Mildmay, R. P. Milnes, W. Taylor, and E. Wilbraham Bootle. Such a group, allied to Rose, Long, and (through Dundas) to the Scottish interest formed a very powerful weapon for Canning to use in the struggle for Pitt's inheritance.

[4] Most active of the royal dukes was Cumberland, who gave opposition dinners, and was described by Richard Ryder as a 'violent party man' (Aspinall, *Politics and the Press*, p. 326). The opposition had a valuable ally in the cartoonist Gillray, who was later rewarded with a pension (M. D. George, *Catalogue of Political and Personal Satires*, vol. 8, Introduction, p. XII).

in the party's efforts and Perceval began to talk significantly of the
'comfort, cordiality, and happiness' of private life.

Meanwhile the government coalition had its own problems. Fox
was first taken ill in April and soon after the end of the session
Auckland admitted that he was unlikely ever to return to the House.[1]
Grenville, fully aware of his own inability to manage men, found it
steadily more difficult to co-ordinate the efforts of the various
ministers. In military affairs he did not even try; each minister who so
desired seems to have picked his favourite general and launched his
own expedition. The percentage of successes was not high. In home
affairs the Talents quickly lost the support of reformers and radicals.

> For twenty years, when out of place,
> Whig Patriots howl'd about Reforms,
> And stoutly swore that, change their case,
> They'd drive the Placemen out by swarms;
>
> When in, they threaten'd general rout,
> But how, good Lord, did they begin?
> For every Placeman they turn'd out
> They brought ten needy Patriots in.[2]

Petty's budget filled Creevey with horror and the only liberal contribution to the debate came ironically from Perceval, who pleaded for
income tax concessions for those with large families and limited
incomes.[3] Even this came dangerously near self-interest. Sheridan was
dissatisfied with his minor office, Tierney got no office at all until after
Fox's death, while Whitbread was entirely ignored. Some ministers
also had uneasy feelings about relations with the prince of Wales.
By June, therefore, Grenville had decided that he was in urgent need
of new recruits.[4]

Pitt's Friends recognised the danger just before parliament was prorogued. At a dinner party given by Castlereagh on 29 June, Lowther

---

[1] *Lonsdale MSS.*, p. 199.

[2] *Sun*, 26 Aug. 1809.

[3] *Parl. Deb.*, vol. VII, 53 and 482; J. Gore, *Creevey's Life and Times*, p. 28.
The property tax was, thought Creevey, the 'most odious' of all existing taxes.
'It is Pitt's child, and it was worthy of him . . . . Upon my soul, Petty! I dread
such a beginning to your reign.'

[4] Moore, *Life of Sheridan*, vol. II, p. 337; H. K. Olphin, *George Tierney*, p. 102;
Gore, p. 33. Professor Aspinall (*Lord Brougham and the Whig Party*, p. 38)
sums up the Talents in words almost identical with those of Perceval—'There
had rarely been, in the history of English ministries, so glaring a contrast between
promise and fulfilment.'

suggested a formal party meeting 'for the purpose of agreeing not to receive any separate overture from Lord Grenville during the recess'. Portland was enthusiastic and offered to hold it at Burlington House. Perceval and Richard Ryder both thought it likely to create more problems than it solved, while Canning commented that he considered himself bound already by having attended with the opposition throughout the session.[1] On the following day Grenville began to make tentative approaches to Canning through Wellesley.[2] On 2 July Wellesley reported that the opposition had held its meeting and would (according to Canning) be willing to accept Grenville as the leader of a new coalition ministry, provided Pitt's Friends entered it as a group.[3] Two days later there seems to have been a second opposition meeting at Lowther's, attended by Castlereagh, Canning, Hawkesbury, Long, Melville, Westmorland, Camden, and 'one or two others'. They discussed possible arrangements for a future Pittite ministry in which Perceval was to be chancellor of the exchequer and leader of the house of commons. Both Canning and Castlereagh (neither of whom wished to give way to the other) 'entirely and cheerfully' accepted the idea, and Hawkesbury saw no reason to object to 'Perceval being Minister if it should be necessary to place him at the head'.[4] Unfortunately no one told any of this to Perceval, and Canning threw his usual spanner in the works by speaking of Camden 'as a person on whom he did not rely' and whose conduct was thought doubtful by the party.[5] Many Pittites were not happy about Canning's, thinking he was too friendly with Granville Leveson-Gower and Lady Bessborough, both of whom tried to edge him away from the opposition. Between the end of July and the middle of September Grenville continued to offer him a seat in the cabinet, but it was a most embarrassing negotiation for both parties. Canning could not forget the recent opposition meetings and disliked the prospect of crossing the floor of the House alone. A single deserter is usually a 'rat'; two or three mean a party split. Grenville was quite eager to have Perceval and Sir William Grant

[1] Harrowby MSS., vol. 4, fols. 40 ff., Richard Ryder to Harrowby, 30 June 1806.

[2] *Hist. MSS. Comm., Dropmore MSS.*, vol. 8, p. 210.

[3] *Ibid.*, pp. 212–13.

[4] Harrowby MSS., vol. 4, fol. 43, Richard Ryder to Harrowby, 5 July 1806; *Hist. MSS. Comm., Bathurst MSS.*, p. 5.

[5] *Dropmore MSS.*, vol. 8, pp. 212–13. Wellesley agreed that Camden, though 'highly respected by many of the party', was not 'numbered among the chiefs'. Eldon protested against being excluded from the party meetings (Add. MSS., 42774, fol. 209).

(the master of the rolls), both of whom would be useful in debate. Rumour had it, however, that Canning wanted a peerage for Mildmay and offices for Huskisson, Long, Sturges Bourne, and Rose. Even Buckingham could not stomach this last recruit, 'so notoriously dipped in all the filth which you and your friends are labouring to remove'.[1] There was some talk of creating one vacancy at the expense of the troublesome Windham, a dangerous method of strengthening any government. For if Grenville, in order to get the few he really wanted, was to take 'all the riff raff and turn out those we now have, it would be ungenerous, dishonourable, and only create a new opposition perhaps stronger than the present'.[2] On 13 September Canning asked Grenville to make all future overtures through the duke of Portland, and there (to the regret of both participants) the negotiations were allowed to rest.[3]

There was, however, no respite for the prime minister. Two days later Fox died and Grenville, fearing a 'strong and active Opposition' as soon as parliament re-assembled, decided that something must be done before that date. The removal of Fox did seem to many to give a new chance of extending the government coalition. Perhaps, sighed Harrowby, it would no longer be considered 'as an unpardonable crime to have been attached to Pitt'.[4] Grenville decided to try a direct approach to Perceval, who was spending the summer at Castle Ashby. Ellenborough called on him at the beginning of October, and began by saying that, now that Fox was dead, he hoped Perceval would be more willing to join the government. Perceval, however, immediately refused even to listen to any proposal which was not part of a general arrangement—'though', he confessed to Rose, 'I own I was not without a little curiosity to have known how they fancied they could have reconciled me to what I should have felt such great degradation and disgrace of character. . . .'[5] Consequently Grenville had to be content

---

[1] *Bathurst MSS.*, p. 53; Ilchester, *Journal of Lady Holland*, vol. II, pp. 208 and 210; *Dropmore MSS.*, vol. 9, p. 4.

[2] Granville, *Private Correspondence of Lord Granville Leveson-Gower*, vol. II, p. 214.

[3] *Dropmore MSS.*, vol. 8, p. 331; Buckingham, *Memoirs of the Court and Cabinets of George III*, vol. IV, p. 72. Wellesley had made a formal offer to Canning on 31 July without success and had then recommended that negotiations be broken off (*ibid.*, p. 252). Canning reported the details to Lowther (*Lonsdale MSS.*, pp. 200–1) and to Harrowby (Harrowby MSS., vol. 9, fols. 163 ff.). Grenville was handicapped throughout by Sidmouth's disapproval of the negotiations with Canning (*Dropmore MSS.*, vol. 8, p. 57).

[4] *Dropmore MSS.*, vol. 8, p. 351; *Bathurst MSS.*, p. 54.

[5] Perceval MSS., Perceval to Richard Ryder, 20 Nov. 1806; Rose, vol. 2, pp. 300–3.

with reshuffling the pack he had already got. Grey (now Lord Howick) succeeded Fox as foreign secretary and leader of the House, Thomas Grenville took the admiralty, and Holland restored the delicate group balance by becoming lord privy seal. Grenville, moreover, immediately asked for and was reluctantly granted a dissolution.[1] The Talents, bewailed Melville, had 'seized on the reins of Government', for the prospects of a general election filled the opposition with alarm. Long (an expert in such matters) admitted that they were taken by surprise —'I hear of the unprovided in all quarters'. Eldon feared that the king was suffering from one of his periodic attacks of insanity and Hawkesbury so far forgot himself as to send a formal protest to Windsor. It would, he wrote, enable the Talents to make full use of the treasury influence in the borough elections; waverers would decide to support the ministry; and 'in the event of your Majesty's feeling it expedient to change your administration, it would deprive their successors of the advantages of that measure that would be essential to the establishment of their power'.[2] The opposition could have been more usefully employed than in writing such fruitless protests. In fact they still had too many unresolved party problems to think seriously of taking office. As late as 14 October, Long was writing to Lowther that, at the next party meeting, the first thing to be done was to elect 'some head to the party without which we shall be no party at all'. Portland was still only a *locum tenens*; a feeble wreck of a politician substituting for a corpse. Among his illustrious rivals were Abercorn, Beaufort, Lowther, Melville, Richmond, and Rutland.[3] It was not difficult to produce a shorter list. Rutland controlled 8 votes, but was inconceivable at the treasury; so were Abercorn and Beaufort; Melville was eager for the

---

[1] *Dropmore MSS.*, vol. 8, p. 382; Bulwer, *Life of Palmerston*, vol. I, p. 52.

[2] *Lonsdale MSS.*, pp. 212–13; Campbell, *Lives of the Lord Chancellors*, vol. 7, p. 494; C. D. Yonge, *Life of the Earl of Liverpool*, vol. I, p. 220. Hawkesbury claimed that 49 county members supported the government, 45 the opposition, 8 were undecided but more inclined to the opposition than to the Talents, and 17 were 'altogether doubtful'. Perceval, though he regretted the dissolution, realised that the king could not have refused it. It was strange if he was taken by surprise 'but still, what could he do? Who could he have gone to that shows himself ready to support him, to have formed a Government for him? These questions we should be ready and able to answer, before we can either condemn him or be justified in concluding that his heart is with his present ministers' (Perceval MSS., Perceval to Melville, 19 Jan. 1807). Portland also thought of sending a protest to Windsor, but got no encouragement from the king (Malmesbury, *Diary*, vol. IV, p. 353).

[3] *Lonsdale MSS.*, p. 204; *Dropmore MSS.*, vol. 9, pp. 53–57; Buckingham, *Court and Cabinets of George III*, vol. IV, p. 43.

role but was ruled out by the Trotter scandal; and Richmond, though
as suitable as most, did not seem to press his application. Lowther had
strong backing and good pretentions. He also had the good sense to
decline. When wanted in parliament, he told Long, he would probably
be hunting at Cottesmore 'and as I can do one better than the other,
you may guess which I should prefer'. The best advice he could give
was to stick to Portland, and so the aged and invalid duke (fortified
by regular doses of laudanum) became the official leader of the
opposition.[1] His new followers were badly in need of guidance, for
they no longer agreed on questions of tactics. Canning and Long in
the Commons and Bathurst, Camden, and Lowther in the Lords still
held to the original aim of bolstering Grenville. Castlereagh, Perceval,
Eldon, and Hawkesbury were now for a war *á l'outrance*.[2]

Fortunately, the general election went better than the opposition had
feared. Although Grenville declared himself quite satisfied with the
results and calculated that the Talents could rely on 480 to 500 votes
in the new House, Lady Bessborough reported ministers to be 'in
great dudgeon'.[3] In fact the government made few outright gains and
there was a good deal of jockeying for position between the various
groups within the coalition, out of which the Sidmouth connection
emerged with the worst bumps. The opposition's statisticians calculated that, at the worst, they had lost less than twenty seats and at
best none at all.[4] In his own election address at Northampton Perceval

---

[1] *Lonsdale MSS.*, p. 217.

[2] *Ibid.*, pp. 214 and 223–4. Lowther still hoped for a coalition with Grenville
as late as October 1806. On the twelfth of that month he drafted a letter to Grenville on the subject, but he never sent it (*ibid.*, p. 221).

[3] *Dropmore MSS.*, vol. 8, p. 430; Auckland, vol. IV, p. 287; Gower, vol. II,
p. 226.

[4] Long calculated that the government made a net gain of 14 from the opposition and that, within the coalition, the Sidmouth group lost 17 to the Grenvillites
and Foxites (*Bathurst MSS.*, p. 54). Canning altered these figures to 10 and 16
respectively (*Lonsdale MSS.*, pp. 223–4). But in a letter to Huskisson three days
later he seems to suggest that the opposition had actually made a net gain. Rose
sent the following calculation to Perceval—'I went over the returns to the new
Parliament with Bourne a few days ago and we made the Administration gain 29,
and the Opposition 22 in England and Wales—with 5 hopeful for us and 14
doubtful; of which 19, all but three were against us in the last Parliament. You
may remember, I gave the Administration a gain of 18 to 30 in the spring by a
dissolution.' This seems to suggest a maximum gain of 10 to the ministry, but the
calculation did not include Scotland or Ireland, where Perceval feared Grenville
would gain 'a good deal'. Feiling (*The Second Tory Party*, p. 251) puts the
government gain at 30. Intrigues between the coalition parties for seats were
reported by Lowther (*Lonsdale MSS.*, pp. 215–16) and Perceval (Walpole,
vol. I, p. 211).

struck a defiant tone. 'I know', he wrote, 'how natural and just a feeling and sentiment it is for Englishmen to entertain at this moment of our country's peril that all party and personal feeling should be sacrificed to the common cause.'[1] Yet the election itself was a party manœuvre. Except on two occasions, argued Perceval, the Talents had been supported in the Commons by majorities of at least two to one, and there had not been any change of ministry to account for a dissolution.[2] Sidmouth had been in office when the late parliament had been elected; he was so at the time of the dissolution. For a short time there seemed likely to be a contest at Northampton as a third candidate began a canvass (directed more against Bouverie than Perceval). It was, reported Perceval, 'an unpremeditated fancy, that struck him after dinner, and the only surprise is that it survived into the following morning'.[3]

Parliament reassembled in December and Perceval seems to have travelled to Westminster determined to act with a self-confidence which he had previously lacked. He had, during the previous session, been as successful as any other Pittite in the Commons. Although he still knew nothing officially of the party decision to make him leader of the House when Pitt's Friends returned to office, Ellenborough's visit had proved his standing with the other side. After November 1806 Perceval's letters to his colleagues were written in a new tone of authority. His message was simple—unity and energy. The dissolution, he admitted to Ryder, had 'flung greater dismay into our ranks than is in any degree reasonable, and required every degree of exertion to counteract it'. The opposition must attend in strength, put 'a good countenance upon things', and show that individuals going to Grenville with tenders of service 'will go unthanked, even unthought of'. He had little patience with Rose's elaborate (and practically unintelligible) calculations of the election results. The truth was, he wrote, 'that the gain on the one side or the other will not be in the new members so much as in the new sentiments of the old ones'.[4] In a long letter to Melville he urged a fuller attendance of the Scottish members. The Talents would be overthrown by votes not by speeches. During

---

[1] Draft election address in Perceval MSS.

[2] The exceptions were on Petty's proposed iron tax and on the third reading of the Militia Bill.

[3] Perceval MSS., Perceval to Arden, 26 and 29 Oct. 1806. At this election Perceval offered to bear half of the election expenses, but the earl of Northampton 'would not hear of it'.

[4] *Ibid.*, Perceval to Richard Ryder, 20 and 24 Nov. 1806.

F

the previous session the opposition had had the best of many debates and was then unable to risk a division because of poor attendance. 'People seem to be waiting till Lord Castlereagh and Canning and Rose and myself, with five or six more in the House of Commons, Lord Hawkesbury and Lord Eldon in the House of Lords, shall overcome the Government and then they will come and shew their goodwill and join us.' Many Pittites refused to attend unless they had decided to take part in the debate or until they were given a positive assurance that the opposition were going to divide. But to give such a positive assurance before one knew who would attend was absurd; and so non-attendance in some produced it in others 'to the extent almost of desertion'. 'Your Lordship's experience will tell you', concluded Perceval, 'that nothing can fling Ministers on their backs in this country, unless there are others forward on their legs, shewing themselves willing and able and ready and in a body of apparent sufficiency to supply their places.' [1]

At the beginning of the session the opposition's ventures showed no sign of such qualities. Perceval made a good party speech against the Address, but no amendment was moved. Then Canning again threatened the group's unity. His conduct became steadily more unpredictable. Immediately after the election he had been sturdily optimistic, rejoicing to Lowther over Sidmouth's losses, and writing to Huskisson 'that *vigour* in Parliament is the only sure and honourable course that is now open'. [2] Yet early in January he told first Perceval and then Richard Ryder that he considered the opposition had been dissolved with the late parliament and that 'every one of the party were now at liberty to take their own line'. The dissolution showed that the king had no desire to change the administration, and even if he had, 'Pitt's Friends were not strong enough to form one'. [3] Canning made his declaration of independence with no ill-will. He spoke highly of Castlereagh's ability, which would make him an acquisition to any government. He knew Castlereagh was not popular, but 'he liked him himself and was on the best footing with him'. But, said Ryder, 'the man he likes best is clearly P[erceva]l though I am not sure whether his feelings are not mixed with some degree of jealousy, which I cannot much wonder at'. The cause of Canning's new attitude soon became

---

[1] Perceval MSS., Perceval to Melville, 19 Jan. 1807.
[2] Add. MSS., 38737, fol. 163, Canning to Huskisson, 26 Nov. 1806.
[3] Harrowby MSS., vol. IV, fols. 46 ff., Richard Ryder to Harrowby, 3 Jan. 1807.

clear. The first Earl Grey could not be expected to live much longer and, when Howick moved to the Lords, the Talents would be left without a leader in the lower House. Canning was already mentioned in government circles as a candidate for that office. 'The real truth', wrote Ryder with uncharacteristic bitterness, 'is, in spite of the attempts he would make to conceal it, that he considers politics as a game, and has no idea of any regard to principle interfering with his object of getting into power'.[1]

All this made Perceval's own brusque rejection of Ellenborough's overture seem a bit hasty. His private finances were a serious embarrassment, and only a pension from his brother saved him 'from feeling the inconvenience of my ex-official situation'. He could not, however, with decency go on for long borrowing Arden's servants each time he gave a party dinner or using Arden's box whenever he took his family to the theatre. In January his brother seems to have suggested that he might reconsider his decision to stay in opposition with Pitt's Friends. 'As to your opinion', replied Perceval, 'of the superiority of my pretentions to influence and weight, as compared with those of others with whom I act, in the sincerity of an honest conscience I do not agree with you. I am ready to acknowledge in the openness of a brotherly confidence to you that I feel that superiority in some respects, but taking all together, talents, connections, know-ledge, and everything, I really have no doubt that they would feel my loss much less than I should feel any of theirs, confining myself of course to the few with whom the comparison would be made— Lord Eldon, and Hawkesbury, Castlereagh and Canning.'[2] More important than this was his opinion of the Talents. He detested their

---

[1] *Ibid.*, vol. IV, fols. 51 ff. Same to same, 7 Jan. 1807. Dissensions amongst Pitt's Friends were noticed by Lady Holland, who in December 1806 wrote of their 'avowed schisms' and that 'Canning is distinct from Perceval and Castle-reagh' (*Journal*, vol. II, p. 193). On Christmas Day Horner wrote to Murray that Canning seemed to be making a bid for the lead, 'the settlement of which seems not yet regulated'. 'I look upon it as a serious misfortune to the country,' he continued, 'that it is for the present deprived of that important part of our politic system; a party arrayed against the ministers, for the purposes of popular vigilance and inquisition, upon fixed and assignable principles' (Horner, *Memoirs*, vol. I, p. 386). Canning was still negotiating with Grenville as late as March 1807. On the seventh of that month he wrote to his wife that he had pressed Grenville to accept Eldon as a cabinet minister without portfolio, only to be told that the Talents could not 'venture to have any person about the king likely to intrigue against us' (A. Aspinall and E. A. Smith, *English Historical Documents*, vol. XI, no. 47).

[2] Perceval MSS., Perceval to Arden, 1 Jan. 1807.

Irish policy and feared their unwillingness to stand up to America in defence of our maritime rights would cause 'more fundamental mischief to our greatness and strength than the whole of the French Revolution together has hitherto done'. He could not forgive Grenville's handling of the Delicate Investigation, nor forget the Seymour case. He felt it to be his duty to try to keep Pitt's Friends together in opposition, 'a most difficult task, since the dissolution specially, I can assure you'. It was, he argued, the widespread belief in the government's 'great and transcendent merit and talents' which filled its benches and emptied the opposition's. Whatever tactics the opposition tried to follow, it ended by offending many whom it would have liked to please. Yet the only fatal policy would be to do as little as possible, for the less it did at present, the smaller would be its influence in the future. Either Pitt's Friends had to be resolutely led into the fight or 'our sandy particles fall away' and there would be no alternative government. The policy was easier to formulate than to put into practice, although Perceval tried hard. Early in January he made an elaborate and (except for some unfortunate personal references to Fox) very effective speech on Yarmouth's peace negotiations.[1] A month later he delivered, during a debate on the Hampshire election petition, what Ryder described as not only 'the best and most impressive speech' he had ever made, but 'one of the best that ever was heard in the House at any period'. 'Long and others told me how much it reminded them of the old times of Pitt and with all my enthusiasm I have no difficulty in saying that I should have thought it good, very good, even for him.'[2] Yet such sporadic efforts never seriously weakened the government. When Lord Henry Petty introduced his new plan of finance at the end of January, the Pittites thought it too popular to be opposed, though Rose attacked it as 'nonsense' and even the independent David Magens called it 'mere moonshine'.[3]

[1] *Parl. Deb.*, vol. VII, 414. There is an elaborate draft of his speech in the Perceval MSS., obviously prepared for publication. Perceval also discussed the negotiations at great length in his letter to Arden of 1 Jan. The personal references to Fox are mentioned in Lady Holland, *Journal*, vol. II, pp. 195 and 196. The debate was opened for the opposition by Perceval's friend Matthew Montague, who convulsed the House by quoting at least ten verses of the *Aeneid*. 'We all thought', wrote Ryder, 'he would never have stopped.'

[2] Harrowby MSS., vol. IV, fol. 73, Richard Ryder to Harrowby, 14 Feb. 1807. Lady Bessborough said of this debate that Perceval spoke 'remarkably well' (Gower, vol. II, p. 242). Cobbett reported that the speech was 'admirable' and that it 'would not have disgraced Sir Francis Burdett himself' (*Political Register*, 24 Feb. 1807, p. 271).

[3] Harrowby MSS., vol. IV, fol. 68, Richard Ryder to Harrowby, 31 Jan. 1807.

Even the final collapse of the Talents was due to the king's resolution and Grenville's inept leadership rather than to the opposition's efforts.[1] On 4 February Bedford, the lord lieutenant of Ireland, warned the cabinet that the Irish Roman catholics would petition for complete emancipation unless speedy action was taken to conciliate them. On the ninth Grenville and his colleagues agreed to introduce a bill allowing Roman catholics to hold commissions in the armed forces, a decision reluctantly accepted by George III the following day. The cabinet itself was not unanimous in favour of the scheme for Sidmouth, sensing royal hostility, was opposed to all concessions. The draft of the despatch to be sent to Bedford only added to the confusion by its ambiguous wording on the extent of the proposed bill. It was, however, returned from Windsor without comment on 2 March and forwarded to Dublin on the third. Only at this late stage did the opposition come into the picture. The proposed concession had first been introduced in the Commons on 20 February as an additional clause to the Mutiny Act, but on 4 March Howick announced that he was to introduce a separate Roman Catholic Army and Navy Service Bill. This was debated on the following day when Perceval, hot from opposing an increased grant to the Roman catholic Maynooth college, rose to denounce the measure as 'one of the most important and dangerous . . . that had ever been submitted to the judgement of the legislature'. 'If it was desirable', he said, 'to preserve anything of our ancient and venerable establishments it could only be effected by making a stand against every fresh attempt at innovation.' [2] The speech rallied anti-catholic opinion in all quarters. Perceval himself began composing anonymous letters to the press while the Speaker wrote to the vice-chancellor of Oxford stressing his opposition to the bill. 1807, bewailed Sydney Smith, was a year 'eminently fruitful in moral and religious scruples (as some years are fruitful in apples, some in hops)'.[3] Finally on 11 March the king told the prime minister of his opposition, and immediately the government coalition began to fall apart.

That same day Sidmouth, having unsuccessfully offered his resignation, decided, although still a cabinet minister, to make secret overtures to the opposition. He saw Arden, admitted he opposed the bill, and

---

[1] For a complete account of the crisis see M. Roberts, *The Whig Party, 1807–1812*, pp. 13–29.

[2] *Parl. Deb.*, vol. IX, 266, and vol. VIII, 931 and 1073; Yonge, vol. I, p. 224.

[3] Perceval MSS., for Perceval's drafts; P.R.O. 30/9/15, Colchester MSS.; Heseltine, *Letters of Peter Plymley*, p. 5.

asked him to arrange an interview with Perceval. The proposal put Perceval in an awkward position. Any meeting, he wrote, 'before some distinct and overt act known to the public (such as your friends in the House of Commons concurring with me in opposition to this bill)' might, if it became known, embarrass all concerned. He therefore suggested that Sidmouth should content himself with contact by letter. He further proposed that Sidmouth might act as an intermediary between the king and the rest of the cabinet by suggesting to George III that he should in 'the most conciliatory and least offensive' way outline his opposition to Grenville. 'This communication may perhaps bring the ministers, if they are not as mad as I fear they will make the King, to reconsider this absurd measure of theirs, and possibly give the King a chance of retaining them in his councils . . . and tho' it may have this effect I must decidedly wish that it may be made.' If, on the other hand, the cabinet refused to withdraw, forcing the king either to veto the bill or use his influence to secure its defeat in parliament, then the approach would make the king's case complete, 'leave no possible charge of duplicity, or underhand dealing, no complaint of political intrigue'. Above all Perceval was anxious that if there was a breach between the king and his cabinet 'they should part with as little contention and mutual ill-will as possible'.[1] Such good sense and moderation, if followed by the party as a whole, would have put the opposition on firm ground. The wilder spirits were, however, in control. The duke of Portland, prodded into unwonted activity by his friend Malmesbury, at last asserted his leadership. On 8 March he ordered Hawkesbury to do what he could to defeat Howick's bill in the Lords: four days later he appealed directly to Windsor. The government, he told the king, could be defeated in the Lords only if the royal opposition were widely known. Even if ministers threatened to resign, there were others 'of sufficient abilities and experience' to replace them. The letter ended with an open invitation to George III to call on Portland to form a new Pittite cabinet, 'and', wrote the duke, 'as for myself, incapable as I know I am from age, infirmity, and want of ability to render Your Majesty any profitable service, should Your Majesty be of opinion that I can be of any use to you I shall do the best I can to serve you to the end of my life'.[2]

---

[1] Perceval MSS., Perceval to Sidmouth, 11 Mar. 1807.
[2] Add. MSS., 38191, fol. 246, Portland to Hawkesbury, 8 Mar. 1807; Windsor MSS., 12706-11, same to George III, 12 Mar. 1807. The king did not even acknowledge Portland's letter until after the cabinet's resignation (*ibid.*, 12746).

Meanwhile Sidmouth continued to press Perceval for a meeting. On 13 March there seems to have been negotiations between Arden and Sidmouth's followers, Bond and Bathurst, during which a meeting between the two principals was arranged at Arden's house in Bruton Street.[1] Secrecy was, however, no longer possible. Perceval, fearful of later misunderstandings, had told his party colleagues while the Speaker and even those at Holland House had also heard rumours.[2] This, and Howick's postponement of the second reading of the bill on 13 March, brought Sidmouth to his senses, for the following day he told Perceval that their interview would be 'premature and improper'.[3] The opposition leaders then met at Malmesbury's house to draft Perceval's reply, which denounced at length any compromise with the catholics' claims.[4] All this was, at best, merely peripheral: the real battle was waged between Windsor and Downing Street. On Sunday, 15 March, the cabinet agreed to withdraw the bill provided that this should not be understood as restraining them 'from time to time from proposing . . . such measures respecting that part of [the] United Kingdom as the nature of circumstances shall appear to require'. On the sixteenth even the *Morning Chronicle* admitted a 'very unpleasant misunderstanding' between Grenville and the king.[5] The following day his majesty demanded a formal pledge that the catholic question should never be re-opened and, when this was refused, sent for the opposition. Grenville, wrote Wilberforce, ran his ship aground 'on a rock above water'. The Talents had, moreover, presented Pitt's Friends with the one issue on which they could rally popular support. 'When there is a public sentiment,' wrote Lord Russell, 'especially if that sentiment is shared or inspired by the Sovereign, there will never be wanting in this country . . . men capable of becoming the organs and the leaders of a popular and powerful party.' [6]

Walter Fitzpatrick (*Hist. MSS. Comm., Dropmore MSS.*, vol. IX, p. XXII) claims that Malmesbury 'had acquired absolute control over the duke of Portland' and set out to embroil the king with the ministry. Burlington House became the headquarters of a cabal, 'of which Lord Eldon, Mr. Perceval, and the Dukes of York and Cumberland appear to have been members'.

[1] Perceval MSS., Sidmouth to Arden, 13 Mar. 1807; Arden to Perceval, 13 Mar. 1807.

[2] Colchester, vol. II, p. 104; Lady Holland, *Journal*, vol. II, p. 217.

[3] *Parl. Deb.*, vol. IX, 109; Perceval MSS., Sidmouth to Perceval, 14 Mar. 1807.

[4] *Ibid.*, Perceval to Sidmouth, 14 Mar. 1807; Malmesbury, vol. IV, p. 368.

[5] *Morning Chronicle*, 16 Mar. 1807.

[6] Russell, *Life*, vol. II, p. 97. 'Gentlemen,' wrote Cobbett on the change of ministry, 'it is the King's prerogative; a prerogative which he possesses, and

In the spring of 1807 that opportunity fell to Perceval, but before he could accept it he had to extricate himself from the unsavoury affair of the Delicate Investigation.

---

which he ought to possess, to change his ministers whensoever he pleases, and without being liable to be questioned or taunted respecting it by any power on earth' (*Political Register*, 4 Apr. 1807, p. 532).

CHAPTER SEVEN

THE DELICATE INVESTIGATION

THERE can have been few British princesses as colourful as Caroline
Amelia of Brunswick. In fact, though she lived through many humilia-
tions and finally died of a broken heart, she was a little too highly-
coloured to make a convincing tragic heroine. She was foolish and
alarmingly indiscreet: in later life her morals were probably little better
than those of her husband. But much can be forgiven a woman who
had the misfortune to marry George III's eldest son. She embarked for
England in March 1795; was married on 8 April; gave birth to a
daughter in the following January; and was turned out of Carlton
House by her husband early in the spring. Observers as varied as
Charles Abbot and Lord Holland agreed that the prince's conduct was
shameful.[1] After their separation the princess lived at Shooter's Hill
and then, from 1801, at Montague House, Blackheath. That winter
she first met Sir John Douglas (a major-general of marines who had
served with credit under Sir Sidney Smith in Egypt) and 'his showy
bold' wife, Charlotte.[2] Soon the princess and Lady Douglas were close
friends. The one was easily bored and liked new faces: the other, a
social climber of doubtful antecedents, was flattered by royal attentions. Together they admired Lady Douglas's young children, danced,
played French proverbs ('in which the Princess always cast the parts'),
musical magic, and forfeits. For a fortnight in February 1802 Lady
Douglas lived at Montague House, and acted as a temporary lady-in-
waiting to the princess. The experiment was not a success, for upon
closer acquaintance Caroline began to suspect that Lady Douglas was
not 'a person whose temper and manners could suit her', while, at
about the same time, Lady Douglas decided that her friend was 'a
very singular and a very indiscreet woman'. In fact, as she later

[1] Colchester, vol. I, p. 52; Holland, vol. II, p. 148. Lady Charlotte Bury
described the princess in 1810 as 'a pretty woman; fine light hair—very delicately
formed features, and a fine complexion—quick, glancing, penetrating eyes, long
cut and rather sunk in the head, which gave them much expression—and a remarkably delicately formed mouth; but her head was always too large for her
body, and her neck too short' (*Diary*, vol. I, pp. 6–7).
[2] Farington, vol. III, p. 292.

claimed, life at Montague House came as a great shock. She found the princess 'a person without education or talents, and without any desire of improving herself', whose conversation was constantly 'very loose, and such as I have not been accustomed to hear'. Most of it she dare not repeat to her own husband. Caroline even tried to embroil her with Prince William of Gloucester and Sir Sidney Smith. 'You see, my dear friend,' the princess was alleged to have replied to Lady Douglas's protests, 'I have the most complaisant husband in the world —I have no one to control *me*—I see whom I please, I go where I like, I spend what I please, and His Royal Highness pays for all.' [1]

It was after this unhappy fortnight that, according to Lady Douglas, the princess first confessed that she was pregnant. No explanation was ever given to account for so unlikely a confession, for Caroline never asked her friend either for advice or for help in concealing her condition. Even if the story were true, Lady Douglas's own conduct was extraordinary. She never mentioned the incident to her husband and she continued to visit Montague House as though nothing unusual had happened. In fact it took one of Caroline's typically tasteless political tirades to provoke their first real quarrel. Lady Douglas made some remonstrance, and the princess (with unusual foresight) called her a liar. But by October 1802 they were fully reconciled, the princess insisting on being present at the birth of Charlotte Douglas's latest child. Sir John and his wife spent that Christmas with relations in Gloucestershire, returning to Blackheath in January 1803. They then found the drawing-room of Montague House transformed into a 'common nursery', with napkins hung round the fire, tables covered with spoons, plates, and clothes, and the princess herself happily looking after a baby boy. Even then Lady Douglas, although believing that the future queen had given birth to an illegitimate child, did nothing about it. The two women remained on close terms for another year, and then only quarrelled because the princess kept her friend waiting for four hours in a draughty corridor in the hope of an audience. There followed a brisk exchange of incivilities and, after a final attempt at a reconciliation made by Lady Douglas, the princess sent word that her friend need not trouble to call at Montague House again. [2]

[1] *Morning Post*, 16 Mar. 1813; *The Book or the Proceedings and Correspondence upon the subject of the Inquiry into the Conduct of Her Royal Highness The Princess of Wales* . . . (Richard Edward's 1813 Edition), App., 53–9.

[2] *The Book*, App., 74–80; Perceval MSS., undated statement by the princess of Wales on her relations with Sir John and Lady Douglas.

Thereafter the affair got progressively uglier. Lady Douglas received a long anonymous letter, written in a tone 'altogether quite shocking', which accused her of spreading rumours about the princess's pregnancy. Both Sir John Douglas and Sir Sidney Smith identified the handwriting as Caroline's, and, after Sir John had closely questioned his wife, she finally told him of the princess's alleged confession. Even then the Douglases decided that, as they had no means of communicating with the king or the prince of Wales, they must 'wait to bring forward her conduct, as there seemed little doubt we should one day be'. Soon after this there arrived two obscene drawings, suggesting adultery between Sir Sidney Smith and Lady Douglas. Smith therefore insisted on meeting the duke of Kent, who acted on behalf of the princess, and who persuaded both parties to keep silent so as to avoid a scandal. Less wisely, he failed to tell the prince of Wales of his mediation.[1] In fact it did little good. In September 1805 the princess succeeded Lady Catherine Pelham as ranger of Greenwich Park, which gave her the right to dispose as she wished of all houses within the estate. One of these was occupied by the Douglases, who, on 23 October, received notice to quit from Lady Anne Townshend, the princess's lady-in-waiting. Sir John's reaction was prompt and violent. The princess herself, he claimed, had advised him to take the house, on the understanding that it should be his for life. He had spent over £2,000 upon it in repairs and threatened to appeal to the king unless the notice were withdrawn. 'At this immediate period,' he concluded, 'it happens, that a division of Marines is formed at Woolwich, of which Sir John Douglas is Lieut[enant] Colonel, and the extraordinary circumstance of his being turned out of his house, might give an idea to his corps (who do not know Her Royal Highness's character so well as Sir John does) that he had acted wrong—and therefore he cannot, nor does he mean to comply. . . .'[2] The duke of Kent immediately advised the princess to appeal to the treasury and added that, from what he knew of Douglas's character, the incident might become much more serious 'if Her Royal Highness did not act with great discretion'.[3] The warning was amply justified. On 9 November Sturges Bourne, one of the joint secretaries to the treasury, confirmed the princess's right to eject, and Caroline left the affair to Lord Chancellor Eldon. Two days later the

---

[1] *The Book*, App., 86–9.

[2] Perceval MSS., Lady Anne Townshend to Sir John Douglas, 23 Oct. 1805 (copy); Sir John Douglas to Lady Townshend, 31 Oct. 1805; Minutes Relative to the Occupation of Houses, etc., in Greenwich Park, 9 Oct. 1805.

[3] *Ibid.*, duke of Kent to princess of Wales, 7 Nov. 1805.

prince of Wales was discussing his wife's alleged pregnancy with Romilly. For Sir John Douglas had finally told his story to the duke of Sussex, knowing that he would repeat it at Carlton House, and on 3 December the Douglases signed a written statement of their charges.[1]

The unofficial Delicate Investigation began on the fifteenth when, at the command of the prince of Wales, Romilly and Lord Thurlow began to consider the sworn statement. Thurlow said bluntly that 'for himself, he did not believe it' but then made the surprising suggestion that the case should be referred not to Pitt but to Lowten, Sir John Douglas's own solicitor, who was asked to collect further evidence. On 31 November Romilly examined Lady Douglas and found that she 'gave her answers with great coolness and self-possession, and in a manner to impress one very much with the truth of them'.[2] A week later the industrious Lowten, assisted by the prince's closest adviser, Lord Moira, began (in great secrecy) to examine Sir John Douglas's servants. But as they proved little help, Lowten fell back on the gossip of former employees at Montague House. William Cole, who had served the princess as a page, was examined four times and provided fresh material in each statement. In the end he had implicated Canning, Sir Samuel Hood, Captain Thomas Manby of the Royal Navy, Sir Sidney Smith, and the painter Thomas Lawrence.[3] The second witness, Robert Bidgood (another page), then told how his wife 'had lately told him, that Fanny Lloyd told her, that Mary Wilson had told Lloyd . . .' a story concerning the princess and Sir Sidney Smith. Unfortunately this chain of gossip broke at Fanny Lloyd, who, in compensation, told how Samuel Mills, the princess's surgeon, had admitted that 'the Princess certainly was with child'. But Mills himself, although bullied by Moira and Conant, a Westminster magistrate, denounced Lloyd's evidence as an 'infamous falsehood'. After this the preliminary inquiries ended. If they had produced no reliable evidence, they had at least rehearsed the witnesses for the prosecution.[4]

On 18 May the results were laid before Romilly and Thurlow, neither of whom was much impressed. Nevertheless the prince, encouraged by the fact that his political friends were then in office, finally decided to lay the charges before the cabinet. On 29 May a royal warrant authorised an official inquiry by Lords Grenville, Erskine,

---

[1] Perceval MSS., Sturges Bourne to princess of Wales, 9 Nov. 1805; *The Book*, App., 90-1; Romilly, vol. II, p. 129.   [2] Romilly, vol. II, pp. 130-2.
[3] *The Book*, App., 98-103.   [4] *Ibid.*, 184-91, and App., 103-8.

Ellenborough, and Spencer, with Romilly, the new solicitor-general, as their legal adviser.[1] On 1 June they heard a shorter and amended version of the Douglases' earlier statement: on the sixth they examined the prurient Cole and Bidgood: and on the seventh they gave the princess her first warning of their inquiries by sending for all the servants then at Montague House. Their testimony, admitted Romilly, 'was very favourable to Her Royal Highness; and Lady Douglas's account was contradicted in very many important particulars'. The story of the princess's pregnancy was denied by Sir Francis Milman, the surgeon, Drs. Edmeades and Mills, Harriet Fitzgerald (a lady-in-waiting), Lady Willoughby, and Mary Wilson (the princess's personal maid). On the evidence of Robert Stikeman (a page), John Sicard (the princess's steward), and Charlotte Saunders (another lady-in-waiting), it was proved that the child seen at Montague House was William Austin, the son of a Deptford labourer, while the fact that he had been adopted by the princess was confirmed by Sophia Austin, the child's mother.[2] The commission's report, largely written by Grenville and issued on 14 July, entirely acquitted the princess on the main charge of pregnancy, but censured her for frivolous conduct, particularly towards Captain Manby. This sop to Carlton House was not unanimously accepted by the cabinet. Both Sidmouth and Windham felt that the inquiry had been too one-sided and even Holland criticised the wording of the report.[3] In fact, although no reliance could be placed on the contradictory and second-hand gossip of Cole, Bidgood, and Lloyd, there was some evidence to support the censure. Hestor Lisle, a moderate and unbiased witness, spoke of the princess's 'flirting conduct' towards Manby. 'I should not have thought', she continued, 'any married woman would have behaved properly who should have behaved as her Royal Highness did to Captain Manby.'[4] The value of the anonymous letters received by Lady Douglas was more open to doubt. The commission examined them and decided they had been written by the princess. But two days after their report had been issued, Lord Cholmondeley (a most competent judge) swore that one of them was not written by her and that the handwriting of the other was too cleverly disguised for him to give any opinion.[5]

[1] *Ibid.*, App., 1; Romilly, vol. II, pp. 134 and 146–8. Romilly had just been offered a safe seat in parliament by the prince of Wales, to whose influence he also owed his office of solicitor-general.

[2] Romilly, vol. II, pp. 148–50; *The Book*, App., 2–46.

[3] *The Book*, 3–10; Romilly, vol. II, p. 161; Holland, vol. II, pp. 149 and 151.

[4] *The Book*, App., 43–4.   [5] Romilly, vol. II, p. 158; *The Book*, App., 47.

The opposition lawyers who took up the princess's cause never lost sight of party advantage: but on the main issue there is no doubt that they were in the right. At the beginning of the inquiry Grenville would have allowed the prince of Wales to be present during the examination of witnesses, and after it was over, Erskine waited a month before he troubled to send one of his footmen to Montague House with a copy of the report.[1] Officially the Delicate Investigation was a secret, but it was common knowledge that the princess was under suspicion. The *Morning Post* began to comment on the case on 20 June. Partisans of the princess claimed that the Douglases had been promised £1,000 in annuities by Mrs. Fitzherbert and that Captain Manby had been offered £20,000 to support their accusations.[2] That inveterate gossip Glenbervie (who had believed the princess to be pregnant as early as 1801) was convinced that William Austin was her illegitimate son, and that he was not her only one. The Douglas faction kept the scandal alive by publishing novels like *The Royal Eclipse*, and were said to have reprinted the most damaging extracts from the commission's report. Even the sober Richard Ryder heard rumours that Canning, Sir William Scott, and the duke of Cumberland had all been lovers of the princess.[3] As long as the true facts were withheld and the princess was excluded from Court, her reputation was at the mercy of every rumour-monger in London. Throughout the inquiry she had the advice and support of Eldon, Gibbs, Plumer, and Malmesbury, but her guiding spirit was Perceval. 'To the Tower,' he was heard to cry, 'or to the scaffold in such a cause.' In his enthusiasm he saw the princess as 'a much injured lady', and even persuaded himself that he preferred her, for all her 'exterior frivolity', to the 'professedly modest and apparently reserved of the sex in high life'. Yet they remained an ill-assorted pair, held together by his disgust at her persecution and by his party's desperate need of a popular cause.[4] Relations between Perceval and Carlton House could hardly have been

---

[1] *Dropmore MSS.*, vol. VIII, p. 168.

[2] *An Admonitary Letter to H.R.H. The Prince of Wales, etc.* (Anon., Tipper and Richards, London, 1806); *An Answer to the Admonitary Letter, etc.*, by *Aristedes* (Johnson and Budd, London, 1806); Farington, vol. III, p. 279.

[3] F. Bickley, *Diaries of Lord Glenbervie*, vol. I, pp. 258 and 285, vol. II, pp. 18–19 and 21; Jackson, *Diaries of Sir George Jackson*, vol. II, p. 143; Harrowby MSS., vol. IV, fol. 43, Richard Ryder to Harrowby, 5 July 1806.

[4] Malmesbury, *Diary*, vol. IV, p. 355; Fitzgerald, *Life of George IV*, vol. I, pp. 412–13; Lady Anne Hamilton, *Secret History of the Court of England*, vol. I, pp. 216–17.

worse. Early in 1806 Perceval had been retained by Lords Euston and Henry Seymour for the house of lords' hearing of the Seymour guardianship case. Their right of ward was contested by Mrs. Fitzherbert, on whose behalf the prince of Wales openly canvassed for votes. According to Brougham, Perceval retaliated by suggesting that the prince was a liar and a bankrupt, which caused his royal highness to swear, 'with most offensive personal abuse, and an oath which cannot be recited, that he felt he could jump on him and stamp out his life with his feet'.[1]

The case for the defence was opened on 12 August when a short letter, drafted at a full meeting of the princess's advisers, was sent to George III.[2] Five days later Perceval drafted a second letter asking for authenticated copies of all the evidence given during the inquiry. These were received by 2 September and Perceval then began to write the formal defence letter.[3] When finished it covered 156 printed pages, the last and greatest production of Perceval's legal career. 'The Answer is finished', wrote Gibbs to Rose on 28 September, 'and I only wish that His Majesty may be prevailed upon to give his personal attention to it, and form his own judgement upon the case. Perceval has done it most incomparably.' Ward thought the letter 'a model of acute argument and eloquent composition'; Robert Huish praised it as 'one of the finest specimens of epistolary writing which the English language can produce'; and even Romilly admitted that it was a work of 'great art and ability'.[4] Grenville, fearing that the opposition was about to raise the matter in parliament, called a special meeting of the cabinet, apparently without reaching any agreed solution. But nine weeks later Perceval drafted a further protest to Windsor, which at length forced the government to act. On 25 January a formal cabinet minute advised George III that it was unnecessary to continue the princess's exclusion from Court, although she was warned that she must 'be more

[1] Colchester, vol. II, p. 69; Brougham, *Statesmen*, vol. II, p. 63.

[2] *The Book*, 10–12. There is a draft of this letter, with Perceval's comments and additions, in the Perceval MSS.

[3] *The Book*, 12–24; Perceval MSS. contain drafts of the letters and copies of most of the evidence.

[4] Rose, vol. II, p. 298; Huish, *Memoirs of Caroline*, p. 257; Romilly, vol. II, p. 171; S. H. Romilly, *Letters to Ivy*, p. 195. Enclosed with the letter of 2 Oct. were depositions by Captain Manby and Thomas Lawrence denying adultery with the princess. The idea, according to Ward, was suggested by Perceval. When his colleagues stressed the danger of perjury, Perceval protested that 'an oath was a very serious matter'. 'You may smile at this,' commented Ward, 'but it is perfectly true. He joined great simplicity to great acuteness. He knew nothing of the wicked world' (*Letters to Ivy*, p. 196).

circumspect in her future behaviour'.[1] The princess's advisers, wisely deciding to accept this limited victory, immediately drafted a letter expressing their client's 'unfeigned happiness' at hearing of the end of her banishment. Yet on 10 February, before a date had been fixed for Caroline's return to Court, George III wrote to say that his son had decided to put the case into the hands of his lawyers. The princess was to stay at Blackheath 'until the further result of the Prince's intention shall have been made known . . .'[2] Six days later the princess threatened to publish full details of the Delicate Investigation.

The idea of an appeal to public opinion was not new. Perceval first mentioned it to Rose on 3 October and Grenville expected it in November. But it was not until the beginning of 1807 that the issue was seriously discussed by the opposition. Perceval, convinced that the prince aimed at a divorce and that the cabinet would not oppose him, began to canvass the idea in January. It met with strong opposition. Charles Long had always believed that the commission's charges of levity were 'perhaps not unfounded'; Richard Ryder agreed that the princess had been 'very imprudent'; and Canning (who was implicated) was strongly against publication.[3] In the same month Melville heard that Caroline had been 'so unguarded and truly German in her manners' that publication would ruin her instead of the prince. 'The subject of such an inquiry', answered Perceval, 'has always appeared to us . . . to be one, which, with a due regard to female delicacy, . . . she ought to be extremely backward to be herself the publisher; our aim has therefore been, by all the means in our power, to procure from the King some act of notice and attention . . . which may satisfy the public . . . But we have not yet been able to accomplish this, and if my judgement had been to be followed [sic] the public would, unquestionably, by this time have been in possession of the case.' In the end the dispute was referred to the duke of Portland, who advised against publication as likely to distress the king and perhaps affect his health.[4]

---

[1] *Dropmore MSS.*, vol. VIII, Introduction, XXV and 431; *The Book*, 193–202; Perceval MSS., draft by Perceval of the princess's letter to the king of 8 Dec.

[2] Perceval MSS., George III to princess of Wales, 10 Feb. 1807; *The Book*, 202–5. The princess's letter of 29 Jan. was drawn up by Eldon, Perceval, and Malmesbury (Harrowby MSS., vol. IV, fol. 66, Richard Ryder to Harrowby, 29 Jan. 1807).

[3] Rose, vol. II, p. 300; *Dropmore MSS.*, vol. VIII, p. 431; *Hist. MSS. Comm.*, *Lonsdale MSS.*, p. 198, Long to Lowther, 5 Aug. 1806; Harrowby MSS., vol. IV, fol. 54, Richard Ryder to Harrowby, 9 Jan. 1807; Perceval MSS., Perceval to Arden, 1 Jan. 1807.

[4] Perceval MSS., Melville to Perceval, 13 Jan. 1807; Perceval to Melville, 19

But Perceval's case was immensely strengthened by the king's letter of 10 February and by the princess's own pleas for publication. On the twelfth she urged that the proceedings should be printed within a fortnight. Four days later she was asking Perceval to promise not to give way even if Grenville tried 'to bully the Princess by making her believe that the King will never more receive her in his presence if the publication should take place'. Lady Townshend heard, from a reliable authority, that the threat of publicity so agitated the prince 'that he could neither speak or sit'. Under such pressure, Perceval was persuaded to draft a long ultimatum to Windsor threatening full publication within a week unless the princess was received at Court and allowed to use her old apartments at Carlton House. Even then his client thought the letter 'too mild and leaving too much chance to her enemies to recall their words and to make a sort of *amende honorable* her last persecution'.[1] Copies of all the documents relating to the Delicate Investigation were sent to Richard Edwards, the printer of Crane Court, off Fleet Street, and on 5 March a short note reached Windsor with the news that *The Book* would not be withheld beyond Monday, the ninth. But on the same day that this final warning was written, Howick introduced the Roman Catholic Army and Navy Bill into the Commons. On the eighth Eldon, who strongly opposed publication, saw the king at Windsor while his anxious colleagues convinced one another that it was still not too late for the cabinet to give way. 'In the meantime', reported Richard Ryder, '1,500 or 2,000 copies of the publication are now ready in Perceval's house to be circulated at a moment's notice.' Ten days later the Talents had fallen on the Roman catholic issue; the king had commanded Pitt's Friends to form a new government; and Perceval was busy destroying most of the copies of *The Book* stored in Lincoln's Inn Fields.[2] The princess herself made the most of her hour of triumph. The Speaker and members of the new government dined by command at Montague

Jan. 1807. Copies of all the papers were also sent to Harrowby (Harrowby MSS., vol. IV, fol. 61, Richard Ryder to Harrowby, 25 Jan. 1807).

[1] Perceval MSS., princess of Wales to Perceval, 12 Feb. 1807; same to same, undated (16 Feb.); Lady Anne Townshend to Perceval, undated; *The Book*, 205–43. On 13 Feb. Richard Ryder reported that Perceval had worked all day 'without intermission and food' on the draft of the princess's letter (Harrowby MSS., vol. IV, fol. 73).

[2] *The Book*, 243–5; Twiss, vol. II, p. 37; Romilly, vol. III, p. 104; Harrowby MSS., vol. IV, fol. 87, Richard Ryder to Harrowby, 9 Mar. 1807; Holland, vol. II, p. 154.

House, and Caroline made her first public appearance in London by attending the House to hear Perceval make his maiden speech as chancellor of the exchequer. On 21 April a cabinet minute, drafted but not signed by Perceval, acquitted the princess on all charges and recommended George III to receive her with 'as little delay as possible'. The old king was not, however, to be rushed, pleading for time to prepare for an interview 'which cannot in its nature be very pleasant'. But that spring the princess was again to be seen at Court, a striking if somewhat vulgar testimony to Perceval's victory in the final and greatest case of his legal career.[1]

There the Delicate Investigation ended, and there it might quickly have been forgotten had it not been for *The Book*, for Perceval's bonfire at Lincoln's Inn Fields had not destroyed all the printed copies. He himself lent one of them to every cabinet minister, to the Speaker, to Lords Harrowby and Elliot, to his personal friends Richard Ryder, Richard Richards (the solicitor-general to the queen), and William Legge (later the fourth earl of Dartmouth), to his brother-in-law, A. B. Drummond, and even to his banker, John Drummond.[2] At the same time Richard Edwards, the printer of *The Book*, was doing a little unofficial lending of his own. On 27 March 1807 the following advertisement appeared in *The Times*—'The Book—Any person having in their possession a CERTAIN BOOK, printed by Mr. Edwards in 1807, but never published, with W. Lindsell's name as the seller of the same on the title page, and will bring it to W. Lindsell, Bookseller, Wimpole Street, will receive a handsome gratuity'. The search was organised by Litchfield, the treasury solicitor, helped by the prince of Wales's private secretary, McMahon. According to Cobbett a total of £3,300 was spent in buying back five copies, while Lady Anne

---

[1] Farington, vol. IV, p. 145; Add. MSS., 38564, fol. 91, George III to Hawkesbury, 23 Apr. 1807; Colchester, vol. II, p. 126; *The Book*, 246–8; *The Times*, 29 June 1807; Yonge, vol. I, p. 244. Perceval's original draft of the cabinet minute of 21 Apr. ended with the following paragraph—'And with respect to what is suggested on the part of His Royal Highness, the Prince of Wales, in regard to a more formal separation between H.R.H. and the Princess, they trust that Yr. My. will excuse them forbearing to submit to your Majesty any opinion upon that most important and delicate subject at the present time . . .' (draft in Perceval MSS.). This passage was omitted before the minute was forwarded to the king.

[2] Colchester, vol. II, p. 105; P.R.O., 30/9/15, Colchester MSS., Perceval to Abbot, 18 Mar. 1807. The Perceval MSS. contain the full list of those to whom copies of *The Book* were sent, as well as the only three known surviving copies of Richard Edwards's original 1807 edition. These are all endorsed by Perceval— '*Most Secret and Confidential*. It is earnestly requested that this book may be kept lockt up, when not in hand; and that it may be returned as soon as read.'

Hamilton claimed that a single copy fetched £15,000.[1] In all Litchfield had recovered by March 1809 fourteen complete copies of *The Book*, as well as quantities of odd proof sheets and manuscript copies of evidence.[2] The most exciting chase occurred in the recovery of a copy which fell into the hands of Francis Blagdon, an enterprising journalist who began life as a horn boy, selling copies of the *Sun*.[3] In July 1805 Perceval (then attorney-general) had secured him six months in king's bench for a libel on the admiralty. But Blagdon was not the sort of man to bear a grudge, for during the 1807 general election he helped the No Popery cry by republishing Fox's *Book of Martyrs*.[4] On 14 February 1808 he published the first issue of a weekly newspaper, the *Phoenix*, in which he announced that he intended to produce, in serial form, a most important publication.[5] Twelve days later Perry, of the *Morning Chronicle*, told Charles Bicknell, the prince of Wales's solicitor, that Blagdon possessed a copy of *The Book*. This news was confirmed by John Budd, a Pall Mall bookseller, who had been in prison with Blagdon after the 1805 libel. Bicknell immediately contacted McMahon who, in turn, wrote to William Adam. McMahon's letter reached Adam at nine o'clock on the evening of Saturday, 27 February, when it was believed that publication was to begin in the *Phoenix* of the following day. 'In this view', wrote McMahon, 'not *one instant* is to be lost, and the Prince is most anxious the situation of matters should this very night be communicated to Mr. Perceval. . . .' Budd had described Blagdon as 'a venal fellow who seeks to be *touch'd*' and it was hoped to use Budd to do the touching. Within an hour Adam had seen both the attorney and the solicitor-general, who assured him that Portland and Castlereagh had already been warned of Blagdon's plans and would 'bear out any suitable person we could

[1] *The Times*, 27 Mar. 1807; Cobbett, *Regency and Reign of George IV*, chapter 3, p. 105; Hamilton, *Secret History of the Court of England*, vol. I, p. 215. 'What do you think', wrote Grey to Grenville on 3 Nov. 1809, 'of Perceval's having avowed to Adam that a fund in the treasury of 10,000 l. for secret service (I don't know what this fund is) has been exhausted in buying up the pamphlet which he had printed when we were in office respecting the Princess's case?' (*Dropmore MSS.*, vol. IX, p. 363).

[2] Perceval MSS., H. C. Litchfield to Lord Arden, 1 June 1812, enclosing two lists of copies recovered. One was surrendered by Peter Stuart, the brother of Daniel Stuart, a proprietor of the *Morning Post*.

[3] *D.N.B.*, Supplement, vol. I, p. 211. There is a short obituary notice on Blagdon in the *Gent. Mag.*, 1819, vol. II, p. 88.

[4] *Letters to Lord St. Vincent, 1801–4*, vol. II, p. 70; Perceval MSS., Joseph Kaye to Perceval, 22 Sep. 1804 and Hawkesbury to same, 24 Sep. 1804.

[5] *Times Handlist*, p. 50; Romilly, vol. II, p. 171; Campbell, vol. IX, p. 281.

find in the means of preventing the threatened publication. . . .'[1]
Therefore on 11 March Eldon granted a chancery injunction against
Blagdon, prohibiting publication on penalty of a £5,000 fine and on
the twenty-first Litchfield received from him four paper parcels
containing unbound copies of *The Book*.[2] He received his reward in
1809 when a treasury subsidy helped to finance his second newspaper
—*Blagdon's Political Register*. But he soon proved an unreliable ally.
'Do you know anything of a man named Blagdon, a publisher?' wrote
Charles Yorke to Perceval in September 1809. 'He has professed an
intention of combatting Cobbett and the other Jacobin publishers;
and I was induced in consequence t'other day to order his papers to
be sent to me; and behold! the very first I have looked at, the *Phoenix*
of Monday last, not content with repeating and re-echoing most of
the vile, absurd, and malignant paragraphs of the other papers, contains
also *Observations* on the transactions in Zealand which are at least as
libellous and mischievous as any of them.'[3] By the following February
the *Phoenix* was officially classed as 'wavering' and before the summer
of 1812 both papers had ceased publication.[4]

Rumours about the Delicate Investigation broke out afresh after
Perceval and the princess had quarrelled. Throughout 1807 and 1808
they had remained on good terms. He gave instructions for repairs
to her apartments in Kensington Palace to be begun immediately,
without waiting for the usual treasury warrants: she acted as godmother
to Ernest Augustus, the Percevals' youngest son.[5] Yet by the winter

---

[1] Blair Adam MSS., quoted by A. Aspinall in *Politics and the Press, 1780–1850*,
pp. 407–8.
[2] Romilly, vol. II, p. 171 footnote; Campbell, vol. IX, p. 282. The hearing
took place in Eldon's private room in Lincoln's Inn Hall before Sir Vicary Gibbs,
Sir Arthur Piggott, and Romilly. Blagdon himself printed the full text of the injunction in his anonymous pamphlet *Chancery Injunction! Letters to the Princess
of Wales* (London, 1813). The surrender of the documents is in the Perceval MSS.
[3] Perceval MSS., C. P. Yorke to Perceval, 12 Sep. 1809. *The Times Handlist*
(page 50) states incorrectly that the *Phoenix* ceased to appear after 25 Dec. 1808.
[4] Westbrook Hay MSS., stamp office list of newspapers (Feb. 1811). On 11
June 1811 Sir John Jervis wrote to Richard Ryder that he had 'attacked, tho' in
the humble and undignified manner of a writer in a mere weekly newspaper, the
enemies of my King and Country, through the only true loyal one, *Blagdon's
Political Register*' (Westbrook Hay MSS.). Cf. Aspinall, *Politics and the Press*,
p. 86, footnote 1.
[5] P.R.O., T1/1030/3134; *The Sun*, 24 Mar. 1808; Bickley, *Diaries of Lord
Glenbervie*, vol. II, pp. 18 and 106. It was Perceval who, early in 1809, arranged
the settlement of her debts, when she wrote that she was 'extremely grateful for
the zeal he has ever shown in her cause' (Perceval MSS., princess of Wales to
Perceval, 21 Jan. 1809).

of 1809 she had decided that she had more to gain from siding with oppositions than with ministers. That December Glenbervie spoke of her as an 'avowed partisan' of the whigs, who dined regularly with Grey and Brougham, and who infuriated ministers by canvassing for Grenville during the Oxford election.[1] 'Even the best of her Royal Highness's advisers,' wrote Lady Charlotte Bury, 'those who were honest and honourable in their intentions towards her, were not free from party spirit—whilst others again used her merely as a ladder on which to climb to power. But then, it must be said in justice to those who tried to serve her and failed, that she frequently marred their endeavours by underhand confidences to persons of opposite principles. . . .'[2] In spite of the warning of the Delicate Investigation, she continued to act very foolishly and to gossip as freely as ever. At her birthday party in 1810 she appeared 'very injudiciously attired—wrapped in a pink dressing-gown', while Miss Berry saw her at Lady Sheffield's ball—'Such an exhibition . . . such an over-dressed, bare-bosomed, painted eye-brow figure one never saw'. 'Aye,' said Horne Tooke, when told of the adoption of William Austin, 'the old story of Moses in the bullrushes.'[3] She openly denounced Perceval as unfit to be prime minister. 'It has also been reported both to Perceval and Mrs. Perceval', noted Glenbervie, 'that she said Perceval was entirely governed by that silly woman his wife. This neither will ever forgive.'[4] By the autumn of 1811 the princess had decided to publish *The Book* and that November there was talk of Leigh Hunt acting as editor, under the supervision of Brougham. But all that actually appeared was Thomas Ashe's *The Spirit of the Book*, based, according to the author, upon a copy of the original, 'which was placed for that express purpose in his hands'.[5] In March 1812 the bookseller, Sir Richard Phillips, asked Moira to support a full publication, and in the following month Grenville and Grey were discussing whether they should raise the

[1] Glenbervie, vol. II, pp. 35–6; *Journal of Miss Berry*, vol. II, p. 409; Faringdon, vol. VI, p. 204; *Dropmore MSS.*, vol. IX, p. 373; Perceval MSS., duke of Cumberland to Perceval, 17 Apr. 1809.

[2] Bury, vol. I, p. 126.

[3] *Ibid.*, vol. I, pp. 15, 51, and 67; *Journal of Miss Berry*, vol. II, p. 380; Faringdon, vol. IV, p. 165.

[4] Glenbervie, vol. II, pp. 128–9. 'Nothing', he continued, 'can be less true. Perceval is a very fond and kind husband, but keeps his wife to her own sphere.'

[5] Bury, vol. I, pp. 73–4, 131–2, and 140; Thomas Ashe, *The Spirit of the Book*, vol. I, Preface, VII–IX. For a typical rumour of the contents of *The Book* see Faringdon, vol. IV, p. 165.

princess's case in parliament.[1] Yet in the end it was left to the adventurer, Andrew Cochrane Johnstone, to defend the princess in the Commons and then not until after Perceval's death. On 8 March 1813 the *Morning Post* ('God knows, with an aching heart!') began to publish the full details of *The Book*; Blagdon hurried into print with 'a mere catchpenny' pamphlet of his own; and at least four booksellers and publishers produced copies for an eager public.[2] Perceval's handling of the Delicate Investigation was, wrote Ward, 'quite a study for lawyers': for politicians it was more of an object lesson in the dangers of hot-headedness.

[1] Aspinall, *Letters of George IV*, vol. I, p. 51; *Dropmore MSS.*, vol. X, pp. 233–4. In April 1809 the duke of Cumberland had reported that either Wardle or Byng was to move a motion (Perceval MSS., Sir Vicary Gibbs to Perceval, 17 Apr. 1809).

[2] *Morning Post*, 8–16 Mar. 1813; Blagdon, *Chancery Injunction*, etc. This began the absurd story, repeated by Cobbett in his *History of the Regency and Reign of George IV*, that Perceval stayed in office after the regency crisis by blackmailing the Regent with *The Book*. For details of the 1813 editions see the *Morning Post*, 17, 18, 20 and 21 Mar. 1813. The Prince Regent was convinced that a copy of *The Book* had been stolen from Downing Street a day or two after Perceval's death, but both Lord Arden and Herries denied this (Herries MSS., commissariat letter books, vol. 4, pp. 148–51).

CHAPTER EIGHT

PORTLAND AND NO POPERY

ON the morning of 19 March 1807 Eldon and Hawkesbury travelled down to Windsor and returned with the news that his majesty commanded the duke of Portland (in collaboration with Chatham and Lowther) to form a new ministry. 'Chaos', wrote Lord Carlisle, 'is come again': Pitt's Friends were to be rallied by an invalid, a sluggard, and a fox-hunter. At least they had a free hand, for although the king 'laughingly' insisted that places should be found for Westmorland and Lord Charles Somerset, he then left his advisers to 'dispose of everything'.[1] It was the one role for which they were all perfectly qualified: Burlington House became a political home of charity with the influential Malmesbury as semi-resident bursar. The duke himself, after one feeble effort on the twentieth to escape office, reconciled himself to the worst, and, fortified by regular doses of laudanum and opiates, steeled himself to play the part of Pitt. He realised the effort might kill him, but would 'by no means regret a few years . . . when he had the inward satisfaction of thinking they were sacrificed in his endeavours to serve his King and his country. . . .'[2]

> 'He totters', jibed the opposition, 'on a crutch,
> His brain, by sickness long depressed,
> Has lost the sense it once possessed,
> Though that's not saying much.'

One cartoonist drew a seated statue of the duke, hewed out of Portland stone and labelled, 'repair'd and whitewash'd in the year 1807'. With remarkable foresight the new first lord entered office on 1 April: it was, as Eldon feared, 'an ominous day'.[3] For two and a half years the

---

[1] Harrowby MSS., vol. XI, fol. 212, Perceval to Harrowby, 19 Mar. 1807; Yonge, vol. II, p. 228; Auckland, vol. IV, p. 301; Malmesbury, *Diary*, vol. IV, pp. 373 and 379.

[2] Windsor MSS., 12733–4, Portland to George III, 20 Mar. 1807; Malmesbury, *Diary*, vol. IV, pp. 366 and 382; *Morning Chronicle*, 23 Mar. 1807.

[3] *Morning Chronicle*, 31 Mar. and 2 Apr. 1807; Twiss, vol. II, pp. 30–1. For an example of Portland's not even being told of a cabinet meeting see Perceval MSS., Portland to Perceval, 27 Dec. 1807.

duke remained prime minister, never once speaking in parliament, rarely attending at the treasury, and often ignored by his own cabinet. Yet neither Portland's incapacity nor his unconquerable silence drew upon him the least criticism from his colleagues. His rank, his wealth, and his genuine devotion to the king placed him above all personal jealousy. He gave his young and ambitious colleagues the shelter of his name, and they neither expected nor wanted more.

The new cabinet contained eleven members, of whom eight were peers. It was largely a resurrection of Pitt's second ministry, with Camden (lord president), Westmorland (privy seal), Eldon (lord chancellor), Chatham (ordnance), Hawkesbury (home office), and Castlereagh (war and colonies) all returning to the places they had held at the time of Pitt's death. There remained vacancies at the foreign office, the admiralty, the exchequer, and the board of trade. Portland, having wisely decided not to re-appoint Mulgrave as foreign secretary, at first thought of Malmesbury. Mercifully the idea did not last. Instead unofficial overtures were made, through Bathurst, to Marquis Wellesley. The king approved, but refused to write a personal invitation: Wellesley was prepared to accept on 21 March, changed his mind the next day, and finally rejected Portland's offer on the twenty-fourth. The reason given was Paul's impending motion in the Commons against Wellesley's conduct in India.[1] This left Canning with a choice between the foreign office and the admiralty. After consulting Malmesbury, he decided to be foreign secretary and left the admiralty to the ubiquitous Mulgrave. Bathurst also entered the cabinet as master of the mint and president of the board of trade, with Rose as his vice-president and treasurer of the navy. Richmond went to Ireland as lord lieutenant after both Powis and Rutland had refused: Arthur Wellesley became chief secretary on the understanding that he should be offered the first suitable army command.[2]

The one to give most trouble was Perceval, who, as always, had to

[1] Malmesbury, *Diary*, vol. IV, pp. 370 and 377; Windsor MSS., 12755–8, Portland to George III, 23 Mar. 1807 and 12770, George III to Portland, 24 Mar.; Add. MSS., 37309, fol. 170; *Bathurst MSS.*, p. 54; *Dropmore MSS.*, vol. IX, p. 124. Within a month Wellesley had again changed his mind and wrote to Portland offering to serve the king 'either at home or abroad' (Add. MSS., 37295, fol. 101).

[2] Windsor MSS., 12755–8, *supra*; 12776–9, Portland to George III, 25 Mar. 1807; 12794–7, same to same, 28 Mar.; 12801–2, same to same, 31 Mar.; Malmesbury, *Diary*, vol. IV, p. 377; *Dropmore MSS.*, vol. IX, pp. 128–9. On 21 Mar. the Speaker had predicted that Castlereagh would go to the foreign office or exchequer and that Canning would be offered the war and colonial office (Colchester, vol. II, p. 107).

think first of his private finances. The clash between George III and his former ministers on the catholic issue had strengthened Perceval's position in the Commons, for he was the only leading Pittite in that House who fully shared the king's views. When Sidmouth decided to 'rat' on his colleagues, it was to Perceval that he made secret overtures. It was also generally thought that Perceval's speech against Howick's Army and Navy Bill had 'inflicted the death-blow' on the Talents: it was rumoured that the duke of Cumberland had read it to the king in order to rouse his delicate conscience.[1] As early as 18 March Grenville shared the 'general opinion' that Perceval was to be chancellor of the exchequer and 'the real minister'. On the following day the same story reached Perceval himself and came as an unpleasant surprise. Arden wrote a letter full of 'solicitude', to which Perceval replied that he would refuse all posts, except that of attorney-general. He repeated this to Eldon, Hawkesbury, Canning, and Castlereagh at a party meeting on the evening of the nineteenth. The following day he 'peremptorily refused' Portland's offer of the exchequer and the leadership of the Commons. It would, he explained, be 'absolute ruin' to sacrifice a steady professional income for an office (of uncertain duration) worth less than £3,700 a year. He also rejected the duke's offer of an arrangement to supplement this income, because, as he wrote to his brother, 'I would not have the administration begin by an increase of the salary of any office, and particularly not by such an increase on my account.' 'I detest the idea', he told Harrowby, 'of reversionary pension or place.' [2] If his colleagues insisted that he must be in the cabinet, he was prepared to accept the home office. This would assure him about £6,000 a year, make him the senior secretary of state, and leave him sufficiently free from departmental duties to concentrate on managing the Commons.[3] The exchequer had none of these attractions. Its status was still undefined. It had become more important since 1761 when Holland spoke of it as 'this insignificant employment': but it was not, as Spencer Walpole supposed, 'the most important office in the cabinet'. It was not even certain that the

---

[1] *Gent. Mag.*, June 1812, 591; *Journal of Lady Holland*, vol. II, p. 224; Perceval MSS.

[2] Buckingham, *Court and Cabinets of George III*, vol. IV, p. 144; Perceval MSS., Perceval to Arden, 19 Mar. 1807 (2 letters) and 20 Mar. 1807; Harrowby MSS., vol. XI, fol. 214, Perceval to Harrowby, 21 Mar. 1807.

[3] 'A Secretary of State,' wrote Hawkesbury to Arthur Wellesley in June 1808, 'I know from experience, cannot live for less than double the amount of his salary' (Wellington, *Civil Despatches, Ireland*, p. 457).

chancellor of the exchequer need be in the cabinet. Thus when Perceval himself offered the post to the untried Palmerston in 1809, he left open the question of a cabinet seat. Palmerston might have one if he wished: Perceval 'thought it better' (but not essential) that he should. It was the type of office thought suitable for promising juniors. Lord Henry Petty held it under Grenville and Perceval offered it to young Milnes.[1] As long as the first lord continued to preside at treasury board meetings, there could not even be any certain definition of the chancellor's duties. In theory the chancellor was responsible for 'ways and means' and the first lord for deciding how the money should be spent. But between 1783 and 1806, when the first lord was in the Commons, the two offices had been combined, which alone must have blurred all nice distinctions. In the last resort, the division of duties depended on the characters and abilities of the individuals involved. Grenville had been interested in the day-to-day business of the treasury and so intervened in it; Portland was not and stayed away. Yet at the best the chancellor of the exchequer was finance minister on sufferance. He came last in the cabinet list of precedence and could never speak as the acknowledged head of the treasury. 'As for myself,' wrote Perceval to Harrowby on 21 March, 'I think you are all mad. My sober opinion is that I can do them as much good, if not more (and certainly much more good to myself) as Attorney-General, than in any other situation.' A second interview with the duke again ended in a deadlock. The following day Portland was so exhausted that Chatham took charge of the negotiations, and, characteristically, made no progress. On the twenty-third, while Richard Ryder reported that Portland had given way and was to appoint Perceval as attorney-general, Hawkesbury made a direct appeal to the king. 'Lord Hawkesbury', he wrote, 'is thoroughly convinced that under the present circumstances he is the only person fully competent to conduct your Majesty's Gov[ernmen]t in the House of Commons, that the support of many respectable individuals depend[s] upon this choice being made, and that he will have great advantages in his situation from his being of an old English family and from his sentiments being known to correspond so entirely with those of your Majesty on the subject of the Catholick claims.'[2]

---

[1] Holland, *Memoirs*, vol. I, p. 40; *Bathurst MSS.*, p. 54; Walpole, vol. I, p. 242; Malmesbury, *Letters*, vol. II, pp. 155–9.

[2] Harrowby MSS., vol. XI, fol. 214, Perceval to Harrowby, 21 Mar. 1807; vol. IV, fol. 82, Richard Ryder to Harrowby, 23 Mar.; Windsor MSS., 12747–8,

The same day Perceval, persuaded by 'the pressing urgency of *all* my friends', agreed to accept the exchequer. 'I shudder', he wrote to Arden, 'as much as you do at the financial and other labours. . . .' He was offered either the chancellorship of the duchy of Lancaster for life (with a special 'additional salary' to make it worth £4,000 a year) or the first reversion to one of the tellerships of the exchequer. Without any hesitation he chose the duchy: his eldest son, he joked, 'might perhaps if he understood it like the other better'.[1] The following evening the matter was raised in the Commons during the debate on Bankes's motion against reversions. After Howick had hinted that the House should 'come to a resolution against the granting of any office for life, not usually so granted', Plumer of Hertford denounced Perceval by name and Henry Martin, a member for Kinsale, gave notice of an address. This was debated, before a full House, on 25 March. Both Canning and Castlereagh (having kissed hands) were standing for re-election and so the defence rested on the Pittite backbenchers. They made a sorry mess of it. Martin and his seconder, J. W. Ward, carefully avoided all personalities: their address, they argued, was moved on constitutional not party grounds. Perceval then made a short statement, in which he assured members that whatever the result of the division he would accept office in a government formed to 'preserve the establishments of the country, and perhaps the religion of it'. There was, reported Bathurst, 'but one opinion of the judgement and spirit of his speech'. Sturges Bourne then tried the effect of a panegyric, but was howled down as soon as he reached the word 'disinterested'. After this Perceval's old school companion, Matthew Montague, lost his temper, as usual, and denounced the opposition as 'not fair nor disposed to be so', while that wayward reactionary Johnstone began a brisk exchange of incivilities with Sheridan. But Wilberforce, Henry Thornton, and General Graham, an ex-Pittite, all supported the address, which was finally carried by 208 votes to

---

Hawkesbury to George III, 23 Mar.; 12754, Chatham to George III, 23 Mar. Walter Fitzpatrick wrongly claims that Perceval became leader of the House 'by his Majesty's particular desire' (*Dropmore MSS.*, vol. IX, p. XXVI). 'In March 1807,' wrote J. L. and Barbara Hammond, 'the Whig Ministry fell and Perceval became Prime Minister' (*The Skilled Labourer*, p. 74). Perceval wrote M. D. George of the 1807 change of ministry, 'made an unimpressive Premier' (*English Political Caricature*, vol. II, p. 99).

[1] Perceval MSS., Perceval to Arden, 23 Mar. 1807; letters patent and indenture appointing Perceval chancellor of the duchy of Lancaster, 30 and 31 Mar.; *Bathurst MSS.*, pp. 54–5. Lord Chichester, an 'old official man', also wanted the duchy for life (Malmesbury, *Diary*, vol. IV, pp. 376 and 378).

115. 'I regret excessively what has passed about Perceval', wrote
Harrowby to Bathurst. 'He seems to have spoken perfectly well, and
acted as he always will act, nobly. . . . I wish he had taken the Home
seals, with the decided lead in the House. In his present situation he
has not that advantage, and will be too much occupied with the details
of his new business to take all the share he ought in debate.' [1] The
Portland ministry had got off to a bad start: even its own supporters
admitted that. Eldon, who wished for an alliance with Sidmouth,
found the change 'no joy' and thought the government could hardly
last a month without a dissolution; Bathurst would have tried to
persuade the king to put up with the Talents; Richard Ryder, certain
that the Pittites could not survive a debate in the Lords or a division
in the Commons, advised his brother to do all he could for their
Tiverton constituents before the whigs got back. 'The battle which
we shall have to fight', confessed Perceval to Harrowby, 'will be a
very hard one, and between ourselves, I think with the present
Parliament quite desperate.' [2]

The cabinet certainly did look thin compared with all the talent on
the opposition benches. 'It is', Tom Moore told his mother, 'all a bad
business for the country. Fine times, to be sure, for changing ministry,
and changing to such fools too!' Portland at least never tried to hide
his deficiencies: that would have been a labour of Hercules. Westmorland, although personally affable and a favourite at Windsor, had little
else (besides his broad acres) to commend him. In cabinet he wrote a
few incomprehensible memoranda and thought nothing of carrying
on discussions there with his feet on the table. Camden, popularly
known as Lord Chuckle, was not a great deal better. Canning thought
little of him and there seems no good reason to disagree.[3] Chatham,
according to Rosebery, was most useful in cabinet discussions. Even
if this were so (and the evidence is not abundant), he was still discreditably lazy, quarrelsome, and indiscreet. He had all his family's lack of
grace with about half its usual ability. The best that can be said for all
four is that they each filled a place and were content to let their col-

---

[1] *Bathurst MSS.*, p. 57; *Parl. Deb.*, vol. IX, 198–219; Harrowby MSS., vol.
IX, fol. 79, Bathurst to Harrowby (undated); Add. MSS., 38190, fol. 11, George
III to Hawkesbury, 27 Mar. 1807. Perceval immediately accepted the duchy
during pleasure.

[2] Twiss, vol. II, pp. 30–2; Harrowby MSS., vol. IV, fol. 82, Richard Ryder to
Harrowby, 23 Mar. 1807; vol. IX, fol. 77, Bathurst to same (undated); vol. XI,
fol. 216, Perceval to same, 26 Mar.

[3] *Dropmore MSS.*, vol. VIII, pp. 212–13; Moore, *Memoirs*, vol. I, p. 222.

leagues get on with the work. Mulgrave had greater gifts, but little more energy. He once sat up all night planning the Copenhagen expedition and then suffered from the after-effects for the rest of his public life. In the end even Eldon began to complain of the difficulty of getting him out of bed, while the *Sun* was forced to assure its readers 'that the Noble Lord is prompt, strenuous, and active, in the arduous situation he fills'. By 1807 the admiralty was just settling down to live off a tradition: Mulgrave was not the type of first lord to object.[1] Bathurst was a reliable, energetic party man. He did much useful work in his own department, and was always ready to sacrifice his personal ambitions to what he considered the public good. But the real core of the ministry consisted of Hawkesbury and Eldon in the Lords and Canning, Castlereagh, and Perceval in the Commons. Hawkesbury's reputation has only just been rescued from the double misfortune of having been smothered in three stout volumes of Victorian biography and demolished, in two words, by Benjamin Disraeli. Between 1807 and 1812 Hawkesbury completed his long apprenticeship, and, by his successes first as home secretary and then at the war and colonial office, made amends for that unhappy period as foreign secretary under Addington. Eldon's defects have been more apparent to historians than they were to contemporaries. Once, in his old age, he had, as high steward, to attend a ceremony at Oxford university. When it was all over and he was about to enter his carriage, someone in the crowd recognised him and shouted, 'There's old Eldon! Cheer him for he never ratted!' 'I was', wrote the old man, 'very much delighted, for I never did rat. I will not say that I have been right through life; I may have been wrong; but I will say that I have been consistent.' He may have confused consistency with stagnation and thought delay 'the very essence of justice', but he was personally likeable, level-headed, and experienced. With his 'almost rustic simplicity and honesty of appearance', he was an invaluable adviser to his younger cabinet colleagues.[2] Canning was the cleverest man in the cabinet: the only one with a touch of genius. He was an excellent administrator, and the only natural orator the group possessed. Yet although no one questioned his ability, many doubted his integrity. He had grossly deceived Grenville, his departmental chief, in 1797; he had been embarrassingly violent in opposition to Addington, and unpredictable in opposition to Grenville. During the formation of the Portland

[1] Rosebery, *Pitt*, p. 246; Twiss, vol. II, p. 96; *Sun*, 21 Apr. 1808.
[2] G. H. Jennings, *Anecdotal History of the British Parliament*, p. 192.

ministry he spoke 'as if the choice of cabinet places was to be at his disposal': Lawrence thought him 'sometimes in the air' while Malmesbury wrote, more bluntly, that 'his ambition rises above this visible diurnal sphere'.[1] After Pitt's death Canning thought he owed nothing to the rest of Pitt's Friends. Instead he concentrated on recruiting his own group of personal followers, not all of whom in 1809 were prepared to follow him into the wilderness. Castlereagh in 1807 was not popular: but then he never was. There was no duller speaker in the government and few in parliament, but he was able, trusted by his colleagues, experienced, and so was Canning's closest rival in the Commons. Perceval was a stop-gap, put in to hold the balance between the two. He had done well as attorney-general and was as successful as any of his colleagues while in opposition to Grenville. In March 1807 Mulgrave spoke of him as 'the ablest man in the House of Commons'. But he still had his reputation to make, for only his closest friends already recognised his true worth. If, wrote Richard Ryder to Harrowby, 'the new government is like to resist the fiery ordeal it has to go through it must be in great measure through his means. I doubt whether our political friends are as sensible of that as they should be, and as you and I are, but I am quite sure that we are right.'[2]

On 26 March, after Howick had made a long statement on the fall of the Talents, parliament went into recess until 8 April. The whigs, encouraged by their success on the duchy issue, were full of self-confidence. 'I have heard in the course of the morning', wrote Grenville to Auckland on 19 March, 'so much of the strong current of opinion in our favour in the public, that I much doubt the possibility of a Government being formed on the ground the King has taken'. The *Morning Chronicle* was convinced that 'the co-existence of the present Parliament and the present Administration is impossible' and that the Pittites 'dare not dissolve Parliament'; *The Times* deplored the

---

[1] Farington, vol. IV, p. 103; Malmesbury, *Diary*, vol. IV, pp. 367–8; Sir Charles Petrie, *Canning*, p. 42.

[2] Farington, vol. IV, p. 103; Harrowby MSS., vol. IV, fol. 84, Richard Ryder to Harrowby, 25 Mar. 1807. 'In the Duke of Portland's last administration the distribution was between three persons of equal pretensions, two of them being Secretaries of State and agreeing to allow the precedency to the third as Chancellor of the Exchequer: originally, perhaps for the very purpose of preventing competition between themselves . . . . Perceval's precedency was, to a certain degree the result of a compromise between Castlereagh and me' (Canning to Liverpool, 25 July 1812, Yonge, vol. II, p. 414). 'If', wrote Sir Thomas Plumer of Perceval in 1807, 'he has fair play he will unquestionably be found the ablest and most upright minister the country ever saw' (Perceval MSS.).

change as 'equally unexpected and unwished for by the country at large'; and even the *Sun* regretted the loss of Grenville, though it shed no tears for his colleagues.[1] Howick was confident that he could muster at least 220 votes in the Commons, even if the Sidmouth group deserted, while Grenville was assured that the opposition would have a majority in the Commons and would be defeated only by about 130 to 90 in the Lords.[2] In order to retain as many floating votes as possible, the opposition put up Thomas Brand, one of the members for Hertfordshire, to move the party motion on the change of administration. They even re-wrote Brand's own draft to bring it 'to the taste of the weakest palates', until Sheridan joked that its whole strength lay in Brand's arms, 'which he usually waves about with great vehemence'.[3] The cabinet relied mostly on the fact that about 200 of the members elected in 1806 had not yet voted, and so existed as potential recruits. The duke of Portland and Manners Sutton, the archbishop of Canterbury (a fervent Pittite), both wrote to the duke of Newcastle urging him to instruct his members to vote for the new government.[4] 'Everyone', wrote the bishop of Meath to Perceval, 'must put their shoulder to the wagon, and I have not been idle amongst those I am acquainted with.' Captain William Gore, a member for County Leitrim, had authorised the bishop to forward his name to London. 'His objects, I should hope, are easily to be obtained, and not embarrassing to you. He has been eight years in the cavalry, and is high among the Captains of the First Dragoon Guards. A majority of cavalry, and some staff appointment would amply satisfy him, but he would be content with the former, if it could be promised him at no very distant time.' [5]

Perceval himself did good work in wooing the Saints. On 18 March, when Wilberforce first heard that the Talents were on their way out, the Slave Trade Abolition Bill had still not passed its final stages in the

---

[1] Auckland, vol. IV, p. 299; *Morning Chronicle*, 4 Apr. 1807; *The Times*, 21 Mar. and 11 Apr.; *Sun*, 2 Apr.

[2] Auckland, vol. IV, pp. 302 and 306.

[3] *Sun*, 8 Apr. 1807; Gower, *Private Correspondence*, vol. II, p. 243.

[4] *Diary of Sir George Jackson*, vol. II, p. 91; Windsor MSS., 12834-5, Perceval to George III, '¼ before 7 o'clock. Friday morning'. (10 Apr. 1807). For the archbishop's views on the collapse of the Talents see Lady Holland, *Journal*, vol. II, p. 226.

[5] Perceval MSS., bishop of Meath to Perceval, 31 Mar. 1807. The letter ends— 'He is certain of being returned upon a future occasion, but as a very principal part of his interest is Roman Catholic he will expect to be left at liberty to vote as he thinks right, in the event of any question upon the petition'.

Lords. Alarmed lest the Bill might 'fall between the two ministries' and be rejected in a snap division, he appealed to Perceval, 'whose attachment to the cause was beyond a doubt'. Perceval therefore persuaded Eldon, Hawkesbury, and Castlereagh to safeguard the measure and also wrote to the duke of Cumberland 'who [is] the King's confidant, and takes on him to be the leading man'. Once satisfied that the Abolition Bill was safe, Wilberforce soon warmed to the new ministry. 'It is', he decided, 'in one grand particular the same question as in 1784. My then principles, to which I still adhere, would govern my vote, even if I did not think so favourably of their leader, Perceval, as I do.' Because of the illness of his wife, Perceval decided to get away from Hampstead and rented Lord Teignmouth's house at Clapham. It kept him conveniently near to the Saints during the crises.[1]

Even more important was Perceval's address to his Northampton constituents, written at Lincoln's Inn Fields on 27 March. In it he appealed to 'every subject attached to the Crown, the Establishment, and the Constitution' to rally round the king, who was making 'so firm and necessary a stand for the religious establishment of the country'. The address was published only in the local *Northampton Mercury*, and contained nothing that Perceval had not already said, more strongly, at Westminster. The by-election itself went off quietly: Perceval in his final speech did not even mention the religious issue.[2] But at the dinner held to celebrate Perceval's re-election, someone suggested sending an address of congratulations to the king upon the change of administration. A requisition for a town meeting was accepted by the mayor, Joshua Gooch, in spite of whig protests. Although neither Perceval nor Bouverie seems to have intervened, party feeling in the town ran high. Whig doors were chalked with 'No Popery' signs while 'the most inflammatory hand-bills, tending to excite the most dangerous riots' were circulated among 'the ignorant and illiterate people.' The town meeting itself was pure Eatanswill. John Buxton, the whig spokesman, began it by moving that no address

[1] Wilberforce, *Life*, vol. III, pp. 301, 307, 308 and 310–11; Wilberforce, *Correspondence*, vol. II, pp. 17–18; Lord Teignmouth, *Life*, vol. II, p. 124. Perceval later became a founder member of the African Institution, formed to safeguard abolition (Wilberforce, vol. III, p. 360). On 16 April a meeting was held at the Freemasons' Hall, London, to safeguard 'innocent commerce and civilisation in Africa'. The meeting was sponsored by the Saints and ex-members of the Talents ministry attended in force. Perceval was the only leading Pittite present (*The Times*, 17 Apr. 1807).

[2] Perceval MSS., *Anonymous Memoir*, pp. 18–19; *Northampton Mercury*, 28 Mar. and 4 Apr. 1807.

be sent, in order to preserve the peace of the borough. After a show of hands both parties claimed a majority, but the mayor ruled against Buxton. There followed a long and unruly discussion on the wording of the address during which the whigs claimed they were prevented from speaking and their opponents accused them of deliberately trying to break up the meeting.

At first the incident aroused little interest in London. Romilly alone of the leading whigs attached much importance to it. The optimistic *Morning Chronicle* actually thought it one of the best symptoms of the times 'that this indecent attempt to excite religious phrenzy has utterly failed'.[1] On 7 April Romilly, attending an opposition party dinner at Howick's, noted that his colleagues were still 'very sanguine' and expected to carry Brand's motion 'by a considerable majority'. The general opinion on the morning of the debate, as reported by the Speaker, was that the government would scrape through in the Lords and be beaten in the Commons, and at White's members were betting not on the result but on the size of the opposition's majority.[2] Ministers met Brand's motion by moving the orders of the day. Perceval spoke early and was supported by Wharton (on behalf of the Lonsdale interest), General Craufurd (for the duke of Newcastle), and the fanatical Irish tory, Duigenan. Canning, who summed up, openly used the threat of dissolution, and the House finally divided at six o'clock in the morning of the tenth. Even while their own side was telling, ministers believed that they were beaten, and in the opposition lobby Howick lectured his followers on the tactics to be pursued as soon as the orders of the day were rejected. But Pitt's Friends who, when in opposition, seldom rallied 100 votes, now polled 258 against 226 for the whigs, a majority of 32.[3]

'What! what in all the world', asked Cobbett, 'could have produced this sudden change! What could have induced so many members, who

---

[1] *Northampton Mercury*, 11 Apr. 1807; Markham and Cox, *Records of the Borough of Northampton*, vol. II, p. 508; *Parl. Deb.*, vol. IX, 529 (Earl Spencer's speech); Romilly, *Memoirs*, vol. II, pp. 198–9; *Morning Chronicle*, 31 Mar. 1807.

[2] Romilly, *Memoirs*, vol. II, p. 199; Colchester, vol. II, p. 118. 'I have not yet had', wrote Howick to Grenville on 4 Apr., 'one unfavourable answer from any of the members of the House of Commons to whom I have applied. Some have not answered at all, which you may consider as pretty near the same thing' (*Dropmore MSS.*, vol. IX, pp. 132–3). A. Bourke, *The Betting Book of White's Club*, p. 45.

[3] *Parl. Deb.*, vol. IX, 284–349; Colchester, vol. II, p. 119; Windsor MSS., 12834–5, *supra*; Malmesbury, *Diary*, vol. IV, p. 382; Romilly, *Memoirs*, vol. II, pp. 201–2.

H

constantly voted with the late ministers, now to vote with their successors?' In fact Howick was beaten not by desertions from his own side so much as by new recruits to the ministry's. The Sidmouth group, as Howick had feared, went over on the catholic issue, but the total opposition vote was fully up to its leader's expectations. Forty-nine of the British knights of shire had generally supported the Grenville ministry. Forty voted against the orders of the day.[1] The new government could rely on the hard core of party members who had attended during the period in opposition. There were others who, though they preferred Pitt's Friends to the whigs, still thought it indecent to be active in opposition, especially in time of war. As long as Grenville remained in office such members tended, in spite of all remonstrances, to stay away from the House. But once the Pittites returned to power, they came back to support the king's government. Genuine waverers and members who had bought their seats at the last general election were bullied by the threat of a dissolution. And to these were added over half the 115 British knights of the shire, the Saints, and the Sidmouth connection. In the Lords' debate, attended by a record number of peers, the result was very similar: Grenville got exactly the 90 votes he had predicted, but ministers polled 171 instead of 130.[2] On 15 April the opposition tried again in the Commons, when W. H. Lyttleton of Worcestershire moved that the House regretted the change of ministry. Pitt's Friends, having expected a majority of only ten, were surprised to win by 244 votes to 198.[3]

In spite of these successes the cabinet decided to go to the country. 'I say nothing on your division,' Buckingham wrote to Thomas Grenville on the 10 April, 'save that, if your 240 hang together, no ministry can stand against that opposition, nor even against 200.' Canning and Huskisson had from the first argued for a dissolution: Eldon and Hawkesbury agreed with them. On 23 April Portland told Malmesbury that Pitt's Friends had 'only a sure majority of twenty-three, and with that there was no going on'. The following day the

[1] *Political Register*, 18 Apr. 1807; Yonge, vol. I, p. 220. The figures include English, Welsh, and Scottish county members. 27 out of the 76 English county members voted against the orders of the day, 5 of the 12 Welsh, and 8 of the 27 Scottish county members. 1 English and 1 Scottish county member also paired off on the whig side.

[2] *Parl. Deb.*, vol. IX, 352–423; Yonge, vol. I, pp. 236–7; Windsor MSS., 12784, Hawkesbury to George III, 26 Mar. 1807.

[3] *Parl. Deb.*, vol. IX, 435–47; Colchester, vol. II, p. 121; Horner, *Memoirs*, vol. I, p. 402.

duke wrote to Windsor asking for a dissolution, which was granted
on Saturday, the twenty-fifth. That evening the news was forwarded
to 'the confidential friends of Government', while Perceval saw the
Speaker and wrote a special letter to Wilberforce.[1] On Monday
27 April parliament was prorogued and then dissolved by proclamation
on the thirtieth. The King's Speech was drafted by Perceval. His first
version, a long-winded affair which sounded like one of his own
outbursts on the catholic question, was wisely rejected by the cabinet:
his second was shortened and softened before being accepted. The
king was made to speak of his resolve 'to recur to the sense of his
people, while the events which have recently taken place are yet fresh
in their recollection'. The electors were to be given an opportunity
'of testifying their determination to support him in every exercise of
the prerogative of his crown'.[2] Buckingham, indignant at 'the wicked
and atrocious charge' made against Grenville 'almost by name',
thought the Speech 'an invitation to the mob to destroy you'. The
whigs he thought, for all Grenville's optimism, would have many
'heavy pills to swallow': 'I am satisfied that the cry is completely against
us, and that we shall lose wherever it can be usefully employed against
us'. Public opinion had swung sharply against the Talents. The
common council of the city of London voted by 123 to 49 to send an
address of congratulations to the king: the S.P.C.K. was so active in
the 'No Popery' cause that Grenville had to write an open letter to its
secretary. Loyal addresses flooded into Windsor and Pittites did all
they could to swell the tide. Cumberland, violent as ever, sent a
suitable draft to Trinity college, Dublin, of which he was chancellor.
The fellows, however, declined to accept it and the copy was returned
to London with a letter announcing its refusal. The home secretary,
in his zeal, failed to read the letter, mistook the copy for an address
and published it in the *Gazette*.[3] The government had decided to strike,
Hawkesbury explained to his father, 'before the country had time to
cool'. Howick, 'in great wrath', tried to address the Commons immediately after the announcement of the prorogation: 'the deed is

---

[1] *Dropmore MSS.*, vol. IX, pp. 134–5; Windsor MSS., 12866–7, Portland to
George III, 24 Apr.; 12868, George III to Portland, 25 Apr.; Malmesbury, *Diary*,
vol. IV, pp. 385–6; Twiss, vol. II, p. 49; Colchester, vol. II, p. 123; Wilberforce,
Life, vol. III, p. 315.

[2] Perceval MSS., 2 drafts of King's Speech; Romilly, *Memoirs*, vol. II, p. 205;
Parl. Deb., vol. IX, 552; Moore, *Memoirs*, vol. I, p. 226.

[3] *Dropmore MSS.*, vol. IX, p. 138; *Sun*, 14 Apr. 1807; *Political Register*, 9 May
1807; Leveson-Gower, vol. II, p. 256.

done', wrote Grenville to Buckingham, 'and in the most violent of all possible ways'.[1]

In fact the dissolution could hardly have taken the opposition by surprise. Cobbett had publicly forecast and welcomed one on 21 March; Canning had threatened one in the Commons on 9 April; Malmesbury spoke of a general election at the levee held the same day; the *Sun* reported rumours on the eleventh; the Speaker on the seventeenth; and *The Times* on the twenty-first.[2] By 27 April the whigs were fully prepared. They had their own press headquarters, run by Brougham, and their own fund for the purchase of seats, subscribed by 'the most distinguished persons in Opposition' and administered by Tierney.[3] In answer to 'No Popery' they raised the cry of 'No Corruption', using the Commons' finance committee to try to discredit their opponents. The committee, under the chairmanship of Henry Bankes (an independent and moderate reformer with Saint connections), was first appointed in February 1807 on the motion of Myddleton Biddulph. It consisted of twenty-four members, nineteen of whom generally voted with the Talents while three were independents and two Pittites. It had authority to examine all regulations designed to control national expenditure and to suggest any further economies which could be adopted without detriment to the public service. At first, claimed Cobbett, it made slow progress, but after 19 March its whig majority became much more zealous. Bankes, studiously refusing to rush the first report for party ends, retired to his country seat and was temporarily replaced as chairman by the more accommodating Giles. The committee's inquiries, reported Thomas Grenville to Buckingham on 20 April, 'have found in Steele, and are expected to find in Huskisson, ample matter to excite the curiosity and the discussion of the public'. By the twenty-seventh the report was ready and Giles was about to read it to the House when Black Rod entered to announce the prorogation. The *Morning Chronicle* made the best use it could of the incident. The committee, it assured its readers, was 'daily making discoveries of the greatest importance, and if they sat but a month longer, it is impossible to say who might not be affected'.

[1] Yonge, vol. I, p. 237; Colchester, vol. II, p. 123; Buckingham, *Court and Cabinets of George III*, vol. IV, p. 172.

[2] *Political Register*, 21 Mar. 1807; *Parl. Deb.*, vol. IX, 347; Malmesbury, *Diary*, vol. IV, p. 382; *Sun*, 11 Apr.; Colchester, vol. II, p. 121; *The Times*, 21 Apr. 1807.

[3] Aspinall, *Politics and the Press*, p. 284; Romilly, *Memoirs*, vol. II, pp. 206–7 and 243.

There were rumours that £100,000 of public money remained 'wholly unaccounted for'. 'It is absolutely necessary for certain persons', concluded the paper, 'that inquiry should be quashed.'[1] But, as *The Times* pointed out, the real issue before the electors was neither 'No Popery' nor 'No Corruption', but the change of administration. Sydney Smith's *Letters of Peter Plymley* were excellent and entertaining party propaganda: they were also irrelevant. In 1807 the Talents suffered at the polls for their own sins. It was they who first raised the catholic issue and then 'under the pretence of defending their own conduct, arraigned that of their sovereign'. 'They wanted', wrote the *Sun*, 'to make the cabinet a body independent of the King; they appealed to the people against their Sovereign, they have now no right to complain, when their Sovereign appeals to the people against them.' The same point was made in the new government's appeal *To the electors of Great Britain* first published in the *Morning Post* on 28 April. Much was made of the Talents' inept handling of the Roman Catholic Army and Navy Bill, of Windham's unpopular recruiting plans, and of our defeats in South America and the Dardanelles. But the first charge (and the longest) was that a 'cabinet junta' had menaced the 'prerogative and independency of the Monarch'.[2] Yet, to the majority of the electors, it undoubtedly remained a 'No Popery' election. The words were painted and chalked on the walls not only of London but of many country towns and villages; the electors of Bristol, mistaking Charles Bragge Bathurst for a pro-catholic, bombarded him with mud and oysters; clergy and corporations vied with each other in voting 'Protestant' addresses; and 'even the cottages on the skirts of the commons and the forests heard fervent blessings poured out on the head of the "good old King, for preserving the nation from a rekindling of the fires in Smithfield" '. Had poor Lord George still been alive, joked Henry Erskine to the Duchess of Gordon, he would have stood a good chance of being in the cabinet instead of in Newgate.[3]

Was one by-election advertisement ultimately responsible for all this? In the opinion of a recent historian of the period Perceval's address and his handbills 'amounted to an appeal to the passions which

---

[1] *Parl. Deb.*, vol. IX, 693; *Political Register*, 2 May 1807; L. C. Sanders, *Lord Melbourne's Papers*, p. 42; Buckingham, *Court and Cabinets of George III*, vol. IV, p. 169; *Morning Chronicle*, 27 and 28 Apr. 1807; *Courier*, 29 Apr. 1807. For the report see *Parl. Deb.*, vol. IX, xvii.

[2] *The Times*, 29 Apr. 1807; *Sun*, 28 and 29 Apr.; *Morning Post*, 28 Apr.

[3] *The Times*, 8 May 1807; Sanders, *op. cit.*, p. 44; Cobbett, *Regency and Reign of George IV*, chapter II, p. 86; Romilly, *Memoirs*, vol. II, pp. 198–9.

had set London on fire in 1780'.[1] No copies of the handbills survive,
their contents can be guessed only from whig speeches. But the address
to the Northampton voters was reprinted by Perceval himself in the
local paper during the general election campaign. In Northamptonshire itself 'a long and respectable list' of freeholders, having asked
the sheriff to call a county meeting, had passed an address of congratulations to the king by a 'decided majority', in spite of the efforts
of Lord Spencer, the late home secretary. 'Can he, can any man
believe', wrote Perceval, 'that an advertisement of mine in the public
paper of your town misled all these gentlemen, counteracted all his
natural influence, overpowered all his exertions, and created the sentiment that did all this? It is ridiculous to urge it!' The election of 1807
was a 'No Popery' election because the great mass of voters were
terrified of the idea of catholic emancipation: Perceval shared rather
than created these fears.[2] 'The spirit of the whole country', wrote
Malmesbury, 'is with the King; and the idea of the Church being
in danger [perhaps not quite untrue] makes Lord Grenville and the
Foxites most unpopular. . . .' The most sanguine of Pitt's Friends
predicted sweeping gains, but Perceval told the Speaker that the new
parliament would still contain 200 opposition members.[3]

In all 92 of the 374 constituencies went to the poll and of the 658
members returned 476 had sat in the previous parliament. Perceval
(having resisted an offer to stand for Cambridge university) was returned unopposed for Northampton.[4] In the English counties Howick
lost his seat to Earl Percy at Northumberland, Lord William Russell
was heavily defeated at Surrey, Sir Henry Mildmay and Perceval's old
friend, William Chute, unseated Herbert in Hampshire, but the Pittite

[1] Fremantle, *England in the 19th Century, 1806–10*, pp. 198–9.
[2] Perceval MSS., drafts of Perceval's general election address to his constituents (with marginal notes by Lord Harrowby); *Parl. Deb.*, vol. IX, 473–4;
Political Register, 9 May 1807. The *Sun* (22 May) tried to argue that the whigs
themselves had encouraged the 'No Popery' riots in order to 'stir the Rabble, and
deter the Loyal from coming forward'. 'The cry of "No Popery",' said Windham,
'had only been heard in remote and comparatively unenlightened places' (*Parl.
Deb..*, vol. IX, 639). Freeling, the postmaster-general, seems to have used official
post office channels to circulate 'No Popery' pamphlets (Aspinall, *Politics and
the Press*, pp. 177–8).
[3] Malmesbury, *Diary*, vol. IV, p. 386; Colchester, vol. II, p. 123.
[4] There was a movement to oppose Bouverie, but it led to nothing (Markham
and Cox, vol. II, p. 508). For the Cambridge offer to Perceval see Malmesbury
Diary, vol. IV, p. 382; Perceval MSS., draft of 1807 general election address and
earl of Northampton to Perceval, 24 Apr. 1807. Perceval had previously thought
of standing for the University at the time of Pitt's death (Perceval to Redesdale,
23 Jan. 1806).

Sir Christopher Baynes failed to win Middlesex. In the great York-shire election Perceval canvassed for Wilberforce, who was returned as senior member: but to the delight of the whigs Lord Milton, the heir to Fitzwilliam, narrowly defeated Lascelles for the second seat. Elsewhere Pitt's Friends retained three of the four seats for the city of London, General Gascoyne defeated William Roscoe at Liverpool, while Cam-bridge university returned the new attorney-general, Sir Vicary Gibbs, in place of Lord Henry Petty.[1] At Westminster the radicals Burdett and Cochrane were returned with large majorities over Sheridan and Eliot, in spite of the combined exertions of the government and the opposition press. It was by far the most significant victory of the entire election.[2] The Irish contests were managed for the government by Arthur Wellesley and Charles Long. The change of administration, reported Wellesley, was almost as popular there as in England. The *Sun* even claimed that the Dublin protestants 'could easily have dis-placed Mr. Grattan had they not been unwilling to expose the city to the trouble of a contest'. 'We are going well,' wrote Wellesley to Hawkesbury on 13 May. 'I think we shall have 75 of the 100 Irish members.'[3] By mid-summer most of the opposition's leaders had conceded defeat. Holland admitted that 'the general result of the struggles in the populous places proved, that if the Court had not gained, the whigs had lost the people'. On 22 June the *Morning Chronicle* published a list of 182 members who, it stated, would vote against the government in the new parliament and Tierney, the opposition's chief statistician, managed, by juggling with the 'doubt-fuls', to reduce the Pittites' majority to 60. But Grenville deplored 'losses that we did not expect' and was discouraged by 'so many unexpected disappointments'. 'The returns', wrote Perceval to Harrowby on 14 May, 'as far as they have gone have rather improved upon our expectations than failed them.'[4] The stock whig explanation

---

[1] For results see H. S. Smith, *The Parliaments of England, 1715–1850*; Wilberforce, *Life*, vol. III, p. 317; Wilberforce, *Correspondence*, vol. II, p. 124.
[2] Patterson, *Sir Francis Burdett*, vol. I, pp. 192–218; *Sun*, 13 and 14 May 1807.
[3] Wellington, *Civil Correspondence, Ireland, 1807–9*, pp. 6 and 45; *Dropmore MSS.*, vol. IX, p. 130; *Sun*, 1 June 1807. Fremantle, pp. 199–200, claims, without citing any authority, that forty-three Irish members continued to support the whigs. But only twenty-five voted for the amendment to the Address on 26 June (cf. *Parl. Deb.*, vol. IX, 657).
[4] Holland, *Memoirs of the Whig Party*, vol. II, p. 230; Olphin, *George Tierney*, p. 115; Feiling, *Second Tory Party*, p. 257; Harrowby MSS., vol. XI, fols. 217–19, Perceval to Harrowby, 14 May 1807. The *Sun* (22 June) denounced the publica-tion of a list of opposition members as 'a gross violation of decency'.

was that they had been defeated by electoral corruption. In the
Commons Howick denounced ministers for using treasury influence
'not in the detail but in wholesale, and such as they ought to have been
ashamed of'. The influence of the Crown had been exercised 'in a
most unexampled manner': in England 'to a great degree' and in
Ireland 'most unblushingly'. Tierney told Romilly that the price of
seats was higher than ever before; that his offer of £10,000 for the two
seats at Westbury had been refused; and that as much as £6,000 was
being paid for single seats. Romilly firmly believed that the Pittites
had bought up all available boroughs, regardless of price, with money
advanced by the king out of the privy purse.[1] But during the election
Cobbett claimed to have read fifty-seven advertisements in the London
press for the sale of seats, and Romilly himself bought Horsham for
£2,000. In the 1807–12 parliament Howick sat for Appleby, Petty for
Camelford, and Sheridan for Ilchester.[2] The Talents had been defeated
in the counties and in the large as well as the rotten boroughs. They
fell because they had lost the confidence of the king: they failed at
the general election because they had also lost the confidence of the
electorate. Henceforth both government and opposition had to reckon
with a more vocal and intelligent public opinion. Neither was well
prepared for the task.

[1] *Parl. Deb.*, vol. IX, 616 and 622–23; Romilly, *Memoirs*, vol. II, pp. 206–7.
For an interesting comment on the Westbury offer see Walpole, vol. I, pp.
340–1; Harris, *History of the Radical Party*, p. 89.

[2] *Political Register*, 9 May 1807; Romilly, *Memoirs*, vol. II, p. 243; Sanders,
op. cit., p. 44.

CHAPTER NINE

PARLIAMENT AND PUBLIC OPINION

THE period 1807 to 1812 was one of constitutional shibboleths, and in its parliamentary debates is embalmed a golden age of political platitudes and memories. From the government benches rose the hymns in praise of 'the good old King' and Pitt; from the other side came constant eulogies of Fox and freedom; and from both the sanctified phrases about our 'balanced constitution', the product of the 'Glorious Revolution' of 1688. Whigs could think of little but the growing influence of the Crown, while ministers were obsessed by the need to defend the royal prerogatives. No age can hope to be entirely free from political cant and most constitutional theories explain not how we are governed to-day, but how we were governed yesterday. Danger arises only when the gap between theories and reality becomes too wide, and when politicians persist in trying to apply the theories. Such was the basic danger in the parliament of 1807 to 1812.

The procedure of the Commons was badly in need of reform. The House normally sat for about six months in every year, assembling about the third week in January and being prorogued at any time between June and August. Each week of the session was divided into 'Order Days' and 'Notice Days'. Since on the 'Order Days' (Mondays and Fridays) it lay with the majority to decide which orders should be taken, precedence was always given to government business. This led Whitbread to complain in 1811 that 'the portion of the week claimed by the Minister was much too large, and curtailed greatly the space allotted for the discussion of all the multifarious relations of national policy. . . . It went to deprive the House of its vitality.' [1] In the previous summer Romilly had tried every day for three weeks to bring on the third reading of one of his legal reform bills, only to be frustrated by previous notices and by 'the orders of the day for business taken up by the Government having always precedence, and lasting till two or three o'clock in the morning'. There were often as many as thirty items on the day's order paper: once there were forty-two orders and six notices of motions. In spite of constant long sittings, lack of

[1] Mackenzie, *The English Parliament*, p. 129.

time killed many private members' bills, while government legislation
was rushed through a thinly-attended House in the early hours of the
morning. The opposition, constantly on the watch for 'juggling' in
matters of procedure, put the blame on government. 'The truth is',
wrote Romilly, 'that the Ministers do not suffer Parliament to sit half
the time which is necessary to do the business which comes before
it.' But the second popular opposition argument was that ministers
deliberately held back important bills until near the end of the session
when many members had left Westminster 'and when the independent
country gentlemen, in particular, are almost to a man withdrawn from
attendance'.[1] The two criticisms were mutually destructive. It was
useless for professional politicians like Romilly and Whitbread to
denounce ministers for not extending the session as long as lusty
knights of the shire insisted on being back at their country seats in
good time for the first day of grouse-shooting. Longer sessions would
have been equally unpopular with the lawyers, the Scottish, and the
Irish members, who were so important to the government in divisions.
The majority of members of the house of commons were self-avowed
amateurs, who thought six months in twelve ample time to be devoted
to politics. In 1810 Perceval and the Speaker discussed relieving the
pressure by introducing regulations designed to reduce the number of
private bills.[2] But in the end nothing was done.

The party position in the Commons was confused. The old terms of
whig and tory were still used in the constituencies, on the hustings,
and even occasionally at Westminster. 'Bred up', William Hanbury
told the cheering electors of Northampton, 'as I have been in Whig
principles, which placed the present illustrious family on the throne,
those principles I shall ever steadily maintain.' [3] So, his political
opponents might have added, would they. But the so-called tories
had even less to distinguish them in the way of principles. Instead they
relied on Pitt and patriotism. Each year they met on the anniversary
of their dead leader's birthday to sing and recite countless doggerel
verses to his fame, to drink toasts to the royal family, to 'the best and
most perfect constitution the world ever saw', to the 'wooden walls
and brave tars of old England' and to 'the trade and commerce of Great

---

[1] Romilly, *Memoirs*, vol. II, p. 340; *Dropmore MSS.*, vol. IX, p. 205; *Sun*, 21
June 1808; Brougham, *Memoirs*, vol. I, p. 380. On 11 Aug. 1807 Whitbread
solemnly protested against the prorogation of parliament because of the critical
state of national affairs (*Parl. Deb.*, vol. IX, 1170).

[2] Perceval MSS., Abbot to Perceval, 4 Jan. 1810.

[3] *Northampton Mercury*, 13 Oct. 1810.

Britain'. The songs they sung were 'God save the King', 'Britons' bulwarks are our wooden walls', 'Britons strike home', and 'There's a health to Old England'. They abused the whigs because they might tamper with the constitution or compromise with Napoleon. 'He, for his own part', said one of Houblon's supporters at the Essex by-election of 1810, 'was a Tory; a blue ribbon was pinned to his cradle, and he hoped one would be nailed to his coffin.' [1] When, in the autumn of 1809, Grenville refused the cabinet's offer of coalition because he could not accept the 'principles' of the duke of Portland's ministry, Perceval could think only of catholic emancipation as an issue of principle between them. And even that divided Perceval as much on principle from Canning and Castlereagh as it did from Grenville and Grey. Whig and tory might be convenient labels to distinguish family and local interests in the country, but they were not very helpful in the house of commons. Until 1806 the most popular names had been Pittite and Foxite, although they had never been strictly applicable to more than a small minority of members. Ministers in the Portland government called themselves 'Pitt's Friends': never once throughout his life did Perceval speak of himself as a tory.[2] The opposition, even more heterogeneous than the government, could not make the same use of Fox's name. For Grenville had never been a Foxite and made a queer sort of whig. 'I look upon what has been called Mr. Fox's party,' wrote young Horner in September 1806, 'the remains of the old Whig faction, as extinguished entirely with him.' [3] But the old party name lingered on: it was familiar if largely meaningless.

To attempt to divide the 1807–12 parliament neatly into whigs and tories would, therefore, be about as helpful as trying to group members according to the colour of their hair. Nor can the political position in the Commons be treated statistically, although some of the members themselves attempted to do so. The Roses, the Longs, and the Tierneys drew up their lists, with columns for friends, foes, and neutrals, and then tried to estimate party gains at an election or to forecast the result of some crucial division. But they nearly always contradicted one another, and frequently contradicted themselves. The most compact block on the government benches, and the hard core of its strength in divisions, was the treasury group, those who held political, legal, or

[1] *Day*, 8 May 1810.
[2] The only cabinet minister who appears to have done so was Canning.
[3] Horner, *Memoirs*, vol. I, pp. 373–5.

military office under the Crown. According to McCallum's radical *Livre Rouge* published in 1810, there were then eighty placemen in the Commons, but this probably exaggerates their voting strength. In the vital division on Lord Porchester's motion on the Walcheren expedition in April 1810 the government had a majority of 275 to 227, with thirteen members paired off on each side. Sixty-six English county members divided: thirty-two for the ministry and thirty-four against. Twenty-five Irish county members supported each side, while the Scottish knights of the shire voted twenty to eight in favour of the government. The English and Welsh borough members were split by 170 to 156 against the motion; the Scottish by fifteen to nine; and the Irish by twenty-three to nine. Finally three university members voted with the ministry and one against.[1] In such a critical division the treasury block could be expected to vote in force. From the English ministry there were the first lord of the treasury, a secretary of state (and the cousin of another), the attorney-general, two under-secretaries of state, the joint secretaries to the treasury, four lords of the treasury, the secretary to the admiralty and four lords of the admiralty, the president, the secretary, and three members of the board of control, the clerk, the solicitor, and the principal store-keeper to the ordnance, the secretary-at-war, the treasurer of the navy (and his son), a comptroller of the navy, the joint paymasters to the forces (with a close relative), the paymaster of marines, the keeper of the state papers, and the king's printer.[2] The Irish sent their chancellor of the exchequer (together with a son, a son-in-law, and a secretary), the chief secretary, and four lords of the Irish treasury.[3] The Scottish list is surprisingly short—the lord advocate, the solicitor-general for Scotland, and a son

[1] Note the government's dependence on the Scottish vote and Irish borough members. List taken from the *Day*, 4 Apr. 1810. The analysis into county and borough members includes the 2 tellers for the motion, but not those against. *The Edinburgh Review* (April 1810, p. 207) gives a slightly different analysis for the county members.

English, for ministry	37	Against	39
Irish, ,, ,,	26	,,	26
Scottish, ,, ,,	20	,,	5

For full lists of office holders see P. F. McCallum, *Le Livre Rouge, Designed as a Companion to the Court Kalendar* (printed J. Blacklock, 92, Royal Exchange, London, 1810) and the *Black Book* (1820 edition).

[2] There was also a son of the postmaster-general and a brother of one of the tellers of the exchequer.

[3] Also a brother of the Irish postmaster-general, a son of the auditor-general, and a brother of a commissioner for Irish stamps.

of the receiver-general of Scottish customs. But the Royal Household was strongly represented by the treasurer, and the chamberlain to the king (and the chamberlain's secretary), the first equerry to the king, two grooms of the bedchamber, and the vice-chamberlain to the queen.[1] The armed forces contributed the governors of the Isle of Wight and of Cork, the English and Irish muster masters general, a deputy quartermaster general, and three staff officers: the law, the judge advocate, a Welsh judge, a judge of the admiralty court, a judge of the arches, and a judge of the Irish prerogative court. Finally there were the chairman and deputy-chairman of the East India company. In all 63 placemen and 13 of their close relatives voted with the ministry. And in the majority of divisions, when the numbers voting were not so large, the support of the treasury block was relatively more important. Immediately after its victory on the Walcheren issue, the government had to face the Burdett riots and so inept was the conduct of ministers that the government's reputation sank even lower. On 17 April Romilly moved for the release of Gale Jones (whose imprisonment had led to the riots). The House did not divide on the usual party lines, for both Windham and Lord Porchester voted against any concessions to 'the spirit of democracy' while most of the Carlton House and Grenville groups abstained. On the other hand, the Saints, the Canning and the Sidmouth connections, even the master of the rolls and Sir William Curtis, one of the members for the City, all supported Romilly. The motion was lost by 161 to 111, 52 of the treasury group dividing with the majority.[2] A fortnight later Romilly's bill to make stealing above forty shillings from a private dwelling no longer a capital offence was rejected in a 'shameful House' by 33 votes to 31. Twenty-three of those who opposed the bill held office under government.[3] The under-secretaries and the junior lords had the great virtue of usually being in their places, ready to vote.

By 1807 the character of the treasury group was slowly changing. The old 'official' men, who had tended to stay in office whatever political connection held power, were gradually disappearing. For, with the emergence of an embryonic higher permanent civil service, the administrators were being taken out of parliament. In October 1803 Redesdale had attributed much of the weakness of the Addington

[1] Also a son of the lord steward of the Household, and a son of the queen's treasurer.

[2] Windsor MSS., 15091, Perceval to George III, 17 Apr. 1810; *Day*, 18 Apr. 1810.

[3] Romilly, *Memoirs*, vol. II, p. 323; Wilberforce, *Life*, vol. III, p. 444.

ministry to the fact that it had replaced the knowledgeable subordinate officials in the various departments by political nominees. Later cabinets did not repeat the mistake. George Harrison of the treasury, although appointed by Pitt, was retained throughout the Talents ministry, and John Becket of the home office, a protégé of Fitzwilliam and Spencer, survived the return of Pitt's Friends in March 1807.[1] It was men like these, as well as Henry Bunbury at the war office and Hamilton at the foreign office, who were in future to supply the essential needs of administrative continuity. None of them were members of parliament: new administrative posts, like that of commissary-in-chief, were created with the stipulation that their holders were ineligible for the house of commons. The rise of this class allowed the party politicians to take control of such posts as secretary-at-war and secretary to the admiralty, previously the two strongholds of the 'officials'. When Sir James Pulteney, a typical member of the old group, resigned the office of secretary-at-war in 1808 he was succeeded by Lord Granville Leveson-Gower, a diplomat by profession and a Canningite in politics. A year later the political crisis caused by Canning's withdrawal left both offices vacant, and Perceval filled them with two young and inexperienced politicians. Palmerston became secretary-at-war and Croker, a lawyer and a pamphleteer, secretary to the admiralty. Like most innovations it was not well received. Huskisson, almost an 'official' himself, considered Palmerston's 'a very bad appointment' and thought 'not much better of Croker's'. 'Till lately', wrote Brougham to Grey of Croker's post, 'that office, which is one of the most important, and requires great experience in the business to which it relates, was not made subject to party changes.' *The Times* suggested that Perceval might just as well nominate a boatswain as clerk of king's bench. 'For shame's sake, Gentlemen,' it added, 'have some regard to decency and common sense, and public utility, in your distribution of offices.' [2] In fact both Palmerston and Croker were successful: the treasury group was to be composed increasingly of politicians instead of civil servants.

[1] Perceval MSS., Redesdale to Perceval, 27 Oct. 1803; Harrowby MSS., vol. IV, fol. 90, Richard Ryder to Harrowby.

[2] Herries, vol. I, p. 13; Brougham, *Memoirs*, vol. I, pp. 466–7; *The Times*, 13 Oct. 1809. Rose (vol. II, p. 48) thought Croker's appointment 'not a desirable one at all'. The idea that the two offices were not subject to party changes still survived. When the opposition was expected to come to power in the early days of the Regency, Wilberforce denounced a report that they would replace Croker by Brougham (another party man and a lawyer) as 'surely *infra dig*' (*Life*, vol. III, p. 493).

Behind the treasury block on the government benches sat the followers and nominees of those magnates who supported the ministry. The 'best feathers', according to Buckingham, were the Lonsdale members and the duke of Rutland's eight. The Newcastle electoral influence still survived; Robert Dundas led Melville's important Scottish interest; and the chief secretary was responsible for the government's Irish supporters. A clear distinction was usually drawn between membership of a particular group, however loyal it might normally be to the interests of government, and outright membership of the government 'party'. Thus, in November 1810, Lord Melville wrote to his son, Robert Dundas, then president of the board of control, warning him not to mistake the nature of his obligations to his fellow cabinet ministers. It was Dundas's duty to concur with them in all measures designed to protect the rights of the crown, 'but I must guard you against every idea of embarking with your colleagues on the footing of a party man'. 'They have', ended Melville, 'no claims upon you of any kind to form such a connection with them, and I think I know enough of the state of the country to know that if you were to place yourself in so unnatural a predicament, you would soon find yourself insulated, and destitute of that honourable and natural connection in politics which circumstances have prepared for you, and which seems to be almost within your grasp.' Thus, for the heads of politically powerful families, and for their heirs, the duty of leading their personal groups still came before any claims of loyalty to the government of the day. Of the cabinet ministers only Canning, with his group of seventeen, had any appreciable personal following although Marquis Wellesley was said in 1812 to control eleven votes. Had Perceval lost office he would probably have been able to rely on only three or four close personal friends: Castlereagh, in 1809, found he could count on three.[1]

The opposition side of the House was filled with a similar patchwork. The old Foxites, now led by Howick, formed the largest single group, but was steadily losing its more radical members, who looked

---

[1] *Dropmore MSS.*, vol. IX, pp. 134–5; Harrowby MSS., vol. IV, fol. 46; Buckingham, *Court and Cabinets of the Regency*, vol. I, p. 405; Add. MSS., 37309, fol. 152; Aspinall, *The Canningite Party*, pp. 222–3 (for a complete list of the Canningites see *supra* chapter 6, p. 63 footnote 3); Bagot, *Canning and his Friends*, vol. I, p. 368; Aspinall and Smith, *English Historical Documents*, vol. XI, no. 48. Perceval's closest friends in the House were Richard Ryder, Matthew Montague, and James Stephen. In addition Denis Browne pledged himself in June 1811 to 'more zealous' support if Perceval lost office (Perceval MSS.).

to Whitbread for inspiration. The Grenville connection in the Commons was small in numbers (probably about a dozen) and weak in debating strength. The Carlton House group, the potential 'King's Friends' of the future, has been estimated at thirty peers and approximately the same number of members in the Commons. Between it and the rest of the opposition there was a loose and somewhat unsatisfactory alliance.[1] The two radicals, Burdett and Cochrane, with the occasional support of members like Wardle, Madocks, and Lord Folkestone, formed a miniature opposition of their own, equally hostile and embarrassing both to the ministry and to the official opposition. Between the two main groups, and courted by both, floated the Sidmouth connection and the Saints. Before the general election of 1806 Sidmouth was said to control thirty votes, but he lost about half that number at the dissolution and by 1807 Professor Roberts calculated that he could rely on only six.[2] The group's policy was recognisably opportunist, consistent only in aiming to please the king and get into office: everyone, joked Canning, had to have Sidmouth once, like the measles. The position of the Saints was exactly the reverse. They were an independent pressure group, not a set of unemployed placemen. 'Nor place nor pension e'er got he', cried Henry Thornton's supporters at Southwark,

> For self or for connection;
> We shall not tax the Treasury
> By Thornton's re-election.[3]

Their leader, Wilberforce, had just seen the final triumph of his Slave-Trade Abolition Bill: as one of the members for Yorkshire he could claim to represent a tenth part of the electors of England. But the Saints had no common policy on party questions. They each voted according to their consciences and were, accordingly, roundly abused by the

[1] Roberts (*The Whig Party, 1807–12*, p. 333) lists the Grenvillites as Thomas Grenville, Sir John Newport, Earl Temple, the Wynn brothers, Lords Althorpe and Kensington, Sir John King, Plunket, Francis Horner, Fremantle, and (after 1810) Sir John Anstruther. They could also probably count on Windham, Henry Martin, and the diplomat, William Wickham. For the Carlton House group see Aspinall, *The Formation of the Canning Ministry* (*Camden Soc. third series* LIX, p. XXVI).

[2] *Lonsdale MSS.*, p. 230; Roberts, *op. cit.*, p. 339, gives the Sidmouth group in the Commons in 1807 as Vansittart, Bragge Bathurst, Hatsell, Charles Adams, Bond, and Hiley Addington.

[3] F. A. Hayek (Ed.), Henry Thornton's '*An Enquiry into the Nature and Effects of the Paper Credit of Great Britain*', Int. 30.

warmer partisans on both sides.[1] The politics of most of the remaining members of the Commons can best be described by the couplet—

> In moderation placing all my glory
> When Tories call me Whig and Whigs a Tory.

It was more 'respectable' to support the king's government than to be in systematic opposition, but it was most 'respectable' of all to be independent of both, especially if the member was one of the seventy-six English knights of the shire. During the Staffordshire election of 1806 one of Lord Granville Leveson-Gower's proposers had the temerity to say that he did not know to which party the candidate belonged. 'Notwithstanding this invitation to declare whether I was with Gov[ernmen]t or in Opposition,' wrote his lordship to Lady Bessborough, 'I abstained from saying anything which could give you the most remote idea upon the subject.' [2]

It was no easy job for the leader of the House to control such an assembly. Many members were virtually permanent absentees, like M.P. Andrews of Bewdley, who in a political career extending over five parliaments, made one speech and took part in two divisions. Before the beginning of each session Perceval sent a circular letter requesting the attendance of known government supporters. Yet the practice, although long established, was still not accepted as a constitutional convention. The leader of the opposition now sent his own circular letter, but the opposition press still thought it worth while to print the text of the government's circular or copies of alleged hostile replies to it.[3] No leader of the House would dare send a circular letter

[1] The 'Saints' group in the Commons included Babington, Bankes, the Grants, Lord Muncaster, James Stephen, Henry Thornton, and Wilberforce. Cf. J. C. Colquhoun, *William Wilberforce, His Friends and His Times*, pp. 225–6 and 279.

[2] *Day*, 3 Feb. 1810; Leveson-Gower, *Correspondence*, vol. II, p. 219. Isaac Milner expressed a common view of opposition politicians in a letter to Perceval suggesting a reform of the leasehold property tax. 'I cannot but request,' he wrote, 'that as nothing can be further from my mind than an intention to teaze or harass in the smallest degree, you would have the goodness to furnish me, in the way that will give you the least trouble, with some sort of answer to the numerous sincere and hearty friends of Government, who see the matter as I freely own I do. In regard to systematic objectors, I never think them worth much notice' (Perceval MSS.). When, in 1808, the Portland ministry clashed with and narrowly defeated the majority of the knights of the shire on the Distillation from Corn Bill, Coke of Norfolk suggested that the cabinet should still withdraw the bill because its majority was small and the minority was 'so respectable' (*Parl. Deb.*, XI, 819).

[3] *Day*, 2 Dec. 1809; *Sun*, 15 June 1807 and 20 Dec. 1809; *Quarterly Review*, Feb. 1809, p. 133.

to a county member: if he were canvassed at all, it was in the most
deferential language. 'With respect to your being in town at the meeting of Parliament', wrote Perceval to one of the members for Mon-
mouthshire, 'it would be the height of presumption in me to mention
another word on the subject; I hope that communicating to you my
sense of the importance of a full attendance, when business of the
utmost importance would certainly come under discussion, you would
have the goodness to excuse that liberty.' [1] Greater pressure could be
brought to bear, through the chief secretary, to compel the attendance
of the ministry's Irish supporters. 'My present impression', wrote
Perceval to Wellesley Pole in December 1811, 'is that whatever person
in Gov[ernmen]t refuses to come over on this occasion must, if we
continue in our places, lose his.' [2] In the critical month of December
1809 Wellington was asked to send home all members serving in the
Peninsula who could be spared from active service and who were
likely to support ministers in the House. Even in the relatively docile
Lords the government was occasionally defeated in divisions. In
February 1808 (and again in June) Hawkesbury was forced to remind
the king 'that your Majesty's Gov[ernmen]t is not adequately supported
in the House of Lords either by your Majesty's Household, or by the
Bishops, and that it is of the utmost importance that your Majesty should
communicate your wishes and expectations on the subject to the Lord
Chamberlain and the Archbishop of Canterbury'.[3] But although many
members owed their offices to ministers, few owed them their seats.
According to Oldfield (who was never given to under-estimates) the
government's electoral influence by itself controlled only sixteen seats:
the treasury was said to return eleven members, the admiralty four, and
the ordnance one. There was, in addition to this, the general influence of
government in other constituencies which, though nowhere decisive in
itself, could be effective if allied with one or more of the local interests.[4]

---

[1] Perceval MSS., Perceval to Sir Charles Morgan, 23 Dec. 1807.

[2] *Ibid.*, Perceval to Pole, 26 Dec. 1811; Westbrook Hay MSS., Pole to
Ryder, 9 July 1811; Wellington, *Civil Correspondence, Ireland*, p. 323. The
Irish representative peers could also be bullied to attend critical divisions in the
Lords. Thus before the first day of the new session after the formation of Per-
ceval's government, Liverpool instructed the lord lieutenant that no excuses
ought to be accepted for absence from the debate on the Address (Aspinall and
Smith, *English Historical Documents*, vol. XI, no. 163).

[3] Add. MSS., 38244, fol. 120; Windsor MSS., 13397–8, Hawkesbury to George
III, 18 Feb. 1808 and 13731–2, same to same, 23 June 1808. The *Sun* reported on
25 Oct. 1808 that there were forty M.P.s serving in the Peninsula.

[4] Oldfield, *Representative History*, vol. VI, p. 202.

This vital alliance was largely cemented by government patronage, which, as long as the structure of politics was based on the group system, was the most effective means of controlling parliament. Ministers had at their disposal a large if diminishing number of political and administrative posts as well as limited opportunities of granting pensions and peerages. In 1810 George Rose tried to argue in his *Observations respecting the Public Expenditure of the Crown,* that the use of patronage was on the decline and illustrated his thesis by drawing up lists of non-essential offices abolished by Pitt. But how, asked the *Edinburgh Review,* could government influence have decreased when the annual national expenditure (including loans) stood at about £70 million compared with £24 million at the end of the war of American independence? The whig and radical propagandists had a simple case, which they put before the public with persistence and skill. Ministers kept themselves in power by means of a great wen of patronage: they relied in parliament on placemen and pensioners and they tried to corrupt the electorate by a lavish use of minor offices. Against them stood 'a small band of patriots' the friends of economic if no longer of parliamentary reform. It is true that occasionally whig apologists fell below this high moral tone by appealing to the place-hunters among the Outs. 'We now see no such thing' wrote a contributor to the *Edinburgh Review* in 1810 'as an opposition man in any office;—no such thing as an opposition member having the power to provide for a single friend or dependant. . . .' Even this was untrue as a charge against Perceval himself who, on several occasions, used his influence as a minister in favour of known political opponents. Thus in 1807 he secured a lucrative barrackmastership for the son of the whig Lord Crew, three years later he accepted one of Ellenborough's nominees for a vacancy in the Scottish court of exchequer, and just before his death he advised the appointment of the duke of Grafton as vice-admiral of Suffolk. In 1810 the young James Mackintosh was anxious to join the *Crown and Rolls* debating society, but the majority of members, being supporters of the ministry and of the war, looked askance at an application from the radical author of *Vindiciae Gallicae.* Scarlett, who had proposed Mackintosh, was reconciled to defeat until Perceval, out of admiration for the young radical's talents, helped with the canvass and so ensured success. Later that year, Perceval again intervened to persuade the benchers of Lincoln's Inn to allow Mackintosh to use their hall for his series of lectures on the laws of nature and nations. In 1812 Perceval engineered Mackintosh's return from India, and, in April, offered to help him win a seat in parliament.[1]

Ministers, however, too rarely tried to put the facts about patronage before the public, until, by constant repetition, the opposition's charges of profusion and corruption came to be accepted without question. The majority of ministers honestly tried to fill vacancies with the most efficient rather than with the politically most important candidate. 'The age has its vices, no doubt,' Perceval once told the Commons, 'and persons in high rank are not exempt from them. But the vice of pecuniary corruption in the higher ranks of society is not (on my conscience I state it) the vice of the present day.' There were still some, like Redesdale, who thought of palmier days and wrote of jobs worth £3,500 a year, plus valuable perquisites, 'and very little business'; 'a friend would find it a comfortable post, and make me very happy'. Lord Kenyon could still, in 1810, apply for his 'deserving cousin' for 'any appointment of a general description consistent with his living as a private gentleman of about £800 a year in Caernarvonshire', while one of the bishop of London's chaplains so far forgot himself as to offer Perceval £3,000 for a deanery.[2] Certain cabinet ministers like Westmorland, Chatham, and even Eldon still occasionally misued their authority, but when they did so they annoyed their colleagues as much as they offended the opposition. Liverpool, while at the war and colonial office, always tried to appoint 'the person best qualified, whoever he might be . . . without any regard to favour or political arrangement', and Mulgrave, the first lord of the admiralty, refused to make 'justice in the service subservient to the objects of Parliamentary influence'. Junior ministers in the Perceval government who ran up against vested interests in their attempts to end corruption could always rely on the support of the prime minister, even when this meant causing displeasure at Windsor.[3] For Perceval was, in many

---

[1] *Edinburgh Review*, April 1810, pp. 188–207; Perceval MSS., Mulgrave to Perceval, 9 Dec. 1807; Perceval to Ellenborough, 15 Oct. 1810; duke of Grafton to Perceval, 11 May, 1812; *Quarterly Review*, July 1835, p. 227; R. J. Mackintosh, *Memoirs of Sir James Mackintosh*, vol. II, pp. 277, 279, and 347–8. Mackintosh was just about to write to Perceval on the evening of 11 May 1812, declining the offer of a seat because of differences over catholic emancipation when Josiah Wedgwood entered with news of the prime minister's assassination.

[2] *The Substance of a Speech delivered by the Rt. Hon. Spencer Perceval in the debate on the Inquiry into the conduct of H.R.H. the Duke of York* (London 1809), p. 14; Perceval MSS., Redesdale to Perceval, 21 May 1802; Lord Kenyon to same, 26 Sept. 1810; *Annual Register*, 1809, p. 143.

[3] Yonge, vol. I, p. 265; Perceval MSS., Mulgrave to Perceval, 5 Mar. 1808; Croker, vol. I, p. 23.

ways, the herald of the Victorians; a professional politician who
scorned to take public money for himself. Compared with even the
best of his predecessors, his record is remarkable. Pitt, a bachelor,
accepted an income of a little over £10,500 for each year he held office.
Perceval, with a wife and twelve children to support, received £8,323
a year between 1807 and October 1809, and from then until his death,
£9,651.[1] He might have had more, but he refused to accept it. For
as soon as he had kissed hands as first lord of the treasury he decided
that, as long as he held that office and the duchy of Lancaster, he would
not draw his salary as chancellor of the exchequer. He made the gesture
without the slightest parade or publicity by announcing his intention
at a treasury board meeting, but saying nothing in parliament and
allowing nothing to appear in the press. It was not until more than six
months later, after Whitbread had attacked him in the Commons as
a placehunter, that he allowed the story to be made public.[2] And he
sacrificed a sinecure for his children as proudly as he had rejected
£2,500 a year for himself. In January 1810 William Eden, one of the
tellers of the exchequer, was found drowned in the Thames. The
ministry seemed at that time on the verge of collapse and loss of office
would have left Perceval in serious financial difficulties. The tellership
was worth about £2,700 a year: its few duties might be performed by
deputy. Cornwallis, who wanted it himself, thought it 'highly probable' and 'perfectly reasonable' that the prime minister should keep it
or give it to his eldest son. George III was about to suggest the same
plan when Perceval wrote to Windsor nominating Charles Yorke, a
brother of the third earl of Hardwicke. 'The King', replied George III,
'has no hesitation in saying that few men would be capable of so
disinterested an act': 'all candid and liberal minds', wrote Yorke to the
Speaker, 'must do him justice'. For, as Palmerston assured his sister,
he knew of no opposition leader who would, in similar circumstances,
have given away such a place.[3]

Unfortunately Perceval combined with his personal integrity a

---

[1] Rosebery, *Pitt*, pp. 295–7; *Political Register*, 18 Mar. 1809. Perceval's net
income before October 1809 consisted of £2,452 as chancellor of the exchequer,
£1,220 as a lord of the treasury, £4,525 as chancellor of the duchy of Lancaster,
and £126 as surveyor of the meltings. After October 1809 he drew £3,780 as
first lord of the treasury in place of his salary as chancellor of the exchequer.

[2] P.R.O., T29/303/170; *Day*, 18 May 1810.

[3] Perceval MSS., Cornwallis to Perceval, 25 Jan. 1810; Windsor MSS., 14917,
Perceval to George III, and 14918, George III to Perceval, 26 Jan. 1810; P.R.O.,
Colchester MSS., 30/9/15 C. P. Yorke to Abbot, 27 Feb. 1810; Lytton-Bulwer,
Palmerston, vol. I, p. 268; P. Treherne, *The Rt. Hon. Spencer Perceval*, pp. 115–16.

distaste for the minor manœuvres of group politics which often drove
his followers to despair. If only, urged James Stephen, he would give
'a small portion of civil notice' to independent members: 'a mutual
friend of ours', continued Stephen, 'who is not too fond of party
making, thinks you negligent of your own interest as a Minister . . .'
'This,' sighed Robert Ward after one unsatisfactory talk about patronage, 'was in his usual negligence of these matters. He trusts too much
to his character and excellent intentions.' 'I do not like to teaze you
with repeated applications,' wrote John Owen, an M.P. for Pembroke,
in a typical letter, 'but at no distant period, if I live, I shall certainly
be a candidate for the representation of the county, which the obliging
of two or three gentlemen in my neighbourhood would undoubtedly
secure to me.' [1] Many such opportunities for group building were
missed by the Perceval ministry. Yet even if Perceval himself had been
more interested and less scrupulous in questions of patronage he had,
in fact, far fewer opportunities for effective bribery than his opponents
imagined. The halcyon days of Sir Robert Walpole had long since
passed and by the first decade of the nineteenth century it was no longer
easy to reward faithful supporters at Westminster. A prime minister
could still command the golden trinity of peerages, places, and pensions. Yet the great excess of candidates over vacancies usually meant
that he disappointed many in satisfying one.

The position with regard to peerages was the most embarrassing
of all. When Pitt's Friends returned to office in 1807 they found a list
of fifty-three unsatisfied claims, all of them blocked by the king's
refusal to add any more members to the already inflated Lords.[2]
Portland's position was not enviable: supporters of his government
continued to write for new creations or promotions, and George III
as steadily refused to grant them. The duke therefore tried to solve his
immediate difficulties by promising each disappointed applicant that
his claim would receive priority whenever the king decided to withdraw his ban. The policy was sufficient for the day, but fatal for the
morrow. For as soon as Perceval succeeded to the treasury he was
overwhelmed by the duke's promise-crammed friends. The pledges
were, he explained to Lord Harewood, 'very inconveniently numerous'.
'Under no circumstances of the Government', he wrote, 'would I

---

[1] Perceval MSS., James Stephen to Perceval, 31 Aug. 1808; R. P. Ward,
Memoirs, vol. I, p. 466; Westbrook Hay MSS., John Owen to Richard Ryder,
14 Dec. 1809.
[2] Malmesbury, *Diary*, vol. IV, p. 389.

incur the responsibility of making a *lavish* use of the prerogative of the crown upon the subject either of advances or creations in the peerage.'[1] He refused to be bound by his predecessor's promises, rejected new applications, even when they were supported by cabinet colleagues or by members of his own family, and, when the Regency restrictions had expired, he advised the Prince Regent to deal strictly with all claims. Changes in the Irish peerage were equally few: during the first four years of the duke of Richmond's tenure of office in Dublin only eleven new Irish baronets were created, all of them 'respectable' men 'with great property'.[2] Such a policy was not implemented without a struggle against those used to the younger Pitt's largess. Late in 1809 Catherine Gordon Byron, the mother of the poet, began to pester him for a peerage. Portland, she claimed, had agreed to make her Viscountess Byron of Rochdale, with remainder to her son. She was a descendant of Sir William Gordon, the third son of George, the second earl of Huntley and his wife, Princess Anabella Stewart, daughter of James the First of Scotland. 'It has long been a source of much vexation to me,' she wrote, 'that I am deprived of that rank in society I am so well *entitled to* by my *own birth*. . . . I am better entitled to these honours than the late Lady Bath and many others to whom higher titles have been granted.' Her son, she ended, who had just taken his seat in the Lords, approved of her claim and would himself have forwarded it had he not been travelling in the Mediterranean. Perceval's curt refusal only produced a more violent outburst. Portland, she wrote, 'thought me (even had titles been seldomer granted) *fully entitled* to the dignity of a viscountess of the Kingdom of Great Britain from my illustrious birth and *royal descent* . . . and being of course a relation of His Majesty's (all that I assert can be very easily proved)'. The Byrons, she had reminded Portland, had stood still for one hundred and fifty years and had been 'peers of England before his *own* family or *name was ever heard of*'. All this was 'my son's opinion whose judgement *never* can *err* whatever mine may do'. 'But I can assure you, sir, that my son would *not accept* the dignity of a viscount for himself. His *brilliant* and splendid talents cannot fail to procure for him, whenever he chooses to exert himself, either as a politician or an orator, the highest honours and the first situation that it is possible for

[1] Add. MSS. 38191, fols. 154 and 157.
[2] *Ibid.*, fols. 165, 174 and 214; 38243, fols. 216 and 217; 38244, fols. 69, 169 and 184; 38362, fol. 47; Westbrook Hay MSS., Richard Ryder to duke of Richmond, 23 Nov. 1809.

His Majesty to confer. . . .' And so, 'yielding to none in point of birth and never forgetting what is due to myself', Mrs. Byron continued fruitlessly to bombard the prime minister.[1] Sir William Manners, the heir to the Scottish earldom of Dysart, who controlled parliamentary seats at Ilchester and Grantham, was even more troublesome. On 3 March 1812 he wrote demanding an English peerage which, he said, had been promised to him in writing by the Prince Regent. A fortnight later a further letter asked brusquely 'whether I am to expect a reply or not'. Perceval then demanded to see a copy of the Regent's promise, reminding Manners that the Crown 'could not exercise any of its prerogatives, but under the advice of some responsible minister'. He met with a blank refusal to show the pledge 'which could not be written in stronger language' and a claim that 'the promise ought now to be fulfilled in me, a person of family, Parliamentary interest, and great property. I shall in a short time hope to receive from you an explicit answer on this subject, that I may know how to proceed, for I am not to be trifled with by you or any other man'. Such bluster had little effect. 'I have not', replied Perceval, 'the slightest intention of trifling with you and have no hesitation in complying with your desire for an explicit answer.' Sir William, for all his parliamentary influence, failed to get his English peerage.[2] The powerful magnates grumbled, but they could not change the policy.

It was widely believed that ministers had much more room for manoeuvre in the distribution of places of profit under the Crown. 'The great patronage', wrote the Scottish lord advocate in 1810, 'is in the gift of the Treasury, where from the vast number of places at the disposal of Mr. Perceval vacancies are occurring every day.' It is

[1] Perceval MSS., Mrs. C. G. Byron to Perceval, 22 and 29 Dec. 1809.
[2] *Ibid.*, Sir William Manners to Perceval, 3, 16 and 20 Mar. 1812; Add. MSS., 38191, fols. 220 and 232. An earlier account by Sir William Manners of his claim for a peerage can be found in Aspinall and Smith, *English Historical Documents*, vol. XI, no. 153. For other cases of claims for peerages see Add MSS., 38191, fols. 161, 176, 178, 180, 181, 183, 195, 197, 206, and 218; 38243, fol. 192; 38244, fols. 151, 175, 183, 197, 213, and 286; 38245, fols. 168 and 238; 38247, fols. 118 and 148. One of the most interesting patronage letters sent to Perceval was one from Sir Walter Scott about his post as principal clerk of the court of sessions. The letter begins—'Sir, it is with equal diffidence and regret that I venture to obtrude upon your recollection a name and a subject very unworthy of mingling with the important matters committed to its charge, but as in my limited intercourse with persons of distinction I have always found them most patient of intrusion where wisdom and power were least doubted, I venture to add one to the number of selfish applications to which your eminent situation so peculiarly exposes you.'

known, on the authority of George Rose, that by 1811 there were 2,000 customs appointments alone at the disposal of the first lord.[1] Yet in all types of posts there were rarely enough vacancies to go round. When, in 1811, the cabinet was rallying all the friends it could for the critical Regency Bill debates, Perceval asked William Dundas to try and attend more regularly. 'My income', replied Dundas, 'is £600 per annum, and as I live with my brother most of the year, I feel no inconvenience. But unless you can throw me in, say, £800 more, I shall not be able to be in London all the session or give you all the support in my power.' Yet, as Dundas himself had foreseen, Perceval had 'the inclination but not the means' to help.[2] The scramble for office was so intense that when Goulburn, the under-secretary at the home office, met with an accident late in November 1811, Sir John Sinclair did not even wait to hear the extent of Goulburn's injuries before recommending his son George Sinclair, a member for Caithness, for the possible vacancy.[3] Even the earl of Northampton, for all his claims on Perceval, could not get one of his connections appointed to so paltry an office as landing waiter at the customs. All that Perceval could do was to add another name to the waiting list and warn the earl that the roll was 'so long and some of the applications on it of so old a date that your friend's prospect must be considered a very distant one'. 'I have in no instance, except the present,' lamented the duke of Newcastle in February 1810, 'yet obtained for any of my friends even the most trifling situation, and this I must confess is so different from what I expected that I could not help feeling considerably hurt at the result of my applications'.[4]

Some disappointed applicants took refusal very badly. Thus, early in 1812, the countess of Glencairn claimed £15,000 from the treasury as recompense for money said to have been spent in the public service by her late husband, William Hamilton, while serving as attorney-general in the Leeward Islands. After pestering Perceval by letter without success, she saw Wilberforce, who arranged an interview for

---

[1] Perceval MSS., Rose to Perceval, 24 Dec. 1811; Westbrook Hay MSS., A. Colquhoun to George Skene, 6 June 1810. 'Mr. Arbuthnot . . .' continued Colquhoun's letter, 'has the arrangement of this immense patronage, which since the late frauds have been discovered by pretended procurers of places, is conducted very cautiously and the vacancies are kept secret.' 'Nothing', commented Perceval, 'can be much more unjust both to me and Mr. Skene . . . .'

[2] Perceval MSS., W. Dundas to Perceval, 6 June 1811.

[3] Westbrook Hay MSS., Sir John Sinclair to Richard Ryder, 26 Nov. 1811.

[4] Perceval MSS., Perceval to the earl of Northampton, 27 Mar. 1811 and the duke of Newcastle to Perceval, 11 Feb. 1810.

her with the prime minister at Downing Street. During her conversation there with Perceval, Lady Glencairn urged that Nelson had always supported her claim, but the prime minister was still not impressed and gave no promise of relief. Lady Glencairn then published her version of the interview as a pamphlet, alleging that Perceval told her 'not to rest so much on the force of Lord Nelson's opinions; with me you could offer no name of less weight. I never thought of the late Lord Nelson and his services as the world has; so far otherwise, that I consider his death was the salvation of the country, since, had he lived, he, in one way or another, would have ruined the nation and emptied the treasury'. The accusation, wrote Perceval to Wilberforce, was as astonishing 'as having damned the King and blasphemed My Maker in the same conversation'.[1] Less dangerous, though more grotesque, was Olivia Wilmot Serres, the daughter of Robert Wilmot, a mural painter, who claimed amongst other things to be related to the royal family through Henry Frederick, duke of Cumberland, the brother of George III. In 1791 she had married John Thomas Serres who was connected with the Royal Coburg theatre, but she left him after alleging that the duke of Cambridge had made improper advances to her. Royal scandals attracted Mrs. Serres as a lamp draws moths. In 1809 she published *Observations and Strictures on the Conduct of Mrs. Clarke*, the prosecution's star witness in the duke of York inquiry. In the summer of 1810 she assured Perceval that 'whatever papers or memorandums I might possess relative to the Royal Family, I have committed to the flames, determined that no advantage or emolument I might have derived from a contrary conduct by publications or otherwise should induce me to give one moment's pain to my exulted patron, His Royal Highness the Prince of Wales'. Eighteen months later she forwarded a plan for pacifying Ireland by giving state salaries to Roman catholic priests, but, wrote Perceval, 'there is not an idea that your note contains that has not occurred to almost everybody who ever thought upon the subject'. Ten days later a specimen of a special type of bread arrived which would solve any shortage of wheat: 'I doubt exceedingly', replied Perceval, 'whether the people in London would eat it.' Thereafter she concentrated on getting a pension by threatening to publish details of the Delicate Investigation and on gaining an interview with Perceval: 'could you, sir, wrap yourself in

---

[1] Isabella, Countess of Glencairn, *A Letter to the Rt. Hon. Spencer Perceval . . . . containing an appeal to the British nation* (Bristol 1812); Add. MSS., 38191, fol. 226 and 38247, fol. 136.

a great coat and honour me with a very private visit. . . . Mr. Pitt, sir, in private has honoured me with several visits—also Mr. Fox. . . .' [1] But Olivia Serres had no better luck than Lady Glencairn.

There was the same embarrassing surfeit of candidates for church appointments. Perceval, who controlled rights of presentation both as chancellor of the duchy of Lancaster and as first lord, found 'from the very early applications which I have for anything which falls, that it is necessary to say at once that a thing is promised in order to preserve the presentation of it to oneself'. His earliest efforts had been to get his old friend and college tutor, Mansel, appointed to the bench, and although he disapproved of bishops holding livings, he offered Mansel the rectorship of Barwick-in-Elmet, the most valuable benefice in the gift of the chancellor of the duchy of Lancaster. He made similar efforts on behalf of Drury, his old schoolmaster, whom he presented to the prebendal stall of Dultingeot in Wells Cathedral, and whom he pressed Portland to appoint as dean of Canterbury.[2] Yet he never thought of preferment merely as an object of patronage. Whenever possible he appointed rectors who promised to reside in the parish, and where this was impossible, he insisted that the absentee should set aside an adequate salary for his curate. Unfortunately, only one minor English bishopric fell vacant during his period at the treasury, but one of his last acts was to recommend the worthy evangelical, Henry Ryder, for future promotion. Yet he never allowed his own opinions to influence him in favour of evangelicals as such: 'pre-eminence of clerical merit and character' were the tests by which he judged all candidates. As soon as he became prime minister he decided that 'the plan of this administration is to be a total neglect of Parliamentary influence in ecclesiastical arrangements' and even his bitterest critics had to admit that in that instance he acted up to his professions. 'I would rather be driven from my post tomorrow,' he told one political magnate who sought to influence the appointment

---

[1] Perceval MSS., Olivia Wilmot Serres to Perceval, 26 June 1810, 9, 19, and 27 Jan., 2 and 23 Feb. 1812. For details of Mrs. Serres see M. L. Penderel and J. Mallet, *Princess or Pretender* (London, 1939).

[2] P.R.O., Chatham MSS., 155, W. L. Mansel to Pitt, 11 Apr. 1797; 166, Perceval to Pitt, 22 Jan. 1805; Windsor MSS., 13723–7, Portland to George III, 20 June 1808; Perceval MSS., Perceval to Mansel, 10 May 1798 and same to same, 28 May, 1807; Farington, *Diary*, vol. V, p. 75; *Annual Biography and Obituary*, vol. XIX, pp. 1–36. George III, according to Portland, raised 'such a variety of objections' to Mansel's promotion that the matter was only settled after a series of interviews between the king and the duke (Perceval MSS., Portland to Perceval, 16 June 1808).

to an Irish bishopric, 'than purchase my continuance in it by breaking through so wise and proper a determination.'[1]

Some of those closest to the source of power thought that the government did too little to co-ordinate and concentrate the use of patronage in its own hands. Under Portland, in particular, ministers often failed to pull together. Thus, early in 1807 a contested election for a vacancy on the East India company court of directors found Dundas and Huskisson supporting one candidate, Mulgrave, a second, while Canning canvassed for a third. In vain Dundas urged Portland to sponsor a united government candidate in future contests. Two years later the elections were still 'completely thrown loose, and persons of all descriptions, fit for the situation and unfit (generally the latter) got themselves chosen in the scramble'.[2] Perceval always made it 'a sort of grace to a lord lieutenant of a county to attend to his recommendation' for local revenue offices and, in all other cases, consulted the local knights of the shire.[3] On 9 June 1809 Canning 'sadly discomposed' Wilberforce by attacking him in the Commons for recommending one of his constituents for a local vacancy and yet voting against the government. Wilberforce's notion, wrote Stephen to Perceval, 'whether right or wrong, was that recommending in that line was no impeachment of a member's independence; that it was even serving Government to point out the proper persons for provincial appointments such as would be generally acceptable, and thereby maintain the popularity of the existing administration in a distant part of the kingdom as far as county feelings are concerned'. After Canning's jibes, Wilberforce called a meeting of the Saints and decided to make no further recommendations, but was persuaded to relent by Perceval, who entirely accepted Wilberforce's definition of the county member's rights.[4]

Perceval's best efforts were usually devoted to helping promising young men to find their feet in politics. Palmerston and Croker both owed their introduction to office to him and in both instances he showed an unusual talent for spotting promising material before his

[1] Perceval MSS., Perceval to Mansel, 13 Oct. 1810; bishop of Clonfert to Arden, 24 Mar. 1810; marquis of Ely to Perceval, 7 Jan. 1810; Harrowby MSS., vol. V, fol. 107, Henry Ryder to Harrowby, 22 May 1812. For an attack on Perceval's use of church patronage see the *Morning Chronicle*, 9 Oct. 1809 and the *Sun*, 10 Oct. 1809.

[2] Perceval MSS., Robert Dundas to Portland, 25 Apr. 1807 and same to Perceval, 19 Dec. 1809. [3] *Ibid.*, Camden to Perceval, 16 July 1810.

[4] Wilberforce, vol. III, p. 410; Perceval MSS., Stephen to Perceval, 12 June 1809; *Parl. Deb.*, vol. XIV, 981.

contemporaries. Croker, who had previously been associated with Perceval's private secretary, Herries, in producing two short-lived newspapers, first entered the Commons in 1807. In his maiden speech he stressed that he had no connection at all with any minister, but Perceval soon remedied that. In April 1808 he offered any financial help he could give and asked Croker to take temporary charge of the parliamentary business of the Irish secretary while Arthur Wellesley was in Spain.[1] His choice of young Palmerston as secretary-at-war in the autumn of 1809 and his earlier dramatic offer of the exchequer was unpopular even with his own supporters. One junior minister, Lord Lovaine, offered to resign because he felt he had a better claim to office. 'As for the promotion of Lord Palmerston,' replied Perceval, 'I certainly do think that I have brought forward into a more prominent and useful situation a young man of considerable parliamentary promise, and one whom in my judgement has given proof of such talents as I conceive will be of great use to His Majesty's service. . . .'[2] That December he chose young Robert Peel, who had still not finished his legal studies, to second the Address at the opening of the 1810 session. 'If', wrote the elder Peel to Perceval, 'he has the good fortune to be honoured with your confidence, I flatter myself he will be found deserving of the trust reposed in him. He possesses capacity, industry, and virtuous habits and under the guidance of a judicious and well-informed friend he may become a useful member of society. Allow me to take the liberty of recommending my son to your patronage.' Two years later Perceval offered Peel full government support in the borough of Weymouth, but Peel declined on grounds of expense.[3] Herries was first brought out of obscurity by Perceval and James Stephen owed him not only his seat but the mastership in chancery which allowed him to concentrate on politics.[4]

Patronage could be supplemented by pensions. But the largest pension which could, by English law, be paid to any individual out of the civil list was £1,200 a year, which after deductions for tax, amounted to about £800 net.[5] Scottish pensions were limited not by

[1] Croker, *Correspondence*, vol. I, pp. 8 and 14–15.
[2] Perceval MSS., Lord Lovaine to Perceval, 24 Nov. 1809; draft of Perceval's reply.
[3] *Ibid.*, Sir Robert Peel sen. to Perceval, 27 Dec. 1809; Robert Peel jun. to same, 29 Dec. 1809; same to same, 10 Sep. 1811.
[4] *Ibid.*, James Stephen to Eldon, 2 Oct. 1810; Zachary Macaulay to Perceval, 2 Nov. 1810; Stephen to same, 6 and 7 Nov. 1810.
[5] *Parl. Deb.*, X, 795.

any regulation but by the extent of the disposable funds. In May 1808
Bankes complained in the Commons that the Scottish pension fund
was constantly increasing and had reached a total of £40,000 a year.
But, as Melville wrote to Robert Dundas, all Scottish pensions were
paid out of the income from the king's private possessions in that
kingdom whereas, under the English system, parliament was often
obliged to make good deficiencies in the civil list. Government spokesmen in the Commons, urged Melville, ought to take a 'more manly
tone' on the issue instead of giving way 'for the sake of a little precarious support from very whimsical characters on whom no dependence can be placed'. The majority of pensions went to 'very loyal and
very indigent subjects', to 'men eminent for their literature or piety',
and 'to people of rank whose small incomes . . . called for an exercise
of the King's bounty, dealt however with a very sparing hand'.[1]
Typical of the majority of pensioners was the dowager Lady Trimilstown, who in August 1810 returned her 'defective tho' grateful
acknowledgements' for a pension of £100 a year. Perceval, she hoped,
would 'accept the broken sentences of a sinking mariner, blessing the
hand which lifts him from destruction': her gratitude would 'reach
beyond this world reverting doubled to Mr. Perceval in long contentment of never-ending happiness'. Alongside decayed dowagers went
the poor relations of grandees and borough owners. A small number
were held by government supporters in parliament, but so hostile
was public opinion to all pensions, that members holding them were
constantly on the defensive. When in July 1807 Cochrane moved for
an inquiry into all sinecures and pensions held by M.P.s both
Huskisson (a pensioner) and Rose (an inveterate sinecurist) felt compelled to set themselves 'right with the House'. So strong had become
the public reaction by 1810 that the government could find no way of
rewarding Thomas Sydenham, a client of Marquis Wellesley, for his
valuable political services. 'It would be dangerous in the extreme,'
wrote Arbuthnot to Perceval, 'in times like the present, to grant any
contingent pension. The pension given to R[ober]t Ward has, as I
know, been a constant source of uneasiness to himself; and certainly
it has been canvassed enough by the public to prevent its being a
precedent which a minister w[oul]d be anxious to follow.' Two
months later, when Charles Yorke stood for re-election in Cambridge-
shire after accepting a tellership of the exchequer, he was howled
down from the hustings and forced to concede the election to his whig

[1] Perceval MSS., Melville to Robert Dundas, 9 May 1808.

opponent without risking a poll.[1] Immediately after his return to the
House for the borough of St. Germains he again outraged public feeling by his conduct in the Gale Jones affair and did much to cause the
Burdett riots. Yet Perceval at once invited him to enter the cabinet,
brusquely dismissing his unpopularity as 'the squib of the day'.[2] In
the day-to-day business of controlling the house of commons ministers
had often to take into account the effect of outside opinion on the
conduct of members. But in theory both cabinet ministers and whig
grandees denied that such an influence should or could exist: when,
during the Burdett riots, democrats challenged the privileges of the
Commons, the two front benches quickly joined forces to resist the
threat. 'Public opinion', said one Westminster radical during the duke
of York inquiry, 'would have it's due weight in this country, whatever
might be the decision of Parliament.' Public opinion, answered the
political theorists, could create or destroy governments, but could
play no part in influencing their policies. Parliament was the constitutional depository and organ of public opinion; 'to represent it as
the antagonistic power before which Parliament must bend and the
constitution bow down is the essence of Jacobinism'.[3] 'It were better',
Perceval told his fellow members, 'there should be no House of
Commons at all; it were better at once to accept as our constitution a
wild, unrepresented democracy . . . than to degrade ourselves by consenting to become the mere instruments of that democracy, to adopt
its opinions, and to register its laws.'[4] But by seeking, wherever
possible, to deny the authority of the new and better-informed electorate, ministers did not strengthen their control over parliament. They
only weakened their own position both within and outside the House.

Much more could and should have been done to influence public
opinion through a more intelligent handling of the press which, as
Arthur Wellesley wrote in 1808, had come to 'rule everything in this
country'.[5] The average expectation of life for the contemporary newspaper was as low as its own circulation or as the literary value of its

[1] *Parl. Deb.*, IX, 753–737X; Perceval MSS., Arbuthnot to Perceval, 9 Jan.
1810; *Day*, 15 Mar. 1810; Perceval MSS., dowager Lady Trimilstown to Perceval,
2 Aug. 1810.
[2] Add. MSS., 37295, fol. 384.
[3] Henry Dundas, *Cursory Remarks on the Correspondence between Lord Melville and Mr. Perceval* (London, 1810), p. 11.
[4] *The Substance of a speech . . . . by . . . . Spencer Perceval*, etc., p. 137. Cf.
Parl. Deb., XXX, 810 ff. for Liverpool's views.
[5] Wellington, *Supplementary Despatches*, XI, p. 185, A. Wellesley to Castlereagh, 14 Nov. 1808.

contents. According to a survey made by the stamp office in 1811, there were then 60 papers published in London, 112 in the provinces, 40 in Ireland and 27 in Scotland.[1] Twenty years previously there had been only about 60 English provincial papers, while London, in 1760, had only 22. The most popular of the London dailies was the pro-government *Courier*, with a circulation of about 5,800. Just before the collapse of the Portland ministry there were some doubts about the *Courier's* loyalty, and the treasury appears to have withdrawn a number of official advertisements usually given to friendly papers.[2] But in 1809 T. G. Street, its joint proprietor, was (according to Canning) given £2,000 to support the Perceval ministry.[3] On the whole the *Courier* was the most influential and the most intelligent of the government press. *The Times*, traditionally the organ of the Sidmouth group, had an estimated sale of 5,000 copies a day. It was, in 1811, officially classed as 'wavering' although in fact it seems for some time to have been generally hostile to the ministry. 'You are losing', wrote James Stephen to Perceval in October 1808, 'or have lost that paper, which has great influence on the public mind, especially on the mercantile world. Till of late it was much more with you than against you, and at the same time, from the independent spirit which it breathed, and the broad British ground which it took, did you more good than any other newspaper. In a national view this is to be regretted. I do not think that your colleagues and you attach as much importance to the press as Bonaparte and I do.' [4]

The circulation of the chief opposition newspaper, the *Morning Chronicle*, was given as about 3,500, but, because of its excellent reports of debates, its circulation was much higher while parliament was in session than during recesses.[5] On or near the 3,000 mark stood the

[1] Westbrook Hay MSS. Most of the following is taken from six documents drawn up in the stamp office, presumably in February 1811, for the use of the home secretary. They were: (A) A list of 53 London papers, with their political allegiance, (B) Total number of papers published in Jan. 1811, (C) Estimated circulation of 13 London papers, (D) Total number of papers published in London during 1715, 1747, 1760, 1775 and 1811, (E) A list of ex-officio informations, 1761–1810, (F) List of results of ex-officio prosecutions 1807–1810.
[2] Harrowby MSS., vol. IV, fol. 155, R. Ryder to Harrowby, 15 Nov. 1808; P.R.O., T1/1061/364.
[3] Add. MSS., 38737, fol. 413.
[4] Perceval MSS., Stephen to Perceval, 26 Oct. 1808.
[5] Once early in 1811, its parliamentary reporters nearly let the *Morning Chronicle* down. Two of them were ill while the third arrived so late that he found himself locked out of the gallery. In desperation he finally broke in through the smoking room window. 'I was told', he later wrote to Abbot by way of apology,

ministerial *Morning Post*, 'a terrible hack in politics', as well as *The British Press* and the *Globe*, both attached to the opposition.[1] Two more hostile papers, the *Morning Herald* and the *Statesman*, had circulations in the region of 1,500, as did the tory *Traveller*. The *Day*, founded on 2 January 1809 and run by a committee of fifteen, most of whom were London merchants, set out as a rival to *The Times*. Two years later it had an estimated sale of 1,100 copies and was officially but unjustly classified as hostile. Its tone was more often than not friendly to the Perceval ministry: it even occasionally printed the routine treasury releases. The circulation of the *Sun*, once one of the more important of the ministerial journals, was, by 1811, too small to be included on the stamp office list. It remained as venal and as hysterical as ever, but it was, undeniably, setting. In contrast the *Pilot* —'a good paper, and gaining ground, and on the right side'—was, in the winter of 1808, recommended to Ryder in place of the back-sliding *Courier*.[2] But it needed uncommon skill or good luck to steer a paper clear of the financial shoals: the *Pilot*, like many of its kin, failed to avoid the rocks. The most important of the thrice-weekly papers was probably the London *Evening Mail*, which was said to sell 5,000 copies each issue, in spite of its wavering political line. There were also at least thirty weekly journals, most of them undistinguished and obscure. By far the liveliest were the two radical papers Leigh Hunt's *Examiner*, and Cobbett's famous *Political Register*. Even the *Edinburgh Review* (which strongly disapproved) admitted that Cobbett had 'more influence than all the other journalists put together'.[3] After the early spring of 1807, when Cobbett turned a neat somersault from bellicose anti-Jacobinism to a whole-hearted advocacy of reform, he was relentlessly hunted by his former colleagues, who used every means, legitimate and otherwise, to discredit him.

In all the stamp office gave the political allegiance of 53 London papers—17 were pro-government, 18 hostile, 15 neutral, and 3 wavering. But the opposition had a majority of 8 to 5 among the dailies (excluding *The Times*) and could also rely on the higher standard and greater prestige of its press.[4] The whigs were well aware of their

---

'that others had sometimes made their way through the smoking room into the gallery' (P.R.O., Colchester MSS., 30/9/15, John Black to Abbot, 22 Jan. 1811).

[1] Moore, *Memoirs*, vol. I, p. 251.

[2] Harrowby MSS., vol. IV, fol. 155, Richard Ryder to Harrowby, 26 Oct. 1808.

[3] *Edinburgh Review*, July 1809, p. 277.

[4] George, *Catalogue of Political and Personal Satires*, vol. 8, p. XI.

advantage. Shortly before the 1807 general election they started a subscription and opened a press-headquarters in Ryder Street, under the management of Brougham. Three years later, when there seemed every chance that they would soon return to power, they set up a similar establishment in St. Alban's Street.[1] Government interference was widespread but seldom well-directed. Proprietors and editors could be bribed with secret service money, with favourable quotas of official advertisements, or with priorities in news items. The direct subsidy method was frequently the least rewarding, for it tended to attract the most unscrupulous hacks who were often neither talented nor reliable. There were too many Blagdon's existing on pensions from the treasury. While Perceval was minister he had two competent press advisers in Herries (an experienced journalist) and Arbuthnot, who as patronage secretary to the treasury was primarily responsible for controlling the ministerial papers. Shortly after Arbuthnot accepted office the treasury suggested a logical scheme to centralise press control. 'It should seem,' began an unsigned circular, 'that priority of intelligence should more than anything else distinguish the Government papers from those that are opposed to it, *but the contrary is notoriously the case.*' [2] There was no co-operation between the various departments, which each gave what information they had to their favourite paper while the treasury (with all the ultimate responsibility if things went wrong) rarely had any news to pass on except that of some insignificant appointment. It was, therefore, suggested that, in future, the secretary to the treasury should be solely responsible for the press relations of the foreign office, the war office, and the admiralty. There ought in each of these departments to be one person whose duty it was every morning to read the principal newspapers and to note any hostile reference to his own office. He should then (if necessary after consultation with his superiors) send to the treasury either a statement of facts or 'a hint of the line which it wished should be taken'. Unfortunately the idea never seems to have been adopted and Arbuthnot and Herries relied on the traditional methods. In January 1811 they gave secret service money and advice to Lewis Goldsmith when he founded his violent *Anti-Gallican Monitor* while the prime minister himself sponsored Hughes' bi-weekly *National Adviser.*[3]

[1] Aspinall, *Politics and the Press, 1780–1850,* pp. 284 and 293.
[2] P.R.O., F.O. 83/16, 11 Dec. 1809.
[3] Aspinall, *op. cit.,* pp. 89 and 92. A good example of the effect of a treasury

There seems to have been little need for much interference with the opposition and radical press until the duke of York scandal in 1808 and the consequent revival of the reform movement. Even before Wardle gave notice of his motion in the House, the duke had been under fire from a series of scurrilous novels and pamphlets, written 'by a set of miscreants, who began in the practice of extortion, and ended in foul-mouthed and desperate abuse'. Many of London's green-grocers' shops 'were ousted of their honest tenants, to be converted into book-stalls, where these vile productions were sold under the protection only of their insignificance'.[1] Throughout the winter of 1808 and the following spring and summer the hostile press carried out a full scale assault on the disintegrating Portland ministry. In January 1809 Canning denounced in the Commons 'the system of abuse and aspersion' which disgraced the London press and hinted that it might make even the most enthusiastic liberal doubt 'whether its liberty was not on such terms too dearly purchased'. But so great was the outcry at this threat that Eldon had to make a conciliatory statement in the Lords while the *Sun* assured the public that there was no intention of stifling criticism of the convention of Cintra.[2] The campaign continued so strongly that public opinion became 'more bold, more ungovernable, more mad every day'. 'Rely upon it', wrote Charles Yorke to Perceval in September, 'that if honest men cannot by some means or other, combat, overthrow, or suppress the existing Jacobinism and tyranny of the daily press, it will very soon become master of the whole commonwealth'.[3]

The most effective method of repression (although one of the most unpopular) was the ex-officio information—'a formal written sugges-tion on behalf of the King of a misdemeanour committed, filed by the Attorney-General in the King's Bench . . . without the intervention of a grand jury'.[4] During the first 50 years of George III's reign it

---

subsidy can be seen in the pages of the *Sun* at the time of the fall of the Talents ministry. On 5 Mar. 1807, when Grenville was still in office, the *Sun* wrote, 'The Government really deserve great credit for abolishing the office of Barrack Master General.' On 3 Apr., after receipt of a subsidy from the Portland ministry, the paper wrote, 'We do not see that any saving could be effected by the change which has been proposed.'

[1] *Day*, 30 Jan. 1809. For a violent attack on the violence of the press see the anonymous letter of Sept. 1812 printed in Aspinall, *Letters of George IV*, vol. 1, no. 148.

[2] *Sun*, 8 Feb. 1809.

[3] Perceval MSS., C. P. Yorke to Perceval, 12 Sep. 1809.

[4] Archbold, *Pleading, Evidence and Practice*, (28th edition), pp. 129-30.

was used only 164 times, principally in 1770 (15 times), 1775 (12), 1781 (11), and 1792 (19). But it was not before 1808 that it seems to have been widely used as a method of intimidation. In that year the attorney-general, Sir Vicary Gibbs, 'a little irritable, sharp-featured, bilious-looking man', began 20 ex-officio informations and a further 22 during the following two years.[1] Occasionally an information was lodged and then held *in terrorem* over some unfortunate proprietor. In the cases where it was decided to prosecute, the percentage of convictions was high. Of the 42 cases handled by Gibbs between 1808 and 1810 25 had, by 1811, led to convictions, 14 were still at issue, while one defendant had not been traced and only 2 acquitted.

Such tactics did little to add to the ministry's popularity: outside the house of commons it was constantly on the defensive. By 1809 it took considerable courage and a good pair of lungs to try and put the government's case in public. In London the common hall of livery-men was completely dominated by the radicals, under the energetic leadership of Robert Waithman. The City's three Pittite M.P.s, Curtis, Price, and Shaw, were constantly under attack for their voting record in the House. When Curtis tried to explain why they had voted for the duke of York's acquittal he was 'assailed with such a storm of groans and hisses as to be altogether inaudible'.[2] At a similar meeting after the Burdett riots, Combe, the only opposition member for the City, was received with great applause while most of Price's speech was drowned by cat-calls. 'Nobody', shouted Price above growing uproar, 'ought to call a member of Parliament to account for his conduct.'[3] In December 1809 the liverymen unanimously passed an address denouncing 'the imbecility of ministers' after sheriff Atkins, who alone attempted to oppose it had been howled down, and on lord mayor's day Perceval's carriage was surrounded by a hostile mob outside the guildhall.[4] After the Burdett riots a group known as the Loyal Liverymen of London drew up a petition affirming their confidence in king and parliament, copies of which were left in the Old London Tavern and the London Coffee House. Over 1,500

---

[1] Westbrook Hay MSS., *op. cit.*; Leigh Hunt, *Autobiography*, vol. 2, p. 80. It should be remembered that Hunt had a personal grudge against the attorney-general. Gibbs preferred to use ex-officio informations instead of prosecutions for libel, where 'one prejudiced and obstinate' juror often could block a conviction (Aspinall, *Letters of George IV*, vol. I, no. 33).

[2] *Day*, 3 Apr., and *Sun*, 4 Apr. 1809.

[3] *Day*, 5 May 1810.

[4] *Sun*, 11 Nov., and *Day*, 15 Dec. 1809.

signatures were claimed within a week and the organisers, encouraged by the news of similar movements at Canterbury, Liverpool, and Manchester, arranged a dinner at the Old London Tavern to celebrate their success. But while the Loyal Liverymen toasted the constitution within, a mob had collected without, 'who rent the air with their discordant shrieks and cries of disapprobation' and covered with mud anyone who tried to leave by the front door. In the end most of the company escaped by the back, so chastened by the experience that they apparently never met again.[1] The position was little better in the home counties. The freeholders of Berkshire decided, with only three or four contrary votes, to petition for an inquiry into the Walcheren expedition. 'I never knew', admitted Matthew Montague, who opposed the motion, 'any Ministry so little supported by the strength of party as the present.' After the electors of Middlesex had passed a petition in April 1810 calling for the release of Burdett, the county's two members were asked to present it to parliament. One of them, Byng, agreed to do so, but the other, Mellish, who refused, was loudly booed and not allowed to speak.[2] Only in the London common council did the Pittites make any sustained attempt to stand up to radical agitators. On 1 August 1809 they failed by only 5 votes in a division of 113 to rescind a previous vote of thanks to Wardle for his services in the duke of York inquiry. When Waithman proposed the usual petition for an inquiry into Walcheren, Sir William Curtis moved the previous question and polled 76 votes against the radicals' 77. Later, by majorities ranging from 9 to 17, Curtis succeeded in defeating the original wording of the petition and substituting a more moderate version. Even in June 1810, when the government's stock was at its lowest, a motion for parliamentary reform was carried by only 86 to 81: a year later the radicals were heavily defeated on a proposal to use the guildhall for a reform meeting.[3] But elsewhere the government case went by default: its spokesmen, lacking self-confidence, were too easily intimidated and were too slow to organise counter-demonstrations. Both in and out of parliament the government, by 1807, was on the defensive: three years later it seemed that unless ministerialists showed more spirit and determination, the situation might get entirely out of hand. But the story of this deterioration is that of the fumblings of the Portland ministry and of the revival of the agitation for parliamentary reform.

[1] *Day*, 7, 14, and 23 May 1810.   [2] *Day*, 17 Jan. and 27 Apr. 1810.
[3] *Day*, 2 Aug., 6, 14, and 16 Dec. 1809, 7 June 1810, and 1 June 1811.

CHAPTER TEN

THE SESSIONS OF 1807 AND 1808

WHEN the new parliament first assembled on 26 June 1807 there were many observers who felt a sense of depression and of anti-climax. Within so short a period the country had lost Pitt and Fox, Nelson and Cornwallis. 'We are', wrote Horner that April, 'no longer in the heroic ages': the debates, thought Wilberforce, were 'poor compared with former times'.[1] The opposition was generally unpopular and there was no one on the treasury benches capable of stirring or guiding public opinion. The debate on the Address (carried by the government by 350 votes to 155) degenerated into mutual accusations of corruption. Howick charged Pitt's Friends with having revived the useless office of militia inspectors in order to gain votes at the general election: Perceval retorted that the Talents had been about to appoint 300 new revenue officials when they had lost office. The radical Cochrane could only add that he hoped both charges would be investigated, and that 'some third party would arise, which would keep aloof from selfish interest, and sinecure places and pensions'. Cobbett christened the new assembly the 'Dog Day Parliament', as much for the warmth of its party debates as for the day on which it assembled.[2] And the public, hardened by the constant charges and counter-charges of corruption, began to believe both. Government and opposition became generally known as the Ins and the Outs. 'That all public men are corrupt', wrote Romilly that July, 'and that the true interests of the country are disregarded in an unceasing struggle between contending factions for power and emolument, is an opinion spreading very fast through the country.' The same signs were noticed by Holland and by Cobbett: the *Edinburgh Review*, alarmed by 'a very general spirit of discontent, distrust, and contempt for public characters among the more intelligent

---

[1] Horner, *Memoirs*, vol. I, p. 398; Wilberforce, *Life*, vol. III, p. 360; *Gent. Mag.*, 1806, vol. LXXVI, Preface 1; *Letters of the late Rt. Hon. Earl of Brooke and Warwick* (London, 1819), p. 340; Farington, *Diary*, vol. IV, p. 196. The division of 505 M.P.s was the largest ever for a debate on the Address (Aitken, vol. II, p. 222).

[2] *Parl. Deb.*, IX, 623, 635 and 642; *Political Register*, 11 July 1807; Colchester, vol. II, pp. 123–4.

portions of the inferior ranks of society', saw 'the seeds of revolution in the present aspect and temper of the nation'.[1] One observer noted that the ten leading ministers in the Commons had been returned by a total of 1,214 electors, or a little over 120 apiece. Even this did not present a true picture, for Perceval's constituents alone accounted for over half the total: no other minister on the list represented as many as 100 voters.[2] Calculations for the opposition front bench would have yielded similar results. The leaders of both major parties seemed content to try and ignore public opinion: the Westminster election of 1807 should have taught them that the radicals would quickly fill the gap.

The remainder of the short 1807 session was equally disappointing. The whig leaders had not had time to recover from their election disappointments while Grenville entered into opposition convinced that it was far more dangerous to do too much than to do too little.[3] Consequently the real leadership of the opposition fell to Whitbread. On 6 July he introduced a motion on the state of the nation, only to be overwhelmed by 322 to 136, but later successfully piloted his Parochial Schools Bill through all its stages in the Commons.[4] The more liberal wing of the party also opposed the renewal of the Irish Insurrection Act and the third reading of the repressive Irish Arms Bill, but they only offended their own leaders who, when in power, had passed the first and drafted the second. Sheridan's motion on the condition of Ireland, introduced in the finest speech of the session, polled 33 votes while a mere 28 members could be persuaded to oppose the Irish Arms Bill.[5] In fact so ineffective were the whigs that ministers had more to fear from the small but energetic group of radicals. Cochrane, who acted as their spokesman in the absence of Burdett, attacked placemen

[1] *Annual Register*, 1807, p. 235; Romilly, *Memoirs*, vol. II, p. 217; Holland, *Memoirs of the Whig Party*, vol. II, p. 21; *Political Register*, 18 July 1807; *Edinburgh Review*, July 1807, p. 421; Oldfield, *op. cit.*, vol. II, p. 286.

[2] *A Biographical Index to the present House of Commons* (London, 1808). The figures given were Canning (Newton) 36, Castlereagh (Plympton) 82, Rose (Christchurch) 24, Long (Haslemere) 55, Huskisson (Liskeard) 80, Sturges Bourne (Christchurch) 24, Sir Arthur Wellesley (St. Michael) 42, Sir James Pulteney (Melcombe Regis) 98, Dundas (Edinburghshire) 83, and Perceval (Northampton) 740.

[3] Buckingham, *Court and Cabinets of George III*, vol. IV, p. 149.

[4] *Parl. Deb.*, IX, 734-40, 797-804, 853-7, 1050X-1055X and 1067. For Perceval's attitude on education see chapter 2, p. 25. Whitbread's bill was defeated in the Lords—*Parl. Deb.*, IX, 1178.

[5] *Ibid.*, 572X, 911, and 1086-95. Grattan himself supported both bills (*ibid.*, 1201-8). Sheridan's speech on his own motion has been called 'the bouquet or last parting blaze of his eloquence' (Moore, *Life of Sheridan*, p. 352). Roberts, *The Whig Party*, p. 36.

in parliament and jobbery at the admiralty. Neither motion had any chance of success in the House: both were intended instead for public consumption.[1] The performance of ministers was equally bad. When, on the eve of the session, Perceval gave the King's Speech dinner to government supporters, Canning excused himself and dined with Wilbraham Bootle, one of his personal followers.[2] In debate the foreign secretary was as brilliant as ever, but Perceval, too over-worked and distracted by Jane's persistent ill-health, was not at his best. For the first time he had to speak regularly without the help of copious notes and often found himself at a loss for words. 'I think', wrote Fremantle, 'that Perceval seems to want nerves; he has not yet attempted that sort of boldness and decision which were the features of his former speeches, but he hesitates and stammers, and certainly as yet, is quite different in his manner': it was, rejoiced Temple, the usual story of 'a chattering lawyer in Opposition' proving unequal to the demands of office. By the end of the session many ministers looked worn out. Castlereagh, reported Richard Ryder, seemed 'very ill' while Portland and Mulgrave looked 'wretched'.[3] In fact some of the best speeches on the government side came from back benchers, par-ticularly from Croker in support of the Address and from Milnes on 6 July.

The cabinet, conscious of its own weakness, had from the first been casting round for new recruits. The king had his eye on Melville and had to be told by Hawkesbury that his return would weaken, not strengthen, the Pittites in the Commons. Perceval favoured his old friend Harrowby, whose accession would reinforce his own position in the cabinet. He sounded Harrowby, unofficially, late in March. In May he proposed to Portland that Harrowby should be admitted to the cabinet without portfolio, only to be reminded that 'it would im-mediately occur to Lord Melville and his friends that he should do the same'. The accommodating Bathurst then offered, 'in the handsomest manner', to make a vacancy at the board of trade, but even Perceval opposed this solution. In the event nothing was done and the session ended with the cabinet unchanged.[4]

[1] *Parl. Deb.*, IX, 746–742X and 754–68.

[2] Colchester, vol. II, p. 123; P.R.O., 30/9/15 Perceval to Abbot, 4 Apr. 1807.

[3] Wilberforce, *Life*, vol. III, p. 342; Buckingham, *Court and Cabinets of George III*, vol. IV, pp. 167, 250; Harrowby MSS., vol. IV, fol. 87, Richard Ryder to Harrowby, 3 Sep. 1807. Perceval's youngest son was born on 17 May 1807 (*Gent. Mag.*, 1807, vol. I, p. 482).

[4] Windsor MSS., 12989–90 Perceval to George III, 27 June 1807; 13003 same

PLATE 4

Spencer Perceval

(*from a miniature by Samuel Shelley*)

Parliament was prorogued on 14 August and did not reassemble until 21 January. The recess brought little relief to Perceval, who was fully occupied drafting the Orders-in-Council and clearing away the arrears of treasury business. The benchers of Lincoln's Inn elected him dean of the chapel and ordered his coat of arms to be displayed in their hall.[1] The little free time the chancellor had left was spent hunting for a country house to replace the unsuitable Belsize. One owner asked £15,000 and, although Jane liked the house, her husband disliked the price. The Ardens found a bargain at Little Merton, but this was too far from town. Then Elm Grove, Ealing, came up for auction on the death of its owner Lord Kinnaird and was sold to Sir James Earle for 6,700 guineas. Within a month Earle had decided to sell it again, and, as Jane was eager to buy, Perceval instructed his agent to make a bid. Ealing, although only seven miles from London, still retained 'a desirable air of retirement and country quiet'. Elm Grove itself, which had been built in the seventeenth century, was detached from the village and stood on the edge of Ealing common. The property included 36 acres of ground, 10 of which were laid out as a formal garden while the rest was left as meadow or pasture. Unfortunately the house itself was in such a state that Perceval calculated that he would have to spend £4,000 on decorations and repairs. All that interested his wife, however, was the fine view of the Surrey hills from the end of the lawn on the south side of the house. Finally Perceval paid £7,500, a great deal more than he could really afford. Although Arden, as usual, offered a loan, Perceval decided to borrow instead from the trustees of Jane's dowry and so, after the necessary alterations and additions, turned Elm Grove into 'a commodious family residence of a plain but desirable character'.[2]

Before parliament reassembled, the death of Earl Grey and Howick's consequent removal to the Lords left the opposition in the Commons leaderless. 'The hour that made you an earl', wrote Tierney dramatically, 'made the power of the Crown during the present reign at least absolute, for it set the House of Commons adrift. . . . I quite despair

---

to same, 7 July 1807; Harrowby MSS., vol. XI, fols. 216, 217–19. 'I learn', wrote Thomas to Lord Grenville in November, 'that Canning and Perceval are very ill together, and Lord Melville dissatisfied with them all'. (*Dropmore MSS.*, vol. IX, p. 149).

[1] *Black Book of Lincoln's Inn*, vol. IV, pp. 103 and 107.

[2] Perceval MSS., William Agar to Perceval, 12 Apr. 1808; Perceval to Arden, 18 and 20 July 1808; Brewer, *London and Middlesex*, vol. IV, pp. 335–6.

and look upon the party of the late administration as split, or as soon about to be split, into a thousand pieces.' [1] Not that there was any shortage of candidates for the succession. One government paper listed Temple, Petty, Sheridan, Whitbread, Ponsonby, and Tierney himself, but added, virtuously, that it could 'hardly suppose that in the present unexampled situation of this country and of Europe, any set of gentlemen could be found who would enter into a systematic opposition to His Majesty's Government'.[2] But the opposition was not put to shame. At the beginning of the session it held an official dinner and even invited Pinckney, the American envoy.[3] Meanwhile the radicals did what they could to beat up petitions for peace, much to the embarrassment of the Grenvillites.[4] The government press, heartened by seeming opposition disunity, faced the new session with confidence. 'Never', wrote the *Sun*, 'was there a period when unanimity so generally reigned throughout the country; the party that for so many years harrassed the measures of the Executive Government . . . . are now most fortunately broken, degraded, and dispersed—their adherents are few, and confessedly without hope.' [5] Events soon shattered such illusions. The main attack came, as Redesdale had predicted, on the Copenhagen and Orders-in-Council issues. There the government was prepared and stood its ground well.[6] What did confound the ministers was the pertinacity and resource with which the motley opposition found and pressed home other embarrassing questions.

The first draft of the Speech was written by Perceval, but George III thought it too long and rewrote part of it himself.[7] Even then it made grim reading. The Copenhagen expedition had been launched with 'the deepest reluctance' after the breakdown of negotiations with the Danish government; Russia, Austria, and Prussia had withdrawn their ambassadors from London; and Anglo-American commercial relations had seriously deteriorated. Against this catalogue of gloom, the Speech emphasised our continuing prosperity and hinted that no new taxes would be imposed during the current year.[8] The discussions on the Address went well for Pitt's Friends, for the opposition, having

[1] Olphin, *George Tierney*, p. 117.   [2] *Sun*, 18 Jan. 1808.
[3] *Romilly*, vol. II, p. 239.   [4] *Sun*, 5 Jan. 1808.
[5] *Ibid*, 1 Jan. 1808. Petitions for peace, presented by Colonel Stanley, one of the members for Preston, came from Bolton, Oldham and Manchester (*Parl. Deb.*, XI, 35).
[6] Colchester, vol. II, p. 135. For the Copenhagen expedition and Orders-in-Council see chapter 11, pages 161–71.
[7] Windsor MSS., 13345, George III to Lord Hawkesbury, 20 Jan. 1808.
[8] *Parl. Deb.*, X, 1–5.

no agreed policy, failed either to move an amendment or to make much impact on the debate. Viscount Hamilton, who moved the Address, made much of the country's financial and military strength. After fifteen years of war Great Britain had 'gained everything and lost nothing', for war, 'the curse of every other nation, had to Great Britain been a comparative blessing'. Our trade flourished, our wealth increased, our possessions multiplied, and our navy had swept all rivals from the high seas. There now existed but two world powers— Britain and France. 'Fortunately, these powers were too unequal to alarm us for the consequences, even should America be added to the number of our foes. . . .' Ponsonby, in his first speech as leader of the opposition, could make nothing of such robust optimism, and Whitbread only added to his embarrassment by pleading for peace negotiations. Milnes again spoke well from the back benches while Canning and Perceval put the government's case. Canning, wrote Lady Holland, was 'heavy and obscure. Perceval excelled him much.' The ministry had indeed got off to an excellent start. Fuller, speaking for the country gentry, praised the chancellor of the exchequer as 'a man of honour and integrity . . . and he should conclude by saying to him, as some gentlemen on the opposite side would never cease to urge objections to the measures of the existing government, "never mind them, pursue your duty and leave them where you find them".' The night's proceedings, Perceval told the king, could be taken 'as a good earnest of the support which His Majesty's Government is likely to meet with in the House of Commons in the present session'.[1] But such high hopes were not fulfilled.

The government did best on war policy, where the defeatist and pacifist wing of the opposition played into its hands. Late in January Windham, Tierney, and Burdett forced a division against a vote of thanks to Gambier, who commanded at Copenhagen, and were overwhelmed by 100 votes to 19.[2] A month later the persistent Whitbread again openly split the opposition by moving a formal motion for peace, only to be opposed by both Ponsonby and Wilberforce and defeated by 217 to 58.[3] In March the Mutiny Act, including a clause to revise Windham's recruiting plan, was passed by 169 to 100.[4] But on both

[1] *Ibid.*, 38–90; Lady Holland, *Journal*, vol. II, p. 279; Windsor MSS., 13361–2, Perceval to George III, 22 Jan, 1808. Romilly (vol. II, p. 239) thought the opposition should have moved an amendment.

[2] *Parl. Deb.*, X, 178.

[3] *Ibid.*, X, 801–56; Colchester, vol. II, p. 140.

[4] *Ibid.*, X, 991.

Copenhagen and the Orders-in-Council the opposition fought long and vigorous parliamentary campaigns, keeping the debates going until five or six in the morning three times in one week early in February.[1] In the end even Arthur Wellesley, for all his iron constitution, began to feel the strain. 'We keep up our numbers tolerably well,' he wrote to Clancarty, 'the opposition astonishingly.' [2] Perceval himself was directly involved in two further issues that played into whig hands. On 20 February he told the treasury board that he intended to ask parliament to prohibit the unlicensed export to France of jesuits' bark, the source of quinine.[3] Two days later he introduced a bill in the Commons, explaining that jesuits' bark was badly needed by the French army and that its price had recently risen by ten shillings to seventy shillings a pound in Paris. There was at first no opposition. On 23 February, however, Whitbread, who had not been in the House on the previous day, rose to give notice of his objections to 'that detestable species of warfare'. On the following day he moved a motion condemning 'war with the helpless, the sick, and the hospitals —one at which the feeling of all mankind would revolt'. The same principle, he claimed, would lead to the encouragement of 'pestilence, poison and assassination'. If Britain ran short of corn while the Baltic ports were closed and relations with the United States were bad, the French might retaliate by prohibiting the export of their corn and causing starvation in Britain. In vain Perceval explained that jesuits' bark could still be exported under licence and that the object of his bill was to break down French commercial restrictions by forcing the French to take other goods if they wanted jesuits' bark. The tender consciences of the Saints had been aroused and Wilberforce joined the 78 members who voted against the government.[4]

[1] Colchester, vol. II, pp. 138, 140, 147. For the debates see chapter 11, pages 172–4.   [2] Wellington, *Civil Correspondence, Ireland*, p. 357.

[3] P.R.O., T 29/93/344.

[4] *Parl. Deb.*, X, 696, 710, 728–31. The jesuits' bark issue was later widely used against Perceval. Sydney Smith in his *Letters of Peter Plymley* denied that the people could be 'so degraded as to look for their safety to a man who proposes to subdue Europe by keeping it without Jesuits' Bark'. The Continent was to be reconquered 'by the want of rhubarb and plums' (Smith, *Works*, vol. III, p. 452). Napier, in his *History of the Peninsular War*, wrote that Perceval's bigotry 'taught him to oppress Ireland; but his religion did not prevent him from passing a law to prevent the introduction of medicines into France during pestilence'. But D. M. Perceval showed in *Remarks on the Character ascribed by Col. Napier to the late Right Hon. S. Perceval* (London, 1825, p. 14) that there was no pestilence in France in the summer of 1808. Cobbett (*Political Register*, 1808, p. 368) supported the bill.

Perceval's second tactical mistake was over the case of Major Palmer, a member of the Commons who had a private claim against the exchequer. In 1782 Palmer had submitted a plan for the reform of postal services which had been accepted by Pitt. For two years Palmer struggled to introduce his scheme against the opposition of local postmasters, inn-keepers, and coach-owners. In 1784 Pitt agreed that, as a recompense for his earlier losses, Palmer should be appointed surveyor and controller-general at £1,500 a year and receive $2\frac{1}{2}\%$ of all profits above £240,000 resulting from the introduction of his reform. In 1788 a parliamentary committee reported in favour of his scheme, but four years later, after renewed disputes with the post office, Palmer was suspended by the postmaster-general for alleged disobedience of orders. The treasury then offered Palmer £7,000 a year compensation, but Palmer held out for the original agreement and had his claim upheld by a second committee in 1797. In May of that year, however, the committee's report was opposed and defeated in the Commons by Pitt himself. Finally in March 1807 Palmer tried again and, on 12 May 1808, backed by a third committee report, moved that the terms of the 1784 agreement be honoured.[1] In spite of strong opposition from Perceval, Rose, and Long, the motion was carried by 137 votes to 71.[2] Perceval then, most unwisely, tried to block Palmer's claim in the Lords. On 17 June he told the Speaker that he meant to hold back the Appropriation Act until the Lords had considered the committee's report. If they rejected it, he would not insert the claim into the Appropriation Act but would put it into a separate bill, which could be rejected by the upper House. This was, as the Speaker protested, 'a manifest departure from the uniform practice of Parliament, and an abandonment of the highest privileges of the Commons'. On 20 June Perceval, armed with four possible precedents, introduced a separate bill, but, in the face of opposition from the Speaker and the disapproval of the House, had to withdraw it on the second reading.[3]

The ministry fared even worse on the Irish and Roman catholic issues, where the cabinet itself was badly split between the ultra-protestants, led by Perceval, and moderates like Canning, Castlereagh, and Hawkesbury. On every major issue the Perceval group, backed by the king and the duke of Cumberland, was able to carry the day.

[1] *H. of C. Journal*, 1806–7, pp. 284–8.

[2] *Parl. Deb.*, XI, 170–231; Colchester, vol. II, p. 149; *Dropmore MSS.*, vol. IX, p. 207.

[3] Colchester, vol. II, pp. 153–6; P.R.O., 30/9/15 Colchester MSS.; *Parl. Deb.*, XI, 956, 1084.

Perceval's policy, as he explained in a letter to Wilberforce, was 'to let the Roman catholic know that he has got as much as a Protestant Parliament can give him, and that he must be contented'.[1] Unfortunately the Irish catholics were not. In October 1807 Arthur Wellesley, the Irish secretary, had to use troops to quell unrest in Limerick, Tipperary, and Waterford. 'I entirely agree in opinion with you', he told Perceval, 'respecting the inexpediency of making any concession to this country in consequence of the turbulence and disturbances of the moment'.[2] Even Redesdale's plan to remove the worst of the Irish tithe grievances was shelved. It was, wrote Perceval, 'breaking in upon an ancient and extensive system, not upon the grounds of a certain conviction that you are reforming and improving that system, but on the importunity of unjust and exaggerated complaint. . . .' Any concession would only repeat 'the unfortunate lesson which has been too often and too successfully taught in Ireland, that if discontent will but be turbulent enough, it will force its object from a yielding government'.[3] The only positive acts he would consider were those to reform the Irish police and to build more Anglican churches.[4] Such rigidity paid neither militarily nor politically. Wellesley had already warned the cabinet that if French troops landed the Irish would rebel: Ireland, he wrote, 'in view to military operations, must be considered as an enemy's country'.[5] In the Commons the opposition pressed Irish affairs whenever possible. On 29 April Sir John Newport, Grattan, and Parnell tried to increase the grant to Maynooth, the training college for Irish Roman catholic priests, from £9,250 to £13,000. 'It was', said Perceval in opposing the amendment, 'no part of religious toleration to make a provision for the education of the clergy of the tolerated sect. All that toleration required . . . was that no difficulty should be created to any measures they might take for their own education.' Even moderate Pittites could not stomach this for, in the division, the government vote dropped to 93 and its majority to 35.[6] A week later the opposition returned to the attack, claiming that the cabinet had accepted a £13,000 grant 'till they went to St. James' Palace, and were closeted for several hours with a royal duke'. Neither

---

[1] Wilberforce, *Life*, vol. II, pp. 17–19.

[2] Wellington, *Civil Correspondence, Ireland*, pp. 158 and 162–5.

[3] *Ibid.*, pp. 167–73.

[4] *Ibid.*, pp. 330 and 390.

[5] *Ibid.*, p. 30.

[6] *Parl. Deb.*, XI, 93. For a hostile view of Perceval's position see Sydney Smith, *Works* (1840 edition), vol. III, p. 398.

Portland and Camden nor Canning and Castlereagh, both pointedly absent, had, it was said, accepted the cabinet's policy. Perceval made the best he could of a bad case, only to be confounded by Duigenan, the most fanatical of all protestants. Roman catholics, he declared, were 'bad subjects and hostile to the state. . . . If anyone would move to withdraw the public aid altogether from Maynooth, he would second the motion.' To make matters worse, Duigenan, the Irish advocate-general, had just been made a privy councillor 'at the express desire of Lord Hawkesbury'. After this the government survived by a slender majority of 24 in a division of 188.[1] On 11 May the opposition struck again at the tottering ministry by moving a vote of censure against Duigenan's appointment. Barham, in proposing the censure, made great play with Perceval's definition of toleration. Ministers, he claimed, 'were as intolerant as the age would allow them to be'. After Wellesley had made a lame defence of the appointment, his colleagues sat firmly in their seats while a succession of opposition speakers taunted them on their silence and reliance on the votes of the specially-mustered placemen. The censure was finally defeated by 179 votes to 107, but, wrote Wellesley, it had been 'a very bad scrape'. Ministers had refused to be drawn into the debate, reported Perceval to the king, in order to avoid a general discussion on the Roman catholic issue.[2] A fortnight later the opposition forced this when Grattan presented another catholic petition. This time they failed to take the government by surprise. Perceval rallied every possible vote and, through Wellesley, ordered Duigenan to 'avoid speaking at all, or . . . if you should speak . . . confine yourself within very narrow limits, and deliver yourself in very moderate language'.[3] After Grattan had introduced the petition, the treasury bench tried to force an immediate division, but

[1] *Parl. Deb.*, XI, 123–9; Colchester, vol. II, p. 148; Wellington, *Civil Correspondence, Ireland*, p. 256; Wilberforce, vol. III, p. 361; Perceval MSS. Hawkesbury to Canning, (undated)—'Dr. Duigenan applied about a year ago to be made a Privy Councillor in Ireland upon the ground of holding the same office there as Sir Wm. Scott holds here'. For Duigenan's views see *Parl. Deb.*, IX, 324 and 498. In 1810 Duigenan published *The Nature and Extent of the Demands of the Irish Roman Catholics fully explained*, in which he argued that all Irish Roman catholics were potential rebels. As further concessions would only make rebellion easier, the penal laws ought to be made more not less stringent. 'Dieu me garde', wrote the *Quarterly Review*, 'de mes amis' (Feb. 1810, p. 138).

[2] *Parl. Deb.*, XI, 148 ff.; Wellington, *op cit.*, p. 419; Windsor MSS., 13650, Perceval to George III, 11 May 1808.

[3] Wellington, *op. cit.*, p. 440. The cabinet was so confident of a majority that it allowed one supporter, Denis Browne, who sat for a catholic constituency, to vote for the petition (*ibid.*, p. 426). For the veto issue see chapter 21, p. 414 ff.

the opposition, amid prolonged confusion, managed to force a debate which ended at six in the morning with a government victory by 281 votes to 128. 'Grattan', admitted Wellesley, 'made an excellent speech. The rest of the debate bad.' Perceval put the best possible gloss on things in his report to the king, but the government had been badly shaken.[1]

Towards the end of the session the government began to meet growing difficulties over reform. Romilly's early attempts to amend the criminal law aroused little enthusiasm on either side, but economic reform stirred deep passions.[2] Moderate economic reform had long been generally popular both in the House and the constituencies. 'The shortest and surest road by which a private individual can now ascend to popularity and influence', admitted the *Edinburgh Review* in July 1809, 'is to denounce some peculator to public justice, or to bring to light some instance of official abuse. Discoveries of this sort are now at a higher premium with us than they ever were in the history of the world.'[3] Nor had the government shown any sign of trying to stifle useful inquiries: to have made the attempt would have weakened not strengthened its influence. Immediately parliament had re-assembled after the 1807 election, ministers, stung by whig charges of corruption, gave a pledge to revive the Commons' committee of finance. Some changes in its composition were inevitable. The original committee had been 'packed' by the Talents and used for party ends at the election; five of the twenty-four members had since lost their seats; a sixth, Sturges Bourne, had become ineligible by accepting office; and another, Sir Henry Mildmay, was suspected of making an illegal bargain with government. Perceval therefore proposed to re-appoint eleven of the seventeen surviving members and to add fourteen new ones. Bankes was to remain as chairman, and to have the assistance of such experts as Biddulph, Petty, Henry Thornton, Grattan, and Thomas Baring. The new members, although scarcely equal in ability to the old, included Richard Ryder, Wharton, and the very promising young Milnes. It seemed a perfectly reasonable proposal which restored the party balance in the committee and left all the various interests and areas their representatives, without seriously weakening its personnel. But the opposition, supported by the Saints and the

[1] *Parl. Deb.*, XI, 638; Wellington, *Civil Correspondence, Ireland*, p. 441; Windsor MSS., 13680–1, Perceval to George III, 25 May 1808.
[2] Colchester, vol. II, p. 158; *Parl. Deb.*, XI, 887.
[3] *Edinburgh Review*, July 1809, p. 282.

Sidmouth group, denounced any changes, taking the issue to a division, which they lost by 244 votes to 145.[1]

The committee issued its first report, dealing with the accounts of the pay office, on 22 July. The findings, although not as sensational as the earlier rumours in the opposition press, were bad enough to confirm the public distrust of all politicians. It was discovered that in May 1799 and again in July 1800 Thomas Steele (then one of the joint paymasters-general) had drawn bills totalling £19,800 on army extraordinaries in order to balance his own private finances. The money had been replaced, together with the accumulated interest of over £7,000, between February and April 1807. Steele's evidence before the committee did even more harm. He had 'no hesitation' in admitting that the sums had not been used for the public service: he had borrowed the money because of 'private considerations of a very peculiar nature'. He had, he ended, hoped to repay the loan 'in a very short time, but it was not in my power to accomplish it'.[2] Ministers did what they could to repair the damage. Within ten days of the report's publication, the treasury board had debated its recommendations, decided on the necessary reforms, and circularised the departments concerned.[3]

The recommendations of the second report, on the management of the national debt, were included in Perceval's budget of 1808.[4] This honeymoon period was ended by the third report on the contentious issue of places and pensions. The question was first raised in parliament on 7 July 1807 by Lord Cochrane, who wished the inquiry to be restricted to M.P.s and their relatives. The idea traditionally appealed to the country gentlemen (who knew they had little to fear from it) and Lethbridge, Lyttleton, and Sir John Sebright all spoke for the motion. The debate put ministers in a delicate position: they had no intention of encouraging an official list of placemen and pensioners, but were equally afraid to offend the knights of the shire and perhaps to endanger their majority by seeming to oppose all inquiry. Fortunately Bankes himself opposed Cochrane, on the grounds that it was 'invidious and improper' to suggest that members were influenced solely by considerations of private advantage. Perceval, with the

[1] *Parl. Deb.*, IX, 693–707; Romilly, *Memoirs*, vol. II, p. 211; Windsor MSS., 12995–6 Perceval to George III, 1 July 1807; Roberts, *The Whig Party*, p. 186; Wellington, *Civil Correspondence, Ireland*, p. 103.

[2] For the report see *Parl. Deb.*, IX, p. lxvii ff.

[3] P.R.O., T29/91/453–8; *Parl. Deb.*, X, 184.

[4] *Parl. Deb.* IX, lxxxvii–cvi. Cf. chapter 17, pp. 321–2.

approval of Wilberforce, immediately rose to say that if the House would reject the original motion, he was prepared to introduce a modified plan which would receive the support of government. A significantly thin House then divided against the motion by 90 to 61. Many of the government's usual supporters obviously abstained, but so, on the other side, did the Grenville connection and the right-wing Foxites. Perceval next proposed that the committee of finance should be instructed to inquire into *all* pensions, places, sinecures, and salaries (except those of military officers and certain minor revenue officials). Bankes, baffled by this strategy, protested that his committee could not present such a report that session or even probably in the next, while Whitbread, Sheridan, and Calcraft denounced Perceval for wishing to smother the investigation. But Wilberforce again supported the minister, and so did the House by 101 votes to 60.[1]

For the next ten months the finance committee was occupied collecting material for its report. By April 1808 Bankes had begun to draft a preface which, according to one government supporter who examined it, read 'not very unlike some of the productions of Mr. Horn[e] Took[e]'. The ministerialists on the committee, led by Denis Browne, therefore decided to delay the publication of the report as long as they could. They joined with certain reformers who disagreed with Bankes 'as to modes and expressions' in the preface, with the result that they deleted by eight votes to five the most objectionable parts of it and postponed others. Friends of government (like Ellis, Mills, and Leycester) who had not previously bothered to attend, were pressed into service to support Browne.[2] These tactics were so successful that twelve months later the committee was still unable to agree on its report. Bankes, unable to make any progress, lost interest and the leadership of the committee passed to Henry Martin, the Grenvillite member for Kinsale. On 8 May 1809 Martin gave notice in the Commons of motions based on the committee's still unpublished findings. Having been warned by Grenville not to stress embarrassing sinecure and pension issues, he was so studiously moderate that Perceval accepted almost all his proposals. Once more the progressive whigs had reason to lament their stifling alliance with Grenville. Even if Bankes 'were a man of iron' Whitbread told the Commons that June, 'if he were to live to the years of Methuselah, from the mode in which that Committee were proceeding, little good was to be hoped

[1] *Parl. Deb.*, IX, 746–742X.
[2] Perceval MSS., Denis Browne to Perceval, 9 Apr. 1808.

for'.[1] In September the treasury introduced the necessary new regulations, and later adopted others on the basis of the committee's fourth and fifth reports. But the third report itself was not issued until the summer of 1810, when it recommended economies estimated at a minimum of £81,000 a year.[2] Perceval had handled relations between the government and the committee with great skill. But his policy of concessions and delay was too mild for court circles and for the ultra-tories. 'Mr. Bankes and his Committee', wrote the duke of Richmond, 'are to the full as great enemies to us as the Talents.'[3] And when the finance committee threatened reversions, the ultras decided to stand their ground, and, in the process, exposed the government's essential weakness in both houses of parliament.

It was on 24 March 1807 (the last day in the life of All the Talents) that Bankes proposed, 'That no office, place, employment, or salary, in any part of his majesty's dominions, ought hereafter to be granted in reversion'. In the debate that followed only Yorke, Johnstone, and Gascoyne were critical: both the retiring ministers and Huskisson, the future financial secretary to the treasury, spoke in favour of the resolution, which passed without a division.[4] On the following 29 June (immediately after the general election) Bankes obtained leave to introduce a Reversions Bill, under the supervision of Petty, Henry Thornton, and himself. Neither then nor during its later stages was the bill opposed by ministers: by 9 July it had completed its third reading. Perceval, wrote Lord Holland, decided not to risk his popularity by opposing the measure in the Commons. 'He knew in the dusk of the session the Lords, like a faithful Penelope, would unravel the web.'[5] On the second reading in the Lords, Perceval's own brother denounced the bill as 'an unnecessary and indecent attack upon the King's lawful prerogative'. Holland tried to save the bill by moving the adjournment, but was beaten in a discreditably thin House by 15 to 9. Amongst those voting with the majority were the duke of Cumberland, Eldon (the only cabinet minister present), Melville, and

---

[1] Windsor MSS., 14459–60, Perceval to George III, undated (8 May 1809); *Sun*, 9 May 1809; *Parl. Deb.*, XI, 1009.

[2] For the 3rd report of the finance committee see *Annual Register*, 1810, p. 478 ff. and P.R.O., T 37/64/530–5. For the 4th report, on the commissioners for Dutch prizes see T 29/100/361 and T27/64/12. For the 5th report, on exchequer bills office, see T29/106/403–4 and T27/66/537.

[3] Perceval MSS., duke of Richmond to Perceval, 25 Sep. 1810.

[4] *Parl. Deb.*, IX, 178–85.

[5] *Commons Journal*, vol. 62, pp. 588, 596, 614, 621, 646, 661, and 668; Holland, *Memoirs of the Whig Party*, vol. II, p. 255.

Redesdale.[1] Perceval, having been previously reproached by Arden for allowing the bill to pass through the Commons, was prepared for its defeat. He immediately saw Bankes and assured him that no new reversions would be granted before the Commons had again debated the subject. He was, he explained, surprised by the passions aroused both for and against the bill, which he thought would neither endanger the prerogative nor do much for economic reform. When on 10 August Bankes proposed an address to prevent the granting of reversions until six weeks after the beginning of the following session, Perceval gave it 'his sincere support' and it was passed without a division.[2]

As soon as parliament re-assembled in 1808 Bankes introduced his second bill, which passed through the Commons as smoothly as its predecessor. 'Mr. Perceval trusts', reported the leader of the House to the king, 'that he is not mistaken when he expresses his belief to his Majesty that the fate of this bill now, if it should succeed in the House of Lords, instead of weakening the means of your Majesty's servants to resist any measure which may really be found objectionable as proposed by the Finance Committee, will rather have strengthened them: altho' undoubtedly, the thinness of the House does not shew any disposition on the part of the friends of Government to give their active support to it upon a measure connected with the subject of reform.' [3] The ultras were, however, still determined to wreck the bill in the Lords. When it came up for its second reading there Arden renewed his opposition, and was supported by Redesdale, the duke of Montrose, and by Auckland, a Grenvillite and former member of the Talents cabinet. Against them were the combined front benches —Hawkesbury, Westmorland, and Eldon for the government and Holland, Lauderdale, and Grosvenor for the Foxites. Together they saved the bill by the narrow majority of 69 to 61.[4] But the unexpected strength of the ultra opposition, and their known determination to continue the fight in committee, alarmed the cabinet. Consequently on 2 March the prime minister wrote to Windsor asking that the king should make known his approval of the cabinet's policy on the bill. He met with a flat refusal. George III had not opposed his ministers' policy, 'although he can never deny that he regrets that it should have

[1] *Parl. Deb.*, IX, 1044X–1049X; *The Times*, 7 Aug. 1807.
[2] *Parl. Deb.*, IX, 1158–1168; Roberts (*Whig Party*, p. 192) writes of the debate on this address that 'only Perceval ventured to speak against it'!
[3] *Parl. Deb.*, X 96–100 and 194–5; Windsor MSS., 13384–5 Perceval to George II, 9 Feb. 1808.
[4] *Parl. Deb.*, X, 870–2.

been adopted'. Therefore the king had decided not to intervene on either side, 'and has no intention of departing from a course which has appeared to him most consistent with propriety and with his own dignity, whilst it is no less fair to those concerned'.[1] The duke of Portland thus found himself neatly impaled between supporters in the Commons who would not vote against Bankes and ultras in the Lords who would do nothing else. The cabinet had a week between the king's declaration of non-belligerency and the date of the committee stage in the Lords in which to decide what to do. They used it for the novel experiment of canvassing in favour of a reform bill. Camden was sent out looking for votes; the prime minister (who made a rule of never attending debates) gave his proxy to Chichester; and attempts were made to reclaim hostile bishops. But the ultras, now confident that they were fighting the king's battle, were equally active. 'The D[uke] of Y[ork],' wrote Portland to Hawkesbury, 'who I had reason to hope would absent himself, has been prevailed upon to attend, and 26 persons who met to-day at Lord Arden's determined to vote against the House going into a committee.' [2]

The decisive debate finally got under way with Arden invoking memories of Charles II on the scaffold and Redesdale reminding the peers that the French Revolution began as a movement for economic reform. Again Pittites and Foxites joined forces to oppose them: Eldon, Harrowby, and Hawkesbury as well as Holland and Grey all spoke in favour of the bill. The division actually ended in a tie (84–84), which allowed the bill to go immediately into committee. Hawkesbury, supported by Mulgrave, then moved the official government amendment to limit the prohibition of reversions to 1 June 1810. As the Foxites refused to vote for this, ministers were left in a straight fight with the ultras. In the division Eldon (who always disliked the bill) shabbily deserted his colleagues, who found themselves in a minority of 21 to 59. After this the cabinet conceded defeat. When the measure came up for its third reading ministers voted with the ultras for rejection and the second Reversions Bill was lost by 120 to 48.[3] Arden, supported by the royal dukes, the bishops, and the Carlton House group, had proved that, in the Lords, the court was still more than a match for the cabinet.[4] But the court's victory only added to the

[1] *Windsor MSS.*, 13463–6, Portland to George III, 2 Mar. 1808 and 13467, George III to Portland, 3 Mar.

[2] Add. MSS., 38191, fol. 248, Portland to Hawkesbury, 9 Mar. 1808.

[3] *Parl. Deb.*, X, 1044–53 and 1087.

[4] For the groups who supported Arden see *Parl. Deb.*, X, 1047 (Moira's

government's difficulties: the city of London petitioned against the rejection of the bill, fourteen opposition peers, led by Grey and Holland, entered a strong protest in the *Lords' Journal*, and Bankes gave notice in the Commons that he would try again.[1]

On 20 March Perceval wrote to his brother suggesting a compromise 'to reconcile feelings, principles, and opinions on all sides'. The cabinet was prepared to abandon Hawkesbury's original amendment and, instead, to sponsor clauses enacting that all reversionary grants should in future be published in the *London Gazette* and should be subject to 'alterations, reform, and even abolition where the King and Parliament might within these two years think proper'. Arden's reply was not encouraging. He accepted the idea of publication, but thought the cautionary clause 'absolutely takes from the King the power of granting any certain reversion for 2 y[ea]rs'. Why should all offices be rendered insecure because a few were still unreformed? The Commons should draw up a list of places subject to abuse and then petition the king not to grant reversions to these. 'We in the House of Lords,' he ended, 'have contended for and successfully supported the right of the Crown, and allow me to say—you, the servants of the Crown in the House of Commons, are bound to support us . . . in return.' [2] But the following day Perceval told the duke of Portland that he was not prepared to resist Bankes in the Commons and that he preferred to try the effect of his own compromise clauses. The duke therefore agreed to recommend them to the king. 'The majorities', wrote the prime minister to Windsor, 'by which your Majesty's Government is enabled to carry its measures at present in the House of Commons, are unquestionably very considerable; but he thinks himself indispensibly called upon to state to your Majesty that the number in those majorities which consists of persons whose opinions are influenced in a great degree by considerations which lead them to coincide in such a measure as Mr. Bankes will propose, is very great. . . .' If the government attempted to reject the bill its majority would certainly be 'very much diminished' and the moderate Bankes himself 'soured'.[3] Two days

---

speech)—1050 (Grey's speech), and 1335 (Whitbread's speech); Grey, *Life and Opinions*, pp. 202–6. 'This business', wrote Camden to Malmesbury, 'will have given the Government a considerable shake' (Aspinall and Smith, *English Historical Documents*, vol. XI, no. 236).

[1] *Parl. Deb.*, X, 1087; *Political Register*, 16 Apr. 1808.
[2] Perceval MSS., Perceval to Arden, 20 Mar. 1808 and Arden to Perceval, 20 Mar.
[3] Windsor MSS., 13515–24, Portland to George III, 21 Mar. 1808.

later the king appears to have told Eldon that he would rather accept
Arden's ideas than Perceval's. This produced a unanimous cabinet
minute in favour of Perceval's clauses and an assurance that the Reversions Bill could not be opposed in the Commons without 'great
prejudice to your Majesty's service'. After this the king reluctantly
accepted the idea of concessions.[1]

Unfortunately the Commons, stung by Arden's previous success,
did not. As soon as Bankes had introduced his third bill on 28 March,
Perceval rose to say that he would move two amendments to it
in committee. The idea of any alterations was immediately opposed
by Ponsonby, Porchester, and Bankes himself, while, on the eve of
the second reading, the sheriffs of London presented a strongly-
worded petition in favour of the original measure.[2] All the advantages
in the debate lay with the reformers. Ward spoke of 'a secret but
irresponsible power' able to thwart the cabinet: 'they were ministers,
and no ministers', having the title but not the privileges of office.
Tierney denounced 'a dark junta behind the throne' and Porchester
recalled the days when the Commons was still 'undaunted by the
frown of princes'.[3] Perceval, conscious of the silent and half-empty
benches behind him, knew that his own amendments had no chance
of success as long as Bankes opposed them. For, as he warned the king,
too many of the government's supporters—'especially those who are
representatives of populous places'—would never risk offending their
constituents by voting against an economic reform bill. If the government challenged Bankes and lost, it would be practically impossible
ever to control the finance committee in the future. Fortunately on
4 April (the day before the committee stage) Bankes unexpectedly
offered a compromise. The whole question of sinecures and reversions
was to be the subject of the finance committee's third report. Therefore, if Perceval would withdraw his clauses, Bankes agreed to limit
the duration of the bill to just over one year. After a hurried con-
ference with Canning and Castlereagh, Perceval agreed to put the idea
before the cabinet on the afternoon of 5 April. On the same day the
king consented to this further concession. But he remained 'satisfied
that Mr. Perceval will agree with him upon the incalculable mischief
which attends the existence of a Committee of Finance originally instituted for bad purposes, and whose influence is such as to become

---

[1] *Ibid.*, 13539, Hawkesbury to George III, 24 Mar.; 13540–3, cabinet minute,
24 Mar.; 13539, George III to Hawkesbury, 25 Mar.
[2] *Parl. Deb.*, X, 1259–68 and 1300–2.   [3] *Ibid.*, X, 1329–45.

formidable to Government, and to assume a controul in the House of Commons'.[1] Consequently when the House went into committee Perceval withdrew his amendments, which had, he claimed, been 'misunderstood and misrepresented', and pledged the government to support the revised bill. The public had been encouraged to believe that its success would lead to great economies: 'he wished to be no party' to that 'delusive' promise. It would, in fact, destroy 'a cheap mode of rewarding public service' and rather increase than diminish the king's prerogative. Logically Perceval's arguments were correct, but in politics logic itself is rarely enough. As Petty himself admitted there were, in 1807, only two important places still held in reversion. George Rose drew a little over £3,250 a year as clerk of parliament and was to be succeeded by his son. But the greatest sinecure of all, that of registrar to the high court of admiralty and to the court of appeals for prizes, was held by Arden, with reversion to Perceval. None of Bankes' proposals would have affected Perceval's inheritance of his brother's office: the minister was in no sense an interested party. Yet the opposition and the public only cared to remember that Perceval (if he lived long enough) would succeed to a sinecure worth between £38 and £39,000 a year. If he spoke against the bill he was thinking of his pocket: when he suggested compromises, he was only intent on staying in office. Emotionally, as long as public opinion was hostile to all placemen, there was no effective answer to his critics.[2] The whigs, confident of public approval, pressed for the original unlimited bill. Whitbread gave notice (but later withdrew it) of an amendment to extend the time-limit to ninety-nine years, which, wrote Perceval to the king, would be 'a little help to open people's eyes to what these measures may lead to'. On the third reading the opposition divided on Porchester's motion to substitute 'prohibit' for 'suspend' in the preamble, but were beaten by 112 to 60. And so the third Reversions Bill was sent up to the Lords where, as a temporary measure, it was allowed to pass without opposition.[3]

A year later the whole wearisome business was revived again. In April 1809 Porchester attempted to introduce a perpetual bill: the government's independent supporters, as usual, stayed away, and

---

[1] Windsor MSS., 13586–8, Perceval to George III, 4 Apr. 1808; 13589, George III to Perceval, 5 Apr.

[2] *Parl. Deb.*, X, 1331–3 (Perceval's speech); Roberts, p. 184; *Black Book*, (1820), pp. 15 and 73.

[3] Windsor MSS., 13591, Perceval to George III, 6 Apr. 1808 and 13598–9, same to same, 7 Apr.; *Parl. Deb.*, XI, 18–29.

Perceval thought himself lucky to carry the division by 121 to 106.[1] Bankes himself waited until after the collapse of the Portland ministry before returning to the attack. On 21 January 1810, four days after the motion for the Walcheren inquiry had been carried against the government, he proposed a permanent Reversions Bill. Perceval did his best to oppose by arguing that since the finance committee had still not published its third report, another temporary measure would be sufficient. But the treasury bench had now lost all control over the Commons. Bankes' motion was carried 'by acclamation, in one voice, by the whole House' while the prime minister's 'and one other voice were all that could be heard' for the amendment. Perceval 'saw with certainty' as he told the king, 'that if he pressed the question to a division that he should have been beat by at least two to one'. Immediately after this the opposition divided the House three times on the election of new members for the finance committee. They carried the first vote by 107 to 98: the second, 108 to 103: and the third, 117 to 104. 'We then,' wrote Creevey, 'stuffed Sir John Newport and Sir George Warrender down their throats, without their daring to oppose us. There never was a more complete victory, and the majority of the committee is now so good, anything may be done with it.' Members 'generally friendly to the Government' had, explained Perceval to the king, stayed away in the afternoon because of 'the dislike which was entertained to the idea of opposing Mr. Bankes' bill for abolishing reversions . . . and with all the exertions which could be made they could not be brought down to the House in the course of the evening.' Even young Peel, who had recently seconded the Address, voted against the government in one division.[2] Bankes' fourth bill subsequently passed through the Commons without further opposition: it could, predicted the king, be safely left to the Lords. On 16 February it was thrown out by Eldon on a technical point, but was speedily reintroduced and only survived its first reading because of a vote of adjournment. Ten days later it came up for its second reading when Arden's motion of rejection was carried by 107 to 67.[3] Bankes then suggested another temporary address, but the Commons insisted on a fifth bill, which was rejected without a division on its second reading

[1] Windsor MSS., 14371, Perceval to George III, 24 Apr. 1809.

[2] *Ibid.*, 14923-4, Perceval to George III, 31 Jan. 1810; Maxton, *Creevey Papers*, vol. I, pp. 126-7; Colchester, vol. II, p. 231; *Parl. Deb.*, XV, 251-262.

[3] Windsor MSS., 14294, George III to Perceval, 1 Feb. 1810; *Parl. Deb.*, XV, 436-7, 493-5, and 587-600.

in the Lords.[1] After this the government finally lost patience and many reformers lost interest. By April 1811 a sixth bill had passed the Commons only to be opposed by Liverpool in the upper House and again rejected without a division. When, in February 1812, a seventh came up for its second reading in the Commons, the attendance was so poor that the prime minister decided to risk dividing against it and carried the House by 56 to 54. Perceval had, as he reported to the Regent, succeeded 'beyond his expectation': after five years of deadlock all parties were getting tired of debating reversions. But there were still many independents who, like Wilberforce, regretted 'that Perceval should so cross the public feeling about economy and reform'. 'I lamented', confessed even the faithful Robert Ward, 'Perceval should so often make it a point of honour to resist all reforms on the ground of defending the prerogative of the Crown, that if he would only give into a few, and moderate reforms, he would not only do good to the country, but would take the only game they had out of the hands of opposition, and play it infinitely better, since he was a far better favourite with the people.' [2] The reversions issue itself ended in a compromise. On 10 March 1812 the heroically persistent Bankes introduced another temporary bill, prohibiting the granting of reversions before February 1814, and this, as expected, passed both Houses without opposition.[3]

The session of 1808 had gone very badly for the Portland ministry. It had been, wrote the Speaker, 'the most laborious session for hours of sitting ever known within living memory of the oldest members or officers of the House'. Altogether, in 111 days, the Commons had sat for 829 hours and rarely met for less than 10 or 11 hours a day between Easter and 4 July, the day of prorogation. Wilberforce thought the debates poor, 'though Perceval improved, and Canning extremely clever'.[4] Yet the cabinet, weakened by internal strains, was clearly losing ground in public opinion. Right at the beginning of the session Glenbervie heard rumours of changes which would have made Chatham prime minister, Lord Wellesley secretary of state for war and the colonies, and removed Castlereagh to the Lords and a minor office.

[1] The cabinet's policy in this debate was to propose a temporary bill. Windsor MSS., 15324–5, Eldon to George III, 3 May 1810.
[2] *Parl. Deb.*, XVI, 12X–10; XX, 18X–19X, 1065–77; XIX, 712–14; XXI, 691–700; Windsor MSS. (Regency file), 19184, Perceval to Prince Regent, 7 Feb. 1812; Wilberforce, *Life*, vol. IV, p. 16; R. P. Ward, *Memoirs*, vol. I, p. 444.
[3] *Parl. Deb.*, XXI, 1240; Aspinall, *Letters of George IV*, vol. I, p. 66.
[4] Colchester, vol. II, p. 158; Wilberforce, vol. III, p. 360.

'I am convinced', wrote Arthur Wellesley in July, 'that unless ministers draw better together . . . than they have done . . . they will not only be unable to hold their offices, but they will entirely ruin the King's affairs.' The greatest fault, he felt, was 'a want of concert in private and of apparent co-operation in public. They are losing the confidence of the House of Commons very fast.'[1] As early as 19 February and again on 14 March, the *Sun* had officially to deny rumours of splits in the cabinet; in June Sheridan openly mocked ministers in the Commons for their lack of co-operation; and in July Bathurst renewed his offers to resign in favour of Harrowby.[2] That autumn Thomas Grenville heard that Portland, Canning, and Castlereagh were at loggerheads with their colleagues, and that there were 'more divisions among them than ever existed in any cabinet'.[3] 'It is singular to see how changed the public sentiments about ministers are' a jubilant Brougham told Grey in December. 'Everyone of all parties (and I have met more Tories than Whigs) admits they are damaged to the greatest degree. . . .' Canning made no effort to hide his disagreements with his colleagues while Harrison of the treasury criticised ministers for 'blind-folding the country'. Such rebellious talk within the treasury was ominous. The government was in poor shape to meet the renewed reform agitation of 1809. 'I do not think', wrote Auckland as parliament began to reassemble, 'that the ministers can survive the first fortnight of the session and I have reason to believe that some of them are of that opinion.'[4] Meanwhile the cabinet had as many problems over war policy.

[1] Bickley, *Diaries of Lord Glenbervie*, vol. II, pp. 12–13; Wellington, *Civil Correspondence*, p. 447.

[2] *Sun*, 19 Feb. and 14 Mar. 1808; *Parl. Deb.*, XI, 886; Harrowby MSS., Main series, IX, fol. 83 Bathurst to Harrowby, 30 July 1808.

[3] *Dropmore MSS.*, IX, 237; Buckingham, *Court and Cabinets*, vol. IV, p. 283.

[4] Brougham, *Memoirs*, vol I, pp. 422–3; *Dropmore MSS.*, IX, 248.

CHAPTER ELEVEN

TOTAL WAR

WHEN Pitt's Friends returned to office in March 1807 the prospects of victory over Napoleon had never seemed more remote. On 26 December 1805 the unfortunate Austrians, stunned by the disaster of Auster-litz, signed the treaty of Pressburg and handed over both Italy and Germany to the French Emperor. In the following autumn the re-nowned Prussian army was crushed at Jena and Auerstadt in a single day and while the armies of the young Tsar Alexander retreated steadily eastward, his British allies were wasting their precious strength in a series of unco-ordinated raids far from the European battleground. For the Grenville ministry thought it more important to please the City merchants than to relieve the pressure on our remaining friends. On 13 September 1806, the day Fox died, news reached England that 1,600 British troops, under Sir Home Popham, had captured Buenos Aires, one of the largest commercial centres in Spanish South America. Dazzled by the prospect of new and unlimited markets for British goods, the prime minister immediately sent re-inforcements to the river Plate. Whitehall was full of grandiose plans for seizing the entire continent of South America. Grenville decided to send Sir Arthur Wellesley to take Mexico: Windham outbidding even this, sent Colonel Craufurd with 4,000 men to sail round Cape Horn, occupy Valparaiso and Chile, and then march across the Andes to join forces with the British army in Buenos Aires, a thousand miles to the east.[1] Meanwhile the navy was asked to force the passage of the Dardanelles and an army of 6,000 men to invade Egypt. By the time the Talents fell there was a British expeditionary force nearly every-where, except where there ought to have been one. Our exertions, said the *Morning Post*, 'as far as the real objects of the war are con-cerned, are totally lost'—lost in small-scale raids which Grenville him-self had once stigmatised as 'foolish, wild, and romantic'. All we had done to help our allies in Europe was to advance £80,000 to Prussia, 'a sum not equal to the yearly emoluments enjoyed by the Grenvilles

---

[1] Bryant, *The Years of Victory*, p. 207.

alone when they were in office'.[1] The new ministry, thanks mainly to Canning's intelligence and Castlereagh's energy, did what it could to remedy the situation. The cabinet still flirted with the idea of a Mexican expedition, and Castlereagh wrote a memorandum suggesting the duke of Orleans for the command, with the exiles Miranda and Dumouriez to advise him on military affairs. Miranda actually got as far as the West Indies on a fact-finding reconnaissance, where he enlisted the aid of Hislop, the martinet governor of Trinidad, and the inevitable Andrew Cochrane Johnstone. But soon after Miranda's return to England the news of Whitelocke's ignominious surrender at Buenos Aires put paid to all hope of a new British American Empire. Castlereagh sent his schemes of paper armies to Windsor, and there they stayed.[2] Meanwhile frantic efforts were made to raise a force of British and Hanoverian troops for a Baltic expedition to help the Russians. But, as usual, the effort came too late. For on 14 June 1808, two days before the first British contingent sailed from Yarmouth, the Russian army was defeated at Friedland. Ten days later Alexander, disgusted with his dilatory allies, decided to sue for peace and to leave the unfortunate British expeditionary force marooned at Stralsund. By 25 June the two Emperors had begun negotiations on a raft moored in the middle of the river Niemen: on 7 July they signed the treaty of Tilsit. Secret clauses in the treaty provided for a Russian offer of mediation between France and England. If the islanders still persisted in the war, the two Emperors were to bully Denmark, Sweden, Portugal, and Austria into a grand alliance to destroy them. Yet Alexander solemnly assured the British diplomat, Sir Robert Wilson, that there were no secret articles in the treaty prejudicial to his allies. 'He had perhaps,' he admitted, 'sacrificed the interests of his own country: but he had agreed to nothing unfavourable to Great Britain.'[3] Fortunately the British cabinet never believed him: instead they decided to seize the Danish fleet at Copenhagen, thus frustrating Napoleon's hopes of again challenging British naval supremacy.

[1] *Morning Post*, 28 Apr. 1807. 'Whilst in England', wrote Leveson-Gower from Memel that July, 'politicians are occupying themselves in squabbles in Parliament, and the people in following Sir F. Burdett's chair, the most deadly blows are aiming at the very existence of the country; for be assured that the dangers that threaten England at this moment infinitely exceed what we ever before apprehended' (*Private Correspondence*, vol. II, p. 272).

[2] Castlereagh, *Correspondence and Despatches*, vol. VII, pp. 314–24, 386, 403–5; Windsor MSS., 13625–8, Portland to George III, 21 Apr. 1808; 13688, Castlereagh to George III, 1 June 1808.

[3] Windsor MSS., 13123–6, Canning to George III, 16 Sep. 1808.

No satisfactory explanation has ever been given of the nature of the information which prompted the attack on Copenhagen. The knowledgeable earl of Malmesbury affirmed that the first warning came from the prince of Wales, who had been told of the enemy's plans by the Prince Regent of Portugal.[1] But the prince was never one to underestimate his own contribution to the British war effort. Had he really been the first to sound the alarm, he would certainly have boasted of it later. One passage in the memoirs attributed to Fouché suggests that Talleyrand, the French foreign minister, betrayed his Emperor by sending the vital information to London.[2] Claims have also been made in favour of the diplomat Sir Robert Wilson, but he was with Lords Hutchinson and Gower at Memel while the treaty of Tilsit was under discussion.[3] The fourth and most romantic possibility is that the talks between the two Emperors were overheard by Colin Mackenzie, a British soldier of fortune who had served with the Russian army in the Crimea. There was for long a family tradition that Mackenzie bribed the Tsar's personal attendant to let him take his place on the raft on the Niemen. Mackenzie, who spoke fluent Russian and was sufficiently ugly to be mistaken for a Cossack, learnt of Napoleon's plans and succeeded in escaping with the secret to England.[4] Canning himself never gave the least hint which, if any, of these stories was true and recent searches among foreign office records have produced nothing decisive. It is certain that intelligent guesses about the enemy's intentions reached Canning from British diplomats at Memel, Copenhagen, and Ancona. Early in June Leveson-Gower reported menacing French troop concentrations near the Danish frontier; Garlike and the earl of Pembroke warned the foreign secretary that the Danish court was hostile and its fleet prepared for sea; further information was certainly received from British merchants then in Denmark. There was also a strong pro-British party in Russia which disapproved of the negotiations with Napoleon. On 25 June Bennigsen, the Russian commander-in-chief, told Mackenzie that the Tsar was about to sign an alliance with the French. Mackenzie reached Gower at Memel with this news on the twenty-sixth and the ambassador wrote to London the same day. This despatch reached London on 16 July.[5]

[1] Malmesbury, *Diary*, vol. I, pp. 391 and 400.
[2] Duff Cooper, *Talleyrand*, p. 161.
[3] G. Costigan, *Sir Robert Wilson*, Univ. of Wisconsin Studies no 16, p. 39.
[4] Farington, vol. VI, p. 236.
[5] *Cambridge History of British Foreign Policy*, vol. I, p. 361; Windsor MSS., 13016–7, Canning to George III, 15 July 1807.

On the following day Castlereagh first broached the proposed Copenhagen expedition with the king while Canning sent his under-secretary, Fitzharris, to fetch the diplomat Francis Jackson from Northamptonshire. Fitzharris reached Lord Spencer's country seat at one o'clock on the morning of 18 July, dragged Jackson straight out of bed and got him back to Downing Street by eleven the same morning.[1] When the pair reached Canning's house they found the cabinet already in session there, debating the king's reply to Castlereagh's message of the seventeenth. For George III, although admitting that preparations for the expedition must be made, begged his ministers to consider 'the necessity of proceeding with temper and caution' so as not to drive Denmark into the arms of France or to cement the new Franco-Russian alliance.[2] Yet later that morning Canning instructed Jackson to be prepared to leave for Copenhagen within a few days, while Mulgrave ordered a fleet of sixty-four vessels to be made ready for action under Admiral Gambier's command.[3] By 18 July ministers had clearly decided that preventive action was imperative: but George III had not. When the cabinet met again on the following day it was suggested to Portland that the king had failed to give his 'unqualified approbation' to the plan. The prime minister immediately asked for an audience in order to explain the government's decision.[4] This took place on the twentieth. The following day Mackenzie reached London with Leveson-Gower's latest despatches and on 2 August Jackson embarked at Yarmouth, six days before the terms of even the innocuous public articles of the treaty of Tilsit were received at Downing Street.

How much could Canning at that time have known of the secret clauses? Holland Rose believed that he knew nothing of them and relied on Leveson-Gower, Garlike, and speculation.[5] But this theory, although it explains Rose's own failure to find any written proof of the existence of secret information, is certainly inadequate on several counts. Perhaps Canning himself was temperamentally capable of gambling on such inconclusive evidence. But the foreign secretary could never have acted unless both his cabinet colleagues and the king were convinced beyond all reasonable doubt that the situation required desperate remedies. As late as 19 July George III hesitated to

[1] Windsor MSS., 13022, Castlereagh to George III, 17 July 1807; Sir George Jackson, *Diaries*, vol. II, pp. 187–8.
[2] Windsor MSS., 13024, George III to Castlereagh, 18 July 1807.
[3] Jackson, *loc. cit.*; *Cambridge History of British Foreign Policy*, vol. I, p. 362.
[4] Windsor MSS., 13026–7, Portland to George III, 19 July 1807.
[5] *Eng. Hist. Rev.*, Jan. 1896. J. H. Rose, *Canning and Denmark 1807*.

give his full consent and insisted that if any demands were made against Denmark they must be justified 'only out of the conduct of the enemy'. Consequently Perceval, an inveterate scribbler, drew up a memorandum presumably designed to overcome the king's doubts. Great Britain, argued Perceval, had every right to send a fleet to the Baltic in order to protect her trade and to safeguard the British troops trapped at Stralsund. 'But for the justification of a hostile armament against Denmark we must look for other reasons. I trust however that the world will feel that we have them.' France had already violated the rights of neutrals in Italy, Switzerland, Hesse, and Hamburg; in the preamble to the Berlin Decrees Napoleon had made it clear that he would be bound by no form of international law which hindered the French war effort. Portugal had so far escaped attack because the enemy knew that Britain would retaliate by trying to seize Brazil, an invaluable market for her trade. Similarly it had been in Napoleon's own interests to respect Danish neutrality as long as France had to face Russia, Prussia, and Sweden in north-east Europe. That coalition had now collapsed and the Danish fleet lay at his mercy. 'The intelligence', continued Perceval, 'from so many and such various sources of B[ounaparte]'s intention to force or to seduce D[enmark] into an active confederacy against this country, leaves no doubt of his design. Nay, the fact that he has openly avowed such intention in an interview with the E[mperor] of R[ussia] is brought to this country in such a way as it cannot be doubted. Under such circumstances it would be madness, it would be idiotic . . . to wait for an overt act.' [1] This memorandum proves beyond doubt that the cabinet did receive secret information other than the usual diplomatic and mercantile reports. But three important questions remain unanswered: how detailed was this secret information? when did it reach London? and who sent it? During the later parliamentary debates on the Copenhagen expedition both Perceval and Mulgrave denied that the government had ever pretended to possess written copies of the secret clauses of the treaty of Tilsit.[2] Had they received a copy of the text they could have disarmed their critics by publishing the information, without specifying who sent it.[3] All ministers ever claimed was knowledge of the substance of 'secret projects and agreements' designed 'to employ the navies of Denmark and Portugal against this country'.[4] The wording of Per-

---

[1] Perceval MSS.   [2] *Parl. Deb.*, X, 71–2 (Perceval's speech) and 31 (Mulgrave).
[3] This was suggested by Lauderdale in the Lords (*Parl. Deb.*, X, 30).
[4] *Parl. Deb.*, X, 28 (Hawkesbury's speech). For the details of the Franco-

ceval's memorandum makes it clear that what finally persuaded the cabinet to act was some sort of verbatim report of conversations between the two Emperors, which may have reached England by word-of-mouth. The conduct of both the cabinet and the king makes it inconceivable that it could have been received before 18 July. Unfortunately the Perceval memorandum is undated but internal evidence suggests that it was written on or before the twenty-second.[1] Colin Mackenzie may have brought the secret information with him when he arrived on 21 July. But this does little to confirm the story of his adventures on the raft. For after his stay at Tilsit Mackenzie had joined Hutchinson and Leveson-Gower at Memel. If he then knew of secret conversations between Napoleon and Alexander he would surely have told this to the two British diplomats. Yet Hutchinson later denied in the house of lords that he had received any evidence sufficient to justify the attack on Denmark.[2] In any case would Mackenzie's unsupported account of the proceedings at Tilsit have been accepted as beyond doubt? Or would ministers have so consistently refused (contrary to their own interests) to give parliament full details of their evidence for fear of endangering 'the lives of individuals friendly to this country' if that information had come from a British subject who was then safely back in London? All the available evidence seems to suggest that some high-ranking Russian or Frenchman (who was himself present at the meetings between the two Emperors) found the means to communicate directly with the British cabinet, probably between 18 and 22 July. Beyond this there is nothing to support further speculation and little hope that important new evidence will ever come to light.

Once the British government had made up its mind it acted with

---

Russian secret treaty of alliance of 7 July see Vandal, *Napoleon et Alexandre*, vol. I, pp. 505–7.

[1] Perceval's memorandum ends with a discussion of the demands which could legitimately be made against Denmark. But this issue was settled in Canning's letter to Brooke Taylor on 22 July (*Cam. Hist. of British Foreign Policy*, vol. I, p. 362). Canning's letter to Brooke Taylor began, 'Intelligence reached me yesterday directly from Tilsit, that at an interview which took place between the Emperor of Russia and Bonaparte, on the 24th or 25th of last month, the latter brought forward a proposal for a Maritime League against Great Britain, to which the accession of Denmark was represented by Bonaparte to be as certain as it was essential.' The Tsar, commented Canning, met this proposal with silence, probably because of 'the presence of persons before whom he was not likely to speak with perfect openness' (P.R.O., F.O. 22/53).

[2] *Parl. Deb.*, X, 354.

unusual speed. Jackson arrived at Kiel on 6 August and had his first interview with the Prince Royal of Denmark on the ninth. The Danes were offered a British alliance and an annual subsidy of £100,000 in return for the surrender of their fleet for the duration of the war. Unfortunately Jackson made the worst of a poor brief: the Danes refused to make any concessions and, after a series of stormy interviews, negotiations broke down on 15 August.[1] On the following day a British army under Cathcart began to disembark ten miles north of Copenhagen. But Cathcart (better at making bows at Court than leading armies in the field) made slow progress even against one of the worst armies in Europe, commanded by a seventy-year-old Hanoverian. On 2 September, Admiral Gambier began naval bombardment of the Danish capital: on 6 September Copenhagen surrendered.[2] Only then was it found that, in spite of Pembroke's warnings, the Danish fleet was quite unfit to put to sea. It took Gambier until the end of October before he was able to tow the captured warships back to England and then he so mismanaged his withdrawal that the irate Danes were able to seize great quantities of property belonging to British merchants. The treasury was overwhelmed with claims for compensation (all of which were refused) and Canning wanted to disown Gambier, but was over-ruled by the rest of the cabinet.[3] Ministers had also hoped for a permanent occupation of the island of Zealand, but gave up the idea when told that it would take an army of at least 30,000 men and a naval squadron to defend it. Yet in spite of these disappointments the government was satisfied with its own performance. 'I do not believe', wrote Perceval to his brother, 'there ever was an expedition executed more completely in respect of the temper and moderation of the commanders . . . or more to the approbation of their employers.'[4] The majority of independent observers agreed. *The Times* was warm in praise of all concerned, while Cobbett denounced the idea that Denmark could have maintained her neutrality as 'vile

---

[1] Jackson, vol. II, p. 196.

[2] Mulgrave reported the success of the expedition to the king on 16 Sep. (Windsor MSS., 13122).

[3] P.R.O., T29/101/209; Perceval MSS., Canning to Perceval, 17 Sep. 1808— 'I stood nearly alone last winter in my opinion that Lord G[ambie]r ought to have been severely censured for his scandalous mismanagement of the Baltic Fleet, after the affair of Copenhagen. It was thought better to hush the matter up. . . .' Gambier was, in July 1809, court martialled for failing to engage the enemy while commanding the channel fleet. (*Day*, 26 July 1808 and Windsor MSS., 14443–6, Portland to George III, 28 May 1809.)

[4] Perceval MSS., Perceval to Arden, 18 Sep. 1807.

mockery', 'hypocrisy', and 'mere party cavilling'.[1] As soon as parliament reassembled both Windham and Sheridan denounced the expedition, but the opposition thought it prudent not to divide the House. Had they done so, jibed Cobbett, they would have been beaten by a majority of four to one.[2] Instead the whigs concentrated on motions for the production of papers, hoping to embarrass ministers who could not divulge the source of their secret information. Ponsonby moved the first motion on 3 February and was supported by the Sidmouth group, who sensed lingering doubts at Windsor. But the Carlton House members voted with the government and the motion was lost by 253 to 108. Five days later Whitbread polled 73 votes in a division of 230; a third attempt, led by Sheridan, was defeated by 184 to 85; and only 19 bold spirits opposed the vote of thanks to Gambier.[3] By the time the whigs got round to moving a formal vote of censure even the *Edinburgh Review* had to admit that the public had lost interest in the issue. Richard Sharp, one of the members for Castle Rising, spoke brilliantly in proposing the motion, but was answered by a 'very odd, blundering, bold, and witty speech from an Irish gentleman of the name of Croker'. When the House divided the attempted censure was overwhelmed by 224 to 64 and an amendment praising the expedition carried by a majority of 155.[4] In the end even Wilberforce confessed that 'after much (I trust impartial) reflection, I am convinced that under all the circumstances of the case, the Danish expedition was just'.[5]

The military stalemate had already led to a further widening of the struggle. For on 21 November 1806 Napoleon had issued the Berlin Decrees, by which the British Isles were declared to be in a state of complete if fictitious blockade. In fact all the land-locked Emperor could do was to blockade his own subjects by prohibiting the admission of British goods into any port controlled by France, and to

[1] *The Times*, 22 Sep. 1807; *Political Register*, 22 Aug. 1807, p. 28 and 19 Sep. 1807, p. 425.

[2] *Parl. Deb.*, X, 70-1 and 72-82; *Political Register*, 30 Jan. 1808, p. 167. 'I cannot help feeling', wrote Thomas to Lord Grenville, 'that in their situation we should very probably have given the same order without being able to publish to Parliament the grounds on which we had believed in the hostile mind of Denmark' (*Dropmore MSS.*, IX, 145).

[3] *Parl. Deb.*, X, 178, 388, and 744; *Sun*, 5 Feb. 1808; Colchester, vol. II, p. 138.

[4] *Parl. Deb.*, X, 1187-1231; Colchester, vol. II, p. 147; *Edinburgh Review*, Jan. 1809, p. 489; Bickley, *Glenbervie Diaries*, vol. II, p. 17. For the Lords debates on Copenhagen see *Parl. Deb.*, X, 6-36, 156-62, 348-79, and 646-58.

[5] Wilberforce, *Life*, vol. III, p. 345; Yonge, vol. I, p. 252.

bully the weaker neutrals by threatening to seize all ships found trading with Great Britain.[1] As a piece of sabre-rattling it was remarkably
effective. The American minister in Paris was assured that his country's
trade would not be ruined and, thanks to British naval superiority, the
promise was honoured.[2] But British merchants were so alarmed that
even the Grenville ministry had been forced to act. Howick, the
foreign secretary, told an approving Commons that Britain reserved
the right to take full reprisals and the same threat was repeated in the
preamble to the Order-in-Council of 7 January 1807. This decree prohibited all seaborne trade between one port and another, 'both which
ports shall belong to or be in the possession of France or her allies,
or shall be so far under their control as that British vessels may not
freely trade thereat'.[3] Braggadocio was answered by humbug. Although the British navy was asked to intercept all coastal shipping,
nothing was done to check direct colonial trade with France. A neutral
merchantman might sail unharmed from the West Indies or New York
to Amsterdam, but was liable to capture if it then tried to leave for
Rouen. It was a useless and senseless compromise which did more to
irritate neutrals than to embarrass the French. Twice Perceval tried to
raise the question in the Commons by moving for the production of
the Order-in-Council. Yet each time the treasury bench opposed the
motion, thus refusing to lay before the House a document which had
previously been printed in the *London Gazette*.[4]

Once in office Perceval pressed home the case for revision. 'The
more I have had time to reflect on our future prospects in this war,'
wrote Castlereagh on 1 October 1807, 'the more impressed I am with
the conviction that neither peace nor independence can be the lot of
this nation, till we have found the means of making France feel that
her new anti-social and anti-commercial system will not avail her
against a power that can for its own preservation, and consequently
legitimately, counteract at sea what she lawlessly inflicts and enforces
on shore.' On 5 October the cabinet began, after a series of preliminary discussions, to consider possible methods of more effective
retaliation.[5] A week later Perceval circularised a long memorandum

---

[1] *Cam. Hist. of British Foreign Policy*, vol. I, p. 356.
[2] *Parl. Deb.*, X, 556.
[3] *London Gazette*, 6–10 Jan. 1807.
[4] *Parl. Deb.*, VIII, 451, 620–33, and 655.
[5] Perceval MSS., 'Draft of a confidential paper', dated 5 Oct. 1807. The
memorandum is unsigned and the handwriting unidentified. Internal evidence
proves that its author was not a member of the cabinet.

on the ethics and expediency of adopting new commercial regulations.
Most of the arguments used can be found in the pamphlet *War in
Disguise*, written by his friend James Stephen in 1805.[1] The early
friendship between the pair had been based on common interests in
evangelicalism, the abolition of the slave trade, and the law; after
August 1807 they were in regular correspondence on political questions. Soon after he entered the cabinet Perceval offered to find Stephen
a seat in parliament. The offer was repeated in January 1808 and, on
Wilberforce's advice, accepted. Stephen, wrote Wilberforce, 'agrees
with Perceval *passim*, and with the Government as to their grand
scheme of policy—Orders-in-Council; indeed it is his measure'.[2] But
although Stephen obviously inspired the general ideas behind the
cabinet's policy, there is absolutely no evidence that he played any
part in framing the revised Orders-in-Council. That was done largely
by the chancellor of the exchequer. His colleagues, thanks to persistent 'lobbying' by shipping interests, were unanimous in accepting
the principle of full retaliation. But no one really wanted to apply it.
Portland, mindful of 'the unpopularity which it cannot be denied we
are held in throughout the Continent', advised restricting our counter-
blockade to France itself.[3] Canning 'would rather confine the measures
to a part of the countries in the occupation of the enemy (a large part
to be sure—France and Holland for instance) and apply it in all its
vigour to that part, than extend it to the whole, and relax it generally
by complicated exceptions and regulations'.[4] Against these two were
the supporters of a strong line—Hawkesbury, Castlereagh, and, with
some reservations, Westmorland. Hawkesbury argued that Perceval's
original proposals 'would have no other effect than to raise the price of
colonial produce in France to a small degree'. He therefore suggested
a complete ban on all neutral trade with France, Holland, and Spain,
designed 'to destroy at once all the remaining commerce of France,
which by means of neutrals is not inconsiderable, and to strike a most
important blow against her agriculture by preventing the exportation
of her wines. . . .'[5] Westmorland, although terrified of the economic

[1] *Ibid.*, Memorandum by Perceval, 12 Oct. 1807. For a resumé see Walpole,
vol. I, pp. 264–8. Castlereagh, *Correspondence and Despatches*, vol. VIII, pp.
87–8.

[2] Wilberforce, *Life*, vol. III, p. 358. Stephen was returned for the Irish
borough of Tralee in 1808. For Stephen's early life see M. E. Bevington, *The
Memoirs of James Stephen*.

[3] Perceval MSS., Memorandum by Portland (undated).

[4] *Ibid.*, Memorandum by Canning (undated).

[5] *Ibid.*, Memorandum by Hawkesbury (undated).

consequences of war with the United States, was in favour of extending our blockade to all countries involved in Napoleon's continental system.[1] But the most vehement member of the cabinet was Castlereagh. The war, he wrote, 'is no longer a struggle for territory or for point of honor, but whether the existence of G[rea]t Britain as a naval power is compatable with that of France'. It was time we took decisive measures in defence of our commerce, for either we destroyed the continental system or faced defeat. 'The sooner the true issue is joined the better. It will render the answer to every proposition either of mediation or negotiation very simple, namely that no terms can be listen'd to which do not terminate the social and commercial warfare between the two states, as well as the contest in arms. The nation is alive to the truth of this principle. They will stand by the Government in maintaining it. We shall escape the embarrassment of a peace party and favourable terms in the ordinary sense. The contest may be a long one, but if we succeed in successfully sustaining it, we may hope for a real instead of a nominal peace.'[2]

After this initial exchange of views Perceval and Bathurst, the president of the board of trade, began to draw up the new Order-in-Council. Perceval wrote the first draft, but Bathurst amended it and rewrote the preamble. The draft order was then referred back to the cabinet, where Eldon denounced the preamble as 'too argumentative' and Westmorland in a long incoherent memorandum appeared to denounce everything, including his own previous views.[3] At the last minute Bathurst also changed his mind. 'Our ability to continue the war,' he argued, 'depends on our commerce; for if our resources fail from a diminuation of our commerce, additional imposts will only add to the evil. The enemy forms one great military empire. The extent of country he covers does not render him so dependent on an export and import trade. The whole of that trade might perish and he could still continue the war. If one-third of our's were to fail, we should be soon reduced to a peace.' For Bathurst realised that any large-scale blockade would offend the United States and Russia. The Americans would probably resist it, 'and an American war would be severely felt by our manufacturers, and even by the very class of merchants now so eager for some measure of relief'.[4] But it was too late to check the forward

[1] Perceval MSS., Memorandum by Westmorland (undated).

[2] *Ibid.*, Memorandum by Castlereagh (undated).

[3] *Ibid.*, Drafts of Order-in-Council of 11 Nov. 1807; Memoranda by Eldon and Westmorland (undated).

[4] *Ibid.*, Memorandum by Bathurst (undated).

party in the cabinet. On 26 October Castlereagh wrote to Portland urging that the new policy should be published within a fortnight and the Order-in-Council appeared on 11 and 25 November. All harbours from which British ships were excluded were declared to be under blockade. Neutrals were still permitted to trade with enemy colonies, to sail from them to certain free ports in the British empire, and to carry British produce to Europe. But most foreign cargoes had first to be landed at a British harbour, where a duty was levied on the re-shipment of freight. Concessions, which Stephen regretted, were made in favour of Russian and Portuguese trade, but these did little to offset the general stringency of the policy. The impression must not be created, Stephen urged Perceval, that the system of Orders-in-Council was simply a measure of retaliation. 'If retaliation were not necessary to prevent our own ruin, if it were merely a matter of *revenge* our defence would be as difficult as it appears to me to be easy, simple, and decisive.' [1] Either France should trade through Britain or she should have no trade at all. 'This', wrote Perceval to the Speaker, 'is a formid-able and tremendous state of the world; but all the part of it which is particularly harrassing to English interests was existing through the new severity with which Buonaparte's decrees of exclusion against our trade were called into action. Our proceeding does not aggravate our distress from it.' [2]

He was soon proved wrong. Before the year was out Napoleon, 'very angry and very sore', had struck back in the Milan Decrees, de-nationalising and making liable to capture any neutral vessel which submitted to a British search or landed at a British port. Europe had its first experience of total war and international trade was virtually at a standstill. That winter Lloyds ceased to quote insurance rates for voyages between Britain and the Continent, while the rate for American ships trading with Britain rose from $2\frac{1}{2}\%$ to $3\frac{3}{4}\%$.[3] Anglo-American relations steadily deteriorated and the strain on British industry in-creased. On 18 April 1806 the United States Congress had passed a Non-Importation Act prohibiting all trade with Britain in a variety of goods, ranging from leather, tin, brass and cloth products to 'nails, pikes, hats, millinery, pictures and prints'. The Act was enforced that November, but speedily withdrawn in the face of protests from

[1] *Ibid.*, Castlereagh to Portland, 26 Oct. 1807 and James Stephen to Perceval, 25 Nov. 1807. For the text of the Order-in-Council see *Parl. Deb.*, X, 126–48.
[2] Colchester, vol. II, pp. 134–5.
[3] *Ibid.*, p. 136; Bryant, *Years of Victory*, p. 220.

American merchants who suffered from the rupture of trade. The Talents did try to reach a sensible agreement with the United States over British maritime rights, only to be frustrated by the jingoism of Pitt's Friends in opposition, and relations were further strained by the shortcomings of successive British diplomats in Washington. Merry ended all social intercourse with Madison, the American president, because he failed to escort Mrs. Merry from table after an official dinner; Erskine, inexperienced and indiscreet, was recalled after exceeding his instructions, and Francis Jackson was as haughty with the Americans as he had been with the Danes. 'I came', he reported from Washington, 'prepared to treat with a regular government, and have had to deal with a mob and mob leaders.' [1] There were, as a legacy of the war of American Independence, strong bodies of opinion in both Britain and the United States hostile to any form of conciliation. In Britain this feeling cut across the usual party divisions. The antediluvian earl of Galloway implored the Portland ministry not to concede 'one point more to that illiberal and prejudiced people'; Sidmouth spoke of the United States in 1808 as 'a country in which there is little authority in the rulers, and as little public spirit and virtue in the people'; even Cobbett preferred war to concessions. [2]

The Orders were, however, strongly opposed in the Commons. On 5 February 1808 Petty challenged their legality and argued that the cabinet should have first waited to see whether the French decrees were enforced against America. But Perceval contended that the

---

[1] *Bath Archives*, vol. I, p. 45; *Political Register*, 23 Jan. 1808, pp. 158–9.

[2] *Parl. Deb.*, X, 6–11; Colchester, vol. II, p. 132; *Political Register*, 16 Jan. 1808, pp. 77–82. Cobbett's views on the commercial effects of a breach with the United States are worth quoting. 'If', he wrote, 'England were cut off from all communication with foreign nations, she would, in point of strength and of happiness, suffer nothing at all' (*Political Register*, 15 July 1809, p. 35). By far the wisest words on Anglo-American relations appeared, surprisingly, in the *Quarterly Review*—'Let but the American Government abstain from war and direct its main attention to the education of the people and the encouragement of arts and knowledge, and in a very few generations their country may vie with Europe. Above all let not that anti-Anglican spirit be cherished, for which there no longer exists a cause. With whatever indignation they may think of the past, they ought to remember that it was from England they embibed those principles for which they fought and by which they triumphed. There is a sacred bond between us of blood and of language, which no circumstances can break. Our literature must always continue to be theirs, and though their laws are no longer the same as ours, we have the same Bible, and we address our common Father in the same prayer. Nations are too ready to admit that they have natural enemies; why should they be less willing to believe that they have natural friends?' (*Quarterly Review*, Nov. 1809, p. 337).

Orders had been drawn up with the aim of doing as little injury to American trade as possible. 'He was', he added, 'far from entertaining the mistaken idea that we might redeem our own losses by the sufferings of America. Loss to America was loss to Great Britain.'[1] The opposition, however, divided against the second reading, polling 94 votes against the ministry's 214.[2] A week later Tierney moved for the appointment of a special committee on trade and navigation to examine the effect of the Orders, but was defeated by 118 votes to 55.[3] Even then whig ingenuity was not exhausted. On 3 March Gascoyne, against the Speaker's advice, tried to introduce a petition from Liverpool against the Orders. He was supported by the Barings and Tarleton, his fellow member for Liverpool, as well as by the opposition front bench, but failed by 128 votes to 80. The following day Tierney tried to reintroduce a slightly amended version and lost by 111 votes to 57.[4] The final struggle took place on 10 March. Alderman Combe, one of the members for the City, opened the debate by trying to present a petition against the Orders-in-Council from the merchants and manufacturers of London. The discussion then degenerated into a squabble between London M.P.s as to what happened at the meeting convened to consider the petition. Sir William Curtis and Alderman Shaw both contradicted Combe's account, claiming that the majority had voted against the petition. This was confirmed by Alexander Baring, who had chaired the meeting. Sir Charles Price then produced a petition in exactly opposite terms signed by London merchants trading with the Continent who approved of the Orders. In the end, after an acrimonious discussion, both petitions were left to lie on the table.[5] Immediately the indefatigible Gascoyne presented another Liverpool petition, forced a further debate, and gained 66 votes in a division against Perceval's 99.[6] Although it was then late at night, the government insisted on pressing on to the third reading of the Orders-in-Council Bill. An amendment was moved to defer this till 'Monday s'ennight' and lost by a majority of 63. At three in the morning Petty and Windham moved the adjournment because of the hour and the number of members still wanting to speak. This was lost by 145 to 71, but in the division lobby Ponsonby had urged his supporters to stay in the House and move repeated adjournments while Sheridan reminded them that he had done this seventeen times on the suspension

---

[1] *Parl. Deb.*, X, 328–30; Wilberforce, vol. III, p. 360.
[2] *Parl. Deb.*, X, 666–76. [3] *Ibid.*, X, 715.
[4] *Ibid.*, X, 895 and 898. [5] *Ibid.*, X, 1058–62. [6] *Ibid.*, X, 1064.

of habeas corpus. Finally at five-thirty in the morning, after two more divisions, Perceval gave way and agreed to adjourn. Later that day, when the House re-assembled, the bill was at last approved by 168 to 68.[1] In the Lords the opposition put up an even longer fight, defeating the government once in a thin House on a motion for the production of papers and even digging out a standing order of 1702 to add to the delay.[2] Britain and France, argued Auckland, seemed intent on 'mutual destruction. Such conduct could only be compared to the insanity of two maniacs ... cutting each other with knives across the veins.' The Orders, predicted the *Edinburgh Review*, would reduce British trade with the United States from £12 million to £4 million a year, thus eliminating at one blow two-thirds of our remaining foreign trade. Such articles, grumbled Stephen, were sheer distortion and showed that the opposition 'like their teacher Bounaparte' knew the value of 'incessant false assertion'.[3]

The first to suffer were the northern cotton operatives. In February 1807 their petition for a Minimum Wages Bill, presented by Colonel Stanley, one of the members for Preston, was referred to a select committee. Before this had time to report parliament was dissolved and the summer taken up with the general election. By the autumn Lancashire was in the middle of a slump as manufacturers began a wholesale attack on wages. In a single month the Bolton operatives reported reductions of between $7\frac{1}{2}\%$ and 15% while, in other areas, wage rates were almost halved. 'Your Honour knows', wrote the Bolton leaders to Rose, 'there is a point beyond which overburthened nature cannot go. . . . Idleness is not the characteristic of Lancashire people—it is quite common to find persons in their damp cellars at their loom during winter before day and until midnight. The haggard looks and skeleton frames of many show their privation and excessive toil; but when all this will not do what must be the consequences?' That winter incendiary notices began to appear on employers' houses, threatening their lives and property.[4] The shortage of both magistrates and troops in the area only aggravated the position. Rose, while urging the men's

---

[1] *Parl. Deb.*, X, 1068 and 1076. Brougham prolonged the issue still further by acting as counsel and presenting evidence to support the petitions against the Orders. Stephen took charge of the government case. *Parl. Deb.*, X, 1182, 1305 and 1315.

[2] *Ibid.*, X, 465–85, 641, 929–71, 1154 and 1255.

[3] *Ibid.*, X, 1501; *Edinburgh Review*, Apr. 1808, pp. 240–1; Perceval MSS., Stephen to Perceval, 23 May 1808.

[4] P.R.O., T1/1015/8277, James Draper and James Nisbet to Rose, 21 Oct. 1807.

leaders to preach moderation, pressed their claims on the treasury. He got little sympathy from Huskisson who thought the minimum wage agitation one 'which ought to be discouraged and which can lead to no good'. Perceval himself shared the laissez faire attitude and explained to his old tutor 'that all things should be permitted to find their own level; the price of labour should be left to be settled between the labourer and the master. . . .' [1] He did, however, receive a delegation of nineteen employers who professed to support the workers' case and suggested to them that they should meet the operatives' leaders at Manchester and pledge themselves to pay an agreed basic wage. Perceval then promised that if the liberal employers found themselves undercut by less scrupulous rivals, the cabinet would sponsor minimum wage legislation.[2] The proposal seemed fair and sensible, but was rejected by the delegation whose spokesman, Thomas Ainsworth, fell back on prophecies of impending calamity. Rose, therefore, decided to test the sense of the Commons. On 19 May 1808 he gave notice of his intention to introduce a Minimum Wage Bill, not, he naïvely confessed, because he believed in it in theory, but in answer to the pleas 'of a numerous and respectable class of persons who were now suffering peculiar hardships . . . .' The House was unmoved. Davies Giddy, Horner, Lord Milton, Tierney, and even the elder Sir Robert Peel, who had been a member of the employers' delegation to Perceval, all denounced the idea. In the end Rose meekly withdrew his motion amidst general applause, leaving Perceval to point the moral to the starving operatives. He was, he said, glad parliament had debated the motion and hoped the cotton weavers would realise that their case 'failed not from any indifference to their sufferings, or any indisposition to relieve them' but from a conviction that legislation 'could do no good and might do much harm'.[3]

The speech did more good at Westminster than in Lancashire. Disturbances began as soon as news of Rose's failure reached the north. Late in May troops had to be called out in Manchester and on the last day of that month the *Sun* reported that troops 'were busily employed in scouring the country . . . dispersing the several bodies of weavers who had assembled at Blackley, White Moss, Middleton, and Kersell Moor'.[4] A week later soldiers were still 'pouring into

[1] T1/1015/8035; Perceval, *Letter to the Rev. Dr. Mansel*, p. 24. For the shortage of troops and magistrates see J. L. and Barbara Hammond, *The Town Labourer*, pp. 81-94.

[2] Barbara and J. L. Hammond, *The Skilled Labourer*, p. 425.

[3] *Parl. Deb.*, XI, 425-8.   [4] *Sun*, 31 May 1808.

Manchester from all quarters', although even the local authorities sympathised with the rioters' claims. Farington, a Manchester magistrate, assured the home office that there was nothing of 'a disloyal or seditious nature' in the outbreaks, while one of his colleagues, Henry Norris, wrote privately to Perceval in support of the workmen's claims.[1] Average daily earnings, reported Colonel Fletcher from Bolton, had fallen from 2s. 4½d. in 1805 to 10½d. and the price of basic foods had lately risen. Early in June Perceval's original idea was finally accepted when 300 Manchester employers agreed on an immediate 20% wage increase and promised further advances in August. Disturbances continued at Stockport and Blackburn: at Rochdale rioters burnt down the town's new gaol while at Wigan the mayor swore in 200 special constables and called out the Volunteers as the mob smashed shuttles and roamed the streets crying, 'Give us bread, we are starving!' [2] In June the operatives, deprived by the Combination Acts of organisation and money, slowly drifted back to work. 'In Manchester', reported the government press, 'all is tranquil', but it was the peace of exhaustion not contentment.[3] The riots had done little to improve the operatives' conditions, but they had shaken Perceval's faith in the Orders-in-Council as originally drafted.

Accordingly in March 1808 the chancellor of the exchequer circulated a memorandum to his cabinet colleagues suggesting revisions in the system of Orders-in-Council, designed to induce the American Congress to relax the Embargo Act. Public opinion in the United States, he thought, only accepted the embargo because it feared the sudden capture of American ships should war break out with Great Britain. Perceval therefore suggested, and drafted, an Order pledging the British government not to seize any neutral vessel found on the high seas or in a British controlled harbour if war should be declared between Great Britain and the country of origin of the ship concerned.[4] The proposal had a rough passage in cabinet. It was plain, wrote Canning, that, however comprehensive the new Order might be made in words, in fact it would apply only to the United States. The American Embargo Act was doing more damage to its authors than to Britain, and Canning had 'no apprehension whatsoever of a war with the United States'. President Jefferson had just proposed to the

[1] Aspinall, *Early English Trade Unions*, pp. 96–7, and 102.
[2] *Sun*, 3 and 8 June 1808; Aspinall, *op. cit.*, pp. 95 and 103.
[3] *Sun*, 11 June 1808.
[4] Perceval MSS. Memorandum and draft Order-in-Council by Perceval, 26 Mar. 1808.

Senate the appointment of William Pinckney as resident minister plenipotentiary in London and Pinckney himself had told Canning that he expected instructions to open fresh negotiations with the British government. The foreign secretary therefore opposed Perceval's attempt at concessions both because they would be better made as a bargaining point in the expected negotiations and because they marked 'a public and unprovoked condemnation and retraction of the principles upon which this country had acted at the breaking out of all her wars with other countries'. 'Above all things,' ended Canning, 'I feel that *to do nothing now*—at this precise moment—*absolutely nothing* is the wisest, safest, and most manful policy. The battle about the Orders-in-Council is just fought. They are established as a system. We have reason to hope that they are working much to the good, and very little to mischief. Every day may be expected to bring additional proofs of this.' [1] When Perceval still refused to withdraw his memorandum Castlereagh added his own to Canning's criticisms. The Embargo Act was, he thought, operating more powerfully in our favour than any hostile measures which we ourselves could adopt should war break out with the United States. We should not, therefore, give the American government any pretext to withdraw the Act, but 'leave them to the full measure of their own difficulties to lower and degrade them in the estimation of the American people'. This view was later echoed by Westmorland and accepted by both Mulgrave and Bathurst.[2] In the face of such united opposition Perceval was forced to drop an idea which might have helped to check the deterioration of Anglo-American relations.

Fortunately the war had already taken a more favourable turn. The cold hard winter of 1807 was followed by a glorious spring and summer. Between the end of April and the beginning of October there was scarcely one cold day: the farmers grumbled, as usual, but the majority had no complaints.[3] And with the spring came, at last, good news. In February Napoleon ordered full military occupation of the Spanish Peninsula, Godoy fell from power, and Charles IV abdicated in favour of his son, Ferdinand. Then over-confidence spoilt the French game. Napoleon summoned both Charles and Ferdinand to Bayonne and, by a mixture of threats and bribes, compelled both to surrender their

[1] *Ibid.*, Memorandum by Canning, 28 Mar. 1808.
[2] *Ibid.*, Memoranda by Castlereagh (undated), Bathurst (26 Mar. 1808), and Mulgrave (undated); Westmorland to Perceval, 1 Apr. 1808.
[3] Smart, *Annals*, vol. I, p. 182.

right to the Spanish throne. In their place the Spaniards were to have Joseph Bonaparte. But the Spaniards refused to acquiesce. Late in May there were risings in Badajoz, Cartagena, Valencia and, most important, in Asturias, where a meeting of the local squirearchy and priesthood declared war on France and ordered the raising of an army. On 30 May six Asturian delegates left for England with a formal appeal for help, arriving at Falmouth on 6 June. In the Commons Sheridan moved a motion urging full British support and Canning, straight from a dinner in honour of the delegation, pledged 'every practicable aid in a contest so magnanimous'.[1] Never was a delegation more certain of success, for the cause of the Spanish patriots had united all England in a surge of enthusiasm and hope. In that flaming June all party differences were forgotten as the nation fêted and lionised the Asturian emissaries. Perceval gave a special dinner in Downing Street, invited Lady Arden, the family radical, and allowed Jane to cut short her latest confinement in order to join the party. The prince of Wales was 'most ardent in the cause' while poor Sheridan, determined to 'electrify' the country, insisted on making a set speech in the House although 'manifestly and disgracefully besotted'.[2] 'I have', confessed Francis Horner, 'been dreaming wild. . . . I cannot but rejoice that a people, who bear such a name as the Spaniards, should make a struggle, at least, for their independence; the example cannot but be beneficial, even if they should entirely fail, to their posterity at some future day, and to all the rest of mankind.' 'I suppose', wrote Wilberforce to Hannah Moore, 'it is with difficulty you restrain sister Patty from going as a volunteer, while you are rubbing up your Spanish that you may assist in diffusing patriotic sentiments through the whole Peninsula.' Only the pusillanimous Westmorland struck a discordant note. 'The Spaniards', he told Lord Holland, 'had got into a d———d scrape, and if we did not look sharp they would drag us into it too.'[3] The opposition leaders saw the Asturians, for all their provincial manners and appearance, as Spanish whig grandees. The patriots, prophesied the *Edinburgh Review*, would never again bow to a corrupt monarchy and nobility who had deserted them at the crisis. If they maintained

---

[1] *Parl. Deb.*, XI, 889; Moore, *Life of Sheridan*, p. 356. The only jarring note in the debate was struck by Ponsonby who emphasised that Sheridan spoke only for himself and was not committing the opposition to a policy of aid.

[2] Colchester, vol. II, p. 163; Wilberforce, *Life*, vol. III, p. 367; *Annual Register*, 1808, pp. 124-5.

[3] Horner, vol. I, p. 424; Wilberforce, vol. III, p. 321; Holland, *Further Memoirs*, p. 13.

their independence they would have struck a blow for liberty throughout the world, 'and who then shall ever presume to cry down popular rights or to tell us that the people have nothing to do with the laws but to obey them—with the taxes, but to pay them—and with the blunders of their rulers, but to suffer them?' 'We shall hear in the language of Cervantes', wrote Thomas Campbell, 'all the great principles of British liberty; they will become a free people and have, like us, their Sidneys and Chathams. Oh sweet and romantic Spain! If the Spanish plume and beaver succeed I shall die of joy—if not, of grief.' [1] But the steady ministerialists were more cautious. 'The Spanish temper', Perceval assured his brother, 'certainly appears at present to be as good as possible. . . . How far this great struggle against French tyranny in Spain shall be effectually carried on without notions of independence and reform arising out of the success of that very struggle itself, must at present be only a matter of conjecture. . . .' [2]

No time was lost in organising military aid to the insurgents. On 16 June Castlereagh ordered the instant release of all Asturian prisoners in British hands and sent Colonel Sir Thomas Dyer and two other officers to obtain first-hand information on the state of affairs in the Peninsula.[3] A day previously Canning had assured the Commons that all possible help would be given to any nation resisting the common enemy of mankind. Thanks to Castlereagh's policy of recruiting from the militia, the strength of the regular army had been increased by 22,000 men in little over a year. The *Edinburgh Review* might denounce Castlereagh's 'puerility and mismanagement', but Windham and the Talents had never done as well.[4] On 14 June Arthur Wellesley, eager to escape from Irish politics, heard that he was due for a command. Within a month he had sailed from Cork and on 1 August began to disembark, with a force of 15,000 men, at the mouth of the Mondega river in Portugal. The news from Spain, wrote a delighted Cobbett, seemed 'too good to be true . . . . Our ministers seem to be using great promptitude in giving them assistance.' [5] But behind the scenes all was far from well. It had originally been planned to send to

[1] Berry, *Journal*, vol. II, p. 354; *Edinburgh Review*, Oct. 1808, p. 27; Beattie, *Life and Letters of Thomas Campbell*, p. 110.

[2] Perceval MSS., Perceval to Arden, 20 July 1808.

[3] Castlereagh, *Correspondence*, vol. VI, p. 371.

[4] *Ibid.*, vol. VIII, p. 61; Fortescue, vol. VI, p. 83; *Edinburgh Review*, Oct. 1807, pp. 171–4.

[5] Wellington, *Civil Correspondence*, pp. 67 and 444; *Political Register*, 18 June 1808.

the Peninsula 10,000 men then under Sir John Moore's command
in Sweden, and Moore, as senior officer to Wellesley, would automatically have assumed supreme command of the combined armies.
Unfortunately Castlereagh and Moore were at loggerheads over
strategy and on 26 July Castlereagh, apparently with Perceval's
approval, formally reported the dispute to the king.[1] From then on
Castlereagh was determined that Moore should not be given the command. Lieutenant-General Sir Harry Burrard, senior to both Wellesley
and Moore, and Lieutenant-General Sir Hew Dalrymple, senior to all
three, were both hastily ordered to Portugal. It was later even widely
rumoured that the duke of York himself was about to set sail and an
alarmed Wilberforce wrote a special letter of protest to Perceval.[2]

The new appointments hardly strengthened the expeditionary
force. Dalrymple, fresh from his comfortable retreat as governor of
Gibraltar, had not seen active service for fourteen years. Burrard,
wrote one observer, was 'a very good sort of man, and if he was unfit
to command an army, they who gave him the command ought to have
known that, for I am sure everyone else knew it'.[3] Meanwhile Wellesley
ordered his troops to advance without waiting for either reinforcements or senior officers. The military position in the Peninsula was
reasonably encouraging. On 23 July General Dupont's army had surrendered to Spanish irregulars at Baylen, while in Portugal Junot's
French army held only Lisbon and a few fortresses. By 20 August,
after two minor skirmishes, the main British and French armies met
at Vimiero. On the same day Sir Harry Burrard assumed the command,
without actually troubling to disembark. On the following day Junot
attacked, only to be heavily beaten by Wellesley's troops. As soon as
the battle was over Burrard landed and over-ruled Wellesley's order
for an immediate advance on Lisbon. Early next day Sir Hew Dalrymple arrived to assume the command. Vimiero, wrote Wellesley to
the duke of Richmond, would have been a rout had not Burrard inter-
fered. 'Indeed, since the arrival of the great generals, we appear to have
been palsied, and everything has gone on wrong.'[4] In the afternoon

[1] Windsor MSS., 13808-9, Castlereagh to George III, 26 July 1808; Farington, *Diary*, vol. V, p. 112.
[2] *Political Register*, 20 Aug. 1808; Wilberforce, *Life*, vol. III, p. 374.
[3] Jackson, vol. II, p. 379.
[4] Wellington, *Despatches*, vol. III, p. 102, 'I do not know', wrote Wellesley
on 1 Sep., 'what Sir H. Dalrymple proposes to do, or is instructed to do, but
if I were in his situation I would have 20,000 men at Madrid in less than a month
from this time' (*ibid.*, p. 109).

of 22 August things went even worse. The French General Kellerman arrived with a flag of truce and proposed a convention for a French evacuation of Portugal. Dalrymple, very properly, accepted the idea, but then made sweeping and unnecessary concessions in drawing up the terms. The French were to be evacuated in British transports, together with all their arms and equipment and all other 'property' legitimately acquired in Portugal. They were to be landed at a western French port, and were to be free to re-enter the war immediately. Dalrymple even originally agreed to allow a Russian fleet in the Tagus to sail to the Baltic under French protection, but, fortunately, Vice-Admiral Cotton had refused to allow mere soldiers to settle naval matters.[1] Thus slightly amended, the convention was officially signed at Cintra on 30 August by Wellesley, acting under Dalrymple's orders, and by Kellerman on behalf of the French. Dalrymple, in accordance with his instructions, had cleared Portugal of the French and that without the difficulty of capturing Lisbon and storming the Portuguese fortresses. 'I was', confessed Napoleon, 'about to send Junot to a council of war, when fortunately the English tried their generals, and so saved me the pain of punishing an old friend.' [2] Wellesley himself generally approved of the convention: it was the individual clauses which caused the trouble.[3] On the last day of August the news of Vimiero reached London, causing unparalleled excitement. Soon garlanded mail coaches set off with the glad tidings to all corners of England, the London radicals actually passed a vote of thanks to the king and his ministers, while the *Political Register* handed out bouquets to all concerned. 'The merits of the ministers in sending out this expedition, in their plan of operations, in their choice of a commander, and in every part of the enterprise, no man of a just mind will ... attempt to deny.' [4] To a country buoyed up with the most extravagant hopes, the news of Cintra sounded like a catastrophe.

The first ministers heard of its term came from an indignant Souza, the Portuguese envoy in London, on the afternoon of 4 September. Camden, in panic, called for Portland's immediate resignation and for Castlereagh's retirement from the war and colonial office, while Canning hurriedly sent the news to Windsor, where the king could 'hardly bring himself to believe' that either Dalrymple or Wellesley

[1] See Wellington, *Despatches*, vol. III, pp. 104 ff., for the full text of the convention.
[2] Robinson, *Wellington's Campaigns*, p. 59.
[3] Wellington, *Despatches*, vol. III, p. 103.
[4] *Political Register*, 10 Sep. 1808.

N

could have signed such a document.[1] 'I know not how', wrote the
duke of Portland from Bulstrode, 'to express my astonishment and
perplexity at the contents of the paper. . . .' Souza's draft could only
be the original French demands which were pretty steep at that. Poor
Castlereagh thought it all 'a base forgery somewhere, and nothing can
induce me to believe it genuine'.[2] As late as 13 September the *Courier*
was repeating that there had in fact been no treaty at all: the rumours
were the work of Junot, desperate to avoid annihilation. Two days later
Dalrymple's despatches reached London, and Castlereagh, although
in 'deep disappointment', assured the king that there seemed no valid
excuse to repudiate the treaty.[3] On 16 September its terms were published in an extraordinary *Gazette*; ministers hopefully ordered the
Tower guns to be fired, and decided in cabinet that day to inform Dalrymple that they approved of his conduct. They were practically the
only individuals in London who did. As soon as the terms of the convention were known church bells were rung in muffled tones; Cobbett
lost little time in blackening Arthur Wellesley; the *Courier* became
openly hostile; even the faithful *Sun* could not disguise its disappointment.[4] Twice within a year bewailed Francis Jackson 'have we had the
game completely in our own hands and twice has it been wantonly
thrown away'.[5] 'What a convention they have made,' wrote Lady
Arden to Perceval. 'Really Spencer I quite feel for your disappointment. In everything Kellerman has outwitted them and got the
advantage. I should almost be led to think that none of them understood French, by their signing articles so extravagantly against their
own interest. If it rests with you Spencer, another time do order these
generals to draw up their treaties in English. It may prevent another
such disaster.' [6] The general mood of embittered idealism caught even
that tory proselyte, Wordsworth. Had parliament not been in recess
the government might easily have been swept away in the first flood
of public indignation.

Even the cabinet itself was divided on the issue. When Dalrymple's
despatches arrived Canning was on holiday at Hinckley and only
heard a garbled version of the news from the guard on the London
mail. Immediately 'the place was in an uproar, bells ringing and mobs

[1] *Bathurst MSS.*, p. 67; Windsor MSS., 13857-8, Canning to George III and
reply, 4 Sep. 1808.   [2] Castlereagh, *Correspondence*, vol. VI, pp. 42 and 423.
[3] Windsor MSS., 13871-2, Castlereagh to George III, 15 Sep. 1808.
[4] *Political Register*, 1 Oct. 1808; *Courier*, 28 Sep.; *Sun*, 16 Sep.
[5] Jackson, vol. II, p. 381.
[6] Perceval MSS., Lady Arden to Perceval, 20 Sep. 1808.

shouting, before I had the means of confirming or qualifying one word of what they all took for certain'. When, two hours later, a special messenger arrived from Perceval the local celebrations were in full swing. The Hinckleyans, thought Canning, were not likely to enter into nice distinctions: the surrender of an army and a fleet was a good enough excuse for making a noise. 'And accordingly', he wrote to Perceval on the sixteenth, 'I am about to make the bell-ringers here drunk. They cannot ring worse after that encouragement than they have been doing of their own accord.' [1] Not that Canning himself ever accepted the convention, for that same afternoon he was de-nouncing it to Bathurst as 'utterly, manifestly, shamefully unjust'.[2] The next day, having received a copy of the *Gazette*, he wrote twice to Perceval and once to Castlereagh developing his criticisms. The government was now too unpopular to risk shielding its officers as it had previously shielded Gambier. 'This Convention must be distinctly *ours*, or our *commanders'*. We must judge *them*—or the public will judge *us*.' He objected most strongly to article five, which guaranteed the right of the French army to take all its 'private property' out of Portugal. This Canning interpreted (in spite of Perceval's protests) as allowing enemy troops to retain goods originally looted from the Portuguese. If our allies took steps to recover their rightful property were we to cut them down in honouring the convention? 'It makes one sick with shame to think of it. And in what country, after this—in what party of Italy—of Spain—or of the north shall we be received with open arms as deliverers?' Under the eighteenth article it was agreed that all French civil and military subjects taken prisoner in Spain should be exchanged for Spanish troops then held by Junot in the Tagus. Yet throughout the war we had refused to barter troops for civilians, in spite of the many English tourists seized by Napoleon after the rupture of the Peace of Amiens. If the Spaniards refused to surrender French civilians were we to use force or merely ship the Spanish prisoners back to France? 'Pleasant allies to the Spaniards we are too!' In addition articles sixteen and seventeen protected the rights of all Portuguese who had collaborated with the French. Any French soldier could sell the plate he had stolen from a loyalist to a known traitor before the rightful owner's eyes, 'and the traitor's side-board will display it ever after with the British army as the guarantee of the transaction! and we went there as allies!' In future all Europeans would be convinced that it was better to be a partisan of the defeated

[1] *Ibid.*, Canning to Perceval, 16 and 17 Sep.   [2] *Bathurst MSS.*, p. 75.

French than of the victorious British. 'Struggling as the two nations are in the eyes of the world against each other, this single trait is enough to decide the preponderance.' Once this heart-breaking convention was ratified 'we shall have lost Portugal, Spain, Sweden, and our character'.[1]

Exaggerated and wrong-headed as many of the Canning outbursts were, they undoubtedly put his colleagues in a very awkward position. The king himself was known to be uneasy about accepting certain parts of the convention, even after the news of Cotton's agreement with Siniavin, by which the Russians surrendered their fleet until six months after a peace had been signed.[2] On Sunday, 18 September, Perceval forwarded Canning's letters to Castlereagh and argued that, under no circumstances, should the cabinet disown Arthur Wellesley. 'I am sure', replied Castlereagh, 'I do not wonder that Canning in his turn, should have the *hot*, as well as the *cold* fit of this desperate ague which has visited us all so lamentably, but I quite agree with you that we ought to deal with the past, now that it is irrevocable, only as it bears on our future means of rendering service and that in this sense we ought well to weigh how we can best save, together with our own characters and that of the country the *Instrument*, which of all others seems capable, if we can rally round him the requisite amount of support, of consoling us and the world for any fault either he himself or others have committed. In this view I quite agree with you that we can only justify ourselves to Spain by increased and accelerated exertion, and I follow all your reasoning as to the mode.'[3] On the main issue there can be no doubt that Castlereagh and Perceval were right. They remembered that Vimiero had been a victory and that Cintra was a bad beginning rather than an end of the Peninsula campaign.

In essence Canning's advice to sacrifice Arthur Wellesley to save the government was the most squalid he ever gave. An enraged public had already damned the young general for signing the convention. Had the cabinet disowned him, Wellesley's career would not have been worth a month's purchase. Fortunately those who had the insight and the courage to defend him realised just in time that a rash acceptance of the convention might ruin their cause. On 17 September

[1] Perceval MSS., Canning to Perceval, 17 Sep. 1808.
[2] Windsor MSS., 13873–4, Mulgrave to George III, 15 Sep. 1808.
[3] Perceval MSS., Castlereagh to Perceval, 'St. James's Sq. Sunday Evening' (18 Sep.). Walpole incorrectly dates this letter the 27 Sep., which was not a Sunday but a Tuesday.

Canning sent to Castlereagh his version of the answer to Dalrymple's despatches. The cabinet immediately amended its draft and Castlereagh wrote privately to Dalrymple that he must, on no account, allow French troops to retain looted Portuguese property.[1] That evening Dalrymple's son set off for Plymouth with the official despatch. The following afternoon Castlereagh received Perceval's letter and realised that an irate foreign secretary would be back in town on Monday evening. He therefore hurried to the admiralty where Mulgrave telegraphed Captain Dalrymple not to sail without further orders.[2] The following week was given up to ministers' squabbles. On the twentieth it was decided to recall Sir Hew Dalrymple, who was loudly booed when he landed at Portsmouth.[3] But Canning and Chatham (who thought that Wellesley ought to face a court martial) were not satisfied. 'I fear', wrote Canning on 24 September, 'that we have lost Portugal for ever instead of gaining it now.' Junot was about to leave Lisbon with ninety-six wagon loads of stolen plate; we had incurred 'a heavier loss and a heavier disgrace than any that a British army or British faith ever sustained'.[4] In vain Castlereagh reminded his colleagues that Kellerman had promised upon his honour that the French would surrender all Portuguese property and that Dalrymple had been told 'very distinctly, do anything and everything but break the treaty to prevent plunder from being carried off'.[5] By the twenty-sixth the majority of the cabinet had agreed that only Dalrymple should be held responsible for the convention: if public opinion forced an inquiry, Wellesley's reputation was to be defended at all costs.[6] Two days later Canning sent a formal protest to the king, repeating his detailed objections to a convention which should have been repudiated on the grounds that military officers had no authority to make political decisions.[7]

The public continued to share Canning's view. Early in October the

[1] Castlereagh, *Correspondence*, vol. VI, pp. 439–41.

[2] Perceval MSS., Castlereagh to Perceval, *op. cit.* Holland Rose printed a version of this story in which Canning himself returned to town just in time to order Capt. Dalrymple not to sail. In fact Canning was still in Hinckley when Castlereagh and Mulgrave made their decision.

[3] Windsor MSS., 13887–8, Castlereagh to George III, 21 Sep. 1808; *Political Register*, 22 Oct. 1808.

[4] Wellington, *Supplementary Despatches*, vol. XI, p. 402; Perceval MSS., Canning to Perceval, 24 Sep. 1808.

[5] Perceval MSS., Castlereagh to Perceval 28 Sep. 1808.

[6] Castlereagh, *Correspondence*, vol. VI, pp. 453–4; Wellington, *Supplementary Despatches*, vol. XI, p. 174.

[7] Windsor MSS., 13914–9, Canning to George III, 28 Sep. 1808.

London court of common council unanimously approved a strongly-worded address calling for a rigorous inquiry.[1] Even the *Sun* admitted that the terms of the convention had caused 'great anxiety and disgust'. 'Indeed, according to the present information which the public mind possesses, it appears to have been one of the most disgraceful events that has ever sullied the page of British history.'[2] 'I suspect', wrote Redesdale to Abbot, 'some of the cabinet talked rather indiscreetly, and encouraged the public censure. A most unwise conduct, if truly imputed, and which they will have great reason to regret.' In county after county honest freeholders met to draw up petitions to parliament and at Carlton House the prince of Wales waited for the king to throw out his ministers.[3] Only the *Morning Post* stood out boldly against the universal clamour, publishing a long article on 'The Incompetency of Persons who have not deeply studied the art of war to judge the conduct of Generals'.[4] Meanwhile the cabinet was busy deciding how to do its own judging. Richard Ryder, the new judge advocate general, recommended a board of inquiry rather than a court martial. Had the latter been adopted specific charges would have had to be framed against the officers concerned. This led the cabinet into immediate difficulties. Certain articles in the convention might have been made the foundation of charges against Dalrymple, yet he could only have been made responsible for what took place after he took command of the army. The merits of the convention, however, depended on the previous operations of the British army and the exact military position when Dalrymple first arrived. Other charges would therefore have been necessary against the other generals in order to inquire into their conduct during their respective commands. Burrard might have been charged with not advancing after Vimiero: Wellesley could only be accused of having won victories at Rolica and Vimiero.[5] Therefore, late in October, Castlereagh informed the king that the government recommended a court of inquiry, consisting of Sir David Dundas, Lord Moira, Lieutenant-General Sir James Craig, Lord Heathfield,

[1] *Sun*, 5 Oct. 1808. On 14 Oct. the same paper rebuked the London tories for their failure to oppose the address. Perceval himself drafted the king's answer. 'A propos of answers,' wrote Huskisson on the 13 Oct., 'I cannot but congratulate you on that to the City. It was time to teach Mr. Waithman that the Govt. is not in the common hall and that we are not to have a supreme council of war made up of the tradesmen of London' (Perceval MSS.). Canning, according to Brougham, 'disapproved of it' (*Memoirs*, vol. I, pp. 422–7).

[2] *Sun*, 20 Sept. 1808.   [3] *Dropmore MSS.*, IX, 222; Colchester, vol. II, p. 159.

[4] *Morning Post*, 4 Nov. 1808.

[5] Perceval MSS., undated memorandum by Richard Ryder.

the earl of Pembroke, Sir George Nugent, and Sir Jasper Nicholls.
The terms of reference were very wide, giving the court full power to
impeach ministers' conduct and at least two of those appointed, Moira
and Nugent, were politically opposed to the government.[1]

The inquiry opened at Chelsea on 17 November and the final report
was published on 22 December, approving the armistice after Vimiero
by six votes to one and the terms of the convention by four to three.
Moreover the board unanimously recommended that no further
military proceeding was necessary against any officer concerned. For
the rest the report was full of masterly ambiguities designed, it seemed,
to please all sides at once.[2] There, but for Canning's stubbornness, the
matter might have rested as Castlereagh and Perceval clearly intended
that it should. 'To throw the report loose upon the table of the House',
wrote the foreign secretary to Perceval, 'is at best only adjourning the
difficulty, for the question will then arise—does Government propose
to do anything upon it? If it does, that proposition cannot be made too
early. If it does not, the reason for not doing so must be that it is
satisfied with the report. If satisfied with the report, it must be so for
one of two reasons—either, that thinking ill of the Convention it
thinks also that the results of the Inquiry is sufficient to check such
Conventions in future, or, that thinking well of the Convention, it is
glad that the report acquits of blame.' [3] And so, with misplaced logic,
Canning re-opened the whole unhappy issue and the cabinet settled
down to drafting a paragraph on the convention for the King's Speech.
Little good came of it. Perceval, Castlereagh, Mulgrave and Westmorland, reported the Speaker, were ranged against Canning, Eldon,
and Chatham.[4] At first the protesting party had the better of the argument. On the eve of the new session Abbot attended the usual King's
Speech dinner at Perceval's and listened to a draft which spoke of the
convention 'with strong expressions of disapprobation. . . .' It was,
thought the Speaker, likely to produce much 'warm and troublesome
discussion'. But, at the last moment, a new and much softened version
was substituted.[5] Wellesley had been saved, but only by again offending Canning. Already it was being whispered in whig country houses
that the foreign secretary disavowed the government's military and
naval plans.[6]

---

[1] *Sun*, 3 Nov. 1808.
[2] *Sun*, 2 Jan. 1809. For Wellesley's opinion of the report see *Civil Correspondence*, p. 526. [3] Perceval MSS., Canning to Perceval, 4 Jan. 1809.
[4] Colchester, vol. II, p. 163.
[5] *Ibid.*, pp. 163–4. [6] *Dropmore MSS.*, IX, 248.

CHAPTER TWELVE

REFORM

PARLIAMENT reassembled in January 1809 in an atmosphere of great
political tension. Rumours of a change of government and a dissolution were so widely believed that canvassing began in many constituencies. Meanwhile both government and opposition sent round
urgent circular letters to rally support. The whigs hoped for 170
votes and Perceval for a good many more, but, reported the *Day*,
'there are many cautious members who will wait for further intelligence
before they come up'.[1] The *Sun*, as optimistic as ever, announced that
Grey and Grenville had decided to abandon their system of 'teazing,
fretful, persevering hostility' for a more moderate policy.[2] Fortunately
for the cabinet, the opposition was distracted by party squabbles.
Ponsonby, their new leader in the Commons, had failed, as Holland
had predicted he would, to hold his followers together. Indiscipline,
disorder, and cross-purposes were rife on the whig benches. Some,
like Romilly, despaired of ever returning to power while George III
lived, and, by the session of 1808, even the fiery Lady Holland had
grown 'sick of and indifferent to the measures of a hopeless opposition'.[3] There were many signs that session of a lack of co-ordination
between those members of the party who usually agreed on major
political issues. Thus, at the end of May, the attorney-general, Sir
Vicary Gibbs, introduced a bill to amend sections of the Seditious
Meetings Act. Both Ponsonby and Petty welcomed the measure, only
to be denounced by Romilly for supporting 'a most insidious attack
on the liberties of the people'.[4] By the end of the year Tierney had
lost all hope and wrote such discouraging reports to Grey and Lauderdale that both declined to come up for the new session. 'The d——d
faulty half-secession', grumbled Brougham, 'will not only finish the
ruin of the party, but deservedly exclude them from all public
confidence'.[5]

[1] *Day*, 16 and 17 Jan. 1809.
[2] *Sun*, 18 Jan. 1809.
[3] Romilly, vol. II, p. 209; Lady Holland, *Journal*, vol. II, p. 240.
[4] Romilly, vol. II, p. 290.
[5] Gore, *Creevey's Life and Times*, p. 40.

When parliament re-assembled the opposition was so split that it could not even move an agreed amendment to the Address. At bottom its troubles sprang from the growing antagonism between grandees and radicals on reform issues. As Whitbread, Folkestone, and Madocks used the cry of 'No Corruption' with growing recklessness to discredit the cabinet, their own official leaders came more and more to fear its effect on public opinion. Auckland, convinced that the ministry must collapse, dreaded lest the government be thrown into the hands of 'wild democrats'.[1] In the last resort Grey and Grenville preferred Portland to 'the patriots'. Ponsonby, reported Thomas Grenville, 'always repeats to me that everyone with whom he converses agrees with him in thinking that this is not the time for very active opposition'. But Ponsonby was then scarcely on speaking terms with his own left wing: the leadership of the opposition in 1809, wrote Creevey, was 'to the last degree contemptible'.[2] By the summer the state of the party was chaotic. In April Grey, Grenville, and Petty broke with Whitbread and sent Auckland and Hardwicke on their rounds to spread the news. The grandees, reported the Speaker, were 'very desirous' of supporting ministers in keeping down 'the wild spirit of Sir Francis Burdett, Lord Folkestone, etc., and their inquiries'.[3] Whitbread, said Holland, was too vain and too rash to lead 'independent and well-educated men', but, though unfit to lead, he was one of the most necessary followers.[4] But the party did not break into two clean halves for Whitbread, like Mahomet's coffin, remained suspended in space, kept there not by the attraction but by the repulsion of two equal forces. The extreme radicals would not accept him because he had not gone far enough: the grandees disowned him because he had gone too far. Meanwhile moderates, thought Horner, deluded the public about the extent of corruption and the efficacy of their reforms, while the official leadership, by its timidity and inconsistency, was losing all hold over opinion within and without parliament.[5] 'The dissolution of the party', wrote Grey to Tierney, 'I regard as a great misfortune, but there was no help for it.'[6]

The session of 1809 was dominated by the issue of reform and the question embarrassed the opposition as much as it did the government. The confusion and contradictions in orthodox whig thinking

[1] *Dropmore MSS.*, VIII, 248.
[2] *Ibid.*, VIII, 256; *Creevey Papers*, vol. I, p. 107.
[3] Colchester, vol. II, pp. 177–8; Auckland, *Journal*, vol. IV, p. 319.
[4] Holland, *Memoirs of the Whig Party*, vol. II, pp. 237 and 241.
[5] Romilly, vol. II, p. 461.   [6] Olphin, *Tierney*, p. 128.

can best be seen in the pages of the *Edinburgh Review*. In July 1807 a long article attacking Cobbett's new-found radicalism came perilously near to an apology for the *status quo*. It was easy, argued the *Review*, to imagine something a great deal worse than the existing constitution, for all its electoral corruption, sinecures, pensions, and placemen. There was too much scrambling for office, but this was caused neither by the presence of placemen in parliament nor by the interference of peers in elections. Placemen were better in parliament than anywhere else; the electoral influence of great families was 'rather beneficial than pernicious', and the sale of boroughs, though dishonourable to those who engaged in it, 'is in no danger of going to such an extent as to put the constitution in any hazard'. The ideal assembly would include the highest possible proportion of 'the effective aristocracy', those who through birth, wealth, or ability were accepted as the natural leaders of public opinion. Universal suffrage would then make little difference as the multitude would still follow and vote for its natural leaders. In the meantime the existing house of commons adequately represented all local and national interests in politics.[1] Two years later the *Edinburgh Review* had shifted its ground. If the people generally wanted reform, 'we think the time is come when it ought to be no longer withheld'. Inequalities in the electoral system ought to be lessened ('but not entirely destroyed') by disenfranchising rotten boroughs and giving their members to new industrial towns. The duration of parliament might be shortened if the property qualification for M.P.s was raised and the tumult of contested elections eliminated by introducing 'a written vote'. Any measures which excluded M.P.s returned 'by the interest of the ministry or noble families' would 'deprive us of all the practical blessings of our constitution' and 'we should think it our duty to strive against it'. At best electoral reform itself could only tinker with the essential problem. M.P.s and voters alike were bound to the majority by the power of patronage. Therefore the opposition's first aim must be to reduce government patronage by calling for decreases in the national debt and establishments. This, at the crisis of a world war, was a policy easy to outline in theory but almost impossible to apply in parliament.[2] Such reform in the interests of a 'natural aristocracy', besides its practical difficulties, was politically unrewarding. For, as Hazlitt later saw, it put the opposition 'on bad

[1] *Edinburgh Review*, July 1807, pp. 387–421. For Cobbett's vitriolic answer see *Political Register*, 17 Oct. 1807, pp. 577 ff.
[2] *Edinburgh Review*, July 1809, pp. 280–300.

terms with the Government and not on good ones with the people'. Trapped between Pitt's Friends and the radicals, Grey and Grenville and their followers were in danger of becoming 'fag ends of a Tory'. 'A Whig', thundered Hazlitt, 'is properly what is called a Trimmer— that is, a coward to both sides of the question, who dare not be a knave or an honest man, but is a sort of whiffling, shuffling, cunning, silly, contemptible, unmeaning negation of the two.' [1] The *Edinburgh Review*, in its famous article 'The State of the Parties', recognised the same problem. The nation was dividing into two factions—'the courtiers, who are almost for arbitrary power, and the democrats, who are almost for revolution and republicanism'. Between them stood 'a small, but most respectable band—the old constitutional Whigs of England—with the best talents and the best intentions, but without power or popularity—calumniated and suspected by both parties and looking on both with too visible a resentment, aversion, and alarm'. Should the two factions come to blows the British constitution and British liberties would be at an end. Therefore the respectable opposition, like the sabine women of old, must throw themselves between the combatants and save the state.[2] Unfortunately the modern sabine women were too busy throwing themselves at each other's throats to make much of their job of mediation. The field was left clear for the radicals.

The cabinet's troubles began as soon as it got down to producing the King's Speech. Canning wrote a draft late in December, just 'to see how the speech would look of which I took charge', and found it 'the most difficult task of my life'.[3] Perceval himself had decided not to reduce the speech to milk and water, but a finally acceptable version was not found until the very day parliament met.[4] During the debate on the Address Ponsonby concentrated on denouncing the convention of Cintra and, ominously, 153 members supported a whig vote of censure moved on 21 February.[5] Ministers were, moreover, sorely harrassed by the extravagance and indiscretions of the royal dukes and of the band of professional place-hunters who looked to them for patronage. The royal family's finances were so chaotic that Perceval

---

[1] Hazlitt, *Works, Political Essays* (1819), preface, XXX-XXXIII.
[2] *Edinburgh Review*, Jan. 1810, pp. 504-20.
[3] Perceval MSS., Canning to Perceval, 31 Dec. 1808.
[4] P.R.O., Colchester MSS., 30/9/15, Perceval to Abbot, 19 Jan. 1809; Colchester, vol. II, pp. 160 and 163.
[5] *Parl. Deb.*, XII, 897-971. The Address was moved by young Frederick Robinson, another of Perceval's protégés (Add. MSS., 40826, fols. 29 and 31).

spent many hours juggling with civil list accounts, 'that *insolvent* or at least *inadequate fund*'.[1] Late in 1805 the treasury had estimated that between them the princess of Wales and the dukes of Gloucester, Clarence, Kent, Cumberland, and Sussex owed £144,000.[2] Three years later Perceval reported to the cabinet that the combined debts of the queen, the princess of Wales, and the dukes of York, Clarence, Kent, and Sussex had reached £200,000, while the civil list itself was a further £200,000 in arrears. In July 1808 a group of tradesmen to whom the princess of Wales owed £26,000 threatened legal action, the duke of Sussex's carriage and horses were publicly seized by bailiffs because of an unpaid debt of less than £900, and young Princess Charlotte could not even start on her summer holidays until the government sent the money to pay her fare.[3] The duke of Kent, who constantly bombarded the cabinet with claims for a larger allowance and the payment of his debts, spent so much on unnecessary alterations to his apartments in Kensington Palace that the treasury finally refused to pay the bill.[4] Finally Sussex, vigorously supported by his royal brothers, tried to persuade the cabinet that a £25,000 debt to his former 'wife' ought to be paid out of public funds.[5]

By far the greatest millstones round the government's neck were Cumberland and York, the only two of George III's sons who really shared his political views. Cumberland, whose reputation was as ugly as his face, exercised considerable power behind the scenes, particularly in the disposal of patronage. In 1808 he was responsible for the appointment to the key post of ambassador at Lisbon of John Villiers, a man turned fifty who had spent all his life doing nothing, 'a mere courtier,

[1] Windsor MSS., Regency file, 18052–3, Perceval to Prince Regent, 22 May 1811.

[2] Perceval MSS., Memorandum by Huskisson (1805). The individual debts were—duke of Gloucester, £19,000; Clarence, about £30,000; Kent, £25,000; Cumberland, £15,000; Sussex, about £12,000; princess of Wales, £43,433.

[3] *Ibid.*, Memorandum by Perceval, 12 July 1808. The individual debts then were—the queen, £25,000; princess of Wales, £40,000; duke of York, £40,000; Clarence, £40,000; Kent, £30,000; Sussex, £25,000. For droits of admiralty see P.R.O., T29/93/214 and T29/103/507. On 29 June 1810 Arden was instructed to transfer £200,000 from the droits to the civil list, T29/106/178; Windsor MSS., 15442; Perceval MSS., Portland to Perceval, 27 June 1808, George III to Portland, 30 June 1808. The treasury had had to find £1,000 to pay for Princess Charlotte's holiday in 1807. For Charlotte's opinion of Perceval see Aspinall, *Letters of Princess Charlotte*, p. 3; Windsor MSS., 15442–3, Perceval to George III, 5 June 1810.

[4] P.R.O., T27/65/347 and T27/66/22 and 176; Perceval MSS., Perceval to Arden, 3 Aug. 1810.

[5] Perceval MSS., George Harrison to Perceval, 2 Feb. 1808.

famous for telling interminably long stories'.[1] Another of the duke's
protégés, while acting as paymaster of marines, managed to mislay
£280,000 of public money and would even, with Cumberland's help,
have stifled all inquiry had not Perceval intervened in the affair.[2] Of all
the royal dukes, Cumberland alone inspired hatred and fear. Even
those nearest the king suffered from his intrigues, and while the general
public knew little of his villainy, it suspected much.[3] On the night of
30 May 1810 the duke's private life came dramatically into the news
when he was found severely wounded in his bed, while Sellis, his
personal valet, lay dead in a neighbouring room. The inquest jury
decided, on the basis of the evidence presented, that Sellis, after an
unsuccessful attempt to murder his master, had committed suicide.
But not everyone was satisfied with the verdict and certainly the home
office was at this time sending 'most secret and confidential' despatches
to Ireland about both Cumberland and his valet.[4] Like so many other
episodes in the duke's life, the Sellis incident remained a centre of
gossip and suspicion.

In contrast, the duke of York's sins were debated in parliament
amidst a blaze of publicity. Fortune never dealt kindly with the duke,
who alone of the king's sons had the capacity for hard and sustained
work. During the early stages of the war he had commanded British
forces in the field at a time when the French were winning spectacular
victories on all fronts. His royal highness did nothing to spoil their
record. It was only when he was appointed to the horseguards that he
showed his true merits. 'Never', said Sir Arthur Wellesley in 1809,
'was there an army in a better state, as far as depended on the Commander-in-Chief. . . .'[5] Perhaps, as his colleagues often complained,
York was over-fond of interfering in things which did not strictly
concern him, but that was a family failing and excessive zeal was the
least of sins in the British army of his day. Less forgivable was his
neglect of his own financial affairs. In October 1807 Perceval and
Charles Long made a special investigation into the duke's position,
following ugly rumours that he owed vast sums to Greenwood and

[1] Jackson, *Diary*, vol. II, p. 302; Perceval MSS., duke of Portland to Perceval,
13 Nov. 1808.
[2] Croker, vol. I, p. 23; Windsor MSS., 14878-9, Perceval to George III,
15 Jan. 1810; Perceval MSS., Cumberland to Portland, 17, 28 Apr., and 11 May
1807, Portland to Cumberland, 18 Apr. 4 and 13 May 1807; George Villiers to
Perceval, 5 and 7 Jan. 1810.
[3] Westbrook Hay MSS., Herbert Taylor to Richard Ryder, 5 Mar. 1810.
[4] *Ibid.*, E. B. Littlehales to W. W. Pole, 13 June 1810.
[5] *Annual Register*, 1809, p. 123; Yonge, *Life of Liverpool*, vol. I, p. 40.

Cox, the agents for his regiment. They found that he had received £21,500 in advances, most of which was covered by a mortgage on Oatlands, the duke's country house.[1] A year later the duke's debts had reached a grand total of £40,000. Worse still he was the butt of constant lampoons in the radical press, inspired, according to Lord Holland, by 'a little knot of discontented officers' who were anxious to discredit the commander-in-chief.[2]

They eventually found a suitable tool in Gwyllm Wardle, M.P. for Okehampton, an old Harrovian, a colonel of Volunteers, and a man 'of mean capacity and meaner disposition'. A radical proselyte he had bought his seat in parliament out of the proceeds of a fortunate marriage, but he made little mark there until on 20 January 1809 he rose to give notice of a motion on 'appointments, promotions, exchanges, the raising of levies, and the general state of the army'. A week later, after a long declaration of the purity and patriotism of his motives, Wardle first made specific charges of corruption against the duke of York and was promptly seconded by the ubiquitous Sir Francis Burdett. The principal witness for the prosecution was to be Mary Anne Clarke, one of the duke's former mistresses.[3] The government was taken completely by surprise. Perceval hurriedly contacted the duke, who denied all charges and demanded a full inquiry. The secretary-at-war therefore accepted Wardle's challenge and William Adam, the royal duke's legal factotum, supported by Perceval, Castlereagh, and Canning, insisted on 'a public investigation before the world at the bar of the House'. Only Charles Yorke and Wilberforce, rightly scenting a scandal, argued that a private inquiry by a select committee would be sufficient. Then, replied government spokesmen, it would be said that the committee had been packed and the duke acquitted by the votes of his own friends. A committee of the whole House might interrupt other public business, but it was essential because of the nature of the charges and the person of the accused. Wilberforce, sneered J. W. Ward, was terrified at the thought of 'this Babylonish person', Mrs. Clarke, 'being brought into his holy presence'. Less reverent members rather enjoyed the prospect. 'Perceval and Castlereagh', wrote Lord Bulkeley, 'take the whole thing very coolly; Mulgrave and Westmorland bawl out faction; Camden shakes

[1] Perceval MSS., duke of York to Perceval, 31 Oct. 1807; undated report by Perceval and Charles Long.
[2] *Day*, 30 Jan. 1809; Holland, *Further Memoirs of the Whig Party*, pp. 27–8.
[3] *Parl. Deb.*, XII, 92 and 179–203.

his head like Lord Burleigh in the *Critic*; Canning is like a madman
they say; Bathurst and Chatham full of *sang froid* and so is Eldon;
Liverpool, they say, looks sad, wretched, and thoughtful.'[1]

From the first the government, firmly supported by the king, was
confident of refuting the charges, although those who knew all the
facts about York's morals and finances might have had cause for
doubt. 'Of Mr. Wardle', wrote Perceval to George III on 27 January,
'Mr. Perceval can say nothing. He is entitled to be considered as
acting on public grounds, and it is possible he may have been imposed
upon by His R[oyal] Highness' enemies to believe what he has undertaken to prove.'[2] Whether he believed it or not, Wardle had undeniably taken great pains in preparing his case. His star witness, Mary
Anne Clarke, the wife of a Northamptonshire stonemason, owed her
success in life entirely to her own exertions. Born in Bowl and Pin
Alley, off Chancery Lane, she graduated by way of Hoxton to the
regal splendours of Park Lane and Gloucester Place. There she lived
under the duke of York's protection, spending annually, according
to Cobbett, enough to have provided for 645 agricultural labourers
and their families or to have paid the poor rates of at least fifty Hampshire parishes.[3] She had an establishment in Gloucester Place with a
staff of eight and a country cottage, she ran two pairs of horse and
carriage and ate off plate said to be valued at £2,000. All this, the
defence claimed, the duke fondly imagined came out of his allowance
to her of £1,000 a year. He had as a youth, his tutor once confessed,
been quick to learn most things, except the value of money.[4] In fact
Mrs. Clarke had supplemented her income by a lucrative trade in
army and church patronage. Her price list for commissions undercut
the official rates, while her percentage of successes was just high
enough to attract a steady flow of clients. But by 1807 Mary Anne
Clarke was a mature beauty: the duke drifted into the arms of a Mrs.
Carey while his discarded mistress descended to a Hampstead boarding house, and the protection of James Dowler, a satisfied customer
of her recent patronage agency. Dowler, however, soon proved a
broken reed and the duke's £400 a year pension, being primly dependent upon her future good conduct, failed to reach its second
instalment. When, in August 1808, she was first introduced to Wardle,

[1] *Ibid., loc. cit.; Letters to Ivy*, p. 65; Buckingham, vol. IV, p. 311.
[2] Windsor MSS., 14107-9, Perceval to George III, 27 Jan. 1809.
[3] *Political Register*, 18 Feb. 1809.
[4] *Annual Register*, 1809, p. 134.

her fortunes were at a very low ebb. Within a month she had a new house in Westbourne Place which, she claimed, Wardle promised to furnish in exchange for information against the duke. 'I was', she later explained, 'rather fearful of doing what he wanted of me with him alone, because he was not much known in Parliament.' [1] Her scruples were, however, soon overcome by Major Dodd, private secretary to the duke of Kent, whom many suspected of wishing to replace his brother at the horseguards.[2] Consequently towards the end of November 1808 a select little party, consisting of Mrs. Clarke, Wardle, Dodd, and James Glenie, the engineer, set out on a three-day tour ostensibly to 'view the Martello Towers' but probably also to discuss military topics of more immediate interest. Unfortunately none of this was known to the government when the inquiry started.

The Commons went into committee for the first time at five p.m. on 1 February and examined witnesses until two o'clock the following morning. Perceval himself was not impressed by Mary Anne Clarke. Her behaviour, he reported to the king, 'was so extremely impudent, not to say audacious, that Mr. Perceval does not believe that any member in the House could fail to see that she did not deserve any credit'.[3] In fact the majority of members saw nothing of the kind. Even Wilberforce was forced to admit that she was 'elegantly dressed, consummately impudent, and very clever' and that, after two hours of cross-examination 'in the old Bailey way' she had 'clearly got the better of the struggle'.[4] Very soon she had charmed a packed Commons. Her bows to the chair were 'in the highest style of theatrical grace' and her wit would have made her fortune on the stage. When she was tired the entire House called for a chair: when she pleaded exhaustion the Commons immediately adjourned. But although throughout the inquiry Mrs. Clarke scored a notable personal triumph, Wardle's attempts to implicate the duke of York at first made little headway. Mrs. Clarke seemed to glory in admitting her own corrupt practices. What Wardle and his supporters had to prove was either that the duke was influenced by his mistress in army matters or, equally as bad, that he knew she was accepting bribes. Mrs. Clarke claimed that, in return for a £200 fee, she had persuaded the duke to authorise an exchange between two colonels, Brook and Knight. It

---

[1] *Annual Register*, 1809, p. 136; *Parl. Deb.*, XII, 647 ff.

[2] The duke of Kent denied all complicity in the affair.

[3] Colchester, vol. II, p. 106; Windsor MSS., 14132–3, Perceval to George III, '½ p' 2 o'clock. (2 Feb. 1809).

[4] Wilberforce, *Life*, vol. III, p. 402.

was, however, proved that the exchange had been approved even before Mrs. Clarke had been approached and Colonel Knight's brother testified that she had begged him not to mention any payment of money 'lest it should come to the Duke's ears'. This secrecy was denied by Mrs. Clarke, but, significantly, it took her butler, David Peirson, a fortnight to remember that he had handed over the bribe in the duke's presence. He had, he explained, failed to mention this when first examined because he was then suffering from a bad headache and loss of memory. Unfortunately he was also patently drunk on his second appearance, with the result that the House wasted nearly an hour debating whether to punish him for disrespect.[1] Mary Anne Clarke then alleged that she had been responsible for the promotion of a Captain Malings, but, as Perceval wrote to Windsor, her case amounted to 'literally nothing'.[2] By far the most serious charge concerned a certain Colonel French, who had been instructed to raise recruits for the army. Mrs. Clarke and the colonel arranged that she was to have the patronage of a certain number of officers in the levy in exchange for her assistance in his promotion. Perceval countered by proving that the duke himself had put a stop to the levy when he learnt that it was costing the country £150 a recruit.[3]

Thus far the inquiry had gone very well for the duke. Perceval's daily reports to the king remained entirely optimistic. On 8 February he thought the case was going excellently; on the tenth he claimed that, although money had undoubtedly been offered for promotions, there was not a shred of evidence against the commander-in-chief; the following day he was still convinced that the feeling of the House was 'very much to the prejudice of the accusers'.[4] The Speaker thought his royal highness was clear of corruption, while Arthur Wellesley argued that the inquiry might do good by proving that bribery was confined to 'the scum of the earth'.[5] The case certainly did not lack publicity. The House frequently sat until the early hours of the morning and the press reported the evidence in great detail. Fantastic rumours circulated in the city, it being 'notoriously known' that Sir Francis Baring and Sir Robert Peel had both paid Mrs. Clarke £5,000

---

[1] *Parl. Deb.*, XII, 271–7, 389–9 and 512–21; Lewis, *Administrations of Great Britain*, p. 311.
[2] *Parl. Deb.*, XII, 342 ff.; Windsor MSS., 14142–3, Perceval to George III, 3 Feb. 1809.
[3] *Parl. Deb.*, XII, 399–409, 446–9 and 524–7.
[4] Windsor MSS., 14150–6, Perceval to George III, 8, 10 and 11 Feb. 1809.
[5] Colchester, vol. II, p. 166; Wellington, *Civil Correspondence, Ireland*, p. 567.

o

for a peerage.[1] Poor Wilberforce lamented that the public should hear of 'such shameless violations of decency', while Fremantle found the scenes within the Commons 'disgusting' and 'alarming' beyond description.[2] But worse was to come. On 13 February two of the duke's love-letters 'expressive of great affection for Mrs. Clarke in terms little calculated to meet the public eye' were produced in evidence and, as Perceval admitted to the king, 'undoubtedly made an unfavourable impression'.[3] On the same day Mrs. Clarke proved that, through the duke's agency, she had nominated one of her clients, a Dr. O'Meara, to preach before the royal family. Appropriately he took as his text a passage from chapter twelve of the Epistle to the Romans—'He that giveth let him do it with liberality'.[4] When the case of Colonel French's levy was reconsidered, a Miss Taylor, a close friend of Mary Anne Clarke, testified that she had dined with the duke and his mistress and she had heard his royal highness say, 'Colonel French continually worries me about the levy business and is always wanting something more in his own favour. How does he behave to you, darling?' 'Middling —not very well,' answered Mrs. Clarke. 'Mister French', replied the duke, 'must mind what he is about, or I shall cut up him and his levy too.' But Miss Taylor, the illegitimate daughter of a stockbroker, was a most unsatisfactory witness. She kept what she claimed was a boarding school for young ladies in Chelsea, she lied about her father's name, and she admitted being in debt, although Lord Folkestone, Wardle's chief lieutenant, managed to turn this into something to her credit. When Perceval handled her roughly in cross-examination he was quickly called to order by the House.[5]

Opinion had swung violently against the duke. Mrs. Clarke was cheered by the mob whenever she appeared in public, children in the London streets tossed their pennies crying 'duke or darling' instead of 'heads or tails', and they burnt his royal highness in effigy in Suffolk and Yorkshire.[6] Perceval's young children, staunch partisans of the duke, seethed with indignation. 'Do not think by my silence on the subject', wrote Maria to her brother, 'that I am an unconcerned spec-

---

[1] Perceval MSS., John Whyte to Perceval, 22 Feb. 1809; Samuel Dalton to same, 9 Feb. 1809.

[2] Wilberforce, *Life*, vol. III, p. 402; Lewis, *loc. cit.*

[3] Windsor MSS., 14159–60, Perceval to George III, 14 Feb. 1809; *Parl. Deb.*, XII, 582–3.

[4] *Annual Register*, 1809, pp. 143–4.

[5] *Parl. Deb.*, XII, 1024.

[6] *Colchester*, vol. II, p. 174; Wellington, *Civil Correspondence*, p. 575.

tator of what is passing in the House of Commons. I assure you I am
not, but I have no remarks to make on it at present except that it is
evidently false, that I hate and detest Mrs. Clarke, a nasty toad, and
that I am not over-partial to the Honourable Gentleman, Mr. Wardle.'
'I think', added her sister, Fanny, 'it was as clear as possible from the
beginning, that the Duke knew nothing about it, and that it was all
an invention of that nasty wretch Clarke to get some money. Don't
you hate her? What a fool Lord Folkestone must be to think her
evidence worth a farthing, she contradicts herself every word she says
and don't you think since he makes such a fuss about Miss Taylor's
debts (who by the way I am not very fond of notwithstanding all he
says about her) and that he says they are only £150, he had better pay
them himself?'[1] Night after night Perceval predicted in his reports to
the king that the inquiry was about to end, but Wardle who, wrote
Perceval bitterly, thought of himself as a 'walking committee', constantly produced new charges. It was admitted that a Captain Tonyn
had paid Mrs. Clarke £500 for a majority, but only after his promotion had been granted on the application of his father. Colonel Shaw
had paid the same amount for a staff appointment and to be put on
half pay. He got his first wish but not his second. Even more damaging,
at first sight, was the fact that one Samuel Carter, who had been Mrs.
Clarke's footboy, had been given a commission. Perceval was, however, able to prove that he was an officer's son, that he had been
brought to the duke's attention before he even met Mrs. Clarke, and
that he had made a good officer.[2] Yet in spite of all Perceval's efforts,
the case continued to slip away from the duke. On 17 February Lord
Folkestone revived the Tonyn case when a Captain Sandon, who was
said to have acted as a go-between, surrendered a note alleged to have
been written by the duke to Mrs. Clarke. If the note was in York's
hand it seemed very likely that he at least knew of Mrs. Clarke's
dealings. All Perceval could do was contest its authenticity. Witnesses
from the Bank and post office were called, and although they did
their best to avoid giving any definite opinion, they left the majority
of members convinced that the note was genuine. When the inquiry
finally closed on 22 February, the duke's position was precarious.
Perceval, fearing an impeachment, assured the king that the feeling of

[1] Perceval MSS., Maria Perceval to Spencer Perceval jun. (undated), and
Fanny Perceval to same, 14 Mar. 1809.
[2] *Parl. Deb.*, XII, 611–12 and 629; Windsor MSS., 14165–70, Perceval to
George III, 15 and 16 Feb. 1809.

the Commons was more hostile to York than would appear from reading the debates as there was a general impression that Mary Anne Clarke did influence the duke in matters of promotion. Francis Horner thought impeachment would be 'the death-knell of the constitution', but was prepared for the worst.[1]

The formal debate did not begin until a fortnight after the end of the inquiry, and both front benches were thankful for the delay. The inquiry had done nothing towards re-uniting the opposition. Wardle, Folkestone, Whitbread and the more daring spirits in the party were soon lost in the excitement of the chase and even talked the prince of Wales into shabbily deserting his brother. Grey, in contrast, could not believe 'that anything more can be imputed to the Duke of York than might have happened to any man who had the misfortune to keep a mistress', found the scenes in the Commons 'disgusting' and wished the whole inquiry had been 'immediately and publically disclaimed by the Opposition'. In the event, complained Holland, the whigs took 'no distinct or manly tone whatever'; 'Snouch' Ponsonby, their nominal leader in the Commons, 'sunk in the estimation of the party, and the party sunk yet more in the estimation of the public'.[2] Ministers, however, had little chance to gloat over their opponents' misfortunes. As early as 18 February Perceval, who in the early stages was practically in sole charge of the defence, had decided that only a solemn public declaration of innocence by the duke himself could save the day. The Speaker was consulted and agreed that Perceval should draft a letter and submit it for the cabinet's approval.[3] A day later Lord Melville had a similar idea, sending Portland a rough draft of an address which the government could submit to the Commons. The first two paragraphs exonerated the duke on the charge of corruption; the third censured him for his 'unworthy connexion' with Mary Anne Clarke and hoped that the inquiry would convince 'all the branches of His Majesty's illustrious family that nothing can conduce so much to the prosperity of His Majesty's reign and the welfare of his people,

---

[1] Windsor MSS., 14178–81, 14183–6, 14189–92, 14193–5 and 14198, Perceval to George III; 17, 18, 19, 20 and 23 Feb. 1809; Horner, vol. I, p. 452; *Annual Register*, 1809, p. 128. Captain Sandon was later, on cabinet advice, cashiered from the royal wagon corps—Perceval MSS., Sir David Dundas to Perceval, 6 Apr. 1809.

[2] Buckingham, *Court and Cabinets of George III*, vol. IV, p. 325; Auckland, *Journal*, vol. IV, p. 318; Holland, *Further Memoirs of the Whig Party*, vol. I, p. 29; Colchester, vol. II, p. 169; Horner, vol. I, pp. 454–5.

[3] P.R.O., 30/9/15, Colchester MSS., Perceval to Abbot, 18 Feb. 1809; Colchester, vol. II, p. 167; *Sun*, 20 Feb. 1809.

as that those nearly connected with the throne should exhibit in their own persons the same bright examples of decorous and regular conduct which has characterised His Majesty's reign'. The princess of Wales, urged Melville, must return to Carlton House and the public hear nothing more of Mary Anne Clarke and her kind.[1] Meanwhile Perceval had produced a draft letter in which, at great length, York denied corruption, regretted his adultery, boasted of his services to the army, and asked to be acquitted or put on trial before his peers. The two drafts were circulated together and both were, deservedly, roughly handled. Mulgrave, with sturdy common sense, pointed out that Melville's address amounted to a gratuitous and futile public censure of the royal family's morals. Perceval's draft letter was condemned as far too long and was revised, sentence by sentence, in full cabinet.[2] Even then the duke himself raised further difficulties by refusing to accept the revised version. He was willing to make all reasonable sacrifices, including that of Mrs. Carey, his reigning mistress, but thought the letter too humiliating. Willoughby Gordon made the necessary alterations and, unwillingly, ministers had to accept them.[3] On 23 February the Speaker finally read the letter to the Commons, but with so little apparent effect that Perceval began to lose heart. On the twenty-eighth he confessed to the king that he was 'more and more' convinced that the House would insist on York's removal from office. Members felt that if they voted for acquittal they would only be overwhelmed with petitions and so give impetus to the movement for parliamentary reform. But George III would not hear of any compromise: the 'interests of the Crown' were at stake and his son's name must be entirely cleared. Perceval's first draft of the resolutions to be presented to the Commons cast a 'stigma' on the duke and was returned with instructions that it must be re-written in 'more mild and more general' terms. Not until the day before the debate began was a version produced which satisfied all concerned.[4] Perceval, tired and dispirited, admitted that he did not approach the debate 'with any confidence'. Even the trusty Stephen gave notice that he would vote

[1] Walpole, vol. I, pp. 316–18. These documents are no longer among the Perceval MSS.

[2] Colchester, vol. II, pp. 167–8; Walpole, vol. I, pp. 319–20; Windsor MSS., 14202, Perceval to George III, 23 Feb. 1809.

[3] Perceval MSS., duke of York to Gordon, 20 Feb. 1809; Colchester MSS., P.R.O., 30/9/15, Perceval to Abbot, '¾ p. 3 o'clock' (21 Feb. 1809).

[4] Windsor MSS., 14214–15, 14222–3, 14227, 14233–4, and 14240–1, Perceval to George III, 28 Feb., George III to Perceval, 1 Mar.; Perceval to George III, 2, 3, and 7 Mar. 1809; Colchester, vol. II, p. 168.

(but not speak) against the government. Many other of the ministry's supporters and a majority of the lawyers in the House, he warned Perceval, would also desert on the issue.[1] Worse still, Canning had begun to quarrel with his cabinet colleagues, thinking that the duke ought to retire voluntarily before being compelled to do so by a hostile vote.[2]

The crucial debate opened on 8 March before a packed House, when Wardle spoke for three hours in introducing an address for the removal of the duke. Perceval had intended to speak second but, at the last minute, gave way to Francis Burton, one of the members for Oxford, who, although blind and nearly seventy, had not missed a meeting of the committee and had later had the evidence read over to him two or three times. It was hoped, wrote Perceval to the king, that his 'respectable character, his great experience, and his judicial situation' would impress the Commons. He was followed, on the other side, by Curwen, who was always listened to with respect. Perceval then rose to move that the duke be acquitted of corruption and that an address be sent to the king, regretting York's association with Mrs. Clarke, but praising his past services as commander-in-chief and expressing confidence in his future good behaviour. Perceval began his speech shortly before midnight, was still on his feet when the House adjourned at three o'clock in the morning, and finished what he had to say the following evening. It was, wrote Arthur Wellesley, 'the best speech I ever heard in Parliament': 'I can', said Whitbread, 'with truth say that, in my opinion, a better speech has never been delivered by any living member of the House of Commons.' The Speaker called it 'masterly' and the prime minister sent a special report of it to the king.[3] At 10, Downing Street all was jubilation. 'You may have read Papa's speech,' wrote Fanny. 'Don't you think it excellent? Everybody thinks so, even some of the Oppositionists. Mr. Ryder said they could not even get out their spiteful "Hear Hears". I have just done reading the newspaper, and I think Sir F[rancis] Burdett's speech is the stupidest thing I ever read. He is the only one yet who said Papa's speech was not excellent. He said it was not candid and not fair, and all that.

[1] Perceval MSS., Stephen to Perceval, 3 Mar. 1809.
[2] Walpole, vol. I, pp. 321–4.
[3] Windsor MSS., 14243–4, Perceval to George III, 9 Mar. and 14249, duke of Portland to George III, 9 Mar. 1809; Colchester, vol. II, pp. 170–2; Wellington, *Civil Correspondence*, p. 604; Fremantle, *England in the 19th Century, 1806–10*, p. 261. Perceval's speech was later published as a pamphlet. For Francis Burton see O. B. Cole, *A Biographical Sketch of Francis Burton.*

I am sure there is no candour, or fairness, or anything else *good* in
his speech. Now Whitbread was much better, though (bad's the best)
he owned that it was a very good speech though *he* was not convinced
by it. I don't think it shows very much wisdom in any of them to
doubt about it.' [1] Yet as the debate continued, it became clear that the
main danger threatened from the outraged consciences of the Saints.

On 10 March Wilberforce, Bankes, and Henry Thornton combined
to frame an amendment which cleared the duke of corruption but
called for his removal because of his immoral conduct.[2] Immediately
Perceval reported to Windsor that he feared it would be carried if put
to the vote, and thenceforth government supporters bent their energies
to avoiding a division, except on Wardle's original address. Charles
Yorke suggested a six months' period of suspension, and, when this
was rejected, hinted that the duke ought to resign. Windham, in one
of his best speeches, took the same line in the Commons on 15 March
and, in his report that evening, Perceval finally put the issue plainly
to the king. If, he argued, the duke resigned immediately after the
defeat of Wardle's address, he could be re-appointed as soon as the
excitement had died down. If, however, the Saints' amendment were
carried, he might be excluded from the horseguards for life.[3] The
situation was becoming increasingly involved, for the cabinet's fate
seemed linked with that of the duke, who had let it be known that he
would not resign, even if advised to do so by ministers.[4] A cabinet
meeting in the afternoon of 16 March decided to try to defeat Wardle,
then delay further debate while an attempt was made to persuade the
duke to change his mind. Perceval therefore kept the Commons up
until six in the morning of the seventeenth, defeating Bankes' amendment by 294 votes to 199 and Wardle's original address by 364 to 123.
When the House re-assembled that evening, amidst the tumult of
Irish members fresh from celebrating St. Patrick's day, Perceval's
own motion was finally carried by 278 votes to 196.[5] It was a pyrrhic
victory, for Bathurst had already tabled another hostile motion for

[1] Perceval MSS., *loc. cit.* Wilberforce said Perceval's 'capital speech greatly
changed my opinions as to his guilt, softening though not quite turning me'
(vol. III, p. 403).

[2] Wilberforce, vol. III, p. 404; Colchester, vol. II, p. 173.

[3] Windsor MSS., 14253-4, 14256-7, 14260-1, and 14262-3, Perceval to George
III, 10, 11, 14, and 15 Mar. 1809; Perceval MSS., C. P. Yorke to Perceval,
7 Mar. 1809. On 15 Mar. the *Sun* first reported that the duke was to resign.

[4] See Canning's letter to Perceval of 5 Mar.—Walpole, vol. I, p. 323.

[5] Windsor MSS., 14265-9, Perceval to George III, and George III to Perceval,
16 Mar. 1809.

debate on the following Monday. 'Upon the last vote of the House of
Commons', wrote the independent *Day*, 'we have merely to remark,
that since of 478, the total number of members present, 196 refused
to concur in his complete acquittal, it is high time for His Royal Highness to resign his office of Commander-in-Chief.' Cobbett announced
that he would publish a list of the minority 'printed upon fine and stout
paper, capable of being framed'.[1] Wilberforce was confident of carrying Bathurst's motion, and Perceval gloomily made the same predic-
tion to the king. The government had lost control of the Commons.
On Saturday, 18 March, York at last agreed to resign, George III,
although still convinced of his son's innocence, gave his consent, and
Perceval broke the news to the House on the twentieth.[2]

Public opinion and the Saints had won the day. Constitutional
theorists could still argue that an M.P. was not accountable to anyone
outside the House, but the important division lists hardly supported
the theory. On questions like economic reform and alleged corruption,
members voted under growing pressure from their constituents and
from public feeling in general. The very fact that it was decided to
hold the inquiry before a committee of the whole House reveals how
sensitive all groups had become to public opinion. Beyond this, the
investigation clarified little. It had virtually put a stop to all other
parliamentary business for two months without either establishing or
rejecting the charges against the duke. The final verdict amounted to
one of 'not proven'. Even the method of conducting the inquiry was
unsatisfactory. Mrs. Clarke appeared at the bar twelves times and was
detected in twenty-eight falsehoods, but, under the rules of procedure,
no witness could be examined under oath.[3] The investigation suffered
from excessive publicity and was inevitably very prolonged when
every member had the right to cross-examine witnesses. Neither
government nor opposition emerged with great credit. Perceval,
apart from his final set speech, did not handle the defence well, and
the duke's cause was often best served by backbenchers like Croker,
Denis Browne, and Beresford. Canning disagreed with his colleagues'
tactics in the House and added the case to his growing list of grievances.
The opposition's leaders, horrified by the conduct of their radical
allies, stood irresolutely aside and displeased everyone by their timidity.

[1] *Political Register*, 1 Apr. 1809; *Day*, 20 Mar. 1809.
[2] Windsor MSS., 14272, 14277, 14282-3, Perceval to George III, 17 and 18
Mar. and George III to Perceval, 18 Mar. 1809; Wilberforce, *Life*, vol. III,
p. 405.
[3] *Sun*, 16 Mar. 1809.

Wardle and his supporters, although heavily defeated in division, at first appeared the sole beneficiaries. For several weeks after the inquiry it rained votes of thanks. The common council of the city of London, Westminster, Southwark, Bristol, Liverpool, Manchester, Nottingham, Sheffield, thirty smaller boroughs, and eight counties formally recorded their appreciation of Wardle's efforts. Only in conservative Oxford and in Wardle's own home town of Montgomery, where they knew him too well, were votes of thanks decisively defeated.[1] A special dinner was held in his honour at the London Tavern when he most unjustly accused Perceval of having 'goaded and ill-treated' him during the inquiry.[2] But his hour was brief. That summer he was sued for non-payment of Mrs. Clarke's furniture bill and that star witness turned her talents against him in open court, gaily admitting that she had been bribed to appear against the duke. Her evidence, said Wardle, was worthless, which, presumably, could also apply to that given at the bar of the House.[3] After this, quipped the *Day*, the petitioning counties and boroughs might not get back their votes of thanks or presents of gold, silver, and oak, 'but they will get back their senses'.[4] Most serious in the long run was the bad feeling aroused between fervent government supporters and the Saints. Melville was furious, Eldon, who had 'seen so much of injustice', was still surprised at the hard-heartedness of 'the bloodhounds of St. Stephen's', and even Perceval's own family were shocked. 'Mr. Wilberforce', complained Fanny, 'I do not think has behaved well at all. Papa has hardly proposed a single thing that he has not objected to, and all for the pleasure of contradicting, for he never proposed anything half so good. I wish he would not "Friend" Papa any more and go over at once. It would be much better than as he is now, always ready to contradict anything that is proposed, and never to be of any use.'[5]

Success inspired the reformers to great efforts. Perceval did what

---

[1] *Political Register*, 15 Apr. 1809; *Sun*, 3 Apr. 1809; *Day*, 4 May 1809. For Canning's disapproval see Colchester, vol. II, p. 179.

[2] *Day*, 24 Apr. 1809; Perceval MSS., G. L. Wardle to Perceval, 29 Jan. 1809.

[3] *Annual Register*, 1809, p. 354 ff. Lord Folkestone's reputation suffered even more severely—Creevey, *Life and Times*, pp. 48 and 50; *Creevey Papers*, vol. I, p. 115. When the new Covent Garden theatre was opened in September 1809 the mob still hissed the duke and greeted him with cries of 'Mrs. Clarke' (*The Times*, 19 Sep. 1809).

[4] *Day*, 5 July 1809.

[5] Twiss, vol. II, p. 71; Perceval MSS., Fanny Perceval to Sp. Perceval jun. On 1 Apr. the Percevals defiantly gave 'an elegant dinner' at Downing Street in the duke's honour (*Day*, 1 Apr. 1809).

he could to smother the cry of 'corruption' by ordering the prosecution of Messrs. Kylock, a firm alleged to be trafficking in the sale of public offices and by introducing a bill 'for the further prevention of the brokerage of offices'.[1] But the agitation continued. On 10 February the Commons appointed a committee to inquire into the existence of corrupt practices in East India company patronage.[2] On 17 April Folkestone went much further by proposing a committee to investigate abuses in the army and all departments of state. He succeeded, however, only in alarming his own leaders, all of whom, except Whitbread, either spoke or voted against the motion. For once the *Sun* was full of praise for the whig leaders, stressing that the nation would now see that the Cavendishes, Russells, Grenvilles, and Greys 'do not agree with the Burdetts and Folkestones and Whitbreads in their wild notion of reform'. Folkestone's motion, reported the *Day*, would have established an English Committee of Public Safety, more powerful than the house of commons itself. Yet in radical eyes the debate, like the famous coalition recorded in Hudibras, showed,

> how perfectly the rump
> and Commonwealth, in nature jump.

Moreover the *Morning Chronicle* defied the grandees by supporting Folkestone.[3] More fuel was added to the fire at a meeting on 1 May of the Friends and Advocates of Parliamentary Reform, held in the Crown and Anchor Tavern in the Strand. When the doors were opened at 5 o'clock the struggle for admission was so hectic that all 680 places at table were filled in a few minutes and an overflow meeting had to be held nearby. The radical leaders Burdett, Major Cartwright, Lord Cochrane, Madocks, William Smith, Townshend, Wardle, and Waithman were all present. Burdett in his speech ridiculed Perceval's 'partial measure' against the sale of public offices as 'worse than useless' while Madocks entertained the company with election statistics. Eleven thousand voters returned 257 M.P.s; English and Irish peers created during George III's reign influenced nearly

---

[1] *Day*, 15 July 1809. The bill was re-printed in full in the *Day* on 27 Apr. 1809. The maximum penalty was a fine of £500 (*Parl. Deb.*, XIV, 573).

[2] *Parl. Deb.*, XII, 503. The committee's report implicated Castlereagh. See chapter 13, pp. 214–15.

[3] *Ibid.*, XIII, 822, XIV, 47, 113, and 268; Colchester, vol. II, p. 178; *Sun*, 18 and 19 Apr. 1809; *Day*, 19 Apr. 1809; C. V. Williams, *Perceval*, p. 139. For Perceval's report on the debate see Windsor MSS., 14342–3, Perceval to George III, 18 Apr. 1809.

200 elections; 91 borough-mongers returned 139 members, while peers or the treasury controlled 17 constituencies. 'The whole borough-faction', he ended, amidst cries of 'shame' and 'disgrace', 'returned 327 English members in the House of Commons. There were only 186 tolerably uninfluenced men'.[1]

Three days later Madocks followed up his case by charging Perceval and Castlereagh 'of having, through the agency of the Hon[ourable] H[enry] Wellesley, late Secretary to the Treasury and a late member of this House and also by other agents, been guilty of corrupt and criminal practices in order to procure members to be elected to this Parliament' and moved that the charges be heard at the bar. Perceval, 'rising under evident agitation', said that he could make no reply to the nothing that had been said, and then withdrew. After a heated debate the motion was negatived without a division, but Madocks still threatened to renew the case.[2] 'Mr. Perceval', wrote the chancellor of the exchequer to the king that night, 'must wait, not without some anxiety, till he hears the nature and extent of the statement made against himself and Lord Castlereagh.' Instances 'do unquestionably some-times occur', he admitted, 'in which more communication is had upon such subjects by the Secretaries of the Treasury (under the authority doubtless of the Chancellor of the Exchequer or the First Lord) than what it would be desirable to make the subject of public discussion in Parliament. . . .' The charges, replied the king, were unfair, but 'His Majesty is perfectly convinced that no man can meet them with a clearer conscience than Mr. Perceval'.[3] That Sunday Perceval saw Wilberforce and learnt that Madocks intended to allege corruption at Rye, Queenborough, Cashel, Hastings, and Cambridge.[4] Rye and

---

[1] *Day*, 2 and 4 May 1809; *Sun*, 2 May 1809. Neither *The Times* nor the *Morning Chronicle* reported the meeting. 'I utterly deny', wrote J. W. Ward, 'that the people do wish for parliamentary reform. If they could be polled upon the question, I would stake my existence upon the poll being ten to one against it' (*Letters to Ivy*, p. 93). William Smith, straight from the Crown and Anchor meeting, convulsed the Commons by saying 'And now, gentlemen' (*Parl. Deb.*, XIV, 377).

[2] *Parl. Deb.*, XIV, 381, Colchester, vol. II, p. 181.

[3] Windsor MSS., 14396-9, Perceval to George III, '½ past 11 p.m.' (4 May 1809); George III to Perceval, 6 May 1809. On the eve of the debate Perceval had written to Clive asking him to attend. 'As for the question itself,' replied Clive, 'I have no doubt as to what should be done. A more mischievous subject was never started in the House of Commons. . . . You will be happy to hear that the country, as far as I can learn, thinks as we do on this question of reform' (Perceval MSS., Perceval to Clive, 3 May 1809).

[4] The members concerned were: Rye, earl of Clancarty and Sir John Nicholl;

Hastings, Perceval told the Speaker, had 'always been more or less on the recommendation of the Treasury, which Henry Wellesley might very possibly know about'. Both Queenborough and Cambridge meant nothing to him, but the case of the Irish borough of Cashel was more dangerous. One of its former members, Quintin Dick, had applied for the chiltern hundreds immediately after refusing a hint from the treasury that he should vote for the duke of York's acquittal. Yet Perceval claimed that, far from forcing Dick to vacate his seat, he had seen him after the debate and urged him to continue in parliament. He had therefore decided that he 'must plead not guilty to the whole'.[1] On 11 May Madocks renewed his accusations, but produced nothing more damaging than the resignation of Quintin Dick. When Foster, the Irish chancellor of the exchequer, read a letter from Dick himself denying that the treasury had brought pressure to bear even this looked very thin. In fact Madocks and his supporters had gone too far and quite lost the sympathy of the House. Burdett, in one of his most intemperate speeches, completed their rout. 'Buonaparte', he said, 'has a strong ally in this House.' Immediately the Commons was in an uproar so loud that the boats passing on the river lay upon their oars with surprise at the sudden noise. Tierney then suggested that the case against Perceval was so vague that it should be dropped and the House then divided by 310 to 85 against Madocks' motion.[2] The accusation, reported the *Day*, had been so undefined that every member in succession might just as well have been put on trial as the two ministers concerned and Perceval wrote his report to Windsor in high glee.[3] Yet the Saints had again deserted the government, Wilberforce, Babington, Grant, and Henry Thornton all voting with the minority. The verdict, said Romilly, would do more to hasten parliamentary reform than all the mass meetings in London taverns.[4]

Never, since the turn of the century, had the prospects for reform seemed so bright. There was not a single cabinet minister, wrote the *Day*, who would venture to claim 'that the people of the United Kingdom are adequately represented', while Wilberforce, 'always a

Queenborough, Joseph Hunt and J. C. Villiers; Cashel, Quintin Dick; Hastings, George Canning and Sir Abraham Hume; Cambridge, Edward Finch and Robert Manners.

[1] Colchester, vol. II, pp. 183–4.
[2] *Parl. Deb.*, XIV, 486 and 527; *Day*, 20 May 1809; Colchester, vol. II, p. 186.
[3] *Day*, 6 May 1809; Windsor MSS., 14407–9, Perceval to George III, 12 May 1809.
[4] Wilberforce, vol. III, p. 408; Romilly, vol. II, p. 287.

friend to moderate and temperate reform', was discussing a new series
of Yorkshire county meetings with the old campaigner Christopher
Wyvil.[1] There seemed every chance that a limited bill might pass the
Commons when on 4 May the country gentleman, J. C. Curwen, gave
notice that he intended to introduce such a measure. Perceval, forced
on the defensive, met the notice with 'manly frankness' and 'honourable candour'. The temper of the House, he reported to the king,
was 'very good against reform', but he still feared that the proposal
'termed a regulation, but certainly leading too nearly to reform, will
have a support which, if the details of the bill are what Mr. Perceval
expects them to be, in his opinion it ought not to have'.[2] The terms
of the bill fulfilled his worst fears. Candidates, as well as electors,
were to take an oath against bribery and corruption; it was to be an
offence to sell or to offer to sell any seat in the House; the bribery
laws were to be extended so as to punish any agent or candidate for
giving and any elector for accepting a bribe for his vote, not only
immediately before and during an election, but at any time. All this
moved Windham, the most fervent anti-reformer of them all, to fury,
but Perceval clung to a waiting game and hoped for better things in
committee.[3] In fact, according to the Speaker, ministerialists themselves were divided on the issue, for while Liverpool, Harrowby, Long,
Yorke, Huskisson, and Vicary Gibbs supported it, Rose, Castlereagh,
Perceval, and Arden were hostile.[4] Later Perceval outlined his own
views at length to Abbot. Although he wished that the bill had never
been introduced, 'yet after all that is passed the question cannot remain
as it *was*. It will in future be a perilous thing for a Secretary of the
Treasury to be an agent between a seller and a purchaser of a seat in
Parliament'. What, he asked, would be the verdict of the House on
motions similar to that just moved by Madocks if Curwen's bill
became law? 'In future elections, therefore, it may be questionable
whether prudence may not require that the Treasury should abstain

---

[1] *Day*, 4 May 1809; Wilberforce, vol. III, pp. 408 and 444.

[2] Windsor MSS., 14390–2, Perceval to George III, 4 May 1809; *Day*, 5 May
1809.

[3] *Parl. Deb.*, XIV, 353, 367, and 374; Windsor MSS., 14439–40, Perceval to
George III, 27 May 1809. Windham, once wrote the *Sun*, 'hardly agrees with
anybody for an hour to-gether, as if he thought it a degradation of character to
entertain any notions likely to rise in any mind besides his own' (*Sun*, 17 June
1808). For Windham's views on 'the general tendency to turn the country
into a democracy' see Aspinall, *Lord Brougham and the Whig Party*, p. 38.

[4] Colchester, vol. II, p. 186. Canning was 'disposed towards it, but not
declared'.

from meddling with any interference as to sales of boroughs, and yet whether the practice will not be so far safe that individuals not in office will continue so to deal. Therefore the government will be nearly excluded from the market instead of being, as it is at present, the most favoured customer. Had I no other feeling, therefore, than what the most job-loving minister could have, I should be anxious to find some way out of the difficulties which the recent discussions have created.' Fundamentally he opposed the bill because it threatened to upset the balance of our mixed constitution. Whether, he wrote, 'it should increase the ministerial, or the aristocratical, or the popular influence, I equally should object to it as producing a practical alteration. For tho' a minister, and connected with the aristocracy, I am as a subject of the country more interested in that character for the welfare and permanency of the constitution as it exists with all its admired practical results than I am in any increase of weight to that part with which I may feel at the moment such a connexion, as may give me an interest in its strength; and therefore I should as much dread any increase in ministerial or aristocratical influence, as I should any increase to the democratic weight in the scale of that internal balance which prevails in the House of Commons at the present moment. And it is *change upon any extensive principle* under the expectation of theoretical improvement which I consider as a *reform* and dread as such. Mr. Bathurst says the proposed measure is no reform in the sense in which reform is obnoxious to him, because it does not alter the elective franchise. But why dread the alteration of the elective franchise, except as that alteration might alter the state of the House of Commons? If therefore the law now proposed would exclude in any degree any description of monied interest or any proportion of it which now exists, if it would increase or diminish any other existing interest or influence which now in its degree prevails in the House of Commons, it will in such degree vary the general result from the motley combination of different interests and influences as they at present prevail.' 'I wish', he ended, 'to keep things as they are, or rather as they were before these late discussions.' The bill might, by preventing 'people of character' from buying seats, 'give the monopoly to the less scrupulous'.[1]

In essence Perceval's case was pure conservatism. The constitution,

---

[1] Perceval MSS., Perceval to Abbot, 23 May 1809. The remainder of this interesting letter is printed in Colchester, vol. II, pp. 188 ff. The full text may also be seen in the P.R.O., Colchester MSS., 30/9/15. For a hostile view of Perceval's attitude to reform see J. C Earle, *English Premiers*, pp. 119–20.

evolved by time and the wisdom of our ancestors, had attained perfection. Change, in any form, would only disfigure its beautiful but
fragile form. Yet even Perceval knew that change must come. His role,
as he saw it, was to limit the damage. On 24 May he saw the Speaker
and admitted that some bill must be passed. Already Curwen's draft
had been through its second reading and had gone into committee.
There Perceval proposed a number of amendments, aided by Abbot
himself, who took the unusual course of outlining his own attitude to
the bill in committee. On one point Perceval was adamant. The bill,
as originally drafted, would have made it 'implied' corruption for an
M.P. or minister to promise or offer any office to an elector who voted
for him. The disposal of offices, argued Perceval, must rest somewhere
and nowhere better than in the Crown. This power, he admitted,
created influence, but without it the business of government could not
be carried on. After the amendment had been passed, the opposition
divided against the third reading, polling 83 votes against 98 and then
mustering 85 votes to 97 in a second division that the bill do pass.
Finally Folkestone proposed to amend the preamble so that it read,
'a Bill for more effectually preventing the sale of seats, and for promot-
ing a Monopoly thereof to the Treasury by means of patronage'.[1] The
Act as it emerged from parliament, grumbled the *Edinburgh Review*, was
so much a changeling that Curwen himself would not find a feature
whereby to recognise it. The Saints had, however, been so anxious
to have a bill of some kind that, like an ancient husband longing for
an heir, they were not very curious about the pedigree of their child.[2]
But the *Edinburgh Review*, obsessed by party feeling, failed to see the
real importance of the bill. In its original form it would have undermined the whole system of patronage before the extension of the
franchise and the consequent organisation of disciplined political parties had created the conditions for new methods of government. Even
as amended the bill made vital alterations in the structure of politics.
'Mr. Curwen's bill', wrote Liverpool to Sir William Scott in 1812, 'has
put an end to all money transactions between Government and the
supposed proprietors of boroughs.' Thereafter the treasury controlled
only Harwich and two more boroughs given to it by supporters.
Members who looked for government assistance had to stand for open
boroughs and rely on the 'general influence' of the ministry, 'combined with a reasonable expense on their own part'. Seats were no

[1] *Parl. Deb.*, XIV, 338; Colchester, vol. II, pp. 192–3.
[2] *Edinburgh Review*, Feb. 1811, p. 256.

longer advertised in the press or bought and sold on the open market.[1]
The old order was passing and Perceval, in this instance, saw it more
clearly than the reformers themselves.

The remainder of the 1809 session was equally dominated by reform.
The cabinet got into further stormy water when Sir David Dundas,
the new commander-in-chief, foolishly approved the irregular promotion of Westmorland's son, Lord Burghersh. Colonel Shipley immediately moved a motion of censure in the Commons, the government was defeated, and Westmorland himself had to write to the king
asking him not to sign the warrant.[2] On 15 June Burdett proposed a
radical reform bill, including equal electoral districts with uniform
qualifications, voting to be based on the parish and to be completed in
one day. 'His speech', reported Perceval to Windsor, 'was in every
respect very moderate. It made no impression at all.'[3] He got only
sixteen members to vote with him. Finally Wardle introduced an
economy plan, calculated to save £16½ million a year. But his list
included a one-third cut in the naval estimates and a saving of £2 million by passing catholic emancipation. Huskisson, in one of his most
forceful speeches, soon demolished the scheme as relying on sweeping
changes of policy rather than on administrative reforms.[4]

Altogether it had been a grim session for Pitt's Friends. 'The times,'
wrote Wilberforce, 'are highly alarming. The Duke of York's case,
and Parliament's conduct in it, has infused a general jealousy of public
men. The House of Commons has lost the public confidence; there is
no man of such talents as to take the ascendency like Pitt or Fox.'
'The storm', said Auckland, 'is gathering round us within and with-

[1] Yonge, vol. I, p. 444; Roberts, *The Whig Party*, p. 215. Fremantle, *England
in the Nineteenth Century, 1806–10* (p. 265), argues that Perceval rendered
Curwen's bill 'harmless'.

[2] *Parl. Deb.*, XIV, 670, 671, and 694; Windsor MSS., 1448–9, Westmorland
to George III, 29 May 1809; Perceval MSS., Westmorland to Perceval (undated). 'Great dissatisfaction appeared in the House, Mr. Perceval is sorry to
say, upon this subject' (Windsor MSS., 14426, Perceval to George III, 24 May
1809).

[3] Windsor MSS., 12966–7, Perceval to George III, 15 June 1809 (this letter is
incorrectly endorsed in the Windsor MSS. as '1807'); Earle, p. 121. Harris,
History of the Radical Party (p. 96), gives the list of those who voted with
Burdett as the radical group then in the Commons. They were: Charles Adams,
G. Campbell, G. Knapp, W. A. Madocks, Sir Thomas Turton, H. Combe, Sir
Francis Burdett, C. S. Lefevre, G. L. Wardle, C. C. Western, W. Maxwell,
J. Wharton, S. R. Cuthbert, P. Moore, C. Hutchinson, Tracy Hanbury, and
Henry Thornton.

[4] *Political Register*, 8 July 1809, p. 6. Huskisson's speech was printed in full
in the *Sun* on 27 June 1809.

out, and, instead of having a man like Pitt to defend us, we are in the hands of a set of people who neither know what they mean, nor if they did, have either talent or spirit to pursue it.' [1] Malmesbury thought the session had been the worst attended and most insignificant he could remember, while Carlisle considered that of all the cabinet only Liverpool 'stood respectable'. Perceval had shown himself during the duke of York debates to be 'an evading lawyer, without principle'.[2] The government's weakness in the Commons became daily more apparent. In April Richmond, the lord lieutenant, wanted Huskisson to succeed Sir Arthur Wellesley as Irish secretary but the idea was dropped after both Perceval and Liverpool had objected that such a change might prove fatal to the ministry.[3] Worst of all was the growing indiscipline of government supporters. Early in June the Irish chancellor of the exchequer moved a bill to indemnify excise officers who, by accepting bribes, had defrauded the revenue of £850,000. When the House divided a number of junior ministers abstained and the bill was lost by six votes. 'I have', wrote Perceval to one who offered to resign, 'suffered my political friends, in various departments, to hang loosely round me in the House of Commons, without even a syllable of remonstrance. . . . The experience of this session must have taught, I think, us all that the Government has but little chance of existence through another, if there is not a stronger impression amongst our friends of the necessity of uniform attendance and support.' [4] But soon the restless Canning had put the cabinet beyond salvation.

[1] Wilberforce, vol. III, p. 407; Auckland, *Journal*, vol. IV, p. 319.
[2] Malmesbury, *Diary*, vol. IV, p. 411; Farington, *Diary*, vol. V, p. 170.
[3] Add. MSS., 38737, fol. 307; Huskisson, *Speeches*, pp. 50-1.
[4] Ward, *Memoirs*, vol. I, p. 204; *Parl. Deb.*, XIV, 787-8 and 966; Perceval MSS., Robert Ward to Perceval, 9 June 1809.

CHAPTER THIRTEEN

THE COLLAPSE OF THE PORTLAND MINISTRY

IT was on 24 March 1809, just before the Easter recess, that Canning brought matters to a head by complaining to Portland that the government was no longer equal to the tasks it had to perform. It had forfeited public confidence by its handling of the convention of Cintra, of Moore's last campaign, and of the duke of York case: the cabinet was paralysed by 'a spirit of compromise'. The duke must either reshape his ministry or begin looking for a new foreign secretary.[1] Canning was therefore invited to visit Bulstrode, where, between 4 and 8 April, he discussed his grievances with the prime minister. Castlereagh was unfit to control war policy and Canning 'thought it desirable that changes should also be made in some other departments'—preferably before parliament reassembled for the new session. The duke agreed with so much of this that he offered his own resignation to the king, who, without even asking for an explanation, firmly rejected it.[2] Canning's attack on Castlereagh was unfortunately timed, for a report of the East India patronage committee, presented early in March, had disclosed that in 1805 Castlereagh (then president of the board of control) had placed a writership at Lord Clancarty's disposal to help him gain a seat in parliament. Although the *Sun* immediately denied the charge 'on authority', the independent Scottish member, Lord Archibald Hamilton, gave notice of a motion of censure. The evidence against Castlereagh looked so strong that even the Speaker thought there was a *prima facie* case of breach of privilege, although 'it seemed to be as slight as any supposable case within that description. . . .'[3] Castlereagh was mediocre in debate and was suspected of corruption: Canning was perhaps the best speaker in the Commons and was one of the most successful ministers in the cabinet. There

[1] Colchester, vol. II, p. 220; Ward, vol. I, p. 241; *Annual Register*, 1809, p. 577.

[2] *Bathurst MSS.*, pp. 112–19.

[3] *Parl. Deb.*, XIII (App.), cxxvii and XIV, p. 204; *Sun*, 7 Mar. 1809; Colchester, vol. II, p. 170. The Saints Henry Thornton and Babington voted for the motion and Wilberforce himself was 'long doubtful' before deciding to vote against 'as too severe to turn him out for such an offence' (Wilberforce, vol. III, p. 406).

could be little doubt which of them the duke would choose if he could not keep both. But characteristically Portland sought to avoid making any choice at all. He did nothing until 16 April when, having returned to town, he took Bathurst into his confidence, under the strictest pledge of secrecy. A few days later Bathurst met Canning, stressed that it would be very difficult to reorganise the government while parliament was in session, and urged him not to press his resignation until the next recess. This Canning refused to do, although he agreed to take no further steps before the Commons had debated Hamilton's motion on 25 April.[1] The debate went badly for the government. E. W. Bootle, a Canningite, had promised Perceval and Richard Ryder that he would move the orders of the day, but, at the last moment, he excused himself on the grounds that he was known to be the brother-in-law of Herbert Taylor, the king's private secretary. Canning himself made the most effective speech in Castlereagh's defence. Yet the temper of the House was so hostile that Perceval was forced to accept a conciliatory amendment proposed by the inevitable Bankes, which was carried by the small majority of 214 votes to 167.[2]

Three days later Portland (on Bathurst's advice) broke the news to Camden, again under a pledge of secrecy. Camden agreed that the only solution likely to save the ministry was to sacrifice Castlereagh (as gently as possible) to Canning's demands. Bathurst and Camden therefore tried to approach Canning directly, only to be reminded that all overtures must come through the prime minister.[3] But the duke, too feeble to do anything constructive, remained the apostle of silence. He thought he could solve problems by ignoring them himself and forbidding others to speak of them. Perceval and Liverpool were kept in complete ignorance: Bathurst and Camden were told and then gagged. Only Canning was left free to act and he made full use of his opportunity. Early that spring the foreign secretary began a series of 'confidential communications' with Marquis Wellesley, a known critic of Castlereagh's war policy. Canning listened to and applauded Wellesley's lectures on strategy; repeated the complaints he had made to Portland; and loftily stated 'his desire to introduce Lord Wellesley into the cabinet'—particularly into the war office. In return Wellesley

[1] *Bathurst MSS., loc. cit.; Annual Register, loc. cit.*
[2] *Parl. Deb.,* XIV, 527; Perceval MSS., E. Wilbraham Bootle to Perceval, 23 Apr. 1809; Windsor MSS., 14372-4, Perceval to George III, 'Wed. Morng. ¼ p. 4 A.M.' (26 Apr. 1809). Bootle, although unwilling to move the orders of the day, pledged himself to 'do what I can in mitigation of Lord Castlereagh's punishment'! [3] *Bathurst MSS., loc. cit.*

promised not to support any government from which Canning resigned on the war issue. The Marquis even 'stated to Mr. Canning
that he could cheerfully serve his Majesty in the cabinet if Mr. Canning
should be placed in the situation of First Lord of the Treasury . . .' [1]
Wellesley was the first volunteer in Canning's recruiting campaign.
Late in April the foreign secretary got a pledge of support from Rose,
while after Easter Huskisson began to complain of the want of authority at the treasury and to hint that if Canning resigned he would not
go out of office alone.[2] On 30 April Canning called on the Speaker and
insisted that Portland should resign 'whilst he could bequeath a strong
Government to his successors and to the country'. Castlereagh, he
thought, should have retired after the close vote on Hamilton's motion;
Westmorland and Camden were 'useless lumber'; Chatham, 'perfectly
unmanageable, though a good officer in his department'; Wellesley
might make a good colleague, but not a good prime minister. In fact
both Abbot and Canning agreed that 'the First Lord could never be
so well anywhere as in the House of Commons. . . .' [3] In the same
month Robert Dundas was nominated to succeed Sir Arthur Wellesley
in Ireland, thus creating a vacancy at the board of control. Portland
decided to offer the place, together with a cabinet seat, to Harrowby,
and Perceval was so anxious to have his friend accept that he unconstitutionally sent the news to Staffordshire before George III had approved the overture. But Harrowby refused on grounds of ill-health,
in spite of Bathurst's offer to exchange the board of control for the
less arduous board of trade.[4] This gave Canning a further opportunity of strengthening his position. Before Dundas left for Dublin
Canning told him of his grievances and was assured 'that if I quitted
the Government he should be prepared to do so too'. In May Portland
had almost decided to offer the board of control to the Canningite,
Granville Leveson-Gower, but hesitated because he knew that Canning would press Gower's claims to a seat in the cabinet. Then Sir
James Pulteney asked to be relieved of the office of secretary-at-war.
Harrowby refused the post; C. P. Yorke did the same (on the instructions of his brother, the earl of Hardwicke); but Leveson-Gower

---

[1] Perceval MSS., copy of a statement by Marquis Wellesley forwarded by
W. W. Pole to Perceval, 30 Oct. 1809 and presented to the king 4 Nov.

[2] Add. MSS., 37416, fol. 107; Rose, vol. II, p. 368.

[3] Colchester, vol. II, pp. 179–81.

[4] Harrowby MSS., XI, fols. 222–3, Perceval to Harrowby, 10 Apr. 1809; XII,
fol. 105, Portland to Harrowby, 12 Apr. 1809; IX, fol. 95, Bathurst to Harrowby
(undated).

accepted and was admitted to the cabinet. And finally in July Harrowby consented to forget his ill-health by accepting the board of control, together with a seat in the cabinet and an English earldom.[1] It was becoming increasingly difficult for the Portland ministry to make any major decisions without upsetting the delicate balance of forces within the cabinet.

The situation was already beyond the duke's powers, and he realised it. On 10 May Portland (on the advice of Bathurst and Canning) renewed his offer of resignation to George III. This time the king demanded an explanation and so learnt the full story of Canning's discontent. It was rumoured that the duke proposed Chatham as his successor as first lord with Wellesley as secretary of state for war and the colonies. But, reported Canning to the Speaker, the king 'did not seem much to give in to it', preferring to find his own solution.[2] For in the last resort he was still the chief executive, with the power to settle disputes between his own servants. On 24 May Portland confided in Eldon, who was thought to be the fittest person to consult with the king. There was little scope for further delay. Canning was rightly beginning to get impatient and pressed for some decision before the year's military plans were approved. The idea of an attack on Walcheren was already so far advanced that Castlereagh had provisionally offered the command to Chatham. On 25 May Canning saw the duke, told him that he was more than ever determined to force the issue, and that he would lay his resignation before the king at the next levee. 'If it cannot be prevented,' wrote the alarmed duke to Eldon, 'I see nothing but ruin to the country and to Europe, and so I told him most plainly and distinctly.'[3] A week later the foreign secretary had his audience with George III, who commanded him to remain in office until his majesty had had time to suggest a solution. The royal plan, as outlined to Portland on 5 June, was ingenious but hardly sound. Responsibility for the war in Europe was to be transferred to the foreign secretary, while Castlereagh was to remain colonial secretary and was to be offered the then vacant board of control. These

---

[1] Add. MSS., 38737, fol. 364, Canning to Huskisson, 2 Oct. 1809; Perceval MSS., Portland to Perceval, 18 May and 3 July; Windsor MSS., 14490–1, Portland to George III, 18 June; Harrowby MSS., II, fol. 69, George III to Portland, 3 July 1809; *Dropmore MSS.*, IX, p. 311.

[2] *Bathurst MSS.*, *loc. cit.*; Colchester, vol. II, pp. 185–6.

[3] Twiss, vol. II, pp. 79–80; Castlereagh, *Correspondence and Despatches*, vol. IV, p. 256. On 18 May the *Day* reported rumours that both Castlereagh and Mulgrave had resigned.

changes were not to take effect until the end of the session, nor were they intended to deprive Castlereagh of control of any expedition then under discussion. Worst of all the king and Portland again 'directed that they who were acquainted with what passed should not disclose it before the prorogation to anyone, not even to any of their colleagues'. 'I wish you to impress upon His Majesty', wrote Portland to Eldon on 7 June, 'that if this storm is laid, it must be his act; it must be his authority alone that can keep everything quiet.' [1]

Canning, although flattered by the king's attention, was disappointed by the terms of the royal plan. It took until the thirteenth to persuade him to accept it and then he did so with misgivings and '*simply* out of deference to a suggestion of the *King's*'.[2] Two days later Castlereagh outlined the plan of the Walcheren expedition to George III, at the same time formally proposing Chatham for the command.[3] If the expedition were a success, it seemed possible that Portland might still be succeeded by another Pitt. But Canning was not prepared to wait for that. On 18 June, three days before the end of the session, he wrote to the prime minister asking that the king's plan be put into execution. The duke hedged until the twenty-first before assuring him that the plan would be carried through and that Camden had been commanded to prepare Castlereagh for the change. That afternoon the cabinet met, considerd Mulgrave's decisive report on the chances of landing troops on Walcheren, and unanimously decided to go ahead with the expedition.[4] Only five out of the eleven cabinet ministers who took that decision could have realised how grossly unfair it was to Castlereagh. But the king had ordered them to remain silent and they all loyally obeyed.

As soon as the cabinet meeting had ended Portland asked Perceval to call on him the following morning, when he outlined all the negotiations since 24 March. Perceval immediately insisted that, after the cabinet decision of the previous day, the king's plan would have to be abandoned.[5] On Sunday, 25 June (after having seen both Bathurst and Eldon), he protested to Canning against the 'extreme hardship

[1] *Annual Register*, 1809, p. 579; *Bathurst MSS., loc. cit.*; Twiss, vol. II, pp. 80–1.

[2] Perceval MSS., Canning to Perceval, 26 June 1809.

[3] Windsor MSS., 14478–9, Castlereagh to George III, 15 June 1809.

[4] *Annual Register*, 1809, p. 580; Windsor MSS., 14498–9, Castlereagh to George III, 21 June 1809.

[5] Colchester, vol. II, pp. 201–4. Lord Sidmouth told the Speaker on 24 June that Castlereagh might go as envoy to Spain and be succeeded as secretary of state by Wellesley (Colchester, vol. II, p. 198).

not to say injustice' of any reshuffle before the conclusion of the Walcheren campaign. Castlereagh would never accept the royal plan —'if he does it is no business of mine to suggest, nor shall I suggest to him, any opinion that he should not acquiesce in it'. But if Castlereagh resigned on the issue, 'I shall certainly not be able to withhold from him, if he asks it, my opinion of the extreme hardship of the proceeding, a hardship to which I must say, . . . I cannot, with my feelings of what is due to a colleague, consent to appear to be a party . . .'[1] Canning's reply was frigid and concise. He liked the king's plan as little as Perceval and had always protested against the policy of secrecy. Portland, he argued, had taken Camden into his confidence as the fittest person to break the news to Castlereagh. 'If Lord Camden has not done this, I dare say he has had good reasons for it. But it is needless to say that it is no fault of mine, and I cannot believe it to be any fault of the Duke of Portland's.' All this, as Perceval emphasised in return, did nothing to explain the concealment from other leading members of the cabinet. Had he been the one to insist on Castlereagh's removal, wrote Perceval, he would have urged the prime minister to consult Canning before any decision was reached. Already Perceval had realised the threat to his own and to his supporters' positions if a cabal within the cabinet could take such vital decisions in secret. For the moment, however, he refrained from pressing the point. On Canning's suggestion they both outlined their ideas to the duke. Perceval repeated his protest against the king's plan, adding pointedly that he could not but feel that what had happened to Castlereagh 'might happen to me or any other of the King's servants when they least expected it': Canning remonstrated against the continued concealment and delay.[2] He saw the king on 28 June and again unsuccessfully tendered his resignation. Camden, he was assured by the duke, was to break the news to Castlereagh as soon as the expedition had sailed. Yet within a week Camden was explaining to Portland why he felt unable to propose the king's plan to Castlereagh.[3] In the face of such marked lack of enthusiasm from all concerned the royal plan was quietly forgotten.

In order to find an alternative the duke of Portland had, early in July, taken Chatham, Liverpool, and Harrowby into his confidence.

[1] Perceval MSS., Perceval to Canning, 'Sunday Morning' (25 June 1809).
[2] *Ibid.*, Canning to Perceval, 26, 27 and 28 June 1809; Perceval to Canning, 26 and 28 June 1809; Perceval to Portland, 26 June 1809; *Annual Register*, 1809, p. 580.
[3] Perceval MSS., Portland to Perceval, 3 July 1809.

Only Mulgrave, Westmorland, and the unfortunate Castlereagh himself appear to have remained in complete ignorance. But the wider became the circle of the prime minister's advisers, the further he got from finding a generally acceptable solution. Liverpool was furious at not having been consulted earlier and wrote a letter of protest to Windsor, while Chatham insisted that Castlereagh should be told nothing until after the Walcheren expedition. Beyond this the duke received little but offers of resignation. Liverpool suggested that if he retired, Castlereagh could be made home secretary and leader of the house of lords; Bathurst wished to be succeeded by Westmorland at the board of trade so that Castlereagh could be offered the privy seal; and Camden was willing to resign and try and persuade his brother-in-law to become lord president of the council on condition that no change was made during the expedition. The king and Portland finally decided to accept Camden's plan, with the important addition that Wellesley was to be the next war and colonial secretary.[1] It was a compromise which satisfied neither Perceval nor Canning.

'This cursed business haunts me,' wrote Perceval to Harrowby on 13 July. 'Why? Because I have been endeavouring to reconcile myself to it by some expedient which is not satisfactorily justifiable and honourable towards Castlereagh.' The war minister was to be sacrificed because his colleagues feared the ruin of the government. They had therefore approved a conclusive arrangement for Castlereagh's removal, and pledged themselves to stand by it, before the victim himself knew anything about the matter. The same day Perceval wrote to the duke clarifying his own position. 'My pledge', he wrote, 'cannot as at present advised go further than this—that I will do anything in my power, submit *to any* arrangement, however affecting myself (I mean by that contentedly remain with any First Lord of the Treasury over me, from amongst ourselves, not excluding Wellesley) provided Castlereagh by such arrangement can be kept amongst us, but cannot pledge myself to consent to any arrangement decisive of Lord C's fate, until I know how Lord C. himself will receive it. And I will pledge myself to use my best endeavours to prevail upon him to acquiesce in it.'[2] Canning discussed the new scheme with Portland on 5 July, and again late on the evening of the eleventh when he left apparently

[1] Perceval MSS., Camden to Perceval, 11 July 1809; *Bathurst MSS.*, pp. 91 and 98–9; Windsor MSS., 14521–4, Liverpool to George III, 11 July 1809; Add. MSS., 38243, fols. 124–7.

[2] Harrowby MSS., XI, fols. 224–5, Perceval to Harrowby, 31 July 1809; Perceval MSS., Perceval to Portland, 13 July 1809.

'satisfied with the state to which the business is brought. . . .' Therefore at the levee held on the twelfth Camden offered his resignation to the king. But the duke had again been involved in a failure of communication. The foreign secretary discovered, too late, that Camden's plan was not to take effect until after the end of the expedition. For a week Canning argued against this further delay. On 18 July he formally reminded the duke that he neither suggested nor supported the idea of concealing the negotiations from Castlereagh, and that 'so far from desiring it, I conceived, however erroneously, Lord Camden to be the sure channel of communication to Lord Castlereagh; and that up to a very late period I believed such communication to have been actually made'. On the main issue of responsibility for the concealment Canning was, as Portland admitted, quite right. But how could Canning ever have really believed that Camden had broken the news to Castlereagh? 'From whom indeed', asked the duke, 'would it have been necessary to conceal it when it was once made known to him?' On 30 July Canning finally 'most reluctantly, and I confess against my better judgement' accepted the Camden plan.[1]

Thereafter negotiation (however ineptly handled) gave way to intrigue. The duke's strength was fast failing: soon Pitt's Friends would have to face the problem of finding his successor. Canning, still in search of possible allies, renewed his informal talks with Wellesley. As early as 28 April the foreign secretary had proposed the marquis as special envoy to Spain. News of the appointment appeared and was welcomed in the press on 1 May. But the ambassador's departure was long delayed by ill-health, aggravated by his wife's refusal to let him take to the Peninsula his 'common whore', Sally Douglas.[2] And the longer Wellesley delayed leaving England, the less inclined he felt to leave at all. He had never wanted to go to Spain in the first instance and had only consented because Canning insisted that the embassy would prepare him for admission to the cabinet. Consequently, during the discussions on the new plan Canning argued that Wellesley should be told before he left England that he was to be the next war and colonial secretary. But his colleagues opposed the request, Perceval giving his qualified pledge on 13 July only on condition that Wellesley should be kept in ignorance. This was already

---

[1] *Annual Register*, 1809, pp. 565 and 581-2; Perceval MSS., Portland to Perceval, 11 July 1809; Add. MSS., 38243, fol. 128.
[2] Windsor MSS., 14377-9, Canning to George III, 28 Apr. 1809; *Sun* and *Day*, 1 May 1809; Lord Hylton, *The Paget Brothers*, p. 143.

impossible, for Canning had then told him 'that an arrangement was in contemplation for vacating the seals held by Lord Castlereagh, and for calling Lord Wellesley to that situation'. On the eighteenth the foreign secretary renewed his demand that Wellesley should be officially informed of his impending promotion. Portland therefore referred the matter to the king, who decided in favour of silence and Canning promised the duke that he 'implicitly' accepted that decision.[1] Yet immediately before Wellesley left London, Canning assured him 'that it was positively determined to make the proposed arrangement for the War Department. . . .' The pair further decided that the Spanish embassy should not last more than two months and that 'if Mr. Canning should resign, Lord Wellesley should be favoured with the earliest notification of His Majesty's permission to return to England'.[2] Nothing of this was mentioned either to the king or the cabinet. The scramble for the leadership of the party had begun: the first victim was Canning's good faith.

On 28 July the Walcheren expedition sailed from England, carrying with it the ministry's fading hopes of survival. Ministers hoped for a brief respite while Chatham tried to beat the French and Camden tried to conciliate Castlereagh. Neither made much progress. During the first week of August Portland repeatedly saw Camden, 'who endeavoured by every argument he could adduce to convince the Duke of Portland of the disadvantages to which the measure would be exposed by his being entrusted with the management of it'. In the end Portland, although unconvinced, had to write to the king offering to break the news to Castlereagh himself. He suggested that it should be done before the result of the expedition was known, for if it failed, the time would be very 'inauspicious' for reshaping the cabinet. The king, anxious not to 'become a principal' in the affair, gave the duke full authority to act as he thought best, as long as he consulted the waverers in the cabinet before taking any major decision.[3] But within a week the unhappy duke had a paralytic stroke while in his carriage near Bulstrode. For a time he lost consciousness and all power of speech, and, although he rallied surprisingly well, it was obvious that he could not go on much longer. At a levee on 16 August the king warned both Bathurst and Liverpool that ministers must begin looking

[1] Perceval MSS., Portland to Perceval, 11 July and Perceval to Portland, 13 July 1809; Windsor MSS., 14540–1, Portland to George III, 21 July 1809.

[2] Perceval MSS., undated copy of Wellesley's statement.

[3] Windsor MSS., 14556–7, Portland to George III, 6 Aug. 1809; 14558, George III to Portland, 7 Aug. 1809.

for a new first lord while Perceval discussed the same delicate subject with Eldon.[1] Two days later Huskisson's sudden threat of resignation forced Perceval to act.

'It is not because the Duke of Portland is at our head,' he told Huskisson, 'that the Gov[ernment] is a Gov[ernment] of departments; but it is because the Gov[ernment] is and must be essentially a Gov[ernment] of departments that the D[uke] of P[ortland] is at our head, and is the best head possibly that we could have. I very much doubt us continuing long under any other.' The existing cabinet was composed of so many members of equal or nearly equal importance to its continuance that there was little scope for a 'strong' prime minister. Any powerful member of the cabinet could, by a threat of resignation, create a situation likely to end in the collapse of the entire government. The prime minister could himself use similar tactics, provided that he thought the issue under discussion sufficiently important to risk the continuance of his ministry. In such circumstances he could persuade, manage, and, in the last resort, blackmail his colleagues: but he could have little effective or consistent authority over them. 'It is a state of things certainly', confessed Perceval, 'which makes the principal situation in Government, the place of Prime Minister, very far from desirable, and it makes it one in which I cannot conceive any man desirous of having it, except it was with the perfect conviction that his leading colleagues wished him there. . . . Such a persuasion of itself would alter the situation. . . .' But the immediate problem was to find some successor to the duke. 'After what I have said you will be prepared readily to believe that I am not desirous of being a candidate to succeed him.'

The most acceptable nominees seemed to be either Harrowby or Bathurst. Huskisson however quite legitimately reserved the right to make his own decision when Portland retired. Canning had not yet stated his intentions: until he did so nothing definite could be decided.[2] Therefore on 28 August Perceval made the first direct approach to the foreign secretary. 'The principal question is,' he wrote, 'is it desirable

[1] Buckingham, *Court and Cabinets of George III*, vol. IV, p. 348; Twiss, vol. II, pp. 77–8.

[2] Perceval MSS., Perceval to Huskisson, 21 Aug. 1809; Huskisson to Perceval, 24 Aug. 1809. It is impossible to discover how much Huskisson knew of the crisis in the cabinet. He had been in close contact with Canning since Easter (Add. MSS., 37416, fol. 107) and as Canning had discussed his grievances with Wellesley, Abbot, Robert Dundas, Rose and Bagot, it is unlikely that he would have kept Huskisson in ignorance. For the reasons given by Huskisson for his threat of resignation see chapter 18, pp. 343–4.

to preserve the present Government with as little alteration as possible? If we all think it is, and are all really desirous that it should be
done, I feel pretty confident that it may; but we certainly have little
strength which we can afford to lose; and I do not think much time
can safely be lost in considering the necessary arrangements.' Dundas, disgusted by the government's weakness, had given 'conditional
notice to quit'; the news from Walcheren got steadily worse; and
although Castlereagh still did not know that he was under sentence of
removal, he could hardly be kept in ignorance much longer. Yet if
ministers could agree on a successor to the duke, Castlereagh's removal
from the war department could be represented as part of a general
cabinet reshuffle. Perceval had originally intended to suggest Harrowby as the new prime minister, but when Harrowby himself learnt this
'he so peremptorily declined having anything to do with it' that
Perceval was forced to redraft his letter. In this second version he
pledged himself to serve 'under anyone, whom it appears to me at
present to be at all likely you and the rest of my colleagues would be
satisfied to see at our head'—provided that such candidate would 'par-
take a little more of the responsibility of the Treasury, than I conceive
the D[uke] of P[ortland] to do'.[1] But Canning was not easily drawn.
After the first exchange of letters, he declined to discuss the question
of Portland's successor, until commanded to do so by the duke himself. Canning's personal position was strong. His seventeen personal
followers in the Commons included Leveson-Gower, a cabinet minister, Huskisson of the treasury, and two junior ministers, Bagot and
Sturges Bourne. In addition he had pledges of support from Wellesley,
Rose, and Robert Dundas, who controlled the vital Scottish votes.
If this coalition held together, no Pittite ministry could hope for a
majority in the Commons, unless it had Canning's support. Portland's
disastrous policy of silence had handicapped everyone except Canning,
who ignored it whenever it conflicted with his own interests. Now he
felt reasonably secure the foreign secretary refused to stray one inch
from the paths of constitutional rectitude.[2] But once assured that Perceval was not plotting with his cabinet colleagues and that the king
himself had recommended such discussion, Canning agreed to break
his silence. 'I have for some time been convinced,' he wrote on

---

[1] Perceval MSS., Perceval to Canning, 28 Aug. 1809 and 'Tuesday Morning'
(28 Aug.).
[2] *Ibid.*, Canning to Perceval, 28 and 29 Aug. 1809; Aspinall, *The Canningite
Party*, pp. 222–3.

31 August, 'and every month's experience tends to confirm that conviction more and more, that a *Minister*—and that Minister in the *House of Commons*—is indispensable to the well-carrying on the King's Government in these times.' [1] He was no longer prepared to accept any member of the house of lords as Portland's successor. For, as he later confessed to Rose, had he agreed to the appointment of any third person, 'he should have given up the lead in administration almost for ever, as Lord Bathurst and Lord Harrowby were very little older than himself'. Both Wellesley and Chatham (Canning's earlier nominee) were also out of the running. The choice lay between Perceval and himself, and, he added, 'I should not think it possible to remain in office, under the change which would necessarily be produced in my situation by the appointment of a First Minister in the House of Commons, even in your person.' Canning, in brief, would serve as prime minister or he would not serve at all: seldom can a claim to the treasury have been more concisely and bluntly stated. Perceval, distracted by his wife's illness after she had given birth to a still-born child, and surprised and uncertain of his own position, declined to comment before he had consulted his brother and Liverpool. 'I always thought it actually out of the question', he confessed', 'that you would acquiesce in the choice falling on me. . . .' [2]

On Saturday, 2 September, the news reached London that Chatham had abandoned the idea of attacking Antwerp and that Sir Arthur Wellesley's army had retreated across the Tagus. That afternoon Perceval showed his recent correspondence with Canning to Liverpool, who refused to give any decisive opinion until he had had time to consider the issue more fully. But in the evening Canning wrote to the prime minister demanding the immediate fulfilment of the king's promise to appoint Wellesley to the war office. This letter reached Bulstrode early on Sunday morning, when the duke, alarmed by the speed with which Canning had acted, immediately sent for Bathurst. Together they decided that the duke should not mention the matter to George III until the next levee to be held on the following Wednesday. They then forwarded the news to Perceval, Eldon and Camden. [3] The chancellor of the exchequer was spending the day at Elm Grove, Ealing,

---

[1] *Ibid.*, Perceval to Canning, 30 Aug. 1809 and Canning to Perceval, 31 Aug.; Campbell, vol. VII, p. 223.

[2] Rose, vol. II, p. 379; Perceval MSS., Perceval to Canning, 31 Aug. 1809; *Gent. Mag.*, Aug. 1809, p. 787.

[3] *Annual Register*, 1809, p. 582; Perceval MSS., Portland to Perceval, 3 Sep. 1809.

trying to decide what he should do about Canning's claim to the premiership. In the afternoon he received a long letter from Liverpool urging him to stand firm and hinting that Canning would never be accepted by the rest of the cabinet. Perceval however remained undecided. 'My own conviction is', he wrote to Arden that evening, 'that to attempt to form a Government of our present friends with myself at the head of it, without Canning, would be to deceive the King and do injustice to the country and to ourselves. I know it is the opinion of many of us (in which I however do not agree) that it would be equally hopeless to make the same attempt under Canning without me.' Either Canning must be brought to accept a peer as first lord or Perceval would have to accept the home office leaving Canning as prime minister, chancellor of the exchequer and leader of the House. 'I think', continued Perceval, 'that I am ready for the King's service to sacrifice every feeling of personal pride or vanity which might be wounded by such an event. But public men are, for their means of public utility, the creatures in great measure of public opinion; and if, as I fear would be the case, such a sacrifice would be felt by my friends and by the public as a degradation, which I ought not to submit to, the submitting to it might much abridge any means of future service to the King, the country and myself.' [1]

Later that evening Portland's letter reached Ealing and Perceval realised that unless he acted quickly the game would be lost. On the following morning he saw Arden, who finally persuaded him not to give way to Canning. At the last minute Bathurst, Liverpool, and Perceval agreed to act together and to run the risk of losing Canning. Perceval therefore wrote to the foreign secretary renewing his offer to serve under any third person, but refusing to accept the 'degradation' of having to surrender both the exchequer and the leadership of the House of Canning. Then, with Bathurst's and Liverpool's approval, he tactfully and successfully suggested that Portland should renew his offer to resign. On 5 September Perceval saw Bathurst who agreed that, as the duke was now bound to resign and the government seemed likely to collapse, it would be useless and foolish to sacrifice Castlereagh. The anti-Canningite group in the cabinet was at last risking a decisive stand. Twenty-four hours later Bathurst saw the king, told him that Portland was to offer his resignation at the levee that day, and urged him to accept it in spite of the risk of a cabinet

---

[1] Perceval MSS., Liverpool to Perceval, 3 Sep. 1809; Perceval to Arden, 3 Sep.

crisis. George III, wrote Bathurst, 'was anxious to keep Mr. Canning, who he thought essential to his Government, but if he was driven to choose between the two, he would choose Mr. Perceval, who was the most straightforward man he had almost ever known'.[1] While Bathurst was closeted with the king, the duke met Canning to tell him that the Camden plan could not be carried through without destroying the ministry and that he was about to resign. The foreign minister immediately hinted that he himself would retire and refused to attend the cabinet held the following day. At this meeting several topics were discussed which particularly affected the foreign office. Over dinner that evening Castlereagh pressed Camden so strongly to explain Canning's absence that he finally learnt the story of the negotiations. 'I flatter myself', wrote Camden to Perceval, 'I set his friends right with him, tho' I fear I have not succeeded in doing so with respect to myself. . . .' The following morning Castlereagh saw Portland and then sent his resignation to Windsor.[2] The inglorious Portland ministry had finally blundered to destruction. It had been an unconscionable time dying and it left a legacy of frustrated ambitions and suspicion which threatened to split Pitt's Friends from top to bottom.

[1] *Ibid.*, Perceval to Canning, undated (4? Sep.); Perceval to Portland, 4 Sep.; Portland to Perceval, 4 Sep.; *Bathurst MSS.*, *loc. cit.*; Yonge, vol. II, pp. 288. Liverpool wrote to Wallace on 23 Sep.—'It occurred to *me* that the best means of obviating the various difficulties . . . was by persuading the Duke of Portland to retire.'

[2] *Annual Register*, 1809, p. 582; Colchester, vol. II, pp. 201–4; Perceval MSS., Camden to Perceval, 'Friday morning 2 a.m.' (8 Sep.); Windsor MSS., 14597–8, Castlereagh to George III, 8 Sep.

CHAPTER FOURTEEN

THE DUEL

ALTHOUGH by 8 September the government had lost its first lord, its
secretary of state for war and the colonies, and seemed likely soon to
lose its foreign secretary, the public had no clear idea of the gravity
of the political crisis. There were rumours of resignations after the
news got round that the king had granted audiences to every member
of the cabinet on 6 September, but reliable information about events
was scarce. The ministerial press remained discreetly silent and the
rest relied largely on guess-work. *The Times* still blandly assumed that
Chatham was about to become first lord: as late as the twelfth it was
calling on Perceval and Canning, the only two ministers of talent,
to quit so hopeless a cabinet. The *Day* began to print rumours on
the seventh, but a week later could do no better than suggest that
Harrowby was to become prime minister, Tierney chancellor of the
exchequer,[1] Leveson-Gower secretary of state for war, and Perceval
lord chancellor. Castlereagh, it informed its readers, was to stay in the
cabinet, 'where his influence has been strengthened by the Wellesley
interest'. Chatham was said to have resigned, but there were no candidates for the vacant ordnance, perhaps, it was suggested, because it
was deemed impossible 'to find one equal to his Lordship in vigour
and promptitude'. The following day it was 'confidently stated' that
Whitbread was to enter the cabinet, as the most likely person to
improve relations with the United States.[2] On 9 September even so
close a supporter of Perceval as James Stephen was still in the dark
and forced to rely on odd paragraphs in the *Morning Chronicle*. The
ministry, he warned his friend, was steadily losing ground in public
opinion; if Perceval's personal reputation was not also to suffer, he
must persuade his colleagues to support 'liberal and humane measures
to conciliate the country'.[3]

In fact ministers were in complete confusion and Perceval himself

---

[1] On 25 September Tierney was still writing to Whitbread that 'I do not
even know, what a number of my friends are sure of, that I am Chancellor of
the Exchequer and have been so this last week' (Creevey, *Life and Times*,
pp. 44–5).　　[2] *The Times*, 6, 7 and 12 Sep. 1809; *Day*, 7 14 and 18 Sep. 1809.
[3] Perceval MSS., James Stephen to Perceval, 9 Sep. 1809.

fully occupied in trying to hold together as many of Pitt's Friends as possible. George III accepted Portland's resignation on the sixth 'in the kindest manner', stressing that only concern for the duke's health made him willing to accept the offer and asking the prime minister to stay in office until arrangements had been made to appoint his successor.[1] On 8 September Castlereagh insisted that he too must go, although he hoped that his resignation would not 'be the means of preventing the King from keeping his present servants'. Thereafter hopes of averting a complete collapse depended on Canning's attitude and on the last-minute efforts being made to keep him and Perceval together in the same cabinet. Canning, in a letter to Portland written on the morning of the seventh, formally withdrew his demand for the execution of the Camden plan because of the 'unexpectedly increased difficulties' of fulfilling it. The duke immediately forwarded the letter to Perceval and had a long interview with Canning, urging him not to resign, but making no visible impression upon him. That afternoon Perceval wrote direct to the foreign secretary to assure him that he had never threatened to quit the government if the Camden plan were put into operation. The duke's resignation, argued Perceval, far from increasing the problems, opened 'a reasonable way out of the difficulties which might otherwise have attended the arrangement proposed with respect to Lord Castlereagh and Lord Wellesley'.[2] The following day Canning again met Portland and told him that he had 'deliberated very anxiously' on all that had passed between them at their previous interview before deciding to send the duke a full disclosure of his attitude to the crisis. This, Canning stipulated, must be shown to the king before any other member of the cabinet was allowed to see it. In the meantime there seemed to be little that the foreign secretary's colleagues could do except wait and hope. Eldon, summoned to town by the king, arrived late that evening and immediately called on Perceval and Liverpool.[3] All that Perceval could show him was a letter he had received that afternoon from Canning, written in the coldest and most discouraging terms. Perceval's letter of 7 September, argued Canning, showed that he would only have accepted the Camden plan on condition that it formed part of a much wider reshuffle of the cabinet following the first lord's resignation. Yet the king had assured Canning

[1] *Ibid.*, Perceval to Arden, 9 Sep. 1809.
[2] *Ibid.*, Perceval to Canning, 7 Sep. 1809 and Perceval to Arden, 9 Sep. 1809.
[3] Windsor MSS., 14599, Eldon to George III, 9 Sep. 1809; *Bathurst MSS.*, *loc. cit.*

Q

two months previously that the Camden plan would be put into operation at the end of the Walcheren campaign and had given the assurance without adding any conditions for its fulfilment. Canning did not impute 'the slightest blame' to Perceval, who had every right to stipulate terms under which alone he would accept a plan to whose adoption he was not originally a party. Equally Canning reserved the right to withdraw his demand for its execution.[1] In spite of Canning's negative attitude, Perceval made one more effort to avoid a final breach. He would not object under any circumstances, he replied, to Wellesley's joining the cabinet. He had, throughout, opposed any scheme to remove Castlereagh from the war office under conditions which would not have placated Castlereagh himself: a wholesale cabinet reorganisation gave the best chance of accomplishing this. How, asked Perceval, could such a view be said to have increased the difficulties of executing the Camden plan? He had certainly not produced his arguments at the last minute for he had first put them to Canning as early as 25 June and had repeated them, at greater length, in his letter to Portland of 13 July.[2] In confirmation of this Perceval enclosed a copy of his letter to the duke. Once more, however, the unfortunate Portland had bungled matters. Perceval's letter of 13 July, wrote Canning, was clearly crucial, but the duke had neither shown him a copy nor even mentioned it. There now seemed, Perceval told the Speaker on 9 September, little hope of preventing the government's collapse: such slender chances as remained all depended on the tone of Canning's promised statement to the duke. 'What will be done', wrote Perceval to his brother, 'in the event of Canning's not consenting to some third person is as yet undetermined. I rather conceive, but this is quite between ourselves, that the King will be advised to direct me to write to Lord Grey, and to endeavour with him to arrange some Government upon a proper understanding. This I confess I do not like, but what is there in any part of the business that one can like at all?'[3]

For three more days the surviving ministers waited for Canning's decision. On 10 September he met Perceval and left him with little doubt of his intention to resign. 'When you are First Lord as well as Chancellor of the Exchequer', he assured his harrassed colleague, 'you will be double yourself in strength in the House of Commons, and

[1] Perceval MSS., Canning to Perceval, 8 Sep. 1809.
[2] *Ibid.*, Perceval to Canning, 8 Sep. 1809.
[3] *Ibid.*, Canning to Perceval, 9 Sep. 1809 and Perceval to Arden, 9 Sep. 1809; Colchester, vol. II, p. 200.

you may go on without me.' This, wrote Arbuthnot to Huskisson,
was nonsense, for without Canning 'the business of Parliament could
not be carried on'. Canning, fumed Eldon, was 'vanity in a human
form'.[1] Finally on the twelfth Portland received the foreign secretary's
statement. The first lord's resignation had deprived the Camden plan
of 'all its benefit'. It would be useless to attempt to patch up the
government 'by merely filling up your Grace's situation', since no
one else could hope to carry on the duke's role. Moreover an administration of departments with an elective head was inadequate for the
country's needs. As a prime minister in the house of commons was
essential, Canning recommended 'the devolution of your Grace's
office on Perceval'. 'I should', he ended, 'see this arrangement without
the smallest dissatisfaction or regret.' Canning himself must resign,
but he would retire with 'the most sincere and undiminished personal
goodwill' towards the new prime minister.[2] The next day George III
handed Canning's letter to Perceval with instructions to lay it before
those of his colleagues who had not or who were not about to resign.
In order to stiffen their resolution the king granted audiences on
14 September to all cabinet ministers then in London, urging them,
wrote Eldon, 'in language that makes my heart bleed for him', not to
leave the Crown at the mercy of the opposition. That evening Perceval,
Liverpool, Eldon and several junior ministers held an informal meeting at the treasury without reaching any decision. There seemed not a
ray of hope, Eldon told his wife, that any satisfactory or lasting solution could be found.[3] Even the holding of a full cabinet meeting
proved unexpectedly difficult. Perceval had written on the evening of
the thirteenth asking all concerned to return to London, but had to
admit to the king on the fifteenth that Harrowby had not left Staffordshire and that Eldon had just set off for Berkshire to attend his sister-in-
law's funeral. The lord chancellor, commented one observer, seemed
destined to return from his relative's graveside to his own political
burial service. Indeed Eldon himself seemed inclined to agree. The
morning of 15 September was spent in fruitless discussion of every
possible type of coalition government, most of which the lord chancellor 'greatly abhorred'. His last act before setting off for Berkshire

[1] Colchester, vol. II, pp. 201-4; Add. MSS., 38737, fol. 321; Twiss, vol. II,
p. 90.
[2] Canning's letter is printed in full in Colchester, vol. II, pp. 207-9. There
is a copy in the Perceval MSS.
[3] Perceval MSS., marginal note by Perceval on copy of Canning's letter to
Portland of 12 Sep. 1809; Add. MSS., 38737, fol. 333; Twiss, vol. II, p. 92.

was unsuccessfully to offer his resignation to the king.[1] Perceval, less easily cast down, tried a mild bit of recruiting on the twelfth when he suggested to the Speaker, Charles Abbot, that he might like to fill one of the vacant secretaryships of state. The prompt refusal can hardly have added to Perceval's self-confidence, although he generously admitted that Abbot had judged 'perfectly right'.[2]

In the end 18 and 19 September proved to be the crucial days in the negotiations. Early in the afternoon of the eighteenth the cabinet met in Perceval's house in Downing Street for a discussion which lasted until one o'clock the following morning. Only six ministers were present—Eldon, Camden, Liverpool, Bathurst, Harrowby, and Perceval—although a seventh, Mulgrave, later endorsed all the decisions taken. The duke of Portland, Castlereagh, Canning, and Granville Leveson-Gower were not summoned as they had all either submitted resignations or announced their intention to do so, while Chatham, although invited, thought it 'not proper' for him to attend in view of the impending Walcheren inquiry.[3] The six survivors began by trying to assess their chances of rallying a majority in parliament if they tried to carry on the government without appealing for outside aid. In the Lords the opposition was already 'a most formidable party', 110 or 112 strong. Yet, although the latest crisis would add to their numbers, ministers could still expect to control the House in future sessions. The outlook in the Commons was, however, bleak. Throughout the session of 1808 'the strength of Government did scarcely at any time appear more than equal, and on some occasions not sufficient to oppose the difficulties to which they were exposed'. When the House reassembled, ministers would have to defend the unfortunate Walcheren expedition and persuade the Commons to vote new taxes without the active support of either Canning or Castlereagh. Moreover the foreign secretary's resignation seemed likely to be followed by those of Huskisson, Sturges Bourne, Rose, and Charles Long. 'Their characters for efficiency,' continued the cabinet minute, 'as men of business, justly give great consideration to them. Long and steadily as they have been connected in government with Mr. Pitt and his friends, and particularly acquainted as they are known to be

[1] Windsor MSS., 14606–7, Perceval to George III, 15 Sep. 1809; *Morning Chronicle*, 16 Sep. 1809; Twiss, vol. II, p. 93.

[2] Colchester, vol. II, pp. 204–5 and 209.

[3] Windsor MSS., 14611–5, Cabinet minute of 18 Sep. 1809 and 14610, Perceval to George III, 18 Sep. 1809. Walpole, vol. II, pp. 7–21 incorrectly gives Mulgrave as present at the meeting.

with the state of the House of Commons, their retirement will be
considered as indicating a well-informed opinion of an almost total
disunion of Mr. Pitt's old connections, and of a want of strength in
Your Majesty's administration; and, it is to be feared, it will be followed to a considerable extent, and will guide the judgement and
conduct of others.' Against these likely defections, ministers had few
hopes of recruiting appreciable fresh strength. Charles Abbot would
refuse to leave the Speaker's chair for cabinet office; Charles Yorke
and the Hardwicke group were unlikely to accept any offer; Wellesley
was still in Spain and had given no sign of his intentions; Robert
Dundas, the chief secretary in Ireland, had been asked to return to
London, but the future conduct of the Melville connection was as yet
unknown. Negotiations might be opened with Sidmouth and his supporters, although their voting strength was so slight and their unpopularity with many of Pitt's Friends so great, that such a coalition
might weaken rather than strengthen the cabinet. Without help from
some quarter, the meeting finally decided, the remaining ministers
had little hope of ensuring a stable majority in parliament: the king
must either send for Canning or allow the cabinet rump to offer a
coalition to Lords Grey and Grenville.

Perceval enclosed this minute to the king in a letter in which he
offered to attend at Windsor the following day. At noon on 19 September, therefore, the cabinet survivors reassembled to continue their
policy discussions just as Perceval began his attempt to persuade his
majesty to accept a coalition.[1] As early as 10 September Arden had
advised his brother that, if forced to look for fresh recruits, he ought
first to approach Lord Grey. There would, he agreed, be those in his
train who would try to wreck such negotiations. Therefore Perceval
'ought not to write as if the cause were at all hopeless without his
assistance, for if you do he will assuredly require *carte blanche*'.[2] In
fact many of those on the government benches in parliament shared
the king's doubts about the wisdom of a coalition. Only Liverpool
seemed genuinely enthusiastic. Eldon wrote a formal letter of protest
to Perceval, who himself was not completely happy at the prospect.
Sturges Bourne thought the cabinet proposed 'surrendering at discretion', while Charles Ellis decided that Liverpool, even with Perceval's help, would make as bad a job of negotiations with opposition
grandees as he had of his dealings with the French in 1800. In the end,

[1] Perceval MSS., Perceval to Portland and Portland to Perceval, 19 Sep. 1809.
[2] *Ibid.*, Arden to Perceval, 10 Sep. 1809.

he predicted, Perceval and Liverpool would be forced 'to waive almost every point' to Grey and Grenville.[1] Sir Thomas Plumer had written to Perceval on the fourteenth asking him to weigh very carefully the possible effects of negotiations with the opposition on party strengths in the Commons. Perceval, he urged, should list and classify every member 'with the aid of experienced Parliamentary jockies' to see how many likely defections by former government supporters would have to be set against possible gains. Above all Perceval must guard against the dangers of a general election while the country was 'still to a certain degree under the influence of the Wardle mania'.[2] The idea of a coalition, however, found more favour amongst the uncommitted groups. Sidmouth was a strong supporter of negotiations while Robert Dundas and the Melville connection generally approved of sounding the opposition. In contrast Henry Wellesley, who refused to commit himself until his elder brother returned from Spain, feared that if a coalition offer were made 'there is an end of Pitt's Friends, for the division of offices and power will be the *partage du lion*'.[3] There was little enthusiasm for the idea on the opposition benches. Any offer, Grenville assured Tierney, would be a trap to involve the grandees in negotiations which could at any time be broken off on the alleged extravagance of the opposition's demands. Perceval could then appeal to the country to support the protestant religion and rely on finding colleagues 'willing to share in the glorious reward of martyrdom whenever the Pope shall be enthroned in St. Paul's'.[4] The religious issue seemed to many an insuperable barrier to any coalition. Grey and Grenville, wrote Francis Horner from Birmingham, must stand firm for catholic emancipation as dissenters and radicals throughout the midlands already had the lowest possible opinion of the parliamentary opposition. Only a firm adherence to principle could rally opinion against the Court.[5] Yet in spite of the distrust of both friends and foes, Perceval had little option but to press the idea of negotiations. Any offer would certainly be taken as a sign of weakness, but the fact was too obvious to even try to hide. Worst of all, the policy might arouse old fears and doubts in the king

---

[1] Malmesbury, *Letters*, vol. II, pp. 134, 135–6; Twiss, vol. II, pp. 88–90.
[2] Perceval MSS., Sir Thomas Plumer to Perceval, 14 Sep. 1809. William Eliot of the treasury wrote to Perceval supporting a coalition on 28 Sep. (Perceval MSS.).
[3] Twiss, vol. II, pp. 99–100; Pellew, vol. III, p. 5; Add. MSS., 37295, fol. 131.
[4] Olphin, p. 181.
[5] Horner, vol. I, pp. 468–9.

and the thought of Grey and Grenville back on the treasury benches could even throw George III into the arms of Canning.

Perceval's audience on 19 September quickly revealed the extent of his majesty's fears. It was, began the king, 'a decision for life; everything was at stake'. If there had to be negotiations he would prefer them to be with Lord Grey only and on the basis of clear assurances that the issue of catholic emancipation would not be pressed. When Eldon had last advised him to recall Pitt he had insisted upon and obtained 'the most direct assurance from Mr. Pitt in writing' that the catholic issue would be left in abeyance. Nothing less than this, argued the king, would now satisfy either Perceval's honour or his own. The advice in the cabinet minute, explained Perceval, was the best means of protecting his majesty on this issue, for if Grey and Grenville agreed to form a coalition with the existing ministers they would know that catholic emancipation could never be supported by such a cabinet. This would 'be *implied* from the very formation of the Government'. Perceval was, in essence, making the first suggestion that the issue should be left as an open question in the cabinet, a device which Lord Liverpool was later to use successfully for many years. But the king refused to be satisfied by anything less than a formal written pledge, even though Perceval insisted that, to require one, would doom the negotiations from the outset. 'Then,' said George III in a moment of real tension, 'they should take the Government to themselves; he would have nothing to do with it, they should not have his name.' 'Oh! Sir,' said Perceval, 'what an extremity Your Majesty is contemplating! What would become of your Majesty's country?' 'No country', replied the king, 'had the right to expect a man should give up his own honour; his honour was in his own keeping; if his country deserted him, he could not help it.' Only repeated assurances by Perceval of his personal loyalty and of the unanimity of the cabinet in its determination to protect the king on the catholic issue so lowered the temperature that the two were able, fairly calmly, to discuss the contents of a possible letter to the opposition leaders.[1]

On the following day, during a levee at Windsor, his majesty spoke to Eldon, Liverpool and Bathurst on the same subject.[2] 'What we are to do is not finally settled,' wrote Perceval to the Speaker that evening. 'It must end in an attempt to form a united Government

[1] Perceval MSS., Perceval to Liverpool, 19 Sep. 1809; Yonge, vol. I, pp. 290–4; Colchester, vol. II, pp. 211–12.
[2] Colchester, vol. II, p. 209.

with our opponents. But it is a bitter pill to swallow for more than one.' Two days later ministers had their answer. In a long and emotional minute the king authorised Perceval and Liverpool to sound both Grey and Grenville on the understanding that, although his majesty should not be asked himself to meet the opposition leaders, he should yet have power to veto or alter any term that might be agreed. The king wrote again at length of his concern for his honour and of his fears on the catholic question. This paper, said Eldon, 'was one of the finest compositions, and the most effecting I ever saw or heard in my life'. 'It is written', added the more practical Rose, 'with great energy and spirit, and upon the whole, if published, would do incalculable good, except as to the manner in which he speaks of the Opposition.' [1]

In fact the terms of the king's consent could scarcely have left Perceval and Liverpool less room for manœuvre. On 23 September the two ministers travelled once more to Windsor in order to get royal approval for their draft letters. The next day two official exchequer messengers, Turner and McGrath, left London carrying brief and identical notes to Grey and Grenville. Both were informed of the recent resignations from the cabinet and asked to return to town 'for the purpose of forming an extended and combined administration'. [2] Initial press comments were surprisingly favourable. The *Sun* warmly welcomed the offer, the *Day* hoped to see Grenville as first lord and Grey at the foreign office, and even the *Morning Chronicle* called on the opposition leaders to accept a coalition. [3] That very day, however, Grey despatched a dusty answer from his country seat at Howick. He would have been pleased to journey to London if the king 'had any commands for me personally' but he saw no reason to undertake the trip in order to negotiate with the survivors of the Portland ministry. Grenville, however, construed Perceval's letter 'as an official signification of His Majesty's pleasure' and promptly left Boconnoc for London. This more encouraging note was addressed to and reached London at nine-thirty on the evening of 27 September. The following day the cabinet considered both answers and agreed to take no further action until Grenville had travelled up to the capital. If, Perceval told Abbot that afternoon, Grenville was still willing to

[1] Twiss, vol. II, p. 98; Rose, vol. II, p. 395. The king's minute is printed in full by Walpole, vol. II, pp. 27–30.

[2] Perceval MSS., Perceval to Arden, 23 Sep. 1809; Perceval to Lords Grey and Grenville, 24 Sep. 1809; *Sun*, 28 Sep. 1809.

[3] *Sun*, 25 Sep. 1809; *Day*, 26 Sep. 1809; *Morning Chronicle*, 26 Sep. 1809.

negotiate in spite of Grey's refusal 'we shall sincerely endeavour to make a Government with him; and I think we may do it effectually'.[1] But when Grenville arrived on the twenty-ninth he soon showed his solidarity with his colleague, declining to open negotiations which could 'not be productive of any public advantage'. The refusal was not grounded on any feeling of personal hostility towards Perceval nor on any desire to prolong political difficulties. Grenville wished 'to compose, not to enflame, the divisions of the Empire' but thought that his acceptance of office in the existing government would generally be considered 'a dereliction of public principle'.[2]

The failure of the negotiations came as a relief to many on both sides. Holland thought their lordships' refusal 'highly creditable to their disinterestedness' and predicted widespread public support for statesmen who showed that they would not sacrifice their principles for office. Westmorland, for different reasons, was equally content. 'What an escape', he rejoiced, 'the country has had.' Even Wilberforce, who had expected a refusal from the first, felt relieved that the public had been spared a coalition and the prospect of more expensive continental expeditions.[3] Zealous ministerialists prepared to gird their loins and fight to the last. 'So be it!' thundered the *Sun*. 'His Majesty is not without servants who will conduct his affairs with fidelity, zeal and talent.' If, wrote Arden to Perceval, the king asked the surviving ministers to stand in the breach 'you must do so to the utmost and at all risks, and be but firm and you will do it with success. For bad as the times are and lowered as the king's authority and influence is, I still think that the constitutional prerogative, His Majesty's character and steady resolution will (as they have often proved before) be sufficient to uphold an administration of his own choice that means nothing but the public good and are [*sic*] resolved to stand by and support the Crown.' In the last resort Perceval was to fall back on the basic influence of the Crown. 'But', warned Arden, 'there must be no wavering—no more concessions to Levellers and Reformers. At any rate, my dear brother, I think your own line of duty is clear, and when a man follows that his conscience at least will be at ease, let

[1] Windsor MSS., 14681, Camden to George III, 27 Sep. 1809; 14683 and 14686, Perceval to same, 28 Sep. 1809; Colchester, vol. II, pp. 210–11; Perceval MSS., Portland to Perceval, 28 Sep. 1809.

[2] Perceval MSS., Grenville to Perceval, 29 Sep. 1809; Windsor MSS., 14688, Perceval to George III, 29 Sep. 1809; 14693, George III to Perceval, 30 Sep. 1809.

[3] Holland, *Further Memoirs*, p. 38; Wilberforce, vol. III, pp. 426–8.

what will happen. If your bodily health and strength is equal to all the labours and fatigues of such a contest, I should have but few fears about anything else.' [1]

At first the opposition was equally confident of its own rectitude, for only Tierney, it seemed, had doubts about Grey and Grenville's refusal. Brougham was full of congratulations to Grey on his victory over 'these miserable intriguers'; Grenville's self-righteousness knew no bounds and Grey at first seemed well satisfied although, on reflection, he began to be disturbed by the memory of his own hasty refusal even to return to London and more so by Grenville's incautious allusion to the catholic question in his second letter.[2] In fact there can be little doubt that the opposition leaders had acted unwisely. By their haughty refusal to enter into negotiations they left Perceval with the alternative of resigning and leaving the king with the choice of Canning and the whigs or of limping on with what remained of the old ministry. Moreover Grey and Grenville had, in their haste, misunderstood the coalition offer itself. Perceval's original invitations were certainly vaguely phrased. The *Quarterly Review*, which strongly opposed the overtures, thought that Perceval's letters amounted only to the proposition that, certain members of the cabinet having resigned their places, the survivors, being anxious to retain theirs, invited Grey and Grenville's assistance in order to facilitate this.[3] On the same day that he received the offer Grenville told Auckland that he would never consent to 'treat with these people as an existing Government, and to submit to the King through them our views of men and measures'. Yet Perceval had never intended that this should be the case. In his final letter to Grenville Perceval explained that the offer was 'not for the accession of Your Lordship to the present administration, but for the purpose of forming a combined and extended ministry'. Routine enquiries could easily have established this before Grey and Grenville sent their final refusals.[4] Nor can there be doubt of the ministers' good faith in suggesting negotiations and of the share of offices which they anticipated offering to the opposition. Harrowby assured Wilberforce that the offer was a *bona fide* attempt to form a real coalition, while Sydenham told Wellesley that the new govern-

---

[1] *Sun*, 30 Sep. 1809; Perceval MSS., Arden to Perceval, 30 Sep. 1809.

[2] Olphin, p. 130; Brougham, *Memoirs*, vol. I, p. 461; Auckland, *Journal*, vol. IV, pp. 323 and 327; *Dropmore MSS.*, IX, p. 330.

[3] *Quarterly Review*, Nov. 1809, pp. 412–26.

[4] Auckland, vol. IV, p. 323; *Day*, 12 Oct. 1809; Perceval MSS., Perceval to Grenville, 29 Sep. 1809.

ment would have an equal division of offices between Perceval's supporters and the whigs. Rose claimed that Grey and Grenville could have had concessions 'beyond anything they can have formed an expectation of' and the *Sun* spoke of the creation of a new Ministry of all the Talents.[1] Perceval never thought of himself as the first lord in such a coalition. His first act, after he had later accepted the premiership, was to assure the prince of Wales that he would 'have gladly seen that office in the hands either of Lord Grey or Lord Grenville' had either consented to serve. Perceval's own wishes, as in 1807, centred on the home office and he went so far as to ask Croker to be his undersecretary there if a coalition were formed.[2] Late in October Grenville himself realised his mistake and confessed that he would have at least opened negotiations 'had he not totally mistaken the meaning of Perceval's letter'.[3] By then it was too late to repent. 'We have no option', wrote Perceval to Arden on 30 September, 'but to surrender the King, or stand as we can. We expect the king's commands tomorrow as to the person under whom the attempt is to be made. I think these commands will fall upon me. If it is so, it will be necessary to put a good face on the thing and therefore I will not say what my expectations are.'[4]

Meanwhile Canning himself had not been idle. He was still an active candidate for 10, Downing Street in spite of his letter to Portland of 12 September. Until the very end Eldon still thought the foreign secretary would finally agree to the appointment as first lord of some peer of his own choice.[5] In fact Canning had the tired and wavering duke's ear and was aiming at higher things. For Portland, unpredictable and misguided to the last, had, within a week, begun to regret his resignation. 'I believe now', wrote the lord chancellor on 13 September, 'such is the imbecility of man, that the old D[uke] is trying in vain to get back.'[6] Thereafter Portland's views swung steadily against Perceval. He opposed the idea of coalition and resented the failure to invite him to the cabinet meeting of 18 September, protested to Arbuthnot that he was kept in ignorance of all that

[1] A. M. Wilberforce, *Private Papers of William Wilberforce*, pp. 140–2; Add. MSS., 37295, fol. 120; Rose, vol. II, p. 397; *Sun*, 2 Oct. 1809.

[2] Windsor MSS., 41277–8, Perceval to the prince of Wales, 2 Oct. 1809; Buckingham, vol. IV, p. 380; Croker, vol. I, p. 22; Rose, vol. II, p. 397.

[3] Malmesbury, *Letters*, vol. II, p. 173. For Canning's strictures on Grenville's 'foolish letter' see Add. MSS., 38737, fol. 368.

[4] Perceval MSS., Perceval to Arden, 30 Sep. 1809.

[5] Twiss, vol II, pp. 88–90.

[6] *Ibid.*, pp. 90–1.

Perceval proposed to do to try and strengthen the government, and, having consequently been told of the idea of coalition, immediately rushed to Canning with the news.[1] In vain the duke's family bewailed that 'their father was so entirely in Canning's hands'. Portland, strongly opposed to any approach to Grey and Grenville and still hoping that the old ministry could somehow be brought back to life, was the ideal emissary for Canning's last bid for power. The two met at Bulstrode on the morning of the nineteenth, just as the cabinet rump reconvened to approve the final draft of their memorandum to the king. While Perceval and his colleagues counselled coalition, Canning was hot for no surrender. 'Even now', he told the duke, 'he could form a pure Pittite ministry.' He could 'have done it with ease a week ago; it became from day to day more and more difficult'.[2] Certainly as Perceval distributed copies of his earlier correspondence with the foreign secretary, Canning's laboriously recruited army showed increasing signs of desertion. But, reported Sydenham to Wellesley the same day, rumours were spreading that Canning had sealed his alliance with Robert Dundas and now had the vital Scottish votes in his pocket.[3]

Canning was clearly playing every card he possessed. The king, he told an admiring Portland, should never be forced to sanction any overture to the opposition.[4] When the two parted, the duke set out for London to meet Perceval while Canning went straight to Windsor for an audience with the king, determined to play on George III's fear of Grey and Grenville. But the king was too experienced a politician to be thus stampeded. The audience, he told Perceval later, was 'the most extraordinary he ever heard'. Canning began by admitting that the duke's health made his resignation unavoidable. His successor, he argued, must be a commoner who could exercise full authority over all other government departments. Thus the choice lay only between Perceval and himself, since there was no other potential prime minister on either the government or the opposition benches in the house of commons. Should the king choose Perceval—'the most natural thing of the two'—Canning would be neither surprised nor displeased, but he would 'readily undertake' to form a government

---

[1] Perceval MSS., Perceval to Portland, 21 Sep. 1809; Arbuthnot to Perceval, 20 Sep.; Rose, vol. II, pp. 387–8.

[2] Perceval MSS., Arbuthnot to Perceval, 20 Sep. 1809; Portland to Perceval and Perceval to Portland, 19 Sep. 1809.

[3] Add. MSS., 37295, fol. 120.

[4] *Bathurst MSS.*, pp. 112–19.

himself if called upon to do so by the king. 'Not', the astonished monarch told Perceval, 'that he would consider of it, that he would advise with others, as you or any other person would have said, but that he was fully prepared to undertake it.' Moreover with Canning as first lord there would be no talk of coalition. The very same ministers now meeting in London, he reminded the king, had timidly resigned immediately Pitt died and left George III to face All the Talents alone. Had Canning been in the cabinet in 1806 there would have been at least one servant unwilling to desert the Crown.[1] Thereafter Canning pressed home his last chance with vigour. The following day he sent Portland to Windsor with a complete list of a Canningite ministry. No copy of the list was ever published: even the duke himself admitted, when questioned by the king, that he knew nothing of the names in it and that he 'believed Mr. Canning had not consulted anybody'.[2] Canning himself later told Rose that he had suggested that Perceval should be given a peerage, made lord president of the council in place of Camden, and appointed chancellor of the duchy of Lancaster for life, in defiance of the Commons' rejection of an identical proposal in 1807.[3] Later, according to both Bathurst and Eldon, Canning changed his mind and told the duke that Perceval must be the lord chancellor, an idea that Portland, 'in the simplicity of his heart', actually proposed to Eldon himself, 'who was outrageous at it'. Canning, said Perceval to Arbuthnot, however he tried 'to gild and decorate the ornament . . . meant only to put an extinguisher on my head in the shape of a coronet'.[4] In fact the majority of Pitt's Friends had already rejected Canning's claim to the treasury and George III knew it. The king, wrote the Pittite back-bencher William Broderick, might fear the consequences of a coalition but a cabinet dominated by Canning would be far worse.[5] Although he continued to be closeted almost daily with the duke, Canning's last chance had gone.[6] When George III finally called on Perceval to form a new government, Canning was full of congratulations. 'I have', he wrote, 'at least the King's sanction for the advice which I humbly presumed to offer': now, he ended, perhaps the government press would cease

[1] Perceval MSS., Perceval to Liverpool, 19 Sep. 1809; Yonge, vol. I, pp. 290–4.
[2] *Bathurst MSS.*, pp. 112–14.
[3] Rose, vol. II, p. 379.
[4] *Ibid.*, vol. II, p. 382; Twiss, vol. II, p. 90; Ward, vol. I, p. 280.
[5] Perceval MSS., William Broderick to Perceval, 21 Sep. 1809.
[6] *Day*, 25 Sep. 1809.

'the nonsense and the calumnies' recently printed about him.[1] At best, on this issue, Canning was the victim of gross self-deception: at worst his congratulations to Perceval could be interpreted as sheer hypocrisy.

Soon, however, Canning was in worse trouble, for, since 7 September, Castlereagh had been brooding on his complaints against his former colleague. On 19 September, without any warning or demand for an explanation, he called Canning out, charging him with having secretly intrigued to remove him from office. Edward Cooke, the under-secretary at the war office, delivered the challenge that morning to Willoughby Gordon of the horseguards, who tried vainly to persuade Castlereagh to withdraw it. Two days later the two principals met on Putney Heath. Castlereagh rode to the duel with his second, Lord Yarmouth, humming snatches of opera, but poor Charles Ellis, Canning's second, was so nervous that he could not load the pistols. Both missed with their first shots, yet Castlereagh, his honour still unsatisfied, insisted they should fire again, and this time put a ball through the fleshy part of Canning's thigh. The affair, wrote Cooke to Perceval, passed off 'with mutual civilities and in a manner in every way becoming their respective situations'.[2] Few observers shared Cooke's satisfaction, for the news of the challenge shocked even those who had at first sympathised with Castlereagh. 'Thank God Canning is not seriously hurt,' wrote Perceval to the Speaker, 'and Castlereagh is not touched. Terrible, all this, for public impression.' Wilberforce, resting at Newport Pagnall, found the news humiliating and hoped the king would exclude both participants from ever holding public office again. 'In what spirit', he added, 'must our national counsellors have been deliberating?'[3] What made matters worse was the tone and contents of Castlereagh's challenge. It would not, wrote Cobbett in the *Political Register*, 'have got him a job in a London counting house at £150 a year', while Wilberforce, shocked that Castlereagh had waited twelve days to write it, called it 'a cold-blooded measure of deliberate revenge'. 'Surely', wrote Perceval to Portland, 'Castlereagh misconceived the case very much.' When Castlereagh sent copies of his subsequent correspondence with the king to Perceval, the new prime minister refused to circulate them to other members of the cabinet. George III himself, although sent letters of self-justification

---

[1] Perceval MSS., Canning to Perceval, 2 Oct. 1809.

[2] Croker, *Correspondence*, vol. I, pp. 20–1; Perceval MSS., Edward Cooke to Perceval, 21 Sep. 1809.

[3] Colchester, vol. II, pp. 209 and 228; Wilberforce, vol. III, pp. 426 and 428.

by both parties, refused all comment, except to express regret that the
duel should have taken place at all.[1]

Perceval had himself made a vain last-minute effort to avoid the
duel. For just before Castlereagh set off for Putney Heath Perceval
had sent him copies of Canning's letters to Portland of 24 March and
18 July. These, wrote Perceval, clearly showed that Canning was not
personally responsible for and never accepted the policy of secrecy.
The same point was made by Charles Ellis on the Heath itself just
before the first shots were fired. Twice Castlereagh brushed it aside.
He would always, he said, date the dissolution of the Portland ministry
from 24 March, when the duke, instead of circulating Canning's letter
to members of the cabinet, received it 'with effusions of tenderness'.
Both the king and Portland had forbidden Canning, as they had subsequently forbidden all others who came to share the secret, from
saying anything to Castlereagh about the transaction. Yet on this
issue of concealment, Castlereagh still thought that 'a dispensation
from the Head of Government, or even from His Majesty, to be in-
operative to justify visible deception between colleague and colleague,
as any authority from the See of Rome in matters relating to Protestant conduct'.[2] Such reasoning, intended to prove Canning's guilt,
equally convicted every member of the cabinet who knew anything
of the negotiations and who obeyed the king's and Portland's commands to remain silent. Canning, lamented Charles Ellis, had 'been
fighting the poor old Duke's duel, or Lord Camden's, or Hawkesbury's, or almost anybody's but his own'.[3] If Castlereagh was justified in challenging anyone, he should, logically, have fought a series
of duels instead of concentrating all his malevolence on Canning.

The duel itself, as Perceval predicted, led to a series of public
statements, accusations and self-justifications from all concerned. On
1 October Castlereagh submitted a long formal statement to the king,
a shortened version of which was published under Edward Cooke's
signature in the *Morning Post* on the third. Camden's statement appeared in the *Day* on 20 October, and this provoked a reply from
Canning which was forwarded to Windsor on 24 November and
printed in the *Sun* four days later.[4] The great majority of contemporary

---

[1] Wilberforce, vol. III, p. 430; *Political Register*, 14 Oct. 1809, p. 518; Perceval
MSS., Perceval to Portland, 21 Sep. 1809; Castlereagh to Perceval, 3 Oct. 1809;
Add. MSS., 38243, fol. 158; Windsor MSS., 14663–8 and 14696.
[2] Perceval MSS., Castlereagh to Perceval, 'Thursday Night' (21 Sep. 1809).
[3] Malmesbury, *Letters*, vol. II, pp. 135–6.
[4] *Morning Post*, 3 Oct. 1809; *Day*, 20 Oct. 1809; *Sun*, 28 Nov. 1809; Perceval

observers condemned Canning. Everybody, wrote the opposition
M.P., J. W. Ward, seemed against him 'except just his own particular
cronies' and even they lost their cohesion as details of the affair became
available.[1] William Broderick thought Canning's conduct 'exceeded
in duplicity everything that I ever thought possible, even in a politician', while William Eliot, a junior lord of the treasury, thought him
'rash and overbearing, which perhaps was not to be wondered at'.[2]
Lord Grey, although 'against proscription in forming an administration', dismissed Canning as 'the last man that he would unite with'.
'Talking of shuffling', wrote Brougham in an aside, 'naturally brings
to one's mind Canning.' Observers as far apart as Cobbett and
Malmesbury were at one in denouncing his ambition and duplicity.[3]
On all sides the affair was discussed in terms of generalisations and
hyperboles. Contemporary opinion searched for one individual who
could be blamed for all the intrigues that had led to the collapse of the
government and the spectacle of a duel between two members of the
cabinet. Canning was their favourite quarry. 'On the major issue',
Sir Charles Petrie has written, 'Castlereagh was surely in the right.' [4] In
fact the entire affair was too involved and the issues too complex to
admit of one simple verdict. At least four major sets of questions must
be answered before any attempt is made to assess blame. Who was
responsible for the secrecy surrounding the whole affair from 24 March
to 7 September? Why did Castlereagh challenge Canning when he did,
and was he justified in doing so? What were the motives behind
Canning's behaviour after 24 March and particularly at the time of his
resignation? Did Perceval or any other member of the cabinet use the
crisis, at any stage, as a weapon against Canning?

The issue of concealment is the least complicated of the four.
Castlereagh, in his written challenge, blamed Canning for concealing
the proposed cabinet changes from him. This was plainly unjust.
Canning had urged throughout that Castlereagh should be told and
finally on 18 July had been assured in writing by Portland that, if he

---

MSS., Lt.-Col. Taylor to Perceval, 26 Nov. 1809, enclosing copies of Canning's
letter of 24 Nov. 1809.

[1] *Letters to Ivy*, p. 87. For the attitude of the Canningites to the crisis see
chapter 15 pp. 264–8.

[2] Perceval MSS., Wm. Broderick to Perceval, 21 Sep. 1809; Wm. Eliot to
Perceval, 19 Sep. 1809.

[3] Brady, *Huskisson and the Liberal Party*, p. 13; Brougham, *Memoirs*, vol. I,
p. 479; Malmesbury, *Letters*, vol. II, p. 186; *Political Register*, 28 Oct. 1809,
p. 626.   [4] Petrie, *George Canning*, p. 108.

would accept Castlereagh as secretary of state for war until the end of the Walcheren campaign, 'in the meantime, and certainly the sooner the better, Lord Castlereagh's friends should take opportunities of preparing him for the change'. Unfortunately the duke failed to show this letter to any of his colleagues, so that as late as 17 September Perceval could still believe that Canning, though not solely responsible for the secrecy, was 'at least a passive, unremonstrating accomplice in that concealment'. But as soon as Canning sent him copies of the letters, Perceval admitted that the charge against Canning was 'unquestionably false' and promised to show them to others who had been similarly misled.[1] Until the final adoption of Lord Camden's plan on 30 July, therefore, the duke of Portland and the king alone were responsible for concealing the suggested changes from Castlereagh. Thereafter Camden must take a major share of the blame. The duke was now anxious that Castlereagh should be told of Canning's demand before the end of the Walcheren campaign and looked upon Camden as the natural person to break the news. In his public statement of 20 October Camden made two points in his own defence. He had, he wrote, never undertaken 'to prepare Lord Castlereagh's mind' for any change of office until after the expedition had ended: and, far from being asked to tell Castlereagh, he was throughout 'absolutely restricted from doing so'. In this he was supported by Bathurst, who argued that both the duke and Camden had always talked to him as though the proposal to remove Castlereagh from control of the war effort had 'been a communication which Lord Camden had engaged himself not to disclose'. Moreover, Bathurst added, Canning always gave him the impression of accepting the same interpretation of the affair.[2] In fact Canning seems genuinely to have expected Camden to act as an intermediary, and after reading Portland's letter of 18 July he had every reason for such hopes. Yet the first of Camden's two assertions may well still be true, for he seems at no point to have given an unqualified pledge that he would definitely break the news to Castlereagh before the end of the expedition. In brief the duke

[1] Perceval MSS., Canning to Perceval, 1 Oct. 1809, enclosing copies of Canning's letter to Portland of 18 July and of the duke's reply. Perceval kept his promise to show the copies to others by sending them to Castlereagh immediately before the duel (see above), by showing them to the Speaker (Colchester, vol. II, pp. 220–3) and by sending them, through Arbuthnot, to Wm. Broderick. They proved, Broderick replied, that Castlereagh had as much ground for complaint against Camden and Portland as he had against Canning (Perceval MSS., Broderick to Arbuthnot, 'Sunday Night').

[2] *Day*, 20 Oct. 1809; *Bathurst MSS.*, pp. 112–19.

R

appears to have given a promise to Canning on 18 July without first ensuring that he would be able to carry it out. Certainly throughout the first week in August Portland was trying and failing to persuade Camden to break the news to Castlereagh.[1] The second of Camden's assertions in his public statement of 20 October was, therefore, false. After 30 July Camden, far from being forbidden to approach Castlereagh, was under pressure from the duke to do so. The policy of concealment was instigated by Portland, approved by the king, and continued after the end of July through the moral weakness of Camden and the blunders of the duke. If anyone was deceived after the adoption of the Camden plan, it was Canning. In a wider sense every member of the cabinet must, from the moment he heard of the crisis, take part of the blame for not insisting that Castlereagh be let into the secret, and this, on reflection, was the verdict that both Perceval and Eldon gave on their own roles in the affair.[2]

At no point could Castlereagh himself have known all the intricacies about the policy of concealment. Yet on the morning of the duel he saw copies of the crucial letters of 18 July. That he still persisted in his challenge and was not even appeased after the first abortive exchange of shots is both the measure of his rage and the final condemnation of his conduct. Why, asked contemporaries, was he brought to this pitch twelve full days after having been told of the affair by Camden? On 7 September, according to Camden, Castlereagh took the news of the plan for his removal from the war office perfectly calmly. But again Camden told only half the truth. He never mentioned that such an arrangement had been under discussion since the previous March, but left his brother-in-law with the impression that the idea had only recently been raised.[3] Not until Perceval later innocently showed him copies of his correspondence with Canning of 26 to 31 August did Castlereagh realise for how long his own demotion had been concealed. 'I shall', he wrote to Perceval on 5 October, 'always feel personally grateful to you for the candour with which you ultimately put me in possession of my real situation, and enabled me to decide, under a fair and full knowledge of the whole of the case, upon the line which it became me to take.'[4] Perceval therefore, un-

---

[1] Windsor MSS., 14556–7, Portland to George III, 7 Aug. 1809.
[2] Perceval MSS., Perceval to Canning, 29 Sep. 1809; Twiss, vol. II, p. 103.
[3] Rose, vol. II, p. 422.
[4] Perceval MSS., Castlereagh to Perceval, 5 Oct. 1809; in a letter of 21 Oct. Castlereagh specifically thanked Perceval for being 'so kind as to allow me to peruse' copies of his correspondence with Canning.

aware that Castlereagh had never been told the whole story, was unwittingly responsible for bringing his colleague to the point of issuing a challenge. Portland's policy of piecemeal and partial confidences ended in confusing all concerned. The events explain, but do little to justify, Castlereagh's blood-thirsty behaviour.

Wider judgements on Canning's conduct depend ultimately on the interpretation of his motives in pressing for Castlereagh's removal and on deciding the real issue on which he finally resigned. His case was not helped by the *Letter to Lord Camden* which appeared in the press on 28 November. 'Never', wrote Cobbett, 'was there so dull, so stupid, so despicable a publication. One can make neither head nor tail of it.' The most important fact established by Canning's own statement, commented the *Day*, was that, although he had demanded Castlereagh's removal on public grounds as early as 4 April, he had continued to sit with him in cabinet and to defend his policies in parliament for a further five months. It was a confession 'not very favourable to his patriotism and his zeal for the public good'.[1] Equally unconvincing was Canning's insistence that the idea of removing Castlereagh did not originate with him, but was put forward by Portland after consultation with Lord Camden and the king. The duke certainly was the first to broach the possibility of moving Castlereagh to another office, but he only did so because he knew that Canning wished for this and in consequence of the foreign secretary's letter of 24 March threatening resignation. Such clear equivocations obscured the stronger parts of Canning's position. There was little, for example, to justify an argument popular with his detractors that the timing of Canning's demands for Castlereagh's removal from the war and colonial office showed that he sought to ruin his colleague's political career. The first complaint, Broderick emphasised, coincided with the damaging report of the East India patronage committee and the final demand came immediately after the Walcheren disaster. Yet Canning was to blame for neither of these unfortunate coincidences. He made his first complaint at Easter in a sensible attempt to settle the issue before the year's military campaigns began. It was Camden and the king who insisted that Castlereagh's removal must be delayed until the end of the Walcheren campaign. Even Portland realised at

---

[1] *Political Register*, 28 Oct. 1809, p. 612 and 2 Dec. 1809, p. 843; *Day*, 28 Nov. 1809. For a favourable view of Canning's statement see Ross's account in Malmesbury, *Letters*, vol. II, p. 143. The *Quarterly Review* exonerated Canning on the secrecy issue, but withheld judgement on his motives for demanding Castlereagh's removal (Oct. 1809, pp. 412–26).

the time that this could add greatly to the difficulties of finding a solution if the expedition failed. He therefore promised Canning on 18 July that 'no time should be lost' in breaking the news to Castlereagh, precisely so that his removal from the war office 'may not appear to be the event (be that what it may) of the expedition'.

In the last resort, three valid charges and one serious query can be made about Canning's conduct between March and September. From as early as April he was busy canvassing for support amongst M.P.s and other political leaders although he knew that many of his cabinet colleagues, and Perceval and Liverpool in particular, were unaware that he had made any specific complaints about the composition of the existing ministry. He was not responsible for the policy of secrecy, but he did not scruple to make unfair use of it for his own political advantage. Not once between March and June did he protest against the fact that Perceval and Liverpool, two of the key ministers in the cabinet, were being kept in ignorance of proposed changes in the government. Secondly, Canning told Wellesley, before he left for Spain in July, of the intention to promote him to the war and colonial office although he had been expressly forbidden to do this by the king and had pledged himself to remain silent. Again, during the third week in September Canning acted equivocally towards Perceval in that, while still ostensibly recommending Perceval as prime minister, as he had done in his letter to Portland of 12 September, he was in fact using the duke and his own audience with the king to press his own claims to 10, Downing Street. It was this behaviour which raises the final query about Canning's motives throughout the whole affair. Why, in Canning's view, did Portland's decision on 4 September to resign destroy all the value of the Camden plan? Canning never explained either in his letters to Perceval of 7 and 8 September or in that to Portland of 12 September why the duke's retirement should have altered the entire situation. If, as Canning argued in his letter to Portland and during his subsequent audience with the king, the continuance of a government of departments was fatal to the interests of the country, he should have welcomed the duke's departure. On 10 May he had raised no objection either to Portland's offer to resign then or to the suggestion that Chatham might be his successor. Between May and September it seems possible that Canning's main object had become to secure the office of prime minister for himself.[1]

---

[1] Support for this interpretation can be found in Canning's own admission to Rose that if he had accepted Perceval's offer in September of their joint service

Canning thought of himself throughout as the victim of a cabinet intrigue led by Perceval whose behaviour, he fumed, was 'treacherous, hypercritical, mean and jealous'. For Perceval, after opening on 26 August 'an unsolicited and unreserved correspondence' on possible political changes in the event of Portland's retirement or death, had drawn from Canning an admission of his 'unwillingness to act a secondary part in the House of Commons' and had later shown these letters, without first asking Canning's permission, to 'all the world, by sending copies to distant people'. Moreover, Perceval, armed with written proof of Canning's views, had then on 4 September suddenly called for the duke's resignation, again without giving his cabinet colleague any warning of his intentions. Thereafter he had built up his government on the twin assertions that Canning's real aim had been to make himself prime minister and that he had refused to serve jointly with Perceval under Wellesley's leadership, 'both of which facts were untrue'. Thus Perceval's whole conduct, Canning told Wilbraham Bootle, was 'irreconcilable with any principle of good faith, public or private'. The final crisis, wrote Ross, could have been avoided had not the chancellor of the exchequer 'played a lawyer's trick' and had not the failing old duke given way to it.[1]

Canning first raised the question of the use of their earlier correspondence in a letter to Perceval on 15 November. He had, he wrote, heard from an unspecified source, 'which carries some weight', that copies of the letters were then in circulation and were intended for publication. Perceval immediately admitted that he had 'privately and confidentially' shown copies of the letters 'to several of my friends' and, he added, 'I have understood that you have done the same.'[2] The letters had undoubtedly been shown, during September and October, by Perceval to Abbot, Broderick, Castlereagh, Croker, Long, Matthew Montague, Rose and Ward: Croker later told Charles Greville

---

under a third person as prime minister, he would have 'given up the lead in administration almost for ever, as Lord Bathurst and Lord Harrowby were very little older than himself' (Rose, vol. II, p. 379). For Canning's canvassing for political support see chapter 13, pp. 215-16; for his dealings with Wellesley, chapter 13, pp. 216 and 221-2; for his conduct during the third week in September, chapter 14, pp. 239-42. Wellington, who had his version of the crisis from Lord Fitzroy Somerset, also thought Canning broke up the government because he wished to be first lord (*Supplementary Despatches*, vol. XI, p. 387).

[1] Colchester, vol. II, pp. 228-30; Malmesbury, vol. II, p. 145; Feiling, *Second Tory Party*, p. 265; Bagot, vol. I, pp. 336 and 344-7; Add. MSS., 38738, fol. 92.
[2] Perceval MSS., Canning to Perceval, 15 Nov. 1809 and Perceval to Canning, 16 Nov. 1809.

that the new prime minister had extended his circle of confidants 'to all of us who then took part with him'. In doing this Perceval was fully justified in claiming that he was but matching Canning's own conduct. In his letter of 15 November Canning added an assurance 'in the most solemn manner, that I have not given copies of the correspondence to anyone'. He had, however, as Castlereagh avowed, shown if he had not given copies to many of those whose support he was seeking. Robert Dundas, Milnes, Henry Wellesley and the Speaker were all certainly among this number.[1] In the prevailing atmosphere of recrimination and self-justification, all parties had used the best weapons at their command. Perceval was, to the best of his knowledge, telling the truth when he assured Canning that he had no intention of publishing the letters and that the only copies he had allowed to go permanently out of his possession were those he had sent to Wellesley in Spain. In fact he had already refused requests from both Castlereagh and Croker to be allowed to make abstracts. What he did not know was that Ward, without asking permission, had secretly done so.[2] Yet this alone neither proved nor justified Canning's accusations, for Perceval himself had acted in good faith and Ward's version of the letters was not published by Phipps until many years after the event.

Equally groundless was the charge that Perceval, as part of a deliberate intrigue against Canning, advised and was primarily responsible for Portland's resignation on 6 September. The duke himself told Malmesbury in mid-October that he retired solely on grounds of ill-health and in order to satisfy the pleas of his family. Moreover Liverpool assured Wallace on 23 September that it had occurred to him that the best solution was for Portland to resign and it is known that Bathurst knew and approved of the scheme. Perceval must bear a share but was certainly not solely responsible for the duke's decision.[3] Perceval defended his conduct on this point in a marginal note which he scribbled on his copy of Canning's letter to Portland of 12 September. His solution of merging the Camden plan with the duke's

[1] Perceval MSS., Broderick to Perceval, 21 Sep. 1809 and Castlereagh to same, 12 Oct. 1809; Rose, vol. II, pp. 353–4; Ward, vol. I, pp. 227–33 and 363; Bickley, Diaries of Lord Glenbervie, vol. II, p. 41; Colchester, vol. II, p. 228; Camden Soc., LXV, Aspinall, Correspondence of Charles Arbuthnot, p. 52.

[2] Aspinall, op. cit.; Perceval MSS., Castlereagh to Perceval, 12 and 21 Oct. 1809.

[3] Malmesbury, vol. II, p. 181; Yonge, vol. I, p. 288. On 23 Sep. Arbuthnot told Croker, 'The Duke of Portland's state of health made his resignation necessary' (Croker, Diaries, vol. I, pp. 15–16).

retirement and his succession by some third party was not, he admitted, ideal. It was, however, the only way of keeping all Pitt's Friends
together. 'If without making the attempt to save Castlereagh, the duke
had proceeded immediately to remove him, I could not have acquiesced
in that, and I thought my cession from the Government would have
broke it up, and I am now convinced that it would, as completely as
Canning's. Therefore I suggested the Duke's resignation.'[1]

Even greater misunderstandings resulted from Perceval's dealings
with Wellesley in Spain. On 5 October Perceval wrote to the marquis
offering him the foreign office and enclosing copies of his correspondence with Canning. The packet was taken to the Peninsula by Thomas
Sydenham, a client of the Wellesley family. A fortnight later Wellesley
sent home a long formal statement of his position which included the
assertion that Perceval had proposed him for the office of prime
minister, 'to which arrangement all Mr. Perceval's friends had acceded,
and no dissent had been expressed by any of His Majesty's ministers;
but Mr. Canning, being of the opinion that the office of First Lord
of the Treasury must be occupied by a commoner, and that his own
claims to that situation could not be postponed to those of Mr. Perceval, had resigned His Majesty's service'. Canning immediately protested to Perceval about this garbled version of the negotiations,
affirming, as he also did in a second letter to Wellesley himself, that
no proposal of Lord Wellesley as prime minister had ever been made
to him by any member of the cabinet. This was confirmed by Perceval
in a statement to the king in which he stressed that he had mentioned
Wellesley's name informally to Canning (together with those of
Bathurst, Harrowby, and Liverpool) as a possible first lord, but Perceval had neither made any formal proposal nor consulted any other
of his colleagues. Canning's protest, however, carried little weight with
Wellesley. 'His denial', wrote Wellesley to Wellington, 'bears every
mark of equivocation. . . . Perceval's words are, "if it should be
thought desirable to place Lord Wellesley at our head, we will cheerfully assent".' 'This', wrote Perceval in despair, 'certainly is incorrect
in the words. I never spoke them, for I never had authority to speak
in the plural number.' In the end W. W. Pole cleared up the mystery.
He had, he admitted, seen Sydenham before he left England and dictated to him 'as nearly as I could recollect' a passage from a letter shown
to him by Arbuthnot and written, as he supposed, by Perceval to

---

[1] Perceval MSS., marginal note by Perceval in copy of Canning's letter to
Portland of 12 Sep. 1809.

Canning. In fact the letter proved to have been addressed to Harrowby. Wellesley's misinformation resulted not from any intrigue by Perceval but from Pole's perfectly innocent mistake.[1] That Perceval was never moved by feelings of malice towards Canning was further shown in November when he ordered Arbuthnot to do all he could to suppress newspaper articles hostile to the former foreign secretary. Perceval had acted towards Canning throughout, concluded Sturges Bourne, with 'strict honour and integrity', a verdict which was echoed by both Vicary Gibbs, another close associate of Canning's, and by the level-headed Wilberforce.[2]

With this the long series of accusations and counter-accusations ended. One of the best features of the behaviour of all concerned was a tenderness towards the dying Portland. Canning, in his public statement, could not conceal that the duke had been primarily responsible for the fatal policy of secrecy, but he was careful to put it 'in such a way that this seemed, at the most, . . . an unfortunate though well-intentioned error'. George III's answer to the cabinet memorandum of 16 September included a special tribute to the duke's long services. 'A testimony', wrote Perceval in forwarding this to Bulstrode, 'more honourable, and more truly deserved by the servant to whom it was given or more sincerely felt by the Master who pronounced it, was never, I believe, delivered by a grateful King to a retiring Minister.' Rarely indeed can so unfortunate a prime minister have been treated with such loyalty and consideration by those who had suffered from his ineptitude.[3]

Mulgrave believed, to the end, that there had been no intention in any quarter to act dishonestly or to compromise the interests of the public.[4] The Portland administration, he claimed, collapsed rather from general muddle and stupidity than because of the evil designs of any one minister. In fact it was, largely, a combination of Portland's

[1] Perceval MSS., Wellesley to Wellington, 18 Oct. 1809 (copy); Canning to Perceval, 28 Oct. 1809 and Perceval to Canning, 30 Oct. 1809; W. W. Pole to Perceval, 30 Oct. and 5 Nov. 1809 and Perceval to Pole, 2 Nov. 1809; Perceval to George III, 4 Nov. 1809 and George III to Perceval, 5 Nov. 1809; copy of Wellesley's statement (undated); Add. MSS., 37296, fol. 135 and fol. 379; Harrowby MSS., XI, fols. 224-5; Bagot, *George Canning and His Friends*, pp. 339-40.

[2] Aspinall, *Politics and the Press*, p. 207; Rose, vol. II, p. 349; Perceval MSS., Vicary Gibbs to Perceval, 5 Oct. 1809; Wilberforce, *Life*, vol. II, p. 428.

[3] Perceval MSS., Lt.-Col. Taylor to Perceval, 26 Nov. 1809 and Perceval to Portland, 24 Sep. 1809.

[4] Ward, vol. I, p. 215.

gross inefficiency, Camden's moral cowardice, and Canning's vaulting ambition that finally destroyed the government. The dying Portland, whatever his defects, at least never sacrificed his honour. It would be difficult to make the same claim for either Camden or Canning.

CHAPTER FIFTEEN

PRIME MINISTER

BY the end of September 1809 the political position could scarcely have been worse. The country had been without an effective government for over three weeks, during which time former colleagues on the treasury bench had engaged in public recrimination and abuse while the leaders of the opposition had flatly refused to consider a coalition. Nerves were so generally strained that even the king was reduced to summoning Eldon to Windsor at 3 o'clock in the morning to emphasise that he would not hear of further cabinet resignations.[1] There seemed little hope of a way out of the impasse unless a successor to Portland as first lord could be appointed. Accordingly on the afternoon of 30 September Eldon, Westmorland, Bathurst, Harrowby, Camden, Chatham, Liverpool, Mulgrave, and Perceval met at the latter's house to draw up an official minute urging his majesty to choose a new prime minister. Eldon was given the job of laying this minute before the king and was asked to add the unanimous opinion of the cabinet that the first lord should be a member of the house of commons. It was a clear nomination of Perceval for 10, Downing Street. George III's reply arrived from Windsor Castle on 2 October. 'Mr. Perceval's conduct', wrote his majesty, 'has so fully confirmed the impression which the King had early received of his zeal and abilities, and of the honourable principles by which he is invariably activated, that His Majesty cannot pause in the choice of the person to whom he should intrust a situation at all times most important, but particularly so under the present arduous circumstances; and His Majesty trusts that the warm and zealous attachment, which Mr. Perceval has manifested towards him on former trying occasions, will now ensure to His Majesty the acceptance of an office in which he may rest assured that he will possess His Majesty's entire confidence.'[2] 'The business', wrote Perceval to his brother, 'is settled': the office of prime minister, he told the Speaker, was one 'which for my sins, or the sins of the

[1] Twiss, vol. II, p. 102.

[2] Windsor MSS., 14695, cabinet minute, 30 Sep. 1809; 14707, George III to cabinet, 2 Oct. 1809; 14711, Perceval to George III, 2 Oct. 1809. Walpole (vol. II, p. 35) incorrectly dates the king's nomination of Perceval as 4 Oct.

PLATE 5

Spencer Perceval as prime minister

(A posthumous portrait painted by G. F. Joseph from a death mask
by Joseph Nollekens)

nation, or both, I am to fill'.[1] 'His eminence', wrote Wilberforce, 'was not of his own seeking.' On 4 October the new prime minister kissed hands.[2]

As first lord, Perceval still faced a political jig-saw many pieces of which, it seemed, would hardly fit into a convincing pattern. He had to find at the very least a new foreign secretary, a secretary of state for war and the colonies, a chancellor of the exchequer, and a president of the board of control, as well as filling the important second-rank offices of secretary to the treasury and secretary-at-war. His only obvious sources of fresh strength to bolster a likely shaky position in parliament were Wellesley, who was thought to be pledged to Canning, the Sidmouth connection, whose support was sure to offend many old Pittites, and the Melville group, whose leader was anathema to the Saints and to most independents. Characteristically Perceval began by offering Portland a cabinet seat without portfolio, but within three weeks of accepting it the long-suffering duke was dead.[3] Far more important were the negotiations with Wellesley, who was still engaged on his special embassy in Spain, and whose attitude to the new government was widely thought to be crucial. So important indeed was the marquis's decision that during the political confusion at the end of September Canning seems to have taken the outrageous step of trying to recall Wellesley to London and deliberately concealing this from his former colleagues. Canning still had in his possession Wellesley's letter of 18 July in which he authorised the foreign secretary to recall him if Canning felt himself compelled to resign from the ministry. The final paragraph of this letter further authorised Canning to show it to other cabinet ministers. But the foreign secretary in fact failed to do this, for to have shown the letter to his colleagues would also have made plain that Canning had deliberately broken his word to the king by giving details of the Camden plan to Wellesley before he sailed to Spain. According to both Bathurst and Sydenham, Canning, during an audience with the king on 2 October, submitted Wellesley's resignation from his embassy, and asked permission to replace him by Bartholomew Frere. His majesty, imagining that change had been

---

[1] Perceval MSS., Perceval to Arden, 2 Oct. 1809; P.R.O., 30/9/15 Colchester MSS., Perceval to Abbot, 1 Oct. 1809.

[2] Wilberforce, vol. II, p. 426; *Day*, 3 and 5 Oct. 1809. The *Sun* printed on 17 Oct. the version of a letter from Perceval to the princess of Wales in which he stressed that he had never thought of himself as a prime minister.

[3] Perceval MSS., Perceval to Portland, 2 and 4 Oct. 1809; Windsor MSS., 14726-7, Perceval to George III, 12 Oct. 1809. Portland died on 30 Oct. 1809.

agreed to by the cabinet in the normal way, made no objection to the plan. Fortunately, according to Bathurst's version of the event, the king saw Perceval later that same day and casually mentioned Canning's request. This gave Perceval the chance to persuade Pole to delay for twenty-four hours the sailing of the ship which was to carry Canning's letter of recall. In the meantime Bathurst was able to write a private note to Wellesley urging him to remain at his post. Sydenham, in contrast, claimed that Canning's plot was discovered only because Liverpool happened to visit the foreign office and see a signed copy of Canning's despatch lying on a table.[1] The whole story appears so extraordinary that it might be difficult to accept, particularly as coming from sources known to be hostile to Canning, were it not for supporting evidence by both Wellesley and the king himself. On 8 October Wellesley wrote to Pole expressly deploring Canning's attempt to use the letter of 18 July to bolster his bid for the office of first lord.[2] Moreover on 30 October Pole received from his brother, and subsequently forwarded to Perceval, a packet containing a formal statement from Wellesley on his dealings with Canning during the previous summer and of his prevailing attitude to the political crisis at home. In this Wellesley confirmed that 'Mr. Canning with great kindness and attention had obtained for Lord Wellesley His Majesty's gracious leave of absence from his post. . . .' It was only when this statement was shown to the king that his majesty realised Canning had broken his pledge of secrecy about the Camden plan. 'The King cannot help expressing his surprise,' wrote his majesty, 'that Mr. Canning's memory should have been so imperfect in regard to what passed between him and Lord Wellesley; Mr. Canning having positively declared to His Majesty when he gave up the seals of his office that he had not made the most distant communication to Lord Wellesley of any intended arrangement which provided for his appointment to the [War and] Colonial Department.'[3] The story remains in part obscure, but the outlines are surely clear enough to account for the suspicion with which Canning was long treated by his former associates.

With yet another crisis safely out of the way Perceval was able to push forward with his plan of offering Wellesley the foreign office.

[1] Rose, vol. II, pp. 399–400; Add. MSS., 37295, fol. 118. For the details of Canning's dealings with Wellesley and the pledge of 18 July see chapter 13, pp. 216 and 221–2.   [2] Add. MSS., 37295, fol. 133.
[3] Perceval MSS., W. W. Pole to Perceval, 30 Oct. 1809; Wellesley's statement (undated); George III to Perceval, 5 Nov. 1809.

On 5 October he sent Thomas Sydenham to Spain with copies both
of the notorious Canning–Perceval correspondence and of the coalition offer to Grey and Grenville.[1] In the meantime Bathurst temporarily accepted the seals of the foreign office, in which post he gave
such satisfaction to the king that his majesty dreaded the thought of
his withdrawing in favour of Wellesley.[2] Finally on 23 November
Wellesley's acceptance of office was received by Pole and five days
later the marquis himself arrived in London.[3] The new foreign secretary had travelled back from Spain with the diplomat, George Jackson.
'It is possible', he confided, 'I may find the Opposition in before I
can reach England, but if not, notwithstanding all they say, I think
we shall form a very strong ministry.' 'I state fairly', he wrote to Sir
John Anstruther, 'that I expect some strength from my own name,
and I have no reason to doubt, that I shall have a principal lead in the
Government, sufficient to justify those who may think favourable
[sic] of me in supporting the system as being essentially mine.' [4] Such
self-confidence was badly needed in the new government and Wellesley's accession undoubtedly strengthened the ministry. Amid the
general chorus of praise only the *Day* ventured to point out that
Wellesley's brilliant career in India might not have been the ideal
training for the necessary compromises of domestic politics.[5]

The vital war and colonial office was offered first to Robert Dundas,
in the hope that this would rally the support of the Melville group and
its Scottish votes. On 12 September Perceval had written to Dundas,
then in Ireland, giving news of Portland's resignation and asking him
to suspend making any final decision about his future political loyalties.
Dundas replied that the duke's departure had not surprised him but
that he hoped, as there seemed to be no basic differences about either
home or foreign policy, that personal feelings alone would not be
allowed to wreck the ministry. On the fourteenth Perceval suggested
that Dundas should return to London and the two met in Downing

---

[1] Perceval MSS., Perceval to Wellesley, 5 Oct. 1809; Add. MSS., 37296, fol. 135.
The embarrassment caused to Perceval by Pole's well-intentioned addition to
these enclosures is discussed in chapter 14, pages 251–2. Liverpool also wrote to
Wellesley urging him to accept (Yonge, vol. I, p. 300).
[2] Malmesbury, *Letters*, vol. II, p. 148; Windsor MSS., 14798, George III to
Bathurst, 24 Nov. 1809; Add. MSS., 37295, fol. 167.
[3] Windsor MSS., 14788 and 14803–4, Perceval to George III, 23 and 28 Nov.
1809.
[4] *Diaries and Letters of Sir George Jackson*, p. 489; Add. MSS., 37295, fol. 175.
[5] *Day*, 25 Nov. 1809. 'Lord Wellesley', wrote Brougham, 'is useless to the
House of Lords, or nearly so. . . .' (Memoirs, vol. I, p. 462.)

Street a week later.[1] The first interview was far from encouraging. His 'natural and oldest connection', Dundas told Perceval, was with Canning. He agreed that the cabinet rump was too weak to go on without recruiting fresh strength and seemed prepared to support either Perceval or Canning if the king asked either of them to form a coalition. If, however, either tried to form a government purely from his own supporters, then Dundas would retire to Scotland.[2] But news of Canning's conduct throughout the crisis quickly changed his attitude. By 30 September Perceval was assuring the Speaker that Dundas was 'very steady' and on 1 October Dundas himself told Canning that he was to succeed Castlereagh at the war office, only to be curtly reminded of his earlier pledge of support for the former foreign secretary.[3] Two days later Perceval formally nominated Dundas to the king as a secretary of state.[4]

In the event it proved easier to detach Dundas from Canning than to reconcile Melville to his son's elevation while he himself was not offered office. On 5 October Perceval wrote to Melville what he himself called 'perhaps the first letter of the kind ever written with such unreserve and frankness from a person in my situation to one in your Lordship's'. It was, confirmed Palmerston, 'more candid perhaps than cautious'. 'Our party's strength,' argued Perceval, 'dismembered as we are by Canning's and Castlereagh's separation from us, and from the following (more or less considerable) of their respective friends, has lost its principle of cohesion. We are no longer the sole representatives of Mr. Pitt. The magic of that name is in a great degree dissolved, and the principle on which we must most rely to keep us together, and give us the assistance of floating strength, is the public sentiment of loyalty and attachment to the King. Amongst the independent part of the House, the country gentlemen, the representatives of popular boroughs, *we must find our saving strength or our destruction.*' Memories of Whitbread's motion and consequent prejudice against Melville was strongest amongst those very people. Perceval indeed might justly have argued that the antagonism to Melville went even further. On 2 October the *Day* opposed Melville's recall on the ground that, in the new cabinet, purity was needed no less than ability: on the sixth even the loyal *Sun* denied that there was any idea of an approach to

[1] Perceval MSS., Perceval to Robert Dundas, 12 and 14 Sep. 1809; Dundas to Perceval, 15 and 17 Sep. 1809.
[2] *Ibid.*, Perceval to Portland, 21 Sep. 1809.
[3] Colchester, vol. II, pp. 211–12; Add. MSS., 38737, fol. 364.
[4] Windsor MSS., 14717, Perceval to George III, 3 Oct. 1809.

Melville.[1] Such opposition, Perceval conceded in his letter, might have
been overcome by Melville's own eloquence had he been eligible to
serve the ministry in the Commons, which was 'the place of difficulty,
and the scene where the decisive battles must be fought, and where
our fate must be decided'. 'Our first burst', continued Perceval, 'will
be our severest trial; if we can but carry a fair cry out of doors with
us at the first, we may hope to stand and serve the country. . . .'
Melville, therefore, could best serve the king by accepting an earldom
and allowing his son to represent the family connection in the cabinet.[2]
The letter was a bold stroke which, for a while, seemed to have some
hopes of success. Robert Dundas himself, although objecting to the
offer of an earldom as likely to be interpreted as a bribe, generally
approved of the text and returned to Ireland to wind up his business
at Dublin Castle.[3] At first even Melville himself appeared disarmed by
Perceval's candour. On 8 October he sent a friendly reply from
Arniston, politely declining an earldom but adding that 'a return to
office would not have afforded any personal gratification to me'.
Nothing was said about Robert Dundas and the war office. Consequently Dundas, taking silence for consent, set out once more from
Ireland, arriving in London, after a rough crossing, on the fifteenth.[4]
But already Melville had had second and less compromising thoughts.
'I have seen Lord Melville,' wrote Lady Anne Townshend to Perceval
from Scotland on 12 October. 'He is an old fox . . . I do not like
either his or his son's manner to you (having had a peep behind the
curtain). I told him so.' His lordship, Palmerston told Malmesbury,
was now 'in high dudgeon', a prophecy amply borne out by the contents
of two letters in 'an altered and more frigid tone' which Robert Dundas
found waiting for him in London.[5] In these Melville counselled
Dundas, both as a father and a friend, not to accept office in the new
administration as many leading peers, including the duke of Buccleuch
and Lord Lonsdale, had decided not to support it unless Melville

[1] *Day*, 2 Oct. 1809; *Sun*, 6 Oct. 1809.
[2] Perceval MSS., Perceval to Melville, 5 Oct. 1809; Ward, vol. I, pp. 259–60.
[3] Perceval MSS., Robert Dundas to Perceval, 7 Oct. 1809. Dundas at first also
objected to the offer of an earldom on the grounds that he could never afford,
when he inherited the title, to maintain the dignity of an earl. But he withdrew
his argument in a second letter to Perceval on 7 Oct. (Perceval MSS.).
[4] *Ibid.*, Melville to Perceval, 8 Oct. 1809; Robert Dundas to same, 11 Oct.
1809. Perceval sent Melville's reply to Windsor on 12 Oct. (Windsor MSS.,
14726–7).
[5] Perceval MSS., Lady Anne Townshend to Perceval, 12 Oct. 1809; Robert
Dundas to same, 15 Oct. 1809; Malmesbury, vol. II, p. 169.

himself was in the cabinet. The letters ended with bitter attacks on Perceval for seeming to prefer the support of the Saints and independents to the votes of the Melville group.

This new turn of events threw ministers once more into confusion. Dundas immediately forwarded Melville's letters to Perceval, together with a reminder that he could never accept the secretaryship of state against his father's wishes. 'The world is turned topsy turvy,' wrote a despairing Perceval to Eldon that evening: Melville seemed 'determined to knock us all on the head'.[1] Ministers were again uncertain even on questions of fundamental parliamentary tactics. For Eldon himself agreed with Melville 'so far as to think that the support of a certain set of men in the House of Commons—I won't call them Saints, but I mean those gentlemen who are always thinking for themselves and yet never know their own minds—is upon the whole a mischievous support. I am sure it was so to Pitt. I am sure he thought so, tho' he could not disengage himself from them—and I am sure it was so to Sidmouth. You know better than I do what it was to the last administration.'[2] 'What you say about the Independents and the Saints,' replied Perceval, 'or whatever distrust you may have for them may be very true; and if any man can have sufficient support from those who will afford it to him systematically, and upon his own principles, and will prefer the support of such uncertain and precarious Friends, he must be a fool. But what can Lord Melville or anyone mean? Are we in a situation of strength that would justify our throwing away from us even the precarious support of from 15 to 20, perhaps, members of Parliament? It is fine talking to say we will not mind them, but can we do otherwise than mind the means of forming a majority in the House of Commons? This support, nor any other, should not be bought or purchased at the expense of principle or [at] the expense of doing wrong morally or politically; but however it might gratify a great deal of feeling to send all those persons into direct opposition yet I am confident it would be giving to our adversaries a weight which would make their scales infallibly preponderate. I do not think the greatest Saint amongst them ever played so devilish a trick upon us as the arch *anti-saint* is doing at the present moment.'[3] The outburst quickly brought Eldon to heel, but did nothing to lessen the ministry's overwhelming political problems.[4]

---

[1] Twiss, vol. II, p. 106.   [2] Perceval MSS., Eldon to Perceval, 15 Oct. 1809.
[3] *Ibid.*, Perceval to Eldon, 17 Oct. 1809.
[4] 'I feel all your arguments about Saints', wrote Eldon to Perceval on 18 Oct.,

All that Perceval could do, while waiting for Dundas to make a final appeal to his father, was to report depressingly to Windsor that 'our difficulties, however considerable at first, were increasing and not dimishing before us'. Characteristically the king replied that he was fully aware of all difficulties but he had 'drawn his line, and no prospect of embarrassment or opposition shall induce him to stray from it'. 'This', wrote Perceval to Eldon with his customary frankness, 'is certainly very fine, firm and noble—but it is not very helpful.' [1] Even Eldon's spirits so far failed him that he saw 'no chance of standing' if Dundas withdrew 'and the Scotch Legion go against us. . . . My inventive powers are at a loss to suggest to me what is to be done.' [2] Huskisson thought that the ministry must not allow itself to be bullied by Melville, while William Dundas assured Perceval that 'you could not take my uncle into office without laying the axe to the root of your Government'. [3] On 20 October and again on 23 October Perceval had to tell the king that there was still no word from Arniston. Finally on the twenty-fourth Melville sent a blank refusal to reconsider his attitude and Dundas withdrew his acceptance of the war office. [4]

The delay had doubly handicapped the government both by giving fresh evidence of its weakness and, as Perceval grumbled to Arden, by making it less likely that the second choice, C. P. Yorke, would accept the office. In fact Yorke would have agreed to serve had he been approached a week earlier, but although Perceval lost no time in contacting him on 24 October, it was already too late. Yorke's brother, Lord Hardwicke, had persuaded him to refuse all offers. It would be better, urged the king with unconscious humour, not to be too hasty in filling the vacancy as a bad appointment might cause great trouble later. [5] In the end Perceval solved at least one of his

---

'and an administration must begin under very different circumstances that can venture to disregard them' (Perceval MSS.).

[1] Windsor MSS., 14728-9, Perceval to George III, 16 Oct. 1809, and 14730, George III to Perceval, 17 Oct. 1809; Perceval MSS., Perceval to Eldon, 17 Oct. 1809. 'Surely', replied Eldon, 'the world has gone mad! I admire the King's firmness, but I feel with you that the situation is tremendous' (Perceval MSS.).

[2] Perceval MSS., Eldon to Perceval, 19 Oct. 1809.

[3] Herries, vol. I, p. 13; Perceval MSS., William Dundas to Perceval, 22 Oct. 1809.

[4] Windsor MSS., 14733-4, 14739-40, and 14744-5; Perceval MSS., Robert Dundas to Perceval, 24 Oct. 1809.

[5] Perceval MSS., Perceval to Arden, 24 Oct. 1809; Windsor MSS., 14743-4, 14745 and 14746, Perceval to George III, 24 Oct. (2 letters) and 26 Oct. 1809.

difficulties by suggesting that Liverpool should move to the war office and be replaced by Richard Ryder as home secretary. Even then the king objected that Ryder should be put in charge of war and the colonies in order to allow Liverpool to stay at the home office, where he had been so successful. Only Liverpool's personal assurance that Ryder's health would not stand the worry of the war office and the strain of constant attendance in the Commons averted the possibility of this catastrophic distribution of the seals of office.[1]

Perceval's third major set of negotiations was with the Sidmouth group, where he once more had the unenviable task of trying to secure general support in parliament, and the acceptance of office by certain members of the connection, without offering Sidmouth himself any share in the government. Contact was first established, through Chatham, on 5 October, who was sent to Sidmouth 'to intimate a wish on the part of the King and Mr. Perceval that they should all be brought together again'. Unfortunately Sidmouth soon lost interest when the exact terms of the offer were explained to him.[2] Nor was this lack of enthusiasm confined to Sidmouth himself, who had been seen walking down Berkley Street arm-in-arm with the two Grenvilles. In government circles Arbuthnot had already assured waverers that 'the Doctor will not be resorted to', as Perceval thought he would be a source of weakness rather than strength, while Eldon feared that Sidmouth would demand an unfair share of offices for his supporters. Sidmouth's army', he grumbled, 'are [sic] all officers and no soldiers.'[3] Yet Perceval was so eager to have Nicholas Vansittart at the treasury and Bragge Bathurst as secretary-at-war that he decided to try a second and direct appeal to Sidmouth. Consequently on 7 October he wrote to the Doctor in as candid terms as he had already approached Melville. 'One of our great dangers', he wrote, 'is from the defection from among our Friends of the old Pitt connection, who may be disposed to follow Mr. Canning; and not only among those who are the most doubtful but among some of the most determined in our support, there are several who have taken such a prejudice upon the subject of your Lordship's immediately forming a part of the Government that I am most strongly impressed with the opinion, that they would, by that circumstance, be much alienated from us, if not wholly

[1] Windsor MSS., 14750-3, Perceval to George III, 26 Oct. 1809; 14754, George III to Perceval, 27 Oct. 1809; 14758-9, Liverpool to George III, 28 Oct. 1809.   [2] Pellew, vol. III, p. 5.

[3] Day, 2 Oct. 1809; Add. MSS., 38737, fol. 333; Twiss, vol. II, p. 103.

decided in favour of Mr. Canning.' Sidmouth, therefore, would initially best serve the king by staying out of office but persuading certain of his friends to accept.[1] Such political honesty impressed the king who, after seeing the text of the letter, assured his prime minister that 'upon these occasions, as indeed in every transaction, . . . a fair straight forward course is that which must ultimately prove most beneficial.' Unfortunately events soon proved that, in the short run, it did not pay.[2] For on the very evening of 7 October Sidmouth replied that Bragge Bathurst would 'under no possible circumstances . . . accede to such a proposition' as he agreed with his leader that the government's only hope of political salvation lay in pursuing its offer of coalition with Grey and Grenville. This plunged ministers into renewed gloom. The suggestion of further negotiations with the opposition, thought Bathurst, might prove politically very dangerous if it became widely known that Sidmouth had made it after conversations with Grenville himself. Eldon confessed that the advice 'makes me sick' and concluded 'that Lord S will be with you or against you as it may seem most advisable when the time for acting comes'. 'And now, my dear sir,' ended Eldon, 'whether we are to be beaten to dust and ashes, or, what is ten times worse, to be humiliated and disgraced . . . by finally coalescing . . . I will stand and fall with my old master and you, whom I believe to be his most attached servant.'[3]

The probable loss of the votes of the Sidmouth group was immediately followed by a humiliating failure to persuade anyone to accept the exchequer. 'I am', wrote Arden to his brother on 7 October, 'quite happy at your plan of having a Chancellor of the Exchequer, which will relieve you of a great load of business.'[4] On 13 October Nicholas Vansittart refused it out of loyalty to Sidmouth, young Palmerston declined a week later, Robert Milnes rejected an offer on the twenty-third, and finally both George Rose and Charles Long declined on the twenty-fourth. After such a series of rebuffs Perceval felt compelled

[1] Perceval MSS., Perceval to Sidmouth, 7 Oct. 1809; Pellew, vol. III, p. 7.

[2] Perceval MSS., Perceval to George III, 7 Oct. 1809 and George III to Perceval, 8 Oct. 1809; Windsor MSS., 14719–20.

[3] Perceval MSS., Sidmouth to Perceval, 7 Oct. 1809; Bathurst to Perceval, 8 Oct. 1809; Eldon to Perceval, 8 Oct. 1809; Windsor MSS., 14723–4, Perceval to George III, 9 Oct. 1809; Herries, vol. I, p. 12; Pellew, vol. III, pp. 7–9. 'His Majesty is sorry to believe', wrote George III to Perceval on 10 Oct., 'that Lord Sidmouth is more influenced by private feelings than by his concern for the welfare and interests of the public cause.'

[4] Perceval MSS., Arden to Perceval, 7 Oct. 1809.

to remain as chancellor himself.[1] 'The times', wrote the faithful Ward, 'are sadly out of joint, and it is difficult to say who are to set them right; for so strange are they that Perceval, who probably combines more honesty with more ability than any other man alive in his own person, is not equal to it alone, so completely have the disadvantageous parts of our mixed constitution got uppermost in the course of our miserable struggles.' 'Nothing', added Ward a few days later, 'would keep me up amidst such hypocrisy, plots and counter-plots, except the excellent clear character of Mr. Perceval, and the idea of fulfilling a great duty of loyalty as long as he thinks it can be fulfilled.' Yet, in spite of rapidly mounting difficulties, Perceval remained 'particularly calm, collected and open'.[2]

Much of the government's hopes of survival depended on the attitude of the Canningites, who might be able to rally as many as sixteen votes in the Commons. On 16 September Rose, while dining with Canning at Gloucester Lodge, mentioned that he had heard from Perceval the previous day that Canning had no intention of opposing the government. Canning immediately denied making any general pledge of support, although he was prepared to give 'general assurances of good will towards Mr. Perceval' and a guarantee not to take any hostile attitude 'in matters which personally interested the King'. While Rose walked home with Bagot, who questioned him about George III's attitude to the Canningites, Canning himself settled down to write to Perceval. There must, he argued, be no misunderstandings about any pledge of support. 'I have given no such promise. I am not aware of having spoken on the subject to any person except the King. And I am *very certain* that the King cannot have so understood what I said to His Majesty.' There was, replied Perceval, no assumption on his part that Canning had ever given a general pledge of support. What he had repeated to Rose, and to others, was the exchange of views with Canning just before his resignation. He had certainly then understood 'that you were of opinion that a sufficiently strong Government could be formed if I were placed at the head of it, and that the support which I certainly understood you to intend, but as certainly never to pledge or to promise, would in fact be of essential use'. This interpretation had been confirmed by later conversations with Portland. If it were wrong, he would be 'as you may well imagine, for

---

[1] For a full discussion of the attempts to find a chancellor of the exchequer see chapter 19, pp. 360–3.
[2] Ward, vol. I, pp. 271, 273 and 275.

many reasons, very sorry for it'. Canning's reply gave the prime minister ample cause for disquiet. 'My goodwill', wrote Canning, 'towards yourself personally you do not over-rate.' He had not, however, talked, either to Perceval or the duke, of support which would be of 'essential use'. What he had said was that, in the existing circumstances, any support that he might give would be more useful if he were out of office rather than serving under Perceval's leadership. He had told the king of his determination to support, from the back benches, 'not any particular Government, but any Government upon a particular *class of questions* in which the fate of *all* Government is involved'. 'Pray, do not imagine,' ended Canning, 'from my declining to avow any fixed *intention* of general support, that I therefore entertain a *contrary* intention. Nothing is farther from my thoughts. But whatever I may do, I am desirous to do *freely*.' With this entirely noncommittal statement of Canning's intentions Perceval had finally to be content. 'All that I shall now feel myself authorised to state', he wrote in ending the exchange of letters, 'will be that you have indeed given me to understand that you have no fixed intention of opposing the Government, but that you are perfectly free from any pledge, express or implied, immediate or eventual, one way or the other, as to the course which you may think it right to pursue.' [1] Early in October Bagot, after a conversation with his leader, assured Ward that the Canningites would enter into no alliances, but would 'stand alone and act according to circumstances'. It seemed to many that Canning hoped to dominate the parliamentary situation by throwing the votes of his group into either scale. If, William Lamb told Lady Bessborough, he stood aside and acted moderately 'he had a great game to play', as independent members would soon flock under his banner.[2] Certainly Canning himself still had no doubts about the rightness of his action in resigning. 'To remain', he pointed out to Malmesbury on 4 November, 'after such usage as I had experienced would have been to remain degraded, and at the mercy of such men as Lord Camden, bearing all the burden of their unfitness and just unpopularity,

[1] Rose, vol. II, p. 375; Perceval MSS., Canning to Perceval, 16 Sep. 1809 (two letters) and 18 Sep. 1809; Perceval to Canning, 16 and 18 Sep. 1809. Probable Canningite voters in the Commons at the beginning of the 1810 session were:—Lord Binning, C. P. Blachford, Sturges Bourne, Col. George Canning, John Dent, Charles Ellis, G. B. Greenhough, Huskisson, Hylton Joliffe, R. H. Leigh, Granville Leveson-Gower, E. J. Littleton, William Taylor, J. W. Ward and Wilbraham Bootle.

[2] Bagot, vol. I, p. 336; *Private Correspondence of Lord Granville Leveson-Gower*, vol. II, pp. 342–3.

and intrigued against by them in return for that support.' [1] The general hostility of the press still rankled and Canning was full of complaints against Cooke, whom he suspected of being responsible. 'This', he wrote after reading one particularly hostile article, 'is not fair—not like a gentleman—but it is very like Cooke.' [2] Perceval had good cause to be apprehensive about the future conduct of so disgruntled a politician.

Fortunately for Perceval the Canningite group had lost some of its cohesion. After September 1809 Granville Leveson-Gower, Bagot, Charles Ellis, Wilbraham Bootle, John Dent and a handful of lesser lights all remained faithful to their leader. So also, in spite of the blandishments of Perceval and Arbuthnot, did Huskisson, the most able and important of the group. [3] Sturges Bourne, although he disapproved of Canning's conduct, finally resigned his treasury lordship rather than be accused of deserting a leader to whom he owed his introduction to Pitt, to parliament, and to office. [4] Four others, Rose, Charles Long, R. P. Milnes and Lord Fitzharris, had no such fine scruples. Rose and Long, old hands on the treasury benches, had both first thrown in their lot with Canning at the time of Pitt's death. When the cabinet rump met on 18 September, Eldon told his colleagues that Rose would resign with the foreign secretary. But two days later Rose decided, after a sleepless night, that Canning had throughout aimed only at the premiership. His change of mind, he explained, was the result of reading copies of the Perceval–Canning correspondence and of pressure from his family not to desert the king. Charles Long also at first sent a letter of resignation to Perceval on 18 September, stressing, however, that he was 'far from objecting in the slightest degree to any part of the conduct which you have held on the late very embarrassing circumstances'. By 23 September he too had seen copies of the Perceval–Canning correspondence and had broken with his former chief. [5] Fitzharris, who never considered Perceval or Liverpool 'pure Pittites', might not have deserted Canning at all had not his father, Malmesbury, brought intense pressure to persuade him to write 'a mild declaration of war'. More damaging to Canning was the loss of the young and promising Robert Milnes, who began with a 'partiality' to the foreign secretary and an 'aversion to Perceval'. Yet, after interviews with both

[1] Malmesbury, *Letters*, vol. II, pp. 176–7.　　[2] Add. MSS., 38737, fol. 364.
[3] For a list of the Canningites see Aspinall, *Trans. of the Royal Hist. Soc.*, 4th series, vol. 17, *The Canningite Party*, p. 227.
[4] Rose, vol. II, p. 349; Add. MSS., 42774, fol. 282.
[5] Rose, vol. II, pp. 354 and 377; Twiss, vol. II, pp. 94 and 96; Perceval MSS., Long to Perceval, 18 Sep. 1809.

on 23 October, Milnes pledged full support for, though he declined participation in, the Perceval government. Parliament, he later told Palmerston, 'must fix this honest little fellow firmly in his seat, as it is a struggle of principle on the one hand against trimming and political intrigue on the other'.[1] Against these losses the Canningite group made only one new recruit, Charles Brandling, one of the members for Newcastle, although Canning himself also tried unsuccessfully to win over Croker.[2]

Of all the junior ministers Huskisson's loss was most keenly felt, both in the House and at the treasury. Arbuthnot might replace him as a party manager in the Commons, although some influential members, like Sir Thomas Plumer, doubted even this, but there was no one to match his mastery of treasury business. Douglas called him the best financial secretary to the treasury in living memory, Nicholas Vansittart, one of Huskisson's most persistent critics on financial policy, thought he had 'done his business extremely well', while the *Day* wrote of his 'most undeviating attention to business and his perfect knowledge of the financial department, both in revenue and expenditure'. Of greater immediate political importance was Wellesley's grief at the news of his resignation. 'I entertain', wrote Wellesley to Arbuthnot, 'the greatest regard and esteem for his character, and the highest respect for his talents and attainments; in any view which I have ever formed of acting in the King's Councils I have always looked to him as a main source of assistance.' Sturges Bourne, never the greatest of optimists, despaired of Perceval's chances, 'even in his own department, if the report of Huskisson's retiring be well-founded'.[3] Perceval himself seems to have shared such doubts, as his conciliatory letters to Huskisson in August had shown.[4] Throughout the last weeks of the Portland ministry Perceval vainly hoped that Huskisson might put his membership of the government above his personal loyalty to Canning. One of his first acts after accepting the

---

[1] Malmesbury, *Letters*, vol. II, pp. 159, 163-9, 174-5 and 191; Perceval MSS., Perceval to Arden, 26 Oct. 1809. For the offer to Milnes see Sterling, *The Letter Bag of Lady Elizabeth Spencer Stanhope*, vol. I, p. 184.

[2] *Creevey Papers*, vol. I, p. 108; Croker, *Correspondence*, vol. I, p. 17.

[3] Perceval MSS., Sir Thomas Plumer to Perceval, 14 Sep. 1809 ('Huskisson has a knowledge of the state of the House of Commons, and the leanings, connections and opinions of everyone in it superior to what I believe anyone else possesses'); Glenbervie, vol. II, p. 29; Herries, vol. I, p. 11; *Day*, 24 Sep. 1809; Camden Soc., LXV, Aspinall, *Correspondence of Charles Arbuthnot*, p. 6; Herries MSS., Vansittart to Herries, 28 Sep. 1809; Malmesbury, *Letters*, vol. II, p. 134.

[4] For details see chapter 13, p. 223.

premiership was to invite his treasury colleague to meet him and discuss arrangements for the new government. His only reply was a formal letter of resignation. Herries was with Perceval when he read it and saw him throw it down on the table, saying, 'This is the worst and most unexpected blow of all.' [1] At the time of Pitt's death, explained Huskisson, 'the political attachment I then formed was certainly with Canning: and with my ideas on this subject, and my personal feelings towards him, I must beg leave to retire from my present situation if I can no longer hold it without the sacrifice of that attachment'. On this point he remained unshakeable though Perceval wrote letters full of gratitude for past help and Arbuthnot hinted at future prospects of the exchequer and cabinet rank.[2]

Finally even the filling of second rank and junior posts caused Perceval great labours. Wellesley had recommended Sir John Anstruther to succeed the earl of Harrowby at the board of control. When he surprisingly declined, Perceval was overjoyed to hear that Melville had belatedly repented so far as to allow Robert Dundas to accept an office outside the cabinet. And so Dundas became the new president of the board of control.[3] Charles Long was the first to refuse the post of secretary-at-war. Perceval then offered it to Lord William Bentinck, on the understanding that he must immediately find himself a seat in the Commons. 'I very much wish Lord William Bentinck were appointed', wrote Bathurst, 'because we want some men of rank among us.' But Bentinck, after consulting Lord Titchfield, also declined, leaving Perceval to sound both Milnes and Palmerston. Milnes took two days for reflection before deciding that his lack of experience might cause him to do more harm than good in office. He softened the blow a little, however, by pledging constant attendance and steady support in the Commons. Fortunately the last choice, Palmerston, finally accepted, although declining the offer of a seat in

---

[1] Perceval MSS., Huskisson to Perceval, 15 Sep. 1809; Ward, vol. I, p. 353.

[2] Perceval MSS., Huskisson to Perceval, 15 Sep. 1809; Add. MSS., 38737, fols. 338 and 383. Perceval's reply to Huskisson's letter of resignation and Arbuthnot's and Herries' interpretation of the same letter led to a lengthy correspondence between Perceval and Huskisson on the nature of the latter's attachment to Canning (Perceval MSS., Huskisson to Perceval, 24 and 28 Sep. 1809; Perceval to Huskisson, 27 Sep. 1809, and Add. MSS., 38737, fol. 347). The correspondence ended when Canning curtly instructed Huskisson to stop explaining his actions lest Perceval should use the letters as he had used copies of the earlier correspondence with Canning. (Add. MSS., 38737, fol. 354).

[3] Add. MSS., 37295, fol. 171; Windsor MSS., 14750-3, Perceval to George III, 26 Oct. 1809; Perceval MSS., Perceval to Arden, 2 Nov. 1809.

the cabinet. It was, thought Huskisson, 'a very bad appointment', but Pole, more wisely, professed 'a very high opinion of his sense and judgement' and had no doubt of his success in office.[1] Croker's appointment as secretary to the admiralty met with a similar mixed reception, but the acceptance by Manners Sutton, the archbishop of Canterbury's son, of the post of judge advocate was widely acclaimed.[2] Eliot and Broderick, both strong supporters of Perceval, remained as lords of the treasury, but vacancies caused by the resignations of Sturges Bourne and Foster led to refusals by Nepean, Lord Percy, and Lord Brooke before Desart and Snowdon Barne, 'a very steady supporter of Your Majesty's Government', consented to complete the commission.[3] And so, by the end of November, and after two full months of taxing negotiations, Perceval had formed a ministry. Yet the prevailing state of political feeling made it seem doubtful if all the effort had been worth while.

The new ministry had a very bad press, particularly from the influential independent papers. *The Times* had compared Perceval's offer to Grey and Grenville with the courtship of Delilah, 'who solicited the embraces of her hero only to shear him of his strength'. On 28 September it prophesied that the king would send for the opposition: four days later it reported that the duke of Richmond would be first lord with Perceval as foreign secretary. Only Perceval and Canning were exempted from the 'general obloquy' cast on members of the Portland cabinet, but Canning was brushed aside as unfit for the lead on account of his birth and Perceval rejected because he lacked 'political weight'. 'Poor people!' wrote the paper, 'and is it come to this with you, that you can find none to accept what you are ready to bestow?' The final announcement that the choice had fallen on Perceval moved *The Times* to fury, while his cabinet was lashed as a 'Junto of Scheldtites' who had 'jumbled themselves together to govern those whom they have almost reduced to such a state that they deserve no better governors'.[4] The newly-founded *Day*, although

[1] Windsor MSS., 14723-4, 14726-7, 14728-9, 14737-8, 14739-40, Perceval to George III, 9, 12, 16, 21, 23 and 24 Oct. 1809; Perceval MSS., W. W. Pole to Perceval, 5 Nov. 1809 and Bathurst to same, 8 Oct. 1809; Herries, vol. I, p. 13.
[2] Croker, *Diaries*, vol. I, pp. 17 and 21-2; Herries, vol. I, p. 13; Brougham, *Memoirs*, vol. I, pp. 466-7; Windsor MSS., 14756 and 14762-3, Perceval to George III, 28 and 30 Oct. 1809.
[3] Windsor MSS., 14750-3, 14781-2, 14785 and 14800-1, Perceval to George III, 2, 13, 20 and 25 Nov. 1809.
[4] *The Times*, 28 Sep., 2, 3, 4 and 14 Oct. 1809. While Perceval was on his

more moderate in its language, was little more friendly. Portland,
Canning, and Castlereagh, it argued, must not be replaced by 'mere
names', for only a 'complete and radical alteration' would satisfy the
public. 'Those little, paltry, trivial changes of men, but not of measures,
which belong to party . . . should be flung aside, and altogether
exploded. To meet the changes that are ready to burst upon us, it
becomes our duty to collect all that is truly patriotic, to make one
common sacrifice of party feuds and party prejudices, to summon all
the means and resources which the united experience and wisdom of
the country can supply.' [1] After Grey and Grenville's rejection of a
coalition, the *Day* became even more critical. The offer itself had
shown the cabinet's awareness of its own insufficiency and yet Perceval
had decided to stay on with colleagues unfitted 'to ride the whirlwind
and direct the storm'. On 2 October the same paper reported canvassing in places as far apart as Sussex and Lancaster in expectation of an
early general election. [2] The great majority of political observers of all
parties thought the same, although Perceval's closest friends did their
best to put a good face on things. 'I wish', wrote Lord Manners, 'you
may have an equal proportion of friends in the House with those you
possess out of it, and you will be strong enough.' 'Bear up boldly',
urged Lord Abercorn, 'against party factions in Parliament and
Jacobins out.' [3] But generally even ministers themselves were pessimistic about the cabinet's chances. Both Eldon, who laid twenty to one
that the government would not even face parliament, and Harrowby
prophesied a quick defeat, while Wellesley half expected the opposition
to have taken office before he could reach London. 'We may not',
wrote Palmerston, 'remain in long enough to retrieve one's blunders
at the start.' [4]

Leaders of the opposition, in contrast, could scarcely have been
more confident. Grey was torn between admiration for the courage and

---

way to the guildhall on lord mayor's day his coach was surrounded by a mob
(*Sun*, 11 Nov. 1809).

[1] *Day*, 22 Sep. 1809.
[2] *Ibid.*, 2 Oct. 1809.
[3] Perceval MSS., Lord Manners to Perceval, 17 Nov. 1809; Lord Abercorn
to same, 12 Mar. 1810. 'I have', wrote Lady Anne Townshend on 16 Nov.,
'been for some time intending to throw in my hearty congratulations with the
rest of your friends—many of them may say more, but I will be bound, that not
one of them (your own family excepted) will feel more sincerely rejoiced at
seeing you placed in your present situation than your old friend A.T.' (Perceval
MSS.).
[4] Malmesbury, *Letters*, vol. II, p. 159.

rage at the wickedness of Perceval at daring to form a ministry at such a crisis. In the end he decided, predictably, that the new government was bound to collapse shortly without his sacrificing the comforts of life in his northern home. Tierney expected another complete change of administration within three months, while Auckland argued that every member of the existing cabinet, with the exception of Perceval, was simply inadequate for the job on hand.[1] 'In the whole of the list', rejoiced Wynn, after studying the composition of the cabinet, 'there is not one man of old property, weight and influence in the country but that idiot Lord Westmorland.' It was a strange charge to come from such a source, but similar thoughts must have occurred to many an independent country gentleman in the Commons.[2] Wilberforce, whose views might influence the vital votes of some of his fellow Saints, thought the government worthy of a trial, as Wellesley, Liverpool, and Ryder were all 'sensible men' and Perceval was 'better than all the rest'. Sidmouth had a similar high opinion of the new prime minister, but considered the rest of the cabinet unfit to tackle the grave problems ahead. The biggest dilemma faced ambitious young backbenchers like Fitzharris who thought the ministry 'weak and inefficient' although he had broken his connection with Canning under pressure from his father. Now if, in spite of his misgivings, he supported Perceval in the House he might soon be faced with the choice of either following a defeated Perceval into opposition or again tacking about and 'without knowing whither to steer becoming either a courtier or a no-party man'.[3] Uncommitted opinion outside the House was even more pessimistic about the ministry's chances. Dr. Jackson, the late dean of Christ Church, told the Speaker that he doubted whether, in spite of Perceval's 'zeal and goodness', the government would ever dare to face parliament, while Willoughby Gordon was convinced that a chimney sweep of good parts and strong nerves had as much chance as Perceval of controlling the Commons. Wellington, full as usual of non-party calls for national unity, gave Perceval his sympathy but not his hopes. These, he told Pole, rested on Wellesley as prime minister with Vansittart at the exchequer.[4]

[1] Auckland, *Journal*, vol. IV, p. 332; Olphin, p. 136; Colchester MSS., P.R.O. 30/9/15. [2] Nat. Lib. of Wales MSS., 4814, fol. 58.
[3] Wilberforce, *Life*, vol. III, pp. 430–3; Pellew, vol. III, p. 16; Malmesbury, *Letters*, vol. II, p. 172.
[4] Colchester, vol. II, p. 214; Add. MSS., 38737, fol. 340; *Camden Soc., 3rd series, Miscellany*, pp. 18–26; Buckingham, *Court and Cabinets of George III*, vol. IV, p. 389.

In fact, ministers did have certain solid advantages. The new administration need no longer be a government of departments for, as Sturges Bourne foresaw, the cabinet had, in Perceval, 'an avowed and, I hope, a real head'. They had the cement of office to encourage their efforts, and if this proved insufficient, they had a loyal and powerful ally in the king. 'You have', Arden assured his brother, 'the King's most entire confidence, and if you retain it by a free, frequent and unreserved communication, it will be peculiarly gratifying and acceptable to him. His intentions are so pure and his judgement so good that I am sure that it will be for the ease and benefit of your administration. ... Mr. Pitt and likewise most of his Ministers have failed in this respect. I hope you will not be wanting in it.' The opposition was strong in numbers but so confused in aims that the moderates might in a crisis be persuaded to help bolster the government against excessive radical pressure. Finally the cabinet appealed to many uncommitted members of both Houses because, blunder as it might, it would surely never waver in the war against revolutionary France. 'To resist this', cried Malmesbury, 'is all in all. Right principles on this point with moderate talents are safer, much safer for us, than the most brilliant talents with nervous principles.' On precisely this appeal much of Perceval's hopes of survival rested.[1]

The new list of cabinet ministers was hardly likely to bolster public confidence, and it was a sad commentary on their collective lack of talent that Perceval so towered above his colleagues. Much of the prime minister's own strength lay in the general acceptance of his personal integrity. Early in 1810 the *Day*, 'in these times of imputed corruption, when everything is supposed to be vendible', set its own estimate of value on political heads. Sidmouth was listed as a counterfeit guinea and Melville as a forged pound note, while Castlereagh was valued at an Irishman's blessing or a bad shilling and Canning was 'worth a song'. Tierney's price was 'known only to his political friends', but Perceval came third in the whole list (below only Grenville and Grey) at a premium of £1 4s. 0d. He commanded the respect of all groups in the House and honest country gentlemen preferred his simple but clear sentences to all the polished oratory of a Canning or a whig. His high standing amongst government supporters was shown in the spring of 1810 when he was the guest of honour at the London Tavern at the annual dinner held to celebrate the anniversary of Pitt's birthday.

[1] Malmesbury, *Letters*, vol. II, pp. 146 and 181–6; Perceval MSS., Arden to Perceval, 7 Oct. 1809.

As he entered the room he was greeted by 'a spontaneous burst of applause which continued until some time after he had taken his seat'. In his short speech Perceval underlined the two cardinal virtues of the ministry. The cabinet would doubtless make its share of mistakes, but, inspired by the memory of Pitt's example, it would carry on the struggle in parliament against 'democrats and levellers': ministers were now completely united and would share equally in all praise and blame that might fall on the government. Above all they had every con- fidence in Wellington and would continue to reinforce the British forces in the Peninsula in spite of the opposition's defeatism. After he had sat down his friend Beeston Long, of the bank of England, had to wait several minutes for the cheers to die down before he could propose the next toast.[1] The most widely shared fear was that Perceval might, as prime minister, prove too conciliatory in parliament. Old Malmesbury, who lived in perpetual fear of the growing strength of radicalism, thought Perceval 'too candid and conceding . . . , bad ingredients when mixed together, and not suited to the temper of the times'. Fitzharris argued, in November 1809, that Perceval's 'system of concession and candour' would ruin his government, while Faring- ton heard the prime minister described at a literary dinner as 'too yielding'. He too readily granted papers when moved for in parliament, 'which causes vast expense; at the Pay Office there is in consequence as much business on that account as the regular business of the Office requires'. In the end even the king complained that Perceval consented to the production of a greater quantity of papers than any of his predecessors had ever done. Lord Bulkeley, usually among the most temperate of the opposition, came to suspect that the prime minister deliberately made concessions to reformers in order to trap Grey and Grenville between the king and the mob.[2]

In fact, Perceval could hardly take the strongest of lines in the Commons. Eight of his nine cabinet colleagues sat in the Lords. The exception, Richard Ryder, the new home secretary, had little to recom- mend him beyond his unswerving personal loyalty to Perceval, which alone had persuaded him to accept office at all. Under Portland he had

---

[1] Wilberforce, *Life*, vol. III, p. 426; *Day*, 16 Jan. 1810; *Sun*, 29 May 1810; *Gent. Mag.*, 1810 Supplement, p. 600; Perceval MSS., draft of Perceval's speech at the London Tavern. Perceval, said Charles Arbuthnot, 'has the best regulated ambition I ever witnessed' (Croker, *Diaries*, pp. 15–16).

[2] Malmesbury, *Letters*, vol. II, pp. 140 and 191; *Bathurst MSS.*, p. 140; Auck- land, *Journal*, vol. IV, p. 339; Farington, *Diary*, vol. V, p. 196; Add. MSS., 38190, fol. 17.

acted for a short time as a lord of the treasury and then as judge
advocate general, a post recommended by Perceval because it brought
Ryder into frequent and useful contact with the king. Devout,
cautious, and badly lacking in energy, Ryder was never suited for the
responsibilities of cabinet office, while his uncertain health and recurring nervous headaches made him liable to collapse at moments of
crisis. Symbolically, he took as his personal private secretary at the
home office a clerk named Peace, but he was to get little of that until
he thankfully retired to private life in 1812.[1]

In the Lords, Liverpool, a parliamentary speaker of a very high
order, led a largely unchanged team. He got most help, among the old
hands, from Lord Chancellor Eldon and from Bathurst, who remained
at the board of trade. For the rest, Westmorland, the lord privy seal,
and the indolent Mulgrave, at the admiralty, filled two places without
any particular distinction, while the discredited Chatham, at the board
of ordnance, and Camden, as lord president, were more a source of
weakness than strength. The only newcomer on the treasury bench
was Wellesley, who quickly proved the most troublesome member of
the team. As foreign secretary Wellesley was inexperienced, lazy, and
haughty. He soon quarrelled with most of his cabinet colleagues, and
treated them with such condescension that they called him 'the Grand
Lama'. He had the temperament, wrote one observer, of 'a Spanish
Grandee grafted on an Irish potato'. The very qualities that had served
him so well in India and in the Peninsula disqualified him from a
successful career in domestic politics. He had, wrote Holland, more
genius than prudence and more spirit than principle; he was more
capable of doing extraordinary things well than doing routine things
satisfactorily. Above all he found it difficult to compromise and to try
to persuade rather than overbear his colleagues in the ministry.[2] He
began his career at the foreign office by objecting to the under-secretary
Hamilton, whom it was seriously proposed to move to the home office.
Within six months the department was in 'a pretty tolerable state of
disorganisation'. In September 1810 Wellesley fell ill and Hamilton
offered to help clear away the accumulation of official papers at
Apsley House. He found seventy books full of them, most of which
had never been opened: of these Hamilton left only six—'the rest being

---

[1] Harrowby MSS., Richard Ryder to Harrowby, 14 Nov. 1807. 'The King',
reported Perceval, 'seemed much pleased with Ryder's appointment' (Perceval
MSS., Perceval to Arden, 2 Nov. 1809).

[2] Fulford, *George the Fourth*, p. 120; Holland, *Further Memoirs*, p. 113.

now mostly useless'. 'I have not yet seen Lord Wellesley,' wrote
Francis Jackson in February 1811. 'He never goes to the Office, and
is visible nowhere but in his harem': 'I wish', confessed Wellington,
'that Wellesley was castrated; or that he would like other people attend
to his business and perform too.' [1] Stratford Canning at Constantinople was left for long periods without any instructions at all; Lord
Strangford assured the duke of Northumberland in 1812 that 'more
will be done in six months with Lord Castlereagh, than in two years
with his predecessor'; and Perceval himself had, more than once, to
remind his foreign secretary to grant an interview or write a despatch. [2]
At other times Wellesley would suddenly take important decisions
without consulting the cabinet or even the prime minister. On Christmas day 1811 Perceval learnt, quite by accident, that Sir Robert
Wilson was about to leave on a new diplomatic mission: 'and as I
know not whither he is going,' wrote the prime minister to Wellesley,
'whether to Egypt, Constantinople, Palestine or elsewhere, nor what
the object of his mission is, I am sure you will not be surprised at
my request to know something concerning it'. The following day
Wellesley replied that he was sending Wilson to Constantinople to
work for a Russo-Turkish armistice: he thought he had mentioned
the subject 'some time ago' and would certainly have discussed it
more fully 'if I had thought it deserving of your attention'. [3] On
another occasion the foreign secretary high-handedly arranged for a
pension to be granted to Erskine, the former British minister at
Washington, without again mentioning the matter to either the cabinet
or the treasury. When Perceval protested, he received a letter from
Wellesley 'written in a most grand magnificent style like some of his
exordiums at our cabinets and like them most clearly wrong in every
one of the propositions he maintains. . . .' Perceval's attitude was
supported by Liverpool, Eldon, and Richard Ryder, but (because of

[1] Perceval MSS., Arbuthnot to Perceval, 9 Jan. 1810; Add. MSS., 37309,
fol. 325, Arbuthnot to Wellesley; Bath Archives, vol. I, pp. 148 and 216; Harrowby
MSS., vol. V, fol. 21, Richard Ryder to Harrowby, 20 Sep. 1810; Camden Soc.,
3rd series, Misc., 18, p. 31.

[2] Lane Poole, Life of Stratford Canning, vol. I, pp. 91 and 129; Aspinall,
Letters of George IV, vol. I, no. 145; Add. MSS., 37295, fols. 296 and 354, and
37296, fol. 153.

[3] Add. MSS., 37296, fols. 145, 147 and 161. Wellesley also authorised Sir James
Saumarez to sign preliminaries of peace with Russia without first consulting
the cabinet. Perceval (who was alone consulted) regretted that the despatch
should be sent before a cabinet meeting was held and feared that other ministers
'might feel hurt at not having so much as the appearance of being consulted'
(Perceval MSS., Perceval to Wellesley, 9 Aug. 1811).

the Regency Bill crisis) it was decided not to risk an open clash on
such an issue. 'It would be a great point', concluded Ryder, 'to get
an effective head for the Foreign Department. . . .' [1] By the end of
1811 there were so many foreign issues to be decided that Wellesley
had to ask for daily cabinet meetings to clear away the arrears. Bathurst
was 'wholly delighted with that plan because he says it will prove to
the Lama his own utter inefficiency'. But, warned Ryder, Wellesley
was 'absolutely mad with vanity' and perfectly convinced that he
would soon be called to the treasury.[2]

Worse still were Wellesley's constant intrigues with Canning, the
result partly of his failure to dominate his cabinet colleagues as he had
hoped. 'I state fairly', he had written to Sir John Anstruther immediately after his acceptance of office, 'that I expect some strength
from my own name; and I have no reason to doubt that I shall have
a principal lead in the Government, sufficient to justify those who think
favourable [sic] of me in supporting the system as being essentially
mine.' [3] For a month the illusion of dominance had persisted. Bathurst,
it was reported, was 'most devoted to him', Liverpool had pledged to
be 'totally governed by him in the conduct of the war', Perceval was
'as civil and, hitherto, as accommodating as possible', while the remaining members of the cabinet were so insignificant and disunited as to
offer no threat to the foreign secretary's supremacy.[4] At first Perceval
undoubtedly did all he could to satisfy Wellesley's claims for attention.
When Portland's death left a vacancy in the order of the garter, the
prime minister persuaded the duke of Richmond to withdraw his
claim so that the ribbon could be offered to Wellesley. Even then the
foreign secretary rejected a suggestion that his investiture should be
delayed until after he had served in the cabinet a few months. In the
end Perceval had to urge the reluctant king to honour Wellesley
immediately.[5] Thereafter relations between Wellesley and his colleagues deteriorated rapidly. Early in December the *Sun* had formally
to deny rumours of clashes between the foreign secretary and the
rest of the cabinet. Wellesley's disinclination to get down to routine

---

[1] Add. MSS., 37296, fols. 7–33; Perceval MSS., Wellesley to Perceval, 4 and 7
Nov. 1811; Harrowby MSS., vol. V, fol. 75, Richard Ryder to Harrowby, 9 Nov.
1811.
[2] Harrowby MSS., vol. V, fol. 79, Richard Ryder to Harrowby, 21 Dec. 1811.
[3] Add. MSS., 37295, fol. 175.
[4] Buckingham, *Memoirs of the Court and Cabinets of George III*, vol. IV, p. 397.
[5] Add. MSS., 37295, fols. 181, 183, 185, 187, 189 and 191; Windsor MSS.,
14809–10, Perceval to George III, 30 Nov. 1809.

business and his failure to establish satisfactory personal relationships with his colleagues in cabinet added to the difficulties caused by his disagreements with them over two matters of policy. By the beginning of 1810 Wellesley was strongly objecting to the way Perceval was handling the defence of the Peninsula campaign in parliament and was urging that the cabinet itself must be reconstructed and strengthened. There were, admitted the *Sun*, 'jarring elements' in the new government: on new year's day there were even sensational reports in the press of a duel between Perceval and Wellesley in which both had received severe wounds.[1] Neither in talent nor cohesion did it seem that Perceval's government was likely to survive the parliamentary storms of the session of 1810.

[1] *Sun*, 4 Dec. 1809 and 1 Jan. 1810; *Day*, 1 and 2 Jan. 1810. Charles Arbuthnot wrote to Perceval on 9 Jan. 'Of the *Morning Chronicle* attacks upon you and Lord Wellesley it had happened to me, during the last evening of my being in town, to have ample proof of the absurdity. For in speaking to me on various subjects, he had mentioned you in a manner which not only put *duels* out of the question, but which gave me the best earnest of entire and confidential cordiality between you and him. It also rejoiced me to find that those among your colleagues whom, as I think, you prize most, are the persons whom he considers as the most valuable' (Perceval MSS.).

CHAPTER SIXTEEN

INQUIRIES AND RIOTS

'THE tide is rising,' wrote Wilberforce early in 1810, 'the wind, though from a distance, is roaring and by and by it will blow, and the waves will beat with unexampled violence from every quarter of the compass.' [1] It seemed that Perceval would need all his nerve to pilot the frail bark of his new ministry through the political shoals of 1810 in such a storm. The most dangerous rock on which the government might founder was the inevitable inquiry into the Walcheren campaign.

Even the strongest of governments would have been hard put to it to defend the expedition. The idea of a diversion against Walcheren was not new. Malmesbury mentioned it to Canning in March 1807 and that autumn Castlereagh was discussing the scheme with Hawkesbury.[2] Two years later conditions seemed ideal for launching the attack. On 8 April 1809 Austria declared war on France and her army, led by the archduke Charles, checked Napoleon at Aspern on 22 May. News of the battle reached London by 8 June, although the defeatest whig press at first refused to believe any favourable reports.[3] A prompt diversion against the Dutch coast might have seriously embarrassed the French war plans. Preliminary discussions had, in fact, already taken place in London. Sir David Dundas, the commander-in-chief, was called to a cabinet meeting at Burlington House on 24 March, when ministers suggested an attack on the island but had to postpone it because of lack of troops.[4] A chronic shortage of specie ruled out the idea of a landing in north Germany and further hamstrung the Walcheren expedition itself from the very first.[5] Early in May plans were laid for linking the landing with a Prussian attack on Holland from the east, but this never materialised. On 17 May the earl of Chatham, the master-general of the ordnance, was offered the

---

[1] Wilberforce, vol. III, p. 441.
[2] Malmesbury, *Correspondence*, vol. IV, p. 380; Castlereagh, *Correspondence and Despatches*, vol. VI, p. 189.
[3] *Edinburgh Review*, Feb. 1811, p. 331; *Sun*, 10 June 1809.
[4] *Parl. Papers, H. of C., Reports of Select Committees*, 1810 (12), vol. VIII, p. 3.
[5] For the financial side of the expedition see chapter 18, pp. 339–42.

command. Militarily no worse choice could have been made. Although his grace had served in America and Holland, he had, fortunately, never previously held a major command. His laziness and inability to work to any timetable had earned him the nickname of 'the late Lord Chatham'. You might, joked Windham, just as well talk of a *coup-de-main* in the court of chancery as a surprise attack on Antwerp under Chatham.[1] The king approved the general plan of the campaign on 16 June and the cabinet held its crucial and fateful meeting on the twenty-first. Ministers had already seen memoranda by Castlereagh, Sir David Dundas, and Harry Calvert, the adjutant-general to the forces.[2] The cabinet discussion itself seems to have been extraordinary. Castlereagh, still unaware that his own political fate had been decided, was full of optimism and talked of seizing French shipping at Antwerp. Every minister, except Chatham himself, then joined in the conversation until Liverpool, disturbed by the commander's silence, asked him what he felt about the plan. It would be possible, replied Chatham, to force a landing without serious loss and to over-run Flushing and the rest of Walcheren. Any attack on Antwerp, however, could succeed only if carried out before French reinforcements arrived. Castlereagh, said Chatham, must be certain that his estimate of the number of French troops available was correct and the admiralty must give an assurance that the fleet could sail up the Scheldt towards Antwerp while the main attack on Walcheren was still in progress. This last point, added Chatham, was a *sine qua non* of success. Mulgrave, the first lord, then promised to have by the following day 'an opinion signed by the three naval Lords of the Admiralty, which shall settle this point'. What happened to this vital document was never afterwards satisfactorily explained. Chatham later claimed that he never even saw it and its very existence was denied during the subsequent parliamentary inquiry. Castlereagh did send an admiralty report to Windsor on 21 June which was pessimistic about the chances of even landing on Walcheren itself.[3] Thus the effective co-operation between the two services, vital for the success of a combined operation was, from the first, missing. Even worse was the failure to take local

---

[1] *Parl. Papers, op. cit.*, p. 12; Jennings, *Anecdotal History of the British Parliament*, p. 166; Castlereagh, vol. VI, p. 256.

[2] Castlereagh, vol. VI, pp. 257-74 and 276; Windsor MSS., 14478-9, Castlereagh to George III, 15 June 1809. It was after this cabinet meeting that Perceval was first told of the plan to remove Castlereagh. See chapter 13, p. 218.

[3] P.R.O. Chatham MSS., 260, gives Chatham's account of the cabinet meeting. Windsor MSS., 14498-9, Castlereagh to George III, 21 June 1809.

climatic conditions into account. There Castlereagh must take the main blame. As early as October 1807 he knew that Walcheren, 'late in the year, is exceedingly unwholesome' and subject to malignant fever. In fact the most unhealthy period lasted from July to early October, precisely the time when British troops would be on the island. Yet at no stage was the army medical board consulted before the expedition sailed. Sir Lucius Pepys, physician-general to the forces, Thomas Keate, surgeon-general to the army, and Francis Knight, inspector-general of army hospitals, all gave damning evidence about lack of preparation to the later committee of inquiry.[1] Even the king, who gave his final approval on 22 June, wished 'that the information upon which the practicability [of the expedition] has been finally decided had not been so imperfect'.[2] Nevertheless Chatham was given the most ambitious instructions. He was to over-run Walcheren, capture all enemy shipping in the Scheldt and then render the river unfit for navigation, and destroy arsenals, dockyards and ships at both Flushing and Antwerp.

Thereafter the intended surprise attack was left to the tender mercy of the British press. On 2 July the *Day* reported that Sir William Curtis, one of the members for the City, intended to sail with the expedition in his private yacht and hoped to be the first to return to England with the news of victory. Curtis wrote to Perceval asking for permission to accompany the fleet, agreed to put his yacht under admiralty orders, and then 'began to perform his naval duties by storing his vessel with every kind of viands, substantial and luxurious, and an abundance of the finest wines'.[3] Unfortunately more important shipping was less easy to get. The *Sun* reported on 3 July that the government would hire any foreign vessels at twenty-five shillings a ton, provided they would be ready to sail within a week, but less friendly newspapers predicted that the expedition would be seriously delayed. By the 12 July all seemed ready. Orders reached Portsmouth that the first division of the fleet should be ready to sail within three days, while the *Sun* made hay of opposition papers which had accused the cabinet of delay. Never in British history, it claimed, had greater promptitude been displayed: within a month of plans being made 40,000 troops had been made ready for foreign service and embarked,

[1] Castlereagh, vol. VI, p. 189; *Parl. Papers*, *op. cit.*, pp. 16, 21 and 33.
[2] *Ibid.*, p. 282.
[3] *Day*, 2 July and 5 Aug. 1809. There is a parody of the episode in the *Annual Register*, 1809, p. 880.

together with 'an immense train of artillery, ammunition, stores and provisions'.[1] On 13 July the *Day* predicted that the expedition was aimed at Bremen; the following day a general embargo was placed on all ports. But still the fleet failed to sail. By the seventeenth all troops were embarked and rumours spread that operations would begin within forty-eight hours. The *Day* then, 'without the fear of any detriment to . . . the great object in view', announced that Walcheren and Antwerp were to be the army's target. On 19 July departure was again postponed and the *Day* admitted sadly that the enemy seemed to know the expedition's destination. Nine French warships, which had been lying at Antwerp, had been moved inland to Fort Lillo, the strongest position on the Scheldt, while French reinforcements had been sent to the Antwerp area.[2] At noon that day Chatham left his house in Hill Street, called at the ordnance office and on Canning and Castlereagh, left London at four in the afternoon for Rochester and, after a leisurely journey, dined and slept at the Crown Inn, Sittingbourne. The earl, at least, seemed in no particular hurry to sail. In fact he had already, metaphorically, missed the boat. On 21 July news reached London of the Austrian disaster thirteen days previously at Wagram. Even the *Sun* was 'too depressed' to make any comment other than that the 'ulterior object of the Expedition . . . may be either altered or abandoned', but the cabinet was too deeply committed to withdraw. Canning, Castlereagh and Perceval all went down to Deal to watch the departure, and the fleet, victualled for four months, finally sailed on 28 July. Rarely can a surprise attack have had less chance of success. The enemy had had twenty-six days' notice of the preparations in the press and ten of the exact destination of the fleet. On the very day before his departure Chatham heard that Austria had successfully sued for peace on 12 July. He sailed, moreover, without even an adequate plan of the fortifications of Antwerp.[3]

From the first there were many who despaired of the campaign, although for a few days the government press struck a note of almost hysterical optimism. Walcheren was to be permanently occupied by a strong garrison and incorporated in the empire to form 'a sort of

[1] *Sun*, 3 and 13 July 1809; *Day*, 4 and 12 July 1809.
[2] *Day*, 13, 14, 17, 18 and 19 July 1809. A cabinet minute authorising the sailing of the expedition was sent to Windsor on July 14 (Windsor MSS., 14533).
[3] *Day*, 20, 22, 27 and 28 July 1809; *Sun*, 21 July 1809; *Parl. Papers*, *op. cit.*, pp. 183 and 201. The *Sun* (31 Jan. 1810) alleged that the French government had warned its commander on Walcheren of the possibility of an attack as early as April 1809.

maritime Gibraltar, neutralising a very large portion of the enemy's naval and military force'. After its initial shock, the *Sun* did its best to minimise the news of Wagram by arguing that Austrian and French losses had been equal and that the archduke Charles had retired to another strong position. 'Away with this rash despondency! this audacious cowardice, this confident discouragement! How many hours have passed since the noblest armament that has ever sailed from Britain exchanged its last salute with the guns and colours of Portsmouth? Have we forgotten those regions where marches the Conqueror of Vimiera?' But, throughout, *The Times* predicted that the army would get no further than Walcheren, while Cobbett assured his readers that we could no more retain the island 'than we can get or keep Paris'.[1] Meanwhile Wilberforce, on holiday at Eastbourne, watched part of the expedition sail with a heavy heart. 'I have', he wrote, 'seen a sad propensity in men, when they have got a great army, to set it at work, even where the prospect is not very encouraging, as being better than letting it lie idle, and rust for want of exercise.'[2]

Yet, for a while, the news was good. On 31 July, as London sweltered in the sun, rumours spread through the coffee houses that Walcheren had surrendered without a fight. The first official reports, a week later, spoke of delays caused by high winds and surf, but were optimistic about the speedy capture of Flushing. The *Day* printed a long article on the success of the campaign and, on 15 August, the Tower guns were firing salvos to celebrate Talavera, 'one of the most splendid victories that was ever obtained by British valour and discipline over an enemy immensely superior in numbers'. Everywhere news of success in the Peninsula stimulated fresh hope of victories on the continent. On the sixteenth it was said Flushing had fallen; the next day Rotterdam had risen against the French; then Austria had re-entered the war. When Chatham's despatch announcing that Flushing really had been captured reached London on 18 August, the Tower guns were fired again and most people forgot that the campaign was already far behind schedule.[3] By the end of the month the press was

[1] *The Times*, 29 July 1809; *Political Register*, 12 Aug. 1809 (vol. XVI, p. 178). On 25 July Lord Elgin had advised Perceval to stake all on a direct landing in France and a bold march on Paris instead of wasting troops on unhealthy Walcheren (Castlereagh, vol. VI, p. 293).

[2] Wilberforce, vol. III, pp. 414–15.

[3] *Sun*, 27 July and 14 Aug. 1809; *Day*, 1, 6, 8, 15, 16, 17, 18, 20 and 22 Aug. 1809. 'It does not yet appear', wrote Henry Legge to the Speaker on 9 Aug., "that Flushing has surrendered. What good they will do with it when they have got it I cannot tell' (P.R.O., 30/9/15).

openly discussing disagreements between Chatham and Strachan, the naval commander, while more and more troops went down with fever. At the treasury Perceval and Huskisson had been reduced to sending drinking water to the island and struggled to set up temporary hospitals along the south coast to house the sick and wounded. At this crisis the army medical board was so crippled by internal feuds that Perceval had to employ local doctors in the sea-side towns and, on his own intiative, draft in some of the staff of London hospital.[1] On 1 September came the first rumours of total failure, quickly followed the next day by the receipt of Chatham's despatch of 29 August, announcing his intention of withdrawing in the face of 35,000 French troops massed on the mainland. The crumbling Portland cabinet had met immediately and decided to abandon the main attack while trying, for the present, to hold on to the island of Walcheren itself.[2] The *Sun* made one brave attempt to disperse the general gloom by emphasising the commercial and military value of Walcheren, the fact that 2,000 French troops had been captured, and that enemy shipping was now bottled up in the Scheldt. So 'happy and brilliant' a result should cause no disappointment.[3] Less biased sources soon punctured this professional optimism. Why, asked the *Day*, in a detailed criticism of Chatham's despatch, was it necessary to besiege Flushing in so leisurely a manner? Could not an attack on the Scheldt have been carried out during the siege? If not, why, when Flushing fell on 16 August, were the main operations against the Scheldt still delayed until the twenty-sixth? Against such close argument there was little value in the *Sun's* sneer that it was easy to sit in closets and plan victories, 'but are generals and statesmen exempted from all miscarriage and failure? Are wise plans never thwarted, even by accident?' On 6 September the *Day* called for a full inquiry, while *The Times* thundered against Chatham's inefficiency. So great was the public unrest that even the staunch *Sun* itself was forced on the twelfth to confess ominously that 'we, perhaps, have also some fault to find with the conduct of the War Department'.[4]

Meanwhile members of the Portland cabinet had to find time from their own absorbing quarrels to decide whether we could even prolong

---

[1] *Day*, 30 Aug. 1809; P.R.O., T29/102/64; T27/64/453 and 525; T27/65/56, 65, 79 and 85–6.

[2] *Day*, 1 Sep. 1809; P.R.O., Chatham MSS., 262; Castlereagh, vol. VI, p. 319; Windsor MSS., 14594–5, Castlereagh to George III, 2 Sep. 1809.

[3] *Sun*, 4 Sep. 1809.

[4] *Ibid.*, 4, 5 and 12 Sep. 1809; *Day*, 4 and 6 Sep. 1809; *The Times*, 5 Sep. 1809.

our occupation of Walcheren. Castlereagh talked on 18 September with Chatham and other officers who had just returned from the island and decided that an early decision was unnecessary. Five days later he attended another cabinet meeting, only on the understanding that he should have no share in any decision on the evacuation or retention of the island.[1] In fact none was taken and thereafter the political crisis made all hope of one impossible, in spite of an alarming report by the army medical board that the majority of the fiftieth and ninety-first regiments were in hospital and the warning that there might soon be a renewed epidemic of fever.[2] Not until the end of October, when the new ministry had begun to take shape, did the cabinet really come to grips with the problem. On 25 September Palmerston, the new secretary-at-war, told Malmesbury that the position on Walcheren was desperate. Only 3,500 men out of the entire garrison were fit for duty if the enemy attacked. The cabinet seemed unable to reach any decision as officers from the two services gave twenty contradictory opinions while Strachan himself changed his own views with bewildering rapidity. Three days later Liverpool informed the king that ministers would finally make up their minds when they knew definitely whether Austria had made peace with France. In the interval the sick were to be evacuated from the island, all military installations would be destroyed at Flushing, and 5,000 troops moved to Kent to reinforce our coastal defences.[3] On 2 November the *Sun* denied there was to be any evacuation now that the unhealthy season on the island was over: a week later Palmerston was told, in confidence, that all troops were to be withdrawn.[4] For a time news of the impending evacuation was still withheld from the public, but rumours of an army mutiny on the island, which caused a slump on the stock exchange, finally forced an announcement.[5]

Thereafter ministers had squarely to face a torrent of criticism. 'I am ready, of course,' wrote a depressed Yorke to Perceval on 23 November, 'to give credit for the *necessity* of abandoning Walcheren; but my grief and mortification are not the less; and the conclusions to be drawn from the existence of such a *necessity* are sufficiently

---

[1] Castlereagh, vol. VI, pp. 325 and 326–7.
[2] Add. MSS., 38244, fol. 179.
[3] Malmesbury, *Letters*, vol. II, pp. 172–3; Add. MSS., 32423, fol. 269.
[4] *Sun*, 2 Nov. 1809; Malmesbury, vol. II, p. 180.
[5] *Day*, 15 Nov. 1809; *Sun*, 27 Nov. 1809. Total British casualties at Walcheren were given as 5,060 killed, 440 discharged and 609 deserted (Add. MSS., 38244, fol. 105).

unpleasant.' [1] The first of these came within a week when the *Day* supported a call for petitions demanding a full parliamentary inquiry. Early in December the common council of the city of London voted by sixty-six to sixty-three for a petition, after the lord mayor had used his casting vote to defeat a motion for the previous question. Moderates on the council were later able to tone down the original strong wording of the petition, but it still remained so critical of ministers that the cabinet discussed it on 18 December without being able to draft a suitable reply. Eventually, on the advice of the king, who was outraged by its language, they sent a 'short dry answer'. But this was only a preliminary skirmish before the main battle in the Commons. Some respite was gained from this ordeal by allowing parliament to remain prorogued over Christmas. It was, Perceval told the Speaker, 'the boldest thing of all I have done'.[2] Yet even this interval brought only fresh disaster.

In December the government suffered the ultimate indignity of defeat at Oxford, the spiritual home of 'No Popery'. Three candidates stood in the election of a new university chancellor: Eldon, the nominee of the ministry, Grenville for the opposition, and that noble nonentity, the duke of Beaufort. In a straight fight Eldon would probably have carried the day, but Beaufort's intervention split the anti-catholic vote. Never had such an election been so bitterly contested, 1084 votes being cast out of a total electorate of 1274. In the end Grenville polled 406, Eldon 390, and Beaufort 288.[3] The result itself was bad enough in ministerial eyes, but the analysis of voting was even worse. Grenville got the support of all but two of the bishops, who stood by Eldon: Wellesley's private secretary, Vaughan, and Harrison of the treasury both voted for Grenville.[4] 'I give you joy,' wrote Brougham to Grey, 'never was any victory more important or more ominous to the Court. It is better than a majority in Parliament, because it is more permanent and general; it gives "No Popery" a death-blow; toryism and twaddle and

[1] Perceval MSS., C. P. Yorke to Perceval, 23 Nov. 1809.

[2] *Day*, 29 Nov., 6, 14 and 16 Dec. 1809; *Sun*, 21 Dec. 1809; Windsor MSS., 14842–3 and 14846–7, Ryder to George III, 18 and 19 Dec. 1809 and George III to Ryder, 19 Dec. 1809; P.R.O., 30/9/15, Colchester MSS., Perceval to Abbot, 18 Oct. 1809.

[3] *Annual Register*, 1809, p. 404; Windsor MSS., 14776–7, Perceval to George III, 7 Nov. 1809. Perceval suggested that either Beaufort or Eldon should withdraw to ensure Grenville's defeat. Liverpool had earlier been asked to stand, but withdrew in favour of Beaufort (Yonge, vol. I, p. 298).

[4] Buckingham, *Court and Cabinets of George III*, vol. IV, p. 408; Perceval MSS., Redesdale to Perceval, 22 Nov. 1809. For Harrison see chapter 17, pp. 311–13.

illiberality of every kind, such a shake as it can scarcely recover. . . .'
The high church party, exalted Horner, was taken by storm in its
ancient stronghold: it was, added Cobbett, 'the victory of sense over
folly, of piety over cant, of toleration over intolerance, of sincerity
over hypocrisy, of truth over falsehood'.[1] Only the level-headed
Bulkeley saw that Grenville's success was not a sign that the country
was ready for emancipation and warned his colleagues that 'No
Popery' could still win a general election.[2] The opposition, long
starved of electoral success, turned the new chancellor's installation
into a party rally. Oxford was so crowded for the ceremony that many
guests were forced to sleep in their carriages while one who was more
fortunate still had to pay five guineas for a back room in an obscure
lane, with extra fees for all service.[3] Eldon, hurt by his defeat and by
the intervention of that 'fox-hunting Duke of Beaufort', was with
difficulty dissuaded from resigning from the cabinet.[4] Gamblers that
winter were laying heavy odds against Perceval himself remaining at
the treasury for many months. At White's Sir Joseph Copley covered
the stakes of all-comers who would wager on Perceval's survival and
lost heavily for his pains.[5]

In desperation the new ministry made what political capital it could
out of George the Third's fiftieth jubilee. On the morning of 25 October a fifty-gun salute was fired in London and Perceval announced an
amnesty for most Crown debtors and those in prison for offences
against the revenue laws. His majesty also sent a present of £2,000
from his own private purse to the society for the relief of persons
confined for small debts. At Windsor the king, accompanied by
members of his family, took his usual morning ride in the Park and
passed up the avenue lined by rosetted spectators and military bands,
all playing 'God Save the King' with special verses composed for the
occasion. 'The brightness and the mildness of the day,' wrote one
onlooker, 'the magnificence of the avenue, and the occasion of this
Jubilee altogether rendered it one of the most interesting, affecting
and beautiful scenes I ever beheld.'[6] The old king had finally reached
the height of his popularity and his servants were quite ready to reap

---

[1] Brougham, *Memoirs*, vol. I, p. 490; Horner, vol. II, p. 6; *Political Register*,
23 Dec. 1809, p. 971.
[2] Auckland, *Journal*, vol. IV, p. 339.
[3] Jerdan, *Autobiography*, vol. I, p. 126.   [4] Twiss, vol. II, p. 111.
[5] Hon. A. Bourke, *Betting Book of White's Club*, vol. II, pp. 61–6.
[6] *Gent. Mag.*, Nov. 1809, pp. 1070–1; P.R.O., T29/102/539; *Annual Register*,
1809, p. 395; P.R.O., 30/43/25/5, Lowry Cole MSS.; *Day*, 26 Oct. 1809.

the benefits. 'This Jubilee', grumbled Romilly, 'is a political engine of the ministers.' [1]

Certainly the government needed all the encouragement it could get. The cabinet, wrote the Speaker, was weak and uncertain of support while the opposition remained eager and confident. Estimates of the opposition's voting strength varied from 180 to 200, which Tierney thought would make the whigs numerically stronger than the government.[2] Meanwhile Perceval did what he could to rally support. On 28 November he sent a circular letter to likely sympathisers, asking them to let him know whether they would attend on the first day of the new session, only to see the opposition press print the hostile replies. The prime minister next sent drafts of the King's Speech to both Harrowby and Wellesley for their comments, tried to restore his supporters' morale by inserting pro-government paragraphs in selected newspapers, and completed his preparations by holding the customary eve-of-the-session dinner at Downing Street for his most prominent supporters. The cabinet, Liverpool assured Wellington, might be defeated when the House met, but would, at worst, keep 'a respectable party' together to protect the king.[3] 'I should feel', Arbuthnot wrote to Perceval, 'that I were not doing justice either to myself or to you if I conceived it necessary to make at any time a *profession* of *my faith*. Your treatment of me has given you a claim to my most zealous assistance. I only wish that for your sake, the assistance was more valuable; but you shall have the best that I can give.' 'They say', Brougham told Grey, 'only Perceval will be in Parliament at the opening, but that is saying only their whole strength will be there.' [4]

Parliament met on 23 January. The King's Speech made the most of Talavera and the best it could of Walcheren. The Address was moved by Lord Barnard and seconded by Perceval's young protégé, Robert Peel. 'Mr. Peel', reported the prime minister to George III, 'has a very great character for talent and he fully maintained it upon this occasion.' [5] Lord Leveson-Gower then moved the opposition's

[1] Romilly, *Memoirs*, vol. II, p. 305.

[2] Colchester, vol. II, pp. 225 and 227; Olphin, p. 138.

[3] *Day*, 2 and 30 Dec. 1809, 18 and 20 Jan. 1810; *Sun*, 20 and 23 Jan. 1810; Add. MSS., 37295, fol. 211; Yonge, vol. I, p. 297. Ministers had some encouragement when Houblon defeated the radical, Burgoyne, by 2,519 votes to 811 in an Essex by-election in Feb. (*Day*, 4 and 17 Feb. 1810).

[4] Perceval MSS., Arbuthnot to Perceval, 9 Jan. 1810; Brougham, *Memoirs*, vol. I, p. 487.

[5] Windsor MSS., 14909–10, Perceval to George III, 14 Jan. 1810; *Creevey Papers*, vol. I, p. 122.

amendment denouncing the failures and disasters of recent military campaigns, the waste of our national resources and the loss of life 'unprofitably sacrificed in enterprises productive, not of advantage, but of lasting injury to their country'. This was seconded by Lord Dudley's son, J. W. Ward, and supported by Whitbread in one of his most powerful interventions. Perceval summed up for the ministry with a speech which J. W. Ward thought 'very inferior to his usual rate'.[1] In the division, however, the government had a remarkable victory by 263 votes to 167. The Sidmouth group, Canning's and Castlereagh's followers, the Saints and, Perceval told Wellesley, 'probably some others who would have voted for a more temperate amendment' all supported ministers. 'Well, Creevey,' joked Castlereagh as he made his way to the division lobby, 'how do we look?' Perhaps, concluded the king, the division was the first sign that the violence of the opposition would disgust moderates and rally opinion to the government.[2] Such hopes were soon disappointed. Three days later Lord Porchester moved for a committee of inquiry into the Walcheren campaign. Ministers met this by moving the previous question on the grounds that papers on the expedition, to be presented to parliament in the following week, would allow the Commons to make a more realistic assessment of the case for an inquiry. The Canningites again supported Perceval, but the desertion of the Sidmouth group and the abstention of Castlereagh and his four supporters led to a government defeat by 195 votes to 186. His majesty, wrote Perceval to Windsor at two o'clock in the morning of 27 January, would be surprised to find that so many friends of government had, in this debate, voted with the opposition. On less passionate subjects, however, Perceval still hoped that ministers would be able to survive divisions. It was a novel and desperate argument that his majesty's servants could control the Commons on all but the most vital issues. In fact Porchester's success had finally exposed the precariousness of the ministry's majority. It needed only a handful of waverers to desert for the cabinet to face defeat.[3] There followed a harrowing period for ministers. On 28 January they were narrowly defeated in three

---

[1] *Parl. Deb.*, XV, 38–105; R. H. Romilly, *Letters to Ivy*, p. 90. 'In spite of that,' continued Ward, 'he is a very clever man. To those, however, who remember Mr. Pitt . . . such exhibitions in a Prime Minister are rather melancholy.'

[2] Add. MSS., 37295, fol. 219; Windsor MSS., 14911, George III to Perceval; Romilly, vol. II, p. 308; *Creevey Papers*, vol. I, p. 123.

[3] *Parl. Deb.*, XV, 208; Pellew, vol. III, p. 22; *Creevey Papers*, vol. I, p. 124; Windsor MSS., 14919–20, Perceval to George III, 27 Jan. 1810.

divisions on the composition of the finance committee and were subsequently badly mauled by the opposition on a vote of thanks to Wellington for the victory of Talavera.[1] After four defeats in the first week of the session the tottering government badly needed a cause to rally waverers. At the beginning of February a temporary distraction came from a totally unexpected source.

The radical debating societies had for long been an embarrassment to ministers. In November 1808 the Marlborough Street magistrates, urged on by the *Sun* to 'suppress those hot-beds of sedition', had raided and dispersed the British Forum Society. The Forum, said the *Sun*, existed solely 'to fill the pockets of desperate adventurers, who are known to be enemies of the constitution'.[2] Fifteen months later the same society sprang into an unexpected and most unpleasant prominence. On 2 February 1810, when the Commons was about to go into committee on the Walcheren expedition, Charles Yorke moved the standing order which automatically excluded all strangers from the House. On the sixth Sheridan, supported by Burdett, proposed that in future all motions to clear the public galleries should be put to a vote and so produced one of Windham's usual jeremiads on the dangers of democracy and the tyranny of the press.[3] On 12 February the British Forum had unanimously passed a motion that Yorke's enforcement of the standing order 'ought to be censured as an insidious and ill-timed attack upon the liberty of the Press, as tending to aggravate the discontents of the people, and to render their representatives objects of jealous suspicion'. It was then decided, and placarded all over Westminster, that at its next weekly meeting the Forum should debate the motion, 'which was the greater outrage upon the public feeling, Mr. Yorke's enforcement of the Standing Order to exclude strangers from the House of Commons, or Mr. Windham's recent attack upon the liberty of the press?'

On the evening of the nineteenth the Commons, on Yorke's motion, decided that the Forum's secretary, the apothecary, John Gale Jones, should be summoned to the bar of the House. He appeared on

---

[1] *Parl. Deb.*, XV, 265, 445, 453 and 467. For the full story of the struggles over the finance committee see chapter 10, pp. 148–58. Creevey (vol. I, p. 126) gives details of the three divisions on 28 Jan. Robert Peel voted, most reluctantly, against the government.

[2] *Sun*, 2 Nov. 1808 and 24 Nov. 1809.

[3] *Parl. Deb.*, XV, 320. When Yorke's motion resulted in the clearing of the public gallery some spectators 'hissed and behaved in an improper manner' (*Sun*, 3 Feb. 1810).

21 February, made an abject apology, but was immediately committed
to Newgate.[1] As Burdett was ill at the time it was not until 12 March
that he was able to move a motion for Jones' release. When this was
heavily defeated, Burdett wrote a sententious open letter to his constituents, denouncing the House for its arbitrary and tyrannical use
of privilege. This appeared in the *Political Register* on Saturday,
24 March.[2] The next day, while walking home from church, Perceval
showed a copy of the paper to Abbot and told him that, on the following Tuesday, he proposed to move that Burdett be committed to the
Tower and that Cobbett be ordered to appear before the Commons.[3]
In fact the initiative was taken by Thomas Lethbridge, one of the
members for Somerset. When the House met on Monday afternoon
Burdett admitted that he was the author of the letter and Lethbridge
gave notice of his resolutions. On Tuesday, 27 March (after Rose had
hastily redrafted the original 'ill-digested' motion) Lethbridge argued
that Burdett's letter was 'a libellous and scandalous paper, reflecting
on the just rights and privileges of the House'. The new government,
too conscious of its own weakness to adopt a sensible policy, was
determined to force Lethbridge's motion through the House without
delay. Ponsonby wisely suggested that the debate be adjourned for
one week, but was strongly opposed by Perceval.[4] When the House
resumed its discussions on the twenty-eighth many members felt that
Perceval was trying to drive them too fast and too far. The opposition
suspected a deliberate plot to distract attention from the Walcheren
inquiry. Liberals, like Romilly, were alarmed at Perceval's known
desire to send Burdett to the Tower. Burdett, because of his conduct
in the duke of York case and his persistent calls for economy, stood
as high in public estimation 'just in proportion as the House is low'.
Even Charles Yorke, then temporarily without a seat after his Cambridge defeat, hoped that Burdett would only be ordered to the
custody of the serjeant or to receive Abbot's reprimand at the bar and
warned the home secretary, Ryder, that any attempt to send him to
the Tower would 'make him of too much importance and is probably
what is wished by the Democrats'. In the Commons both Brand and
Romilly renewed the demand for a week's adjournment while Croker
and Sir Joseph Yorke made violent speeches in favour of Lethbridge's

[1] *Parl. Deb.*, XV, 497 and 502.
[2] *Annual Register*, 1809, p. 344. Burdett's letter was reprinted in full in the
Sun on 26 Mar.
[3] Colchester, vol. II, p. 240.
[4] *Parl. Deb.*, XVI, 136–94; Colchester, vol. II, p. 241.

original motion. Perceval would certainly have forced a division that night had not Wilberforce, Bathurst and even Grant, the master of the rolls, opposed any hasty action. In the end the government, 'fearful of being beaten', reluctantly agreed to adjourn after the debate had lasted until after midnight.[1] The 'real reason' explained the disgusted Perceval to George III, 'with too many for wishing to delay the question was the fear of meeting it—the fear of Sir Francis Burdett and his followers—a sentiment which Mr. Perceval begs to assure Your Majesty had not the slightest influence upon him'.[2]

Unfortunately the situation required realism and tact, not obstinacy, even though that might pass for courage at Windsor. Before the debate on Lethbridge's motion was resumed on 5 April Perceval had made a further move against Burdett. At a political dinner held some days before the fifth he met Sir Robert Salusbury, the member for Brecon borough. They began to discuss the Burdett affair and Perceval said that, although he did not know what the Commons would do, he thought Sir Francis ought to be sent to the Tower. 'You', he added, 'would be a proper person to move it, being a country gentleman, and not always voting with us, it would not seem to arise from ministerial influence.' When Salusbury objected that, like many a good country gentleman, he never made a habit of speaking in the House, Perceval replied 'a few words will be sufficient, as we shall support you'.[3] On 5 April Sir Robert played his brief but fatal role. For as soon as Lord Folkestone's motion to pass to the orders of the day had been rejected by 191 votes, Salusbury moved that Burdett be committed to the Tower. William Adam then proposed a formal reprimand instead of imprisonment and ran the government to 152 votes to 189. The debate ended at 7.30 on the morning of Friday, the sixth: within an hour Abbot had signed the warrant for Burdett's arrest.[4] That was the last resolute action taken before the capital was virtually in the hands of the mob. The government had ample warning of the dangers at hand. Even while the House was in session on 5 April a crowd had begun to collect in the lobbies and in Palace Yard and had to be dispersed by constables. As soon as the House rose on Friday morning, Jones Burdett, Sir Francis Burdett's brother, and Roger O'Connor set off

---

[1] *Parl. Deb.*, XVI, 258 ff.; Westbrook Hay MSS., C. P. Yorke to Ryder, 28 Mar. 1810; Romilly, vol. II, pp. 313-14. The *Sun* claimed on 28 Mar. that ministers had no prior knowledge of Lethbridge's motion.

[2] Windsor MSS., 15035-6, Perceval to George III, 28 Mar. 1810.

[3] Farington, *Diary*, vol. VI, pp. 51-2.

[4] *Parl. Deb.*, XVI, 547; Colchester, vol. II, p. 245.

for Wimbledon to tell Sir Francis the result of the debate. At nine that same morning Colman and Clementson, the serjeant and deputy serjeant-at-arms, called at Burdett's town house at seventy-eight, Piccadilly. As Sir Francis did not arrive back in town until noon, the two officers returned to Westminster and reported to Abbot. After this Colman wrote a letter to Burdett, 'to consult your convenience as to the time and mode of your removal'. Clementson delivered this before noon when he found a small crowd already gathered outside number seventy-eight. In the early afternoon Burdett acknowledged Colman's letter and arranged to 'be at home to receive you at 12 o'clock to-morrow'. For some unknown reason Burdett's reply had not reached the serjeant-at-arms at four o'clock, when Colman paid a second visit to Piccadilly, only to be told of the interview arranged for the morrow. At five-thirty the unwearied Colman again reported to the Speaker, who bluntly told him to get a move on. And so that evening he again trailed back to Piccadilly to ask Burdett to leave immediately and quietly for the Tower. Sir Francis replied that as the Speaker's warrant was illegal he had no intention of obeying it. Instead he asked Colman to deliver a letter to the Speaker in which Burdett repeated most of the assertions which had originally caused all the trouble. This the serjeant rightly refused to do and so Burdett sent it by his own brother. It reached Abbot at ten o'clock that evening, shortly after Colman had admitted that no arrest could be made that day. There were now large crowds both in Piccadilly and outside the Tower: Colman had no chance of making the arrest single-handed and Ryder refused to send any troops until there had been actual resistance.[1]

Few ministers got much sleep that night. The Guards were finally called out after the mob had broken the windows of the houses belonging to Lethbridge, Yorke, Castlereagh, Chatham, Dartmouth, Perceval, and Sir John Anstruther (who had spoken against Burdett on 5 April). All who passed through Piccadilly without crying 'Burdett for ever' were showered with mud. Westmorland, who should have had enough sense to keep away, was 'covered with dirt from top to toe'. The unfortunate Salusbury was forced to leave for Wales after several hotels, out of fear of the mob, had refused him admission.[2] On Saturday, 7 April the harrassed Colman continued his comedy of

[1] *Sun*, 6 Apr. 1810; Patterson, *Sir Francis Burdett*, vol. I, pp. 255–8.
[2] Windsor MSS., 15059–6, Perceval to George III, 7 Apr. 1810; Rede, *Memoir of the Rt. Hon. George Canning*, p. 235; Farington, *loc. cit.*

errors. At six-thirty in the morning he reached Piccadilly where he learnt that Sir Francis had already gone out. He decided to leave a messenger at Burdett's house with the Speaker's warrant while he rushed back to Westminster to report, before setting off (on mere chance) for Burdett's country house at Wimbledon. In fact his quarry had breakfasted with Roger O'Connor in Maddox Street and afterwards taken a ride in Hyde Park. It was twelve-thirty before Burdett returned to Piccadilly, saw Colman's messenger, relieved him of the warrant and politely showed him the door. Half an hour later the serjeant arrived back from Wimbledon to learn that his messenger had lost the warrant. Every hour the crowds in the city streets got larger and more unruly. Yet it took him four more hours to call on Burdett to recover the warrant. He found the doors locked and had to return to the Speaker, who at seven p.m. signed a fresh warrant, thirty-six hours after he had issued the first. 'The Serjeant's mismanagement of to-day', Abbot complained to Perceval, 'exceeds, if possible, that of yesterday.' [1]

Colman was undoubtedly gravely at fault, but he got little help from his superiors. Had the home office given him an adequate escort on the afternoon of 6 April, Burdett would have been safely in the Tower before the situation got out of hand. But the home secretary was quite unfitted to deal with such a crisis. The best that can be said for Richard Ryder is that he was a born junior minister who, through no fault of his own, ended in the cabinet. Although he had sat in the Commons since 1795, he had never sufficiently mastered his nerves to take much part in debate. Not that he wanted talent, for he was an able lawyer and a shrewd judge of men. The king thought highly of his abilities while Perceval (his next-door neighbour in Lincoln's Inn Fields) relied a great deal on his advice. Rarely can two families have been so close as the Percevals and the Ryders. Some members of the one could always be found visiting the other. Jane advised Frederica on the handling of children while Spencer and Richard had in common their religion, their profession, and their politics. Had Perceval gone to the home office in 1807, Ryder was to have been his under-secretary. Instead Ryder became first a junior lord of the treasury and then, against his own inclinations, judge advocate-general. He was too happy a family man and too conscious of his own defects to be ambitious. When he accepted the home seals under Perceval he made a great personal sacrifice out of loyalty to an old king and a harassed

[1] *Sun*, 9 Apr. 1810; Colchester, vol. II, p. 248; Patterson, vol. I, pp. 258–60.

U

friend. As long as he was not called upon to take immediate and vital decisions, he proved a conscientious and humane minister. Yet in a crisis like the Burdett riots his lack of self-confidence soon became mere timidity and he found himself entirely incapable of controlling events. On that crucial April Friday he made no attempt to support the serjeant-at-arms. By Saturday the seventh he had so lost control of things that Perceval moved to the home office, wrote a detailed report on the day's riots to Windsor, and stayed with Ryder until two o'clock in the morning. On 8 April the prime minister informed Abbot that he would be permanently with the home secretary until the disturbances were over.[1]

There was now no alternative to the use of force to disperse the mob: orders were sent to call out the Volunteers and to concentrate all troops then stationed within marching distance of London. By Saturday afternoon Piccadilly and its approaches were sealed off by contingents of foot and horse guards, the Riot Act having been read at one o'clock. Most of London's shops were shut, the Tower guns were mounted and reinforcements of troops and artillery poured into the capital throughout the following twenty-four hours.[2]

Meanwhile Burdett consulted with such fellow radicals as Coke, Folkestone, Cochrane, Madocks, Cartwright and Wardle before deciding to call upon the sheriffs of Middlesex, Wood and Atkins, to call out the posse comitatus to protect his home, 'at this moment beset by a military force'. Wood, a staunch Burdettite, was eager to act, but when he called on his colleague he discovered the prudent Atkins was 'out of town'. At nine that night Wood visited the Speaker, who refused to say more than that the sheriff should do as he thought best. Therefore at two o'clock on Sunday morning Wood sent a copy of Burdett's letter to the home office to which Ryder (on Perceval's advice) replied that the sheriffs should aid not resist the execution of the warrant. In fact Burdett's refusal to admit the serjeant-at-arms had made the government very uncertain of the legal position. On Saturday afternoon Perceval, unable to assure Colman that he had authority to break down Burdett's door, recommended an appeal to the attorney-general. Sir Vicary Gibbs, called to the home office on Saturday night, confessed that he doubted whether the Speaker's warrant legally

[1] P.R.O., 30/9/15, Colchester MSS., Perceval to Abbot, 8 Apr. 1810; Windsor MSS., 15067–8, Perceval to George III, 8 Apr. 1810. Early in his career Ryder was said to have earned £2,000 a year by auditing Lord Stafford's accounts (S. H. Romilly, *Letters to Ivy*, p. 86).

[2] Romilly, vol. II, p. 318; Patterson, vol. I, p. 261.

justified forcible entry. Throughout that night, while the mob in Piccadilly continued its mud larks and taunted the soldiery, ministers settled down to search for precedents. Perceval for a time favoured a parliamentary address to the king to issue a proclamation for the arrest of Burdett, while the Speaker heard a rumour that Moira, the governor of the Tower, would refuse to hold Burdett 'unless there comes an order by the Sign Manual for the purpose'.[1]

By Sunday, 8 April, the crisis was at its height. In spite of this and of all his previous fatigues, the prime minister went as usual to morning service and then, accompanied by Eldon, called on Abbot 'to talk over the defective power of warrants'. It was generally agreed that the government should stand firm, resist any motion for the release of Gale Jones and, if necessary, introduce 'a general declaratory act to give efficiency to the warrants or orders of both Houses'. At about the same time Cochrane, always a man of action, called on Burdett with a cask of gunpowder, with the idea of placing it under the front wall of seventy-eight Piccadilly 'so that he might blow the invaders to the devil'. Colman had made his own regular call at seven that morning and had again been refused admittance. After this he decided to wait until ministers had made up their minds about the use of force. Gibbs worked on the problem all day. He told both Perceval and Abbot that he had grave doubts about breaking open Burdett's doors and advised that the warrant should not be executed on a Sunday.[2] This was all very well for the little lawyer, but it placed a great burden on the troops trying to keep order in Piccadilly, where, in spite of the bad weather, the crowds got progressively larger and more daring. At three o'clock that afternoon the Riot Act was again read and the magistrates ordered the officer in command to disperse the mob, while Wood threatened him with indictment if anyone was killed. There were in fact several scuffles which once led to a brief burst of shots, fortunately without serious results. At one point the rioters set up two barricades between St. James's church and the end of Piccadilly, made of bricks from a house then under repair. But there was no attempt at resistance when a small party of horse and foot advanced to level them.[3] Elsewhere civil defence was left largely to the Volunteers, who were thought more reliable than the regulars. Pessimists even

[1] Colchester, vol. II, p. 250; Patterson, vol. I, pp. 262–7.
[2] Colchester, vol. II, pp. 251 and 253; P.R.O., 30/9/15, Colchester MSS., Perceval to Abbot, 8 Apr. 1810.
[3] Patterson, vol. I, p. 268.

reported that the foot guards were about to join the riots in spite of promises of extra pay for those on duty in Piccadilly. On Sunday evening Abbot ordered all the passages of the house of commons to be locked as well as the underground exit from Westminster Hall to Old Palace Yard. The St. Mary's Volunteers were under arms in the Hall itself, from where they sent out patrols into the neighbouring streets. A about nine o'clock there was a fire alarm at the back of the Lords, caused by lighted coals which had either fallen or been thrown inside the wooden fence of Parliament Place. Four field pieces and two troops of horse patrolled Bloomsbury Square in the drenching rain while the duke of Sussex and his North Britons guarded the sitting room and wine cellars of Gray's Inn Hall. Portland, the new lord lieutenant of Middlesex, tried to call out Herries' Light Horse Volunteers, only to be told that under the terms of its charter the corps would only obey orders direct from the home secretary.[1] At nine-thirty p.m. the attorney-general delivered his formal opinion to the Speaker. It must be, he argued, Colman's own decision whether or not to use force, for it was not possible to say if the breaking of the door would be held to be legal or illegal. Once performed he thought the action could be defended. The serjeant then decided to risk an arrest on the understanding that he would be given an adequate escort and the promise that government would 'protect and indemnify him to the utmost of their power'.[2]

Immediately after breakfast on Monday, 9 April, Colman set off for the last time to Piccadilly. When he arrived it was still raining heavily and there were few people about. Mused one observer,

> 'For clearing a mob in the streets,
> To save us from all being slain,
> What are Wellesley's brave Cintra feats
> To those of a General Rain?'

A constable fetched a ladder, climbed to the first-floor window through which he saw Sir Francis teaching his son to translate magna carta. According to Graham Wallas, Burdett had held a council of his sympathisers the previous evening at which Place had persuaded the

---

[1] Colchester, vol. II, p. 252; P.R.O., 30/3/1, Bosanquet MSS., Portland, lord lieutenant of Middlesex, to Colonel Herries, 7 Apr. 1810; Hutton, *Letters and Correspondence of Sir James Bland Burges*, vol. II, pp. 316–17; Windsor MSS., 15067–8 and 15069–70, Ryder to George III, 8 Apr. 1810.

[2] Colchester, vol. II, p. 254. The *Day* attacked the ministry on 9 April for the delay in executing the warrant.

hot-heads that armed resistance was out of the question. When, there-fore, the radicals saw the constable at the top of the ladder they merely closed the window instead of pushing him off. But by this time soldiers had broken into the ground floor followed by Colman who, with immense courtesy, finally arrested Sir Francis Burdett. The baronet was then hustled into a waiting carriage which, surrounded by a small army of guards, set off for the Tower. The news of the serjeant's coup soon spread through the capital, but although crowds quickly gathered, they were not able seriously to molest Burdett's captors, who reached the Tower after a long northwards detour. The only major clash with the mob occurred as the troops were returning to the horse-guards when firing began which caused fatal casualties among the crowd.[1]

And so on 9 April Liverpool was finally able to report Burdett's arrest to Windsor. Ryder, after the fatigue of the previous three days, was too indisposed to be able to put pen to paper. The ministry's fumblings boded ill for its efficiency in more important matters. 'I think', wrote Wellington, 'that Gov[ernmen]t and country are going to the Devil as fast as possible; and I expect every day to hear that the mob of London are masters of the country.' Wilberforce, alarmed by mob violence, dwelt on the virtues of withdrawal from worldly problems, while the more mundane Windham lamented the 'terrible disposition to yield to popular opinion, and to give up the House of Commons'.[2] With Burdett safely in the Tower peace was immediately restored to the streets of London. The rioters, concluded the *Day*, had aimed at defending the constitution, not at overthrowing it.[3] Certain legal and constitutional problems, however, still remained when the Commons reassembled on the afternoon of 9 April. Burdett's letter to the Speaker of the seventh, challenging the legality of the warrant for his arrest, led to a warm debate before the House unanimously agreed to defer consideration of it for six months.[4] The following morning the Speaker received notice from Burdett's lawyer that Sir Francis had decided to institute proceedings against him. Abbot, in

---

[1] *Day*, 16 Apr. 1810; Wallas, *Life of Place*, p. 51; Patterson, vol. I, pp. 269-71. At the subsequent inquest on those killed on 9 Apr. the jury brought in a verdict of 'wilful murder against some Lifeguards man unknown' (*Parl. Deb.*, XVI, 746).

[2] Windsor MSS., 15073-4, Liverpool to George III, 9 Apr. 1810; Windham, *Diary*, p. 503; *Camden Soc., 3rd series, Miscellany 18*, p. 34.

[3] *Day*, 10 Apr. 1810.

[4] *Parl. Deb.*, XVI, 630; Colchester, vol. II, p. 258.

great alarm, retained both government law officers and three other barristers, the king sent assurances that the Speaker had the right to order the serjeant-at-arms to break into any house except the homes of princes or princesses, while Perceval persuaded the Commons to set up a special committee on privileges.[1] On the advice of this committee the House itself decided to undertake the Speaker's defence and the court of king's bench ruled against Burdett on 17 May.[2] Fine legal points, however, carried little weight with Burdett's fellow radicals either in or out of parliament. On 17 April a motion for the release of Gale Jones was carried against the government by the combined votes of the opposition, the Canningites, the Saints, the Sidmouth group and even the master of the rolls.[3] Meanwhile petitions for Burdett's own release came from a packed meeting held in Palace Yard, from the freeholders of Middlesex and the liverymen of London, as well as from several provincial counties and towns.[4] Pro-government speeches were once more hissed and shouted down in common hall while rumours spread that the cabinet had decided to suspend habeas corpus. But Perceval was never easily rattled. The most violently worded petitions were rejected and Burdett was not released until late in June, after parliament had gone into recess. Even this crisis went off without further alarms, for the mob's temper had cooled, Burdett himself avoided incitement, and Perceval surrounded London with troops and called out the Volunteers.[5]

Subtler tactics were needed to meet the Walcheren inquiry which had indirectly precipitated the Burdett riots. The inquiry was conducted by a committee of the whole House, under the chairmanship of Sir John Anstruther, which met twenty times between 2 February and 30 March.[6] Sir David Dundas, the commander-in-chief, and Chatham himself were the chief witnesses on military issues, Huskisson and Wharton were questioned on matters of finance, while Sir Lucius Pepys, physician-general to the forces, Thomas Keate, surgeon-general to the army, and Francis Knight, inspector-general of army hospitals, gave evidence on the health of the troops. At first the inquiry went

[1] Colchester, vol. II, pp. 263, 269 (Ponsonby's opinion), 270 (Tierney's), 271–2 (Canning's), 273 (Grenville's); *Parl. Deb.*, XVI, 869; P.R.O., 30/9/15, Perceval to Abbot, 11 Apr. 1810.

[2] Colchester, vol. II, p. 275 (report of committee on privileges), 331 (verdict of king's bench).

[3] Windsor MSS., 15091, Perceval to George III, 17 Apr. 1810.

[4] *Parl. Deb.*, XVI, 818 and 944; *Day*, 23 Apr., 4 and 14 May 1810.

[5] *Day*, 5 May and 21 June 1810.

[6] *Parl. Papers, 1810* (12), VIII, *H. of C. Reports of Committees.*

unexpectedly well for ministers. Castlereagh got them off to a flying start on the first day in a speech which the *Sun* described as the best made in the Commons since the death of Pitt. The opposition, alarmed as usual by radical violence during the Burdett riots, seemed too inhibited to be able to press home even so strong a case. Porchester, who led for them on the issue, showed little skill in examining witnesses, Ponsonby was largely inept, while Brougham, who might have been their most effective spokesman, seemed to some of his friends more intent on ridiculing the cabinet in private than in exposing its errors in public. In fact only Tierney, Whitbread and the old warrior Windham showed any real enthusiasm for the cause.[1] Then, on 20 February, Lord Folkestone electrified the opposition by singling out one of the many papers which had been laid on the table as evidence in the inquiry. This appeared to be a confidential report by Chatham, written on 15 January, and sent direct to Windsor without first being submitted to the secretary of state for war. How, asked Folkestone, could the House accept a paper which had not been presented on the authority of any member of the government and for the contents of which no minister could, therefore, be held responsible?[2] The paper was clearly unconstitutional. Its contents were equally embarrassing, for Chatham's apologia laid the blame for the failure to press home the main attack against the Scheldt partly on the dilatoriness of Sir Richard Strachan and partly on 'changes in the original plan, adopted by the authorities at home in compliance with the views of others, and not from any suggestion of his own'.[3]

This new revelation of disunity in the Portland ministry was bad enough, but the manner in which Chatham's report had been presented would certainly be used as evidence of similar divisions and personal rivalries in Perceval's own cabinet. Chatham had now become a positive liability to his colleagues. Lonsdale regretted that any attempt had ever been made to defend him in parliament, while Mulgrave had already complained direct to Perceval of his 'captious disposition'. 'It will not be possible for me', wrote Mulgrave from the admiralty on 8 February, 'long to support the uninterrupted labour and confinement of this office. I will hold it whilst your Government requires for its strength that it should not exhibit any change or chasm; and this I am ready to do at any sacrifice but that of submitting to personal

---

[1] *Sun*, 3 Feb. 1810; Holland, *Further Memoirs*, pp. 46–7.
[2] *Parl. Deb.*, XV, 493.
[3] Colchester, vol. II, p. 238.

arrogance, to avoid which it is desirable . . . that business with the Master General of the Ordnance should pass through your medium. I was up till past one o'clock this morning clearing away arrears of business; and what with the daily repetition of similar exertions and the pressure of successive family anxieties, I am not in a temper to meet the childish vehemence of a jealous votary of formalities.' [1] The prime minister, who had grappled with a seemingly uninterrupted series of crises for the past six months, now found himself with two cabinet colleagues who could not even safely be left to meet to conduct routine government business. The opposition, scenting the kill, pressed home its attack on 23 February. Whitbread then moved an address to the Crown for 'copies of all reports, memoranda, narrative or papers, submitted at any time to His Majesty, by the Earl of Chatham, relative to the late Expedition'.[2] At a hurried cabinet meeting Chatham explained that the fatal report had been written on the insistence of the king and submitted to him on 15 January after George III had pressed both Camden and General Brownrigg for its presentation. The report had not been made public both because it was intended to be the basis of Chatham's defence at any future court of inquiry and because a similar report by Strachan, called for by the admiralty, had not then been presented. Mulgrave, alleged Chatham, was 'in private connection with those adverse to me'. Chatham had explained these reasons against publication to Perceval and had written to the secretary of war before 15 January asking for a court martial. Finally on 7 February Chatham had seen the king, asked for the return of his statement so that he could alter certain parts of it, returned the amended version on the tenth and had then sent it to Liverpool on 14 February for circulation to the cabinet.[3]

Chatham's colleagues thereupon agreed to try to oppose Whitbread's motion, using the argument that they could not agree to ask the king for the production of hypothetical papers. The House divided shortly before midnight when ministers were defeated by 178 votes to 171. While a large party of opposition members returned to Brooks's 'in great triumph', a weary Perceval sat down to send news of the division to Windsor. 'Mr. Perceval', he wrote, 'laments extremely the loss of this question; but he is in duty bound to state to Your Majesty that the prejudice excited by Lord Chatham's narrative, and all the

---

[1] Ward, vol. I, p. 294; Perceval MSS., Mulgrave to Perceval, 8 Feb. 1810.
[2] *Parl. Deb.*, XV, 564.
[3] P.R.O., Chatham MSS., 260 memorandum in Chatham's defence.

circumstances connected with it, is so great that Mr. Perceval fears
the loss of this question will not be the only inconvenience that paper
will produce.' But the king would have none of such despondency.
How could an answer to the Commons' address embarrass ministers
as 'the plain simple statement will be that *the King has no paper*'? [1]
Perceval, however, knew that the Commons was in no mood to be
treated in so cavalier a fashion. Another cabinet meeting was called to
consider the king's answer and a minute drafted arguing for a reasoned
reply to the address. If the House was curtly told that the king had no
paper from Chatham, members might assume that other statements
had been presented and then removed from Windsor or destroyed in
order to prevent their production as evidence. The whole incident had
'occasioned more prejudice to the character of Your Majesty's administration, has increased the opinion of a want of communication, concert,
and confidence amongst them, and will do more to endanger their
stability than any other circumstance whatever which has arisen out
of the Walcheren Expedition'. This warning, backed by an audience
with Perceval, finally persuaded the king to give the full history of
Chatham's report of 15 January. The dates were identical to those
already offered by Chatham to his colleagues.[2] On the morning of
25 February the prime minister was once more at Windsor to get the
king's consent to a draft reply to the address and a lengthy cabinet
meeting was held in Downing Street on his return. At first the atmosphere was cordial as Chatham was too occupied with the inquiry
and the pressure of other business to attend. Just as ministers were
breaking up, however, Chatham appeared. As soon as he entered the
room, Perceval told him they had discussed the answer to the address
at length and offered to read, as well as he could, the rough notes he
had jotted down. After this had been done, Chatham objected that
he was completely opposed to going into details in the proposed
reply 'and wished only for a general answer' to be given to the House.
This the cabinet refused to accept. After some discussion, therefore,
Chatham said that if the agreed draft was thought best for the king's
sake, he would accept it. He then asked Perceval to give him the draft
so that he might read it carefully, to which the prime minister replied
'that the paper had gone thro[ugh] so many alterations, and was so

[1] *Parl. Deb.*, XV, 587; Auckland, *Journal*, vol. IV, p. 348; Windsor MSS.,
14970–1, Perceval to George III, 23 Feb. 1810 and George III to Perceval,
24 Feb. 1810.
    [2] Windsor MSS., 14972–3, Perceval to George III, 24 Feb. 1810 and George
III to Perceval, 25 Feb. 1810.

blotted and underlined, that he could scarcely read it himself' and thought Chatham would make nothing of it. Chatham then began to object to certain passages in the draft until Perceval was finally compelled to rule that the cabinet must break up in order to give him time to prepare a fair copy to be read to the Commons. Even then the earl was not satisfied. Just before the House reassembled he called on Perceval, only to be told that the prime minister was out, although Chatham himself suspected that 'he would not admit him'.[1]

In this atmosphere of strained personal relations, ministers had, on 3 March, to face two resolutions by Whitbread outlining the history of the secret narrative and claiming that 'the Earl of Chatham, by private communication to His Majesty, accompanied by a desire of secrecy, did unconstitutionally abuse the privilege of access to his sovereign, and thereby afford an example most pernicious in its tendency to His Majesty's service, and to the general service of the state'. The best that Perceval could do was to delay the debate until Monday, 6 March. Hopes of surviving a division seemed slim, for it was now evident that either Chatham must resign or the cabinet faced yet another defeat. That week-end Perceval wrote to Chatham virtually inviting him to retire. 'I have great reason to fear', he confessed, 'that we shall be beat. I have heard to-day of many who will keep away, and not support us.' Both Lascelles and the master of the rolls felt that, on such an issue, the House could not accept a motion for the previous question. If the vote went against ministers then 'it will be impossible that the King's service can go on (particularly in our state of weakness) with the weight of such a vote against any one of his servants. . . .'[2] When Chatham failed to take the hint defeat was certain. On the evening of the sixth Perceval moved the previous question and lost by 188 votes to 221. Whitbread's first resolution was then carried, as was Canning's amendment to the second, declaring Chatham's conduct 'highly reprehensible' and deserving of 'the censure of this House'. After such a humiliation, predicted the *Day*, the government was doomed, an opinion fully shared by Grenville himself, who believed that the cabinet had already told the king that it would resign as soon as the inquiry was completed.[3] Yet, with incredible stupidity, Chatham still sought to cling to office throughout Tuesday, 7 March.

[1] Windsor MSS., 14977, Perceval to George III, 25 Feb. 1810; P.R.O., Chatham MSS., 260, undated memorandum by Chatham.

[2] Walpole, vol. II, pp. 77-8.

[3] *Parl. Deb.*, XVI, 16; *Day*, 5 and 6 Mar. 1810; Auckland, *Journal*, vol. IV, p. 349.

That evening Whitbread asked Arbuthnot privately 'whether Lord Chatham was still Master-General of the Ordnance'. When Arbuthnot replied that he was, Whitbread said, 'Well, I shall wait a day or two, and then I shall put the same question publicly.' Only after Perceval had bluntly reported this to Chatham was the cabinet finally disencumbered of its most embarrassing member.[1]

Chatham's resignation, belated as it was, came just in time to save his colleagues from all having to tender theirs. For, with the late expedition's commander out of the way, waverers in the Commons began to drift back to their normal support of the government of the day. By 29 March an ebullient Perceval felt able to report to Windsor that he was confident of carrying the crucial divisions on the following day. When the House finally divided at 4 o'clock in the morning of 31 March, members decided by 275 votes to 227 against censuring the policy of the expedition. They then accepted a government amendment formally approving of the expedition by 272 to 232, supported the attempt made to retain the island of Walcheren itself by 275 to 224, and excused the delay in ordering the eventual evacuation by 253 to 232.[2] The unexpected defeat threw the whigs into confusion. 'The Opposition', confessed a disappointed J. W. Ward, 'must be considered as completely beat. The truth is that the country is outrageously against them and that it prefers anything to the Grenvilles.' Lord Holland and the *Edinburgh Review*, in contrast, thought the result furnished the strongest practical argument for parliamentary reform, since the votes reflected neither public opinion nor the real feelings of the majority of M.P.s. The opposition had had a good case, strong allies in parliament, and popular support outside it. Yet, in the words of the party's latest historian, it was so distrusted by independent members because of its defeatism in the Peninsula and its indiscipline in the Commons that, in the last resort, the majority of M.P.s 'preferred to take the chance that Walcheren would be a salutary lesson to the Government, than to risk putting the country into the hands

[1] Walpole, vol. II, p. 79; *Sun*, 8 Mar. 1810; Windsor MSS., 15003-4, Perceval to George III, 8 Mar. 1810.

[2] Windsor MSS., 15047-8, Perceval to George III, 29 Mar. 1810; Windham, *Diary*, p. 503; Perceval MSS., Richard Wharton to Perceval, 24 Mar. 1810. The *Sun* (31 Mar. 1810) explained that after Porchester's motion had been defeated by a majority of forty-eight a number of the ministry's supporters left the chamber, thinking that the opposition would not force divisions on the government's amendments. Because of this the ministers' majority was reduced in the last three divisions. In these divisions Canning and Sturges Bourne voted for the government, and Granville Leveson-Gower and Charles Ellis against.

of a party that had neither policy, nor prospect of uniting upon one, nor ability to carry it out'. In the end Perceval's courage and steadiness had pulled it off against the greatest imaginable difficulties and odds. After the Walcheren debates Pittites again knew that they had a leader of resolution and character.[1] Moreover the new prime minister's growing parliamentary reputation was matched by his increasing mastery of business at the exchequer.

[1] S. H. Romilly, *Letters to Ivy*, p. 72; Holland, *Further Memoirs*, p. 47; *Edinburgh Review*, Oct. 1809, pp. 234–5; Roberts, *The Whig Party, 1807–12*, pp. 146–7; Colchester, vol. II, p. 244; Brougham (*Memoirs*, vol. I, pp. 472–3) had predicted a swing of opinion to the new government as early as November 1809.

CHAPTER SEVENTEEN

THE TREASURY

OF all Portland's appointments in the spring of 1807 that of Perceval as chancellor of the exchequer was commonly thought the worst. If, joked Sheridan, Pitt's Friends possessed anything at all 'they were swarming with Chancellors of the Exchequer' and yet they had chosen 'a gentleman who, though a very frequent speaker in the House, had never, to his knowledge, uttered one word on the subject of finance in his life'. There was not, said Howick more briefly and accurately, a department for which Perceval was less fitted, and even the new minister himself agreed. He was, he wrote to a friend, 'without any pretension in his own mind to be called, as he has been, to this office of Chancellor of the Exchequer, the duties of which overwhelm him with alarm'. Before March was out Lady Bessborough was busy reporting Perceval's resignation because he had discovered that some slight knowledge of figures was necessary and that he had none.[1] But Perceval's reaction was rather to learn than to resign: if the duke proved a cypher as first lord, he must rely on the specialised knowledge of his subordinates and on a determination to husband the nation's resources as zealously as he had hitherto managed his own.

The organisation of the treasury would have tried a more highly qualified man. There were, the radical Sir Francis Burdett once told the Commons, 'some who thought there were two seasons improper for reform—a time of peace and a time of war. In peace it was a pity to disturb the general tranquillity, in war the nation had a great deal of other business on its hands.'[2] To this doctrine those at the treasury had clung as to a rock. The oldest clerks could still remember the golden days of the 1760's when the permanent staff never exceeded fourteen and when work never began before eleven o'clock in the morning. In that spacious age even important measures were 'carried into execution by mere oral authority' conveyed to the office by the

---

[1] *Parl. Deb.*, IX, 211 and 217; Gower, vol. II, p. 243; Harrowby MSS., XI, fol. 216; C. V. Williams, *Life and Administration of Spencer Perceval*, p. 28.
[2] *Parl. Deb.*, XIV, 729.

joint parliamentary secretaries. The department under the duke of
Newcastle was content with little business and less efficiency. When
Charles Jenkinson was appointed one of the secretaries to the treasury
under Newcastle's successor, Bute, he found that the board's decisions
were not even regularly minuted. The joint secretaries were still expected to give verbal instructions to all clerks after board meetings and
to take personal responsibility whenever anything went wrong. It was
Jenkinson who, with the help of J. M. Leakes, a treasury clerk, first
began a workable system of board minutes. 'Mr. Jenkinson', wrote
Leakes, 'took short notes during the sitting of the Board, afterwards
detailed at his own house, in which he required my assistance as a
junior clerk.' [1]

The treasury board in the eighteenth and early nineteenth centuries
consisted of the first lord, the chancellor of the exchequer, and usually
four junior lords. All board meetings were attended by at least one of
the joint secretaries to the treasury, both of whom sat in parliament.[2]
The senior secretary was responsible to the board for presenting and
minuting all papers, he supervised the preparation of all non-revenue
parliamentary bills, dealt with merchants' trade problems and interviewed petitioners, maintained contact with most other government
departments, and was responsible to the first lord for all treasury
patronage and for the management of the press. An efficient senior
secretary to the treasury was, in fact, a key member of any administration. His junior colleague was charged with the issuing of all public
money, dealt with the civil list, revenue bills, all colonial affairs and
generally assisted the chancellor of the exchequer in financial matters.[3]
Under a strong chancellor with a firm financial policy of his own, the
junior secretary tended to play a minor role. When the exchequer was
in weak or inexperienced hands, his influence could become vital.
Treasury business, wrote Leakes, 'was conducted theoretically, and
nearly practically, as follows. The Board determined all matters coming before them, as well public as for official Government. The Secretaries received all papers, laid them before and obtained the direc-

---

[1] P.R.O., T1/4306. J. M. Leakes entered the treasury in 1763, became a chief
clerk in 1782, and in 1785 was appointed a comptroller of army accounts.

[2] The 1786 committee of inquiry recommended that one of the secretaries
should be 'stationary' and excluded from parliament. The treasury board strongly
objected and the proposal was withdrawn.—*Parl. Papers, H. of C. Rep. of Comm.*
(*1797–8*), vol. XII, 2.

[3] P.R.O., Chatham MSS., 231, memorandum on treasury organisation; F. S.
Thomas, *Notes on the Materials for the History of the Public Departments*
(London, 1846), p. 17.

tions of, the Board thereon—minuted, shortly, such directions—
which minutes were afterwards detailed, under their immediate
direction, before delivery for execution to the Chief Clerks.'[1] There
were, after 1759, four chief clerks in the treasury. As a group they
were expected to attend board meetings and give all necessary detailed
information to their lordships, to superintend routine office work, and
to interview members of the public who called at the treasury for
advice. In addition they each had specialised duties. One kept a register
of incoming letters and read all petitions and memorials to the board;
a second drafted all warrants, orders, and contracts submitted to the
board; a third kept the office accounts and fee fund; the fourth helped
in all parliamentary business.[2] Finally there were the junior clerks to
whom 'the whole of the executive business of the Office, divided into
different branches was allotted, to some more, to other less, according
to merit or favour'.

This system worked tolerably well until the outbreak of the war of
American independence caused a sudden increase in treasury business.
Between 1767 and 1783 the yearly intake of registered papers was more
than trebled. A special revenue department was set up in 1776 in an
attempt to increase efficiency and the permanent staff was told that in
future ability rather than seniority would be the test for promotion.
Lord North put all junior clerks on fixed salaries, instead of allowing
them to earn what they could from fees.[3] The real pressure of work
fell hardest, however, on the chief clerks, until certain of them resigned and those next in succession refused the offer of promotion.
Fortunately the return of peace averted a major crisis: work declined
and the treasury officials returned thankfully to normal conditions.
In fact the staff had done fairly well financially out of the war. The
department's fee fund leapt and so did treasury salaries. Between 1779
and 1781 the joint secretaries earned an average of £5,114 a year,
compared with a pre-war average of less than £3,500. They were, in
fact, earning more than the salary of the chancellor of the exchequer.
The salaries of chief clerks in the same period went up from £853 to
£1,278. A minute of 1782 fixed the basic salary of the secretaries at
£3,000 a year, plus fees, and that of the chief clerks at £800, plus fees.
By the end of the century these had risen to £4,000 and £1,400

[1] Leakes, *loc. cit.*
[2] Chatham MSS., and Leakes, *loc. cit.*
[3] P.R.O., T1/4306. Memorandum respecting the increase of the business and
of the establishment of the treasury (1820).

respectively. Only the junior staff got no concessions, for the basic starting salary remained at £100 a year, augmented by trivial fees.[1]

The outbreak of war with France finally overwhelmed the old treasury organisation. In 1792 the total permanent establishment consisted of four chief, six senior, six assistant clerks and one copying clerk. These seventeen had to grapple with an intake of registered papers which was exactly doubled in the four years ending in 1796. At first Pitt tried to control the avalanche by increases in staff. By 1797 there were twenty-seven clerks, but the problem could not be solved merely by adding a few inexperienced young men to the department's staff. The old system collapsed at all levels for the lords of the treasury were as overwhelmed as the junior clerks. By 1797 Smyth, a junior lord, could assure his newly-appointed colleague, Douglas, 'You will find the Board quite a sinecure. There are seldom Boards. Mr. Pitt does all the material business at his own house, signs the papers and then two other Lords sign them of course. Other business the Secretaries judge of without carrying it to him, and lay the papers on the table and circulate them for the signature of any of the Lords.' [2] Pitt himself hardly ever entered the treasury chambers and board meetings, in his absence, became an empty formality. Douglas describes one sitting at which only he, Smyth and the secretaries, Rose and Long, were present. Smyth read out a list of points to be discussed, Rose or Long made a brief comment on each, after which Smyth duly ticked off that item in the book before him. Douglas did ask a few questions, mostly out of curiosity, without appreciably delaying the routine. 'In short,' wrote Douglas, 'to an ignorant person Smyth would have appeared to be the Secretary, and Rose and Long the Board.' [3] By 1801 Hiley Addington, then one of the treasury secretaries, could contemptuously dismiss junior lords as 'mere signers of papers', while Long warned Pitt not to let treasury business fall too much into the hands of the joint secretaries. Junior lordships, according to some observers, were already virtually sinecures. 'It appears', wrote Gran-

---

[1] P.R.O., Chatham MSS., *loc. cit.*; *Parl. Papers, H. of C. 15th Report of Committee of Finance*, App. 8, p. 18. The treasury's wage bill was paid out of the department's fee fund, augmented by a deficiency grant from the civil list. This, between 1807 and 1812, varied from about £3,500 to £7,500 a quarter (P.R.O., T29/103/58; T29/106/250). Most of the clerks held additional posts to augment their official salaries. Thus in 1797, the four chief clerks held seven posts between them worth £1,710 a year; the six senior clerks held six offices and one pension; the six assistant clerks another six posts.

[2] Glenbervie, *Diary*, vol. I, p. 128.

[3] Glenbervie, *loc. cit.*

ville Leveson-Gower, 'that in the present constitution and practice of the Treasury Office, the business of the meetings of the Board, which take place twice a week, is merely formal. The duty of the Lords who assist is that of listening to the perusal of minutes on multifarious subjects, on which minutes they are supposed to decide. From their

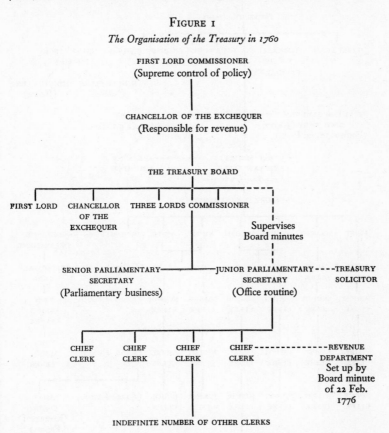

FIGURE 1

The Organisation of the Treasury in 1760

FIRST LORD COMMISSIONER
(Supreme control of policy)

CHANCELLOR OF THE EXCHEQUER
(Responsible for revenue)

THE TREASURY BOARD

FIRST LORD   CHANCELLOR   THREE LORDS COMMISSIONER
              OF THE
              EXCHEQUER
                                          Supervises
                                          Board minutes

SENIOR PARLIAMENTARY————JUNIOR PARLIAMENTARY----TREASURY
        SECRETARY   SECRETARY   SOLICITOR
(Parliamentary business)   (Office routine)

CHIEF   CHIEF   CHIEF   CHIEF------------REVENUE
CLERK   CLERK   CLERK   CLERK   DEPARTMENT
                                                 Set up by
                                                 Board minute
                                                 of 22 Feb.
                                                 1776

INDEFINITE NUMBER OF OTHER CLERKS

ignorance of every matter contained in these papers their decision upon the principle of Sir Isaac Newton would be as necessary and as valuable as a sanction or disapproval.'[1] As confusion within the department grew, there were many complaints against 'the irregular, dilatory and incorrect mode of transacting business' by the clerks, who lost so many state papers that Grenville, at the foreign office, finally

[1] *Ibid.*, p. 210; P.R.O., Chatham MSS., 326, no. 328, Long to Pitt, 8 Sep. 1805.

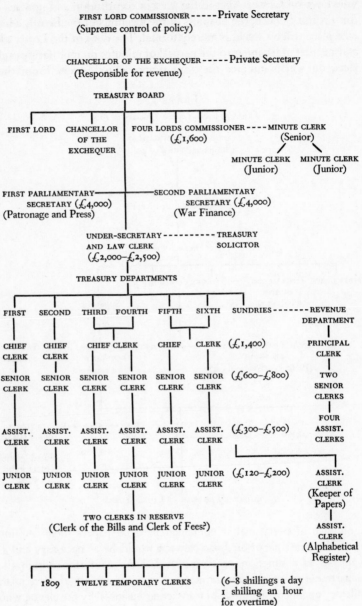

FIGURE 2
The Organisation of the Treasury after 1805

FIRST LORD COMMISSIONER - - - - - Private Secretary
(Supreme control of policy)

CHANCELLOR OF THE EXCHEQUER - - - - - Private Secretary
(Responsible for revenue)

TREASURY BOARD

FIRST LORD   CHANCELLOR   FOUR LORDS COMMISSIONER - - - - MINUTE CLERK
       OF THE   (£1,600)   (Senior)
   EXCHEQUER

MINUTE CLERK   MINUTE CLERK
(Junior)   (Junior)

FIRST PARLIAMENTARY —————— SECOND PARLIAMENTARY
     SECRETARY (£4,000)   SECRETARY (£4,000)
(Patronage and Press)   (War Finance)

UNDER-SECRETARY - - - - - - - - - TREASURY
AND LAW CLERK   SOLICITOR
(£2,000–£2,500)

TREASURY DEPARTMENTS

FIRST   SECOND   THIRD   FOURTH   FIFTH   SIXTH   SUNDRIES - - - - - - REVENUE
                                                     DEPARTMENT

CHIEF   CHIEF   CHIEF CLERK   CHIEF   CLERK   (£1,400)   PRINCIPAL
CLERK   CLERK   CLERK

SENIOR   SENIOR   SENIOR   SENIOR   SENIOR   SENIOR   (£600–£800)   TWO
CLERK   CLERK   CLERK   CLERK   CLERK   CLERK   SENIOR
                                                            CLERKS

FOUR
ASSIST.
CLERKS

ASSIST.   ASSIST.   ASSIST.   ASSIST.   ASSIST.   ASSIST.   (£300–£500)
CLERK   CLERK   CLERK   CLERK   CLERK   CLERK

JUNIOR   JUNIOR   JUNIOR   JUNIOR   JUNIOR   JUNIOR   (£120–£200)   ASSIST.
CLERK   CLERK   CLERK   CLERK   CLERK   CLERK   CLERK
                                                           (Keeper of
                                                           Papers)

TWO CLERKS IN RESERVE
(Clerk of the Bills and Clerk of Fees?)

ASSIST.
CLERK
(Alphabetical
Register)

1809   TWELVE TEMPORARY CLERKS   (6–8 shillings a day
                                           1 shilling an hour
                                           for overtime)

TOTAL STAFF—PARLIAMENTARY 8 and 2 Private Secretaries
                 PERMANENT   30 and 7 in Revenue Department
                 TEMPORARY   12

decided that in future no originals should be sent.[1] On the whole
Grenville's view was probably exaggerated. The board no longer
debated financial policy, but under Portland and Perceval it did much
useful work in supervising the auditing of accounts and deciding the
details of commercial policy. Particularly after 1809 the pressure of
business caused board meetings to get longer and longer.

Major if belated reorganisation came in August 1805. At its lowest
level the treasury was divided into six sections, each responsible for
a particular type of business. The first division, the most important,
dealt with war finance and all American, West Indian, and Mediterranean business; the second controlled customs and excise and all
matters relating to the privy council; the third was responsible for a
great deal of miscellaneous business, mostly relating to taxes, while
the fourth was concerned with crown lands, police matters and correspondence with the secretaries of state; contacts with the Bank, the
South Sea and East India companies, the exchequer, the law officers
and Ireland were made by the fifth division; the sixth dealt with the
civil list, parliamentary business and all matters not specifically assigned
to the other five. Finally the revenue department dealt with the collection of taxes, maintained contact with the clerk of the pells and the
exchequer bill office, and prepared weekly, quarterly, and annual
revenue accounts. There were by 1805 thirty-six clerks working in the
treasury, twenty-two of them in the six divisions, seven in the revenue
department, three responsible for board minutes, and four others with
specialised duties.[2] This total, claimed their lordships, was ample to
control our national finances and run a world war. The treasury board
itself was not affected by the 1805 reform, remaining a formal but
relatively harmless institution. By far the most important move was
the appointment of a new permanent official, George Harrison, as
assistant-secretary and law clerk, at an initial salary of £2,000 a year.[3]

Little is known of Harrison's early life. The son of a former attorney
and advocate-general of Jamaica, he soon conquered a youthful desire
to become a historian and instead entered Lincoln's Inn. His keen

---

[1] Colchester, vol. II, p. 50; Add. MSS., 38749, fol. 89.

[2] See pp. 309–10, figs. 1–2, for the treasury in 1760 and 1805. In 1807 the first
division dealt with two-thirds of the total business of the treasury (T29/95/382).
For the revenue department see T1/4306/3. In 1811 the foreign office consisted
of the secretary of state, two under-secretaries and twenty-one permanent
officials (T1/1230/679).

[3] Harrison's salary was increased to £3,000 a year in 1809 and to £3,500 in
1815. For full details of the 1805 reform see T1/4308.

interest in taxation problems brought him to the notice of Pitt and led
to his appointment, in 1798, as registrar for the redemption of the land
tax and later to the posts of counsel to the war office, the commander-
in-chief's office, and the barrack office.[1] As assistant-secretary at the
treasury Harrison rapidly became one of the most important figures
in the department. He attended all board meetings, supervised the
taking of minutes and was responsible for the efficient execution of all
board decisions by the chief clerk concerned, he had authority to draft
letters and special warrants, to sign all references and directions for
executing orders-in-council, and to accept bills of exchange drawn on
the treasury. He alone could grant leave of absence to treasury clerks
and he was given general powers 'to take care that all regulations for
the conduct of business are punctually attended to'.[2] His appointment
marks the beginning of the modern higher permanent civil service, for
he was forbidden to seek election to parliament and was never involved
in group or party politics. At first such impartiality seemed to many
neither possible nor desirable. When Grenville went to the treasury in
1806 he was urged by the marquis of Buckingham to replace Harrison
by Fremantle, a staunch personal follower. 'Of Mr. Harrison', wrote
Grenville in reply, 'I know nothing, but I learn that his situation is very
considerably inferior to that of the other two Secretaries both in rank
and in emolument, is not tenable with parliament and is rather the
station of a first clerk than of a Joint Secretary.'[3] Relations between
Grenville and Harrison were soon so cordial that the latter took an
active part in the high-level discussions that led to the new government's plan of finance.[4] For Perceval, Harrison had 'the highest personal respect and esteem'.[5] He acted as the first lord's legal adviser on
parliamentary business, was entrusted with confidential negotiations
on the royal family's private affairs and formed, together with Henry
Bunbury of the war office, and Willoughby Gordon of the com-

---

[1] The *Dictionary of National Biography* account of Harrison's life is not
satisfactory. See also *Black Book of Lincoln's Inn*, p. 242; G. Harrison, *Fragments
of History*; P.R.O., Chatham MSS., 642, Harrison to Pitt, Feb. 1793 and Dec.
1797.

[2] T1/4308 (unnumbered).

[3] *Dropmore MSS.*, VII, p. 22; Buckingham, *Memoirs of Court and Cabinets
of George III*, vol. IV, p. 17. Fremantle, described by Rose as 'a gentleman, but
new to business as a child', had been deputy teller of the exchequer under
Buckingham. (*Lonsdale MSS.*, p. 196).

[4] *Dropmore MSS.*, VIII, pp. 469 and 485.

[5] G. Harrison, *Observations in support of the title of the King to all escheats . . .
within the Duchy of Lancaster*, p. 67. Harrison was one of the witnesses to Perceval's will in Oct. 1808 (Somerset House, wills, Oxford, fol. 292).

missariat, an informal committee to advise on supplying Wellington's army in the Peninsula.[1] He was a constant visitor at 10, Downing Street and was consulted over most aspects of financial policy. When, in the autumn of 1809, Perceval offered the exchequer to the inexperienced Palmerston, he assured him he could rely on Harrison for guidance and advice.[2] Two years later, although nearly crippled by gout, Harrison was working as hard 'at home as at the Treasury' and had two full-time private secretaries, 'without whom it would have been utterly impossible for him to have got through the business of the Office'.[3] At the end of the war a board minute formally paid tribute to his 'unremitting labour' in 'a variety of business . . . of a most important and confidential nature' and the knighthood awarded him on his retirement was one of the first recognitions of the increased status of the permanent official.

The 1805 reform professionalised the treasury. Under the new system routine business, wrote William Speer, one of the most experienced of the chief clerks, 'was transacted with as much accuracy as human institutions and performances generally admit of and with as much despatch as is consistent with such accuracy'. William Cotton, who spent twenty-three years in the department, saw the real significance of the reorganisation in its effect on the work of the chief clerks. After 1805 they were no longer responsible for the general supervision of office business and were thus free to concentrate on the work of their own departments. They lost responsibility but gained specialist knowledge.[4] The treasury's work became increasingly complicated, until even the most highly qualified politicians and economists had to rely on the guidance of the permanent staff. In 1808 Perceval called in Robertson, the Savilian professor of geometry at Oxford, and Gilpin of the Royal Society to help with the details of the Life Annuities Act. They were, wrote the treasury clerk who worked with them, 'deeply detailed in algebra and in all formula of the questions to be solved' but 'so utterly unacquainted were they with the financial measures of the country, with the nature of the Sinking Fund, the difference of the

---

[1] Perceval MSS., Strong, Still and Strong to W. M. Taylor, 23 Mar. 1810. Harrison was involved in the duke of Sussex—Lady Augusta Murray affair (Perceval MSS., Grenville to Perceval, 1 Aug. 1808, and Harrison to Perceval, 10 Aug. 1808). For the committee see P.R.O., W.O. 67/173/72–3 and 207.

[2] Malmesbury, *Letters*, vol. II, p. 155.

[3] P.R.O., T29/111/752; Perceval MSS., Harrison to Perceval, 14 Jan. 1812.

[4] P.R.O., T1/4306, memoranda by William Speer and William Cotton (21 Aug. 1828).

nominal and actual value of the Funded Debt and various other matters, that it was not without much time and labour that they gained the
necessary information on these subjects'.[1] The joint secretaries, distracted by their parliamentary duties, lost contact with the details of
treasury business and were increasingly forced 'to learn their duties
from those who in their official characters never die, and though their
names may change their knowledge continues in succession and in
perpetuity'.[2] Even the lowest-paid clerks were often entrusted with
responsible work.[3] From them were chosen private secretaries to the
first lord, the chancellor and the joint secretaries.[4] They could, if
inefficient or dishonest, do serious harm to the public service. Leigh
Hunt, who entered the war office on Sidmouth's recommendation,
made, on his own admission, 'a bad clerk; wasting my time and that of
others in perpetual jesting; going too late to the office'. One treasury
scribe in Pitt's time was paid by Cope, 'the great Exchange broker', for
'information for the purposes of stock jobbing'.[5] In order to check
such abuses Perceval introduced a three months' probationary period
for all treasury officials and, in some departments, ordered reports on
the ability and industry of the entire staff.[6] On the whole, however,
the treasury was well served by its junior staff, who, by the autumn of
1809, were even working from ten in the morning to four in the
afternoon on Sundays.[7]

There was, in the early nineteenth century, ample scope for a
young man with energy and ability to carve out a career for himself in
the department. T. C. Brooksbank, who entered the treasury in 1796
as an extra clerk in the revenue department, rose to be principal clerk

---

[1] T29/95/382 and T1/4306/4.

[2] T1/4306, memorandum by T. C. Brooksbank (Jan. 1831).

[3] Under the 1805 wage rates junior clerks earned from £120–£200 a year,
assistant clerks from £300–£500, and senior clerks from £600 to a maximum
of £800. Overtime was paid at a minimum of 1s. an hour.

[4] P.R.O., T29/117/293. Private secretaries to the first lord and the chancellor
were given leave of absence, but those assisting the joint secretaries had also to
continue their routine office work. All were paid an additional £150 a year.
In 1811, George Harrison, when applying for a second private secretary,
claimed that the practice of drawing private secretaries from the clerks upset
office routine. The board therefore appointed from outside the treasury (P.R.O.,
T29/111/752).

[5] Leigh Hunt, *Autobiography*, vol. II, p. 13; P.R.O., Chatham MSS., 327,
Edward Cooke to Pitt, 24 Apr. 1795. For trouble with foreign office clerks see
Jackson, *Diary*, vol. I, p. 307 and Malmesbury, vol. IV, p. 360.

[6] P.R.O., T29/96/275; T1/1114/332.

[7] P.R.O., T1/4306.

and private secretary to Perceval and then to Lord Liverpool.[1] In 1798 Anthony Rosenhagen was earning £40 a year as a junior clerk of the bills: by 1812 he was private secretary to the chancellor of the exchequer and later became a comptroller of army accounts.[2] Alexander Speerman also began as a junior clerk and became assistant secretary to the treasury, a comptroller of the national debt and was knighted on his retirement. Even more remarkable was the career of John Charles Herries, the Samuel Smiles of Georgian England, who rose from an assistant clerk at the treasury to chancellor of the exchequer. The son of a prosperous merchant, he was educated at Leipzig and seemed destined for a comfortable and successful life when his father suddenly went bankrupt. Consequently in July 1798, at the age of twenty, Herries entered the treasury as a junior copying clerk at £100 a year. The elder Herries, however, though penniless, still had useful connections. As colonel of the Light Horse Volunteers, he commanded a duke, an earl, and a host of rising young politicians.[3] In January 1799 his son was transferred to the revenue department and his salary trebled, a most unusual promotion after only six months in the department. But young Herries had more to recommend him than influential connections. His chief clerk, Joseph Alcock, 'a gentleman who concerned himself as little as possible with the business of his office', soon began to load work upon him. By 1800 he was drawing up resolutions for Pitt's use in the Commons: during the Addington ministry he became private secretary to Vansittart, one of the joint secretaries to the treasury (and a Light Horse Volunteer). He defended government policy in the press, wrote a pamphlet against Cobbett, and translated Gentz's treatise *On the State of Europe before and after the Revolution*, all for nothing more tangible than a length of service rise of £50.[4] In March 1805 he was temporarily seconded to Ireland to assist the chief secretary, returned to Whitehall after Pitt's death, and in December 1806 was offered by Grenville a customs appointment at Buenos Aires worth £1,000 a year.[5] Herries had joined that marginal group of embryonic higher permanent civil servants. But permanence was as

[1] *Parl. Papers, H. of C. Reports of Committees* (1797–8), vol. LXII, App. C, p. 2; P.R.O., T1/4306, no. 4. T. C. Brooksbank had, in 1806, acted as private secretary to Fremantle, one of the joint parliamentary secretaries to the treasury (Add. MSS., 37309, fol. 152).

[2] P.R.O., T1/4305; Herries, vol. I, p. 26.

[3] cf. chapter 1, pp. 12–13.

[4] Herries, vol. I, p. 18.

[5] Herries MSS., William Wickham to Vansittart, 5 Dec. 1806.

yet only an ideal, for a change of ministry could still involve loss of office. Before Herries could take up his customs post the Talents ministry collapsed and his patron, Vansittart, did not join the duke of Portland's government. Once more the Volunteers came to the rescue. Colonel Herries wrote to the honorary treasurer of the corps, Spencer Perceval, and J. C. Herries became private secretary to the new chancellor of the exchequer at a salary of £300 a year.[1] In the winter of 1808 Perceval, who 'was loud in praise of his secretary to all his friends', tried to persuade the prime minister that Herries would make an ideal successor to an aged and ailing comptroller of lotteries. Portland had a 'particular friend and relative' of his own earmarked for the same vacancy, but the ancient incumbent frustrated both by failing to die.[2] The following spring Herries was compensated by the post of secretary and registrar of the order of the bath, a sinecure with an official salary of £144 2s. 6d. a year, but 'worth quite a little fortune' in fees whenever there was an enlargement of the order.[3] When Perceval became first lord as well as chancellor, he offered Herries the joint private secretaryship at £600 a year and for three months Herries held both posts.[4] His salary as a treasury official was still only £400 a year, but with his private secretaryships and sinecure he was in fact receiving £1,144 2s. 6d. plus very substantial fees, a remarkable income for a treasury clerk. In June 1811 he went to Ireland as secretary to Foster, the Irish chancellor of the exchequer, refused Pole's offer to make him a lord of the Irish treasury, but accepted a comptrollership of army accounts worth £1,500.[5] Three months later he was back in London as commissary-in-chief, earning £2,700 a year. There he remained until the end of the war, when he was appointed auditor of the civil list. In 1823 he first entered parliament and became successively financial secretary to the treasury, chancellor of the exchequer, president of the board of trade, secretary-at-war, and president of the board of control. Not only in France were careers open to talent.

The greatest weakness of Pitt's reform was its failure to tackle the problem of public accounting. The system of auditing was still very imperfect. Both the auditors of imprest and their successors, the commissioners for auditing public accounts, accepted the exchequer maxim

---

[1] Herries MSS., Perceval to Colonel Charles Herries, 25 Mar. 1807.

[2] Perceval MSS., duke of Portland to Perceval, 13 Nov. 1808.

[3] Herries MSS., W. D. Adams, private secretary to duke of Portland, to J. C. Herries, 1 Mar. 1809. The fees were said to reach £7,000 on occasions.

[4] P.R.O., T29/111/665. Herries was succeeded by Anthony Rosenhagen.

[5] Herries MSS., T. P. Courtenay to J. C. Herries, 16 June 1811.

that complexity was desirable for its own sake. Long before their abolition in 1785 the auditors of imprest had so perfected this doctrine that it is doubtful if they even fully understood their own system. They exercised no effective control over expenditure, for they only checked the arithmetic instead of querying items in the accounts they were supposed to audit. They left such arrears and chaos that the new auditors of public accounts were quickly overwhelmed. The department started with five commissioners, two inspectors and twenty-four clerks, but by 1801 had a staff of seventy-three, including its own foreign language translators. Even then it failed to keep abreast with its work. Four years later a second and independent board was created and in 1806 the two were amalgamated and further enlarged. Finally, there was the older and smaller office of the comptrollers of army accounts. When Perceval first went to the exchequer he found, in spite of this proliferation of auditors, many accounts outstanding from the war of American independence, the pay office accounts twenty-five years in arrears, and those of the treasurers of the navy untouched since 1799.[1] Inevitably the two departments were co-ordinated by allowing some of the overworked comptrollers to act also as auditors of public accounts and to draw a double salary. All Perceval was able to do was to enlarge the staff of the comptrollers of army accounts in the summer of 1808 and to carry out a partial re-organisation of the public accounts office in the following year.[2]

He did more to tighten the treasury's own internal audit system, which included the colonial agencies and various minor government departments whose work was supervised by the treasury board. In the spring of 1808 Perceval ordered all these to be indexed, and appointed Harrison and Cotton, one of the chief clerks, to act as auditors.[3] They reported to the board twice a year and had, by the beginning of 1810, examined 'the greater part' of accounts for 1802 to 1809.[4] Yet the system remained defective. The records of successive agents for Nova Scotia remained unaudited since 1753, while the board of agriculture was unable to produce a single receipt for 1802.[5] Securities were taken

[1] P.R.O., T1/3423 and 3424; *Parl. Papers, H. of C. Reports of Committees*, 5th report of committee on public expenditure, part 2, 1810, ii, 382. For a full discussion of the auditing of the paymasters-general's accounts see the first report of the Commons' committee of finance (*Parl. Deb.*, IX, pp. lxvii ff., and P.R.O., T29/91/453–8). A bill to speed up the audit was introduced by Charles Long for the government in October 1808 (*Parl. Deb.*, XI, 88–9).

[2] P.R.O., T29/91/77; T29/100/366; T29/103/106–7; T29/110/54–5.

[3] P.R.O., T29/90/316–17; T29/92/490–1; T29/99/141–2.

[4] P.R.O., T29/104/87–8.   [5] P.R.O., T29/92/663; T29/93/290.

from all those who handled large sums of public money, but the method used was not fool-proof.

Even a mere treasury clerk like William Chinnery could live for years beyond his means on the proceeds of fraud. Chinnery, who had once been Rose's private secretary, collected lucrative colonial agencies. He was, wrote George Jackson, 'a perfect cypher; a more complete Jeremy Sneak than I ever saw before'.[1] All his ambitions centred on his son and his gifted daughter who, according to Glenbervie, could 'claim a place among the geniuses as well as with the beauties'. Soon after becoming a chief clerk Chinnery began to give 'select' and 'exquisite' dinner parties to the cream of London society, who listened to Miss Chinnery's violin recitals and sneered at her father's attempts to hide 'under tolerable French and Italian and a profusion of civility, the quill behind his ear'.[2] In September 1810 Rose began to wonder where Chinnery got all his money. Perceval interviewed him, queried the unusually large balances, but could find nothing seriously wrong, especially as Harrison and Cotton had examined and approved many of the accounts. Chinnery agreed to invest all his balances in exchequer bills and Perceval tightened the treasury's system of securities. In future every agent was to deposit a bond equal to the largest balance ever likely to be in his hands at one time, and no further sums were then to be entrusted to him unless his security was also increased.[3] But Perceval was still deceived. Eighteen months later Chinnery fled abroad, leaving a deficit of £70,000 in his accounts. An extent against his estate and the sale of some exchequer bills which were recovered raised £28,000; the balance of £42,000 had to be written off. Chinnery himself was never heard of again, his daughter died shortly after his disappearance, while the son accepted a junior clerkship in the treasury offered by Perceval with characteristic generosity.[4]

The political team at the treasury after 1807 was uncommonly weak. The duke of Portland, the nominal first lord, took practically no part in routine business and was never consulted by his colleagues on a major financial issue. He presided at the first formal meeting of

---

[1] *Bath Archives*, vol. I, p. 293.

[2] Sichel, *Glenbervie Journals*, pp. 143-4.

[3] Rose, vol. II, pp. 492-3; P.R.O., T29/92/491, 513, and 588; T29/104/544. Perceval had earlier tightened the system of securities required from army agents (T29/91/444).

[4] Rose, vol. II, pp. 492-3; *Day*, 21 Mar. 1812; *Bath Archives*, vol. I, p. 351; P.R.O., T1/3535; T29/116/291 and 448. For the similar case of Edward Hunt, treasurer of the ordnance department, see *Sun*, 30 Jan. 1811.

the board on April fool's day, 1807 but thereafter appeared at only 10 of the 196 meetings held during 1807 and 1808.[1] This left Perceval, as he once complained, in the 'essentially unpleasant' position of being generally credited with more authority than he in fact possessed and with 'consequent responsibility far beyond the power which I really have'.[2] The burden of work upon the chancellor was immense, for in Portland's absence, he had to preside at the twice-weekly board meetings in addition to his duties as leader of the Commons and a member of the cabinet. Even during the parliamentary recess he had little rest. 'He could not be more worked if Parliament were sitting,' wrote Ryder in November 1807. 'The only difference is that business is now done which would in that case be postponed.' Frequent cabinet meetings, 'almost day by day, exceeding those which ever occurred in the same space of time' left Perceval 'not a moment for the ordinary official business'.[3] Yet he was most conscientious in his attendance at the board, missing only three meetings out of 196 and being on seven occasions the only member present. He got little help from his junior lords. One of them, Sturges Bourne, had been senior secretary to the treasury in Pitt's second ministry, but 'though with a very clear understanding and to many points very able', was not considered a success in politics. He was, however, the most assiduous of the junior lords and probably the most useful.[4] William Eliot, although reasonably conscientious, was generally 'considered as one of the perfectly inefficient members'.[5] Much the same might have been said of the rest. Titchfield, Portland's son, served until the summer of 1807 when he was replaced, for a short time, by Perceval's old friend, Richard Ryder. But Ryder soon found that board meetings aggravated his headaches. 'I have', he told his brother, 'received a hint from Wellesley that I shall be expected at the treasury . . . at about 5 November. I have returned it by another hint that I should like another week's leave for the waters: but I fear the accumulation of business is such as to give me little chance of having my hint taken.'[6] In December Ryder sensibly resigned. The two remaining junior lords in the Portland ministry, Foster and William Broderick, were both of little account. Foster, the Irish chancellor of the exchequer, never attended a single board meeting: Broderick

[1] Board attendance figures taken from P.R.O., T29/89-99.
[2] Perceval MSS., Perceval to Huskisson, 21 Aug. 1809.
[3] Harrowby MSS., vol. IV, fols. 45-6 and 107, Richard Ryder to Harrowby.
[4] P.R.O., Chatham MSS., 328, Charles Long to Pitt, 8 Sep. 1805.
[5] Harrowby MSS., IV, fol. 109, Richard Ryder to Harrowby, 25 Nov. 1807.
[6] Ibid., vol. IV, fol. 96.

appeared and made no impression. More important were the joint secretaries, Henry Wellesley and William Huskisson. Wellesley, the senior of the two, concentrated on patronage, the press, and the general management of departmental business. In March 1809 he resigned after his wife, Lady Charlotte, had deserted him for Lord Paget, and was succeeded by Charles Arbuthnot.[1] Huskisson, the financial secretary, was the one expert of them all: without him neither Perceval's hard work nor the permanent staff's knowledge of routine could have saved the day.

Both Perceval and Huskisson put great emphasis on minor administrative reforms. In this field their qualities were complementary, Perceval providing the moral drive and Huskisson the mastery of detail. Early in 1808 they began an inquiry into the system of collecting taxes, which finally ranged from the property and assessed taxes to the duties on houses, windows and hats! Perceval himself took particular interest in the customs and excise where 'not the smallest part of the public money could be expended in extraordinaries, without its being submitted to his consideration'.[2] Even anonymous letters denouncing corruption were investigated.[3] In the summer of 1808 he began a survey of the ports at Bristol, Hull and Liverpool in order to extend the provisions of an act abolishing fees to customs officers. He investigated cases of alleged bribery and ordered the abolition of sinecures, a number of traditional holidays, and of certain 'unnecessary forms and official regulations'.[4] In 1811 he sent a collector, three surveyors and six clerks as a roving commission of inquiry into evasions of excise duty. The commission, reported the *Examiner*, had power to question on oath and to consult firms' accounts, which resulted in the collection of £80,000 arrears at Plymouth and £100,000 at Ipswich.[5] Between 1807 and 1809 the treasury also authorised inquiries into the organisation of the barracks department, the board of works, and the paymaster-general, the stamp and the war offices.[6] The army medical

---

[1] Sir George Jackson, *Diary*, vol. II, p. 417; *Annual Register*, 1809, p. 334; P.R.O., T29/100/166. Wellesley was awarded £20,000 damages against Lord Paget.

[2] P.R.O., T29/91/407; T29/96/378; T22/12/49–50.

[3] Perceval MSS., *Anonymous Memoir*; *Sun*, 4 Sep. 1810; P.R.O., T29/90/243; T29/96/206.

[4] P.R.O., T29/90/369; T29/91/461; T29/99/524; T29/106/429.

[5] *Examiner*, 11 Nov. 1811; P.R.O., T29/95/220.

[6] P.R.O., T29/94/56 (barracks); T29/95/75–6 (board of works); T29/94/324 and T29/97/261 (paymasters-general); T27/64/45 (stamp office); T29/96/409 and T29/103/199–217 (war office).

department was reformed on lines suggested in a report of the commissioners of military inquiry and the entire organisation of the state lottery was revised on the recommendation of the commissioners for auditing public accounts.[1] Furthermore both Perceval and Huskisson steadily continued Pitt's policy of abolishing sinecures wherever possible.[2]

Most far-reaching of these minor reforms were those concerned with relations between the treasury and the bank of England. The subject was first raised in the second report of the Commons' committee of finance which dealt with the management of the national debt. The committee found that the Bank levied a charge of about £450 for the management of every £1 million of the unredeemed debt. Although the total of the unredeemed debt had more than doubled since 1786, there had been no reduction in the percentage charged for management. Consequently by 1807 the treasury was paying £265,000 a year in management charges alone. This, the committee felt, was excessive, particularly as the Bank also received percentages for handling the annual loans and the lottery. Finally the Bank was shown to make large profits out of the balances of public accounts deposited with it.[3] In the autumn of 1808 Perceval and Huskisson opened negotiations with the governor and deputy-governor, persuading them to reduce the management charge on the first £550 million of the unredeemed debt to £340 per million and then to £300 for each additional million. This, Perceval told the Commons, would save the public £65,000 a year. Moreover, after prolonged bargaining, the Bank's court of directors agreed to advance the government a £3 million loan, free of interest, as an acknowledgement of the profit made out of the public balances left at Threadneedle Street. The agreement was generally well received in the Commons, though Tierney, in one of the worst of his party speeches, claimed that the Bank ought to have managed the debt free of charge.[4] In the following March Huskisson persuaded Goldsmid and Antrobus, the treasury's agents for the sale of exchequer bills, to reduce their commission from two shillings and six pence to a shilling for every £100 worth sold.[5] Thereafter both the

---

[1] P.R.O., T29/94/360 (army medical department); T29/92/654-8 (lottery).
[2] For examples see T29/91/438 and T29/102/36.
[3] *Parl. Deb.*, IX, pp. lxxxvii ff.; *Sun*, 8 Jan. 1808.
[4] *Parl. Deb.*, IX, 232 ff. for the negotiations with the Bank; 416 ff. for the debate and Tierney's speech. Harrowby MSS., XI, fol. 220, Perceval to Harrowby, 26 Dec. 1807. This gives Perceval's account of the negotiations.
[5] P.R.O., T29/93/426. The editor of Huskisson's speeches claims that

Chancellor and Huskisson were absorbed with the twin problems of war finance and budget policy.

Huskisson alone was responsible for the success of the debt negotiations with the Bank (vol. I, pp. 49–50). There is no evidence in either the Perceval MSS. or *Parl. Deb.* to support this. Perceval in fact successfully negotiated with the Bank on similar lines after Huskisson's resignation (P.R.O., T29/108/42–5). The revised scheme with Antrobus and Goldsmid saved £9,000 a year (*Sun*, 4 Mar. 1808). Randle Jackson, in a speech to a general court meeting of the Bank, expressed 'great uneasiness at the lowering of their dividend' after Perceval's negotiations (*Sun*, 27 Sep. 1808).

CHAPTER EIGHTEEN

THE DOLLAR PROBLEM

MOST difficult of all the treasury's problems was that of financing and supplying British military expeditions abroad. Lord Grenville left office in 1807 convinced that we were capable of waging only a defensive war: any major continental campaign, he told his closest associates, was financially beyond our means.[1] Yet, over the succeeding five years, the Portland and Perceval administrations maintained British garrisons in all parts of the world, subsidised Austria, Portugal, Sicily and Sweden, launched the Walcheren expedition, and supported Wellington's lengthy and expensive campaigns in the Peninsula.

The government had, throughout, only the sketchiest administrative machinery. The treasury often obtained supplies of foreign currency by signing contracts with free-lancers and merchants: their consignments were shipped to and from England in frigates and the captain of each vessel was paid 1% of the value of the cargo.[2] Often strange things happened during the voyage.[3] In September 1809 the treasury had to remind Captain Hayes of H.M.S. *Alfred* that he had signed a certificate for £130,000 worth of currency at his port of embarkation and yet had landed less than £64,000 worth.[4] In contrast when the *Gannet* and *Pompee* reached Portsmouth after the Copenhagen expedition they produced between them nearly 36,000 dollars more than they were supposed to have on board.[5] In disputed cases an official of the Bank or the paymaster-general's office was ordered to weigh and estimate the value of the currency.[6] Even this was most unsatisfactory. In the summer of 1809 T. P. Courtenay, then deputy paymaster to the forces in Spain, refused to produce his accounts as, 'from the investigation he has made, he finds the calculation made by the Bank of the average number of dollars contained in 1,000 ounces

---

[1] Buckingham, *Court and Cabinets of George III*, vol. IV, p. 206.
[2] Perceval MSS., Sir Francis Baring to Perceval, 17 Mar. 1808.
[3] Until the summer of 1808 ships' captains were not required to produce a certificate of the amount of currency embarked. A receipt for the amount landed was sufficient (P.R.O., T27/74/366/).
[4] P.R.O., T27/64/519.
[5] P.R.O., T27/64/484. For a similar case see P.R.O., T27/66/517.
[6] P.R.O., T.27/65/417.

of silver to be erroneous'.[1] In order to avoid similar confusion, the paymaster's office pleaded with the treasury, when ordering shipments of dollars, to state the exact number wanted and not its sterling equivalent.[2] Sheer inefficiency often added to the treasury's difficulties. Early in 1808 the paymaster-general's office protested that it was not always being told when decisions were taken to send specie abroad.[3]

In theory there was a set routine for ordering and sending specie overseas. British commanders sent their requests for money to the war office while demands for allied forces, including the Spaniards and Portuguese, went to the foreign secretary. The military cost of the war was divided into 'ordinary' and 'extraordinary' expenditure. 'Ordinary' expenditure, which had previously been voted by parliament, was handled by deputy paymasters who either received specie from or issued bills of exchange on the authority of the joint paymasters-general to the forces. Foreign 'extraordinary' expenditure went through commissaries-general or their deputies, who reported their dealings direct to the treasury. The original decision on all requests was taken by the treasury board and implemented by the junior secretary to the treasury and the assistant secretary. They either authorised the paymasters-general to buy the required amount from the Bank or, if the Bank had no specie available, entered into a contract with a merchant or private agent to supply the money needed. The Bank always sold foreign currency to the government at the price it had paid for it, if this was lower than the existing market price at the time of sale.[4] If the specie was bought in London, the treasury had to write to the horseguards, asking them to take it by wagon train to the port of embarkation, and to the admiralty to provide a frigate for the voyage. Delays often occurred at this point. The wagon train was notoriously slow, thus either missing the frigate altogether or causing it to be delayed by contrary winds. One vital consignment from London to Portsmouth, which should have taken ten to twelve hours, was actually three days on the road and arrived in the Peninsula six weeks late as a result of missing favourable winds. By 1812 the treasury was reduced to sending sums of up to £100,000 by mail and stage coaches.[5]

---

[1] P.R.O., T27/64/454.   [2] P.R.O., T29/93/368.   [3] P.R.O., T29/93/282.

[4] Herries MSS., commissariat letter books, vol. V, p. 7. For an example of the saving possible see P.R.O., T19/97/214. The treasury bought £75,000 worth of dollars from the Bank at 5s. 4½d. and paid them as the Swedish subsidy at 5s. 6d.

[5] Herries MSS., commissariat letter books, vol. III, pp. 150–1, Herries to Col. Torrens, 9 Aug. 1812; P.R.O., T1/65/123.

Success or failure in the Peninsula depended, in large measure, on the efficiency of the commissariat, for long the last refuge of decayed merchants and rogues. When the Peninsula campaign began Wellesley's commissariat was organised by Huskisson of the treasury. It was not one of Huskisson's happiest assignments. 'This department', wrote Wellesley after one week in Portugal, 'deserves your serious consideration. The existence of the army depends upon it, and yet the people who manage it are incapable of managing anything out of a counting house.' [1] Consequently, in 1808, a new office, that of commissary-in-chief, was opened in Great George Street. Its first occupant, Thomas Aston Coffin, had a total staff of three clerks and one messenger, a skeleton crew with which to try and steer the infant department between the Scylla of the horseguards and the Charybdis of the treasury. [2] For the duke of York claimed the commissariat as his own domain. Early in 1808 there were complaints against his interference at Lisbon and two years later he succeeded in getting the right to pay members of the corps transferred to his own office. [3] Finally in the summer of 1810 Coffin retired and was succeeded by Colonel Willoughby Gordon, the duke's military secretary. Under the energetic Gordon the new department expanded rapidly until there was a deputy commissary-in-chief and a headquarters' staff of twenty-six. The office was then divided into home, foreign, and accounts branches, the third being under the general supervision of the comptrollers of army accounts. [4] But early in 1811 Gordon was offered and accepted the post of quartermaster-general under Wellington as from 1 October 1811. The appointment was not even gazetted until August, but the battle for the succession began long before that, for the duke was determined not to lose his hold over the commissariat. On 11 April a Lieutenant-Colonel Drinkwater called at Downing Street and, with the duke's and the Regent's approval, officially lodged his claim. [5] Perceval was polite and non-committal. His patronage relations with Carlton House at the time were not happy and he thought he had a far more worthy candidate in his own former private secretary, Herries. In July he nominated Herries, then in Ireland, for a vacant comptrollership of army accounts, only to find that the Regent had already

---

[1] Wellington, *Despatches*, vol. III, p. 62; Castlereagh, *Correspondence*, vol. VI, p. 396.   [2] *Royal Kalendar*, 1808, p. 241.

[3] P.R.O., T29/94/170-1 and T27/65/425.

[4] *Royal Kalendar*, 1810, p. 243; P.R.O., T27/64/267 and T29/104/67-84. For the comptrollers of army accounts see chapter 17, pp. 316-17.

[5] Windsor MSS., Regency file, 17922, 13 Apr. 1811, Drinkwater to McMahon.

promised it to someone else. On hearing of this Perceval went immediately to Carlton House, insisted on Herries' appointment, 'saying that it was a question whether he was or was not minister', and returned with the place at his disposal.[1] But such stands could not be taken too often. When the final struggle for the commissariat was joined early in August, Perceval acted with greater caution. Herries, he told the Prince Regent, was 'one of the best men of business Mr. Perceval ever knew'. The Prince was unmoved. Drinkwater, 'still urgent and importunate', laid siege to 10, Downing Street, until Perceval told him that he did not want the corps left under military control. 'I will', wrote Perceval to Herries, 'apply for the appointment for you. I will not promise to urge it as indispensible, but I will propose it strongly and you shall be out of your anxiety speedily. My reason why I wish you to keep it to yourself is that if I meet with a very strong resistance, I shall not think it a ground to quarrel upon.' On 20 August, however, the Prince Regent agreed that if Drinkwater were given a comptrollership of army accounts, Herries should have the commissariat.[2]

At Great George Street Herries found, as he later confessed, 'my natural place which is in the working class of politicians'.[3] In fact he reverted quite naturally to the civil service. 'My interest in party contentions', he wrote to a friend in 1812, 'is quite extinct.' [4] Henceforth he devoted all his energies to hacking through the administrative jungle which choked Wellington's supply lines. Gordon had already begun the job of reforming the department which, in the course of years, had got into a sorry state. Warrants appointing new officers in the corps had traditionally stated the station at which they were to serve, until the claim was made that therefore they were only liable to serve in that one place and could not be moved without their own consent. The commissariat had, in fact, lost control over its own personnel until Gordon altered the form of warrants and compelled dissidents to accept overseas service.[5] Early in 1810 he drew up the first effective service regulations the corps had ever had. No recruits were admitted under sixteen years old; all new entrants started as clerks and no higher; promotion was granted only after one year's

[1] Herries, *Memoirs*, vol. I, p. 17.
[2] Windsor MSS., Regency file, Drinkwater to McMahon, 10 Aug. 1811; Herries MSS., Perceval to J. C. Herries, 8, 15 and 21 Aug. 1811; P.R.O., T.29/113 p. 306.   [3] Herries, *Memoirs*, vol. I, p. 135.
[4] Herries MSS., letter books, vol. III, p. 113, J. C. Herries to John Trotter, 17 July 1812.   [5] P.R.O., T29/94/210.

probation. The service had too many very young gentlemen with very influential patrons. At the same time the home commissariat was completely reorganised and a regulation issued that all supplies were to be ordered only after fair and public competition for the contract.[1] Shortly before he left for the Peninsula, Gordon had even begun to tackle the formidably complicated problem of the department's accounts.[2] But Gordon touched only the fringe of the difficulties. Herries plunged right into the middle. He began by disillusioning those who still thought of a place in the commissariat as a dignified retreat when all else failed. Apparently some genuinely believed that whereas the army and navy sold commissions, the commissariat relied on the more genteel method of bribery. Coffin once received a letter offering £1,000 for an appointment from a respectable merchant, who quoted testimonials from members of parliament. 'The public newspapers', explained the applicant, 'frequently contain advertisements for situations under Government and considerable sums of money have been offered to gentlemen having it in their power to appoint.' As proof of his goodwill he would even 'have no objections to any required duty or attendance'. [3] A second candidate, wishing to express his prospective gratitude 'more fully than by the equivocal criterion of profession', offered Herries 500 guineas, 'supposing that your influence might have been obtained, and an acknowledgement for it with propriety made, as an accepted and honourable perquisite of office'.[4] In fact all patronage rights (except for the choice of clerks for Great George Street) were held by the treasury. It was arranged between Herries and Arbuthnot that all candidates nominated by the board should, before being accepted, take a short examination in English and arithmetic and then be called for interview by the commissary-in-chief. This, one of the earliest experiments in written tests for the civil service, was not well received. Herries gave fair warning to the treasury that he would deal 'very strictly in the examination of the persons they appoint' as he was determined to accept 'none but well-educated young men, and as much as possible, gentlemen into the department'.[5] The first results were chastening. One candidate,

---

[1] P.R.O., T29/104/201–6. This was ignored in cases of urgency (T29/96/40).

[2] P.R.O., T29/109/677–84; Herries MSS., Perceval to Herries, 22 Aug. 1811. In 1808 the treasury ended the system under which commissariat officials acted as bankers to army officers 'thereby blending private accounts with those of the public' (P.R.O., T29/64/241).   [3] P.R.O., T1/1024/1151.

[4] Herries MSS., G. C. Card to Herries, 12 and 14 Feb. 1808.

[5] *Ibid.*, letter books, vol. I, p. 205, Herries to J. Bisset, 30 Jan. 1812.

approved by the treasury, was found to have been previously court-martialled and cashiered from the army: a second, sponsored by Charles Bathurst, produced so 'illiterate and heterographical' an examination paper that he was rejected, but claimed that he had been flurried and should be given another chance. After having several days to collect himself, he had again sat the test when, in a written answer to one of the preliminary questions, he stressed that he was 'a lernging a letel French.' [1] 'I feel', wrote Herries to Arbuthnot, 'that I am getting into terrible hot water in consequence of my endeavours to purify this department.' Disappointed patrons put the blame on the commissary-in-chief instead of on the protégé who had disgraced their patronage. 'But justice', sighed Herries, 'is a rare thing in this world.' [2] Even the examination system, though it improved the quality of the service, was by itself inadequate. One successful candidate was ordered to Lisbon where he arrived 'totally unfit for service in consequence of a desperate venereal complaint' and had to be shipped straight back home again.[3] In the Peninsula Wellington was virtually his own commissary-in-chief. All promotions in the commissariat at Lisbon depended on his recommendation and were based on merit in the service not on personal favour. The treasury meekly accepted the whole of his plan for the organisation of the Portuguese commissariat after he had denounced Huskisson's version as 'absurd'.[4]

By 1812 Herries had a staff of fifty-three in Great George Street, and twenty commissaries-general and over one thousand clerks serving abroad.[5] But his job of supplying the army (and particularly Wellington) with equipment and specie was bedevilled by a chaotic administrative system. In order to lessen financial demands on the treasury, as

[1] Herries MSS., vol. III, pp. 143–4, same to William Bragge, 7 Aug. 1812. Palmerston, as secretary-at-war, put a different scheme into operation in his department. New entrants were placed on probation for two months. At the end of this period a full report on the candidate's work was prepared, which determined whether he should be made permanent or dismissed. Between 1810 and 1833, thirty-three probationaries were rejected (P.R.O., T1/4044).

[2] Herries MSS., letter books, vol. II, pp. 144–5, Herries to Arbuthnot, 1 May 1812. For a later attempt at corrupt use of patronage see L. Bulwer, *Life of Palmerston*, pp. 109–10.

[3] Herries MSS., letter books, vol. II, p. 36, same to Richard Wharton, 9 Mar. 1812. Herries decided to 'overlook a slight indiscretion'.

[4] *Ibid.*, vol. I, pp. 97–8, same to T. P. Courtenay, 20 Nov. 1811; P.R.O., T29/103/36; Wellington, *Despatches*, vol. III, pp. 285 and 314. By 1812 there were 552 on the commissariat staff in Portugal (*Parl. Papers, H. of C. Accounts and Reports*, 1812 (198), IX, p. 111).

[5] Herries MSS., letter books, vol. III, p. 117.

much as possible of Wellington's supplies and equipment was bought in Great Britain and then shipped to the Peninsula. Requests from the British army were sent to the war office, those from the Spaniards and Beresford's Portuguese to the foreign office. Both then went on to the treasury where they were considered, before being sent to the appropriate department for action. Foodstuffs were bought by the victualling board, but fodder for the horses was controlled by the transport commissioners.[1] The commissary-in-chief purchased all clothing for allied troops, but only greatcoats and shoes for the British, the rest being provided by the colonel of each regiment under the system of off-reckonings.[2] Responsibility for buying equipment seems to have been shared between the commissary-in-chief, the ordnance, the paymasters, and the secretary-at-war: all articles for use in barracks were purchased by the commissary-in-chief on the instructions of the barrack commissioners.

Until the spring of 1807 there was not even a place where stores waiting to be shipped or held in reserve could safely be lodged. Each government department made the best arrangement it could or relied on John Trotter and company, a firm of private contractors. Then Trotter was appointed the first storekeeper general and given the use of some empty warehouses on the banks of the Thames, below London Bridge.[3] Trotter was responsible for the custody of all stores: the transport commissioners for packing them. The system of inspection of goods was even worse. All those bought by the commissary-in-chief were examined by the storekeeper general and marked with a reject stamp if they failed in quality. All other departments had their own system of inspection, merely authorising Trotter to store their goods. The system put a premium on fraud. When, early in 1812, Herries decided to inspect one of Trotter's depots, he found several large cases of shoes, bought by the joint-paymasters to the forces. Every pair bore the rejection stamp of the storekeeper general, clumsily erased before the shoes were accepted by the paymasters.[4] Enterprising contractors could often sell their goods in the Peninsula if they failed to get rid of them at home. Stores rejected by Trotter were sent to Lisbon and sold direct to the adjutant-general there. 'I

---

[1] P.R.O., T27/64/397; Herries MSS., letter books, vol. V, p. 103.

[2] For details of a dispute over off-reckonings between Palmerston and Sir David Dundas see Add. MSS., 27598, fols. 1–37.

[3] P.R.O., T29/90/274; T29/93/482. The department began with a total staff of thirty-two, all appointed and paid by the treasury (T29/95/376).

[4] Herries MSS., letter books, vol. II, p. 37.

am', wrote Herries to Trotter in despair, 'quite sick of contractors. They are growing worse and worse.' Wellington denounced the commissariat while Herries damned 'the cursed contractors'.[1]

Frauds were not uncommon in spite of the commissariat's attempt to give orders only to those offering the lowest tenders. One Davison, who was given a contract to supply barrack bedding, defrauded the public of over £22,000 above the $2\frac{1}{2}\%$ profit to which he was legally entitled. On one order he made a profit of nearly 30%.[2] When supplies were needed particularly urgently there was no time for public advertisements for tenders and the commissary-in-chief had to make the best bargain he could on the spot. Occasionally even routine contracts were placed without public competition. In the summer of 1808 the radical Wardle raised one such case in the Commons. In June 1806 Messrs. Scott and company, a firm of contractors, had offered to supply the commander-in-chief with 20,000 greatcoats at fourteen shillings and ninepence each. The offer was refused and the contract given to Messrs. Pearce and company. Scott then took on part of Pearce's contract and sold the identical greatcoats he had offered at fourteen shillings and ninepence for sixteen shillings and sixpence. The same process was repeated in 1808 when the firm offered greatcoats at twelve shillings each, was refused, and sold them indirectly at fourteen shillings.[3] More difficulties were caused by the Spaniards' and Portuguese love of finery and requests for 'round hats', 'cockades' and white waistcoats of unusual design.[4] Finally in the Peninsula itself great quantities of stores were pilfered from depots until Herries and Perceval devised a corps of 'conductors', who were recruited from 'honest, active, intelligent warehousemen, porters and other inferior servants of great mercantile concerns'. 'The men I want', wrote Herries, 'must not be gentlemen.' Slowly the commissary-in-chief was creating a basis for victory in the Peninsula: he was the unsung Carnot of Whitehall.[5]

Even more vital to success in the Peninsula was a regular supply of specie. During the Portland administration Huskisson was largely responsible for war finance. His handling of the task first established his political reputation. He was, admitted Glenbervie, rarely a generous

---

[1] Herries, vol. III, pp. 19 and 113.   [2] P.R.O., T1/1015/8355.

[3] For an example of this see P.R.O., T29/96/40; *Parl. Deb.*, XI, 1002–10.

[4] P.R.O., W.O. 6/172/88; W.O. 6/173/156. These were sometimes supplied deliberately in material of inferior quality to that used for British troops (T29/96/200).

[5] Herries MSS., letter books, vol. III, pp. 45–6 and 66.

critic, 'a very able man and one of the best secretaries for the finance branch of the treasury in the office and in parliament of the many I have remembered. This is the character given him by friend and foe.' Canning called him 'the best practical man of business in England'.[1] For over two years he was a key figure in the treasury who, by his efforts, freed Perceval to concentrate on his work as leader of the house of commons. Yet although Huskisson's ability was beyond dispute, his handling of personal relations was often faulty. His manners were 'reserved, important' and he was liable to ignore or deal unsympathetically with his subordinates' problems. The finance of the war, claimed Fremantle, benefited from Huskisson's resignation in 1809, for though Perceval, who assumed direct responsibility, lacked his colleague's technical knowledge he far excelled him in the management of men.[2]

As the rates of exchange between London and the continent were constantly adverse, often by as much as 20% to 25%, Huskisson at first sought to finance overseas campaigns mainly by shipping specie directly from England. The paymasters' accounts show that in 1808 a little over £2,860,000 was sent to the Peninsula in specie and only £196,000 raised by bills of exchange.[3] The real difficulty, once our bullion reserves had been exhausted, lay in finding a sufficient number of dollars, the only currency acceptable to the Spaniards. One of his first moves was to prohibit any government department, other than the treasury, from buying dollars in order to avoid competition between agents which had, in the past, forced up the market price.[4] In the long run, however, argued Huskisson, the Spaniards would have to sacrifice their monopoly and allow Britain to trade with their South American colonies.

At the beginning of 1809 Perceval and Canning persuaded the Spanish minister, Don Pedro Cevallos, to allow the British treasury to export dollars from Vera Cruz. The combined resources of the Peninsula and of South America would, it was hoped, be sufficient to solve our dollar problem. But the treasury unfortunately had no means of directly purchasing currency in South America, as the British government had no official representative there. Members of the commissariat might have been sent, but it seemed simpler to rely on private

[1] Bickley, *Diaries of Lord Glenbervie*, vol. II, p. 29; Huskisson, *Speeches*, vol. I, p. 40.
[2] Fremantle, *England in the Nineteenth Century, 1806–10*, pp. 338–9.
[3] *Parl. Papers, H. of C. Accounts and Reports*, 1812 (198), IX, 60.
[4] P.R.O., T1/999/2628.

agents, who were expected to negotiate more favourable terms. The treasury seems to have been prepared to take their honesty for granted. The first to be chosen was Andrew Cochrane Johnstone, the eighth son of the eighth earl of Dundonald and a younger brother of Admiral Sir Alexander Cochrane, who had served with distinction in the West Indies. In politics Cochrane Johnstone was a consistent whig and an unmitigated rogue in everything else.[1] After an early career in the army, he was elected as M.P. for Stirling Boroughs. In 1797 he was appointed governor of Dominica, where his rule was marked by 'tyranny, extortion and vice'. He was recalled in 1803 after it had been discovered that he had set up a wholesale business in negresses, many of whom he kept in his private harem. Four years later he was arrested in Tortola for fraud, but escaped to England, sent Perceval a report on the inefficiency of our administration in the West Indies, and then bought his way back to parliament as M.P. for Grampound. In March 1808 he was unseated for bribery, which left him quite free to represent the treasury at Vera Cruz.[2]

By the terms of the original contract Johnstone and his partner, Abraham Atkins, were to buy not more than six million dollars at a maximum price of four shillings a dollar. As soon as these were delivered on board a British ship at Vera Cruz they were to be paid for by issuing thirty day bills on the treasury and after the deal was completed Johnstone and Atkins were to draw a 3% commission.[3] Late in March Johnstone left London bound, so the treasury supposed, for South America. On 20 April he sent them a letter from Seville, explaining that his visit to Spain was one of a number of alterations he had decided to make in the original agreement. The existing value of the dollar in Spain was already four shillings and eightpence and the merchants of Cadiz had written to Vera Cruz urging that the rate of exchange should be further increased before Johnstone arrived. He therefore consulted with Frere, who had recommended a direct deal with the Supreme Junta. Johnstone began this by issuing a bill for £600,000 on the British treasury in exchange for a promise of three

[1] Add. MSS., 37295, fol. 240; C. L. Johnstone, *History of the Johnstones, 1191 to 1909*, p. 277. Andrew Cochrane took the additional name of Johnstone after marrying Georgiana, a daughter of the third earl of Hopetown.

[2] *Defence of the Hon. A. C. Johnstone*, etc. (Edinburgh, 1806); *Public Characters*, vol. X, p. 23; T1/1028/2902; Perceval MSS., Huskisson to Perceval, 27 Dec. 1807; A. C. Johnstone to Perceval, 30 Aug. 1808; *Parl. Deb.*, IX, 689 and 746. For a hostile account see A. Mackenrot, *Secret Memoirs of the Hon. A. C. Johnstone* (London, 1814).

[3] P.R.O., T29/103/383–5.

million dollars at Vera Cruz.[1] The price of four shillings a dollar seemed so favourable that the treasury might have overlooked departures from the original contract. For six days Huskisson believed that Johnstone was then on his way to collect the dollars, until a private letter, still written from Cadiz, gave news of further complications. There had, it appeared, never been any definite agreement on the rate of exchange—four shillings a dollar had been only Johnstone's version. The Supreme Junta had demanded a minimum of four shillings and fourpence, at which point negotiations broke down. But the fertile Johnstone was not dismayed. Early in May he reported that he had signed a contract for six million dollars and hinted that he could get another six million if the treasury were prepared to give him half the profits. The board's response was immediate and violent. Canning was asked to send a formal reprimand to Frere, while Huskisson wrote to Johnstone expressing the board's 'strongest disapprobation' of 'so extraordinary a transaction'. The treasury could not refuse to meet the bills already issued without destroying confidence in all future British agents in both Cadiz and Vera Cruz. They therefore agreed to pay £1,200,000 for six million dollars. It was then found that Johnstone had, without any official authority, arranged that the dollars should be shipped direct to Spain. Harrison immediately wrote to the admiralty who sent orders to the frigates *Wolverine* and *Recruit*, then waiting to collect the specie at Vera Cruz, that they were to land at no port except Spithead.[2]

By the time the two transports reached England Huskisson had resigned, leaving Perceval in sole control of war finance. In December 1809 the first lord began to read through the mass of correspondence dealing with the case. He found that Johnstone had issued altogether £635,800 worth of bills on the treasury, which meant that he had paid four shillings and threepence a dollar. When Perceval refused to go beyond four shillings, Johnstone was full of complaints at such an 'act of injustice'. He demanded an interview with the minister and when this was refused, called at the treasury to see Richard Wharton. As Wharton was out, he saw only the assistant bill clerk, with whom he left a message that the dollars ought to be valued at four shillings and ninepence each. Perceval retaliated by withholding Johnstone's commission and by ordering that the dollars on board the *Wolverine* and the *Recruit* should be counted by the representatives of the paymaster-general. They found only 2,364,000, the odd 636,000 turning up in

[1] P.R.O., T29/103/388–91.   [2] P.R.O., T29/103/395.

Johnstone's private account at the bank of England. These were not, explained Johnstone, part of the public money: they had been entrusted to him by personal friends.[1] Even then the treasury failed, after many threats, to bring Johnstone to trial.[2] He went on to supply the Spanish government with muskets which he manufactured at Birmingham for seventeen shillings each and sold for three guineas. In the end he was caught speculating on the stock exchange on the false news of Napoleon's death, and, having been found guilty of conspiracy, fled the country and was never heard of again.

Some of the treasury's attempts to get dollars were merely comic. In December 1810 they supplied Ignatius Palyart, a merchant, with 1,182 bottles, 373 large boxes, and 27 small boxes of quicksilver which he was to take to and sell in Mexico. This, it was hoped, would produce £25,000 worth of dollars. Unfortunately, some of the quicksilver leaked from its containers and ran loose during the voyage, but it was nearly all recovered and safely landed at Vera Cruz. It was then found that the Mexican authorities had not received permission from the Spanish government to buy the quicksilver and, while Palyart was waiting for this, an unexpectedly large supply of quicksilver arrived direct from Cadiz, causing a temporary glut on the Mexican market. When this was over, it was learnt that the Mexican revolutionaries had seized the mining areas of Guanaxua and Laiateras, interrupting all supplies of silver and ruining many of Vera Cruz's merchants. No one now, wrote Palyart's agent, seemed to be able to afford to buy quicksilver. But it was, he emphasised, quite safely stored in a warehouse and could easily be shipped back to England if the rebels attacked Vera Cruz.[3] In the previous August the treasury managed to buy just over £115,000 worth of dollars from China, which turned out to be so defaced with Chinese insignia that they were sent to Lisbon with orders that they might be melted down if Wellington thought them unfit for circulation.[4]

Fortunately there was never any shortage of merchants willing to

---

[1] P.R.O., T27/65/364–456; Add. MSS., 38737, fol. 360.

[2] Add. MSS., 37295, fol. 256. He even offered his services to the treasury again 'to deliver a quantity of doubloons and dollars', but without success (T.27/66/372 and T1/1122/2782). In April 1812 Johnstone wrote to Perceval suggesting many possible economies in the Peninsula. 250 to 300 Spaniards could be attached to every British regiment, thus increasing Wellington's army by 20,000 men; supplies for the Peninsula army could be bought more cheaply by a British agent resident in New York (Johnstone himself?). No answer was sent (Perceval MSS., A. C. Johnstone to Perceval, 2 Apr. 1812).

[3] P.R.O., T1/1210/11152.   [4] P.R.O., T29/107/156.

act as treasury agents for the purchase of dollars. The profit to be made out of such deals was often fantastic. Thus, in the summer of 1809, when the shortage of specie was at its height, one enterprising merchant offered to deliver at Portsmouth ten million dollars from Vera Cruz at five shillings and sixpence each. They were selling in South America at four shillings and tenpence, which, after deducting freight and insurance costs, would have given the contractor a clear profit of £281,452 on the deal. Yet the original proposal also included the issue of government licences to allow the merchant to despatch and sell in South America fifteen or twenty boat loads of enemy property captured in Spain. This early venture in war surplus would have added a further £360,000 clear profit to the contractor.[1] In the Peninsula itself Murray, Wellington's commissary-general, was responsible for raising dollars locally, although by 1809 he had the help of special agents in Cadiz, Corunna, Gibraltar, and Oporto.[2] He sent reports of his efforts direct to the treasury, who in turn forwarded copies to the commissary-in-chief and to the comptrollers of army accounts. Help also came occasionally from George Bergmann, the commissary-general in the Mediterranean area. His operations were, however, handicapped by 'the cab', a financial combine which deliberately forced up the rate of exchange thus making, wrote Herries, 'an enormous gain from the public and embarrassing our operations so cruelly in the Mediterranean'.[3]

Throughout, the treasury had to contend with Wellington's suspicions and Murray's accounts. Wellington, for all his virtues, was a prince of grumblers. He had a low opinion of Spanish troops: at Talavera, he told Lord Wellesley, they ran away frightened by the sound of their own gunfire.[4] He denounced Cuesta, the Spanish commander until the summer of 1809, as 'obstinate' and 'impractical'; Souza, a member of the Portuguese Regency council and envoy to London, he constantly abused; the Portuguese government, he claimed, was lazy and inefficient; Vice-Admiral Berkeley, the local British naval

---

[1] Perceval MSS., Rose to Perceval, 12 Aug. 1809.

[2] *Ibid.*, Castlereagh to Perceval, 8 Jan. 1809.

[3] Herries MSS., commissariat letter books, vol. IV, p. 241. In June 1810 Bergmann, the commissary-general at Malta, was forced to pay up to 6s. 4d. for each dollar which had then to be issued at 4s. 6d. (P.R.O., T1/1150/9973). In Sept. 1810 Bergmann made the interesting suggestion that the balance of the droits of admiralty, which then stood at £½ million, should be paid into the military chest in exchange for bills on the treasury (P.R.O., T29/103/507 and T29/107/317).

[4] Wellington, *Despatches*, vol. III, p. 447.

commander, in contrast, was too fond of interfering.[1] He was, more-over, hypersensitive of criticism from London while his suspicions of his own government's intentions were almost pathological. 'I suspect the ministers in England', he wrote to Villiers in May 1809, 'are very indifferent to our operations in this country.' [2] In August 1810 he was convinced that 'the Government themselves felt no confidence in the measures which they were adopting in this country' and to this he attributed 'the little exertion which has lately been made in the cause'.[3] That December he told Stuart that it was 'useless to expect more money from England, as the desire of economy has overcome even the fears of the ministers'.[4] 'I am not in general very suspicious', he wrote in August 1811, 'but I begin to suspect the Government of treachery. Nothing can be so fatal to the cause as to distress us for money, and yet all the measures of the Government appear to have that sole object in view.' [5]

Shortly before the British army first sailed for the Peninsula, the paymasters-general suggested that the Bank should try to keep a reserve fund of £100,000 worth of foreign currency always available for immediate use.[6] But overwhelming and insistent demands for specie soon destroyed all hopes of building up a reserve. Even the treasury was carried away by the first generous impulse to give all possible aid to the Spanish insurgents.[7] In March 1808 Sir Francis Baring obtained 1,500,000 dollars from Mexico, but this and all the Bank's stock quickly vanished that summer. Between June and August 1,500,000 dollars were sent to Gallicia, 1,000,000 each to Asturias and Seville, 500,000 to Leon and 300,000 to the Portuguese.[8] The early efforts in Spain were entirely unco-ordinated and haphazard. British envoys, hurriedly sent to the Peninsula, often lacked experience and sent home over-optimistic accounts of the Spaniards' strength and prospects. Hopes in London ran high. In such an atmosphere it was impossible for the treasury, strongly pressed as it was by Canning, to refuse requests for money. Even our own forces in Portugal suffered

---

[1] Wellington, *Despatches*, vol. III, pp. 306, 367 and 422 (criticisms of Cuesta); vol. IV, pp. 278, 439, and vol. V, p. 119 (Souza); vol. IV, p. 560, and vol. V, pp. 71 and 331 (Portuguese troops); *Camden Soc., 3rd series, Miscellany 18*, p. 30 (Berkeley).

[2] Wellington, *Despatches*, vol. III, p. 263.

[3] *Ibid.*, vol. IV, p. 235.   [4] *Ibid.*, vol. IV, p. 471.

[5] *Ibid.*, vol. V, p. 219.   [6] P.R.O., T29/93/368.

[7] For criticism of this see Napier, *History of the Peninsular War*, vol. I, p. 137.

[8] Perceval MSS., Sir Francis Baring to Perceval, 17 Mar. 1808; P.R.O., T29/95/167 and 344; Bagot, *George Canning and his Friends*, vol. I, p. 259.

from the Spaniards' inordinate demands. 'We have not now', wrote Wellington to Murray in September, 'one shilling here, money is due to the officers, to the troops, to the people of the country.' [1] In the summer Perceval and Huskisson had calculated that 5,000,000 dollars was the maximum that could be sent until the end of 1808: by September only 200,000 of this remained.[2] By the first week in October the treasury was faced with a major crisis. The military chest in the Mediterranean was practically empty and Canning was insisting that another 1,000,000 dollars must be sent to Hookham Frere in Spain.[3] The rate of exchange at Lisbon was very unfavourable; there was no news of a frigate sent specially to Vera Cruz to bring back dollars; Duff, the British agent at Cadiz, had been authorised to issue £250,000 worth of bills of exchange for dollars, but had failed to raise the sum. 'I am afraid', Huskisson told Perceval on 2 October, 'we can hardly expect that in the next three months our stores of bullion will be sufficiently kept up or replenished to enable us . . . to continue our present exertions, and much less to increase them. We must therefore be cautious to what we commit ourselves. . . .' [4] On 5 October the treasury board met and decided to send every single dollar available to the Peninsula. Demands from all other areas were to be refused.[5] Huskisson also suggested that all reserves of bar silver should be sent and that this could either be coined at Seville or sold for its full value in dollars at Cadiz.[6] This not only overcame the immediate problem, but also meant an appreciable saving to the public. Thus £82,424 worth of bar silver sent in one shipment from London produced £81,599 in dollars for the British army, a saving of 6% over the cost of buying that quantity of dollars at the existing market price in London and of 12% over issuing bills of exchange in the Peninsula.[7] Unfortunately supplies of bar silver quickly ran out and Moore's campaign in Spain was only saved from financial disaster by Major-General Brodrick, who issued bills of exchange in Corunna in defiance of treasury instructions.[8]

By the beginning of 1809 it had become apparent to those in the

---

[1] Wellington, *Despatches*, vol. III, p. 118.
[2] Perceval MSS., Huskisson to Perceval, 2 Oct. 1808.
[3] P.R.O., T1/1002/138 and T29/97/70.
[4] Perceval MSS., Huskisson to Perceval, 2 Oct. 1808.
[5] P.R.O., T29/97/70.
[6] Perceval MSS., Huskisson to Perceval, 5 Oct. 1808.
[7] P.R.O., T1/1001/11437; T27/64/428.
[8] Perceval MSS., Brodrick to Gordon, 30 Dec. 1808.

Peninsula, but unfortunately not to Huskisson himself, that more specie would have to be raised by bills of exchange. Reliance on shipments of dollars from England had been, at best, a short-term policy: once the Bank's reserves had gone, the treasury could no longer send adequate sums to Wellington. In January Rawlings, the deputy commissary-general in Portugal, asked for greater freedom to deal on the Lisbon money market, claiming that he could raise enough dollars to meet 'the utmost exigencies'. All he got from Huskisson was a lecture on economics. 'The dealers in money, like the dealers in any other merchandise,' wrote Huskisson, 'are always ready to exchange it for that commodity which offers to them, without any risk, the greatest amount of profit, and such in the present case are bills upon England.' [1] When Rawlings took no notice and continued to issue bills, the lecture was repeated in stronger terms.[2] Such tactics silenced Rawlings, but had little effect on Wellington. By May the army's financial position had become critical.[3] On the fifth Wellington reported the position in detail to Huskisson. Before he sailed for Lisbon to resume the command after the Cintra inquiry, he had been told there was £400,000 in the war chest at Lisbon. He found on arrival only £100,000, much of it in unsuitable currency, and all pledged to meet 'monstrous demands'. The army, he calculated, would need £200,000 a month to meet all its commitments.[4] 'If we are to carry on a war in this country,' he wrote to Villiers, the British ambassador at Lisbon, 'money must be sent from England.' [5] On 30 May he renewed his pleas to Huskisson, stressing that £300,000 would only clear debts already contracted. 'Pay is due to the troops, and we have not a shilling, or the chance of getting any.' In desperation he had borrowed £100,000 from the senate and merchants of Oporto, but was still prevented from advancing by lack of money. 'The army', he told Frere on 11 June, 'is two months in arrears; we are over head and ears in debt everywhere.' [6] 'It is very extraordinary', he complained to Castlereagh, 'that I have not received a word from Huskisson upon this subject, notwithstanding that I wrote to him upon it early in May.' [7] But that

[1] P.R.O., T29/99/71–4.
[2] Ibid., p. 179. Huskisson's unfortunate manner is illustrated by the following phrase—'If this view of the subject be correct, and in the nature of things it is impossible that it should be otherwise . . .'
[3] Wellington, Despatches, vol. III, p. 211.
[4] Ibid., vol. III, pp. 212–13.
[5] Ibid., vol. III, p. 246.
[6] Ibid., vol. III, pp. 261–2, 269 and 288.
[7] Ibid., vol. III, p. 318.

spring and summer neither Huskisson nor Perceval had much time for writing letters as the treasury faced the greatest financial crisis of the war.

In March 1809 Austria declared war on France. On 19 May the Baring brothers' company informed the treasury that Messrs. Fermin de Tasket, bankers to the Austrian government, had drawn three bills on them amounting to £37,500. Without either authorisation or warning the Austrian government had relied on a British subsidy.[1] The treasury, realising that to refuse to meet the bills would break the coalition, had no option but to pay. In July Abraham Goldsmid and company presented bills for £10,000 and £6,000; Messrs. Fermin de Tasket one for £23,000; and Baring brothers one for £150,000.[2] Furthermore the British cabinet decided to support the Austrian military effort by launching an attack on the island of Walcheren, a decision which completed the treasury's dilemma.

Marquis Wellesley, then in Spain on a diplomatic mission, argued that the forces used at Walcheren could have been better employed by Wellington in the Peninsula.[3] Militarily the argument was sound: financially, as Huskisson told the Commons, it was nonsense. The acute shortage of dollars ruled out any large-scale reinforcement of Wellington. Had sufficient specie been available, Chatham's army would have landed in north Germany instead of on Walcheren.[4] The purposes and nature of the expedition as finally planned were dictated largely by the financial position. Even then the campaign strained the treasury's resources and upset its other financial commitments. When, in the late autumn of 1808, the decision was finally taken to launch the expedition, Huskisson found that there was, 'strictly speaking', no suitable currency at all at the treasury's disposal. Between October 1808 and the following June he managed to buy from the Bank £60,000 in dollars and £65,000 in Dutch ducats. The entire £125,000 was then forwarded, early in July, to Robinson, the commissary-general who accompanied the expedition. 'This sum,' wrote Huskisson

---

[1] P.R.O., T29/101/82. The total amount of British loans and subsidies to foreign states leapt from £859,000 in 1807 to £2,898,000 in 1808, an amount previously equalled only by Pitt's subsidy policy during the early years of the war with France. Between 1809 and 1811 the total varied between £2,000,000 and £2,500,000 before increasing to nearly £4,000,000 in 1812 (Porter, *The Progress of the Nation*, vol. II, pp. 335–8).

[2] P.R.O., T29/101/163 and T29/64/368, 381 and 392.

[3] Jackson, *Diary*, vol. II, p. 489.

[4] *Parl. Papers, H. of C. Reports of Select Committees*, 1810 (12), VIII, pp. 231–2.

to Robinson, 'their Lordships are aware, will not be sufficient for the
ordinary and extraordinary expenses of so large an army for any
length of time.'[1] The troops had received one month's subsistence
allowance in advance and all officers had been given bat and baggage
and 200 days' forage money. No more specie would be sent from the
treasury: when the initial sum had been spent Robinson would have
to rely on bills of exchange and on requisition. Unfortunately the
Hamburg exchange was then from 18% to 20% against London and
Castlereagh warned the king that every ducat raised by the normal
process of bills of exchange and issued to the troops at nine shillings
and sixpence would cost the treasury thirteen shillings and fourpence.[2]
In desperation Huskisson ordered Robinson to use force. Supplies
were to be compulsorily purchased at the market price obtaining just
before the expedition landed: refusal to sell at such a rate could be met
by seizure without any payment. Similarly specie was to be raised by
compelling the acceptance of bills of exchange issued at four shillings
and sixpence a dollar and nine shillings and sixpence a ducat, regardless
of the prevailing rates of exchange. By such means, wrote Huskisson,
the army ought, with strict economy, to pay its own way without
treasury assistance.[3] But the policy was unjust and unworkable. Never
previously during the Napoleonic war had a British army received
such orders. The French, wrote Herries, boasted that they could
maintain four men in the Peninsula for the cost of one British soldier
there. 'The difference is of course made up by robbery'; now the
British were being told to copy the enemy's methods.[4] Immediately
both Chatham, the commander of the expedition, and Robinson protested that the instructions were unjust towards the local population.
They got scant sympathy from London. The treasury, Castlereagh
told Chatham, 'do not possess the power of sending you from hence
a single foreign coin of any sort'.[5] Poor Huskisson, sorely harrassed
by Wellington's vitriolic despatches and the Austrian subsidy payments, was even more intractable. The Dutch should know, he wrote
to Robinson, that French occupation was far worse. Beyond that he
could offer the commissary-general only the now familiar treatise on
the principles of finance.[6] But this failed to persuade either Chatham

---

[1] *Parl. Papers*, VIII, p. 230; Castlereagh, *Correspondence and Despatches*, vol.
VI, p. 289.
[2] Castlereagh, *op. cit.*, pp. 280 and 290; P.R.O., T27/64/377–9.
[3] P.R.O., T27/64/379.   [4] Herries MSS., letter books, vol. III, p. 89.
[5] Castlereagh, *op. cit.*, p. 304.
[6] *Ibid.*, pp. 305–6; Glenbervie, vol. II, p. 29.

or Robinson to withdraw their opposition. The dispute was referred first to the advocate-general, who reported in Huskisson's favour, and then to the cabinet itself. At this level good sense prevailed: bills were not to be issued at par but at the average rate of discount prevailing on the Amsterdam and Hamburg exchanges at the time the expedition sailed.[1]

June to August 1809 was spent in a frantic search for specie for both Wellington and Chatham. Early in June dollars worth £220,000 were despatched on the *Niobe* and *Rosamund*, reaching the Tagus by the end of the month.[2] This shipment, Castlereagh warned Wellington, was definitely the last that could be sent until fresh supplies arrived from South America. In the meantime Murray would have to get what he needed by bills of exchange at Gibraltar and Cadiz.[3] 'How', wrote Huskisson to Wellington in July, 'can you expect us to buy specie here with the exchange thirty per cent against us, and guineas selling at twenty-four shilling?' But those in Portugal were obsessed with their own difficulties. The lack of money was affecting the discipline of the troops, who plundered in the sight of their own discontented officers. Only an improvement in the amount raised by bills of exchange saved the situation that August.[4] The few dollars available in London were needed on Walcheren. A small consignment already loaded for Bermuda was diverted to Robinson, while 184,000 dollars received by the Bank from South America late in August were forwarded immediately to the island. After that Robinson, like Murray, was told to rely on what he could raise locally. In desperation the commissariat suggested in August that dollars should be issued to the forces at the full rate at which they might pass current in that area, instead of at the fixed rate of four shillings and sixpence in the Mediterranean and four shillings and eightpence in America. Altogether the Walcheren expedition cost the treasury £834,275 in extraordinary expenditure alone: Wellington in 1809 received nearly £2,500,000 from England.[5] Militarily the results were negligible. Chatham failed and Wellington made but slow progress. Economically the efforts of

[1] Castlereagh, *op. cit.*, pp. 310 and 312–13.
[2] P.R.O., T27/64/181–2 and 189; Wellington, *Despatches*, vol. III, pp. 339 and 384.
[3] Wellington, *Despatches*, vol. III, p. 341; Castlereagh, *Despatches*, vol. VII, p. 95.
[4] Fortescue, *History of the British Army*, vol. VII, p. 435; Wellington, vol. III, pp. 405 and 439.
[5] P.R.O., T27/64/490, and 502; T29/102/119 and T29/108/372; *Parl. Papers*, H. of C. *Reports of Select Committees*, 1810 (12), VIII, 287.

the summer of 1809 convinced many at the treasury that the country's war effort would have to be curtailed.

The first to stress the lesson was Huskisson. Early in August, rankled by the cabinet's rejection of his scheme for financing the Walcheren campaign, he sent Perceval a long memorandum on war expenditure.[1] The basis of Britain's war policy had, he recalled, long been to fight a defensive war. As long as we maintained command of the seas we could defend our empire, protect our commerce, and husband our resources without risking premature major European campaigns. France was so overwhelmingly strong on land that individual European states only courted disaster by opposing her: British forces could only be thrown into the struggle with decisive effect as part of a great continental alliance against Napoleon. The difficulty was obviously to decide when the right time had arrived to make this supreme effort. The Grenville cabinet had wasted a possible opportunity early in 1807: Portland and his colleagues had failed at Walcheren. The battle of Wagram seemed, for the present, to have ended all hopes of destroying French hegemony in Europe. All that remained was to give what help we could to the Spaniards and Portuguese while preparing for a long defensive war. 'When we speak of peace,' sighed Cobbett, 'it is like speaking of posterity.'

The cost of maintaining an army of 40,000 men in the Peninsula could not be less than £2,500,000 a year, half of which would be extraordinary expenditure, which would not have been required for the same army in quarters at home. A further £1,500,000 a year would be needed to buy military stores in Spain and to support Beresford's Portuguese. In all, ignoring all other commitments, this would entail raising at least £250,000 each month in specie or by bills of exchange. 'I wish', continued Huskisson, 'to be understood as entertaining strong doubts whether it will be practicable to provide the remittances . . . for any length of time, unless we can obtain very great facilities for procuring bullion in [South] America . . . by opening to us the trade of that continent.' There was also, in addition to the problem of getting foreign currency, the internal difficulty of finding new sources of income from taxation in order to balance an ever-increasing national budget. Year by year the financial burden of the war became heavier. Only vigorous military retrenchment could save the nation's economy. The navy cost the treasury £19,000,000 in 1809, an increase of £3,500,000 over the total for 1805, when Napoleon's Grand Army

[1] Add. MSS., 37416, fol. 355 ff.

was encamped at Boulogne. The number of seamen on active service had, in the same period, and in spite of the improvement in our military position, risen from 120,000 to 140,000. Naval expenditure, argued Huskisson, must be reduced to and held at the 1805 level, largely by curtailing the ship-building programme and by economising on the sea fencibles. Annual expenditure on the army had, from 1805 to 1809, risen from under £15,000,000 to £17,500,000. Here £2,000,000 a year might be saved by reducing our strategic reserve and wagon train, by eliminating inefficiency in the recruiting services, and by reducing the cavalry strength by a quarter. Finally £1,000,000 a year could be saved on the ordnance estimates by cutting down the artillery corps and barrack services. 'I will not disguise my opinion', ended Huskisson, 'that unless these measures are adopted, upon an extensive scale, we shall be driven either to make peace or to risk a convulsion in the country. . . . Will any man say that we possess the means of continuing for any permanence our present scale of expense? Whoever does say so, to him be consigned the task of bringing them forth.'

On 18 August Huskisson sent copies of this memorandum to Perceval and Canning. His conclusions, he assured Canning, were not the result of 'any splenetic weariness of office', nor had his judgement 'been warped by feelings of a peevish or gloomy nature'. He had, on the contrary, in his memorandum 'studiously kept out of sight many unpromising features'. He would, he confessed, 'look forward without regret to any circumstance by which I might be honourably released from further participation in the labours of the Government as at present constituted'.[1] The letter to Perceval was more bluntly phrased. 'I can only repeat to you', he wrote, 'that, without being conscious of any abatement in my disposition to make myself useful to the public, without a particle of ill-humour to any one, and with every kind and grateful feeling to yourself in particular, *it would be impossible for me, if the Government remains in its present state and proceeds in its present course, with a reference to the manner in which public expenditure is controlled and directed, to take an active part in bringing forward measures, founded upon a system, or rather perhaps upon a want of system, which I believe, in my conscience, will, if persevered in, lead, at no great distance of time, to consequences most distressing to the King and prejudicial to the country.'* [2] After this Perceval was fully occupied in trying to persuade

[1] Add. MSS., 37416, fol. 107.
[2] Perceval MSS., Huskisson to Perceval, 18 Aug. 1809.

his young colleague to remain in office. The ministry, he wrote on 21 August, could not afford to lose 'a person so important to the Government as yourself': Huskisson was, he admitted, 'essential to its well-being'. Above all Perceval dreaded to 'awake some morning, when the day may perhaps require the greatest exertion, and find myself without *my right hand*'.[1] But in less than a month Huskisson had followed Canning out of office, leaving Perceval to lead the government and tackle the dollar problem alone.[2] For Richard Wharton, who succeeded Huskisson as junior secretary, was a political light-weight. There were few politicians who envied Perceval his job. George Rose, one of the acknowledged financial experts among Pitt's Friends and a man with long experience at the treasury and board of trade, was convinced that it was impossible. 'To carry on the war on the present scale of expense,' he wrote that November, 'with the *ordinary means of the country*, or anything approaching to it, is *utterly impossible*. It is not a question that any man living can conceive will admit of discussion, after an attentive consideration of the actual resources of the country. It follows therefore of *absolute necessity* that unless our expenses can be very greatly reduced, we cannot continue to exist long as an independent nation. This is an opinion not hastily taken up, nor arising from despondency; but is founded on long and mature deliberation on all the circumstances alluded to; with a full knowledge of the wealth of the nation, its prosperous revenue and flourishing commerce; and supposing no check or reverse in any of these.'[3] Altogether it seemed a cheerless prospect for the new prime minister.

Perceval's problems were soon further complicated by inaccurate estimates of military expenditure forwarded from the Peninsula. In September 1809 the position appeared, on paper, most encouraging, although Murray reported that the dollar had reached five shillings and twopence on the Lisbon exchange and that efforts to issue bills at Cadiz and Gibraltar had caused sharp rises in both places.[4] On 23 September Wellington told Castlereagh that he estimated total expenditure from August to November at £654,050, or just over £235,000 a month. Assets included a balance of £250,000 in the war

---

[1] Perceval MSS., Perceval to Huskisson, 21 Aug. 1809.

[2] For details of Huskisson's resignation see chapter 15, pp. 267–8.

[3] Add. MSS., 42774, fol. 182, memorandum by George Rose, 11 Nov. 1809. Huskisson, wrote the *Morning Chronicle* on 4 Oct. 1809, 'boasts of having left them the means of going on, if they have any resources in themselves, till after Christmas'.

[4] P.R.O., T29/102/38; T1/1128/4078.

chest and £150,000 which had just arrived in Lisbon on board H.M.S.
Fylla, while a further £459,000 could probably be raised in the
Peninsula by bills of exchange.[1] The Perceval ministry, boasted
Huskisson, had inherited sufficient specie to pay for the Spanish war
until the end of the year. On 29 August news had arrived that two
frigates had reached Vera Cruz and found 'an abundant supply of
specie' available, while on 22 September Murray reported the arrival
of still more from Gibraltar and Cadiz.[2] A month later the exchange
at Lisbon improved, with a consequent easing of the problem of
raising money locally. 'I am', wrote Murray to Harrison on 21 October,
'inclined to believe that I shall have no difficulty in providing funds
for the general service in this country during the present year.' The
position seemed so much better that Harrison, acting on Perceval's
instructions, actually refused an offer by Sir John Lubbock to sell
100,000 dollars then deposited at Portsmouth.[3] By December they
both must have wished they had bought them. For on the thirteenth
of that month Wellington asked Liverpool (the new secretary of state)
for £100,000 in specie immediately and a similar sum in January, as
the money markets at Cadiz, Gibraltar and Lisbon had taken a sudden
turn for the worse. 'I cannot', Murray told the commissary-in-chief,
'account for it in any satisfactory manner.'[4] The treasury, still relying
on the September estimates, was caught entirely unprepared and had
nothing to send. The government, wrote Wellington to Villiers on 6
January, had undertaken more than it could support in the Peninsula,
while Dunsmore, Murray's deputy at Lisbon, finding only £2,000
left in the military chest, was forced to raise funds by private deals on
most unfavourable terms.[5] It took Perceval until February to collect
500,000 dollars, which were immediately shipped to Portugal on board
the *Comus*. By that time the position had greatly deteriorated and the
treasury was overwhelmed by pleas for aid from Wellington, Murray,
and Stuart. The pay of British troops was a month in arrears and the
Portuguese army needed £80,000 a month if it were not to be forced
to disband.[6] As usual Wellington was full of complaints against the
ministry. On 1 March he told Liverpool that Perceval's cabinet was
bound to fall; in April he repeated the forecast to General Crauford.

[1] Wellington, *Despatches*, vol. III, p. 516. Murray's estimate for the same
period was £705,000 (P.R.O., T29/103/425).
[2] P.R.O., T29/102/218 and 380.   [3] P.R.O., T29/103/505; T1/1113/343.
[4] Wellington, *Despatches*, vol. III, p. 647; P.R.O., T1/1114/186.
[5] Wellington, *Despatches*, vol. III, p. 677; P.R.O., T1/1128/4078.
[6] Wellington, *Despatches*, vol. III, p. 758 and vol. IV, p. 15.

'The Government', he wrote to Vice-Admiral Berkeley, 'are terribly afraid that I shall get them, and myself, into a scrape. But what can be expected of men who are beaten in the House of Commons three times a week? A great deal might be done now, if there existed in England less party and more public sentiment and if there was any Government.' Public opinion in England, he assured Stuart, was very unfavourable to the Peninsula: ministers were as much alarmed as the public or the opposition and feared he would 'fight a desperate battle which is to answer no purpose'.[1] Meanwhile the prime minister tried doggedly to find out how much financial aid from London the duke really did want. By 17 April the treasury had obtained 63,573 dollars from Jamaica and bought just over 400,000 from the Bank at prices varying from five shillings and sixpence to five shillings and seven-pence halfpenny each.[2] A week later Harrison told Bunbury of the war office that the treasury had managed to collect and despatch 670,000. In addition the commissary at Gibraltar had sent 240,000 and Consul Duff had been ordered to raise what he could at Cadiz.

The crisis taught Perceval the need for reliable estimates that would be accepted in both London and the Peninsula. On 27 April he called a full and important meeting of the treasury board to consider future needs. The recent shipments, he explained, would in some degree at least relieve Wellington's immediate difficulties. He would continue to do all humanly possible in the future to get sufficient dollars, but he warned the board, 'from the small quantities that have been offered for sale in the market and the uncertainty as to any early importations, it is not in Their Lordships' power to make any precise statement of the amount of specie which can be procured . . . in the next three or four months'. The treasury would have to rely on such casual supplies as it could buy on the London market, while the commissary-general in Lisbon would have to push his own bills of exchange and get what dollars he could from Duff at Cadiz and Sweetland at Gibraltar. Harrison then presented a full financial account as he and Bunbury had calculated it. Wellington, in his now notorious despatch of the pre-vious 23 September, had calculated the total annual expenditure of the British army in Portugal at £1,756,236. On this basis, the expenditure from 25 August 1809 to 25 April 1810 should have been £1,170,824. The British-subsidised Portuguese army should have spent only £640,000 in the same period, even if the whole force of 30,000 men

---

[1] Wellington, *Despatches*, vol. IV, pp. 2, 8 and 27.
[2] P.R.O., T29/105/213–14.

had been on full pay throughout (which their commander, Beresford, had confirmed was not the case). A further £200,000 had been advanced to the Portuguese government and £50,000 had been needed to meet the arrears of pay to the British army in August 1809. This, concluded Harrison, made the total expenditure until 25 April £2,060,824. Against this Murray had estimated the balance in the military chest on 25 August 1809 at £400,000; Murray, Duff and Sweetland had since raised £1,714,000 by bills of exchange, and £380,000 had been sent in dollars from London. The total of specie made available was, therefore, a little over £2,500,000, or at least £440,000 more than the estimated expenditure.[1]

The figures used were the only ones sent to London by Wellington and his commissary-general. They gave no justification whatever for Wellington's hot-headed attacks on the government, but the army commander remained unabashed. In a despatch to Liverpool of 16 May he argued that the treasury had consistently over-estimated the amount of specie that could be raised in the Peninsula by bills of exchange. Little could be hoped for from Cadiz, as practically every dollar which reached there from South America was imported for the use of the Spanish government. 'If circumstances do not permit the Government', he continued, 'to make the remittances required regularly from England, it is my duty to inform your Lordship that it is impossible for the army to continue in this country on the scale on which we have been hitherto or on which we ought to be to have it in our power to do any good.' Because of the increased cost of transport and a general rise in prices, the estimated monthly expenditure of the army had risen from the £235,000 of the previous September to £300,000.[2] Galloping inflation followed. A fortnight later Wellington forwarded a monthly estimate of £376,120; by the next week it had risen to £421,565, only half of which was to be raised in the Peninsula. 'Fresh letters of Saturday night', wrote Bunbury to Harrison in despair, 'swell the demands higher than ever. But there are many items in the various calculations which appear to me inexplicable.'[3] The £170,000 worth of dollars that Perceval had managed to send in May and June now seemed ludicrously inadequate. Huskisson, in August

---

[1] P.R.O., T29/105/284-91.   [2] Wellington, *Despatches*, vol. IV, pp. 72-3.
[3] *Ibid.*, vol. IV, pp. 96, 106 and 193; P.R.O., W.O. 6/173/6. Stuart, in a despatch from Lisbon on 16 June, argued that the presence of a large force at Cadiz which absorbed a large part of the dollars raised there and an 'exorbitant' increase in the prices of corn, meat and forage were 'satisfactory reasons' for exceeding the December estimates (P.R.O., T1/1142/7802).

1809, had felt unable to raise £250,000 a month: Perceval, distracted
by the labours of leading an exceedingly weak government almost
single-handed, was now faced with demands for over £420,000 a
month. Early in June Liverpool told Wellesley that the Bank had no
reserves and that a consignment of specie from Buenos Aires, expected to contain 9 million dollars, had turned out to be of only
600,000. There was, added Liverpool, unanimity in the cabinet on the
need to continue the Peninsula campaign. Yet as costs soared, and as
there seemed no reliable way of estimating future expenditure, 'both
the cabinet ministers and every person acquainted with the finances
and resources of the country' agreed that retrenchment was unavoidable. It is difficult to see, on the evidence of Wellington's letters, how
Perceval could have realised that the cost of the campaign would
spring at one bound from £3 to £5 million a year. It was, indeed, a
striking example of the prime minister's loyalty to his subordinates
that he accepted such an increase without public protest and with an
emphatic declaration of confidence in the expedition's commander.[1]

Once again the first lord took the unusual step of consulting the
full treasury board. At a very long meeting on 3 July their lordships
ploughed their way through two months' despatches from the Peninsula. It would be necessary, at four shillings and sixpence a dollar, to
raise 11 million dollars a year in Britain in order to meet the latest
demands. This seemed impossible, even if the treasury were able to
buy every single dollar offered for sale in the country and to send the
lot to Lisbon. Unfortunately Perceval had no monopoly on the money
market and the Peninsula armies had none on the treasury's dollar resources. Perceval had repeatedly urged the Bank to try and buy up all
the dollars imported into Britain on private account, but some were
bound to go to merchants. 'No exertion of this Board', admitted
Perceval, 'can prevent it.' The short term position was equally grave,
as no appreciable supply of dollars was expected from Vera Cruz for
at least eight weeks. The only solution was to increase once more the
total raised by bills of exchange in the Peninsula itself. The board had
suggested in April that Murray ought to aim at £300,000 a month:
Wellington, in his despatch of 6 June, had budgeted for a little over
£218,000. This seemed to Perceval unduly pessimistic. Great sums of

[1] Fortescue, vol. VII, p. 437. 'I am afraid', wrote Wellington to Liverpool
on 6 June, 'from the spirit and tone in which the letters from the Treasury are
written, I have not given satisfaction to that department of the Government
which I regret much' (*Despatches*, vol. IV, p. 801); Yonge, vol. I, pp. 335-7
and 365-6; Add. MSS., 37295, fol. 312.

money had been spent in Portugal by the British expeditionary force and more had reached the Peninsula direct from South America. The difficulty found in negotiating bills on London must have been at least partly due to the fact that individuals had been collecting and with-holding dollars from circulation. In order to test this, Perceval pro-posed to send an expert to Portugal with the sole duty of selling bills. He would not be distracted, as was Murray, by other duties and could persuade the hoarders that 'their money would be safer as well as more productive if remitted to London and deposited on their account in our public securities'.[1] Accordingly Commissary-General Drummond was ordered to leave immediately for Lisbon.[2] It was all, grumbled Wellington, the work of John Villiers, the former British minister at Lisbon, who, while in the Peninsula, had constantly urged that greater efforts should be made to raise money locally. 'My answer was', added his lordship, 'that we were neither pickpockets nor coiners.' Even Gordon, the commissary-in-chief, thought little good would come of the idea. Wellington predicted it might do 'a great deal of harm'. 'I attribute this mission', he wrote, 'to a belief prevalent at the Treasury that we have not done our best to procure money, in which they may depend on it they are mistaken.'[3] Drummond reached Lisbon late in August: a month later, in his first despatch, he was able to report that the Lisbon money market had been 'so far productive as to afford a reasonable hope that the Commissary-General may con-tinue to find specie for his bills in sufficient quantity (with such remit-tances as their Lordships may be enabled from time to time to send . . .) to carry on the service in Portugal'.[4] He remained in the Peninsula until the following May when he sailed for Lima to buy three million dollars under a special agreement with the Spanish authorities.[5] Accord-ing to the paymaster-general's accounts a total of £6,066,021 was spent in the Peninsula during 1810. A little over £5,000,000 of this was raised by bills of exchange, compared with £1,220,000 from the same source in 1809. Total expenditure in 1811 reached practically £9,000,000, over £8,500,000 of which was raised by bills.[6]

With so much more specie being raised in the Peninsula, 1811 was,

[1] P.R.O., T29/106/231-8.   [2] P.R.O., T29/107/262 and 438.
[3] Wellington, *Despatches*, vol. IV, pp. 198 and 251. Wellington eventually agreed to give Drummond all assistance on the understanding that he should see copies of all reports sent to London and give prior consent to any alteration in the method of raising money at Lisbon (*Despatches*, vol. IV, p. 230).
[4] P.R.O., T29/107/361-3.   [5] *Ibid.*, T29/111/9 and T1/1346/4817.
[6] *Parl. Papers, H. of C. Accounts and Reports*, 1812 (198), IX, p. 60.

relatively, a year of plenty. In January Robert Kennedy, who had succeeded the much-tried Murray as commissary-general at Lisbon, complained that the war chest was almost exhausted, and in April he was asking for 500,000 dollars from London in order to meet the previous month's expenses. Fortunately, however, £1,100,000 worth of bills were negotiated at Lisbon during March and April, which fully relieved Kennedy's anxieties.[1] Wellington himself seemed satisfied for a while, for until July there was not a single complaint in his despatches of lack of money. In March he was even on the defensive and sought to prove that the treasury was exaggerating the real cost of the Peninsula campaign. 'I shall be sorry', he wrote in unusually chastened tones, 'if Government should think themselves under the necessity of withdrawing from this country on account of the expense of the contest.' If that happened, the French might risk everything on an invasion of England. 'Then indeed would commence an expensive contest; then would His Majesty's subjects discover what are the miseries of war, of which, by the blessing of God, they have hitherto had no knowledge. God forbid that I should be a witness, much less an actor in such a scene.' That May Perceval, distracted by the debate on the bullion report, told Canning that we could not possibly maintain our existing military expenditure. But the mood of depression soon passed and even Wellington agreed that 'His Majesty's Government have done everything in their power'.[2] However great his own difficulties at home, Perceval never forgot those of his colleagues in the Peninsula. There was a new flexibility in treasury policy: the era of Huskissonian lectures had passed.

Perceval still, however, had much to try him. At the end of 1811 Robert Kennedy came home on sick leave, leaving assistant-commissary-general John Bisset to act as his deputy. The two then failed to agree on policy and Kennedy began to badger Herries for copies of all treasury correspondence with Bisset. Early in 1812 Kennedy returned to Lisbon where he became 'every day more and more impracticable', quarrelling with George Harrison of the treasury and opposing all Herries' plans.[3] Yet Perceval wisely continued to allow all those at Lisbon the maximum freedom of manœuvre. When Kennedy

[1] P.R.O., T29/109/128–9 and T29/110/644.
[2] Wellington, *Despatches*, vol. IV, pp. 691–3. For complaints of lack of specie in July and 18 Aug. see *Despatches*, vol. V, pp. 153 and 195; Colchester, vol. II, p. 329. In October the Portuguese Regent accepted a British offer to pay part of the subsidy in goods instead of specie (P.R.O., T29/113/576).
[3] Herries MSS., letter books, vol. I, pp. 137 and 242; vol. III, pp. 39 and 113.

was given fresh instructions on the methods to be used in issuing bills
of exchange, he was told to delay introducing the new system if he
thought it might interfere with the raising of specie. The lords of
the treasury, wrote Perceval, 'placed as they are at such a distance
from the scene of these transactions and in comparative ignorance of
any special or peculiar circumstances' would give no 'peremptory
directions . . . to be considered binding under all circumstances'.[1] The
treasury, wrote Herries to Bisset in April 1812, might on occasions
differ in opinion from those in Lisbon, but they realised 'the impossi-
bility of laying down any fixed rules which should be binding upon
you under all the various circumstances of service in the Peninsula . . .'.[2]
In March 1812 Bisset, with Wellington's approval, bought 400,000
dollars from Gibraltar at five shillings and eightpence each, a figure
higher than the prevailing market rate at Lisbon. The British army,
wrote Wellington, was 5,000,000 dollars in debt and two months in
arrears in pay, while Beresford's Portuguese would have to be practically disbanded if more specie was not forthcoming. When the
treasury protested against private bargains to raise dollars at prices
above the open market rate, Wellington immediately refused an offer
of an additional 500,000 dollars from Gibraltar and then complained
that without this sum he might be prevented from advancing into
Spain before the harvest. Once more his old suspicions of the treasury
were revived. 'It would be very desirable on every account', he wrote
on 12 May, 'that the Treasury should appoint a person here in whom
they would feel confidence to conduct the finances of this army. It
would relieve the Commissary-General and me from much business
and anxiety . . . and the business would be done to the satisfaction of
the Treasury.'[3] But as Wellington wrote, Perceval was already dead.
On the very day of his death he had instructed George Harrison to
reassure Bisset that the lords of the treasury 'feel themselves utterly
incompetent to form a judgement at this distance which should be
opposed to the deliberate judgement of the Earl of Wellington on the
spot, and . . . if his Lordship should continue to think it advantageous
to obtain money by such [private] contracts, Mr. Bissett will follow the
Earl of Wellington's instructions; and their Lordships will be fully
prepared to sanction whatever he directs and be satisfied that it is
determined by the best judgement which can be applied to the

[1] P.R.O., T29/107/605-12; T29/110/397-8.
[2] Herries, *Memoirs*, vol. I, pp. 72-3.
[3] Wellington, *Despatches*, vol. V, pp. 607 and 647.

subject.' [1] By the end of May the treasury had collected the required 500,000 dollars from as far afield as China and the East Indies, thus enabling Wellington to advance into Spain without delay.

'You cannot have failed to perceive', wrote Herries to John Trotter the day after Perceval's death, 'that the objections made against us were levelled partly at the Treasury. Perhaps these complaints will all be buried with poor Perceval. I heartily wish Lord Wellington may not too soon feel the loss of him.' [2] Without Perceval's steady courage and industry, the outcome of the Peninsula campaign might have been very different. In parliament, although leading the weakest of ministries, he never wavered in the face of opposition, defeatism, and scorn: at the treasury he made immense and successful efforts to find sufficient specie, never once remonstrating against Wellington's complaints when things were not going well. His loyalty towards his subordinate was no less than heroic. In the end even Wellington himself recognised this. 'I assure you', he wrote to Herries on 9 June 1812, 'that I am fully aware of Mr. Perceval's kindness, and I must say partiality, towards me.' [3] By the spring of 1812 everyone could see the possibility of victory in the Peninsula. Even Whitbread was converted. 'People', wrote Wellington to Beresford, 'are in great good humour with the affairs of Portugal.' It is to Perceval's credit that he never despaired nor sought to give up in the long years when the final victory seemed very doubtful.

[1] Herries, *Memoirs*, vol. I, p. 73.
[2] Herries MSS., letter books, vol. II, pp. 154–5.
[3] Herries, *Memoirs*, vol. I, p. 48.

CHAPTER NINETEEN

THE PERCEVAL BUDGETS AND THE BULLION REPORT

THE years 1800 to 1815 were, said Gladstone, the heroic age of British war finance. During this period Great Britain raised almost half her annual national expenditure through taxation, a much greater proportion than during the wars of either 1914–18 or 1939–45.[1] The annual national expenditure rose from £17,500,000 in 1792 to £68,500,000 in 1806 while the national debt was nearly trebled in the same period. Yet in 1806 Petty was able to raise a loan of £20,000,000 at under 5%. Public confidence was maintained by a belief in Pitt's sinking fund which, through the miracles of compound interest, was supposed eventually to pay off the accumulated war debts. As long as confidence was maintained in this way, the treasury could continue to meet annual deficits by means of further loans. But by 1807 the sinking fund itself was one of the chancellor's main headaches for he had to raise sufficient additional revenue each year to offset the combined charges and sinking fund, which together amounted to about 10% of every new loan. This had previously been done by raising fresh taxes, but, even before Pitt's death, many thought that the limit had been reached 'without degenerating into a system of the most vexatious and grinding oppression'. 'Toleration', lamented the *Edinburgh Review*, 'never had a present tense, nor taxation a future one.' The direct permanent taxes had been increased nine times between 1793 and 1809 and had risen fivefold in their yield. Stamp duties, in the same period, grew from £800,000 to £6,000,000 per annum.[2] Every year it became increasingly difficult to persuade parliament to vote new taxes which were not opposed by some powerful sectional interest.

In 1806 Petty, free from the embarrassment of a radical opposition, tried first a tax on pig iron, then one on private brewing. Both raised such opposition that he fell back in the end on increasing the assessed taxes and raising the income tax to two shillings in the pound, much to the discomfort of many of his own supporters and of 'the middling

[1] W. H. Hancock and M. M. Gowing, *British War Economy*, p. 3.
[2] *Edinburgh Review*, Oct. 1808, p. 18; Add. MSS., 37416, fol. 355.

class of society'.[1] In the following year the Talents, too weak to risk another unpopular budget, took refuge in a new plan of finance. Instead of borrowing the principal and raising the interest on it by taxation, the government decided to borrow both and to impose new taxes only to meet the interest on the interest. Petty and Harrison calculated that, exclusive of foreign subsidies and other unexpected calls, £32,000,000 a year would finance the war effort. £21,000,000 of this would come from the war taxes and the remainder from annual loans. The 10% needed to cover loan charges and the sinking fund was to be taken from the war taxes. Consequently these would yield less in disposable revenue each year and would be wholly mortgaged at the end of fourteen years. They were, therefore, to be replenished partly by increasing the total of the annual war loan from £12,000,000 in the first three years of the plan to £14,000,000 in the fourth, and to £16,000,000 in the following ten years, and partly by floating a second, supplementary loan. This would need to be for only £200,000 in the first year, but would have, thereafter, to be progressively increased as the war taxes became more heavily mortgaged. Petty hoped, however, at least for the first three years of his plan, to meet the charges and 1% sinking fund on the supplementary loans out of the proceeds of expiring annuities. Not until the fourth year would new taxes have to be raised. According to the treasury calculations, the first annual loan would have been redeemed by the end of the fourteen-year period and so would again be available for the service of the state. Each succeeding year another loan would be redeemed 'so that the plan presents a series of loans and redemptions which is inexhaustible'.[2] Even the *Edinburgh Review*, for all its party fervour, confessed that 'it rather appears to us to be too complicated . . .', while the independent member David Magens thought it 'mere moonshine'. In fact Petty was leading the country in statistical circles, borrowing money to start sinking funds and so accumulating fresh debts as fast as he was raising funds to repay old loans. The details might baffle the public as much as they certainly bemused the majority of the Commons, but everyone seemed to grasp the main point. 'I thank ministers individually and collectively,' wrote Cobbett, 'from the bottom of my heart for three blessed years, without beholding the hideous face of a new-created,

---

[1] *Parl. Deb.*, VI, 580.

[2] *Edinburgh Review*, Apr. 1807, pp. 72–85; *Parl. Deb.*, IX, 813 ff. The plan assumed that the cost of the war could be stabilised at £32 million a year. This soon proved impossible (Aitkin, *Annals of the Reign of George III*, vol. II, p. 207).

gaunt and hungry tax-gatherer.' It would, he forecast, 'snuff out the little court-fed faction of the Roses and the Cannings and the Castlereaghs and the Percevals'. At first some of Pitt's Friends feared as much themselves. George Rose boldly demolished the plan at party dinners, but no one had the courage to force a division in the House. Castlereagh did his best by producing some tortuous calculations of his own which seemed to have perplexed his colleagues as much as they did the government.[1]

The new plan of finance went into cold storage with the fall of the Talents, but the attractive idea of a moratorium of taxation survived. Perceval, never keen on mere juggling with accounts, decided to rely instead on administrative economies.[2] By persuading the Bank to reduce its interest rate for managing the national debt he saved between £62,000 and £65,000 a year. He checked the younger members of the Royal Family in their extravagant plans for redecorating their apartments at the public's expense and cut down the barrack building programme.[3] He reduced the treasury allowance to all state departments for the purchase of almanacks, pocket books, court calendars, and newspapers; he persuaded the treasury board to authorise the planting of potatoes in Marylebone Park in order, as he grandiloquently explained, 'to bring revenue to the Crown and food to the nation'; he even tried, unsuccessfully, to persuade the navy to drink cheap surplus coffee instead of rum.[4] In May 1808 came a revised life annuities plan. Similar schemes had been tried many times since the late seventeenth century, most of them failing because the treasury had had to pay well above the statutory rate of interest to attract subscribers.[5] Perceval's idea was that holders of 3% stock should be given the option of transferring it to the commissioners for the reduction of the national debt in exchange for a treasury life annuity. The amount of the annuity was calculated by the price of the stock on the day of transfer and the age of the applicant. The idea was not well received in the House. William Smith, the Unitarian member for Norwich,

---

[1] *Edinburgh Review, loc. cit.; Political Register*, 7 Feb. 1807, p. 206; Harrowby MSS., vol. IV, fol. 68, Richard Ryder to Harrowby, 31 Jan. 1807; *Parl. Deb.*, IX, 428–32.   [2] For details of these see chapter 17, pp. 320–2.

[3] P.R.O., T27/64/58 and 166.

[4] *Ibid.*, F.O.83/17/22; T29/98/74; T29/114/717. The reduction of the paper allowance was said to have saved the improbable sum of £360,000 a year (*Day*, 15 Sep. 1810).

[5] *Proceedings of Manchester Statistical Soc.*, Dec. 1856, F. Hendrickes, *On the Financial Statistics of British Government Life Annuities*; Colchester, vol. II, p. 148.

protested on religious grounds, while Windham argued that the plan would 'vitiate the morals of the lower orders' by encouraging them to put their own interests before those of their children. It seemed doubtful, however, whether many of 'the lower orders' held the necessary minimum of £100 worth of 3% stock to be tempted by the scheme. The plan did have more serious faults. Perceval himself admitted that, in essence, it was a gamble, for the public could only benefit if 3% stock continued to rise as it had done in the previous year. Were there a depression, the exchequer would have to stand a loss. But it was Tierney who pointed to the gravest weakness; investors were more concerned to increase their capital than to secure a steady rate of interest. The monied interests mostly preferred speculation to insurance.[1]

The budget of 1808 was awaited with great optimism. Huskisson had, at first, wanted to increase the Irish taxes, but was over-ruled by Arthur Wellesley who argued that this would only increase disaffection.[2] On 15 February the *Sun* predicted a 'trifling' loan of £10,000,000 while rumours in the City even halved this.[3] In the event Perceval managed to keep it down to £8,000,000. The total supplies for the year were estimated at a little over £54,000,000, nearly £6,000,000 of which was to be raised in Ireland, leaving just over £48,000,000 to be met in the chancellor's budget. Against this the war taxes were expected to yield £20,000,000; advances from the Bank amounted to £3,500,000; malt and pensions duties would yield £3,000,000 and the lottery £350,000; there was a surplus of over £2,250,000 on the 1807 ways and means, while the consolidated fund had an unappropriated surplus of £726,000 and was expected to yield a further £3,500,000 in the current year. Finally just over £1 million worth of exchequer bills were to be funded and another £6,000,000 worth issued. All this, together with the £8,000,000 loan, would just meet the year's expenditure. It was, in every respect, an honest, workmanlike budget. By consolidating nearly one hundred acts for collecting stamp duties into a single measure, Perceval saved £200,000 in the cost of collection, while another £125,000 was saved by reforming the assessed taxes. The year's loan was raised at an interest rate of

---

[1] *Parl. Deb.*, XI, pp. 261–72 and 697–700. The scheme attracted £588,000 in its first year (P.R.O., T29/105/270). The *Sun* (6 May 1808) attacked the *Morning Chronicle* for suggesting that 'the principal end' of the scheme was to 'afford the means of influence' by creating a new board of commissioners.

[2] Wellington, *Civil Correspondence, Ireland*, p. 239.

[3] *Sun*, 15 Feb. and 4 Mar. 1808.

£4 14s. 6¼d.% per annum, terms which even Tierney admitted far exceeded his hopes and 'were as good for the country as the public could have expected'. By funding exchequer bills when stock stood at 63½ and by borrowing in 4% instead of 3% stock, the chancellor claimed to have saved the state £4,000,000 of debt capital. The total annual charge of the new debt created was calculated at £728,783. £375,000, or over half of this, was defrayed from short-term annuities which had fallen in; £65,000 from the reduction of the management charges on the national debt; and £300,000 by increasing the assessed taxes and stamp duties. This was the only tax increase proposed for the year: if, promised Perceval, the current estimates met all expenses, 'they might in the next and following years resort to the principle which had been so generally approved of [no new taxes]'. The budget was thereafter accepted without any opposition. The new chancellor had again confounded his critics.[1]

The budget of 1809 was on similar lines. Early in January there was a boom on the stock exchange following rumours that the loan would again be less than £10,000,000 and that there were really to be no new taxes.[2] The *Day* predicted a £12,000,000 surplus for the consolidated fund and war taxes: the loan, it reported, would be raised by life annuities.[3] Huskisson, conscious of the government's weakness in parliament, urged Perceval to use the war taxes to offset the interest on the loan, but the chancellor declined to be led into the maze of another new plan of finance.[4] Instead he relied once more on careful management. The total estimates for the year were reduced to just under £54,000,000 which, deducting Ireland's proportion, left him to find £47,500,000. The consolidated fund and the ways and means for 1808 provided a combined surplus of £6,750,000; the war taxes were estimated at £19,000,000; the malt and pensions duties, £3,000,000, and the lottery, £300,000. The remaining expenditure was met by a £3,000,000 vote of credit, a £11,000,000 loan, and a further £4,500,000 raised by exchequer bills. The loan itself was contracted for at

---

[1] The consolidated fund was made up of the produce of all the permanent taxes, except those voted annually, and the surplus consisted of what remained after meeting the interest and other charges on the national debt. For the budget debates see *Parl. Deb.*, XI, 12-18 and 764-7. On 28 Mar. 1808 Perceval agreed to a motion by Scrope Bernard for a committee of inquiry into the evils of the lottery (*Parl. Deb.*, X, 1269). The chairman of the committee was Whitbread. The report, issued on 24 June, condemned state lotteries as creators of 'idleness, dissipation and poverty' (*Gent. Mag.*, Oct. 1808, p. 887; *Courier*, 19 Aug. 1808; *Parl. Deb.*, XI, 1043).　　[2] *Day*, 26 Jan. 1809.
[3] *Ibid.*, 28 Jan. 1809.　　[4] Perceval MSS., Huskisson to Perceval, 5 Oct. 1808.

£4 12s. 10d. %, the most favourable terms negotiated since the outbreak of war. Moreover, by consolidating the methods of collecting the customs and war taxes, all loan charges were met without imposing a single new tax or increasing an old one.[1] All the opposition could do was attack the principle of a state lottery as encouraging 'a spirit of gambling in the lower classes', but even then they polled only thirty-six votes in a division. The budget, said the *Day*, had been 'highly satisfactory to the country'.[2]

Yet Perceval's first two budgets, whatever their limited success, evaded the fundamental issue. The treasury saved odd thousands by careful management and improved methods of tax collection, but these were wasting assets. When all minor economies had been made and the system of tax collection been thoroughly overhauled, the treasury must either find productive new taxes or check the mounting national expenditure. By the summer of 1809 the time of decision was at hand. At first Perceval put his faith in finding fresh taxes. He had been shown a paper in Pitt's handwriting that claimed a further £2,500,000 a year could be raised. But George Rose soon ended these hopes: Pitt's calculations, he told Perceval, 'must not be relied on at all'. 'Mr. Pitt', he added, 'was in the habit of putting on paper the loosest ideas that occurred to him on the subject of finance, as well as on other matters; which he sometimes gave me, and at other times put them into his own drawer or threw them into the fire. Since his death I have destroyed a number of them, not thinking it fit they should be seen.'[3] Pitt hoped to raise £500,000 a year by a tax on private brewing, but Petty had tried in vain to persuade parliament to adopt it in 1806. The proposed duty of one penny a ton on coal had also been tried and defeated by the coal owners and iron masters. A tax on hides and candles, calculated to yield £250,000, would be 'most oppressive to the poor and the middling class'; cotton could not, for all Pitt's optimism, bear another one penny a pound; a tax on farm horses, thought Rose, would yield little revenue but a great deal of unpopularity; tobacco was 'as high as it can safely be carried'; while a tax on broad cloth could not be imposed while the price of cloth was so high. The alternative of reducing national expenditure was largely a political issue.

[1] *Annual Register*, 1809, pp. 80 ff. There was an additional loan of £3 million for Ireland and £600,000 for the Prince Regent of Portugal. For the terms of the loan, see the *Day*, 9 May 1809.

[2] *Annual Register*, 1809, *loc. cit.*; *Day*, 13 May 1809. The *Day* had on 24 Apr. forecast a loan of £15 million.

[3] Add. MSS., 42774, fol. 182, memorandum by George Rose.

By the summer of 1809 the duke of Portland was incapable of transacting any business, for he could neither read despatches nor endure long conversations. Only by drugs and sleep could he get relief from incessant pain. More and more of Perceval's time was spent in trying to maintain the ministry's crumbling majority in the Commons. This virtually left the treasury in the hands of Huskisson and Harrison, both of whom showed signs of discontent. The assistant-secretary, grossly over-worked and gouty, began to wish the Talents were back, while Huskisson had since Easter been dropping hints to the eager Canning that he would be glad of any excuse to resign.[1] The situation rapidly deteriorated for the want of effective leadership. 'I have always been surprised', wrote Willoughby Gordon, the duke of York's military secretary, 'that the Treasury exercised so little control over the other departments in matters of expenditure. Indeed in the manner in which the business has of late years been transacted there, you might almost have at once transferred it over to the Bank of England, upon which all the great offices should draw at pleasure: this sounds absurd, but the practice was not far short of it.' [2] Sturges Bourne, a junior lord, also realised that 'the country has suffered great evils in matters of finance' from the weakness of the treasury, while George Rose argued 'in the strongest language in which I could express myself' that the sole power of controlling the public purse must be in the hands of the first lord. Under the duke he admitted, 'the heads of each department dip their hands into [the public purse] without mercy; each anxious to have the services under his management performed effectually without considering the evil brought upon the country by the expense of the whole'.[3] But they all left it to Huskisson to act. On 17 August he saw Perceval at the treasury and on the following day threatened to resign unless there was some tightening of treasury control.[4] On the same day he sent both Perceval and Canning copies of a long memorandum outlining his ideas on finance.[5] Perceval saw, however, that what was financially desirable was also, under existing conditions, politically unattainable. 'Our administration', he wrote, 'is so constructed that let us change our head how we please, it is

---

[1] For Harrison's discontent with the ministry see Buckingham, *Court and Cabinets of George III*, vol. IV, p. 408. For Huskisson's attitude see chapter 18, pp. 342–3.
[2] Add. MSS., 38737, fol. 340, Gordon to Huskisson, 25 Sep. 1809.
[3] Malmesbury, *Letters*, vol. II, p. 146; Rose, vol. II, p. 432.
[4] Perceval MSS., Huskisson to Perceval, 18 Aug. 1809.
[5] For a summary of this see chapter 18, pp. 343–4.

impossible, or next to impossible, that we should have such a controlling power as you have been used to see exist with advantage, and consequently wish for again. There never can be the sort of acquiescence amongst us in control as there naturally and necessarily was under Mr. Pitt.' Pitt, continued Perceval, had such 'comprehensive talents and powers that he was himself essentially the Government in all its departments': when Pitt formed a cabinet all its members knew that, whereas he could do without any of them, they could not survive without him. Yet Huskisson himself had told Perceval that even Pitt 'could not in all departments control expenditure as he wished'. The Portland government, in contrast, was made up of 'so many of equal, or nearly equal, pretensions with respect to personal weight in the Government, and importance to its continuance . . . that the Government, under whatever head, must, to a great degree, be and remain a Government of Departments'. In these circumstances, claimed Perceval, he could do little to control his colleagues. 'My situation at present,' he wrote, 'with a degree of supposed power in public opinion, and of consequent responsibility far beyond the power which I really have is essentially unpleasant.' In fact all the treasury could hope to do was get its way through 'persuasion' and 'consent'.[1] But the critics were not convinced. Perceval's case, wrote Gordon, was 'trifling and weak and argues unfitness at least for high office'.[2] Within a month Canning had smashed the Portland cabinet, Huskisson had resigned, and Perceval found his position more unpleasant than ever.[3]

One of Perceval's last acts as chancellor of the exchequer under Portland had been to circulate to all ministers a financial statement, based on Huskisson's memorandum on 18 August 1809.[4] In December he sent copies of it to the king and to Wellesley, the new foreign secretary. 'From this paper', he wrote to George III, 'Your Majesty will see how serious a duty is imposed upon Your Majesty's Servants to endeavour to reduce the expenses of the war in every department of Your Majesty's Government within as narrow limits as good faith to Your Majesty's allies and the security of Your Majesty's dominions will allow.'[5] So unpromising was the entire financial position that

[1] Perceval MSS., Perceval to Huskisson, 21 Aug. 1809.
[2] Add. MSS., 38737, fol. 340.
[3] For Huskisson's resignation see chapter 15, pp. 267–8.
[4] He had promised Huskisson on 21 Aug. to make the memorandum 'the groundwork of a financial statement for my colleagues' (Perceval MSS.).
[5] Add. MSS., 37295, fol. 181; Windsor MSS., 14314–5, Perceval to George III, 5 Dec. 1809.

the prime minister failed to find anyone willing to relieve him of the exchequer. As Huskisson had thrown in his lot with Canning and gone into opposition, Perceval first tried Nicholas Vansittart, the pick of the Sidmouth connection. On 7 October he wrote to Vansittart at Torquay, where the latter was staying because of his wife's ill-health. This first offer made no specific mention of the exchequer: Perceval was still toying with the idea of persuading Vansittart to succeed Huskisson as financial secretary. Two days later Vansittart replied that he could not act without first consulting Sidmouth, but Rose was already confident that he would reject the joint-secretaryship as beneath his dignity as a privy councillor.[1] In fact Perceval had thoroughly mismanaged the overture. On 5 October he had sent Chatham to Sidmouth with a hint that 'they might all be brought together again' and to tell him that vacancies would be kept open for some of his friends in the Commons. But, explained Perceval, he could not then offer Sidmouth himself a place in the cabinet because of 'the prejudices of some of the old Pitt connexion' against his lordship. Not surprisingly Sidmouth saw this as a shallow attempt to break up his group and refused the ingenuous offer out of hand.[2] There were, however, rumours that Vansittart was not entirely happy in the Sidmouth group, and so Perceval decided to step up his bid. On the 8 October he sent Herries, a close personal friend of Vansittart, to Torquay with a firm offer of the exchequer. It was, grumbled Rose, 'much more than he is worth, either from talents or experience'. Herries was to go armed with a copy of Perceval's latest financial memorandum and was instructed not to frighten Vansittart 'with the necessity of leaving his wife immediately'.[3] Even so, wrote Perceval to the king on 12 October, there seemed little hope of Vansittart accepting. The following day he had his refusal. The offer, wrote Vansittart, 'required me . . . to quit a connection which has lasted during the whole of my political life for the gratification of I know not *what* and I know not *whose* unexplained prejudice'. It would, he wrote, be said that the bribe of high office had persuaded him to desert his friends.[4]

This left Perceval with the alternative of trying old George Rose

---

[1] Perceval MSS., Perceval to Vansittart, 7 Oct. 1809; Vansittart to Perceval, 9 Oct. 1809; Rose, vol. II, p. 408; Windsor MSS., 14719–20.

[2] Pellew, vol. III, p. 5.

[3] Rose, *loc. cit.*; Herries, vol. I, p. 12; *Dropmore MSS.*, vol. IX, p. 352.

[4] Windsor MSS., 14726–7, Perceval to George III, 12 Oct. 1809; 14728–9, same to same, 16 Oct. 1809; Perceval MSS., Vansittart to Perceval, 13 Oct. 1809. Vansittart even declined to read Perceval's financial memorandum.

or some promising but inexperienced young man. He had mentioned the possibility of approaching Rose to the king as early as 6 October.[1] In the end, however, he decided to try youth first. On 14 October he wrote to Robert Milnes and Lord Palmerston asking them both to see him at Downing Street. Milnes, one of the members for Pomfret, was perhaps the most brilliant speaker on the government back benches, but, thought Palmerston, 'although a man of very brilliant talents', he lacked 'steadiness'. He had, moreover, a 'partiality for Canning and [an] aversion to Perceval'. 'He will not', wrote Perceval to Eldon, 'be of the same use to me as Vansittart, but he will be of great service, if we can secure him entirely with us.' [2] Palmerston, a member of the admiralty board, was equally inexperienced, but Plumer Ward already thought highly of 'the talents and excellent understanding, as well as the many other good qualities and accomplishments of this very fine young man'.[3] Early on 16 October Palmerston reached town, having interrupted 'a pleasant sailing holiday' at Broadlands, and called on Perceval at the treasury. There he was 'infinitely surprised' to be suddenly offered the exchequer with a seat in the cabinet, 'if I chose it'. When Palmerston protested that he lacked both knowledge of finance and experience in debate, Perceval assured him that 'he should of course take the principal share of the Treasury business both in and out of the House; that, in the office, Harrison and his own secretary, [Herries] would be able to afford me great assistance'. As the astonished Palmerston hesitated, Perceval then proposed that he should become a junior lord 'and afterwards, if upon fagging at the business between this and the meeting of Parliament, I found it likely I could take the Chancellorship, I should be promoted to it'. Perceval then finally offered the post of secretary-at-war. Still Palmerston pleaded for time to make up his mind. In the end it was agreed that he should have until 18 October, on the understanding that, in the meantime, Perceval should be free to approach Milnes.[4] Few young men could have resisted so tempting a bait, but Palmerston, to his credit, kept his sense of proportion. Vanity and ambition, he told Malmesbury, urged him to accept the exchequer: 'but it is throwing for a great stake, and where much is to be gained very much also may be lost'. The new

[1] Perceval MSS., Arden to Perceval, 7 Oct. 1809.
[2] Malmesbury, *Letters*, vol. II, p. 159; Twiss, vol. I, p. 105. Wilberforce was horrified by the offer to Milnes (Wilberforce, *Life*, vol. III, p. 433).
[3] P. R. Ward, *Memoirs*, vol. I, p. 250.
[4] Malmesbury, *Letters*, vol. II, pp. 155–9; Windsor MSS., 14728–9, Perceval to George III, 16 Oct. 1809.

cabinet would be weak and the financial position of the country was critical. Therefore, with Malmesbury's blessing, he opted for the secretaryship-at-war and again refused the offer of a place in the cabinet.[1]

Three days later Milnes finally reached town, saw Canning, and then called on Perceval at Downing Street. After a long inverview he asked for two days' grace to make up his mind, but that evening Perceval wrote despondently to the king that he was prepared for a further refusal. Again the prime minister's fears were realised. On 23 October Milnes rejected all offers of office because, with his lack of experience, he might do more harm than good. All he would promise was his constant attendance and support from the back benches.[2] In desperation Perceval fell back on sixty-six years old Rose. The king was full of doubts until reassured that the appointment would be only temporary, Arden objected that Rose was already clerk to the house of lords which he would have to resign if he took the exchequer, while Plumer Ward wrote in horror to Lonsdale that he was finally convinced 'the times are sadly out of joint'.[3] Rose himself was as terrified as anyone. He seemed, Perceval reported to Windsor, 'much to dread the change of his situation and to apprehend that at his time of life to embark on such an office as that of the Chancellor of the Exchequer might expose himself and the Government to some ridicule'. The next day Rose added to the long list of refusals, pleading his age, his lack of talent in debate, and the difficulty there would be in replacing him at the board of trade. A fortnight later he sent Perceval a long memorandum stressing the critical state of the nation's finances: the prime minister lacked help, but not advice.[4] Even then Perceval did not give up hope. On 24 October he offered the exchequer to that old party campaigner, Charles Long. Fortunately Long had the sense to refuse. After the fifth refusal Perceval reluctantly decided, at least temporarily, to keep the exchequer himself, although he declined to draw the double salary.[5]

At the end of the year Perceval was at least able to give a little more of his time to financial problems. From then on his troubles

[1] Malmesbury, Letters, vol. II, pp. 161 and 164.
[2] Windsor MSS., 14737-8, Perceval to George III, 21 Oct. 1809; 14739-40, same to same, 23 Oct. 1809; Malmesbury, Letters, vol. III, pp. 167-9; Perceval MSS., Perceval to Arden, 24 Oct. 1809.
[3] Malmesbury, vol. III, p. 164; R. P. Ward, Memoirs, vol. I, p. 275; Perceval MSS., Arden to Perceval, 27 Oct. 1809.
[4] Add. MSS., 42774, fol. 276; Windsor MSS., 14739-40, Perceval to George III, 23 Oct. 1809; 14743-4, same to same, 24 Oct. 1809; Rose, vol. II, pp. 413, 420, and 432.   [5] Windsor MSS., 14743-4, Perceval to George III.

multiplied rapidly. Governments, even Pittite governments, were no longer the mouthpieces of the landlords of England. Both the financial needs of the war and the growing influence in the Commons of the members for the large towns began to affect cabinet decisions. Pitt's Friends, writes Professor Roberts, were, by 1807, the party of trade while the opposition, which later made *laissez-faire* its own, supported the agricultural interest. Many of the old guard thought Pitt's Friends had gone too far. 'I wish the landed interest was a little more considered,' wrote Redesdale to the Speaker, 'for I am sure it is the stay of the nation.' 'We must not act', Bathurst warned Perceval, 'as if we prefer'd the colonial to the landed interest of the country.' Late in 1809 Wynn was criticising the new Perceval cabinet because it contained 'not one man of old property, weight and influence in the country but that idiot Westmorland'.[1] The first direct clash between the Portland administration and the landed interest came early in 1808 after the appointment of a select committee to investigate the widespread distress in the West Indies. In order to help the planters, the committee recommended that distillation from grain should be prohibited in order to give a monopoly to sugar and molasses. This immediately aroused the country gentry, led by Sir Henry Mildmay and Charles Western, one of the members for Maldon in Essex. 'The landed interest', claimed Perceval's old school companion, William Chute, 'was sufficiently depressed, and the influence of members whose consequence arose from trade was already sufficiently great, without striking a general blow at an extensive branch of the agriculture of the country.' In the end only a formal disclaimer from Perceval of any intentional government hostility towards landlords prevented the agriculturalists from dividing against the presentation of the report.[2] There followed a series of hostile petitions from the shires and favourable ones from the towns. By the time Lord Binning, the chairman of

---

[1] M. Roberts, *The Whig Party, 1807–12*, p. 237; Colchester, vol. II, p. 160; Perceval MSS., Bathurst to Perceval, 14 Oct. 1810; Nat. Lib. of Wales MSS., 4814, fol. 58. In June 1810 Sir John Sinclair asked to be made a privy councillor, 'not only as a compliment to the landed interest which might in different respects be of service, but also to enable me to bring agricultural matters more effectually under the consideration of the Board of Trade' (Perceval MSS., Sir John Sinclair to Perceval, 26 June 1810).

[2] *Parl. Deb.*, XI, 56–9. For the report of the committee on the commercial state of the West Indies (1807) see *Parl. Deb.*, IX, *Parl. Papers*, LXXXI ff. For comments on the report see the *Quarterly Review*, Aug. 1808, pp. 8 ff. (For Huskisson's comments see Add. MSS., 38737, fols. 219–20; *Edinburgh Review*, Jan. 1809, pp. 383–94.)

the committee, was ready to introduce resolutions based on the report the country gentry were up in arms.[1] Great Britain, argued Binning, now depended on foreign grain to feed its population, but European supplies were cut off. The 1807 harvest had been so poor that there was a distinct threat of famine, particularly in Ireland. Prohibition would save 470,000 quarters of wheat, or half the loss due to the stoppage of imports. He proposed that prohibition should, therefore, last from 1 July to 1 October 1808, and that the privy council should be empowered to extend this period at its discretion. Immediately the debate became acrimonious. Gascoyne, one of the members for Liverpool, was constantly interrupted by deliberate coughing and one by one the knights of the shire rose to condemn the proposal. Sensing victory in the lobbies, the opposition rallied to the country gentry. Amidst jeers Perceval tried to argue that this was a temporary measure to fight the threat of starvation: if faced with a straight choice between agricultural and West Indian interests the ministry would never have sacrificed the landlords. Finally Foster, the Irish chancellor of the exchequer, caused a sensation by attacking the resolutions as 'contrary to all the acknowledged maxims of agriculture' and by announcing that he would vote against his colleagues. When the House divided at four in the morning, the government scraped through by 122 votes to 108.[2] During the committee stage, taken before the whole House four days later, the agriculturalists again forced a division and, backed by the opposition, polled 127 votes against the ministry's 163.[3]

The cabinet had pushed through its policy, but by defeating not convincing the country gentry. The measure, indeed, fell with particular severity on Scotland, where oats and barley were the only grain cultivated over three-fourths of the country. It was doubtful, grumbled the *Farmers' Magazine*, 'whether the bill would enable West Indian planters to pay their taxes': 'it is certain that Scots farmers will not be enabled to pay theirs'.[4] The harvest of 1808, however, fully justified the government's policy. Eight months of stormy winter were followed by an exceptionally hot, dry summer and a wet and foggy autumn. Wheat crops were of poor quality and reduced by a quarter; peas and beans were short; barley and oats only average. The following year Britain had to import 1,500,000 quarters of wheat under licence

[1] *Parl. Deb.*, XI, 252, 392 and 412; *Political Register*, 21 May 1808, p. 823.
[2] *Parl. Deb.*, XI, 431–46.
[3] *Ibid.*, XI, 493–537 and 706. On the third reading the voting dropped to 74 to 34 in favour of the proposals (*Ibid.*, 870).
[4] Smart, *Economic Annals of the Nineteenth Century*, pp. 172–3.

from France and in 1810 the ban on distillation from grain still continued, 'much to the indignation of those who witnessed in the autumn
a public thanksgiving ordered for the plentiful harvest at the same
time as the distillation from grain was prohibited on account of the
scarcity'. But, as the *Day* pointed out, only 400,000 quarters of barley
was used in distilleries and this was not one-thousandth of the total
grain production of the country. Why did not the landowners set
about growing at home the millions of tons of grain that had been
imported from Europe to feed the population? 'Considerable but insensible changes', it concluded, 'have taken place in the different orders
of the community during the last century; and it is not impossible that
the landed interest of the present day may not be exactly what the
landed interest was a century since and that the change has been so imperceptible as to escape the notice even of the individuals themselves who
compose that respectable class.'[1] The cabinet's policy on the bullion
issue and on Lord King's letter only underlined the same lesson.

By the summer of 1809 there were clear signs of an impending
internal financial breakdown, due to the depreciation of the bank of
England's paper money. Ever since cash payments had been suspended, under an order in council by the Pitt ministry in 1797, successive governments had faced recurring currency problems. In 1797
the shortage of coin had forced the Bank to issue captured Spanish
dollars, with a small head of George III superimposed on that of the
Spanish monarch. Although the bullion value of the dollar was only
four shillings and eightpence, they were issued at four shillings and
ninepence with the result that unscrupulous dealers bought dollars in
the open market, stamped them, and made a profit of a penny on every
dollar. In 1805 a sudden rise in the price of copper made one and twopenny pieces worth more than their face value, causing a grave shortage
as so many were illegally melted down. Fluctuations in the value of
silver had a similar effect on the circulation of dollars, in spite of
savage laws and frequent death penalties for counterfeiting and forging. In October 1808 a deputation of bankers met the cabinet and
stressed the damage caused to trade by the wretchedness and shortage
of silver coin. In the end ministers decided to order a new issue of
half-crowns, shillings, and sixpences.[2] Until 1808 however there was
little cause to suspect the soundness of the Bank's paper pound notes,

---

[1] *Parl. Deb.*, XI, 182, 198 and 213; *Day*, 13 Apr. 1811.
[2] Phillips, *Token Money of the Bank of England*, pp. 1–19; *Sun*, 22 Oct. 1808.
In 1803 it was decided to defer the resumption of cash payments until six months

although there were always many counterfeits in circulation, many of them produced by French prisoners of war to relieve the tedium of captivity. One pamphleteer claimed, as early as 1797, that the suspension of cash payments would lead to an excessive issue of paper notes and consequently adversely affect the rates of exchange and drive up the price of food.[1] Only in Dublin were these worst fears realised. There the bank of Ireland recklessly quadrupled its note issue in six years: the rate of exchange on London fell by 30% while the London–Belfast exchange (which had a coin and local bank note circulation) remained at par.[2] The directors of the bank of England resisted such temptations. The Bank was free of all government control and no ministry sought to persuade it to increase its paper issue to back war expenditure as long as £20,000,000 could be raised annually through the funding system. The Bank, moreover, regularly published the total of its paper issue as a further safeguard against excess. The total value of notes in circulation increased between 1793 and 1808 from a little under £13,500,000 to just over £17,500,000, a very moderate expansion in view of the country's growing population and the replacement of gold by small bank notes. 'If', wrote Henry Thornton in 1802, 'there has been any fault in the conduct of the Bank of England, the fault, as I conceive, has rather been . . . on the side of too much restricting its notes in the late seasons of alarm, than on that of too much enlarging them.'[3]

By 1808 the position had, however, become more serious. After Napoleon's Continental System, the British Orders in Council, and the American Non-Intercourse Acts, the nation's economic life became feverish and uncertain while the sudden opening of South American markets led to reckless and fundamentally unsound commercial speculation.[4] The Bank's annual commercial discounts, which in 1797 had been less than £5,500,000, leapt between 1808 and 1810 from £13,000,000 to £20,000,000.[5] Bank of England notes began to depreciate and all gold to disappear. 'The scarcity of gold', wrote the *Sun*

after the ratification of a definitive treaty of peace. For a summary of the situation which led to suspension see J. J. Grellier, *Terms of all the Public Loans*, London, 1812.

[1] W. Anderson, *The Iniquity of Banking, or Banknote proved to be an Injury to the Public, and the Real Cause of the Exorbitant Prices of Provisions*, 1797.

[2] Henry Parnell, *Observations upon the State of Currency in Ireland*, 1804, p. 7.

[3] Henry Thornton, *An Enquiry into the Nature and Effects of the Paper Credit of Great Britain*, p. 127.   [4] Clapham, *The Bank of England*, vol. II, p. 18.

[5] E. Cannan, *The Paper Pound*, Introduction, xliii.

in July 1809, 'exceeds that of any period for many years past.' There were rumours that itinerant Jews were buying all types of gold coin for illegal export at from $1\frac{1}{2}\%$ to 5% premium. In November Perceval told the treasury board that a certain Dutchman was purchasing seven-shilling pieces at eight shillings and large quantities of guineas for twenty-seven shillings each. A month later Harrison of the treasury was instructing the mint to report all persons 'purchasing current gold coin of this realm at a price above its current value' to the government law officers, who would proceed against them under 'the statute of 5th and 6th Edward 6th c. 191'. But such measures were useless. Guineas, Lord Folkestone reported to Creevey, were passing for twenty-two shillings in paper at Winchester while the press claimed that £1 notes fetched only eighteen shillings at Flushing. That August coast-guards seized one consignment of chests containing 30,000 guineas bound for the continent.[1] By the end of the year there were even rumours that the Bank intended to try and relieve the shortage of currency by issuing ten-shilling notes. A generation that had seen the spectacular career of the French assignats began to have doubts about the stability of its own paper currency. David Ricardo, in a series of letters to the *Morning Chronicle*, argued that the total notes issue should slowly be reduced as soon as the difference between the mint and market price of gold disappeared.[2]

The issue was first raised in the Commons on 1 February 1810 when Francis Horner, an opposition member, moved for the production of papers relating to the shortage of bullion, and suggested the appointment of a select committee. He had, he said in a conciliatory speech, no wish to attack country banks or to suggest 'that the explanation of the cause of the present evils must be referred wholly to an undue issue of notes by the Bank of England'. Only the splenetic George Johnstone was prepared to denounce the Bank out of hand, but Davies Giddy, Magens, and Henry Thornton all supported the idea of a committee. Perceval then admitted that he could not see how a reduction of the total of Bank notes in circulation could affect the price of bullion. More likely causes of the crisis, he thought, were our great war expenditure, interruptions in our trade, and hoard-

[1] *Day*, 15 July, 3 Aug., and 16 Oct. 1809; P.R.O., T29/103/167; *Creevey Papers*, vol. I, p. 97; P.R.O., T1/1114/160.
[2] *Day*, 13 Dec. 1809; David Ricardo, *The High Price of Bullion a Proof of the Depreciation of Bank Notes* (1810), pp. 117–18; P.R.O., T27/65/280. On 3 June 1808 Huskisson had introduced a bill to forbid the issuing of notes below ten shillings in value (*Parl. Deb.*, XI, 810).

ing, suggestions which he threw out 'with great diffidence, as he was aware that he was not as well informed on the question as he hoped yet to be'.[1] Both Horner and Perceval seemed intent on avoiding a party debate, for Horner wanted a full inquiry while the prime minister feared to risk his majority in a division. Although the session was only a fortnight old, the Perceval ministry had already been defeated four times in the House and still had to face the crucial vote on the Walcheren expedition. In these circumstances Perceval had little time to study currency problems. The prime minister, according to Sir John Sinclair, having consented to the appointment of a committee, 'took hardly any concern in the nomination of its members'.[2] The result was a committee strong in both economists and whigs, but notably weak in ministerialists and spokesmen for the Bank. Twenty-one members, under the chairmanship of Horner himself, were appointed on 19 February. Only two of these, Perceval and Rose, were ministers and two others, Alexander Baring and William Manning, members of the Bank's court of directors. Perceval was too busy to attend the early sessions of the inquiry, Rose withdrew his name before the committee met, while Manning only accepted membership after consulting the Speaker. This left the ministry for a while without a single member on the committee. Not until 12 March, when the committee had met eleven times and the outline of its eventual report was already clear, did Perceval realise his mistake and nominate Charles Long as an additional member. Politically the committee had a majority of roughly two to one against the ministry. On the very question it was appointed to examine it had four of its most influential members who had already publicly prejudged the issue against the Bank. The committee, in short, was packed by Horner and his friends.[3]

[1] *Parl. Deb.*, XV, 269–77.
[2] Sinclair, *Observations on the Report of the Bullion Committee*, 1810, p. 5.
[3] The members of the committee were: Francis Horner (chairman), Perceval, Tierney, Earl Temple, Davies Giddy, Huskisson, Henry Thornton, Sheridan, Thomas Brand, William Dickinson, James Abercromby, J. L. Foster, Henry Parnell, Alexander Baring, William Manning, Richard Sharp, David Magens, John Irving, Pascoe Grenfell, Thomas Thompson, George Johnstone and (after 12 Mar.) Charles Long.
Six members—Perceval, Long, Manning, Irving, Foster and Johnstone—usually voted with the ministry. Nine—Brand, Dickinson, Grenfell, Horner, Parnell, Sharp, Sheridan, Temple and Tierney—always voted with the opposition. Three more—Abercromby, Baring and Thornton—tended to support the opposition at this time. The remaining four—Giddy, Huskisson, Magens and Thompson—could be classed as independents. Ten—Baring, Giddy, Grenfell, Horner, Huskisson, Magens, Manning, Parnell, Perceval and Thornton—

The inquiry lasted from 22 February to 25 April, the committee meeting thirty times to hear evidence from financiers, merchants, Bank and mint officials. Horner acted as chairman on nineteen occasions, Huskisson on seven, Thornton on three, and Davies Giddy once. From the first the bullionist majority dominated the proceedings and sought to prove that the high price and scarcity of bullion was the result of an excessive issue of paper money. The majority of witnesses, although closely pressed, doggedly denied that the total of paper notes in circulation had any connection with or influence on either the price of gold or the rates of exchange. It was, however, an untenable thesis and began to crack in the committee's third session, when Samuel Burns, a bullion broker, admitted that he preferred even light guinea pieces to a guinea's worth of notes. Witnesses like Aaron Goldsmid, a partner in the firm of brokers to the bank of England, and J. L. Greffulhe, a wealthy merchant, argued that our difficulties arose from an adverse balance of trade, caused by the fact that British imports and subsidies exceeded her exports, and aggravated by the American embargo as well as by the use of foreign shipping with high freight rates.[1] But by the end of February the inquiry had begun to take an ugly turn for both the government and the Bank. In the Commons both Huskisson and Rose publicly elaborated their previous memoranda to Perceval, causing 'no small degree of alarm throughout the country'. 'The spell', wrote the independent *Day*, 'is now dissolved; the danger which threatens the country stands revealed to every eye. . . . Stamped with ministerial authority, the imminent failure in our finances no longer seems the idle creation of party spirit.'[2] Meanwhile N. M. Rothschild, appearing modestly before the bullion committee as Mr. ——, a continental merchant, claimed that Bank notes had depreciated from 15% to 20% and that the adverse rates of exchange were caused by the use of an inconver-

---

specialised on finance. Four members—Parnell and Thornton (in pamphlets), Huskisson (in a memorandum) and Johnstone (in the Commons) had previously adopted a bullionist point of view. Thomas Thompson was himself a country banker. See *H. of C. Journal*, 1810, pp. 105, 111 and 166; P.R.O., Colchester MSS., 30/9/15, Manning to Abbot, 16 Feb. 1810.

[1] *Bullion Report*, Minutes of Evidence, pp. 17, 23, 30–5, 76.

[2] *Day*, 28 Feb. 1810. Huskisson's and Rose's gloomy prophecies had at least one good result; within a week Perceval received an anonymous letter containing £1,600 'the amount of certain duties which had been omitted to be paid, and of which the person who sent it was anxious not to defraud the public' (*Sun*, 6 Mar. 1810).

tible paper currency. Even worse damage was done, inadvertently, by
John Whitmore and John Pearce, the governor and deputy governor
of the Bank. Both admitted that, as in their view 'the amount of our
paper circulation has no reference at all to the state of the exchange',
the Bank had not regulated its note issues either in relation to the state
of foreign exchanges or to the difference between the mint and market
price of gold. The only check they accepted was that all discounts of
merchants' bills should be 'confined to paper of undoubted solidity,
arising out of real commercial transactions, and payable at short and
fixed intervals'.[1] In fact their evidence was not as foolish as it seemed
to the dogmatic bullionists on the committee. The Bank only advanced
credit to discount authentic mercantile bills, payable after a maximum
of sixty-one days, and at a rate of interest of 5 % a year. This, together
with the government policy of periodically reducing the floating debt
by funding, did limit the total issues of the Bank, as the market rate
of interest on bills did not for long or to any great extent exceed 5 %
a year. But Whitmore's claim that the rate of interest could be lowered
to 4 % or even 3 % and his tacit approval of a perpetual suspension of
cash payments did irreparable harm. When Perceval, finally realising
the danger of a hostile report, intervened in the inquiry the battle
was already lost. In vain Perceval emphasised, in a memorandum presented to the committee, that any reduction in the total currency in
circulation would hit government and merchants alike. After long and
fierce debates in the committee Horner and Thornton carried their
bullionist motions against the prime minister by eleven votes to four.[2]

Six weeks after the inquiry closed the bullion committee had completed its report.[3] It was, admitted Horner, 'very clumsily and pro-
lixily drawn' for Huskisson, Thornton, and Horner himself each wrote
sections 'which we tacked together without any care to give them a
uniform style or a very exact connection'. In essence the report claimed
that an excessive note issue had caused 'a general rise of all prices, a
rise in the market price of gold, and a fall of the foreign exchanges'.
'The suspension of cash payments', it continued, 'has had the effect
of committing into the hands of the directors of the Bank of England,

---

[1] For Rothschild's evidence see *Bullion Report*, Minutes of Evidence, p. 101.
For Whitmore's and Pearce's evidence see *ibid.*, pp. 110, 126, 173.

[2] Tooke, *A History of Prices*, p. 159; J. C. Colquhoun, *William Wilberforce,
His Friends and His Times*, p. 301; Sinclair, *op. cit.*, p. 5; Perceval's memorandum
is in the Perceval MSS. The minority was probably composed of Perceval, Long,
Manning and Thompson.

[3] *H. of C. Journal*, 1810, p. 478.

to be exercised by their sole discretion, the important charge of supplying the country with that quantity of circulating medium which is exactly proportioned to the wants and occasions of the public. In the judgement of the committee, that is a trust, which it is unreasonable to expect that the directors of the Bank of England should ever be able to discharge.' The report therefore recommended a resumption of cash payments within a period of two years.[1] The committee's opinion was nothing if not dogmatic: it stated as 'most clear' theories formed 'decidedly' on incomplete evidence on the most speculative topics. E. V. Morgan and Sir William Beveridge have since shown that during the whole period of suspension there was very little correlation between the general level of prices and the volume of Bank notes in circulation. In general, price changes preceded changes in note issues.[2] In fact, although the bullion committee took no evidence on prices, they assumed a rise and blamed this on 'the state of the currency of this country'. But Tooke proved that, with the exception of some food prices which rose after the failure of the 1809 harvest, prices were falling rapidly at the time the report was issued. Between 1810 and May 1811 even corn prices fell from an average of 115 to 110 shillings to 86 shillings a quarter.[3] Similarly the committee grossly over-simplified the relation between total note circulation and the state of the exchanges. Even the bullionists disagreed among themselves on the issue, for Huskisson, Thornton, and Baring argued that the depression was originally caused by an adverse balance of trade and only perpetuated by an excessive note issue, while Horner put the whole blame on over-issue.[4] None of them was concerned with the effects of war expenditure. Yet Tooke was later able to demonstrate that rates of exchange invariably improved whenever expenditure in gold diminished abroad. When the payment of foreign subsidies finally ended, both the exchanges and the price of gold were restored to par, although the total of Bank notes in circulation was then higher than

[1] *Annual Register*, 1810, pp. 127 ff.

[2] E. V. Morgan, *The Theory and Practice of Central Banking*, pp. 23 ff.; *Oxford Economic Papers 1940*, Sir William Beveridge, *Trade Cycles in Britain before 1850*; Jevons, *Investigations in Currency and Finance*, p. 144; *British Association Trans.*, June 1865, Jevons, *On the Variations of Prices and the Value of the Currency since 1782*, p. 303.

[3] Tooke, *A History of Prices*, p. 309. Prices fluctuated on the continent as much as they did in England.

[4] Horner, vol. II, p. 61. For a detailed summary of movements in the exchanges see Robert Mushet, *An Inquiry into the Effects of . . . the Bank Restriction Bill*, 1811. (Particularly the tables on pp. 104 ff.)

ever before. 'In the divergence between the paper and the gold', concluded Tooke, 'it was the gold that by increased demand departed
from the paper, and not the paper by increased quantity from the
gold.'[1]

The publication of the report coincided with and deepened a depression on the stock exchange. Throughout July omnium varied from
$1\frac{1}{2}$% to $2\frac{1}{2}$% discount and there were 'many strange fluctuations' in
the price of other stocks. August saw a steady improvement, but the
appearance of the report early in September caused a serious slump.
On the eighteenth the market was 'in a dreadfully depressed state'
with omnium quoted at $5\frac{1}{2}$% discount. By the following day omnium
touched rock bottom at $7\frac{1}{4}$% discount while consols fell to $65\frac{1}{4}$. That
afternoon Randle Jackson, a Bank director, in a speech to a quarterly
meeting of the proprietors, opened the public attack on the report.
It was, he claimed, forced through by the opposition majority on the
committee and was, moreover, 'at variance with, nay in contradiction
to, the evidence given before that committee'. It was yet another
attack on 'those great capitalists, upon whom it seemed to be so much
the fashion in these days to cast a slur'. The Bank's note issue, far from
being excessive, was 'parsimonious in the extreme'.[2] Jackson's speech,
rapturously applauded in the ministerialist press, rallied anti-bullionist
opinion, but, reported the independent *Day*, 'it appears to us rather
to have opened the discussion than to have settled it'.[3] Throughout the
parliamentary recess of 1810 the controversy raged in the press, in
periodicals, and, most fiercely, in a flood of pamphlets. 'Every day I
hear of converts', wrote Horner to Duguld Stewart in November.
The bullionists' arguments were gaining ground 'against the prejudices of a large part of the English public' and in spite of the Bank's
and the government's 'acts of misrepresentation'.[4] For once even the
Edinburgh and *Quarterly Reviews* could agree, for both strongly
backed the report. As early as the autumn of 1808 the *Edinburgh Review*
had suggested that all advances on taxes should be borrowed by the
government from money dealers and private banks rather than from
the bank of England. Sums advanced from private sources represented only a temporary withdrawal and subsequent re-issue of the

---

[1] Tooke, *op. cit.*, pp. 144, 157–8, 172.

[2] *Day*, 18, 19, 24 July, 18, 19, 21 Sep. 1810; *Sun*, 20 and 21 Sep. 1810. The day
after Jackson's speech there was an improvement on the stock exchange (*Day*,
22 Sep. 1810).

[3] *Day*, 22 Sep. 1810.

[4] Horner, vol. II, pp. 59–60.

sum concerned from the total of notes in circulation. The bank of
England, in contrast, often printed new notes to cover advances to
the government, thus adding to an already excessive issue.[1] After the
publication of the bullion report the *Edinburgh Review* campaigned
for the establishment of one or more other national banks to reduce
the exorbitant power of Threadneedle Street. Even French assignats,
it claimed, were more worthy of trust than bank of England notes,
and unless parliament enforced the recommendations of the bullion
committee, 'the disorder in our currency which we have at present
experienced will be absolutely nothing compared with that which we
must then look forward to'.[2] The *Quarterly Review*, under strong
Canningite influence, was equally alarmist. The trading world, it
admitted, would suffer from a restriction in the note issue, but the
alternative was financial chaos.[3] The anti-bullionist case, thanks to
treasury influence, got more support in the daily press. The ever-
faithful *Sun* boasted of Britain's commercial prosperity under the
restriction of cash payments while the *Day*, forgetting its earlier impartiality, pointed to the increasing surplus of the consolidated fund.[4]

Meanwhile pamphlets on the currency question poured from the
presses, doing as much to obscure as to clarify the real issues.
The ablest defence of the bullion report was made in Huskisson's
*The Question Concerning the Depreciation of Our Currency Stated and
Examined*, intended as a simple exposition of the bullionist case for
lay readers. Huskisson began by sketching the development of his own
views. As secretary to the treasury his 'incessant occupations and
multiplied duties' left him little time for economic theory, 'and this is
far from the only instance in which the studies and self-examination of
retirement have shown me how great in every respect (assiduity
perhaps excepted) were my own deficiencies in office'. Even after his
resignation he remained convinced that Napoleon's commercial policy
and the Anglo-American trade dispute accounted for the adverse
exchanges. His conversion began after hearing Whitmore and Pearce
admit that the Bank paid no attention to the mint and market price of
gold or to the state of the exchange in regulating its note issue.[5]

---

[1] *Edinburgh Review*, Oct. 1808, p. 60.

[2] *Ibid.*, Feb. 1811, pp. 351–70. The *Edinburgh Review* suggested that the Bank
should be forced to reduce its total note circulation by £1 million a year.

[3] *Quarterly Review*, Feb. 1810, p. 161.

[4] *Sun*, 27 Apr. 1811; *Day*, 9 Mar. and 12 Apr. 1811.

[5] Huskisson, *The Question Concerning the Depreciation of Our Currency Stated
and Examined*, Preface XVII–XIX.

Thereafter he became increasingly convinced that Bank notes had depreciated. By law one pound of gold was divided into 44½ guineas or £46 14s. 6d. By this division, which was made at the public expense with no charge for coinage, nothing was added to or taken away from the value of the gold. Consequently £46 14s. 6d. worth of currency ought to be exchangeable at will for one pound of gold. Yet, at the time the bullion report was issued, £46 14s. 6d. in paper was exchangeable for only 10½ ounces of gold, while one pound of gold would produce £56 in paper. Therefore, concluded Huskisson, the difference between £56 and £46 14s. 6d. or between one pound and 10½ ounces of gold resulted from the depreciation of paper notes, and was the measure of that depreciation.[1] The argument was, theoretically, unassailable, but Huskisson wrote as though victory in a world war were an irrelevance.[2]

Perceval, though less able an economist, at least saw the basic weakness immediately. On 28 October Huskisson sent his former chief a copy of the preface to his pamphlet straight from the press, modestly apologising for having taken so little trouble 'to lick this burbling into a shape which may fit it to meet the public eye'. He was most anxious that the issue should not be 'claimed or used in Parliament as a party question and that Government may not be driven or expected to meet it as such'. 'I shall', replied Perceval, 'read your pamphlet with every attention in my power. I must confess, however, that I retain all the ignorance and [remain] under all the prejudice which influenced me on the committee before the publication of the report ... and certainly neither the reading of that report nor the circumstances which have since occurred have in any degree diminished my apprehensions of the ruinous consequence of which that report recommends.'[3] In a letter to Croker, Perceval frankly outlined his objections to Huskisson's work. 'It is in many parts very able,' he wrote, 'in all very specious, in many, however, I presume to think, very fallacious, and particularly unfair in keeping out of sight so much as it does the ... interrupted commercial intercourse with the continent. . . .' The truth in the dispute for and against the report, he thought, 'probably lies between the two

---

[1] *Ibid.*, pp. 12–13.
[2] The only reference to the war in the pamphlet occurs on p. 148. Most of Huskisson's friends, wrote Herries to Gentz, were annoyed with him for the attitude he took in the bullion controversy (Herries MSS., letter books, vol. I, pp. 86–90).
[3] Perceval MSS., Huskisson to Perceval, 28 Oct. 1810; Perceval to Huskisson, 30 Oct. 1810.

extremes of opinion'. Yet the prime minister's own attitude was clear. The practical danger and difficulty of adopting the report so outweighed the alleged mischief caused by a depreciated paper currency 'that I should consider the measure [Huskisson] proposes as tantamount to a Parliamentary declaration that we must submit to any terms of peace rather than continue the war, which I apprehend, under his project would be found utterly impossible'.[1] From the first Perceval had grasped the essential point of the debate: once he had done so no subtlety of argument could confuse or confound him. Less able bullionist pamphleteers only played into Perceval's hands. Sir Philip Francis in his *Reflections on the Abundance of Paper in Circulation* argued that the state was 'essentially impoverished' and 'going headlong into real beggary'. His remedy was to 'stop your foreign expenses. Sell more than you buy; and then the wealth that has left you will gradually come back again.'[2]

Those who rejected the committee's report weakened their case by trying to attack its economic theory instead of concentrating on its political impracticability. George Chalmers, one of Perceval's family friends, was content to laud 1809 as the greatest year of national prosperity, while John Grenfell in *A Defence of Bank Notes* argued that the wealth of a nation consisted not in gold and silver but in 'the industry, skill and abilities of its workmen, the excellence of its machinery for shortening hours and the magnitude and application of its accumulated capital'.[3] Robert Mushet, an official of the mint, broke more promising ground by studying the course of foreign exchanges since the suspension of cash payments; even Herries wrote a pamphlet, but decided to publish it anonymously because of his close connection with Perceval.[4] More important, and unintentionally more harmful to the Bank's case, were pamphlets by Sir John Sinclair, the member for Caithness, and by Charles Bosanquet. Sinclair, a born publicist, sent a copy of his *Observations on the Report of the Bullion Committee* to every M.P. It is doubtful if many of them managed to read it. An abundant paper currency, claimed Sinclair, was 'a mine of national

---

[1] Croker, *Correspondence*, vol. I, p. 34. Horner (*Memoirs*, vol. II, p. 61) thought Huskisson's pamphlet 'excellent'. The *Quarterly Review* (Nov. 1810, pp. 414–53) also praised it very highly.

[2] Sir Philip Francis, *Reflections on the Abundance of Paper in Circulation* (London, 1810), pp. 3, 18 and 26.

[3] George Chalmers, *Considerations of Commerce* (London, 1811), p. 228; John Grenfell, *A Defence of Bank Notes* (London, 1810), p. 9.

[4] Robert Mushet, *An Inquiry into the Effects of . . . . the Bank Restriction Bill* (London, 1811); Herries MSS., letter books, vol. I, pp. 86–90.

prosperity'. 'The wonder is, not that provisions are high, but that with such a war, against such an enemy, with armies in every quarter of the globe and fleets commanding every ocean in it, we should be able at the same time to carry on our agriculture, manufactures and commerce in the manner and to the extent we are doing.' [1] Adverse rates of exchange were not caused by an excessive issue of paper. There were, according to Sinclair, seventeen reasons, eight of them commercial, two mixed, three political, and four miscellaneous.[2] Charles Bosanquet's *Practical Observations* was most useful in its examination of price changes since suspension and weakest in searching for a standard by which to prove that paper notes had not depreciated at all.[3] The bullion report, said the *Quarterly Review*, was attacked by 'a numerous musquetry, and by a few light field pieces, but . . . not by anything of a larger calibre'. In fact, for want of concert, the Bank's apologists were inclined to pour in their fire upon each other.[4]

During the pamphlet war of the parliamentary recess, Perceval spent most of his time with Jane and the children at Ealing. But on 28 September he was forced to return to town by news of another crisis. Abraham Goldsmid, the chief contractor for the 1810 loan, cut his throat after finding he faced bankruptcy. The *Sun* reported depressingly that he held £2,000,000 worth of omnium, while the stock exchange experienced 'the greatest fluctuation that ever was known'. Three per cent stocks opened at $65\frac{1}{2}$, only to fall to $63\frac{3}{4}$; omnium began at a discount of seven and dropped to ten; exchequer bills, which had recently been at a premium, closed at a discount of three shillings. Rumours circulated that the Bank might refuse to pay instalments of the loan for omnium holders, thus leaving the government without the means of meeting routine monthly expenditure. 'We think this', reported the *Day*, 'one of the most trying circumstances in which the Government of this country was ever placed.' Perceval immediately asked three leading merchants, John Barrett, Thomas

---

[1] Sir John Sinclair, *Observations on the Report of the Bullion Committee* (London, 1810), pp. 23 and 42.

[2] *Quarterly Review*, Nov. 1810, pp. 518–36.

[3] Charles Bosanquet, *Practical Observations on the Report of the Bullion Committee* (London, 1810), pp. 42 and 100. Both Sinclair and Bosanquet published direct answers to Huskisson's pamphlet. See Sir John Sinclair, *Remarks on a pamphlet entitled 'The Question concerning the Depreciation of our Currency'* (London, 1811), and Charles Bosanquet, *Supplement to Practical Observations* (London, 1811). For a review of Sinclair's reply see the *Quarterly Review*, Feb. 1811, p. 139.

[4] *Quarterly Review, loc. cit.*

Bainbridge, and J. P. Kensington to examine Goldsmid's books. They found that he held just over £466,000 worth of exchequer bills, mostly on account of the treasurer of the navy. On 30 September Perceval called a meeting at the treasury of all leading financiers, when Goldsmid's business associates announced that their late colleague also owed £1,775,000 to private creditors, making a total deficit of £2,243,000 against estimated assets of £2,104,000. Perceval had arrived at the meeting with a process against Goldsmid's estate which he had decided to issue so as to safeguard the exchequer. He was, however, soon convinced that the greater part of the dead man's estate consisted of government stock that was mortgaged to other creditors and consequently was out of reach of a Crown process until those creditors had been satisfied.[1] Had the stock been sold at current prices it would not have produced sufficient to meet the demands of both private creditors and the exchequer. It would have left creditors who had no security to a 'certain and total loss' and, by suddenly throwing a large quantity of stock on the market, it would have deepened the existing depression. Accordingly Perceval proposed the appointment of thirty-eight managers, nominated by the lords of the treasury and the governor of the Bank, who would 'ensure to all the creditors a judicious management of the funds and an honest application of their proceeds'. He even agreed to waive the priority of the Crown's debt and allowed all creditors to come in *pari passu* with the Crown itself for a dividend on a legal debt.[2] As soon as news of the settlement was released both consuls and omnium rose sharply on the stock exchange: the threat of a major collapse had been averted by prompt and generous action. The prime minister's handling of the case, wrote one creditor, after Perceval's death, was sufficient 'to cover [his] memory . . . with honour and gratitude'.[3]

When parliament re-assembled early in 1811, the bullion report had already been published for five months. A speedy debate was essential to end the prevailing uncertainty. On 14 February Horner moved for various accounts and papers, but refused to reply when challenged by Sir John Sinclair to name a date for the debate.[4] The king's illness and Horner's own legal duties then delayed action for another seven weeks. On 5 April Horner announced that he would

[1] *Sun*, 29 Sep. 1810; *Day*, 29 Sep. 1810; P.R.O., T29/107/480–91; Windsor MSS., 15500–7, Perceval to George III, 28 and 29 Sep. and 2 Oct. 1810.

[2] *Day*, 1 Oct. 1810; Add. MSS., 38245, fol. 203.

[3] *Day*, 3 and 12 Oct. 1810; Add. MSS., 38247, fol. 260.

[4] *Parl. Deb.*, XVII, 1212 and 1215.

move certain unspecified resolutions before a committee of the whole House on the twenty-ninth. A week later he gave details of his proposals in sixteen resolutions.[1] The first fifteen gave a bullionist analysis of the existing position, while the last, and most important, called for a resumption of cash payments within two years. Even his own supporters were divided on the sixteenth resolution: there had, admitted Henry Thornton, been 'many shades of opinion in the committee' on the resumption issue.[2] The anti-bullionist resolutions were tabled on 24 April by Nicholas Vansittart, the financial specialist of the Sidmouth group. His seventeen resolutions included the now familiar mass of figures on rates of exchange and on prices. Parliament was asked to confirm that the war-time interruption of trade, rather than a depreciated currency, had caused the unfavourable state of the foreign exchanges and the high price of bullion. Cash payments should be resumed 'whenever the political and commercial relations of the country shall render it compatible with the public interest'.[3] Much of Vansittart's theory was ludicrous: his third resolution invited the House, in the face of all the facts, to pledge themselves that bank notes were regarded as equivalent to the legal coin of the realm. But Vansittart himself saw no weak links in the chain. His resolutions, he told the Speaker, 'appear to me to make a strong case and, though I cannot flatter myself that it will be generally thought conclusive, I hope it will in some instances place the zeal of our friends upon better grounds of knowledge. . . .' [4] Finally, after yet another week's delay, the vital Commons debate began on 6 May.

For seven days members sat through a series of lengthy speeches, most of them models, said Tooke, of 'ingeniously perplexed and elaborately unintelligible general reasoning'. 'Thus,' said Henry Parnell in one passage from his speech, 'the standard of a pound sterling is 3 ozs. 11 dwts. $14\frac{22}{31}$ grains troy of fine silver, which is equal to 3 ozs. 17 dwts. $10\frac{2}{3}$ grains of silver 11 ozs. 2 dwts. fine, which is our standard of fineness. The standard of a shilling is $73\frac{29}{31}$ grains troy of fine silver, or $80\frac{28}{31}$ grains of silver 111/12 fine.' [5] It says much for the tenacity of the House that over 220 members stuck it out and were

[1] *Ibid.*, XIX, 726 and 757.
[2] *Ibid.*, XX, 80–1. Thornton himself had 'expressed a wish to soften the terms used in that part of the report which suggested that the restriction should cease in two years'.
[3] *Annual Register*, 1811, pp. 44 ff.; *Parl. Deb.*, XIX, 758.
[4] P.R.O., Colchester MSS., 30/9/15, Vansittart to Abbot, 24 Apr. 1811.
[5] *Parl. Deb.*, XIX, 1031.

still present to vote on Horner's resolutions. Both sides bolstered their
case with a mass of statistics, by no means all of which were either
accurate or relevant. Nor did the anti-bullionists have a monopoly of
patently absurd theory. Sir Francis Baring said he thought a paper
circulation of £11,000,000 would be excessive, although to have attempted deflation on anything like this scale in time of war would
have been suicidal. In fact the entire debate, tedious as it was, did little
to clarify the issue. On many vital points there was no generally accepted basic evidence; the two sides, for instance, could not agree
whether we had a favourable or unfavourable balance of payments.
At the end of it all many a perplexed and dazed country gentleman
must have decided to rely on his original prejudices to guide him in
the divisions.

Francis Horner opened the debate with a speech which filled thirty-
two columns of the *Parliamentary Debates*.[1] From the start he was on
the defensive, paying a tribute to the Bank and protesting against 'a prejudice that represents us as mere theorists, and as setting up our theory
against the conclusions of practice and experience'. The bullion committee had worked with a firm determination to make 'the most ample,
accurate and impartial scrutiny into the subject, and to suspend judgement till that scrutiny was accomplished'. The market price of gold,
he claimed, was 20% above its mint price and a £1 note would purchase only 15*s*. 10*d*. worth of gold. At Amsterdam guineas were selling for twelve guilders while a paper pound would fetch no more than
seven. He then quoted figures for the price of corn to support his
argument for depreciation and denounced the Bank for having issued
an additional £2,000,000 worth of notes since the committee's report
had been issued. But as soon as he returned to his own resolutions he
fell back on to the defensive. This was, he admitted, a remedy that
ought to be administered with great caution: even an admission that
depreciation existed would do much good. His opponents would
argue that this was impossible in time of war, but this should not deter
the legislature from trying to restore the currency to a sound and legitimate state. There followed a marathon effort by George Rose which
filled sixty-two columns of print.[2] He treated the House to a detailed
examination of the report, which, he claimed, was contrary to the
evidence and contained more errors than any that had ever been
presented to parliament. Unfortunately he was soon firmly bogged
down in a welter of quotations, trade, currency, and price statistics

[1] *Parl. Deb.*, XIX, 798–830.   [2] *Ibid.*, XIX, 833–95.

by means of which he sought to deny that the amount of notes in circulation was directly linked to either the market price of gold or the state of the exchanges. The bullionist Henry Thornton who spoke next was, by the standards of the debates, remarkably brief, confining himself to 'great and broad principles'.[1] His preliminary lecture on economic theory far surpassed both Horner's and Rose's efforts, but he was less effective when he came to deal with the resolutions before the House. A return to cash payments, he said, amidst cries of assent from the treasury benches, might lead to 'considerable pressure' on the economy. 'What degree of pressure might result', he continued, 'was not the main point now under consideration. He did not care at this moment what gentlemen said as to this point. He was in search of a principle.' This, to non-specialists in the House who were more concerned with such mundane matters as the effect on the country's war effort, was a most damaging admission. When the Commons adjourned at one-thirty in the morning Perceval must have been well content with the way the debate had gone.

The following day's discussion began with a speech by Nicholas Vansittart which rivalled Rose's in length and complexity.[2] Vansittart was at his best in ridiculing the bullionists. They spoke about the loss of our standard as though it were 'something visible and tangible, which had been accidently mislaid, and that we ought to offer a reward for bringing it back again'. Horner had sought to establish premises while hesitating about his own conclusions. 'He asserts the existence of an enormous evil, for which he says, we have a safe and certain remedy in our hands, yet he desires us to recognise the existence of the evil, but to postpone the remedy.' Thereafter Vansittart plunged into figures which were far less effective than his earlier debating points. Huskisson, who followed, was, like most bullionist speakers, at his best when expounding theory.[3] He 'certainly would allow there were inconveniences' attached to Horner's resolutions, but if the Bank used its profits to buy bullion, he 'hoped and trusted' they could accumulate enough to resume cash payments by 1813. Castlereagh, the last main speaker that evening, defended the suspension of cash payments as a 'conservative' measure, similar to the suspension of habeas corpus and

[1] *Ibid.*, XIX, 895–919.
[2] *Ibid.*, XIX, 919–67.
[3] *Ibid.*, XIX, 967–85. He made very effective play with Vansittart's discussion of an 'abstract standard'. Most of the supporters of this idea were employed by the government 'and it would be worth their while to consider how they would be satisfied by an abstract payment of their salaries' (*Ibid.*, XIX, 978).

the proclaiming of martial law: it had 'solved the problem of reconciling national prosperity with a state of war'. If, as the bullionists
suggested, we were to regulate our note issue according to the state
of the foreign exchanges, we should virtually be surrendering our
economy to enemy control. 'The value of property would become so
uncertain, that no man could judge one day what it would be worth the
next. The quantity of circulating medium must be so enormously and
rapidly reduced as to throw everything into confusion.' [1] As economic
theory it was mostly arrant and alarmist nonsense: as a vote-catching
speech it was probably the most successful of the night. At two in the
morning the House rose.

When the Commons reassembled on 8 May members showed clear
signs of exhaustion and impatience. Henry Parnell, who began with
one of the best statements of the bullionist case, was frequently interrupted when he launched at length into more 'silly calculation'. At
one point members were entertained by the spectacle of Parnell reading passages from a pamphlet to prove his case and being loudly
cheered by both Rose and Vansittart.[2] He was followed by Sir Thomas
Turton and William Manning, who both defended the Bank, and by
Sir Alexander Baring, who in a singularly stupid speech contradicted
friend and foe with nice impartiality.[3] When Perceval rose the House
was clearly in no mood for yet another technical disquisition. In the
shortest of the major speeches, he avoided getting lost in statistics
and concentrated on driving home one supreme point. Unlike Rose and
Vansittart, he made no attempt to dispute the bullionists' theory. A
reduction of Bank paper would, he admitted, tend to diminish the
adverse balance of exchanges, but only at a great cost. For the adoption
of Horner's resolutions 'would be tantamount to a declaration that
they would no longer continue those foreign exertions which they had
hitherto considered as indispensable to the security of the country'.
Was it, he asked the House, better to have the 'balance of exchange
nicely adjusted' or to continue the Peninsula campaign? Huskisson,
he reminded the Commons, had spoken without once mentioning the
war. 'The proposition', he concluded, 'came to this—whether, in the
existing state of affairs, having proceeded for four or five years in . . .
the carrying on of a war by a foreign expenditure to a very considerable amount, it was advisable to supply the domestic deficiency in
circulation, which that expenditure must occasion, by a paper cur-

[1] *Parl. Deb.*, XIX, 986-1011.
[2] *Ibid.*, XIX, 1021-51.   [3] *Ibid.*, XIX, 1051-63.

rency. This was a plain question of policy.' The bullionists argued that the Bank's issues had been excessive, but they could not even agree amongst themselves on a definition of what constituted an excessive issue. Huskisson had argued that there could be no excess of paper before the suspension of cash payments: Parnell had stated that there already was a surfeit.[1] Perceval's, reported the *Day*, was 'the only speech which gave either variety or interest to the continued debate', for it was 'at once eloquent, argumentative and convincing'.[2] This was certainly unjust to Canning, the last speaker before the House rose, who made perhaps the best contribution to the entire debate.[3] Parliament, he suggested, must accept the bullionist theory, but diverge from it in practice. He, therefore, proposed to support the first fifteen of Horner's resolutions, but to vote against the last, which set a definite date for the resumption of cash payments. The House finally divided on 9 May after nine more speeches by back-benchers. Horner's first resolution was defeated by 151 votes to 75, a majority of two to one, and resolutions two to fifteen were then rejected without a division. When Horner insisted on a vote on the last resolution, calling for a resumption of cash payments in two years' time, only 45 members went into the aye lobby against 180 noes.[4] 'The divisions', wrote Horner to his father, 'were better than I expected, particularly upon the last; that division I took at a venture, contrary to the wishes of some who left me: but I am satisfied that good has been done by getting the forty-five names which I shall have to show for that.'[5] But neither Perceval nor the Bank had cause for alarm. Omnium rose on the stock exchange to a premium of $1\frac{1}{4}$ and the prime minister was able to send a very satisfactory report on the debate to the Prince Regent.[6]

The Commons had, as Horner said, listened to 'so tedious a debate upon so uninviting a subject' with 'much attention and without any impatience'. But when Vansittart very unwisely decided to put his own counter-resolutions, members' self-control was tested to the full. Vansittart's opening speech, the most tedious and involved of all, filled

[1] Ibid., XIX, 1063–76.
[2] *Day*, 9 May 1811. For an interesting bullionist comment on Perceval's argument see the *Edinburgh Review*, Aug. 1811, p. 461.
[3] *Parl. Deb.*, XIX, 1076–1128. 'The best speech', wrote Horner, 'was Canning's, which astounded everybody by the knowledge he showed of the subject' (*Memoirs*, vol. II, pp. 85–6).
[4] *Parl. Deb.*, XIX, 1169.
[5] Horner, *Memoirs*, vol. II, pp. 85–6.
[6] *Day*, 21 May 1811; Windsor MSS., Regency file, 17989–90.

seventy-four columns of the *Parliamentary Debates*.[1] Canning then
moved a bullionist amendment which was again lost by a majority of
two to one in a thin House. Finally 14 and 15 May were taken up by
the report stage and more speeches, mostly by back-benchers. In the
end Fuller, always the least temperate of the country gentlemen, could
stand it no longer. He said his friends had had more than enough of
this 'tiresome question' and could spare no more time for 'labour and
sweating about this bullion'. 'Mr. Speaker,' he said, 'I don't like this
business at all. I think that it is a humbug.' If we lost all our gold, we
must use a currency that nobody would take from us: in a crisis tallow,
leather or oyster shells would do.[2] When the last division was called
only twenty-four stalwarts remained to vote for the resumption of
cash payments.[3]

In essence the Commons had decided that in time of war a certain
degree of inflation was inevitable. For all the bullionists' dialectical
triumphs in parliament, on the ultimate issue Perceval and his allies
were in the right. They may have failed to grasp Horner's and Huskisson's nice points of theory, but at least they never forgot that Great
Britain was in the middle of a world war. For once even Cobbett could
cheer the government: a bullionist victory, he wrote, would have
ended in 'putting a stop to the war . . . and plunging the whole kingdom into confusion'.[4] Compared with this, wrote Sir Keith Hancock
and Mr. M. M. Gowing, the debating points of the bullionists seem
'pitifully irrelevant'. Monetary theory has outgrown their 'one-sided
cocksureness'. Worse still was their 'political irresponsibility' which,
had Horner's resolutions been approved, 'would have forced the nation
back to gold and a restricted war effort in the very month—so it
turned out—when Napoleon was winning the opening battles in the
great campaign in Saxony'. Had the report been adopted, wrote
Professor Silberling, there would in all probability be no British empire
to-day.[5] Certainly the publicity given to the bullionist case hampered
the British war effort. Thomas Murphy, a treasury agent at Vera Cruz,
reported great difficulty in negotiating bills of exchange on the
Mexican money market. These bills, he was told by a leading local

---

[1] *Parl. Deb.*, XX, 1–74.
[2] *Ibid.*, XX, 140.
[3] *Ibid.*, XX, 172.
[4] Cobbett, *Regency and Reign of George IV*, chapter II, p. 117.
[5] W. K. Hancock and M. M. Gowing, *British War Economy*, p. 7; *Quarterly
Journal of Economics*, XXXVIII, Silberling, *Financial and Monetary policy of
Great Britain during the Napoleonic Wars*.

merchant, were certainly promptly met, but in a badly depreciated paper currency instead of in gold. The man, wrote Murphy, had with him a copy of the bullionist *Morning Chronicle*.[1]

Even after this Perceval's currency troubles were not over. Towards the middle of June Lord King, a large landowner, a convinced bullionist, and a relative of Grenville, issued a notice to his tenants that, because bank of England notes were depreciated, his rents must in future be paid either in gold or in paper estimated by the price of gold. The ultimatum was, as the *Day* pointed out, 'absurd and impracticable': if his lordship would only value his tenants' pound notes at sixteen shillings, then he too could expect to receive only sixteen shillings for his.[2] It soon, however, became clear that Lord King intended to enforce his claim and that other landlords might follow his example. Lord Stanhope immediately introduced a private member's bill in the Lords to make bank notes a legal tender and Perceval agreed to pilot it through the Commons. In spite of hot opposition from Grenville and Holland in the Lords and Tierney and Whitbread in the Commons, the bill had passed all its stages by 19 July.[3] The government was then further embarrassed by claims from Dublin that the provisions of the bill should extend to Ireland. Many landlords in northern Ireland, argued Pole, had long demanded rents in gold, including the marquises of Hertford, Donegal, and Downshire. The practice was general in Belfast and counties Down and Antrim, while everywhere guineas were sold openly and legally for what they would fetch. There would certainly be trouble if Irish tenants were not protected. The Irish government was thoroughly alarmed and Richmond, the lord lieutenant, the Irish law officers, and the governor of the bank of Ireland all backed Pole's demands. This put the cabinet in an awkward position. Stanhope's bill, wrote Richard Ryder, was intended merely to maintain the *status quo* between landlord and tenant. If applied to those parts of Ireland where rents had previously been paid in guineas, it would be denounced as an attack on landlords' rights. On 12 July the cabinet decided against any extension, giving as its reason the lateness in the session and the consequent absence of many

---

[1] P.R.O., T1/1210/11151.

[2] *Day*, 4 July 1810. For the text of Lord King's letter see *Annual Register*, 1811, Chronicle, p. 76.

[3] *Parl. Deb.*, XX, 960, 980 and 1106; *Annual Register*, 1811, pp. 80 ff. Romilly reports that ministers only finally decided to support the bill after consultations between Perceval and Liverpool during the second reading in the Lords (vol. II, p. 411).

Irish M.P.s from Westminster. The decision failed to please Dublin Castle and Pole predicted growing resentment against the Union.[1]

Victory in the bullion debates did little to lessen the prime minister's other financial worries. The main point made by Rose in his memorandum of 11 November 1809 had been the need for large-scale retrenchment. Economies must be made, he wrote, 'not in the reduction of paltry places and pensions . . . but in the great branches of public expenditure'. This meant, in practice, as Perceval realised, cuts in the armed forces. Huskisson had called for this before his resignation. Rose proposed that war office, admiralty and ordnance expenditure should be based on the totals for 1800, which would have involved a 33% reduction in military expenditure. In order to enforce this Rose first made the revolutionary suggestion of requiring all departments to submit annual estimates. At first Perceval toyed with the idea and on 20 December 1809 the treasury went so far as to send out a general circular asking for estimates for 1810.[2] But the scheme, in advance of its time, was soon abandoned. Instead Perceval planned to put a paragraph about the need for economy in the King's Speech which was to open the 1810 parliamentary session. As originally drafted by Perceval and Liverpool the paragraph would have pledged all government offices to prune their expenses and thus reduce total national expenditure. At the last moment, however, the prime minister withdrew this. It would, he explained to Wellesley, lead the public to expect economies which could only be made at the cost of crippling our war effort. 'This', he wrote, 'is a most terrible truth, but at least as far as this year's expense is concerned, I believe it to be an indisputable one.'[3] Such honesty alarmed even his best friends. The decision, wrote Harrowby, 'has disturbed my sleep. If you omit it entirely you lose your only hold over all departments. . . . While the Duke was at the head, where the authority existed the wish was wanting and where the wish existed the authority was wanting. Now they ought to be and are united, and if nothing results from this union, I am almost afraid of owning to myself how completely I despair of the existence of the administration, the constitution and the country itself.'[4]

Altogether prospects for the 1810 budget looked bad. Rose estimated that Perceval would need a £22,000,000 loan and so be

[1] Westbrook Hay MSS., W. W. Pole to Ryder, 10 and 15 July 1811; Ryder to Pole, 12 and 13 July 1811.
[2] Add. MSS., 42774, fol. 182; P.R.O., T27/65/260.
[3] Add. MSS., 37295, fol. 227.
[4] Harrowby MSS., vol. XVII, fol. 94, Harrowby to Perceval, 22 Jan. 1810.

forced to raise £1,250,000 in new taxes to meet the interest and sinking fund.[1] Late in February Rose and Huskisson, now joint prophets of gloom, warned the House of the dangers of complete financial collapse.[2] For a while even Perceval's self-confidence was undermined. He had, since his arrival at the treasury, opposed the idea of anything like Petty's new plan of finance. Such ingenuity, he thought, verged on dishonesty. There was no doubt, he told Harrowby, 'that if we want to borrow money, we or our posterity must in some manner pay for it; any plan therefore that eases the present day must affect the future, and that, at least, in proportion to the ease which it affords at present'. By the beginning of 1810 he became increasingly disturbed by the thought that too great a burden might ruin the present generation and so also affect posterity. Therefore, he decided, 'out of mercy and consideration for them, we should take care of ourselves'. He had, with great difficulty, reduced the estimates for 1810 by £3,000,000 and so hoped to manage with a loan of £16,000,000 for the current year. Yet loans at least as large would be needed every year as long as the war lasted. 'How long that may be, whether five, ten, fifteen, twenty or thirty years, God only knows.' If it lasted only five years the treasury would have to raise £4,800,000 in new taxes to meet all charges on a £16,000,000 annual loan. The alternatives were either to pledge the war taxes to meet loans or revise the sinking fund system. On the whole Perceval preferred to try the second. 'I think it is clear', he wrote, 'that it was never Pitt's original intention that we should go on accumulating [the Sinking Fund], without any view to diminishing the growing burden on the country. I have been credibly informed that when Pitt was last in Government, he had made up his mind to this proposition; that if the annual loans could have been reduced so low as only to equal the amount of the Sinking Fund, he would have ceased to borrow, and ceased also to redeem; applying the Sinking Fund in some way or other to the service of the year. In other words he would have been contented to leave the Sinking Fund stationary, leaving the work of further reduction to . . . peace.' By 1810 the sinking fund total did not equal the annual loan, but Perceval decided that it would be only a logical extension of Pitt's idea to adopt a plan which kept the sinking fund and the debt at their existing proportion to each other. And so the idea was born of raiding the sinking fund, thereafter the stock resource of harassed chancellors. Herries was put to work

[1] Rose, vol. II, p. 420.
[2] *Day*, 28 Feb. 1810.

making the necessary calculations, after which Perceval devised the new scheme.

'The plan', he wrote exultantly to Harrowby, 'has this advantage, that it is extremely simple and easily intelligible. Whatever, therefore, may be its defects, they will be easily open to detection, and I do not believe there is any fallacy whatever belonging to it.' Loans would be raised as usual, but without a sinking fund. The interest on these loans would be taken out of the war taxes. A supplementary loan would then be floated to make good the deficiency in the war taxes and a $1\frac{1}{2}\%$ sinking fund raised on this supplementary loan by new taxes. The new sinking fund, added to the fund previously accumulated, would release the pledged war taxes in two years. Consequently a new plan could be started every two years, 'and so on from two years to two years until the end of time', as long as the treasury could raise each year the amount needed in new taxes to provide the $1\frac{1}{2}\%$ sinking fund on the supplementary loan. Therefore 'whether the war lasted two years or 200 years', the war taxes would be unpledged at the end of every second year and the sinking fund would bear the same proportion to the debt as it did when the plan came into operation. Finally the burden of extra taxation would be slightly more than halved.[1] The scheme was certainly an improvement on Petty's ideas: but, like them, it had many weaknesses. Petty's plan assumed that the cost of the war could be stabilised at £32,000,000 a year: Perceval's that the annual loans need not exceed £16,000,000. Neither assumption was valid. Furthermore all Perceval's calculations hinged on the treasury's ability to raise loans at $4\frac{1}{2}\%$ and redeem them at the same rate. Fortunately Perceval's own enthusiasm for the plan quickly waned. By May he had decided to rely once more on orthodox policies.

Total estimates for 1810 were slightly over £52,000,000 which, when the Irish contribution was deducted, left Perceval to find £46,000,000. Against this the war taxes produced £19,500,000, the malt and pension duties £3,000,000, the lottery £350,000; the 1809 and 1810 surpluses of the consolidated fund just over £6,000,000, and the vote of credit £3,000,000. This left a deficit of £13,300,000, which was met by issuing £5,300,000 worth of exchequer bills and by floating a loan of £8,000,000. In the event Perceval had done better than either his critics or friends had expected. The method of raising the loan was complicated, but the practical result was that the country

[1] Harrowby MSS., XVI, fol. 286; Herries, vol. I, pp. 13–14; Herries MSS., Perceval to Herries, 24 Feb. 1810.

had to pay only £4 15s. 3d. per cent for the sum required. Even Huskisson was impressed, while Rose was at a loss to account for the country's apparent prosperity.[1] The budget, wrote a jubilant Perceval to the king, 'was very well received in the House': Tierney alone was critical and he got little support, even from his own colleagues.[2] The budget of 1811, in spite of the current bullion debates, had an equally smooth passage. Owing to the increasing cost of the war, the estimates for Great Britain exceeded £54,000,000 which, excluding the total for Ireland, left Perceval to raise £49,500,000, or £3,500,000 more than in the previous year. The combined war taxes, malt and pension duties, and the lottery produced £23,300,000; accumulated surpluses from the consolidated fund a little over £6,000,000; a vote of credit £3,000,000. The balance remaining was made good by funding £4,000,000 worth of exchequer bills and by raising a loan of £12,500,000 at an interest rate of £4 14s. 11d. per cent. Finally the additional loan charge thus created was met by raising taxes on spirits, Baltic timber, pearl, potash and American cotton. Only the last of these met with vocal opposition in parliament and all were finally approved without a division.[3] The last of Perceval's budgets was delayed by the government crisis following the chancellor's assassination in May 1812 and was therefore not introduced until 7 June when Vansittart, who had succeeded Perceval at the exchequer, made his first budget speech in commending the dead minister's proposals. The estimated expenditure for the year reached a new record of over £62,000,000, of which a little more than £55,000,000 fell on the English budget. The annual loan exceeded £15,500,000 and a further £6,800,000 was borrowed from the subscribers of funded exchequer bills. It was the least successful of all Perceval's efforts, but criticism was stifled by the memory of the recent assassination and by Vansittart's moving tribute to his former colleague.[4]

No one could accuse Perceval of originality in finance. At the treasury, as well as in parliament, he took Pitt as his model and so tried, in every crisis, to act as he thought his former leader would have done. Yet the five Perceval budgets, when considered as a whole, stand comparison with those of any similar period during the Napoleonic War as models of sound and cautious finance. Between 1808

[1] *Parl. Deb.*, XVI, 1043; *Annual Register*, 1810, pp. 117 ff.
[2] Windsor MSS., 15371, Perceval to George III, 19 May 1810.
[3] *Parl. Deb.*, XX, 210; *Annual Register*, 1811, pp. 59 ff.; Colchester, vol. II, p. 333. Cf. the list of new taxes with the forecast in the *Day* (9 Apr. 1811); Add. MSS., 38362, fol. 68. [4] *Annual Register*, 1812, pp. 95 ff.

and 1812 the total supplies that had to be raised exceeded those of any previous quinquennium and a greater proportion of these than ever before was raised by taxation. The total of new debt contracted between 1798 and 1801 had exceeded £191,000,000, between 1803 and 1807 it was £156,000,000, whereas from 1808 to 1812 it fell to £123,000,000. In the three remaining war years after Perceval's assassination it rose again to £184,000,000.[1] The little chancellor not only found the means to continue an increasingly costly world war, when experts like Huskisson and Rose began to despair of such a task, but he even did so without adding as much as either his predecessors or his successor to the financial burden on future generations. In the early days of his administration, however, Perceval was obsessed rather by current political crises than by the problems of posterity.

[1] For these figures see the *Extraordinary Red Book* (1821 edition), App., p. 56.

CHAPTER TWENTY

THE REGENCY CRISIS

THE outcome of the Walcheren debates and the consequent deflation of opposition hopes eased the immediate political pressure on the ministry. Yet even this success might have proved a pyrrhic victory, for the government still had no sure majority in the Commons and Perceval was still left as the only spokesman of consequence on the treasury bench. Ryder, through nerves, and Palmerston, through inexperience, were virtually sleeping partners in debate, leaving junior ministers like Arbuthnot, Croker and Wharton to do what they could to support their prime minister. In mid-January the *Day* had predicted a cabinet reshuffle which would have moved Wellesley to 10, Downing Street, made Perceval lord chancellor and brought back Canning as foreign secretary with Huskisson as chancellor of the exchequer. The return of both Canning and Huskisson, wrote the same paper in March, would be 'hailed with joy by every impartial man'.[1] For once press rumours had some basis in fact, for Wellesley had been urging the need to strengthen the ministry almost from the day he accepted the seals of the foreign office. Although the cabinet majority favoured waiting until after the end of the Walcheren debates, Wellesley continued privately to press Perceval to open simultaneous negotiations with Canning, Castlereagh, and Sidmouth. It would not be easy either to persuade these heterogeneous groups to act together or to convince cabinet colleagues like Camden and Eldon of the virtues of such overtures. Yet, argued Wellesley, it was only by sacrificing 'personal animosities and prejudices of the hour' that ministers could prevent Grey and Grenville from seizing power. The foreign secretary himself was willing to serve under Perceval or any agreed successor in an extended administration.[2]

At first Perceval had little sympathy with so grandiose a scheme.

[1] *Day*, 13 Jan. and 10 Mar. 1810. Had Perceval been defeated on Walcheren, wrote Buckingham, Wellesley would have headed a coalition which would certainly have included Canning (*Court and Cabinets*, vol. IV, p. 434). On 24 Mar. Grenville told Auckland that he had heard 'from a quarter which I cannot disbelieve' that he would be asked to form a new ministry within a fortnight (Auckland, vol. IV, p. 350).   [2] Add. MSS., 37295, fol. 244.

When Chatham's resignation created a vacancy at the ordnance he was content to patch up his existing team by offering it to the gouty earl of Pembroke. Fortunately, as George III predicted, Pembroke declined.[1] Only the return of trouble with the Melville group forced the prime minister to think on more ambitious lines. Just before Christmas Melville had sent Perceval a statement of his political position and future intentions which he had first committed to paper on 6 May 1809. This had been done, explained Melville, in order to prove that his reservations toward the new government were not caused by resentment of Perceval's candid letter in October. On Saturday, 14 January, there appeared in the *Courier* a version of the Melville–Perceval correspondence of the previous autumn which was so inaccurate that Robert Dundas immediately lodged a vigorous protest with Perceval. Although the prime minister denied being implicated in these disclosures, relations with the Melville group quickly deteriorated even further. A week later the *Sun* carried a Melvillite version of the exchange of letters while Henry Dundas and 'A Country Gentleman' both came out with pamphlets roundly attacking Perceval's attitude towards Melville.[2] All this put Robert Dundas in an impossible position at the board of control. Although, out of loyalty to the prime minister, he stayed on in office until the cabinet had survived both the Walcheren inquiry and the Burdett riots, he was ultimately forced to offer his resignation on 14 April. His own attitude to the ministry, he explained, remained unchanged, but 'the language which my father now holds in regard to it is of too hostile a character to allow of my indulging any expectation that his conduct will long be restrained even within its present bounds, more especially when I shall have retired. It has come to a crisis in which I must either break off all political connection with him, and endeavour to attach to the present administration as large a portion as possible of *his* friends in Scotland, or I must act inconsistently with my duty to His Majesty and his Government.' The only real hope for the future,

---

[1] Windsor MSS., 15003–4, Perceval to George III, 8 Mar. 1810 and 15012, same to same, 12 Mar. 1810.

[2] Perceval MSS., Melville to Perceval, 19 Dec. 1809; Perceval to Melville, 23 Dec. 1809; Robert Dundas to Perceval, 15 Jan. 1810; and Perceval to Robert Dundas, 15 Jan. 1810; *Courier*, 14 Jan. 1810; *Day*, 22 Jan. 1810; Henry Dundas, *Cursory Remarks on the Correspondence between Lord Melville and Mr. Perceval* (1810); *A Letter to the Rt. Hon. Spencer Perceval upon his reported correspondence with Lord Melville—by a Country Gentleman* (1810). In this anonymous pamphlet Perceval was attacked for refusing to offer office to Melville out of fear of 'a motley junta of Whigs, Tories, Jacobins and Saints' (p. 42).

concluded Dundas, lay in further general attempts to strengthen the ministry.[1] When news of Dundas's letter reached the cabinet offers of resignation suddenly became fashionable. Mulgrave, who could never long tolerate any office which required real effort, reminded Perceval of his hints in February of a desire to leave the admiralty, Camden showed every willingness to quit the privy council, while even Ryder offered to go, if by means of his retirement 'we could secure additional support'. Wellesley promptly took advantage of this atmosphere of self-sacrifice to renew his pressure for renewed negotiations with groups then outside the ministry. 'After all that had passed', wrote Perceval to Richmond, 'there was, as you may imagine, much repugnance felt by most of us to applying to Canning; and for an application to Canning and his friends alone no one was desirous. . . .' Even Wellesley agreed that 'Canning alone would not do'. In the end the cabinet decided to try simultaneous approaches to Canning, Castlereagh and Sidmouth for 'a junction with us, upon the principle of collecting again all the remains of Pitt's Friends . . . at this period of danger'. Perceval was to approach first Sidmouth and then Castlereagh, while Wellesley acted as intermediary with Canning. No one was, however, to be given a firm offer of any particular cabinet office. Perceval and Wellesley were simply authorised to ask the three potential recruits whether they would consent to act with the existing government or whether they would be willing to serve in an administration 'which would comprehend the several persons who had at any time been connected with Mr. Pitt'.[2]

During the Easter recess prime minister and foreign secretary busied themselves with their initial overtures. Neither got very far. Canning had enough political troubles of his own to worry overmuch about those of the government. His original intention, immediately after his resignation, of avoiding entanglements with both ministers and opposition had seemed fine in theory. A compact block of Canningites would hold the balance in the Commons and wait for the most tempting offer of coalition. Reality, however, proved very different from these brave hopes. Canning's hostile amendment censuring Chatham on 6 March only widened the gulf with ministers, while both Grey and Brougham shied away from 'an odious coalition' with the former foreign secretary, in spite of the meddling Lady Holland's attempts to engineer it. It was hard to aspire to play the romantic lead only to find oneself cast

[1] Perceval MSS., Robert Dundas to Perceval, 14 Apr. 1810.
[2] *Ibid.*, Perceval to Richmond, 30 Apr. 1810.

as the wicked uncle. Furthermore the little group of his personal followers showed alarming tendencies to disagree when faced with a choice of division lobbies. In the final divisions on Walcheren, Canning and Sturges Bourne voted with Perceval while Granville Leveson-Gower and Charles Ellis voted against. The sessions of 1810 and 1811, wrote Rede, were 'a mere blank' in Canning's political life.[1] Matters were not improved by his reservations about both Wellesley's capabilities and his tactics in seeking to persuade the cabinet to make an offer to the Canningites. Wellesley, he told the Speaker in May, would make a good colleague 'but not Premier', although there was no objection to using him in order to get back to office 'rich as he is'. If Wellesley tried to bring this about, Canning assured Bagot, without tendering his resignation he would only be baffled by Perceval and despised by the king. Early in April he was urging Wellesley to use the opportunity of an audience with the king on the twelfth 'to take advantage of the present discontents' at the handling of the Burdett riots.[2] When all that Wellesley finally produced was his two questions about future conduct, a disappointed Canning brusquely refused either to be 'quizzed' or to give 'any gratuitous declaration of my opinions upon questions involving matters of so much personal delicacy'.[3] Meanwhile Perceval, having temporarily delayed the probable loss of the Scottish votes by persuading Dundas to make one last appeal to Melville, sent Charles Yorke to sound Sidmouth. But Sidmouth would have nothing to do with a proposal which involved him in serving in any government which included Canning. If, however, 'in the case supposed of C[anning] being out of the question', Sidmouth was willing both to 'unite with you as *the head of the King's Government* in the House of Commons' and to make this 'the permanent and ultimate political connection for himself'. His lordship's only stipulation was that he should be sent for by the king himself, 'it being a mark of honour and confidence to which he thinks himself entitled. . . .'[4]

There, it seemed, the recruiting drive must come to a halt. For if Sidmouth rejected the idea of co-operating with Canning, it was pointless to ask Castlereagh to accept him. Moreover the cabinet had already unanimously rejected the idea of applying to Canning alone, while

[1] Bagot, vol. I, pp. 336 and 346; Brougham, *Memoirs*, vol. I, pp. 461, 475 and 478; Rede, p. 162. [2] Colchester, vol. II, pp. 179–81; Bagot, vol. I, p. 351. [3] Add. MSS., 37295, fol. 401.
[4] Perceval MSS., Perceval to Dundas, 15 Apr. 1810; C. P. Yorke to Perceval, '½ p. 2 Tuesday' (24 Apr. 1810).

Wellesley quickly completed the impasse by vetoing a suggestion for a coalition with Sidmouth and Castlereagh 'upon a more limited principle'.[1] In short, so complex were the personal animosities involved that the cabinet, having failed to recruit all three groups simultaneously, was reduced to trying to carry on without any fresh strength at all. Therefore, on 26 April Perceval advised the king simply to authorise Mulgrave's transfer to the ordnance and his replacement at the admiralty either by Charles Yorke or Lord Gambier. The prime minister admitted that he would have had little hesitation in preferring Yorke had not his action in precipitating the Burdett riots and his recent acceptance of a particularly lucrative sinecure created 'a temporary feeling of hostility against him'.[2] George III stoutly refused to accept such objections and countered with the assertion that Gambier's appointment 'would not be a popular one with the Navy, in which his professional abilities are not held in the highest estimation'. Perceval accordingly tried Yorke, who refused, and then turned to the inevitable Robert Dundas. It was a shrewd move, for Melville was at last placated by the idea that his son should move to the department in which he himself had served for so long under Pitt. Melville marked the more cordial relations by calling at 10, Downing Street on the afternoon of 28 April. 'You will find him', wrote Dundas, 'perfectly disposed to aid your views in strengthening your Government, provided he is not himself required to take office. His supporting it, and of course my continuing in it, will depend upon our all agreeing to sacrifice our predilections in favour of particular individuals. . . .' Although the Dundases immediately went on to break their own principle by ruling out Whitbread and Burdett as threats to monarchy, they agreed not to press their objections to Sidmouth. 'No person', ended Dundas, 'would be more rejoiced than myself to see Canning again in office; but if that object cannot be attained without relinquishing every other connection within our reach, it would be purchased at too dear a rate, more especially when we consider the predicament in which he unfortunately stands at present in public estimation.' After this frank exchange Dundas finally opted to stay at the board of control while Perceval managed to persuade Yorke to change his mind and accept the admiralty.[3]

[1] Perceval MSS., Perceval to Richmond, 30 Apr. 1810.
[2] Windsor MSS., 15102, Perceval to George III, 26 Apr. 1810. For Yorke's acceptance of a tellership of the exchequer see chapter 9, pp. 121 and 130-1.
[3] Windsor MSS., 15103, George III to Perceval, 27 Apr. 1810, 15106-8,

Even after this the unwearied Wellesley persisted in urging the prime minister to renew contacts with Canning. On 3 May he told Perceval that the recent reshuffle had weakened rather than strengthened the government and then sent a copy of this letter to Canning himself.[1] A little over a week later Wellesley, with Perceval's consent, met Sidmouth in a vain attempt to persuade him to withdraw his objections to serving with Canning. Just before the end of the session the prime minister himself interviewed Sidmouth equally fruitlessly, although news of this meeting leaked out to revive rumours that Perceval was intent on a seat in the Lords. Should he leave the Commons, lamented the *Day* in the language of Shakespeare, 'we n'er shall see his like again.' [2] Divisions within the cabinet were clearly hardening as Wellesley became more firmly committed to Canning while the majority of ministers refused to touch him except as part of a seemingly unobtainable broad coalition. On 13 June Canning warned Wellesley of rumours of 'other arrangements' which would mean that 'something is doing unknown to you, which will place you in an awkward situation'. The following day Canning repeated his forebodings and went so far as to ask the foreign secretary whether there were points he would like him to include in a Commons' speech on Spain. Wellesley therefore wrote to Perceval on the fourteenth asking officially that the cabinet should consider making an immediate offer to Canning and his supporters, on the understanding that Wellesley himself was willing to facilitate this either by moving to another post or remaining as a cabinet minister without portfolio until a vacancy could be found for him.[3] Still Wellesley did not push his reluctant colleagues sufficiently strongly to satisfy Canning's eagerness to return to office. After the cabinet had met without reaching any decision, Canning renewed his pressure on Wellesley to 'bring matters to a head'. The issue was to have been discussed at a cabinet on 3 July, but as Wellesley was then indisposed, ministers met only to adjourn.[4] The summer was slipping by and nothing had yet been agreed when

---

Perceval to George III, 27 and 28 Apr. 1810; Perceval MSS., Dundas to Perceval, 28 Apr. 1810; Add. MSS., 37295, fol. 272. The *Day* (3 May 1810) welcomed Mulgrave's move but deplored Yorke's acceptance of the admiralty.

[1] Add. MSS., 37295, fols. 282 and 284.

[2] Perceval MSS., Wellesley to Perceval, 12 June 1810; Pellew, vol. III, p. 27; *Day*, 19 May 1810.

[3] Add. MSS., 37295, fols. 304, 306, 308 and 310; Perceval MSS., Wellesley to Perceval, 14 June 1810.

[4] Add. MSS., 37295, fols. 316 and 320.

Wellesley retired to Dorking and Perceval took his family to Ealing on 17 July.[1]

In an attempt to weaken his colleagues' resistance, Wellesley next proposed joint offers to Canning and Castlereagh, a proposal which Perceval thought futile if made so soon after the duel. In fact the chief mover in all this was Canning, now become the place-hunter *par excellence*. On 24 July he had arranged to see Perceval about some routine treasury business and used the excuse, on the twenty-third, again to remind Wellesley of his claims and to inquire 'how far I was *understood* to be acquainted with what has passed'.[2] The foreign secretary's confidential exchanges with a politician outside the cabinet, and one about whom he knew all his associates had grave reservations, now bordered on disloyalty to his colleagues. In spite of this, Wellesley obediently raised the issue once more in a letter to the prime minister on 23 July. It was, he argued, 'very desirable to bring the matter to a final and positive determination, and (if it is determined to be either useless or dangerous to accept my offer) to apprise Canning distinctly of his situation'. Therefore Perceval should take the opportunity of his meeting with Canning the following day to talk 'freely on the whole subject' with him. This Perceval refused to do until the cabinet had met for dinner at Ryder's house on 26 July.[3] At this meeting ministers discussed a memorandum by Wellesley repeating the arguments for a joint approach to Canning and Castlereagh, both of which the foreign secretary offered to undertake himself. Canning, wrote Wellesley, had heard 'through various channels' of Sidmouth's personal objection to him. 'The result of this information on Mr. Canning's mind has not been to determine him never to act with Lord Sidmouth, but Mr. Canning thinks that it would be injurious to his just pretensions to suffer his admission into the cabinet to be subjected again to the will of Lord Sidmouth. . . .' If Canning and Castlereagh were to be recruited they must be approached before the government had made all major policy decisions and military plans for the next session.[4] Thereupon Liverpool offered to vacate the war office so that both Canning and Castlereagh could be offered their old departments. But the cabinet wisely would have nothing of this, preferring Yorke's and Ryder's suggestions of the admiralty and the home office. The prime

---

[1] *Day*, 17 July 1810.   [2] Add. MSS., 37295, fol. 338.
[3] Perceval MSS., Wellesley to Perceval, 23 July 1810; Add. MSS., 37295, fols. 340 and 346.
[4] Perceval MSS., memorandum by Wellesley, enclosed in his letter to Perceval of 23 July 1810.

minister, rather than Wellesley, it was decided, should be in charge of the overture to Castlereagh. On these terms the cabinet was finally united, although Camden, 'in most perfect good humour', warned Perceval that he would be compelled to resign if Canning rejoined the ministry.[1]

Throughout the fine weather of early August Perceval began leisurely to draft a suitable letter to Castlereagh. By the seventeenth he had, 'after much consideration and reconsideration', produced a version over 2,800 words long which laboriously explained all the negotiations since before Easter. This was sent to Wellesley and Dundas for their approval and finally despatched on 22 August to Ireland, where Castlereagh was on holiday. Perceval was still 'far from sanguine' and events proved him right. On 4 September Castlereagh posted his rejection: the proposed coalition would neither increase public confidence nor inspire the nation with a feeling that its government 'was really united within itself'.[2] Only Wellesley seemed disappointed or surprised. Melville found it exactly what he had expected from the first, Sidmouth automatically approved of any letter that kept Canning out of office, while Mulgrave resolved to 'make the best battle we can, and if necessary "die in the last ditch"'. 'You appear to have done all you can', wrote Richmond to the prime minister, 'to obtain strength. It certainly is not your fault that it has failed.'[3] On 14 September Canning, having received a 'final' letter from Wellesley, was consulting Bagot and Charles Ellis on 'whether anything, or what, remains for me to say or do'. On their advice he wrote to Perceval his version of the lengthy negotiations in order to demonstrate 'that it is not by any personal pretensions of mine that the reunion of the friends of Mr. Pitt in the service of the country is rendered impracticable'. It was, replied Perceval, clearly understood that Canning had raised no personal objections to any individual and had shown himself willing to join a strengthened ministry in which the prime minister himself should 'continue to hold my present situation'. 'What I understood to be proposed to me', replied Canning, 'was . . .

---

[1] Twiss, vol. II, p. 126; Perceval MSS., Perceval to Castlereagh, 22 Aug. 1810.

[2] Perceval MSS., Wellesley to Perceval, 17 and 24 Aug. 1810; Perceval to Castlereagh, 22 Aug. 1810; Castlereagh to Perceval, 4 Sep. 1810; Add. MSS., 37295, fols. 358, 360, 364, 382, and 401.

[3] Perceval MSS., Robert Dundas to Perceval, 14 Sep. 1810; Perceval to Sidmouth, 21 Sep. 1810 and Sidmouth to Perceval, 23 Sep. 1810; Mulgrave to Perceval, 11 Sep. 1810; Perceval to Richmond, 21 Sep. 1810 and Richmond to Perceval, 25 Sep. 1810; Add. MSS., 37295, fols. 388, 390 and 399.

your "continuance at the head of the Treasury" . . . I *always* understood it to be a point settled (not upon any stipulation or suggestion
of mine, but as an original and fundamental part of the proposition
opened to me) that the Chancellorship of the Exchequer was to be,
in some way or other, disposable in any arrangement to which I
might be invited to accede.' A change at the exchequer, argued
Perceval, could not be accepted as a *sine qua non* of any coalition with
the Canningites. He had never wanted the job in the first instance and
had frequently told Wellesley in conversation that he would willingly
vacate the exchequer, 'provided I could satisfy myself with respect to
my successor'. The obvious Canningite candidate was Huskisson, who
had all the necessary qualifications for the post, but who was then a
leading critic of the ministry in the bullion controversy. 'Huskisson's
succession to *that* office', Wellesley assured Perceval, 'was never stated
as an indispensable condition. A suitable arrangement for him was, of
course, always considered and stated to be essential to the whole
arrangement.' [1] By the autumn of 1810 the gulf between Perceval and
Canning seemed as wide as ever while Wellesley, having failed to
carry his point, remained as an increasingly disgruntled member of
the government. 'And so', concluded Eldon, 'ends our negotiations,
and the consequence, I trust will be that we shall all be determined to
stand firmly by ourselves.' [2] Such resolution was quickly tested yet
again for, on the eve of the new session, the cruellest and most unexpected blow of all fell on the unfortunate cabinet.

The sudden return in 1810 of George III's insanity deprived the
tottering government of its staunchest and most powerful friend.
There had in previous years been many groundless rumours about the
king's health. In December 1807 some opposition members were saying that his majesty must be mad because he so rarely left Windsor.
In the following autumn Portland had sought to save him the labour
of travelling by suggesting that cabinet ministers should always go to
see him, while a report of the king's death, early in 1809, was so readily

---

[1] Bagot, *George Canning and his Friends*, vol. I, pp. 344–7 and 354; Perceval
MSS., Canning to Perceval, 25 Sep. and 4 Oct. 1810; Perceval to Canning, 30
Sep. and 5 Oct. 1810; Wellesley to Perceval, 9 Oct. 1810; Add. MSS., 37295, fols.
401, 410, 413 and 415. 'Huskisson, I think,' Fremantle wrote to Earl Temple in
May 1810, 'has taken a decided line of opposition . . . .' (Buckingham, *Court and
Cabinets of George III*, vol. IV, p. 445).

[2] 'You must', wrote Wellington to Arbuthnot on 5 Oct., 'strengthen the
Government if it is intended that it should last.' In future reliance could not be
placed 'upon the casual support of one or other of the loose parties which are
floating about' (Wellington, *Supplementary Despatches*, vol. XI, pp. 611–12).

believed that tailors' shops were besieged by customers ordering
mourning clothes and the price of black cloth rocketed over-night.
At this time Auckland told Grenville that the royal dukes were talking
without reserve to those who had their confidence 'on the subject of
what they call a Council of Regency . . . grounded on the King's
misfortune in the loss of his eyesight'.[1] Consequently in the autumn of
1810 elaborate precautions were taken to keep the news of the king's
illness from the public until his doctors were certain that his condition
was really serious. His majesty's attendants first became anxious at
the beginning of October when Princess Amelia, the king's favourite
daughter, was taken ill. For a time, although it was soon known that
the princess would never recover, there were hopes that her father's
health would withstand the shock. 'Our good King', reported Herbert
Taylor on the eighth, 'is prepared for the melancholy event, and altho'
deeply distressed . . . he is perfectly resigned and his valuable health
is not affected by this severe and painful trial.'[2] The first symptoms
of insanity were detected on the eighteenth when George III had to
be told that his daughter was on the verge of death. In order not to
overtax his strength, the home secretary then agreed that he should
be sent only the most urgent state papers. Even then, had Princess
Amelia died as quickly as those at Windsor expected, the king's sanity
might not have given way, for as late as 19 October Taylor was still
sending reassuring notes to the home office. 'Nothing', he wrote,
'escapes his attention, no direction becomes necessary which is not
given with the utmost decision and clearness.' But on the following
day Perceval decided that he must consult the more important of his
cabinet colleagues and summoned Wellesley from Ramsgate, recommending 'that you should disguise as much as possible the cause of
your return to town'.[3] Slowly during the following week both Princess
Amelia's and the king's condition deteriorated. On 22 October the
princess was said to be 'as bad as she could be to be alive' while his
majesty was much worse on the twenty-fourth and was placed under
full medical supervision on the twenty-eighth.

[1] Gower, *Correspondence*, vol. II, p. 316; Brougham, *Memoirs*, vol. I, p. 426;
Windsor MSS., 14000–3, Portland to George III, 28 Nov. 1808; *Dropmore MSS.*,
IX, 261. The *Day* reported on 29 Sep. 1809 rumours that 'a great party' had suggested a Regency. On 12 Aug. 1805 Perceval had written to Pitt that 'my friend
Carey' was asking for payment of £400 said to be due to him for a secret cure to
restore the King's sight (P.R.O., Chatham MSS., 166).
[2] Westbrook Hay MSS., Herbert Taylor to Richard Ryder, 8 Oct. 1810.
[3] *Ibid.*, same to same, 9, 15 and 19 Oct. 1810; Add. MSS., 37295, fol. 426.

By that time Perceval had already discussed the crisis with Liverpool, Eldon, and Ryder, although Wellesley had, characteristically,
failed to appear in London. That day Perceval sent him a second letter,
stressing that the physicians' reports were alarming and that a group of
ministers was to meet on 30 October 'when we may confer on many
anxious points'. That night the king was very restless and did not fall
asleep until four the following morning. At noon Perceval and Eldon
arrived at Windsor to see if George III was well enough to sign the
commission continuing the prorogation of parliament, which, in the
absence of such an order, was due to reassemble on 1 November. They
found his majesty's conversation coherent but 'prodigiously hurried'
and 'extremely diffuse': the doctors were unanimous that the king was
unfit to undertake any official business.[1] That evening Perceval warned
the Speaker that parliament would probably have to meet and the next
morning he sent this news to the rest of the cabinet ministers who were
out of town, to Castlereagh, and to the Canningites. Efforts were still
made to maintain secrecy, but rumours began to reach the public on
the twenty-seventh and spread quickly when the king failed to take
his usual Saturday afternoon ride or to attend service on Sunday
morning. On the thirtieth the ministerial press finally admitted that all
was not well at Windsor: the king, said the official announcement, had
a severe cold. In fact his condition was so bad that it was decided to
withhold all state papers. The following day Abbot returned to Westminster, saw Perceval at Downing Street, and learnt that ministers
had decided to send Eldon and Ryder to make a final effort to get the
king's signature to the commission proroguing parliament. If they
failed Perceval intended to ask both Houses to agree to a short adjournment and then 'to proceed according to the precedent of 20 November
1788'. By the afternoon of Wednesday, 31 October, the king was
quieter, 'but silly': that evening he suddenly became so violent that
his physicians feared that they would have to use a strait-jacket. The
next day he had again fallen into 'a state of debility and vacancy of
mind'. The two ministers talked to him and decided that he was quite
incompetent to sign the commission.[2]

And so when the Commons met Perceval, seconded by Sheridan,

[1] Westbrook Hay MSS., Taylor to Ryder, 20 and 23 Oct. 1810; Add. MSS.,
37295, fol. 428; Colchester, vol. II, pp. 282–3; *Day*, 22 Oct. 1810. As Perceval and
Eldon were returning from Windsor to Ealing on the evening of 29 Oct. their
coach overturned on Hounslow Heath. Fortunately neither minister was
seriously injured (*Day*, 31 Oct. 1810).

[2] Westbrook Hay MSS., Taylor to Ryder, 30 and 31 Oct. 1810; Colchester,

proposed a fortnight's adjournment. The motion was passed unanimously, for all parties in the House recognised that they could do little but wait on events. In future the most important political news of each day was the wording of the bulletin on the king's health. Between 1 and 4 November there was not much change in his condition: he was feverish and slept little. Private accounts were even less encouraging. Abbot heard on reliable authority that on the second and third the king's insanity was at a 'horrible height'. He had eaten very little for five days and nothing but magnesia for the previous forty-eight hours. By the fourth his doctors, fearing for his life, used coercion to apply medicine and leeches and then issued a bulletin claiming that the king had slept well and was much better. But on the sixth they had to admit that the improvement was not maintained. 'Nor', wrote the Speaker in his diary, 'had any symptoms of returning reason appeared since the beginning of the attack.' [1] In spite of this all the doctors in attendance at Windsor were confident of the king's speedy recovery: there was, said William Knighton, the prince of Wales' physician, 'no just ground of despair'. The king remained very ill until the ninth when he was reported to be 'rather better'. Three days later a bulletin claimed that he was 'better on the whole than he has been since the commencement of his illness', and by the fourteenth his majesty appeared to be 'in a state of progressive amendment'. Parliament met again on 15 November and, in spite of opposition from Sheridan and the radicals, agreed by 343 votes to 58 to adjourn for another fortnight.[2]

During the subsequent week there was little change in the king's condition, although the official bulletins still sought to put the best possible face on things. Inevitably the political sympathies of the royal medical advisers became as much canvassed as their professional skill. The senior doctor, Sir Henry Halford, was suspected by many government supporters of being connected with the opposition because he called so frequently at Carlton House. Meanwhile the faithful Sydenham warned Wellesley that he should have some doctor near the king 'on whom *you can depend*'. In fact, from the government's point of view, the doctors were reliable enough; it suited their own purposes to exaggerate the extent of the king's recovery and rumour had it that,

---

vol. II, pp. 283–4; *Day*, 29 and 30 Oct. 1810; *Sun*, 30 Oct. 1810; Perceval MSS., Lonsdale to Perceval, 3 Nov. 1810.

[1] *Parl. Deb.*, XVIII, 6; Colchester, vol. II, pp. 287–9.
[2] Add. MSS., 37295, fol. 432; *Parl. Deb.*, XVIII, 42.

as early as 18 November, they had decided that if the king heard talk of a Regency the shock might drive him permanently insane. On the twenty-second they assured a delighted Perceval that his majesty had reached the 'second stage of his disorder' and was well on the way to complete recovery.[1] But once again they proved over-optimistic. Princess Amelia had died on 2 November and was buried on the fourteenth. The following day the king was well enough to go through his daughter's affairs. Yet on the seventeenth he was more feverish than ever and, after rallying slightly, remained very seriously ill from the twenty-third to the twenty-sixth. The privy council met on the twenty-eighth and twenty-ninth to hear reports from the medical attendants, each of whom spoke confidently of the soundness of George III's constitution and of the certainty of his ultimate recovery. Consequently the prime minister told a later meeting of his own supporters that when parliament reassembled he proposed to present the minutes of the examination and to propose yet another fortnight's adjournment. This was carried in the Commons, against strong whig protests, by 233 votes to 129: in the Lords the government's majority fell to 32.[2]

At first it seemed possible that the additional time thus gained would solve ministers' difficulties, for the king was reported to be so surprisingly well on 4 and 5 December that Perceval was convinced that a privy council would soon be summoned to prorogue parliament. Yet the following day his majesty had another severe relapse and on the eleventh Leigh Hunt's *Examiner* contained the first public forecast that the king would never recover. Perceval himself had his own doubts: on 12 December he warned the Speaker that he could not ask the Commons to adjourn again. When parliament met the next day the prime minister proposed a committee to examine the king's physicians and then, armed with its report, gave notice that, in a committee of the whole House, he would move the resolutions adopted in 1788.[3] The first and second, establishing George III's inability to conduct state business and parliament's right to supply this deficiency, were

---

[1] Add. MSS., 37295, fol. 432; Colchester, vol. II, p. 292. On 23 Nov. Perceval received the following prescription for the King from Richard Clarke of 11, Beaufort Buildings, Strand—'the camphorated mixture of the London Pharmacopia to be taken as common drink, in any quantity the stomach will bear' (Perceval MSS.).

[2] Perceval MSS., duke of York to Perceval, 2 Nov. 1810; Rose, vol. II, p. 455; *Parl. Deb.*, XVIII, 75 and 188.

[3] *Parl. Deb.*, XVIII, 127 and 179; Auckland, *Journal*, vol. IV, p. 356; Colchester, vol. II, pp. 296–7.

not challenged by the opposition. But the wording of the third caused a revival of the bitter disputes which had aggravated the Regency crisis twenty-two years previously. Perceval, like Pitt, insisted that the authority of the Regent should be based on an act of parliament. The opposition, supported by the City radicals, argued that parliament ought to proceed by an address, thus inviting the prince of Wales to accept the Regency as an indefeasible right. The Commons divided on the issue and agreed by a majority of 111 to accept the government's policy.

Yet this was not the main issue. Dare the ministry, conscious of its own political weakness and distracted by grave financial and military crises, seek to restrict the prince of Wales' authority as Regent? Most of the opposition thought not, for the one restriction the cabinet could not impose was that forbidding a change of ministers. Brougham predicted a servile bill with few restrictions, 'just enough to save the principle as it were': the radical press jibed that the Inns, although devoid of foresight in great matters, could 'at least see a few yards before them at Court' and would soon be converted to the virtues of an unrestricted Regency.[1] But in Perceval they mistook their man. The situation was one which he could understand and in which he could act with self-confidence and decision. He had the precedent of 1788 to guide him and the inspiration of knowing that he was defending the interests of the old king: 'what he had to do', he told an admirer, 'was the merest plain-sailing in the world—his duty had no difficulties' for he acted on Pitt's brief.[2] The government's position was weak, but it had the advantage of being led by one man who knew what he wanted and was not afraid to act. The prince of Wales, in contrast, was so harassed by conflicting advice and so handicapped by his own inherent lack of determination that he drifted from one policy to another, until he lost all command of the situation. As soon as he heard of his father's illness he assured the duke of York that his conduct would be very moderate and, towards the end of November, Cumberland told Rose that the prince had no contact with the opposition and had no wish to dismiss ministers, provided they treated him 'like a gentleman, not like a ruffian'.[3]

On 19 December the prime minister wrote to Carlton House informing the prince that the cabinet had decided on the details of the Regency Bill. The Regent was to be restricted, for a period of twelve

---

[1] Brougham, *Memoirs*, vol. I, p. 512; *Examiner*, 11 Nov. 1810.
[2] R. P. Ward, *Memoirs*, vol. I, p. 335.   [3] Rose, vol. II, pp. 450 and 459.

months from the time of the passing of the Act, from creating peers
and from granting offices in reversion or bestowing pensions: the care
of the king's person, during his illness, was to be entrusted to the
queen, assisted by a special council, and the king's private property
was to be vested in trustees for his majesty's benefit. The prince's
reaction was violent. He immediately assembled all the royal dukes at
Carlton House and persuaded them to sign a joint protest against the
proposed limitations. At midnight they issued a statement denouncing
the ministry's proposals as 'perfectly unconstitutional' and subversive
of the principles 'which seated our family upon the throne of these
realms'.[1] But the public was in no mood to be lectured on constitutional
doctrine by princes of the blood. 'It is', wrote Leigh Hunt in the
Examiner, 'a very weak paper, without meaning and without importance.' Few members, admitted Lady Holland, were bullied into
ratting on the ministry; the country gentlemen, on the whole, were
outraged rather than intimidated. The protest itself, emphasised the
Courier, was strictly unconstitutional, for it sought to influence parliament's decision before it had even begun to debate the Regency Bill.[2]
All groups began to rally their supporters for the decisive struggle.
Both Perceval and Ponsonby sent out circular letters. 'Two or three
Irish members are got over', wrote the lord lieutenant to the home
office, 'and I hope to prevail upon two or three more. A good bulletin
would have much weight.' The more sanguine of the government's
supporters still hoped that the king would recover and dish the whigs.
Bathurst spread optimistic reports of his majesty's condition while the
government press was full of rumours that the prince and Perceval
had agreed to settle their differences, although, in fact, the prince was
too undecided and flustered to settle anything. The *Sun* scored a neat
point by reprinting in full Grenville's 1788 speech in favour of a limited
Regency. As always at a crisis the opposition was uncertain and disunited. Sheridan, still influential at Carlton House, was on bad terms
with both Grey and Grenville; Grey himself stayed in Northumberland
and left the Foxites leaderless; Grenville at least came to town, but,
dogged by his 1788 speech, was more of an embarrassment than a
help.[3]

[1] Windsor MSS. (prince of Wales file), 41514-9; Colchester, vol. II, pp.
299-300.
[2] *Examiner*, 23 Dec. 1810; *Courier*, 22 Dec. 1810; Lady Holland, *Journal*,
vol. II, p. 280; Rose, vol. II, p. 463.
[3] *Day*, 11 and 12 Dec. 1810; *Sun*, 16 Dec. 1810; Westbrook Hay MSS., duke
of Richmond to Ryder, 10 Jan. 1811; Moore, *Memoirs*, vol. I, p. 245.

The decisive struggle began in parliament on the last day of 1810 when Perceval moved the five resolutions on which the Regency Bill was to be based. William Lamb, the future Lord Melbourne, proposed to amend the first resolution by omitting the restrictions on the Regent's exercise of the royal authority. Although Canning voted with the opposition, the government had a majority of 224 to 200. The second and third resolutions, which detailed the restrictions, were then approved by 226 votes to 210 and 233 to 214, while the uncontroversial fourth resolution, vesting the king's private property in the hands of trustees, was accepted without a division. The new year was half an hour old when the House finally adjourned without dividing on the fifth and most vital proposition, which confided the care of the king's person to the queen, assisted by a council.[1] When the debate was resumed on the evening of new year's day Perceval made a major tactical blunder by proposing that her majesty should have full control over the entire royal Household. This seemed so gratuitous an insult to the prince that Granville Leveson-Gower promptly moved an amendment restricting the queen's control to that portion of the Household which was to remain in personal attendance on the old king. In the discussion that evening Castlereagh, Wilberforce, and Canning, with eleven of his followers, all deserted and so ministers lost by 226 votes to 213. The result, wrote an exultant Canning to Bagot, was 'exactly what was most to be wished'. 'I could have changed the majority of thirteen against ministers to one of nine for them with my own forces only, and with those who went with me, into a majority of twenty at least.' [2] But Perceval had little patience with such doubtful political arithmetic. There were, he told Ward, not many rats, 'only a few mice'. Canning's speech in the debate, wrote Ward, contained 'not a single flash of wit, but a dull and laboured argument, on which he was wrong from beginning to end'. Perceval, although suffering from a headache, had answered him 'in his full style of manliness, and beat him to pieces'. More important in the long run than such dialectical triumphs was the steady loyalty of regular government supporters on the back benches. When Lord Huntly arrived in London to take part in the debate, he was immediately beset by the duke of Cumberland

[1] *Parl. Deb.*, XVIII, 348. Relations between Perceval and the prince of Wales were so delicate that the prime minister sent his official report on the debate through the duke of Cumberland (Walpole, vol. II, pp. 173–5).

[2] *Parl. Deb.*, XVIII, 598; *Trans. of the Royal Historical Society, 4th series*, vol. 17, Aspinall, *The Canningite Party*, pp. 188–9; Bagot, vol. I, p. 368. The Canningites Wilbraham Bootle and Sturges Bourne voted with Perceval.

and urged to vote against Perceval's resolutions. There was, admitted Huntly, merit in the duke's arguments, 'but there is an old Highland proverb, never quit a friend in need, and it is so much observed that if I were to comply I should never be able to show my face in the Highlands, which, as I have a house there, would be mighty inconvenient'.[1] The following day the Commons continued its 'sad quarrelling work' on the report stage. Ministers then mistakenly tried to restore the fifth resolution in its original form and, equally unwisely, relied on Ryder and Yorke to answer a half-tipsy but still eloquent Sheridan. When the House divided the government was again defeated, although only by the narrow margin of three votes.[2] The resolutions were then sent on to the Lords where Grenville, burdened by memories of his Pittite days, effectively dished the opposition's hopes of fresh triumphs. In the first division he supported an amendment, moved by Lord Lansdowne, to omit all reference to restrictions and saw the government unexpectedly defeated by 105 votes to 102. This first major rebuff in the Lords was largely due to abstentions, for Malmesbury, having told Camden and Liverpool that ill-health would prevent his attendance, confessed to Perceval that he opposed the idea of limitations, and the disgruntled Chatham also failed to appear. 'In such a moment as the present', wrote Richmond, 'we expected rats, but not such a man as Lord Chatham.' Yet on the second resolution Grenville promptly turned round, voted for restricting the prince's right to create peers and gave ministers a majority of six. 'D——n him,' grumbled an opposition peer, 'after the worst speech that was ever made to pave the way for inconsistency, to on a sudden leave us for the sake of consistency, and ruin the whole game.'[3] By 14 January the resolutions had passed both Houses and were sent down 'for a commission to pass the Great Seal for opening the session. . . .'[4]

The need to set up an effective Regency without delay had been underlined, late in December, by a new crisis at the exchequer. On the twenty-seventh a treasury board meeting, attended by Perceval, Broderick, Eliot, and Snowdon Barne had approved a minute for the issue from the exchequer of two sums of £500,000 for the use of the army and navy respectively. Neither the keeper of the signet nor the

[1] Ward, vol. I, pp. 300 and 304-5.
[2] *Parl. Deb.*, XVIII, 673; Wilberforce, vol. III, p. 491; Colchester, vol. II, p. 302.
[3] Ward, vol. I, p. 317; Perceval MSS., Malmesbury to Perceval, 2 Jan. 1811; Westbrook Hay MSS., duke of Richmond to Ryder, 10 Jan. 1811.
[4] Colchester, vol. II, p. 307.

lord privy seal himself raised any constitutional objection to the use of the privy seal to authorise these advances. A Mr. Larpent, however, the clerk to the lord privy seal, refused to append his signature which was necessary under the terms of a statute of Henry VIII. His oath of office, he argued, forbade him from affixing the privy seal to any bill which did not bear the sign manual.[1] The treasury board was therefore forced to rely solely on the authority of its own warrant to the auditor of the exchequer instructing him to issue the required sums. Such resolution might have overcome all difficulties had not the sinecure of auditor been held by Lord Grenville, who wrote from Camelford House on new year's day to say that he had convenient doubts about the legality of his relying on the treasury warrant alone and to ask for a ruling from the government law officers. The following day Sir Vicary Gibbs and Sir Thomas Plumer formally advised the board that a treasury warrant was not 'a sufficient authority imperative upon the auditor nor consequently a legal sanction for his proceeding to obey the same. . . .' Even then Perceval still refused to admit defeat. At a special meeting of the board on 2 January he told his colleagues that the disputed money must be issued without delay if the business of government was to be carried on, and finally persuaded them to agree 'that they are consequently ready to take upon themselves the responsibility of any act which may be essential for that purpose'. The under-secretary, Harrison, forwarded this decision to Grenville and Larpent, but both still declined to give way. Perceval was therefore finally reduced to submitting a special motion in the Commons. It was extraordinary, wrote Malmesbury, that a clerk earning not more than £150 a year had the power to disrupt the workings of government until over-ruled by a resolution of parliament.[2]

Throughout the bitter January of 1811 rumours of Perceval's impending fall were as thick as the ice which covered the west side of the Thames and nearly blocked the arches of Westminster Bridge. On 8 January Rose heard that Grenville had spent three hours closeted with the prince, who had finally decided on a change of ministers. Later that day Moira, a seemingly reliable source, gave Liverpool the same news. Canning, it was said, was to be a member of the new cabinet, which would ask for a dissolution in March. At White's they were taking many bets that Perceval would not be at the treasury by

[1] P.R.O., T27/67/511–14.
[2] P.R.O., T27/67/515–28; Malmesbury, *Letters*, vol. II, p. 220.

1 April; by the thirteenth almost every wall west of Temple Bar bore
the slogan 'The Prince and No Perceval', while Wilberforce and Henry
Thornton were busy comparing lists of the expected new ministry.[1]
Before January was out the prince had sounded Huskisson about
resuming office and Grenville had informally invited Horner to become
one of the joint secretaries to the treasury on the understanding that
his lordship himself would be first lord and Tierney, chancellor of the
exchequer. Meanwhile nearly every issue of the *Day* contained long
lists of alleged new ministers and went so far as to name even minor
office holders. Grenville, Grey, and Holland appeared to be favourites
for 10, Downing Street with Tierney and Whitbread as the chief rivals
for the exchequer. One version, more bizarre than the rest, gave
Burdett as home secretary and the duke of Kent as commander-in-
chief. Canning regularly appeared as the new first lord of the
admiralty.[2] Throughout all this poor Perceval, although knowing
nothing more than he could glean from opposition rumours and from
the press, fought on with a dogged courage which touched on the
heroic. He got, thought Wilberforce, precious little help from his
colleagues in the Commons whom Ponsonby, with a rare flash of wit,
took to addressing as 'Right Honourable Mutes'. Never, wrote the
Day, had a prime minister been so obviously isolated on the treasury
bench. Fortunately the first lord still proved 'a Hercules in strength
though a pigmy in size': there was, admitted one opponent, no one
on the opposition benches 'that is at all a match for little Perceval'.[3]
Although he had brief thoughts of resigning on 23 January and told
Wellesley that he felt 'very unwell' under the accumulated strain, he
soon rallied to renew the fight, so that Robert Ward, who dined with
him on the twenty-fifth, found him 'never more easy or more cheerful'.
His government's only chances of survival lay, it seemed, either in a
miraculous recovery by the old king or in piloting the final stages
of the Regency Bill through parliament and then relying on Grey's
and Grenville's proved ability to mis-play even the strongest hand.

Hopes of George III's recovery could scarcely have been lower
than they seemed at the beginning of January, when Thomas Tyrwhitt
told the Speaker that his majesty was so violent that his doctors could

[1] Rose, vol. II, p. 469; Bourke, *The Betting Book of White's Club*, pp. 67–71;
Examiner, 13 Jan. 1811; Wilberforce, vol. III, pp. 492–3.
[2] *Speeches of William Huskisson*, pp. 56–7; Horner, vol. II, pp. 35–6; *Day*,
24–9 Jan. 1811.
[3] Add. MSS., 37295, fol. 444; Wilberforce, vol. III, p. 493; *Day*, 21 Jan. 1811;
Letters to Ivy, p. 151; Ward, vol. I, p. 354.

not even get near enough to him to take his pulse.[1] Yet by the eighteenth the king was so much better that he was allowed to walk on Windsor terrace and on the twenty-sixth he granted an audience to Eldon and Perceval, during which he recognised them both and talked intelligibly on state affairs. Three days later he had a long conversation with his prime minister, confessing that he was ready, at the age of seventy-two, to retire, but adding, with all his old defiance, that 'he must still, however, be "King"; he could not part with that name'.[2] Meanwhile, in the Commons, Perceval continued against all odds to fight his way through the later stages of the Regency Bill. On 17 January the opposition attempted to reduce the period of restrictions on the Regent from twelve to six months, but, wrote Robert Ward, 'we beat them hollow'. Perceval, more forceful than ever, routed Canning and Tierney in debate, until the latter confessed that the prime minister had made 'one of Mr. Pitt's speeches'. 'It is amazing', concluded Ward, 'how Perceval fights.' After three unsuccessful divisions the opposition agreed to adjourn, 'though delay is death to them'. Four days' later, during the debate on the report stage, a flagging opposition had to be coerced by Carlton House into dividing against the Household clauses and then could only muster 190 votes against a government total of 212.[3] And so by 29 January the Regency Bill had completed all its stages through parliament. On 4 February it received the Royal Assent. Throughout all the alarms and the ugly debates a seemingly doomed Perceval had been kept afloat by the steady loyalty of government back-benchers and by the clear preference of the great majority of independent country gentlemen for a man of integrity and resolution rather than all the talents but uncertain policies of a heterogeneous opposition. It was a personal and parliamentary triumph worthy of a Pitt.

Both the improvement in the king's condition and the outcome of the debates left the prince of Wales with a difficult decision about a possible change of ministers. Even so he might well have still dismissed Perceval had not the opposition once again thrown the game away. As soon as the Regency Bill had passed through all its stages, the prince asked Grey and Grenville to draft, in co-operation with Moira, an answer to parliament's address. The grandees began by refusing to consult with Moira and then offered a draft which did scant justice to

---

[1] Colchester, vol. II, p. 345; Ward, vol. I, pp. 363-4.
[2] Colchester, vol. II, pp. 302-8, 311 and 313-14.
[3] Ward, vol. I, pp. 336-7; Colchester, vol. II, p. 309.

the prince's objections to the restrictions imposed upon him. Grenville, still groping to reconcile his views of 1788 with those of 1811, was hardly a suitable joint author for such a paper. In the end the prince objected 'to almost every part of it' and adopted instead a version prepared by Sheridan. This in turn was rejected by Grey after 'a warm discussion' at Holland House the very night before the answer was due to be presented to parliament. Both Grey and Grenville then sent a formal remonstrance against the prince's consulting Sheridan, whose lame excuse was that he did not know that the grandees had been asked to prepare the first draft. Personal rivalry and distrust had again baffled the opposition although Sheridan himself had probably only intended his party colleagues 'to feel his power and not to sink under it'.[1] On the evening of 1 February the Speaker heard the first reports that the prince had told Grey and Grenville that he had no intention of changing the government 'at present'. Although the prince had spent nearly all that day with the duke of York, rumour had it that he had finally been swayed by a letter from the queen giving news of his father's continued recovery. Romilly, having read the text of the letter, suspected that it had been drafted by Perceval himself. Yet still the prince made no formal public announcement of his intentions and throughout 2 February ministers still seemed resigned to being dismissed until at tea-time and at the opera that evening stories spread of a final discouraging letter from the prince to Grenville. 'I am now a free man', wrote Grenville after he had received it, 'and shall go to Dropmore.' The following day his royal highness granted one more interview to the grandees and then on the fourth he wrote to Perceval confirming him in office.[2]

The prime minister had spent that morning with Charles Yorke at Windsor talking with the king, who remained 'quite sure that it could never enter into the Prince's mind to change the ministry'. Yet the prince's letter to Perceval was frigid enough in tone. His determination to retain the existing cabinet, he wrote, was dictated 'alone' by a desire to do nothing which might aggravate the king's illness. Romilly thought the letter had deliberately been phrased to try to persuade Perceval to offer his resignation, but, if so, the prince much mistook his man. The prime minister's reply thanked the prince for his frankness in disclosing the real motive for his decision and ended with a

[1] Sheridan, *Memoirs*, vol. II, pp. 387–8, 395–6 and 407.
[2] Colchester, vol. II, pp. 314–15; Romilly, vol. II, pp. 366–7; Auckland, *Journal*, vol. IV, p. 365; Ward, vol. I, p. 375.

spirited defence of the Regency Bill. The prince's letter, Perceval told Ward, was 'not more dry than could be expected' for he had never expected his royal highness to 'jump into his arms'. There was, added Perceval with a laugh, 'a monstrous deal of antipathy to overcome before he could even get to the length of being endured'.[1] Certainly there seemed small hope of close co-operation between 10, Downing Street and Carlton House as the prince abused ministers 'without measure' to opposition leaders and swore he would never 'break bread in the house of any one of them'. He had already, according to Romilly, told Sheridan and Adam that he intended to consult them on all public affairs and had left them with the embarrassing job of convincing him that this was constitutionally impossible. When his royal highness finally took the oath as Prince Regent on 6 February he had a bust of Fox ostentatiously displayed during the ceremony and kept the privy council waiting one and a half hours so that all should have ample opportunity to look at it. Yet, with whatever ill-grace, the Prince Regent had taken the only possible realistic political decision. The news of Perceval's retention, wrote Abbot, would give satisfaction to nine-tenths of the country while Bank stocks rose 8% as soon as it was known that there was to be no change.[2]

[1] Colchester, vol. II, pp. 317–18; Romilly, vol. II, pp. 366–7; Ward, vol. I, pp. 380–1.
[2] Holland, *Further Memoirs*, p. 91; Ward, vol. I, p. 378; *Bath Archives*, vol. I, p. 210.

CHAPTER TWENTY-ONE

PERCEVAL AND THE PRINCE REGENT

WHEN parliament formally re-assembled in the second week of February for the session of 1811 it seemed that the key to the political situation lay in the way in which relations developed between the Prince Regent and his prime minister. Perceval got off to a good start when, on the eleventh, he read a copy of the Speech to 'an absolute mob' of his supporters. 'It could not', said the Regent after reading the draft, 'be done better.' [1] Yet there were still many issues, both political and personal, which might have thrown the Regent back into the arms of his old friends. Beyond the memory of the Delicate Investigation and the Seymour case, there were sufficient clashes over patronage to continue to ruffle relations between Perceval and the Regent. They disagreed over the appointment of Herries as commissary-in-chief and frequently clashed over the Regent's attempts to reward faithful clients of Carlton House. Without consulting any of his ministers, the Regent promised William Adam, his legal adviser, the office of chief baron of the Scottish court of exchequer. It was left to Perceval to persuade William Dundas, the existing holder, to change it for the presidency of the court of sessions. Dundas held out for a peerage as part of the bargain, Melville was furious and threatened to go into opposition, and only Adam's last-minute withdrawal averted a major crisis. If Pitt's Friends were to stay in office, wrote Melville, 'there must really be some explanation and understanding as to other and irresponsible advisers'.[2] The Regent was also personally responsible for the appointment of Colonel McMahon as paymaster of widows' pensions. Perceval protested throughout that the office should be abolished and that its acceptance by the Regent's private secretary would bring the Crown into disrepute. In the end the Commons rejected the vote for McMahon's salary by 115 to 112, the Saints, as Perceval had foreseen, voting against the government.[3] The situation

[1] Ward, vol. I, p. 385; Colchester, vol. II, p. 321.
[2] Perceval MSS., Perceval to William Dundas, 10 Sep. 1811; same to Robert Dundas, 15 Sep. 1811; Melville to Perceval, 4 Oct. 1811.
[3] Windsor MSS. (Regency file), 18266–8, memorandum by McMahon, 25 July 1811; 19313, Perceval to the Prince Regent, 24 Feb. 1812.

was ideal for the whig press who lost no opportunity of painting a flattering picture of an incorruptible Regent checking a job-loving Perceval. In April 1811 the *Day* published a suspiciously long account of an alleged conversation between the Regent and his prime minister on the appointment of General Charles Craufurd as governor of Marlow military college. Although Craufurd already had £3,000 a year from other offices, Perceval was said to have urged the appointment in order to conciliate Craufurd's son-in-law, the duke of Newcastle, 'whose support in Parliament was most essential to His Majesty's administration'. 'I must tell you, once and for all,' the Regent was reported as replying, 'that I never can nor will consent to bestow any place or appointment meant to be an asylum or reward for the toils and services of our gallant soldiers and seamen, on any person on account of Parliamentary connection, or in return for Parliamentary votes.' So unlikely a declaration, wrote one ministerialist, 'struck me as a mere *ruse de guerre* of an experienced partisan'. But such paragraphs added to the general uncertainty and were very effective propaganda for the 'No Corruption' cause.[1] Late in May Wellington still anticipated a breach between the Regent and Perceval and thought it best that ministers should resign 'if the McMahon cabinet should continue to exist'.[2]

The establishment of the Regency also revived the lagging cause of catholic emancipation and so added another possible source of conflict between Perceval and the prince. George III had always been an insuperable barrier while the Regent had, in the past, accepted the whig case. On the whole, Ireland had been relatively tranquil since 1807. 'We are going on so well', wrote Lord Manners at the end of 1809, 'that I hope our tranquillity and prosperity will be a useful topic . . . and will add strength and stability to your administration.' The country, the dean of Waterford told Perceval early the next year, 'is much quieter than it has been at any period for the past eight years'. The duke of Richmond had proved to be one of the best lord lieutenants to cross the Irish channel for a long time. Furthermore, after the 1808 debate, the whigs embroiled themselves with the Irish hierarchy on the 'veto' issue and so gave ample ammunition to the ultra-protestants. Grattan formally announced during the debate that he was authorised by Dr. Milner, the accredited agent of the Irish catholic hierarchy, to state that the Crown should have power to veto the nomination of all catholic bishops if emancipation were granted. As

---

[1] *Day*, 5 Apr. 1811; Perceval MSS., duke of Montrose to Perceval (undated).
[2] *Camden Society*, vol. LXV, pp. 6–7.

early as 1805 Perceval had warned the opposition that any such scheme
would fail, because the Irish catholics would never 'be honestly contented with priests or bishops, polluted in their very creation by the
heretical nomination of a Protestant Government'.[1] When, in spite of
this, the whigs fell into the trap and then made matters worse by
publicly brawling with Milner, Perceval was too skilful a controversial-
ist to let the opportunity slip. Under the pseudonym 'A.B.' he wrote
Six Letters on the subject of Dr. Milner's Explanation to the *Morning
Post* and later published them as a pamphlet. It was by far the most
effective of Perceval's contributions on the catholic issue, for even
Professor Roberts, the most recent historian of the whig party of the
period, quoted extensively from the pamphlet without guessing the
identity of its author.[2] The decision of the Irish prelates to reject the
veto proposal was a major defeat for Grenville and Grey. The proposal, wrote the *Edinburgh Review*, was 'the most sovereign remedy'
and would have produced emancipation 'almost by acclamation' in a
matter of months.[3] In spite of the rebuff the whigs clung to the scheme.
In the autumn of 1809 Grenville published an open letter to Lord
Fingall, the moderate catholic leader, while Grey told Tierney that
the opposition could only take office determined to press emancipation
'emphatically' by means of the veto.[4] In February 1810 Grattan again
presented a series of catholic petitions, but the emancipationists cut
a sorry figure in the debate. Grattan did his best in a brilliant speech,
but had to announce the withdrawal of the veto plan. This, as Horner
told Murray, split the whigs, and Grenville pointedly absented himself
when the petition reached the Lords. In the Commons Wilberforce
hotly attacked the opposition and the petition was rejected by 213
votes to 109.[5]

Rarely had the cause of emancipation looked so hopeless. So heavy
a defeat stung the Irish catholics to self-help. 'I have no reason to
apprehend', wrote Pole to Ryder in July, 'that there is any regular
system of rebellion yet organised. There certainly is mischief on foot,
but we have our emissaries in all quarters, and I hope we shall be

[1] D. M. Perceval, *The Church Question in Ireland*, p. 39; Perceval MSS., Lord
Manners to Perceval, 7 Dec. 1809; the dean of Waterford to same, 20 Mar. 1810.
[2] Drafts of the *Six Letters* are in Perceval's hand in the Perceval MSS.; M.
Roberts, *The Whig Party, 1807-12*, pp. 41 ff.
[3] *Edinburgh Review*, Apr. 1809, p. 63.
[4] Olphin, p. 137; *Quarterly Review*, Feb. 1810, p. 140.
[5] Wilberforce, vol. III, p. 445; Horner, vol. II, p. 24. Brougham had to write
to Grey urging him to support the petition (*Memoirs*, vol. I, p. 492).

sufficiently vigilant to avert any serious mischief. I am not under any apprehension, and the Duke [of Richmond] is as usual as stout as a lion.' Rumours reached the Castle that catholic extremists had been with Fouché in Paris and were in contact with disaffected elements in London. Any agent caught would, promised Pole, be hanged if the cabinet approved: Richmond was for hanging them all with or without cabinet approval.[1] On 19 July Keogh made a violent speech at a catholic meeting, talking of Wolfe Tone as 'his lamented friend' and hinting that he would welcome a French invasion. Government spies all reported talk of rebellion, but could give no details; attempts were made by 'notorious rebels' to suborn the sixth Garrison Battalion while the loyalty of the fifty-ninth Regiment was so doubtful that it had to be moved from Dublin to Newry and replaced by highlanders. Pole reported open unrest in Tipperary, Waterford, and County Down, but was still confident that any rebellion could be quickly suppressed 'provided the French do not appear on the coast'. If, however, the French did attempt an invasion, 'there certainly would, as I conceive, be a very general rising; and in the present state of our military force, of the Catholic mind and of the general feeling among all ranks of dislike to the English connection, my own opinion is that we should have considerable difficulties to cope with even before the enemy landed; and that if he landed in any force, and acted with vigour, the most fatal consequences might ensue'. There were less than 17,000 regular troops in Ireland, led by Lord Harrington who was too infirm to take command in the field. His second-in-command, Lieutenant General Floyd, was nearly seventy years of age and 'very subject to gout'.[2] But the danger of rebellion never materialised. By the beginning of 1811 the country was much quieter after recovering from the effects of a depression in the woollen and cotton industries.[3]

It was then Lord Fingall and the moderates who caused the government real trouble by calling a catholic convention. Early in February the Castle authorities, 'determined to convince the Roman Catholics that this Government was in earnest', and without waiting to consult the British cabinet, issued decrees forbidding the convention to meet. Richmond, who acted under the First Convention Act of 33 George III cap. 29, defended his conduct in a despatch of 12 February. People in Ireland, he wrote, had begun to talk of the government's 'supineness'

[1] Westbrook Hay MSS., W. W. Pole to R. Ryder, 30 June 1810.
[2] *Ibid.*, same to same, 27 July 1810.
[3] *Ibid.*, same to same, 5 July 1810 and 10 Feb. 1811.

in allowing the catholics to assemble in the very heart of Dublin. Pole, Lord Manners, the Irish lord chancellor, and the attorney-general in Ireland all supported the policy, although fully aware that it would be attacked in parliament. 'I desire', wrote Pole, 'no better sport than being left to defend myself.' [1] But the person left really on the defensive was Perceval, who had to justify to the Prince Regent actions taken without his consent. The Irish government, as Manners admitted in a letter to the prime minister, had deliberately acted without first contacting London. Even 'if there had been abundance of time to have made the communication to you, as far as my opinion would have gone, I should have resisted it'. The responsibility rested fairly with the Castle authorities who were more competent to judge the issues than the cabinet itself. Moreover independent action by Dublin had the political advantage of not requiring the Regent either to sanction repression and offend the great majority of Roman catholics or to overrule Richmond, which 'would have been an unfortunate circumstance in the outset of His Royal Highness's Regency'.[2] On 14 February Richard Ryder forwarded the lord lieutenant's crucial despatch to Perceval. The Irish government, thought Perceval, had done right to forbid the catholic meeting and seemed to have acted within the terms of the Convention Act. Yet it was 'by no means a clear question' and the prime minister decided that the decrees must be submitted to the Regent before they were enforced.[3] The next day the home secretary sent Richmond's case to the prince, while in Dublin the impetuous Pole decided that, if the convention dared to meet, he would disperse it without waiting for instructions from London. Richmond's decrees, he wrote, had given 'general satisfaction', particularly to 'respectable' catholics. 'The newspapers as yet have hardly shaped or concerted their attacks. They mean to contend that our proceeding is illegal, but upon this subject if we are not well fortified all our Crown Lawyers are good for nothing.' [4] For three days Perceval's government again seemed on the verge of disaster. On the sixteenth it was generally expected that Fingall would call on the convention to meet and that Richmond would then arrest the catholic leaders immediately. Had this happened before any decision had been taken at Carlton House on Richmond's despatch, the Prince Regent could easily have decided

[1] *Ibid.*, same to same, 12 Feb. 1811.
[2] Perceval MSS., Lord Manners to Perceval, 2 Mar. 1811.
[3] Westbrook Hay MSS., memorandum by Perceval, 14 Feb. 1811.
[4] *Ibid.*, R. Ryder to Prince Regent, 15 Feb. 1811; W. W. Pole to Ryder, 15 Feb. 1811.

to stand forth as a staunch emancipationist and send the cabinet packing. On 17 February an anxious Perceval waited on the prince and, in an ominously quiet Dublin, Pole was busy consulting the Crown lawyers and reading his spies' reports.[1] The next day all was safe. In the morning the Regent, after four hours with Ryder, approved the decrees and only asked that the law be enforced with all leniency consistent with maintaining public peace. 'With a perfect indifference as to office,' wrote a jubilant Manners, 'I really am quite delighted with this specimen of what may be expected from the fairness, the prudence and steadiness of the Prince, whenever we shall have the misfortune to lose the good old King.' [2] The Regent had forsaken his old whig allies and even sections of the pro-catholic English press supported the government. With Pole in yet more defiant mood, Fingall opted for discretion and postponed the convention until the summer.[3] The cabinet had survived without a clash with the Regent, but was so shaken by the unexpected zeal and independence of their colleagues in Dublin that even so rigid a protestant as Eldon could not disguise his misgivings in the Lords.[4]

That summer the whole crisis was repeated in spite of Foster's optimistic report to Perceval that 'I never saw more content nor less disposition to think of politics, or Popery, or Protestantism'.[5] On 10 July Pole sent Ryder news that Fingall intended to form a catholic committee and ten days later Richmond sent an urgent despatch to London. The catholic bishops, wrote Pole, intended to attend the convention, which would increase the threat to the Irish establishment. The home secretary must decide on a policy and send precise instructions: 'but you cannot agree to let this Convention meet without molestation unless you are prepared to allow the country to be thrown into the utmost confusion and disorder'. 'Beware', warned the indefatigable Pole, 'of compromise.' [6] On 21 July reports reached Dublin

---

[1] Westbrook Hay MSS., W. W. Pole to Ryder, 17 Feb. 1811.

[2] *Ibid.*, R. Ryder to duke of Richmond, 18 Feb. 1811; Perceval MSS., Lord Manners to Perceval, 2 Mar. 1811; Colchester, vol. II, p. 322.

[3] *Day*, 23 Feb. 1811; Westbrook Hay MSS., W. W. Pole to Ryder, 21 and 24 Feb. 1811.

[4] Westbrook Hay MSS., duke of Richmond to Pole, 8 Mar. 1811; 'Lord Eldon's speech was very injudicious, and will do us considerable harm in Ireland. The violent men at the meetings will take advantage of it, and we shall I fear have more difficulty in stopping them than I expected.'—Pole to Ryder, 16 Apr. 1811. 'Lord Eldon has done an injury that will not easily be repaired.'

[5] Perceval MSS., John Foster to Perceval, 22 June 1811.

[6] Westbrook Hay MSS., W. W. Pole to Ryder, 10 and 20 July 1811.

that Fingall intended to call on the sheriff of Meath to allow his
country house to be used for a meeting to elect ten local catholics to
the national committee. Again the Castle would have used force had
not Perceval consulted Gibbs and Plumer, the English Crown lawyers,
who ruled that the Irish Convention Act made all sessions of a catholic
committee itself illegal, but could not be extended to suppress meetings
called to elect delegates.[1] Once again Perceval played a difficult role
with great skill, checking the hotheads in Dublin Castle and steering
the Regent into the protestant camp. On 25 July the prime minister
went to Carlton House to persuade the prince of the need to use 'all
the measures which the law puts into our hands to prevent this illegal
and dangerous assembly'. The following day Ryder was able to send
the lord lieutenant full powers to disperse the convention, but warned
Pole 'not to take any strong measure that is not absolutely necessary'.
It was for Perceval a triple triumph, for Richmond was delighted, the
Regent converted, and Pole 'tied hand and foot'.[2] That December the
Irish secretary submitted a long anti-catholic memorandum to the
cabinet calling on the Regent to make some public declaration of his
conversion to the protestant camp. But it needed no public declaration
to convince the English whigs that their game was lost. Both Moira
and Bedford sent strong protests to Carlton House and the opposition
raised the issue again in parliament early in 1812. It looked, as even
the pro-catholic *Day* reported, like an open attempt to 'embarrass
and embroil the Prince Regent with his ministers'.[3] It was the Irish
catholics' own impetuosity, wrote Herries to Pole, that had lost them
the support of Carlton House. The catholic issue, if prudently handled,
would certainly have gravely embarrassed the government 'and most
probably have expelled Messrs. Perceval, Pole and Co. from their
stations. It is fortunate for the country that this powerful organisation
is in unskilful hands.' [4]

Equally firm was Perceval's handling of war policy, for above all,
in spite of political difficulties at home and the treasury's Spanish
dollar problem, the new government continued doggedly to support

[1] *Ibid.*, W. W. Pole to Ryder, 21 July 1811; legal opinions by Sir Vicary
Gibbs and Sir Thomas Plumer, 24 and 25 July 1811.

[2] *Ibid.*, Ryder to Pole, 25 and 26 July 1811; same to duke of Richmond, 26
July 1811; Pole to Ryder, 30 July 1811.

[3] Perceval MSS., cabinet memorandum by W. W. Pole, 31 Dec. 1811. (For
the full text see Walpole, vol. II, pp. 248–54.) Windsor MSS. (Regency file),
18419–24, Moira to Prince Regent, 19 Aug. 1811; Aspinall, *Letters of George IV*,
vol. I, no. 9; *Day*, 31 Jan. 1812.

[4] Herries, vol. I, p. 21.

Wellington's army in the Peninsula. Never, it seemed, had British prospects of victory been at a lower ebb.[1] The opposition, shaken by the many peace petitions of the long hard winter of 1808, had long been barren of constructive ideas about the conduct of the war. Their arguments in parliament, when not purely destructive, frequently cancelled out each other, while the *Edinburgh Review* lurched from outright defeatism to calls for wild military gambles in northern Spain.[2] When the Commons debated a vote of thanks for Talavera, Ponsonby first sent round notes to his supporters saying that the opposition would divide the House and then sent a second to say that they would not. 'The result', wrote Creevey, 'was recrimination and confusion.'[3] Sir John Moore's ill-fated campaign and the subsequent publication of his *Memoirs* further shattered weak nerves. Jeffrey had 'despaired utterly' and had not expected ever to see the bulk of the expeditionary force back in Britain again; Wilberforce found even his most modest hopes disappointed; Nicholas Vansittart, after reading Moore's *Memoirs*, was 'full of anxieties' about the Peninsula and 'by no means easy about Sir Arthur Wellesley'. Even Lord Wellesley himself had told Thomas Grenville of his entire disapprobation of the conduct of the war and of 'the impolicy of sending a regular English army to act permanently in Spain'.[4] In both January and March of 1810 the *Day* printed rumours of a convention under which the British agreed finally to evacuate all their troops from Portugal until even so informed and usually calm an observer as Robert Dundas wrote suggesting that Wellington might succeed Minto in India.[5]

Such widespread pessimism in London combined with the fashionable 'croaking' of army officers on leave from Portugal soon began to affect relations between Wellington and the new ministry. Napier tells of one unnamed member of the Portland Government who, during the political crisis of the autumn of 1809, wrote to Wellington complaining of his inaction and demanding news that would excite interest at home—'anything provided blood was spilt'.[6] The precariousness of the new government's majority in the Commons only added to Wellington's fears of the 'wise gentlemen in the Debating

[1] Sir C. C. Lewis, *The Administrations of Great Britain*, p. 318.

[2] *Sun*, 5 Jan. 1808; Roberts, *The Whig Party*, pp. 3 and 117; *Edinburgh Review*, July 1808, p. 444; July 1809, pp. 463–81.   [3] *Creevey Papers*, vol. I, p. 125.

[4] Horner, vol. I, p. 439; Wilberforce, vol. III, p. 396; Colchester MSS., P.R.O. 30/9/15, Nicholas Vansittart to Abbot, 12 Aug. 1809; *Dropmore MSS.*, vol. IX, p. 268.   [5] *Day*, 11 Jan. and 3 Mar. 1810; Add. MSS., 38244, fol. 131.

[6] Napier, *History of the Peninsular War*, vol. III, p. 218.

Society' who constantly attacked his military policy. 'The Gov[ern-men]t', he wrote, 'are terribly afraid that I shall get them, and myself, into a scrape. But what can be expected of men who are beaten in the H[ouse] of C[ommons] three times a week?' [1] In fact the new government had no intention of abandoning the campaign. Liverpool had, with Perceval's full support, accepted the war office only on condition that all future military efforts should be concentrated on the Peninsula. 'I never knew a question', he assured Wellington, 'on which there was less difference of opinion in the cabinet than upon the subject of Portugal.' [2] Everything possible was done to whip up confidence at home in the final outcome of the campaign. Treasury newspapers teemed with accounts of even minor skirmishes (often written up until they sounded like major battles) and of plans for future operations. The award of the order of the bath to Beresford, the commander of the Portuguese forces attached to the British army, publicly marked Perceval's determination to fight on in spite of all difficulties.[3] Early in 1810 the prime minister was encouraging Nathaniel Wraxall, the author of historical memoirs, to produce a pamphlet on the conduct of the war. Britain's great hope of eventual victory, wrote Perceval to his brother, lay in stimulating 'the resistance of the oppressed peoples of the continent'. Such was our policy in the Peninsula and we had to give these efforts absolute priority. Eventually the same tactics might be tried elsewhere in Europe. 'Yet', concluded Perceval, 'I cannot flatter myself that the minds and condition of those people are so far ripe for the execution of this plan as to make it either prudent with regard to our own interest or justifiable with regard to theirs to be endeavouring at this time to foment any movement amongst them. ... Everyone will agree that an attempt prematurely made would expose to destruction those means, which at a more favourable opportunity, might be exerted with success.' It would be neither prudent nor moral to try and involve other nations in uprisings against the French until we had the means to give them adequate military aid.[4] For the same reasons Perceval refused all entanglements in Spanish

---

[1] *Camden Soc., 3rd series, Miscellany 18, Letters of Wellington to W. W. Pole*, p. 29; Wellington, *Despatches*, vol. V, p. 413 and vol. VI, p. 21; Fortescue, *History of the British Army*, vol. VI, p. 235.

[2] Yonge, vol. I, pp. 330-1; Wellington, *Supplementary Despatches*, vol. XI, p. 591.

[3] Napier, vol. III, p. 247; Add. MSS., 38191, fol. 190. Major-General Beresford was appointed to the command of the Portuguese troops in British pay in Feb. 1809 (Castlereagh, *Correspondence and Despatches*, vol. VII, p. 34).

[4] Perceval MSS., Perceval to Arden, 22 Jan. 1810.

and Portuguese South America. General Miranda pressed the idea on him in the interests of the national independence of the American peoples, mercantile interests in the house of commons supported it for the opportunities of free trade, and Saints like James Stephen had their sights on an extension of the abolition of the slave trade. Yet Perceval realised that it would only weaken the crucial efforts in Portugal.[1] After years of over-ambitious campaigns and ill-digested plans the new prime minister's realism and grasp of essentials promised well for the future conduct of the war.

Although in July 1811 there were press rumours of French troops, under Napoleon himself, massing in the French ports for an attempted invasion of Britain, the war generally was at last going well. Liverpool had instructed Wellington in the Peninsula to invite or avoid engagements with the enemy solely on military grounds without being influenced in any way by the state of public opinion at home, while in the autumn of 1810, 10,000 troops had courageously been sent from Ireland to reinforce the forces in Portugal. 'We are becoming', wrote Wellington to Liverpool in February of 1811, 'a more efficient army every day.' [2] After holding firm behind the lines of Torres Vedras in the winter of 1810, British troops forced Massena to retreat in the following March and by the summer were themselves besieging the key fortresses of Badajoz and Ciudad Rodrigo. Although neither fell that year and the 1811 campaign ended inconclusively, both were in British hands by the following spring and exactly three months after Perceval's death Wellington led his troops into Madrid. Meanwhile in parliament Perceval had lost no opportunity of ridiculing the forebodings and defeatism of the opposition. 'Destroy the web of prophecy in vain', he joked, misquoting Pope, 'The creature's at his dirty work again.' Such courage soon proved infectious with the abler young men on the treasury bench. When in March 1811 Fremantle made a typically gloomy speech on the Peninsula, he was answered by young Peel 'and pulled to pieces in one of the most beautiful as well as argumentative speeches ever delivered in the House'.[3] Finally Perceval, in the spring of 1811, felt able to take the vital step of advising the

[1] Herries MSS., General Miranda to Herries, Mar. 31 and 3 Apr. 1810. For Wellington's views see Fortescue, vol. VI, pp. 214–15 and 221.

[2] *Day*, 29 July 1811; Yonge, vol. I, p. 326; Add. MSS., 38244, fol. 275 and 38246, fol. 47; Perceval MSS., Mulgrave to Perceval, 11 Sept. 1810.

[3] Roberts, *The Whig Party*, p. 163; Ward, vol. I, p. 407. In May of 1811 even Whitbread wrote to Wellington admitting that he had changed his views on the Peninsular campaign (Wellington, *Despatches*, vol. V, p. 43).

reappointment of the duke of York as commander-in-chief. For on 11 April 1811 and again on 13 May Sir David Dundas formally submitted his resignation to the Prince Regent after more than fifty years in the king's service. At the age of seventy-five his faculties began to fail him and he therefore begged to retire from a post which demanded the energy of a much younger man. In fact Dundas had been virtually in retirement when he had been unexpectedly called to succeed the duke of York after the Mary Anne Clarke scandal. During his brief period at the horseguards Dundas served loyally and conscientiously, apart from one bitter and unnecessary dispute with Palmerston, the secretary-at-war, about army clothing.[1] But for two years the war effort had sadly missed the drive of the duke of York. When, on 18 May, the Prince Regent asked the cabinet's advice on the appointment of a successor to Dundas, Perceval did not hesitate to recommend the duke in spite of the danger of reviving 'those heats and prejudices which the Parliamentary inquiry into His Royal Highness's conduct had excited'. In the event the prime minister's boldness was well repaid for the news of the duke's reappointment was generally welcomed. Grenville gave it his full support, though Sheridan wrote to the Regent protesting against its timing. More important was Wellington's approval and the Prince Regent's own satisfaction. 'I have', wrote that fervent young partisan, Fanny Perceval, to her brother Spencer, 'the best thing in the world to tell you, and that is that the dear Duke of York has at last had justice done him, and that he is what (in my opinion) he ought always to have been, Commander-in-Chief. Are not you glad?' The government's firmness on both Irish and war policy was gradually reconciling the Prince Regent to the servants he had inherited from his father.[2]

As the 1811 session wore on it became increasingly obvious that there were small hopes of George III's return to sanity ending the Regency before the expiration of the restrictions on the prince. During May the old king's condition got steadily worse and by the middle of July he either talked in his wild ravings to people long since dead (Perceval's own father and 'some old Hanoverian minister' figured

[1] Perceval MSS., Sir David Dundas to the Prince Regent, 11 Apr. and 13 May 1811; Add. MSS., 27598, fols. 1–37.
[2] Perceval MSS., Prince Regent to Perceval, 18 May 1811, cabinet minute, 19 May 1811; Windsor MSS., 18064, Robert Dundas to Prince Regent, 28 May 1811; 18055–6, Sheridan to same, 24 May 1811; Colchester, vol. II, p. 214; Wellington, *Despatches*, vol. V, p. 124; Perceval MSS., Fanny to Spencer Perceval jnr., undated.

largely in his delusions) or thought himself 'to be shut up in Noah's Ark as an antediluvian'. On 20 May his body was so swollen and his strength appeared to be ebbing so fast that those at Windsor expected him to die within a few days. 'The sad scene', wrote Moira to McMahon on the thirtieth, 'is on the eve of closing.' But although the old man clung as stubbornly to life as his last prime minister clung to office, the *Day* publicly admitted in August that all hope of his recovery had been abandoned. That autumn even Perceval was occupied drafting a proclamation for the accession of George IV.[1] There were still odd rumours throughout the summer and early autumn of major political changes. One, started by that great newsmonger Tierney, included a forecast that Speaker Abbot was to go to the Lords. This so convinced Canning that he told his Oxford friends that he would be a candidate for the vacant chair. Yet the former foreign secretary, although, according to Abbot, 'evidently consulting and co-operating with Adam', was no longer one of Perceval's major worries. Robert Ward noticed 'how well pleased most, whether friends or foes, seemed to be at the little way Canning made. . . . Several observed he had not got an inch since last session.' For although Perceval marvelled 'at the slavery' which Canning exacted from his followers, that little band continued slowly to decline in numbers as Sturges Bourne took to sitting with Perceval's supporters 'and often on the Treasury bench'.[2] More prophetic of real future trouble for Perceval was a rumour in the *Day* that autumn of a coalition headed by Wellesley with Perceval as lord chancellor and Holland, Ponsonby, and Liverpool as secretaries of state. Such a combination, unlikely as it seemed, had far more to commend it than the suggestion which Willoughby Gordon sent to Carlton House of a real government of grandees, to include Bedford, Northumberland, Rutland, Beaufort, Hertford, and Moira.[3] In fact while Canning's fortunes continued to ebb and Grey and Grenville squabbled with Sheridan and began to distrust Carlton House, Perceval's followers were left as the only major united and purposeful group in the Commons. As a result the Prince Regent drifted slowly but surely into closer contact with his

[1] Colchester, vol. II, pp. 333, 343 and 373; Windsor MSS., 18301–2; Moira to McMahon, 30 July 1811; *Day*, 15 and 21 Aug. 1811; Harrowby MSS., vol. XVI, fol. 60.

[2] Colchester, vol. II, pp. 308 and 328; Ward, vol. I, pp. 336–7, 363–4 and 402.

[3] *Day*, 27 Nov. 1811; Windsor MSS., 18839–42, Willoughby Gordon to McMahon, 15 Nov. 1811.

cabinet ministers. As early as 25 February 1811 Perceval had felt
sufficiently confident to appeal to McMahon for support when the
opposition tried to censure Eldon for his conduct during the early days
of the king's illness. The prime minister had, he explained, no wish to
change the politics of the prince's friends but he thought it most proper
for them to vote with the ministry on this occasion.[1] In May Richmond
was assuring Ryder that the great virtue of the Regent's having tried
the existing government was that, 'tho' he will kick us out as soon as he
is King, he will not be so much afraid of employing us hereafter when
the country will probably be tired for a second time of the Talents'.[2]

The Regent could still sorely try his servants' patience. Lady
Spencer took delight in telling how he once sent word from Brighton
calling a special cabinet meeting in the treasury at noon. Ministers
assembled on time and waited for three hours while the prince was
busy choosing uniform patterns at his tailors. Finally he sent a message
to the treasury that there would be no meeting as he had to see the
queen.[3] Such behaviour, however, seemed increasingly the result of
the Regent's naturally wayward disposition rather than a sign of
positive malice. In June Perceval told the Speaker that he did not now
expect any change of government while Lady Donegal, hearing that
the prince had ordered 'a fine street' to lead straight from Carlton
House to his villa on Primrose Hill, feared it was to be one of the
primrose paths of dalliance by which Perceval was finding his way to
the Regent's heart.[4] By July the prince, in spite of his oaths, was at
last dining with his ministers, an event which convinced Richmond that
he would not conceive of turning Perceval out, especially after his
triumphs in the Regency debates. In fact, as Holland realised, the
decision on 4 February to keep Perceval for the time being was bound
to strain relations between the prince and the opposition. When he
tried to consult his old friends behind the cabinet's back they had to
reject such approaches as unconstitutional, and when he showed any
confidence in Perceval they were tempted to accuse him of disloyalty
and deceit. 'The shrewd in our party', wrote Holland, 'left Parliament
in the summer of 1811 with more apprehensions of the Prince Regent's
designs than confidence in his late professions.'[5]

[1] Windsor MSS., 41682–3, Perceval to McMahon, 25 Feb. 1811.
[2] Westbrook Hay MSS., Richmond to Ryder, 15 May 1811.
[3] Granville Leveson-Gower, *Correspondence*, vol. II, pp. 416–17.
[4] Colchester, vol. II, p. 239; Moore, *Memoirs*, vol. I, p. 263.
[5] Westbrook Hay MSS., Richmond to Ryder, 4 and 21 July 1811; Holland,
Further Memoirs, pp. 95 and 108.

When Perceval was finally able to leave town on 9 September for a short visit to Castle Ashby he could feel that his lonely battle throughout the ugly session of 1811 had finally won him universal respect in parliament. His character, wrote Liverpool to Wellington, 'is completely established in the House of Commons; he has acquired an authority there beyond any minister in my recollection, except Mr. Pitt'. His speeches, which practically filled the columns of the *Sun* during the Regency debates, gained new depth and eloquence. On one occasion he recited some very beautiful lines of Sheridan's 'in a manner which charmed the whole House' and drew compliments from the author himself.[1] 'This crisis', exulted Manners Sutton, 'will now make the world understand and approve Perceval as those only who knew him have hitherto done', while the battle-hardened Rose could not help comparing the prime minister's performance with that of Pitt at his best. 'It is pleasant,' wrote Robert Ward at the height of the Regency crisis, 'if you must fall, to fall with such a leader, and in such a cause', for Perceval's fighting qualities had united government supporters in a remarkable way. When Mulgrave, Palmerston, Clive, Lowther, Long, Pole, General Phipps, Holmes, and Ward dined together in January of 1811, the party was struck by 'the union founded upon an esteem of individuals and a general sense of right, which seemed to pervade all'. In the general enthusiasm 'for such a leader as Perceval' it was agreed that, whatever happened, they all 'hoped and expected to keep together'.[2] Even professional placemen like Denis Browne found personal loyalty transcending the desire to stay in office. 'My feelings of devoted and respectful esteem', wrote Browne to Perceval, 'have grown with my observation of your public life and are, I believe, in unison with those of every loyal, rational and honest man in this Empire. . . . During your ministry the French have, after breaking all the great Continental Powers of Europe, been driven (their best armies and their best generals) from the Kingdom of our ally.' It was Perceval's leadership which had made Britain 'beat the beaters and established it as great on land as it has ever been on the seas. . . . You did right at every risk and the consequences were as those should be—fame, honour and public confidence.' 'I take this opportunity', ended Browne, 'of assuring you that my attachment to you will not lessen with your loss of power. If I know myself, the further you are from it, the more zealous it will be. Those same senti-

[1] *Day*, 10 Sep. 1811; Yonge, vol. I, p. 372; Ward, vol. I, p. 350.
[2] Ward, vol. I, pp. 300, 340 and 341; Rose, vol. II, pp. 472–3.

ments I will impress on all those with whom I have connection as the truest patriotism and as the best way of serving their country.' 'The country', added old Malmesbury, 'can never be under the direction of a more honourable and virtuous man.' [1]

Admiration for the prime minister spread, however, well beyond the government benches. Many country gentlemen admitted to Robert Ward that they disagreed with Perceval's policy 'and knew he would be beaten, but devoted themselves to him on account of his manly firmness, integrity, honour and courage'. 'What a wonderful creature he is!' said Fane, one of the members for Oxfordshire, while one of Robert Ward's nephews from the City assured him that Perceval had won favour there beyond anything that was thought possible. Sidmouth so admired the prime minister's handling of the Regency issue that he began to consider a new and permanent political connection with him. 'Whatever may be the changes', concluded the independent *Day*, 'which the revolution of time and affairs may produce, the Chancellor of the Exchequer of the year 1811 can never, during his life, descend from the highest rank among distinguished ministers and statesmen.' [2] Even many staunch opposition members were unstinted in their praise. Perceval was, confessed the Grenvillites, 'a true gamecock' while Greenhill, a talented opposition back-bencher, admitted 'he adores Perceval and hates Canning'. Young whigs like Sir George Warrender and Brand 'even cheered him', waxed eloquent on his talents and character, and wished they could have voted for him. After the Regency debates, thought Brand, Perceval would make a very formidable leader of the opposition, but then he added with a laugh, the Regent would doubtless keep Perceval three months out of loyalty to the old king and then 'fall so much in love with him' that he would retain him permanently. J. W. Ward spoke of the prime minister as 'the most popular man in England' while Fremantle acknowledged him as 'a most determined and gallant fighter' who led 'a steady crew, who will follow him through anything, even worse than this'. Both Clive and Wellesley Pole heard Whitbread admit that he now had such great respect for Perceval 'that he was the only man in the House of Commons whom he would act under'. Even the restrained Holland gave it as his opinion that the prime minister had

---

[1] Perceval MSS., Denis Browne to Perceval, 7 June 1811 and Malmesbury to Perceval, 2 Jan. 1811.
[2] Ward, vol. I, pp. 300, 320 and 391; Pellew, vol. II, p. 73; *Day*, 13 Dec. 1811.

displayed in debate 'some talent and more spirit'.[1] One morning in mid-January Robert Ward walked home from the House with Perceval and told him of the universal praise. He was, replied Perceval simply, pleased to hear it, but 'he could not help wondering that anything he had done should be thought so praiseworthy'. His duty had no real difficulty for 'it was the merest plain-sailing in the world' as long as all he had to do was to speak to Pitt's brief. The prime minister's ultimate strength was his sense of absolute personal loyalty to the king, for this, Abercromby said in the Commons, was 'precisely the difference between us Tories and them Whigs; one was for the person of the King, the other for the kingly office'.[2] To some it seemed in the autumn of 1811 that the gravest threat to Perceval's continuing in office was his ability to stand for much longer the physical and mental strain laid upon him by over two years of virtually unbroken political crises.

In spite of his frail appearance, he stood up to the burden of responsibility and the strain of leading a precarious government remarkably well. 'He is', Long told Farrington, 'as hard as iron.' 'I have', wrote Wilberforce during the 1810 recess, 'to clear away a heavy arrear of unanswered letters, postponed as usual. How you get on I am astonished.' [3] Only those nearest to him realised, as Jane had feared from the first, that the strain was proving too great. 'Perceval', wrote Herries in the autumn of 1811, 'stays more in the country than he used to do'; 'the labour, fatigue and anxiety of his situation . . .' confessed Arden, 'were too much for his strength long to bear.' [4] As his responsibilities grew he found he had less and less time free to spend with his family, and when parliament was in session he rarely saw them, except on Sundays. 10, Downing Street was split into two parts, Perceval working on the ground floor while Jane and the children lived above. Perceval rose early, ate his breakfast alone and then began his day's work. In the evening, after a solitary and single-course dinner, he would again settle down to work, often until the early hours of the morning.[5] Even during the recess, when the family moved to Elm

[1] Ward, vol. I, pp. 300, 315, 336–7, 342 and 345–7; *Letters to Ivy*, p. 149; Holland, *Further Memoirs*, pp. 75–6.

[2] Ward, vol. I, pp. 329 and 335.

[3] Farington, *Diary*, vol. 5, p. 188; Perceval MSS., Wilberforce to Perceval, 26 Apr. 1810.

[4] Farington, vol. VII, p. 83; Herries, vol. I, p. 21; Perceval MSS., Arden to bishop of Bristol, 30 July 1812.

[5] Perceval MSS., *Anonymous Memoir*.

Grove, Ealing, Perceval, if able to leave Downing Street, still had to make daily trips to town. Only Sunday was kept relatively free. In the morning the family and domestic servants would assemble and set out for St. Margaret's, Westminster or Ealing parish church with Jane and Spencer leading the procession while the children, 'their faces washed and their hair pleasingly combed', followed in order of seniority.[1] The family rarely entertained on a grand scale, although a special effort was made in honour of the Persian ambassador, Mirza Abdul Hassan Khan, when 'upwards of 200 persons of distinction' were invited to a concert and ball. 'The concert concluded with "God Save the King", in which all the ladies present joined in the chorus' and afterwards the Misses Perceval led the dancing which continued 'with great spirit till a late hour on Saturday morning'.[2] For the most part, however, Perceval preferred small informal parties when the company, 'never more easy or more cheerful', would find its host in 'bantering humour' and all would sit up 'telling ghost stories with the women till midnight'.[3] All talk of politics on such occasions was forbidden and even the volcanic Matthew Montague had to spend an evening exchanging civilities with Pinckney, the American minister. Only Wilberforce dare defy the ban by lecturing his host on the evils of the slave trade, or engaging him in lengthy discussions on theology.[4]

Because of her husband's many preoccupations Jane took charge of most routine family and domestic affairs. 'Perceval', gossiped the princess of Wales, 'was entirely governed by that silly woman his wife.' Nothing could be further from the truth. 'Perceval is a very fond and kind husband,' wrote Lord Glenbervie, 'but keeps his wife to her own sphere.'[5] All major decisions were taken by Perceval himself. Thus Jane supervised the childrens' education, but her husband laid down the programme to be followed. The first aim must be 'to furnish their minds with right principles and religious truths' and Jane was to be particularly careful to impress such truths on Spencer, their eldest son, that he might grow up to be 'a champion of true religion in a careless world'.[6] Great pains were taken with his education. John Carey, who had once been employed by Thomas Jefferson in America, was engaged, at half-a-guinea a visit, to prepare

[1] Heseltine, *Letters of Peter Plymley*, p. 69.
[2] *Day*, 26 Feb. 1810.
[3] Ward, vol. I, pp. 392 and 476.
[4] Wilberforce, vol. III, pp. 349, 433, 458, 485.
[5] Glenbervie, *Diaries*, vol. II, pp. 128–9.
[6] Perceval MSS., Rev. T. N. Cunningham to Sp. Perceval jnr., 22 May 1812.

'dear Pessy' for Harrow. Carey wrote a special Latin grammar for his pupil while Jane learnt all her son's exercises by heart and examined him on them during their afternoon drive.[1] As soon as he was thirteen young Spencer was sent off to Harrow, taking with him a set of rhyming rules for Latin versification specially composed for the occasion by his proud father.[2] But in spite of all his family's efforts Spencer's school career was not an unqualified success. Lord Teignmouth, on a visit to Harrow, described him as 'a pleasing, interesting youth' and counselled him to seek the spiritual guidance of the Reverend Thomas Cunningham, a most 'laborious, active and zealous' minister.[3] Unfortunately the same adjectives could not be used of young Perceval, who soon proved to be incorrigibly lazy. His headmaster, Dr. George Butler, 'a good disciplinarian and a very pleasing and sensible man', even failed to get his charge out of bed in the mornings. In the end hints had to be dropped to Perceval himself that perhaps his son and heir was 'apt to be a little idle'. 'Do not let that make you uneasy,' was the reply, 'for I can promise you that he is far more advanced than I was at his age.' [4] There were, however, limits to Perceval's patience. 'Papa desired me to tell you', wrote Maria to her brother, 'that, without goading your tender conscience too much, he thinks he might expect when he sends you money to pay your debts, and only desires you to send him a receipt, that you should do so. So pray send it.' In the autumn of 1811 the prime minister bought his son a complete pocket-size set of Bell's *Edition of the Poets* which he sent to Spencer at Harrow. 'The possession of the poets,' he wrote, 'which I conceive to be a very great treasure for you and to make almost a library in itself, may afford you much valuable amusement, if you consult them freely.' It would be particularly valuable to compare the epistles and satires of Horace with Pope's version of them. 'This will improve and enrich your knowledge of the English language which, at least, is the language which you will have most occasion in life to employ, and which perhaps is generally too little attended to in schools. Not that I would have you attend to *that* in preference to the learned languages, but *neither* should be neglected. Remember this is the last year of your schooling and that I have always

[1] Perceval MSS., J. Carey to Sp. Perceval jnr., 29 Apr. 1813; *Gent. Mag.*, Nov. 1809, p. 10.

[2] Walpole, vol. I, pp. 230–1; *Gent. Mag.*, Aug. 1821, p. 111; Perceval MSS., J. Carey to Sp. Perceval jnr., 26 Apr. 1813.

[3] Teignmouth, vol. II, pp. 196–7, 199.

[4] *National Adviser*, 16–20 May 1812.

told you more may be done in the last year than in any of the five years which have preceded it.' Yet, he ended a little sadly, 'from your Mother's account of the heat in which she has twice found you, I fear that football is upon the whole a more favourite pursuit with you than your books'.

Undoubtedly whenever Spencer chose to exert himself he did well. The best of his school exercises were posted off to Downing Street where Perceval, called upstairs to examine them, 'seemed very much pleased at seeing so many, and said they were worth coming up for'.[1] Spencer's performance at the 1810 school speech day was specially mentioned in the press and two years later he was 'without doubt the best speaker in the room'. Mrs. Montague, whose good opinion counted in such matters, was lyrical in praise of his 'elegant action', his 'agreeable voice', and his 'great fire and enthusiasm'. 'I wish', she added wistfully, 'he had spoken in English as I could have better appreciated his merit.' 'Certainly', admitted the headmaster, 'Spencer does not want of talent.' [2]

Frederick, the second son, never enjoyed robust health and so was sent to Rottingdean, a special school for semi-invalids. Henry and Dudley Montague were both at Harrow by 1812, and both 'industrious as usual'. Henry, with his 'unaffected simple heartedness', was 'vastly proper', but Dudley, showing early signs of his violent religious opinions, soon got mixed up in a fight between Harrovians and Anabaptists which resulted in one death.[3] The two remaining sons, the ill-fated John and baby Ernest, and their three young sisters, Isobella, Louisa and Frederica, were still scarcely out of the nursery. There remained only Jane, Fanny and Maria, 'the three Miss Percevals', who had outraged Lincoln's Inn Fields by refusing to play with any children other than Sir John Nicholls' equally exclusive young daughters.[4] The Perceval girls were inseparable and irrepressible. Family friends trembled at their 'quizzing' and all visitors to 10, Downing Street, from cabinet ministers and generals downwards, were critically assessed. 'Fanny and I', wrote Maria to her 'dear Pessy' at Harrow, 'have found a most excellent, ridiculous and striking likeness

[1] Perceval MSS., Frances Perceval to Sp. Perceval jnr., no date; Maria Perceval to same, undated; C. Hassell, *Edward Marsh*, pp. 7-8.
[2] *Sun*, 8 Jan. 1810; Perceval MSS., John Perceval to Mrs. Spencer Perceval, 15 Jan. 1812; Mrs. Elizabeth Montague to same, 15 Jan. 1812, and Dr. George Butler to same, 19 June 1812.
[3] Harrowby MSS., vol. IV, fol. 56.
[4] Strachey, *Memoirs of a Highland Lady*, pp. 72 and 160.

—Mr. Oldham in side face to a fish. Any fish will do, but a cod particularly. He dined here the other day and it was then we saw it. He opens and shuts his mouth just as fish do when they breathe.' By 1809 Jane, aged eighteen, and Fanny, a year younger, were old enough to come out and were presented at the queen's birthday reception. Maria, still only fifteen, had to be content with seeing her mother in a 'most beautiful plume of purple ostrich feathers, with a bird of paradise in front' and then waiting for her sisters' description of all that had happened.[1] Soon Jane was lost in a round of balls, dinners, visits to the opera, ballet and the ancient music while her sister, thinking plain 'Fanny' too undignified for the adult daughter of a prime minister, took 'such a fancy to the name of Eleanor that I intend henceforward to adopt it as my own', and so became Miss Frances Eleanor Perceval. Meanwhile poor Maria had to be content with an odd visit to Drury Lane to see a revival of *Blue Beard*, with 'real horrors introduced in the last scene'. 'It was', she reported, 'really very good.'[2] But such things were quickly forgotten when Jane, Fanny, and Maria all fell in love and all with the same man. 'He', too wonderful to be mentioned by name, was the centre of all their hopes and the standard of male perfection against which all callers at Downing Street came to be judged and condemned. If one sister went out alone the other two suffered agonies waiting at home lest 'He' might be lavishing his attentions unequally. 'Last Friday', wrote Maria, 'Jane went to a ball at Lady Alvaney's and He was there. . . . It was just like our luck.' 'Mama and Jane are gone to the Ancient [Music]; I hope He is not there.' In the end, Mama, perhaps a little weary of hearing of 'His' merits, decided to introduce a rival. 'Lord Granville Leveson-Gower', wrote Maria, 'dines here on Saturday. I am very glad of it for I am anxious to see what sort of a looking body he is. You know Mama says, what is quite impossible, that he is handsomer than Him. I am certain sure he is not a quarter of a thousandth part as handsome, but I shall like to see him very much.' But poor Leveson-Gower, in spite of all his conquests elsewhere, totally failed to impress the Misses Perceval. 'I never was so much disappointed,' reported Maria, 'except with Sir Arthur Wellesley. Having heard that it was *possible* for anybody to think him as handsome as Him, I expected to see an exceedingly handsome man. But I'll tell you just what he really is. He is a tolerably good height, but he slouches horridly—can that be

[1] Perceval MSS., Maria to Spencer Perceval jnr., Mar. 1809; *Day*, 19 Jan. 1809.
[2] Perceval MSS., Fanny to Spencer Perceval jnr., undated.

compared to Him! His face is handsome enough, but his features are too *pretty* for a man and he is rather silly looking—and how can that possibly be compared to Him! Instead of his beautiful, exactly well-proportioned figure he is too slim and slouches, and instead of His lovely, divine, sensible expressive face he has a silly look. There is no more comparison between them than between light and darkness, or to name two things still more unlike one another, between the King and Bonaparte.' After that even Mama acknowledged defeat, deserting her protégé and confessing 'she never really thought him handsomer than Him'.[1]

The Percevals' family life was, for the most part, unpretentious and tranquil. The most constant visitors to Downing Street were a little group of relations and close friends: Lord Arden and his wife, Margaretta, the only radical in the family and a regular reader of Cobbett's *Political Register*; Richard and Frederica Ryder; Matthew Montague, Perceval's warmest political follower; the architect Gally Knight; and Perceval's maiden sister, Elizabeth, who was a great favourite with the children. In such company Perceval could feel 'easy, playful and unassuming' and would often slip quietly into the nursery to see the children, for he 'was never so happy as when playing in the midst of them'.[2] Political crises and the alarms of war had little impact on the family's life. Much more exciting was the fire which, in February 1809, burnt down Drury Lane theatre. The Misses Perceval were taken on to the roof of Downing Street to watch the blaze which could be clearly seen as far as Twickenham and which allowed a family friend, who lived in North Audley Street, to 'read a book by the light of the flames'. The immense blaze of light from the fire shone in at the windows of the house of commons and caused confusion in the middle of one of Canning's speeches on the progress of the war. Perceval himself joined the many members who rushed out to watch the blaze. It was, he told the king, 'a most tremendous and splendid sight . . ., illuminating as it did the river, the bridge, Lambeth Palace and all the surrounding buildings'.[3] There was nothing quite so exciting again until the winter of 1811 when the family's house at Ealing was burgled by 'a desperate gang of thieves', led by a man with a whey-coloured beard. Jane rushed the children back to the safety of Downing Street

[1] *Ibid.*, Maria to Spencer Perceval jnr., undated.
[2] *Ibid.*, *Anonymous Memoir*. Lady Arden, wrote Redesdale on 16 Aug. 1803, 'reads Cobbett till she becomes as mad as Windham himself' (Perceval MSS.).
[3] *Annual Register*, 1809, p. 317; *Journal of Miss Berry*, p. 377; Windsor MSS., 14210, Perceval to George III, 25 Feb. 1809.

while Papa quickly offered a reward. But in the end it appeared that the gang had only succeeded in entering the dairy and stealing butter churns, milk pails and butter-milk tubs.[1]

[1] *Examiner*, 24 Nov. 1811.

CHAPTER TWENTY-TWO

THE BREACH WITH WELLESLEY

In the winter of 1811 it seemed that the country at last had a united government led by a resolute prime minister. The foreign secretary, Wellesley, alone remained disgruntled after the failure of his efforts in the spring and summer of 1810 to reintroduce Canning into the cabinet. During the most critical period of the Regency crisis Wellesley held his fire, only to renew his complaints as soon as the Regency was established. In July he had written to Carlton House asking for an interview with the Regent on matters 'deeply connected with the interests of the public service'.[1] A week earlier he had condemned Perceval's draft of the end of session speech as 'totally inadequate to the occasion' both in substance and style. 'I am satisfied', he told the prime minister, 'that on reconsideration of the draft you will approve of very few words which are now on the paper.' As his foreign secretary objected to 'the whole plan' of his version, Perceval obligingly asked Wellesley to produce his own draft as he had 'no idea' what Wellesley wished it to contain. When the cabinet compared the two efforts they adopted Perceval's, although slightly shortened at Harrowby's suggestion.[2] By the autumn relations between Wellesley and his colleagues were reaching breaking point. 'I will write again later in the week', Richard Ryder assured Harrowby on 22 October, 'and tell you more of cabinets next week. But as they depend on the G[rand] L[ama], who lets everything go its own way, professes himself ready to bring one, two, or three points forward, not being ready on any one, there is no knowing before-hand where one is as to state of business.'[3] The decisive clash came, however, over the composition and financing of the Regent's Household.

The first draft of a scheme for the Regent's Household was produced by Liverpool. The great difficulty facing the cabinet, he argued, was that of separating the government of the state from the personal custody of the king. In all previous cases where a Regency had been

[1] Windsor MSS., 18251-2, Wellesley to Tyrwhitt, 20 July 1811.
[2] Perceval MSS., Perceval to Wellesley, 15 July 1811; Add. MSS., 37295, fols. 475 and 477; Harrowby MSS., vol. 16, fol. 58.
[3] Harrowby MSS., vol. V, fol. 70, Richard Ryder to Harrowby, 22 Oct. 1811.

necessary during the minority of a king, the Regent himself had been entrusted with the guardianship of the young king. Therefore, although there had been problems in previous cases about the degree of political power to be vested in the Regent, there had never been any hesitation in conferring on the Regent full control over the royal Household. The 1811 Regency Act, in contrast, had vested the prerogatives of the Crown in the heir apparent and the custody of the king in the queen. Consequently the royal Household would have to be divided. A superficially attractive idea would have been to attempt to separate that part of the Household established for purposes of state from that devoted to domestic attendance on the royal family. In practice, however, such a division was hardly possible as all the great Household officials—the lord chamberlain, the lord steward, the master of the horse, the groom of the stole, and the master of the robes— were both officers of state and employers of all the servants in the royal Household. The Household was so completely a whole that any hasty division 'might lead eventually to inextricable confusion'. Liverpool therefore suggested that absolute control over the Household should lie with the Regent, with the queen having only the power to choose a given number of peers and commoners who should attend the king and have control over his personal servants. This new group of officials need not be chosen from individuals already attached to the Household. When selected they should be empowered to draw specified sums each year from the heads of the various departments in the Household to whom they should also be financially accountable. Such a scheme, argued Liverpool, would allow the disbanding of the existing Household of the prince of Wales, but the parliamentary allowance to the prince might be continued in order to make good the loss caused by payments to those attending the old king.[1]

Liverpool's ideas were considered at a cabinet on 19 November together with a memorandum produced by Perceval himself. The prime minister objected to Liverpool's draft mainly because it did not leave 'enough of the *dignity* of the Household about the king'. One at least of the principal officers of the Household ought to be allocated to his majesty. When the matter was first considered by parliament late in 1810, Perceval reminded his colleagues, Ponsonby, Castlereagh, and Canning had all supported the idea of seconding a number of the major officers to attendance on the king. His conversations with the Regent, warned Perceval, had already made it clear to him 'that His

[1] Perceval MSS., undated memorandum by Liverpool.

Royal Highness will very frankly state his opinion upon the proposal that shall be submitted to him, if he shall not entirely approve of it'.[1] In fact Wellesley had already reported the Regent's views to the prime minister two days before the cabinet meeting. The old king's Household must be 'a separate Establishment, under a new office of the Highest Rank', thus leaving the Regent with the full civil list and all the state and powers of the Crown.[2] This was far too extravagant a claim for the cabinet which, on 30 November, sent its first agreed scheme to the prince through Adam. The part of the Household under the queen's control should consist, it was suggested, of the groom of the stole, four lords and four grooms of the bedchamber, the privy purse, the master of the robes, and a suitable number of equerries. It was calculated that this establishment would cost £100,000 a year, which would be taken out of the civil list and then made good either by a special parliamentary grant or, as the cabinet preferred, by continuing the allowance already made to the prince of Wales. The privy purse was to be given to the queen to meet the cost of the king's doctors and application would be made to parliament to vote a similar sum as the Regent's privy purse.[3] These suggestions soon got a dusty answer from the Regent. Adam had already drawn up a paper outlining the prince's views after an interview at Oatlands on 28 November and this was forwarded to Perceval on 4 December as the Regent's answer to the cabinet's proposals. It contained typically grandiose schemes. The king's establishment should be headed by a new official, the grand master of the Household, who should have under him a deputy grand master, eight gentlemen of the Household and a full complement of domestic servants. The queen was to have the full establishment of a dowager and all the princesses were also to have separate Households. The suspension of the prince of Wales's allowance from the exchequer of £120,000 a year, argued the Regent optimistically, would 'probably cover or nearly cover' these costs, leaving the prince himself with the full civil list and 'the whole state, dignity and place of the person exercising the Sovereign Power'. Not content with this the Regent also asked the government to raise in parliament the vexed question of his accumulated debts, which he himself estimated at £522,000.[4]

[1] *Ibid.*, memorandum by Perceval, headed, 'cabinet 19 Nov. 1811'.
[2] Add. MSS., 37296, fol. 41.
[3] Perceval MSS., memorandum by Perceval, 30 Nov. 1811.
[4] *Ibid.*, memorandum by William Adam, 4 Dec. 1811; Add. MSS., 37296, fols. 61, 69 and 71–83.

The Regent's counter-suggestions, so different from those envis-
aged by the cabinet, put Perceval in a very difficult political position.
Any attempt to conciliate the prince by adopting all or part of his
ideas would involve ministers in applying to parliament for large sums
of money to set up new royal Households and pay old royal debts.
This would certainly antagonise many country gentlemen in the Commons and might even, on the evidence of past support for economic
reform, lead to a government defeat in the House. An outright rejection of the Regent's scheme might, however, on a matter so near to
his heart, upset the slowly growing intimacy between Carlton House
and the government. Perceval, as usual, decided to risk sticking to
his principles. On 5 December, after a hurried cabinet meeting, the
prime minister wrote to Adam repeating that it was, in his opinion,
best for the real dignity of the Prince Regent and for 'the maintenance
of his popularity and high estimation in the country' that he should
accept a scheme by which his debts 'should be discharged by means of
his own privations and not by means of fresh burdens on the people'.[1]

It was a forthright declaration likely to lead to hard words with
the Regent, but the situation got much worse when Wellesley, with
absolute disloyalty to his colleagues, decided to fish for himself in the
troubled waters. On 6 December Wellesley saw the prince at Oatlands
and told him that he disapproved of Perceval's proposals.[2] In the hard
negotiations which followed the Regent could now hope to exploit
an acknowledged lack of unanimity within the cabinet. He began by
requiring a formal cabinet minute supporting Perceval's blunt letter
of 5 December. This was forwarded on the ninth. It was, ran the
minute, 'the clear, decided and unanimous opinion of Mr. Perceval and
all his colleagues, most reluctantly and unwillingly adopted', not to
bring the question of the prince's debts before parliament. This
minute, wrote Perceval, had been read to a full cabinet on Friday,
6 December and 'was agreed by everyone present correctly to represent the decision of the day before'.[3] On this point, at least, Wellesley
was apparently not prepared to accept the Regent's point of view. At

---

[1] Perceval MSS., Perceval to Adam, 5 Dec. 1811. Arbuthnot scored a neat
point by sending McMahon extracts from speeches made in 1795 on the subject
of the payment of the prince's debts by Grey, Fox, Sheridan and Bankes (Windsor
MSS., 19185–6).

[2] Add. MSS., 37296, fol. 50.

[3] Perceval MSS., cabinet minute, 6 Dec. 1811 and Perceval to Adam, 9 Dec.
1811. There seems no explanation for the three days' delay in forwarding this
minute.

noon the following day Perceval saw the Regent at York House and had to listen to another memorandum before the audience began. In this paper his royal highness again argued that 'all his creditors are entitled to the protection of Parliament—on the soundest principles of equity and fair dealing'. 'This', wrote the prime minister in the margin of his personal copy, 'is the foundation of the great and leading difficulty. As long as the Prince continues to feel, and is persuaded by such persons as he consults out of cabinet to be impressed with this idea, there is no hope of inducing him to believe that Parliament could make any difficulty, or that he could be expected to make any sacrifice.'[1] There followed a strained interview in the course of which the Prince Regent called for an annual parliamentary vote of £196,000 to support the king, queen and the princesses. He could see no reason why M.P.s should not grant this with alacrity to care for a Sovereign 'endeared to them by a reign as unexampled in its length as in its popularity'.[2] As the prime minister refused to give ground the Regent tried a new tack, producing, on 12 December, another scheme involving complicated juggling between parliamentary votes, the civil list, revenues from the duchies of Lancaster and Cornwall, the existing exchequer allowance to the prince of Wales, and a novel proposal to exempt the Regent from property tax as well as all rents, rates, and taxes on Carlton House.[3] At this point Carlton House ran out of fresh ideas. As Perceval was temperamentally far better suited to prolonged negotiations than the volatile Regent it seemed by the third week in December that the cabinet would eventually carry the main points of its original proposal. Gradually the prince came to accept his government's scheme for the composition of the king's establishment and the fact that it should be financed out of the civil list. In the end he was left insisting only that the special parliamentary vote to make good the resulting deficiency in the civil list should be for £150,000 a year instead of his ministers' suggestion of £100,000.[4]

In this the Regent was supported by Wellesley, who argued the case for the larger sum at a cabinet meeting on 18 December. When his colleagues refused to agree to this, Wellesley ended the meeting by giving them to understand that he was finally able to accept the

[1] *Ibid.*, 'Memorandum read to Mr. Perceval at York House 10 Dec. 1811; previous to his seeing the Prince Regent'.

[2] *Ibid.*, 'Paper Delivered by the Prince to Mr. Perceval at York House on Dec. 10th'.

[3] *Ibid.*, Adam to Perceval, 12 Dec. 1811.

[4] Add. MSS., 37296, fols. 112–37.

majority view. He had, he told the prime minister that evening, no
wish to register any formal dissent from a decision taken 'by so many
persons whom I respect and esteem'. Accordingly Perceval was preparing finally to present his government's full proposals to the Prince
Regent when he suddenly learnt that his foreign secretary had sent a
private letter to his royal highness repeating his support for an annual
grant of £150,000. It was, wrote Richard Ryder, thought by all the
cabinet, 'a most shabby proceeding'. Perceval immediately postponed
the presentation of the Household plan and summoned another meeting of ministers for the nineteenth. At this Wellesley promised to withdraw his letter, but struck out the word 'unanimous' in the cabinet
minute. On the whole what might have been a vitriolic meeting went
well, although Charles Yorke 'was very near letting off against the
Lama'. By Christmas eve the cabinet had completed its discussion of
details and a reluctant prince had accepted the advice of his prime
minister.[1] Perceval had won a major victory, for behind the apparently
domestic issues and trifling sums involved, there lay a principle of great
constitutional importance. The controversy had marked a crucial trial
of strength between the wishes of an overwhelming cabinet majority
and a Regent guided by unconstitutional advisers at Carlton House
and abetted by a single disgruntled cabinet minister. The final settlement of the Household problem, wrote Perceval to Richmond on
26 December, was 'as favourable a one as could possibly be expected',
although the Prince Regent still felt 'some little soreness'. Even sorer
was the defeated Wellesley whom rumour had it was, early in the new
year, about to resign.[2]

Perceval first heard of his foreign secretary's resignation through
Bathurst, on 17 January. Wellesley himself made no attempt to contact
the prime minister, to whom the news would have come as a complete
surprise had not the Regent warned him to expect it during an interview that very morning. Wellesley told Bathurst that he had first
decided to resign in October 1810, but had postponed putting his
decision into effect because of the series of political crises. Even on
17 January he did not offer to leave office immediately. He was, in his
own words, prepared to relinquish the foreign office seals at any time
'which would cause the least embarrassment to the Government'.[3]

<hr>

[1] Add. MSS., 37296, fols. 105, 139–44 and 153; Harrowby MSS., vol. V, fol. 79,
Richard Ryder to Harrowby, 21 Dec. 1811.
[2] Perceval MSS., Perceval to Richmond, 26 Dec. 1811; Colchester, vol. II,
p. 355.
[3] Add. MSS., 37296, fol. 175; Bathurst MSS., pp. 160–1.

In fact, as Wellesley must have been well aware, he could hardly have chosen a more discouraging time for his colleagues. The Regency restrictions were due to expire early in February when the prince was generally expected to take a final decision about the composition of his government. Relations between his royal highness and Perceval had just been strained by the Household dispute, during which Wellesley himself had openly supported the Carlton House point-of-view. If the foreign secretary's real motive was to replace Perceval at 10, Downing Street both his actions and their timing were ideally chosen for that purpose. Perceval himself was clearly conscious of the weakness of his position. Early in December he told Lethbridge, of the Burdett riots fame, that he had no means of forecasting his government's future, 'except perhaps that I am better able to judge that there is nothing in the reports of the newspapers'. Wellington still thought at that time that Perceval would be dismissed, although Richmond was confident that no ministry could be formed 'without you that would have any chance of lasting many weeks'.[1] On 5 January even the *Sun*, usually the last to despair, printed a list of the supposed new whig cabinet. Uncertainty as to the Regent's intentions also affected the government's voting strength in parliament, which reassembled for the new session on 7 January. It was, wrote Richmond late in December, very difficult to persuade some Irish members to cross the water until the Prince Regent had given an indication of his intentions. Pole, as usual, was zealous on Perceval's behalf. 'If any persons in office do not attend', he wrote to the prime minister from Dublin, 'it will not be from not being aware of your sentiments.' Yet still the prince's plans, joked Lady Donegal, were as inscrutable as Bonaparte's 'but for a very different reason'. The powder on his royal highness's hair was, she thought, more settled than anything in either his head or his heart.[2] In so uncertain a situation Wellesley's suspended offer of resignation clearly hung over Perceval's head like the sword of Damocles. Fortunately the prime minister was not the type to stand and wait for it to fall. The next day he was with the Regent to warn him that 'he could not be answerable for what might happen in Parliament any day unless he would authorise me to fill up our ranks' and so got immediate permission to offer the foreign office to Castlereagh.

---

[1] Add. MSS., 18191, fol. 199; Wellington, *Despatches*, vol. IV, pp. 512-13; Perceval MSS., Richmond to Perceval, 15 Dec. 1811.

[2] *Sun*, 5 Jan. 1812; Perceval MSS., Richmond to Perceval, 29 Dec. 1811 and W. W. Pole to same, 31 Dec. 1811; Moore, *Memoirs*, vol. I, p. 266.

Castlereagh, however, again refused to return to the cabinet unless Sidmouth were also invited 'and if possible some of the Prince's former friends: men immediately connected with his person'. This answer not only failed to solve Perceval's immediate problem but also unwittingly created a new one. The prince was clearly unwilling to authorise any approach to Sidmouth, mainly, it was thought, because Wellesley had told him that the return of the Doctor would drive both Wellesley and Canning into systematic opposition 'and that they would carry at least twenty votes with them'. Accordingly the Regent expressly countermanded his authority to Perceval to seek fresh strength. The government's position, the prime minister told the Speaker on 25 January, was 'very precarious' and its future prospects were hardly improved on 31 January when Charles Yorke resigned from the admiralty. Yorke had, in fairness, warned the prime minister on 15 December that he wished to be relieved of office as soon as the Regency restrictions ended, both on grounds of ill-health and because he did not relish the idea of serving the prince.[1] Yorke's departure, added to Wellesley's manœuvres, and Castlereagh's refusal of a cabinet place, could only increase the Regent's awareness of the weakness of Perceval's position. The prime minister's sole consolation that day was the news that Eldon and Liverpool had seen George III in one of his more lucid moments and been assured that his majesty would recall Perceval as soon as he recovered if the Regent in fact changed the government.[2]

It was at this point that his royal highness took up the hint dropped by Castlereagh and decided to try another appeal to the opposition. He first discussed the idea of a renewed coalition offer with Eldon on 6 February. The following day he granted an audience to Perceval, who came expecting notice of dismissal, and showed him a letter inviting Grey and Grenville to consider uniting with the existing government. After some discussion both agreed that the opposition leaders would almost certainly reject such an overture and Perceval therefore advised the Regent not to make it, lest the offer should expose him to a charge of insincerity. It was, the prime minister told Lonsdale, 'a hopeless idea'. It would be better, argued Perceval, to write frankly to Grey and Grenville explaining why they could not be called to office. This advice was repeated by the prime minister and

[1] Perceval MSS., C. P. Yorke to Perceval, 15 Dec. 1811 and Perceval to Lonsdale, 19 Jan. 1812; *Bathurst MSS.*, pp. 164–6; Colchester, vol. II, pp. 362 and 366.   [2] Rose, vol. II, p. 477.

supported by Eldon when the pair were again closeted with the prince on Sunday, 8 February. As soon as his royal highness accepted this argument, Perceval drafted a letter which was shown to and approved by the prince on 11 February. The draft was as frank as most of the prime minister's letters. The Regent, he wrote, had originally decided to bear with the existing cabinet out of consideration for the king and in the hope that he would soon recover. A new era had now begun in which the prince found himself 'so well satisfied with the principles upon which my present servants have acted, and with the success which has attended their measures' that he felt he could not change the government without endangering 'the cause of our allies by shaking their confidence in my determination to support them'. The Regent, ended Perceval, would have liked to see a coalition ministry but thought that 'irreconcilable conflict upon certain more important points of foreign and domestic policy made this impossible'.[1] The next morning the Regent changed his mind, decided that Perceval's draft was badly written, and asked Sheridan to produce a new version. This ended with a plea to 'those persons with whom the early habits of his public life were formed' to 'strengthen his hands and constitute a part of his Administration'. His royal highness warned Eldon of this change of plan on the twelfth during an interview in which he assured the lord chancellor that Perceval would remain as first lord in any coalition, that there would be a majority of Pitt's Friends in the cabinet, and that the issue of catholic emancipation would not be raised while the old king lived. Although both Eldon and Perceval still opposed the idea of a coalition offer, the Regent's letter was sent to Grey and Grenville through the duke of York on 14 February. For a while the discouraged Perceval toyed with the idea of resigning. 'Negotiate,' pleaded Arden, 'but do not resign. Your negotiations will be more likely to succeed if you are in office than if you are out of it.'

Opinion generally, even in ministerial circles, was that ministers were within an ace of being dismissed. On the twelfth Charles Yorke indiscreetly told the Canningite, Dent, that 'no-one's place was in his opinion worth 24 hours' purchase' while the usually staunch Robert Ward was busy passing on rumours that Perceval had yielded the entire Household to the Regent's sole nomination, 'which produces long faces from many even of our well-wishers'.[2]

[1] Perceval MSS., Perceval to Lonsdale, undated; Aspinall, *Letters of George IV*, vol. I, no. 1; *Bathurst MSS.*, pp. 164–6.
[2] Aspinall, *Letters of George IV*, vol. I, no. 2; Fulford, *George IV*, p. 119;

Fortunately for Perceval's peace of mind Grey and Grenville flatly rejected the coalition offer on the fifteenth.[1] Holland thought that both friends and foes agreed that the rejection was inevitable and that the terms of the offer demonstrated that the new court was now as intent on keeping the whigs from power as the old one had always been. Some independent observers were, however, frankly critical of the grandees. The *Day* was particularly outraged that 'so liberal and patriotic an offer ... should have been unconditionally and peremptorily refused'. Undoubtedly the Regent's initiative and Grey's and Grenville's reaction to it marked the final breach between his royal highness and his former friends. In March certain Scottish and Irish newspapers published accounts of a dinner party said to have been held at Carlton House on 22 February at which the Regent's guests included the dukes of York and Cambridge, Princess Charlotte, Moira, Erskine, Lauderdale, Sheridan, and Adam. During dinner the prince roundly attacked the grandees' reply, complaining that they had deserted him. Lauderdale took up the point with such heat that Charlotte burst into tears, the ladies retired, and the gentlemen continued their fracas until late at night. In the end Adam patched up a temporary reconciliation, but Lauderdale was so incensed that he insisted on continuing the argument in a formal memorandum.[2]

By 17 February, the day on which the Regency restrictions expired, his royal highness had still given no sign of his political intentions. That morning Wellesley at last made a definite bid for the premiership by seeing the prince and again offering his resignation. The Regent replied that he was 'still at liberty, and was resolved to form his cabinet according to His Royal Highness's own views'. He then asked Wellesley to outline his suggestions on policy, upon which the foreign secretary pressed for a more vigorous war effort and an intermediate position on the catholic issue—neither 'unqualified concession' nor 'peremptory, eternal exclusion'. He would, he conceded, serve in the same cabinet as Perceval, but he would not accept him as first lord, an office 'he was incompetent to fill although sufficiently qualified for inferior stations'. Wellesley then suggested either Moira or Holland

---

Colchester, vol. II, pp. 368–9; *Parl. Deb.*, XXII, 39; Twiss, vol. II, p. 201; Walpole, vol. II, p. 261; Aspinall and Smith, *English Historical Documents*, vol. XI, no. 237.

[1] *Dropmore MSS.*, vol. X, p. 213.

[2] Holland, *Further Memoirs*, pp. 120–1; *Day*, 17 Feb. 1812; *Ramsey's Waterford Chronicle*, 19 Mar. 1812.

as prime minister, adding that both Canning and Castlereagh ought also to be reintroduced into the cabinet, a feat which he gave the Regent to understand only he could perform. Unfortunately Wellesley had chosen the wrong person for his confidences. Later that day his royal highness saw the inevitable Eldon, gave him a full account of the audience with Wellesley, and asked him to pass the information on to Perceval. When Eldon immediately announced that he would refuse to stay in office if Perceval left 10, Downing Street, the prince assured him that there would be no change of prime minister. That evening Perceval, having seen Eldon, called a special cabinet meeting to consider Wellesley's behaviour. Ministers then unanimously agreed 'that Lord Wellesley's conduct had been such as to make it necessary for Mr. Perceval to state to the Prince that Lord Wellesley's resignation must be immediately accepted; and that it should be further represented to the Prince that not one of the present cabinet would continue, if Lord Wellesley remained in office'.[1] On the morning of the eighteenth the final outcome of the political crisis was still generally unknown. That edition of the *Day* wrote of the Perceval cabinet as the 'late ministry' and prepared its readers 'with pain and sorrow' for the news that Perceval himself would not be a member of the new government. 'Whatever may be the destination', concluded the paper, 'of this distinguished statesman, he will bear with him the gratitude and admiration of his countrymen.' In fact, with the cabinet's ultimatum in his pocket, Perceval was at last in a virtually unassailable position. That afternoon the Regent accepted Wellesley's resignation and asked Liverpool to act as a caretaker foreign secretary. There was no one, wrote the *Day* when news of Perceval's retention spread through London, 'more highly or more amply qualified' for the premiership.[2]

The Regent's final decision caused one last outburst of anger in opposition circles. Some spread rumours that he had been influenced by Lady Hertford or Mrs. Fitzherbert, while Cobbett fell back on the absurd suggestion that Perceval had blackmailed the prince by producing a copy of *The Book*. Meanwhile Moira refused an offer of the Garter and pleaded with his royal highness to return 'into the paths of safety'.[3] In fact, as Professor Webster has since written, there can be

[1] *Bathurst MSS.*, pp. 164–6; Colchester, vol. II, p. 370.
[2] *Day*, 18 and 19 Feb. 1811; Windsor MSS., 19275–6, Wellesley to the Prince Regent, 18 Feb. 1811; Add. MSS., 37296, fol. 195.
[3] Rose, vol. II, p. 483; Wilberforce, vol. III, p. 494; Aspinall, *Letters of George IV*, vol. I, no. 23.

no question as to where the political duty of the Regent lay in 1812. Even Horner once admitted that the prince had acted 'with eminent propriety and with perfect honour towards the Whigs'. In the last analysis the opposition had no right to think that he was under any perpetual obligation to them. The prince's early political life can be summed up as faithfulness to Fox, and when he died his royal highness had warned Moira that he would 'cease to be party man'. On vital policy issues he was by 1812 drifting away from the views widely held on the opposition benches, for the prince had never been enthusiastic for parliamentary reform, had never fully shared—and grew less and less sympathetic towards—the desire for catholic emancipation, and much preferred Perceval's honest resolution on war policy to the confusion and pessimism of his former associates.[1]

Wellesley's departure made little difference to the government's strength either in parliament or the country, although Wellington wrote loyally that he was 'very sorry for it'. Late in January the duke of Northumberland had written to McMahon attacking Wellesley for having private not public interests at heart. If he did resign, his grace had concluded, 'I do not imagine either the affairs of the P[rince], or the public will suffer much from it.' The foreign secretary, said F. J. Jackson, at about the same time, was plotting to drop Perceval, 'but he is riveting himself more and more every day in the confidence of the country and in the management of the House of Commons'. The prime minister's own assessment of his former colleague's motives was apparent when he curtly told Wellington that Wellesley had resigned because he had been confirmed as prime minister.[2] Wellesley himself took his fall with ill-grace. He had, he later wrote in his own defence, offered to delay his resignation on 17 January in order to do the least possible harm to the Perceval government. Yet, he alleged, the prime minister had immediately tried, without telling Wellesley, to persuade the Prince Regent to remove him before the expiration of the Regency restrictions. Perceval had 'repeatedly urged the attempt with great earnestness, severally proposing Lord Moira, Lord Castlereagh and Lord Sidmouth or some of his party to supersede Lord Wellesley, without an hour of delay'.[3] Such a charge was, as Bathurst said, 'childish' for Perceval could not do other than try to find a new foreign

[1] Horner, vol. II, p. 74; Fulford, *George IV*, p. 96.
[2] Wellington, *Despatches*, vol. V, p. 545; Windsor MSS., 19154-5, duke of Northumberland to McMahon, 27 Jan. 1812; *Bath Archives*, vol. I, p. 324; Perceval MSS., Perceval to Wellington, 18 Feb. 1812.
[3] Add. MSS., 37296, fol. 201.

secretary without delay if his government was to have the best chance of survival. Wellesley's statement on the reasons for his eventual resignation included many bitter personal attacks on his former chief. He listed four causes of his discontent. He resigned, he claimed first, 'in a great degree, from the *narrow* and imperfect scale on which the efforts in the Peninsula were conducted'. He specifically attacked Perceval for his failure to raise sufficient money to keep more troops in Portugal and claimed that he objected to the practice of subsidising continental allies, sending a few troops to help them, and then leaving both the planning and the execution of the campaign in their hands. This usually led to the adoption of antiquated tactics, often carried out by corrupt or treacherous officers and officials. Wellesley next listed his disagreement with Perceval over the issue of catholic emancipation. The prime minister was opposed in principle to ever conceding the catholic's claim while Wellesley would have preferred the government to take a more moderate position on this issue. There is, in fact, no evidence to support Wellesley's claim of serious political differences within the cabinet, although Perceval and all the other ministers had disagreed with him over the question of recruiting Canning, on the royal Household issue, and over the production of papers in parliament on both America and the Peninsula. None of these, however, was an issue of sufficient importance to justify Wellesley's attitude. Liverpool, a man not given to hasty judgements, later assured Wellington that he knew of no difference of opinion with Wellesley on 'any political question of importance'.[1] Wellesley's two remaining complaints were personal rather than political. When he had first accepted office in the autumn of 1809, he claimed, 'no pretensions to the Supreme Command of the Cabinet (which he afterwards assumed) were at that time advanced by Mr. P.' He soon found, however, that he 'had not sufficient weight' in the cabinet. Finally, Wellesley pointed to lack of talent in the cabinet, which 'neither possessed ability nor knowledge to *advise* a good plan, nor temper and discernment to *adopt* what he now thought necessary, unless Mr. Perceval should concur with Lord Wellesley'. 'To Mr. Perceval's judgement or attainments', the statement ended, 'Lord Wellesley . . . could not pay any deference, without injury to the public service.' [2] Clearly, these personal complaints lay at the heart of Wellesley's failure to fit into the Perceval administration.

[1] Yonge, vol. I, p. 378; Add. MSS., 37296, fol. 181; Perceval MSS., Wellesley to Perceval, 12 Feb. 1810.
[2] Add. MSS., 37296, fols. 201 and 264.

The foreign secretary's early career had not prepared him to work harmoniously as a member of a team, while his hauteur scarcely endeared him to colleagues who were further irritated by his obvious failure to cope with the routine business of the foreign office. In the last resort, Wellesley found himself isolated in the cabinet because his colleagues much preferred Perceval's steady application and courage to his more flamboyant but unpredictable qualities.

With Perceval finally confirmed in office and with both Wellesley, by popular request, and the grandees, by choice, in the wilderness, renewed efforts could be made to strengthen the government. Replacements were badly needed. Wellesley's exit created a vacancy at the foreign office and had also led to the loss of his son Richard, one of the lords of the treasury, who felt compelled to ask for the chiltern hundreds. Young Wellesley held a government-controlled seat for East Grinstead which he vacated even though Perceval generously offered to allow him to retain it 'on which ever side of the House you might sit'. Yorke had already left the admiralty and on 26 March Camden at last placed his office at the Regent's disposal, after assuring himself of 'that step in the peerage which would be very agreeable to me'.[1] Thus Camden became a marquis and Perceval had the lord presidency of the council to offer. The first choice amongst new recruits was clearly Castlereagh. On 16 February Liverpool had written to Perceval reminding him that he had reluctantly accepted the war department in the autumn of 1809 'and that I have not since manifested any particular desire to continue in it . . . but I am fully persuaded that (if the Government is to remain upon its present foundation) the objections to any change in the office . . . are at this particular moment insuperable'. Any move at this point, wrote Liverpool, would cause 'a great degree of personal awkwardness to myself' and might prejudice military operations in the Peninsula. Accordingly Perceval abandoned the idea of offering Castlereagh his old post and wrote instead on the eighteenth suggesting he might take the foreign office, where he soon found 'much employment of a very pressing nature' in clearing away arrears of business.[2]

The prime minister next renewed his overtures to Sidmouth who held out for cabinet places for Lord Buckinghamshire, Bragge Bathurst

[1] Perceval MSS., Perceval to Richard Wellesley, 19 and 27 Feb. 1812 and Camden to Perceval, 26 Mar. 1812.

[2] *Ibid.*, Liverpool to Perceval, 16 Feb. 1812 and Perceval to Castlereagh, 18 Feb. 1812.

and himself. Sidmouth agreed to succeed Camden, who, however, remained in the cabinet without portfolio until the end of the session. Buckinghamshire took the board of control from Robert Dundas, who had succeeded as the second Viscount Melville on the death of his father. This left Melville free to replace Yorke at the admiralty where he also brought with him William Dundas to fill a vacant seat at the board. The difficulty of finding a place for Bragge Bathurst appeared solved when Rose offered to retire two months after the start of the new session in order that Bathurst might both take his place as treasurer of the navy and accept a seat in the cabinet. Rose had originally offered to end his long period of service on the treasury bench on the grounds of ill-health. As soon, however, as he learned that his successor was already chosen Rose began to have second thoughts about the wisdom of retirement. One of the great obstacles to strengthening the government, wrote the *Day* on 11 March, was 'the discovery of the means of prevailing on Mr. Rose Snr. to retire; to which the known love of business and habits of that veteran senator must naturally induce him to object'. Only after hurried meetings between Perceval, Bathurst, and Rose were matters so arranged that Sidmouth, Buckinghamshire, and Bragge Bathurst might be simultaneously introduced into the cabinet.[1] Even then the claims of the Sidmouth group were not fully satisfied. Sidmouth himself was anxious to see Nicholas Vansittart at the exchequer, but Perceval refused to accept him as chancellor. The prime minister offered Vansittart instead the seat at the treasury board vacated by Richard Wellesley, a minor office which he at first accepted in order to please Sidmouth, but later he changed his mind and decided to stay out of office.[2] Finally Sidmouth pressed that Hiley Addington should be found a place at the board of control, thought likely to be vacated by Lord Lovaine.[3] There were some government supporters who felt that the Doctor had driven too hard a bargain. He had, wrote Lonsdale to Perceval, achieved a position 'which all his combined influence, personal and political, does not warrant'. The *Day* even carried rumours that Lonsdale's opposition to the idea of an alliance with the Sidmouthites had delayed the process of strengthening the government. Lonsdale, however, was not alone in his misgivings. Richmond, while conceding

[1] *Ibid.*, Perceval to Bathurst, 6 Mar. 1812; *Day*, 11 Mar. 1812; *Bathurst MSS.*, p. 167.
[2] Perceval MSS., Perceval to Sidmouth, 15 Mar. 1812 and Vansittart to Perceval, 1 May 1812.
[3] Perceval MSS., Buckinghamshire to Perceval, 26 Mar. 1812.

that Perceval had little choice about applying to Sidmouth, still confessed that 'as a steady Pittite I own I feel a little alarmed'. The prime minister was well aware of the extent of these misgivings. 'This proportion in the cabinet', he wrote, '(I may say this in perfect confidence) several of our Friends thought excessive.'[1] The proposed changes, however, undoubtedly strengthened his ministry for, while Castlereagh brought administrative efficiency, Sidmouth and his connection carried with them much needed votes. Only one further round of changes was anticipated. The duke of Richmond hinted at an early return from Ireland. As the faithful Wellesley Pole was anxious to leave Dublin at the same time as the duke, Perceval planned to offer Pole the treasurership of the navy so that Bragge Bathurst might at last relieve Richard Ryder of his burdens as home secretary.[2]

Meanwhile the opposition's main attack during the early days of the 1812 session had been concentrated against the Orders-in-Council. The adoption of the Orders of November 1807, following as they did the *Chesapeake* crisis of that summer, had led the American Congress to pass the Embargo Act and had further strained relations between the two countries. After the minimum wage riots in the north during the winter of 1807, Perceval had tried to persuade his colleagues to make concessions in favour of the United States, only to be overcome by the combined opposition of Canning and Castlereagh.[3] In December 1808, however, the Americans substituted a Non-Intercourse Act for their absolute embargo. Canning accordingly wrote to Perceval on the thirty-first of that month suggesting that, under the changed circumstances, he should re-submit his earlier ideas, while even James Stephen, always the staunchest advocate of the Orders, saw no objection to our amending them in return for the relaxation of the embargo and an undertaking from the American government that it would rigidly forbid all trade with France until that country withdrew the Berlin and Milan Decrees.[4] That April Bathurst circulated a draft of the revised Orders which were then published without delay. The Orders-in-Council, wrote the *Day*, 'exist no more, or at least they are

---

[1] Perceval MSS., Lonsdale to Perceval, 1 Apr. 1812; Richmond to same, 3 Apr. 1812 and Perceval to Lonsdale, 3 Apr. 1812; *Day*, 13 Mar. 1812; Colchester, vol. II, pp. 371–2.

[2] Perceval MSS., Richmond to Perceval, 3 Apr. 1812 and Perceval to Lonsdale, undated.

[3] For details see chapter 11, pp. 167–77.

[4] Perceval MSS., Canning to Perceval, 31 Dec. 1808 and James Stephen to same, 19 Jan. 1809.

now so materially altered in their nature and operation as to be no longer distinguishable by their former characteristics'.[1] Unfortunately the American government, which aimed at the withdrawal rather than the revision of the Orders, failed to take the same view. Wider negotiations had, in fact, already begun between Canning and Pinckney, the American minister in London, on the basis of the simultaneous withdrawal by France, Britain, and the United States of all their restrictions on trade. Little progress was made, partly because of the distaste felt by ministers like Perceval and Westmorland for 'any courting of negotiations or explanation with Mr. Pinckney of what England will do, if America should do this or do that'.[2] A further barrier was the prejudice felt by many cabinet ministers against the very nature of the United States. This was typified by Bathurst's willingness at a most critical point in our dealings with the Americans to show copies of an intercepted American government despatch on Florida to the Spanish Regency Council as 'there may be advantage in exciting jealousy between the two countries'. It was also suggested in 1810 that Miner, the British chargé d'affaires in Washington, might be sent a copy of a secret article on trading policy in a proposed treaty between the United States and France. 'The American Government', wrote Bathurst, 'will probably wish to keep it back at first from the knowledge of Congress; and Mr. Miner might contrive to have it published in the American newspapers without it being traced to him. This would occasion discussions in Congress which would be useful here.'[3] Such basic antipathy to the Americans and 'their foolish constitution' was doubtless emotionally attractive to Perceval himself. Yet both James Monroe and Pinckney, American envoy in London, paid tribute to Perceval's and Canning's 'candid and temperate behaviour' in dealings with Washington.[4] Great pressure was also put on Perceval for a firm line against the Americans by shipping and West Indian interests in the Commons while James Stephen could write thirty-two pages to the prime minister on a *Coup d'œil on an American War*.[5]

Negotiations with Pinckney did not reach their crisis until after Perceval had succeeded Portland as prime minister and Wellesley had replaced Canning at the foreign office. Then the Americans succeeded in persuading Napoleon to publish a statement in the *Moniteur*

[1] *Bathurst MSS.*, pp. 87–9; *Day*, 12 and 28 Apr. 1809.
[2] Perceval MSS., Westmorland to Perceval, 1 Aug. 1808.
[3] *Ibid.*, Bathurst to Perceval, 14 Sep. 1810.
[4] Brougham, *Memoirs*, vol. I, pp. 383–4.
[5] Perceval MSS., James Stephen to Perceval, undated.

rescinding the Berlin and Milan Decrees provided that the British government withdrew both the Orders-in-Council and the new principles of blockade which they had sought to establish. There followed long discussions between Wellesley and Pinckney as to whether the French declaration could be interpreted as an absolute withdrawal of the Decrees or only as a pledge to rescind them if the British government also made the necessary concessions. There the main obstacle was the refusal of the cabinet to link any renunciation of our rights of blockade with the ending of the Orders-in-Council.[1] By the end of 1810 Pinckney had broken off negotiations and left the country. The following year both the bullion crisis and a trade depression, which severely cut British import and export figures, added to the government's difficulty in justifying the Orders. In March the first Luddite riots broke out in Nottinghamshire and then died down during the summer, only to flare up again early in November. On 16 November the *Day* reported riots in Nottingham which it attributed to the high price of bread. A month later the trouble had spread into Derbyshire and by the middle of January 1812 the *Day* was bewailing the failure of a lenient system 'so laudable and humanely adopted'. Widespread criticism of the 'torpor of the magistracy' followed the discharge of eleven men who had been brought before the Nottinghamshire quarter sessions charged with collecting money to support riots. In February the *Day* calculated that 1,000 frames had been smashed in the county and between £6,000 and £10,000 worth of damage done. 'Where it will end', wailed that paper, 'God only knows!' At the following county assizes four rioters were sentenced to fourteen years' and three to seven years' transportation, but by then the trouble had spread from the midlands to the north. By 11 April there were press reports of riots in Manchester while in Birmingham patrols of Scots Greys were hooted in the streets by the hungry mob.[2] Meanwhile at the home office Perceval, as usual in times of crisis, was busy bolstering Richard Ryder's confidence. Reports from local magistrates showed that delegates from the northern towns were in touch with those from the midlands while Perceval urged Ryder to trace an emissary from Nottingham who was said to have left for Scotland and Ireland. In the face of such alarming rumours the authorities

---

[1] For details of Wellesley's negotiations with Pinckney see P.R.O., F.O. 95/378 and R. A. Pearce, *Memoirs and Correspondence of Richard, Marquis Wellesley*, vol. III, pp. 108–205.

[2] *Day*, 16 and 30 Nov., 16 Dec. 1811, 13, 14, 30 Jan., 20, 21 Mar., 11, 14, 18, 23 Apr. and 5 May 1812.

fell back on severer repression. At the Chester assizes held during the last week in May there were fourteen death sentences, eight sentences of transportation, and six more rioters were sent to prison. One of Perceval's own last acts was to set up a special commission in Lancashire during which a further eight offenders were to be condemned to death and twenty-four to transportation or imprisonment.[1]

The unrest at home and the crisis with America spurred on the opponents of the Orders-in-Council. Whitbread first moved for papers in the Commons on 13 February when the Regent had still not finally confirmed Perceval in office. Although Wellesley himself had repeatedly pressed the prime minister to present all available papers to the House, Perceval decided to resist Whitbread's motion. In the division the ministry had a majority of 136 to 23: 'O si sic omnia' joked Perceval when the result was announced.[2] The opposition, however, was not so easily deterred and continued to press the issue until on 3 March Brougham moved his motion for a select committee on the Orders-in-Council. Although Canning, until then one of the chief supporters of the system, spoke in support of Brougham, Perceval still carried the House by 216 votes to 144.[3] Brougham immediately called for petitions against the Orders and got such a flood in response that, on 28 April, the government finally agreed that they should be considered by a committee of the whole House. Public opinion had clearly turned against the Orders-in-Council, but still Perceval fought to the last. Wilberforce, 'sick at heart with the sad prospect of a war with America', spoke against the government on 3 March, only to be answered by his fellow Saint, Stephen, who 'spoke well, and still better, like an honest man'. Perceval, encouraged by a letter from Josiah Spode and thirteen other Staffordshire pottery manufacturers supporting the Orders, pinned his main hopes on the Yorkshire woollen areas. 'You will not run alone,' he warned Brougham, 'there will be counter-petitions from the clothing districts.' Meanwhile the prime minister asked Stephen to write a pamphlet in reply to those of Baring and Roscoe and printed and circulated at the treasury's expense Croker's anonymous work, *A Key to the Orders-in-Council*,

---

[1] J. L. and Barbara Hammond, *The Skilled Labourers*, pp. 290 and 298–300; Aspinall, *Early English Trade Unions*, pp. 116–21; P.R.O., H.O. 42/122, Perceval to Richard Ryder, 10 Apr. 1812 and H.O. 35/25, cabinet memorandum by Ryder, 27 Apr. 1812.

[2] Perceval MSS., Wellesley to Perceval, 29 Jan., 1 and 12 Feb. 1812; *Parl. Deb.*, XXI, 776, 782, 794 and 801; Ward, vol. I, p. 412.

[3] *Parl. Deb.*, XXI, 1163; Ward, vol. I, p. 447.

written at Perceval's own suggestion to explain his government's
policy. The examination of witnesses in committee proceeded throughout the early days of May and the issue was still in the balance when,
on Monday, 11 May, a madman's bullet ended Perceval's last political
struggle.[1]

[1] Wilberforce, vol. III, p. 17; Brougham, *Memoirs*, vol. II, p. 14; *Courier*,
22 Mar. 1812; Aspinall, *Politics and the Press*, p. 154.

CHAPTER TWENTY-THREE

ASSASSINATION

ANYONE entering the public gallery of the house of commons early in May 1812 might have noticed 'a tall, large-boned man, about forty years of age, with a long thin visage and aquiline nose' who scarcely ever took his eyes off the treasury bench below. Once he asked those sitting near him to point out the prime minister and then used a pair of opera glasses to get a better view.[1] The watcher was John Bellingham, a native of St. Neot's in Huntingdon, the son of a land-surveyor who was known to have died in a lunatic-asylum. He had ample time to sit and stare at the king's ministers for he seemed to have no job. As a youth he had been a merchant's clerk and had eventually represented a Liverpool firm at Archangel in Russia. Having got into debt while there he spent five years in prison, a disaster which he had come to blame not on the Russian government but on Granville Leveson-Gower, then British ambassador at St. Petersburg. Since his release and return to England, Bellingham had devoted himself to trying to get compensation from the British government. He moved from Liverpool to London, left his wife and three children to fend for themselves, took lodgings with a Mrs. Roberts at 9, New Milman Street, and began to bombard Whitehall with his petitions. He first pestered Gascoyne, one of the members for Liverpool, then Leveson-Gower, and in the winter of 1809 he petitioned the foreign office. The secretary of state ordered an inquiry but rejected Bellingham's claims on the evidence of Leveson-Gower's private secretary and of Sir Stephen Sharpe (a former consul-general in Russia).[2] In February 1810 the same petition was rejected by the lords of the treasury and a month later by the privy council. On 22 May Bellingham called at 10, Downing Street, when Perceval's secretary told him that the prime minister refused to present his petition to parliament. Four days later Perceval received a long letter from Bellingham to which he replied 'that the time for presenting private petitions has long since passed'.

[1] *Sun*, 12 May 1812; W. Jerdan, *Autobiography*, vol. I, p. 141.
[2] P.R.O., T29/117/205.

But in June the unwearied Bellingham again unsuccessfully forwarded his claims to the treasury.[1] There, for a time, he seemed content to let matters rest, for nothing more was heard of him until early in 1812, when he began to bother the home office and twice petitioned the Prince Regent. By March he had grown desperate and sent a copy of a printed circular to each M.P., asking that his case should be debated in parliament.[2] A fortnight later he wrote to the Bow Street magistrates demanding 'what is right and proper be done in my instance'. 'Should this reasonable request be finally denied,' he continued, 'I shall then feel justified in executing justice myself—in which case I shall be ready to argue the merits of so reluctant a measure with His Majesty's Attorney-General, wherever and whenever I may be called upon to do so.'[3] On 5 May he sent a last petition to the treasury: as soon as he heard of its rejection he began his visits to the Commons' gallery. 'I wish', he wrote to a friend at Liverpool, 'my affairs were come to a conclusion—everything in point of law is in my favour.' He saw in the constant failure of his claims only a vast conspiracy to deny him justice. And so with insane self-righteousness and premeditation he decided to 'play a court-card to compel them to finish the game'.[4] Early in May he began practising daily with his pistols on Primrose Hill.

As he was dressing for dinner on Sunday, 10 May Perceval asked his valet how many guests were expected that evening. The valet answered that there were none. 'Then', Perceval is said to have replied, 'I am happy, for I shall have a pleasure I very seldom enjoy, of dining with all my family alone.' When the meal was over, and the customary passage from the bible had been read, he asked Jane to let the children stay up beyond their normal hour. And then he kissed and blessed each one as they went to bed. It had been altogether a happy week for him. His elder daughters had been confirmed by the bishop of London at St. Martin's-in-the-Fields and he had made all arrangements to hear young Spencer perform at Harrow speech day.[5] The following morning the prime minister spent preparing for

[1] P.R.O., T1/1243/4253 (copies of Bellingham's petitions), T29/104/376 and T29/106/168, T27/65/502 and T27/66/392; Perceval MSS., Bellingham to Perceval, 26 May 1810.
[2] P.R.O., H.O. 42/122/unnumbered (13 Apr. 1812); Perceval MSS., copy of Bellingham's printed circular, 12 Mar. 1812.
[3] *Courier*, 16 May 1812; P.R.O., H.O. 42/122 letter from Bellingham, 13 Apr. 1812.
[4] P.R.O., T29/116/747; *Northampton Mercury*, 1 Jan. 1819.
[5] *Northampton Mercury*, 30 May 1812; *The Times*, 14 May 1812.

PLATE 6

The assassination of Spencer Perceval at the hands of John Bellingham,
11 May 1812

(*from a contemporary print*)

that day's debate on the Orders-in-Council. After lunch Jane went out
to visit Frederica Ryder and Perceval was so absorbed that he was late
starting for the Commons. Brougham moved the order of the day for
going into committee, complained that the prime minister was not
in his place, and then began to cross-examine the first witness. By
this time Perceval had gathered together his papers and set out for the
House. As he hurried along Downing Street he passed Thomas
Babington's home, where Wilberforce and several other Saints had
met to discuss the debate. Wilberforce, who was standing at one of the
windows, saw the prime minister walking past and broke spontane-
ously 'into an affectionate eulogy on his worth and principles'.[1]
Meanwhile Bellingham had spent the afternoon with his landlady,
visiting the European Museum. When they left the Museum at four
o'clock Bellingham suggested that, as it was a mild day, they should
take a stroll. At the corner of Sydney Alley, however, he left her
with the excuse that he was going 'to buy a prayer book'. At a little
past five o'clock, just after Stephen had begun to speak in defence
of the Orders-in-Council, the prime minister, accompanied by Lord
Osborne, reached the St. Stephen's entrance to the palace of Westminster. He left his cloak and stick with an attendant before mounting the stairs which led to the lobby of the old house of commons.
There he was recognised by the journalist William Jerdan, who stood
aside to hold open the swing door. Perceval smiled his acknowledgement and stepped into the crowded lobby as Bellingham raised his
pistol, pressed it against the minister's breast, fired, and then calmly sat
down on a bench by the wall. Perceval gave one faint cry, staggered
forward and fell on his face at the feet of William Smith, the member
for Norwich.[2]

Smith was standing talking to a friend when he heard the pistol
fired quite close to him. He turned, saw a small figure burst from the
crowd just before him, cry, 'I am murdered, murdered!' and then
fall. For a second Smith felt convinced that it was Wilberforce, but
as soon as he bent down and lifted the head he saw that it was Perceval.
With the help of another bystander, he carried the prime minister
into a small room, called the Secretary's Office, and laid him on a
table. A little blood flowed from Perceval's mouth; he gave 'two heavy

[1] Colquhoun, p. 227.
[2] William Jerdan, *Autobiography*, vol. I, pp. 134–6. There are full accounts of
the assassination in the *Courier*, the *Morning Post*, and the *Morning Chronicle*
for 12 May 1812.

groans and no more', for he 'neither showed sense nor feeling but his head dropped and his pulse was still'. A Doctor Lygon was called and could do no more than pronounce him dead![1]

All this time Bellingham sat quietly beside his smoking pistol, until one of the clerks of the vote office pointed to him and shouted, 'That is the murderer!' Immediately he was surrounded by a small crowd and was recognised by General Gascoyne. He put up no resistance: 'a mouse might have secured him with a bit of thread'. Jerdan and Henry Burgess (a friend of Sheridan's) searched his pockets, taking out a second loaded pistol, a pair of opera glasses, and about fifty shillings in change. Then, with the help of Joseph Hume, they brought their prisoner before the bar of the House, where the committee had adjourned in confusion and Abbot had resumed the chair. Bellingham was next taken to the prison belonging to the serjeant-at-arms, examined by White, a Westminster justice, and by the two M.P.s Alderman Combe and Michael Angelo Taylor (who were both also magistrates), and was then ordered to be committed to Newgate for murder.[2]

As news of the assassination spread there were few who did not give way to panic. Eldon (anticipating general slaughter) adjourned the Lords, ordered all the doors to be locked and strangers to be searched. 'Look I', said one peer, turning to his neighbour, 'so pale, Lord Dorset, as the rest?' Arden rushed across to the Commons, found his brother's body lying in the Speaker's picture room, threw himself on his knees and broke into tears. Arbuthnot was 'quite overwhelmed', poor Ryder was so dazed that he could neither speak nor act, while the gentle James Stephen was taken ill. Wilberforce heard the news from Babington and hurried to Downing Street to break it to Jane. But that had already been done by Redesdale. At first she refused to believe it 'and even fancied she heard him coming upstairs'. For hours she was too shocked to cry, but finally she broke down and afterwards grew 'very moderate and resigned'. At one o'clock in the morning of 12 May they brought Perceval's body back to 10, Downing Street and placed it in his old dressing-room, where it was attended by two of the household servants. And there, by candle-light, Jane prayed for her husband and for God's mercy on the soul of his assassin. 'I have seen our poor brother,' wrote Lady Redesdale to

[1] Taken from a MSS. account by one of William Smith's daughters.
[2] Add. MSS., 29764, fol. 12, Henry Burgess to Sheridan; Colchester, vol. II, p. 379.

Margaret Walpole, 'and nothing could be more calm and undisturbed than his countenance is.'[1]

There were many on that night of 11 May who thought that Perceval's assassination was the signal for the English revolution. Within an hour of the prime minister's death a mob had begun to gather in Parliament Square. Just before eight a heavily guarded coach arrived to take Bellingham to Newgate, but as soon as the prisoner and his escort appeared outside, part of the crowd surged forward and succeeded in pulling open one of the coach doors. Bellingham was immediately hustled back into the lobby while the senior police officer told the magistrates that it would not be safe to try to reach Newgate without the aid of a military force. A troop of horse guards was then ordered to the scene, and with their help the prisoner was removed to gaol at about midnight.[2] Fashionable society, unnerved by the Luddite riots and by a recent series of brutal and undetected murders in London, prepared for arson and pillage. The Prince Regent (safe in Brighton) sent orders to secure all arms depots in and around the capital. Walls were placarded with 'Rescue Bellingham or die', and, in a London tavern, Coleridge listened to the mob's exultant, 'more of these damned scoundrels must go the same way, and then poor people may live'. While Perceval's friends recalled that 11 May was the anniversary of Chatham's death, his enemies remembered that it was also the day Madocks moved his motion on corruption. That great alarmist Lady Malmesbury talked of fleeing to the country and young Frederick Robinson prudently left town on the plea of going to join the Volunteers.[3] When the news reached Nottingham and Leicester bells were rung, bonfires lit, and a crowd assembled with drums beating and flags flying; 'there they stood huzaaing and expressing their savage joy'. Even from remote little Donington Tom Moore reported

[1] Perceval MSS., Redesdale to Thomas Walpole, 11 May 1812; Lady Frances Redesdale to Margaret Walpole, 12 May 1812; A. B. Drummond to Thomas Walpole, 12 May 1812; Wilberforce, *Life*, vol. IV, pp. 26–7; *The Times*, 14 May 1812. The *Day* reported that while Perceval's body still lay in the Speaker's picture room 'one of the son's of Mr. Perceval, a fine boy of about thirteen years of age, happened accidently to come down a few moments after the assassination took place'. 'The unhappy child's distress is beyond description.' The two sons nearest thirteen years of age, Henry and Dudley Montague, were both away at Harrow school. The child concerned may have been John, then nine years old. For a fascinating account of John Perceval's later insanity see *Perceval's Narrative* (ed. G. Bateson).

[2] *Courier*, 12 May 1812; Cobbett, *History of the Regency*, chapter III, p. 128.

[3] Windsor MSS., 19620 (Regency file), Liverpool to Prince Regent, 11 May 1812; Malmesbury, *Letters*, vol. II, p. 281.

that 'all the common people's heads are full of revolution'. One of Birmingham's leading manufacturers lamented to Lord Holland, 'with a demure countenance and a subdued voice', the wickedness of such un-Christian joy. ' "It is indeed disgusting, and yet", added he, with an arch, puritanical smile, "it proves the sad condition of the poor manufacturers, and it cannot be denied that, in the present critical state of the question on the Orders-in-Council, the finger of a benevolent providence is visible in this horrible event." ' 'The English character', sighed Romilly, 'seems to have undergone some unaccountable and portentious change.' [1]

The inquest on Perceval was held on the morning of 12 May at the *Cat and Bagpipes*, a public house on the corner of Downing Street. Medical evidence proved that he had been shot just over the fourth rib and that the ball had penetrated to his heart. A number of witnesses then gave evidence against Bellingham, a verdict of wilful murder was returned, and Thomas Brooksbank was bound over to prosecute.[2] At three o'clock that afternoon party leaders met at the Speaker's to discuss some provision for Mrs. Perceval and her children. An hour later the Commons assembled to hear the Regent's proposals. The House was packed: 'in most faces there was an agony of tears'. Ryder was to have moved the address, but found that he was too overwrought to speak. And so Castlereagh took his place. He read the Regent's message recommending an annuity of £2,000 for Jane Perceval and a grant of £50,000 for her children. But before he could finish his speech he was so overcome with emotion that he had to sit down 'amidst the loud cheers and strong sympathy of the House'. He was followed by Ponsonby, Canning, and Whitbread before it was agreed unanimously that the address should be presented to the Prince Regent by the whole House.[3]

Meanwhile, at Charles Long's suggestion, the sculptor Joseph Nollekens called at Downing Street to take a death mask of the prime minister, and later that evening Perceval's body was placed into a soldered lead coffin. Arrangements for the funeral began immediately. There were some who urged that Perceval should be buried with great pomp in Westminster Abbey, but Jane, whose only concern was 'to do everything she thinks he would wish if he could direct her', insisted

[1] *Northampton Mercury*, 23 May 1812; Moore, *Memoirs*, vol. I, p. 277; Holland, *Further Memoirs of the Whig Party*, pp. 131–2; Romilly, *Diary*, vol. III, p. 35; *Quarterly Review*, Dec. 1812, p. 349.
[2] *Courier*, 12 May 1812.
[3] Colchester, vol. II, p. 380; *Parl. Deb.*, XXIII, 172.

on a private ceremony. Members of parliament were asked not to attend in a body and it was decided that, in order to avoid large crowds on the route, the procession should leave Downing Street early in the morning of Saturday, 16 May. There were only six coaches. In the first rode young Spencer (hurriedly summoned from Harrow) and Lord Arden; in the second sat Eldon, Liverpool, Harrowby, and Ryder, who acted as pall-bearers; the third contained Perceval's three brothers-in-law; the fourth his private secretaries, Herries, Brooksbank and Rosenhagen; the fifth and sixth, his closest political friends—Camden, Castlereagh, Croker, Arbuthnot, and Wharton. As the cortège passed down Whitehall the bells of the Abbey and of St. Margaret's rang in muffled tones. Outside the houses of parliament the procession halted for a while, passed slowly over Westminster bridge, and then, escorted by a troop of Light Horse Volunteers, carried Spencer Perceval on to St. Luke's, Charlton, close by the house where he was born. And at the west end of the nave was placed a small white marble bust by Chantrey above an inscription which tells of the assassin's shot that 'Turned a Home of Peace and Love into a House of Mourning and Desolation'.[1]

John Bellingham was tried at the Old Bailey on Friday, 15 May before Sir John Mansfield, Mr. Justice Grose, and Baron Graham. After the attorney-general had examined the witnesses for the prosecution, the only point remaining at issue was whether or not the accused was responsible for his own actions. The defence pleaded unsuccessfully for an adjournment to give time for witnesses to be called from Liverpool: the medical evidence offered at the trial was dismissed as inconclusive. But in the end it was the prisoner himself who was his own executioner. For two hours he addressed the jury, giving a lucid account of his dealings in Russia and of his later failure to secure redress. He disclaimed all personal enmity towards Perceval: he now wished, he confessed, that he had murdered Leveson-Gower instead. 'If', he concluded, 'I am destined to sacrifice my life, I shall meet my doom with conscious tranquillity; I shall look forward to it as the weary traveller looks for the promised inn, where he may repose his weary frame, after enduring the pelting of the pitiless storm. Gentlemen, it now remains between God and your consciences as to what

[1] Farington, *Diary*, vol. VII, p. 83; *Courier*, 13 and 14 May 1812; *The Times*, 18 May 1812; *Northampton Mercury*, 23 May 1812; Perceval MSS., Arden to Thomas Walpole, 15 May 1812; C. V. Williams, p. 233. L. M. May, *Copies of the Inscriptions in the old parish church and churchyard of Charlton* (1908.)

your verdict will be.' In an age which equated lunacy with Bedlam, Bellingham's coherence and self-possession were fatal. It would have needed a jury of psychologists to save him from the rope: he was tried instead by frightened men, obsessed by the dangers of risings in the north and in the midlands. Mansfield's summing up was largely a panegyric on the dead minister and the jury retired for only ten minutes before returning a verdict of guilty. And so Bellingham was condemned to death, his body afterwards to be anatomised and dissected. 'Thank God', wrote the queen, 'that it has ended as it ought.' The execution was fixed for the morning of 18 May, too long a delay for her majesty's liking, 'tho', she confessed, 'it must be owned that two days for recollection and preparation for the prisoner to go out of the world is a grant worthy of a Christian and religious nation.' [1]

James Stephen and other evangelicals visited him in prison, thinking that they might bring him to repent. He remained calm to the end, 'very humble and thankful', but still spoke of himself as unfortunate rather than guilty. Cobbett, from a cell in Newgate, watched him go to his death. Even on the scaffold the sheriffs questioned him about accomplices, but he denied having any. He died without fear or remorse, and was cheered to the last by many of the watching crowd. The execution went off surprisingly quietly: every precaution had been taken to preserve the peace, but the mob showed no desire to riot. Instead they auctioned Bellingham's clothes button by button as souvenirs: his greatcoat alone was said to have fetched £10.[2] But he never became a radical martyr. For a single week in his unhappy life Bellingham and his grievances became as important to the nation as he himself had always thought them to be. He flashed into public view like a meteor and then, except for one second's bloody deed, was soon forgotten.

Meanwhile the Commons debated the intended provision for Jane and her children. The Regent's original proposals, although lavish enough, were attacked as 'utterly unworthy of the national character'. The *Sun* suggested a peerage for Jane while the *Courier* thought the fund to be invested for her children 'totally insufficient to educate and maintain them in the rank they deserve to occupy, insufficient

---

[1] *Gent. Mag.*, June 1812, pp. 660-2; Aspinall, *Letters of George IV*, vol. I, no. 73. Even the *Sun*, which on 12 May had called Bellingham 'a confirmed lunatic', rejoiced at his execution.

[2] Wilberforce, *Life*, vol. IV, pp. 26-7; Cobbett, *History of the Regency*, chapter III, p. 133; *Sun*, 21 May 1812; Aspinall, *Letters of George IV*, vol. I, no. 74; D. Wilson, *The Substance of a Conversation with John Bellingham*, 1812.

even to set them up in any trade!' A series of motions by back-
benchers forced the government to be even more prodigal with public
money and drove some opposition members to divide the House.
'How very low and mercenary people are!' sighed Wilberforce. In
the end Jane was assured of £2,000 a year for life out of the consolidated fund, with £1,000 a year going to her heir after her death.
£50,000, tax free, was taken out of the supplies for 1812 to be set aside
for her children, Arden settled an additional pension on Jane out of
his own money, young Spencer was appointed, in February 1813, to
the lucrative post of teller of the exchequer, while the benchers of
Lincoln's Inn paid for the legal training of both Spencer and Dudley
Montague. It was a generous but not wholly undeserved settlement.
'Poor Perceval!' wrote George Jackson, when he first heard the news
of the assassination, 'poor in every sense I believe; for he was too
honest to enrich himself, however he may have helped to enrich
others.' [1] Like Pitt he died practically penniless, though he might have
made a fortune out of public office. He was, said George III, 'perhaps
the most straightforward man he had ever known'. 'I most anxiously
wish', wrote Queen Charlotte to the Prince Regent, 'that you may be
fortunate enough to replace this loss with a person equally attached
to yourself and the country.' The dead minister, added Princess
Elizabeth, was 'one of the best of men, one of the truest friends of this
family, and one of the most upright characters that ever existed'. Even
the duke of Kent, who had sufficient political reasons to dislike him,
paid glowing tributes to his private virtues, while the princess of
Wales, mindful of past kindnesses, realised that perhaps she had lost
her best friend and cancelled all her public engagements except
attendance at court, 'as that cannot be attributed to any love of
pleasure'. The three basic qualities in Perceval's character, said
William Van Mildert, who preached the memorial sermon at Lincoln's
Inn, were piety, benevolence, and self-control, 'all united by one plain
and simple principle, a never-failing sense of duty'. 'Never', said
Wilberforce, 'had he known any individual die of whose salvation
he entertained less doubt.' [2] There was, amongst those who had known

[1] *Courier*, 14 May 1812; *Sun*, 13 May 1812; Wilberforce, *Life*, vol. IV, pp.
25–6; *Statutes*, 52 George III, cap. 67; *Black Book of Lincoln's Inn*, vol. IV,
pp. 124–7; Add. MSS., 38190, fol. 23; *Bath Archives*, vol. I, p. 375. Jane Perceval
later married Lieutenant-Colonel Sir Henry William Carr. She died on 26 Jan.
1844 and was buried with Perceval in St. Luke's, Charlton.
[2] Aspinall, *Letters of George IV*, vol. I, no. 70; Perceval MSS., Princess
Elizabeth to Arden, (undated); duke of Kent to same, 21 June 1812; Harrowby

him, whether as political friend or foe, a genuine sense of personal loss. He was, said Herries, who knew him as well as anyone, 'the model of a high-minded, high-principled, truthful, generous gentleman, sans peur et sans reproche'. In the treasury they remembered his cordiality and the considerate way he had treated even the most junior of clerks while in the Commons his opponents recalled his fairness and courtesy in debate. Canning, Cobbett, Grattan, Romilly, and Holland all spoke of his personal qualities in glowing terms; he was, wrote Lord Camden, in the true language of panegyric, 'one of the best men who ever existed'.[1]

For Jane the last three weeks in May was a period of continual strain. For a few days she went to stay with Richard and Frederica Ryder while it was being whispered in some circles that Ryder's negligence was partly responsible for her husband's death. On the Sunday after the assassination she took her three eldest daughters to St. Martin's only to find that they had to sit through a sermon on the text 'Thou shalt do no murder.' The London papers vied with each other in their 'paraphanalia of sorrow' while the bookstalls were filled with catch-penny ballads and dirges. Addresses and letters of condolence poured in and the government struck a special medal with Perceval's likeness on the obverse and on the reverse a bowed figure pointing to a broken pillar, the capital of which had fallen to the ground, emblematic of the country's loss.[2] Inevitably the students of divine prophecy had wonders to relate. John Williams, a Cornish mining engineer, afterwards claimed that on the night of 2 May he had had three dreams, in each of which he had seen the assassination scene, realistic even to the colour of Bellingham's waistcoat buttons. And certainly when Jane came to sort her husband's papers she found part of his last message to his eldest son, written early in 1809, in which he wrote of his life 'with a sense of the improbability of its long continuance'. Later still Lord Arden, scarcely an over-imaginative

MSS., vol. V, fol. 107, Henry Ryder to Harrowby, 22 May 1812; Lady Bury, *Diary*, vol. I, pp. 92–5; Melville, *The Berry Papers*, p. 305; *Gent. Mag.*, 1812 Supplement, p. 664.

[1] Herries, *Memoirs*, vol. I, p. 20; *Political Register*, 16 May 1812, pp. 857–8; Romilly, vol. III, p. 37; Holland, *Further Memoirs*, pp. 132–3; *Annual Register*, 1812, p. 79; Perceval MSS., Camden to Arden, 24 June 1812.

[2] *The Times*, 14 May 1812; Malmesbury, *Letters*, vol. II, p. 276; *Northampton Mercury*, 23 May 1812; *Day*, 12 and 18 May 1812; *Notes and Queries*, 7th series, vol. III, p. 445; D. M. Perceval, *Remarks on the Character of the Rt. Hon. Spencer Perceval*, p. 32.

man, claimed to have found a copy of the *Rambler* with a marginal
note in Perceval's hand:

> I do not weep, the springs of tears are dry,
>   And of a sudden I am calm, as if
> All things were well, and yet my husband's murdered.[1]

At first it seemed as though John Bellingham had destroyed both
prime minister and government, for there were few who thought that
the cabinet could survive without Perceval. 'The firm', wrote *The
Times*, 'is entirely broken up by the death of the chief partner. The
survivors cannot carry on the concern.' [2] But the prophets again
underestimated the ineptitude of the opposition. Wellesley, who had
the premiership at his command, allowed the full text of his resignation statement to appear in *The Times* on 20 May and so caused a fatal
revulsion of feeling against himself by publicly attacking Perceval
within a week of his funeral; Canning, as usual, asked for too much;
and the whigs were still too busy quarrelling among themselves to
bother about office. In the end the Prince Regent had to fall back on
the old firm, led this time by Liverpool.[3] The negotiations of May 1812
only underlined the lesson of the autumn of 1809—there was no
immediate alternative to the Perceval government. That same government was still in office when the long war with Napoleon was finally
won. But long before that Perceval himself was generally forgotten.
The court went into mourning for a fortnight and the citizens of
Northampton did the same. All Saints' church was hung with black,
a Chantrey statue was erected in the shire hall by public subscription
and a portrait of Perceval was commissioned to record 'the memory
of a man whose virtues were in no place more justly appreciated'.[4]
The benchers of Lincoln's Inn ordered 'a plain handsome tablet' for
their chapel and asked the bishop of Oxford to compose a fulsome

[1] For a text of the account of John Williams' dream see Walpole, vol. II,
pp. 329–332; *Notes and Queries*, 5th series, vol. XI, p. 256; 7th series, vol. XI,
pp. 47 and 121; Perceval MSS., copy of the *Rambler*. Perceval's youngest daughter
Frederica, kept until her death in 1900 relics of her father, including the blood-
stained rug on which he died. (*Northamptonshire Daily Record*, 14 May 1900).

[2] *The Times*, 22 May 1812.

[3] Liverpool based his refusal to serve with Wellesley and Canning on the
publication of Wellesley's statement (Yonge, vol. I, p. 392).

[4] *Gent. Mag.*, June 1812, p. 585 and Feb. 1818, p. 102; Markham and Cox,
vol. II, pp. 487–8; Add. MSS., 38255, fol. 130. Among the list of subscribers to the
monument were all Perceval's closest political friends, George Harrison of the
treasury, and the William Walcot who had been a candidate at the Northampton
election of 1796.

Latin epitaph for it, and, by order of the Prince Regent, Richard
Westmacott produced a large classical memorial which joined the
rapidly growing collection in Westminster abbey.[1] But once the new
cabinet was firmly in power, there were few men in public life who
really felt his loss, though young Peel long remembered the days when
he had 'seen our little champion go forth with his sling and with his
sword, and bring down the mightiest of his enemies'. On the surface
it seemed that his sudden death had little political significance once his
colleagues were retained in office. But Lord Liverpool, who remained
at the treasury from 1812 to 1827, was never an ultra-tory of the
Perceval school. Only *The Times* realised that Bellingham had shot
the one 'faithful and persevering advocate of a system of opinions,
which however some may think them obsolete, are yet warmly
cherished by many others, as conducive to the support of religion,
and through it to the welfare of the state. Amidst all the political
changes that could have occurred during his natural life, he would
ever have been heard, and not in vain, in their defence.' [2] Only when
the Roman catholics were emancipated and the rotten boroughs swept
away did the friends of the old order realise what they had lost. 'Mr.
Perceval', wrote Robert Southey in 1835, 'was in my judgement the
best minister we have ever had. I looked upon his death, at the time,
as the greatest misfortune that could have befallen this country, and
subsequent events have shown that it was so.' And Arbuthnot,
struggling to save a 'remnant of our Constitution' from whig reforms,
would pray for a Pitt or a Perceval to lead the cause in the house of
commons.[3]

Some biographers, like Midas, turn all they touch into pure gold.
The gift may be divine, but it is dangerous. There have been
few golden kings or statesmen and Spencer Perceval was certainly not
of their number. He died a martyr's death, but no biographer could
make him a political saint. He was not by any standards a great prime
minister. Those historians who have not completely ignored him have
scarcely added to his stature. 'Never', wrote A. F. Fremantle, 'have
England's destinies been presided over by a commoner who had so
little genius to compensate for the absence of the influence accom-
panying title and property.' Professor Roberts, although recognising

---

[1] *Black Book of Lincoln's Inn*, vol. IV, pp. 128–9 and 149.
[2] Croker, vol. I, p. 46; *The Times*, 11 May 1812.
[3] Perceval MSS., Southey to D. M. Perceval, 9 July 1835; *Trans. of Camden Soc.*, vol. LXV, pp. 175–6.

IN MEMORY OF THE RIGHT HON^{ble} SPENCER PERCEVAL
Chancellor of the Exchequer _ First Lord of the Treasury
THIS MONUMENT WAS ERECTED BY THE PRINCE REGENT AND PARLIAMENT
TO RECORD THEIR DEEP SENSE OF HIS PUBLIC AND PRIVATE VIRTUES
AND TO MARK THE NATION'S ABHORRENCE OF THE ACT BY WHICH HE FELL

Born 1 Novr 1762 _ Assassinated within the walls of the House of Commons _ 11 May 1812

PLATE 7

The Westmacott memorial to Spencer Perceval in Westminster Abbey

his many admirable qualities and his great influence over the Pittite
rank and file, thought him 'hardly equal to the responsibilities of his
post'.[1] Professor Aspinall and Mr. Anthony Smith roundly condemn him as 'the most reactionary Prime Minister of the century'.
Perceval, like the great majority of the educated Englishmen of his
time, believed quite simply that the mixed constitution under which he
lived gave the greatest possible measure of happiness and civil liberty
to all classes of his fellow countrymen. He consequently opposed, in
his own typically vigorous and unambiguous way, all those movements which he judged to threaten the basis of that constitution.
Radical proposals for parliamentary reform would destroy the existing
constitutional balance; catholic emancipation would undermine the
established church. Both were intimately linked with the external
threat from France whose rulers, and whose British sympathisers,
espoused doctrines subversive of the rights of property in England
and of the entire *status quo* in Ireland. But Perceval was never simply
opposed, on principle, to all change. He tried hard to work out a
sensible compromise on Henry Bankes' Reversions Bill against the
opposition of the real ultras, led by his own brother. He was equally
moderate in his attitude to Curwen's bill on the sale of seats and more
perceptive than his opponents in seeing its real significance. On
questions of both political and church patronage his own high personal
standards of morality made him a reformer. Sheer ignorance rather
than any innate lack of sympathy accounts for his neglect of economic
and industrial issues, for he had no first-hand knowledge whatsoever
of conditions in the new industrial towns of the midlands and of
Lancashire. He seems never in his life to have travelled further north
than the county towns which were on the midland circuit, with the
exception of one brief visit to Knutsford in the 1790's. Yet his sympathies extended beyond the plight of West Indian slaves and impoverished curates. He refused, as attorney-general, to interpret the
combination acts in the interests of employers, and he wished to widen
the scope of the elder Peel's Cotton Manufacturing Apprentices Bill.
He was less theoretical and more liberal than people like Huskisson
on the minimum wage issue and urged employers in the cotton
industry to offer their operatives an agreed basic wage. The verdict
of posterity is, however, seldom kind to those who defended the
status quo, wasting little sympathy on those whom 'history has proved

---

[1] Fremantle, *England in the 19th Century, 1806–10*, p. 295; Roberts, *The
Whig Party, 1807–12*, pp. 1–2.

to have been wrong'. Reformers, it seems, sometimes get their reward in heaven, if not on earth: those who opposed reform get their deserts in history text books. The best that can usually be said of politicians like Spencer Perceval is that, although misguided in public affairs, they were often 'blameless in private life'.

A great deal might be written to justify such a verdict. Perceval was essentially a 'safe' man, who put the golden age in the past and saw the future not as a challenge but as a threat to the established order.

> Long, Perceval, Brittania's council's guide

wrote a poetasting admirer,

> To wise restrictions make the rabble bow.

He was too limited and too frightened to understand fully the social changes taking place around him. Dickens thought him 'palpably a third-rate professional politician scarcely fit to carry Lord Chatham's crutch'. He wrote, said the Prince Regent, in a style which would disgrace a respectable washerwoman and, in an age of great parliamentarians, he never reached the front rank as an orator. He had indeed almost a genius for missing great occasions for speech-making. Yet all this does little justice to his real contribution, for he alone, particularly during the period from 1807 to 1812, possessed a combination of solid if unspectacular qualities which served his country well. 'He is not', said Grattan, 'a ship of the line, but he carries many guns, is tight-built, and is out in all weathers.' While he was prime minister he had in the Commons no superior and few equals in debate. His language was always 'purely but unaffectedly English, nor ever chargeable with incorrect taste'. He suffered, particularly at the beginning of sentences, from 'a little temporary hesitation', which amounted almost to a stammer, but, as he warmed to his theme, he would speak with a directness and a spirit born of self-conviction. The young Charles Shore heard him give his last major speech on the catholic question. 'His short and slender frame was instinct with spirit and his countenance beaming with animation.' As he warmed to his theme he gradually became almost bent double over the table as he leant towards and looked full at his opponents. Many unsophisticated country members, whose support was so vital to a weakened government, appreciated his plain speaking as much as they trusted his personal honesty. If he was not far-sighted, he was, within his own limits, remarkably clear-sighted. He was, admitted the young Melbourne, 'a very clever fellow at business', while Wilberforce recognised his 'sweetest of all possible tempers'.[1] In public life he was scrupulously fair, often witty but very rarely malicious: once outside the house of commons he tried to forget party differences, thinking that political disagreements need not end private friendships. While in office he handled public money and government appointments with unusual care and with complete disregard for personal financial gain. It can, above all, be said of him that he was one of those prime ministers who developed in office. He had a much firmer control over both the cabinet and the Commons at the end than at the beginning of his period in power. By 1812 he had at last won the confidence of the Prince Regent, was clearly recognised by ministers like Liverpool, Eldon, and Castlereagh as the undisputed leader of Pitt's Friends, had attracted Sidmouth and his supporters into what was to prove their final and permanent political connection, and had driven dissidents like Canning and Wellesley into the political wilderness. He was, moreover, only in his fiftieth year and so seemed destined to a long period at 10, Downing Street.

Even brighter were his achievements and his prospects as a war minister. He brought to the cabinet, at a critical time in the long struggle with France, the essential qualities of steadfastness and coolness. Never once, in spite of whig defeatism and a crippling Spanish dollar problem, did he waver in support of Wellington's campaigns in the Peninsula. Wellington himself often criticised the Perceval ministry's policies during the heat of the struggle, but in later years he paid unqualified tribute to the prime minister's constant support and encouragement. Other expeditions were ill-contrived and their commanders badly chosen, but Perceval never doubted our chances of ultimate success. It was he who, in the years from 1809 to 1812, kept the majority of Pitt's Friends together as a party, taught them to stand fast in parliament, and encouraged the promising young men who were to take the lead in the future. He gave the country a firm government to continue the war when it seemed that no one else could command a majority in parliament.[2] Only a few days before Perceval was shot

[1] Brougham, *Statesmen*, vol. I, p. 32; *Anti-Jacobin Review*, May 1812, p. 69; Wilberforce, *Life*, vol. IV, p. 26; Farington, vol. IV, p. 166; Holland, *Further Memoirs*, pp. 132–3. John Ward thought Perceval the equal of Pitt 'in quickness and dexterity as a debater' (*Letters to Ivy*, pp. 157 and 196).

[2] Add. MSS., 37296, fol. 155. It was Perceval who, in February 1812, persuaded the Prince Regent to mark the beginning of his unrestricted Regency by conferring an earldom on Wellington (Add. MSS., 37296, fols. 183 and 187 and Perceval MSS., Perceval to Wellington, 18 Feb. 1812).

dead, Napoleon left Paris to lead his Grand Army to Moscow—and to destruction. If only John Bellingham had obeyed his first impulse to shoot Lord Granville Leveson-Gower instead of the prime minister Perceval would almost certainly have been in power at the time of Waterloo. For the younger Pitt, with all his titles to fame, was not 'The pilot who weather'd the storm'. He died when the tempest was still at its height, and left Perceval to guide the ship of state to the harbour entrance. He did this by a combination of courage and honesty, two qualities which alone should rescue his memory from oblivion and make him worthy of Fortescue's eloquent tribute:

'His career was cut short by the hand of an assassin before he could share in the credit of having carried the war to a successful issue, but in this place at least his service must not remain uncommemorated, because he endured the dust and heat of the race without gaining the immortal garland.' [1]

[1] Fortescue, *History of the British Army*, vol. VII, p. 330.

LIST OF MINISTERS, 1807–1812

A. CABINET MINISTERS

	Portland Ministry	*Perceval Ministry*
First Lord of the Treasury	Duke of Portland	Spencer Perceval[1]
Chancellor of Exchequer	Spencer Perceval[1]	Spencer Perceval[1]
Lord Privy Seal	Earl of Westmorland	Earl of Westmorland
Lord President of Council	Earl Camden	1. Earl Camden 2. Viscount Sidmouth (Apr. 1812)
Lord Chancellor	Lord Eldon	Lord Eldon
Home Secretary	Lord Hawkesbury (succeeded as second Earl of Liverpool (Dec. 1808)	Richard Ryder
Foreign Secretary	George Canning	1. Earl Bathurst (Oct.–Nov. 1809) 2. Marquis Wellesley (Dec. 1809) 3. Viscount Castlereagh (Mar. 1812)
Secretary for War and Colonies	Viscount Castlereagh	Earl of Liverpool
First Lord of Admiralty	Lord Mulgrave	1. Lord Mulgrave 2. C. P. Yorke (May 1810) 3. Viscount Melville (Mar. 1812)
President of Board of Control	Not in cabinet until July 1809 Earl of Harrowby (July 1809)	1. R. S. Dundas (Viscount Melville, 1811) 2. Earl of Buckinghamshire (Apr. 1812)
Master-General of Ordnance	Earl of Chatham	1. Earl of Chatham 2. Lord Mulgrave (Mar. 1810)
President of Board of Trade	Earl Bathurst[2]	Earl Bathurst[2]
Secretary-at-War	Not in cabinet until June 1809 Lord Granville Leveson-Gower (June 1809)	Not in cabinet
Ministers without Portfolio		1. Duke of Portland (d. Oct. 1809) 2. Earl of Harrowby (Nov. 1809) 3. Earl Camden (Marquis of Camden, Mar. 1812)

---

[1] Also Chancellor of the Duchy of Lancaster.
[2] Also Master of the Mint.

B. MINISTERS NOT IN THE CABINET

	Portland Ministry	*Perceval Ministry*
President of Board of Control	R. E. Dundas (until Apr. 1809) The holder subsequently was a member of the cabinet	The holder was a member of the cabinet
Secretary-at-War	1. Sir James Pulteney 2. Lord Granville Leveson-Gower (June 1809)[1]	Viscount Palmerston
Vice-President of the Board of Trade	George Rose	George Rose[2]
Joint Paymasters-General of the Forces	Lord Charles Henry Somerset Charles Long	Lord Charles Henry Somerset Charles Long
Joint Postmasters-General	Earl of Chichester Earl of Sandwich	Earl of Chichester Earl of Sandwich
Attorney-General	Sir Vicary Gibbs	Sir Vicary Gibbs
Solicitor-General	Sir Thomas Plumer	Sir Thomas Plumer
Judge Advocate General	1. Nicholas Bond 2. Richard Ryder (Nov. 1807)	Charles Manners Sutton
Master of the Rolls	Sir William Grant	Sir William Grant
Junior Lords of the Treasury	Marquis of Titchfield (Apr.–Sept. 1807) William Eliot William Sturges Bourne John Foster (from Sept. 1807) Richard Ryder (Sept.–Nov. 1807) William Broderick (from Dec. 1807)	John Foster (until July 1811) William Broderick William Eliot (until Dec. 1811) Snowdon Barne Earl of Desart (until June 1810) Berkeley Paget (from June 1810) W. W. Pole (from Dec. 1811) Richard Wellesley (from Dec. 1811)
Secretaries of the Treasury	1. Henry Wellesley (until Mar. 1809) 2. Charles Arbuthnot (from Mar. 1809) William Huskisson	Charles Arbuthnot Richard Wharton
Junior Lords of the Admiralty	Admiral James Gambier (until May 1808) Vice-Admiral Sir Richard Bickerton Captain William Johnston Hope (until Mar. 1809) Robert Ward Viscount Palmerston (until Nov. 1809) James Buller Rear-Admiral William Domett (from May 1808) Robert Moorsom (from Mar. 1809) Viscount Lowther (from Nov. 1809)	Vice-Admiral Sir Richard Bickerton Robert Ward (until June 1811) James Buller Rear-Admiral William Domett Robert Moorsom (until June 1810) Viscount Lowther (until June 1810) Sir Joseph Sydney Yorke (from June 1810) Frederick Robinson (from June 1810) Lord Walpole (from June 1811)

[1] Leveson-Gower was a member of the cabinet.

[2] During October and November 1809 Rose performed the duties of President of the Board of Trade while Earl Bathurst was acting as Foreign Secretary.

	Portland Ministry	*Perceval Ministry*
Secretary of the Admiralty	1. William Marsden 2. W. W. Pole (from June 1807)	J. W. Croker
Treasurer of the Navy	George Rose	George Rose
Commissioners of the Board of Control	Lord Lovaine Lord Teignmouth Thomas Wallace George Johnstone	Lord Lovaine Lord Teignmouth Thomas Wallace George Johnstone (until June 1810) Viscount Lowther (from June 1810) John Sullivan (from Apr. 1812)
Clerk of the Ordnance	1. W. W. Pole (until June 1807) 2. Cropley Ashley Cooper (from June 1807)	1. Cropley Ashley Cooper (until June 1811) 2. Robert Ward (from June 1811)

C. THE IRISH GOVERNMENT

	Portland Ministry	*Percival Ministry*
Lord Lieutenant	Duke of Richmond	Duke of Richmond
Lord Chancellor	Lord Manners	Lord Manners
Chief Secretary	1. Sir Arthur Wellesley (until June 1808) 2. R. S. Dundas (from Apr. 1809)[1]	1. R. S. Dundas (until Oct. 1809) 2. W. W. Pole (from Oct. 1809)
Chancellor of Exchequer	John Foster	1. John Foster (until Dec. 1811) 2. W. W. Pole (from Dec. 1811)

---

[1] J. W. Croker temporarily took charge of the business of Chief Secretary after Sir Arthur Wellesley assumed his command in Portugal.

BIBLIOGRAPHY

1. MANUSCRIPT SOURCES

Private Collections:

The Royal Archives at Windsor Castle. I have to acknowledge the gracious permission of Her Majesty the Queen to make use of material from the George III and Regency papers.

Perceval Papers. Two collections of Perceval's papers survive. Both seem to have been available to Sir Spencer Walpole when he wrote his *Life of the Right Honourable Spencer Perceval* in 1874. The papers may indeed have been divided into two collections after that date. The larger and more important collection was owned by Mr. David Holland and was traced by the present writer through the Perceval family wills. The second collection was made available by the National Register of Archives and was then owned by Mr. Dudley Perceval. Neither collection had been used by historians since 1874. Both are now deposited in the British Museum and are catalogued as Add. MSS. 49173–49195.

Harrowby Papers. Volumes 4 to 18 of the main series were studied at Sandon Hall, Staffordshire, by kind permission of the earl of Harrowby.

Westbrook Hay Papers. This collection of the letters of Richard Ryder and of material relating to the home office was discovered during the demolition of the Ryder family's old home at Westbrook Hay, Hertfordshire. These papers, which had not previously been used, were also made available by the earl of Harrowby.

Herries Papers. These papers were traced by the present writer to their owner, Lt.-Col. A. H. Spottiswoode of Sevenoaks, Kent. The letters of J. C. Herries were used in 1880 by E. Herries in writing his *Memoir of the Public Life of the Rt. Hon. J. C. Herries.* The collection, however, also contains important and previously unused material relating to the commissariat.

At the British Museum:

Additional Manuscripts—
Bentham Papers	33537–33564.
Huskisson Papers	38734–38770.
Liverpool Papers	38190–38489 and 38564–38581.
Rose Papers	42772–42846.
Wellesley Papers	36274–37318 and 37414–37416.

At the Public Record Office:

Treasury Papers	T29/89–117	Treasury board minutes, 1807–12.
	T27/64–66	Treasury out letters, 1809–10.
	T22/11–12	Treasury letters, taxes.

Treasury Papers	T1/999–1230	Registered papers, 1807–12.
	T1/3423–3424	Papers relating to the commissioners for auditing public accounts and the comptrollers of army accounts.
	T1/4305–4308	Papers relating to treasury reorganisation.
Audit Office	A.O.10/28	Account of the audit office after Petty's reform.
Foreign Office	F.O.83/15–20	
	F.O.91/485–7	Foreign office to treasury.
	F.O.95/378–9	
Home Office	H.O.40/40	Papers relating to J. T. Perceval.
War Office	W.O.6/172–3	War office to treasury.
Bosanquet Papers	30/3	
Chatham Papers	30/8	
Colchester Papers	30/9	
Lowry Cole Papers	30/43	

2. PRINTED SOURCES

Newspapers:

Cobbett's Political Register.
The Courier.
The Day.
The Examiner.

The Morning Chronicle.
The National Adviser.
The Northampton Mercury.
The Sun.

The Times.

Periodicals:

The Annual Register.
The Anti-Jacobin Review.
Cobbett's Parliamentary Debates.
Cobbett's Parliamentary History.
The Edinburgh Review.
The Monthly Review.
Notes and Queries.
The Parliamentary Register.
The Statutes of the Realm.

The Gentleman's Magazine.
House of Commons Accounts and Papers.
House of Commons Journals.
House of Lords Journals.
The London Gazette.
The Quarterly Review.
The Senator.
State Trials—Howell.

Books and Pamphlets:

ACWORTH, A. W. *Financial Reconstruction in England, 1815–22.* London, 1925.

AIKIN, JOHN. *Annals of the Reign of George III, 1760–1815.* Two vols. London, 1816.

ANDERSON, W. *The Iniquity of Banking or Banknotes Proved to be an injury to the Public.* London, 1797.

ARBUTHNOT, CHARLES. *The Correspondence of.* Edited by A. Aspinall. *R.H.S. Camden Society, 3rd series,* vol. lxv, 1941.

ASHE, T. *The Spirit of 'The Book'.* London, 1811.
ASPINALL, A. *Lord Brougham and the Whig Party.* Manchester, 1927.
— *The Canningite Party. Trans. of the Royal Hist. Soc., 4th series,* vol. 17.
— *Politics and the Press, 1780–1850.* London, 1949.
— *The Letters of George IV.* Three vols. Cambridge, 1938.
— *The Letters of Princess Charlotte.* London, 1949.
ASPINALL, A., and SMITH, A. E. *English Historical Documents,* vol. xi, 1783–1832. London, 1959.
ATKINSON, C. M., and MITCHELL, J. E. *The Life and Principles of Sir Samuel Romilly.* Derby, 1920.
AUCKLAND, LORD. *Journal and Correspondence.* Edited by the bishop of Bath and Wells. Two vols. London, 1861.

BAGOT, J. *George Canning and His Friends.* Two vols. London, 1909.
BAILDON, W. P. *Admissions to Lincoln's Inn.* Vol. i. London, 1896.
— *The Black Book of Lincoln's Inn.* Vol. iv. London, 1897.
BARING, ALEXANDER. *An Inquiry into the Causes and Consequences of the Order in Council.* London, 1808.
BATHURST, LORD. *Report on the MSS. of Earl Bathurst. Hist. MSS. Comm.,* 1923.
BEATTIE, W. *The Life and Letters of Thomas Campbell.* London, 1894.
BERRY, MARY. *Journals and Correspondence of Miss Berry.* Edited by Lady Lewis. London, 1865.
BERRY PAPERS. *The Berry Papers.* Edited by L. Melville. London, 1914.
BESSBOROUGH, LADY. *Lady Bessborough and Her Family Circle.* Edited by the earl of Bessborough and A. Aspinall. London, 1940.
BEVERIDGE, SIR WILLIAM. *Trade Cycles in Britain before 1850. Oxford Economic Papers,* 1940.
BLAGDON, F. W. *Chancery Injunction, Letters to the Princess of Wales.* London, 1813.
BLAND-BURGESS, SIR JAMES. *Letters and Correspondence of Sir James Bland-Burgess.* Edited by J. Hutton. London, 1885.
BOSANQUET, CHARLES. *Practical Observations on the Report of the Bullion Committee.* London, 1810.
— *Supplement to 'Practical Observations',* etc. London, 1811.
BOURKE, A. *The Betting Book of White's Club, 1743–1878.* Two vols. London, 1882.
BRADY, A. *William Huskisson and Liberal Reform.* Oxford, 1928.
BRIGHTFIELD, M. F. *John Wilson Croker.* London, 1940.
BROCK, W. R. *Lord Liverpool and Liberal Toryism.* Cambridge, 1941.
BROUGHAM, LORD. *Memoirs of the Life and Times of Lord Brougham by himself.* Three vols. Edinburgh, 1871.
— *Statesmen of the Reign of George III.* London, 1853.
— *The Speech of Henry Brougham, April 1st, 1808.* London, 1808.
BUCKINGHAM AND CHANDOS. *Memoirs of the Court and Cabinets of George III.* Four vols. London, 1853–5.
— *Memoirs of the Court of England during the Regency.* London, 1856.

BUCKLAND, C. S. B. *Metternich and the British Government, 1809–14.* London, 1932.

BURDETT, SIR FRANCIS. *To his Constituents, denying the power of the House of Commons to imprison the people of England.* London, 1810.

— *Speech ... at the Crown and Anchor Tavern, July 31st, 1810 ...* London, 1810.

BURGHERSH, LORD. *Memoir of the Early Campaigns of the Duke of Wellington.* London, 1820.

BURNE, LT.-COL. A. H. *The Noble Duke of York.* London, 1949.

BURY, LADY CHARLOTTE. *Diary Illustrative of the Times of George IV.* London, 1838.

BUTTERFIELD, H. *George III and the Historians.* London, 1957.

BUXTON, S. *Finance and Politics—an Historical Study, 1783–1885.* Two vols. London, 1888.

CAMBRIDGE. *Cambridge History of British Foreign Policy.* Vol. I. Cambridge, 1922.

CAMPBELL, LORD JOHN. *The Lives of the Lord Chancellors.* Ten vols. London, 1868.

CANNAN, E. *The Paper Pound, 1797–1821.* London, 1919.

CANNING, GEORGE. *Speeches.* Edited by R. Therry. Six vols. London, 1836.

— *George Canning and His Times.* London, 1859.

CASTLEREAGH, LORD. *The Correspondence and Despatches of Viscount Castlereagh.* Edited by the marquis of Londonderry. Twelve vols. London, 1848–53.

CHALMERS, GEORGE. *Considerations on Commerce.* London, 1811.

CLAPHAM, J. H. *The Bank of England—a History.* Two vols. London, 1944.

COBBETT, WILLIAM. *History of the Regency and Reign of George IV.* Two vols. London, 1830.

COLCHESTER, LORD. *The Diary and Correspondence of Charles Abbot, Lord Colchester.* Edited by his son. Three vols. London, 1861.

COLE, G. D. H. *The Life of William Cobbett.* London, 1924.

COLE, O. B. *A Biographical Sketch of Francis Burton.* London, 1827.

COLQUHOUN, J. C. *William Wilberforce—His Friends and His Times.* London, 1867.

COOPER, DUFF. *Talleyrand.* London, 1938.

CORNWALLIS, LORD. *The Correspondence of Marquis Cornwallis.* Edited by C. Ross. Three vols. London, 1859.

COSTIGAN, G. *Sir Robert Wilson.* University of Wisconsin studies, no. 16.

CREEVEY, THOMAS. *A selection from the Correspondence and Diaries of the late Thomas Creevey, M.P.* Edited by Sir H. Maxwell. London, 1906.

CRISP, F. A. *Fragmenta Genealogica.* Vol. IV. London, 1899.

CROKER, JOHN WILSON. *Letters, Diaries, and Memoirs of the Rt. Hon. J. W. Croker.* Edited by J. L. Jennings. Three vols. London, 1884.

DAVIS, H. W. C. *The Age of Grey and Peel.* Oxford, 1929.

DICKENS, CHARLES. *All the Year Round.* 1 December 1866.

DOWELL, STEPHEN. *A History of Taxation and Taxes in England.* Four vols. London, 1884.

DROPMORE PAPERS. *The MSS. of J. B. Fortescue preserved at Dropmore.* Ten vols. *Hist. MSS. Comm.,* 1892–1927.

DUNDAS, HENRY. *Cursary Remarks on the Correspondence Between Lord Melville and Mr. Perceval.* London, 1809.

EARLE, J. C. *English Premiers.* London, 1871.

EGMONT, LORD. *The Diaries of the Earl of Egmont.* Three vols. *Hist. MSS. Comm.,* 1920–4.

ELDON, LORD. *The Public and Private Life of Lord Chancellor Eldon.* Edited by H. Twiss. Three vols. London, 1844.

FARINGTON, JOSEPH. *The Diary of Joseph Farington, R.A.* Edited by J. Greig. Eight vols. London, 1922–8.

FAY, C. R. *Huskisson and His Age.* London, 1951.

FEAVERYEAR, A. E. *The Pound Sterling.* London, 1931.

FEILING, K. G. *The Second Tory Party, 1714–1832.* London, 1938.

FOORD, A. S. *The Waning of 'The Influence of the Crown'.* *Eng. Hist. Review,* lxii, 1947, pp. 484–507.

FORTESCUE, J. W. *History of the British Army.* Vols. V–VII. London, 1910–12.

FRANCIS, SIR PHILIP. *Reflections on the Abundance of Paper in Circulation.* London, 1810.

FREMANTLE, A. F. *England in the Nineteenth Century, 1806–10.* London, 1930.

FULFORD, ROGER. *The Royal Dukes,* London, 1933.

— *George IV.* London, 1935.

GASH, N. *Mr. Secretary Peel.* London, 1961.

GEORGE, M. D. *English Political Caricature, 1793–1832.* Oxford, 1959.

— *Catalogue of Political and Personal Satires.* Vols. 8–9. London, 1947–9.

GLENBERVIE, LORD. *The Diaries of Lord Glenbervie.* Edited by F. Bickley. Two vols. London, 1928.

GLENCAIRN, COUNTESS OF. *A Letter to the Rt. Hon. Spencer Perceval . . . Containing an Appeal to the British Nation.* Bristol, 1812.

GORE, J. *The Life and Times of Thomas Creevey.* London, 1934.

GOWER, LORD GRANVILLE LEVESON-. *The Private Correspondence of Lord Granville Leveson-Gower.* Edited by Countess Granville. Two vols. London, 1916.

GRATTAN, HENRY. *Memoirs of the Life and Times of Henry Grattan.* Five vols. London, 1849.

GRELLIER, J. J. *The Terms of All the Public Loans.* London, 1812.

GRENFELL, JOHN. *A Defence of Banknotes.* London, 1810.

GREY, C. *The Life and Opinions of Earl Grey.* London, 1861.

GUN, W. T. J. *Harrow School Register, 1571–1800.* London, 1934.

HAMILTON, LADY ANNE. *A Secret History of the Court of England.* Vol. 1. London, 1903.

HAMMOND, J. L., and BARBARA. *The Village Labourer.* London, 1911.
— *The Town Labourer,* London, 1917.
— *The Skilled Labourer.* London, 1920.
HARFORD, J. S. *Recollections of William Wilberforce.* London, 1864.
HARRIS, W. *A History of the Radical Party in Parliament.* London, 1885.
HARROWBY, LORD. *Substance of a speech of the Earl of Harrowby delivered in the House of Lords, June 18 1810, upon the clause in the Appropriation Act for granting the sum of £100,000 for the relief of the Poorer clergy.* London, 1811.
HAZLITT, WILLIAM, *Political Essays, with Sketches of Public Characters.* London, 1819.
— *The Spirit of the Age.* London, 1825.
HENDRICKES, F. *On the Financial Statistics of the British Government Life Annuities. Proceedings of the Manchester Statistical Society,* December 1856.
HERRIES, J. C. *Memoir of the Public Life of the Rt. Hon. J. C. Herries.* Edited by E. Herries. Two vols. London, 1880.
HOLLAND, LADY. *The Journal of Elizabeth, Lady Holland.* Edited by the earl of Ilchester. Two vols. London, 1908.
HOLLAND, LORD. *Memoirs of the Whig Party.* Two vols. London, 1852.
— *Further Memoirs of the Whig Party, 1807–21.* Edited by Lord Stavordale. London, 1905.
HORNER, FRANCIS. *Memoirs and Correspondence of Francis Horner, M.P.* Edited by L. Horner. Two vols. London, 1843.
HOWSE, E. M. *Saints in Politics.* London, 1953.
HUISH, R. *Memoirs of Caroline.* London, 1820–1.
HUNT, LEIGH. *Autobiography.* London, 1885.
HUSKISSON, WILLIAM. *The Speeches of the Right Honourable William Huskisson.* Three vols. London, 1831.
— *The Question Concerning the Depreciation of our Currency stated and examined.* London, 1810.
HYLTON, LORD. *The Paget Brothers.* London, 1918.

IVERNOIS, SIR F. D'. *Effects of the Continental Blockade upon the Commerce, Finance, Credit, and Prosperity of the British Isles.* London, 1810.

JACKSON, LADY. *The Bath Archives.* Two vols. London, 1873.
JACKSON, SIR GEORGE. *The Diaries and Letters of Sir George Jackson.* Edited by Lady Jackson. London, 1872–3.
JACKSON, J. S. *The Public Career of Sir Francis Burdett, 1790–1815.* London, 1840.
JENNINGS, G. H. *Anecdotal History of the British Parliament.* London, 1883.
JENNINGS, SIR W. IVOR. *Party Politics.* Vol. II—*The Growth of Parties.* Cambridge, 1961.
JERDAN, WILLIAM. *Autobiography.* Four vols. London, 1852–3.
JEVONS, W. S. *Investigations in Currency and Finance.* Edited by H. S. Foxwell. London, 1884.

JEVONS, W. S. *On the Variations of Prices and the Value of the Currency since 1782. British Association Transactions,* 1865.

JOHNSTONE, C. L. *A History of the Johnstones, 1191–1909.* Edinburgh, 1910.

KEOGH, CORNELIUS. *A Commentary on the Grenville Manifesto.* Dublin, 1810.

KNIGHT, CORNELIA. *Autobiography of Mrs. Cornelia Knight, Lady Companion to the Princess Charlotte of Wales.* Two vols. London, 1861.

KNIGHTON, SIR WILLIAM. *Memoirs.* Edited by Lady Knighton. Two vols. London, 1838.

LANE, POOLE S. *The Life of the Right Honourable Stratford Canning.* Two vols. London, 1888.

LEWIS, SIR G. C. *The Administrations of Great Britain, 1783–1830.* London, 1864.

LIVERPOOL, LORD. *The Life and Administration of Robert Banks, second Earl of Liverpool.* Edited by C. D. Yonge. Three vols. London, 1868.

LONSDALE, LORD. *The Papers of the Earl of Lonsdale. Hist. MSS. Comm.* 13th Report, part 7.

LYTTON-BULWER, E. G. C. *The Life of Lord Palmerston.* Three vols. London, 1870.

McCALLUM, P. F. *Le Livre Rouge.* London, 1810.

MACKENROT, A. *Secret Memoirs of the Hon. A. C. Johnstone.* London, 1814.

MACKENZIE, K. *The English Parliament.* London, 1950.

MACKINTOSH, SIR JAMES. *Memoirs of the Life of Sir James Mackintosh.* Edited by R. J. Mackintosh. Two vols. London, 1835.

MACLAREN, J. *A Sketch of the History of the Currency.* London, 1858.

MALMESBURY, LORD. *Correspondence and Diaries of the Earl of Malmesbury.* Edited by the third Earl. Five vols. London, 1844.

— *The Malmesbury Letters, 1745–1820.* Edited by the third Earl. Two vols. London, 1870.

MARKHAM, C. A., and COX, J. C. *The Records of the Borough of Northampton.* Two vols. London, 1898.

MARSHALL, D. *The Rise of George Canning.* London, 1938.

MAY, L. M. *Copies of the Inscriptions in the old parish church and churchyard of Charlton.* London, 1908.

MELVILLE, L. *The Wellesley Papers.* Two vols. London, 1914.

— *The Huskisson Papers.* London, 1931.

MITFORD, E. B. *The Life of Lord Redesdale.* London, 1939.

MOORE, THOMAS. *Memoirs, Correspondence, and Journal of Thomas Moore.* Edited by Lord John Russell. Eight vols. London, 1853–6.

MORGAN, E. V. *The Theory and Practice of Central Banking, 1797–1913.* London, 1943.

MORISON, STANLEY. *The English Newspaper, 1622–1932.* Cambridge, 1932.

MOULE, C. G. *Charles Simeon.* London, 1892.

MUSHET, ROBERT. *An Inquiry into the effects of the Bank Restriction Bill.* London, 1811.

NAMIER, SIR LEWIS. *The Structure of Politics at the Accession of George III.* Two vols. London, 1929.
— *Monarchy and the Party System.* Oxford, 1952.
NAPIER, W. F. P. *History of the War in the Peninsula.* Vols. II and III. London, 1886.
— *Counter-Remarks to Mr. D. M. Perceval's 'Remarks on the Character',* etc. London, 1835.
NEWTON, J. F. *The Early Days of the Right Honourable George Canning.* London, 1834.
NORTHAMPTON. *Victoria County History of Northamptonshire.* Vol. III.
— *Poll Book of the Northampton Election of 1796.*

OAKES, C. G. *Sir Samuel Romilly.* London, 1935.
OLDFIELD, T. H. B. *An Entire and Complete History of the Boroughs of Great Britain.* Three vols. London, 1792.
— *Representative History of Great Britain and Ireland.* Six vols. London, 1816.
OLPHIN, H. K. *George Tierney.* London, 1934.
OMAN, SIR CHARLES. *A History of the Peninsular War.* Seven vols. Oxford, 1902–31.
OVERTON, J. H. *The English Church in the Nineteenth Century, 1800–33.* London, 1894.
OVERTON, J. H., and WILBERFORCE, E. *Christopher Wilberforce, Bishop of Lincoln.* London, 1888.

PARES, RICHARD. *King George III and the Politicians.* Oxford, 1953.
PARKER, C. S. *The Life and Letters of Sir James Graham, 1792–1861.* Two vols. London, 1907.
PARNELL, HENRY. *Observations Upon the State of the Currency in Ireland.* London, 1804.
PATTERSON, M. W. *Sir Francis Burdett and His Times, 1770–1844.* Two vols. London, 1931.
PELLEW, GEORGE. *The Life and Correspondence of the Right Honourable Henry Addington, first Viscount Sidmouth.* Three vols. London, 1847.
PENDEREL, M. L., and MALET, J. *Princess or Pretender.* London, 1939.
PERCEVAL, D. M. *Remarks on the Character Ascribed by Colonel Napier to the late Right Honourable Spencer Perceval.* London, 1835.
— *Remarks on the Character . . . . Postscript in Reply.* London, 1836.
— *The Church Question in Ireland.* London, 1844.
PERCEVAL, JOHN. *Perceval's Narrative. A patient's account of his psychosis, 1830–1832.* Edited by Gregory Bateson. London, 1962.
PERCEVAL, SPENCER. *A Review of the Arguments in Favour of a Continuance of Impeachments Notwithstanding a Dissolution.* London, 1791.
— *The Duties and Powers of Public Officers with respect to Violations of the Public Peace.* London, 1792.
— *Observations intended to point out the application of a Prophecy in the Eleventh Chapter of the Book of Daniel to the French Power.* London, 1800.

PERCEVAL, SPENCER. *A Letter to the Rev. Dr. Mansel on the Curates' Bill.* London, 1808.

— *The Substance of a Speech delivered by the Right Honourable Spencer Perceval in the debate on the Inquiry into the Conduct of His Royal Highness, the Duke of York.* London, 1809.

'A.B.' (PERCEVAL, SPENCER). *Six Letters on the Subject of Dr. Milner's Explanation.* London, 1809.

PETRIE, SIR CHARLES. *George Canning.* London, 1946.

— *Lord Liverpool and His Times.* London, 1954.

PHILLIPS, M. *The Token Money of the Bank of England, 1797–1816.* London, 1900.

PHIPPS, HON. E. *Memoirs of the Political and Literary Life of R. Plummer Ward.* Vol. I. London, 1850.

PORRITT, E., and A. G. *The Unreformed House of Commons.* Two vols. Cambridge, 1903.

PORTER, G. R. *The Progress of the Nation.* London, 1836.

REDE, L. T. *A Memoir of the Right Honourable George Canning.* London, 1827.

REDESDALE, LORD. *The Catholic Question. Correspondence between . . . Lord Redesdale . . . and . . . the Earl of Fingall.* Dublin, 1804.

RICARDO, DAVID. *The High Price of Bullion a Proof of the Depreciation of Bank Notes.* London, 1810.

ROBERTS, M. *The Whig Party, 1807–12.* London, 1939.

ROBERTS, W. *The Portraiture of a Christian Gentleman.* London, 1829.

ROBINSON, MAJ.-GEN. C. W. *Wellington's Campaigns, 1808–15.* London, 1911.

ROMILLY, SIR SAMUEL. *Memoirs of the Life of Sir Samuel Romilly.* Edited by his sons. Three vols. London, 1841.

ROMILLY, S. H. *Letters to Ivy by Lord Ward and Dudley.* London, 1905.

ROSE, GEORGE. *Diaries and Correspondence of the Right Honourable George Rose.* Edited by L. V. Harcourt. Two vols. London, 1860.

— *Observations Respecting the Public Expenditure and Influence of the Crown.* London, 1798.

ROSE, J. H. *Canning and Denmark, 1807. Eng. Hist. Review,* January, 1896.

— *A British Agent in Tilsit. Eng. Hist. Review,* 1901.

ROSEBERY, LORD. *Pitt.* London, 1892.

ROUSE BALL, W. W., and VENN, J. A. *Admissions to Trinity College, Cambridge.* Vol. III.

RUTLAND, DUKE OF. *Manuscripts of the Duke of Rutland.* Four vols. *Hist. MSS. Comm.,* 1888–1905.

SANDERS, L. C. *Lord Melbourne's Papers.* London, 1889.

SCOTT, SIR WALTER. *Journal.* Two vols. Edinburgh, 1890.

SERRES, MRS. OLIVIA WILMOT. *Letters of the late Right Honourable Earl of Brooke and Warwick to Mrs. Wilmot Serres.* London, 1819.

SHERIDAN, R. B. *Memoirs of the Life of the Right Honourable R. B. Sheridan.* Edited by Thomas Moore. London, 1825.

SILBERLING, N. J. *The Financial and Monetary Policy of Great Britain during the Napoleonic Wars. Quarterly Journal of Economics,* XXXVIII.

SINCLAIR, SIR JOHN. *Observations on the Report of the Bullion Committee.* London, 1810.

— *Remarks on a Pamphlet, 'The Question Concerning the Depreciation of our Currency . . . .'* London, 1811.

— *Memoirs of Sir John Sinclair.* London, 1837.

SMART, WILLIAM. *Economic Annals of the Nineteenth Century.* Vol. I. London, 1910.

SMITH, H. S. *The Parliaments of England, 1715–1850.* London, 1844.

SMITH, SIDNEY. *A Memoir.* By his daughter, Lady Holland. Two vols. London, 1855.

— *Works.* London, 1869.

— *The Letters of Peter Plymley.* Edited by G. C. Heseltine. London, 1929.

STEPHEN, JAMES. *The Memoirs of James Stephen.* Edited by M. E. Bevington. London, 1954.

STERLING, A. M. W. *The Letter-Bag of Lady Elizabeth Spencer Stanhope.* Two vols. London, 1913.

STEVEN WATSON, J. *The Reign of George III, 1760–1815.* Oxford, 1960.

STRACHEY, LADY. *Memoirs of a Highland Lady.* London, 1911.

TEIGNMOUTH, LORD. *Memoir of the Life and Correspondence of Lord Teignmouth.* Edited by his son, Lord Teignmouth. London, 1843.

— *Reminiscences of Many Years.* Two vols. Edinburgh, 1878.

THOMAS, F. S. *Notes on the Materials for the History of the Public Departments.* London, 1846.

THORNTON, HENRY. *An Enquiry into the Nature and Effects of the Paper Credit of Great Britain.* Edited by F. A. Hayek. London, 1939.

THORNTON, P. M. *Harrow School.* London, 1885.

Times, The. Tercentenary Handlist of English Newspapers. London, 1920.

TOOKE, THOMAS. *A History of Prices.* London, 1848.

TORRENS, W. M. *Memoirs of Viscount Melbourne.* Two vols. London, 1878.

TREHERNE, P. *The Right Honourable Spencer Perceval.* London, 1911.

VANDAL, A. *Napoleon et Alexandre I.* Vol. I. Paris, 1891.

VAN MILDERT, J. *A Sermon Preached to the Honourable Society of Lincoln's Inn on the occasion of the Assassination of the Right Honourable Spencer Perceval.* London, 1812.

VEITCH, G. S. *The Genesis of Parliamentary Reform.* London, 1913.

WALLAS, GRAHAM. *Life of Francis Place.* London, 1898.

WALPOLE, SPENCER. *The Life of the Right Honourable Spencer Perceval.* Two vols. London, 1874.

WARD, S. G. P. *Wellington's Headquarters.* Oxford, 1957.

WELLESLEY, LORD. *Memoirs and Correspondence of Richard, Marquis Wellesley.* Edited by R. R. Pearce. Vols. I and II. London, 1846.

— *The Wellesley Papers.* Edited by H. Jenkins. London, 1914.

WELLINGTON, DUKE OF. *The Despatches of the Duke of Wellington in the Peninsula.* Edited by Colonel Gurwood. Twelve vols. London, 1837–8.
— *Supplementary Despatches.* Edited by his son. Fifteen vols. London, 1858–72.
— *Civil Correspondence of the Duke of Wellington—Ireland, 1807–9.*
— *Letters of Wellington to W. W. Pole. Camden Society, 3rd series,* Miscellany 18.
WILBERFORCE, WILLIAM. *The Life of William Wilberforce.* Edited by R. I. and S. Wilberforce. Two vols. London, 1840.
— *The Private Papers of William Wilberforce.* Edited by A. M. Wilberforce. London, 1845.
WILLIAMS, C. V. *The Life and Administration of the Right Honourable Spencer Perceval.* London, 1812.
WILSON, D. *The Substance of a Conversation with John Bellingham.* London, 1812.
WINDHAM, WILLIAM. *The Diary of the Right Honourable William Windham, 1784–1810.* Edited by Mrs. Henry Baring. London, 1866.
— *The Windham Papers.* Edited by the earl of Rosebery. Two vols. London, 1913.

ANONYMOUS BOOKS AND PAMPHLETS

— *The Royal Kalender.* 1797, 1798, and 1810.
— *Defence of the Honourable A. C. Johnstone.* Edinburgh, 1806.
— *An Admonitary Letter to H.R.H. the Prince of Wales.* London, 1806.
'ARISTEDES'. *An Answer to the 'Admonitary Letter',* etc. London, 1806.
— *The Royal and Delicate Investigation into the Conduct of Her Royal Highness, the Princess of Wales.* London, 1807 edition.
— *A Biographical Index to the Present House of Commons.* London, 1808.
— *Public Characters 1809–10.* London, 1810.
'A COUNTRY GENTLEMAN'. *A Letter to the Right Honourable Spencer Perceval upon his reported Correspondence with Lord Melville.* London, 1810.
— *Politics and Public Men for the Year 1812.* London, 1812.
— *The New Whig Guide.* London, 1819.
— *The Black Book or Corruption Unmasked.* London, 1820.
— *The Extraordinary Red Book.* London, 1821.

INDEX

The index attempts to give brief notes on persons who appear in the text. This is done in three ways:

(1) British subjects whose years of birth and death are given in brackets are included in the *Dictionary of National Biography*.
(2) Members of Parliament not included in the first category are identified by the constituency they represented in the 1807–12 parliament. The years for which they were returned for that constituency are also given.
(3) All remaining persons occurring in the text are briefly identified.